HEZBOLLAH

AURÉLIE DAHER

Hezbollah

Mobilisation and Power

Translated from the French by
H. W. Randolph

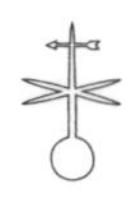

HURST & COMPANY, LONDON

Originally published in French as *Le Hezbollah. Mobilisation et Pouvoir* by Presses Universitaires de France in 2014.
First published in English in the United Kingdom in 2019.
C. Hurst & Co. (Publishers) Ltd.,
41 Great Russell Street, London, WC1B 3PL

Printed in India

A Cataloguing-in-Publication data record for this book is available from the British Library.

ISBN: 9781849046312

This book is printed using paper from registered sustainable and managed sources.

www.hurstpublishers.com

To my parents, my sister and my husband—this book is theirs first and foremost.

CONTENTS

BOXES, TABLES AND FIGURES

BOXES

TABLES

FIGURES

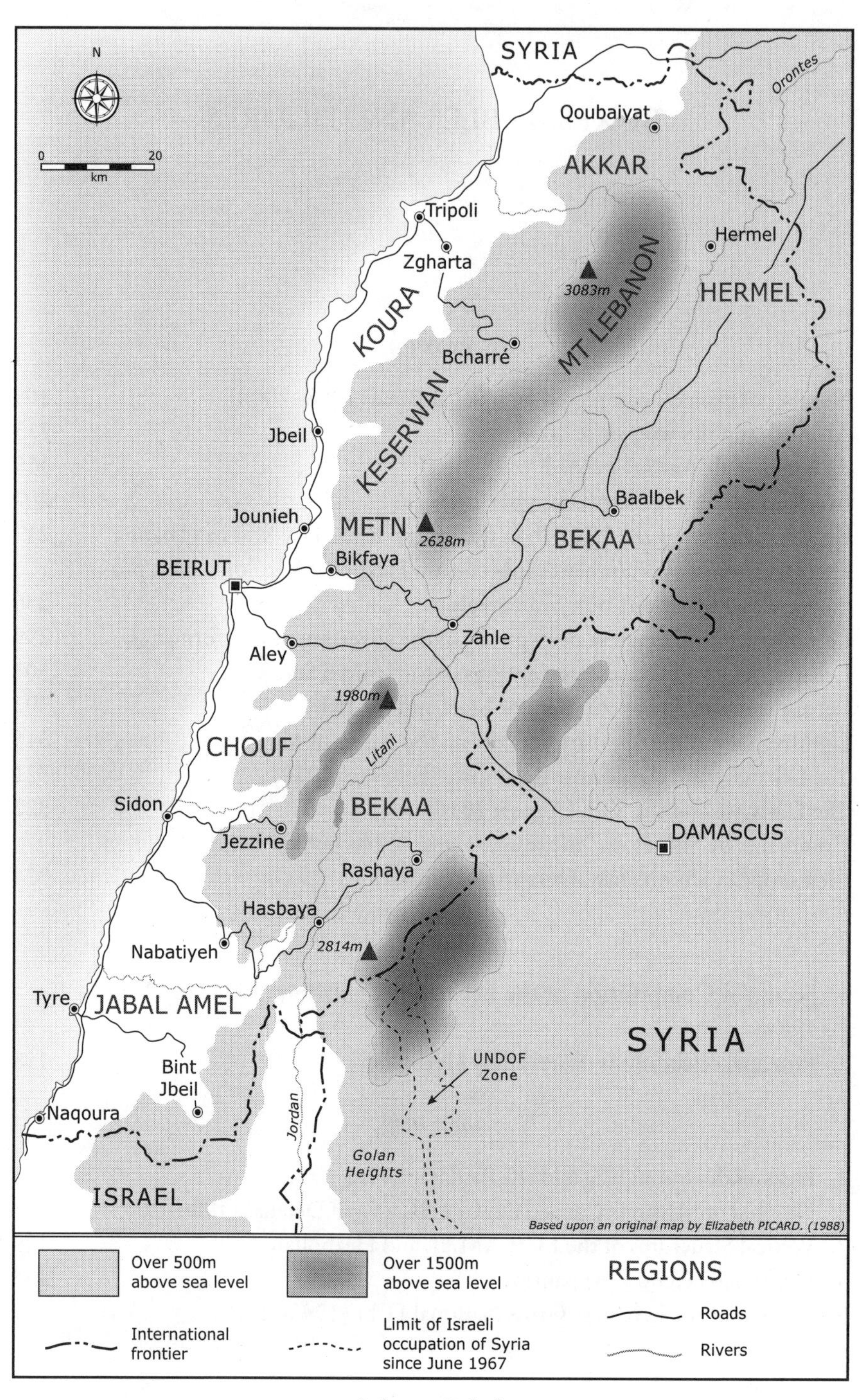

Lebanon Relief

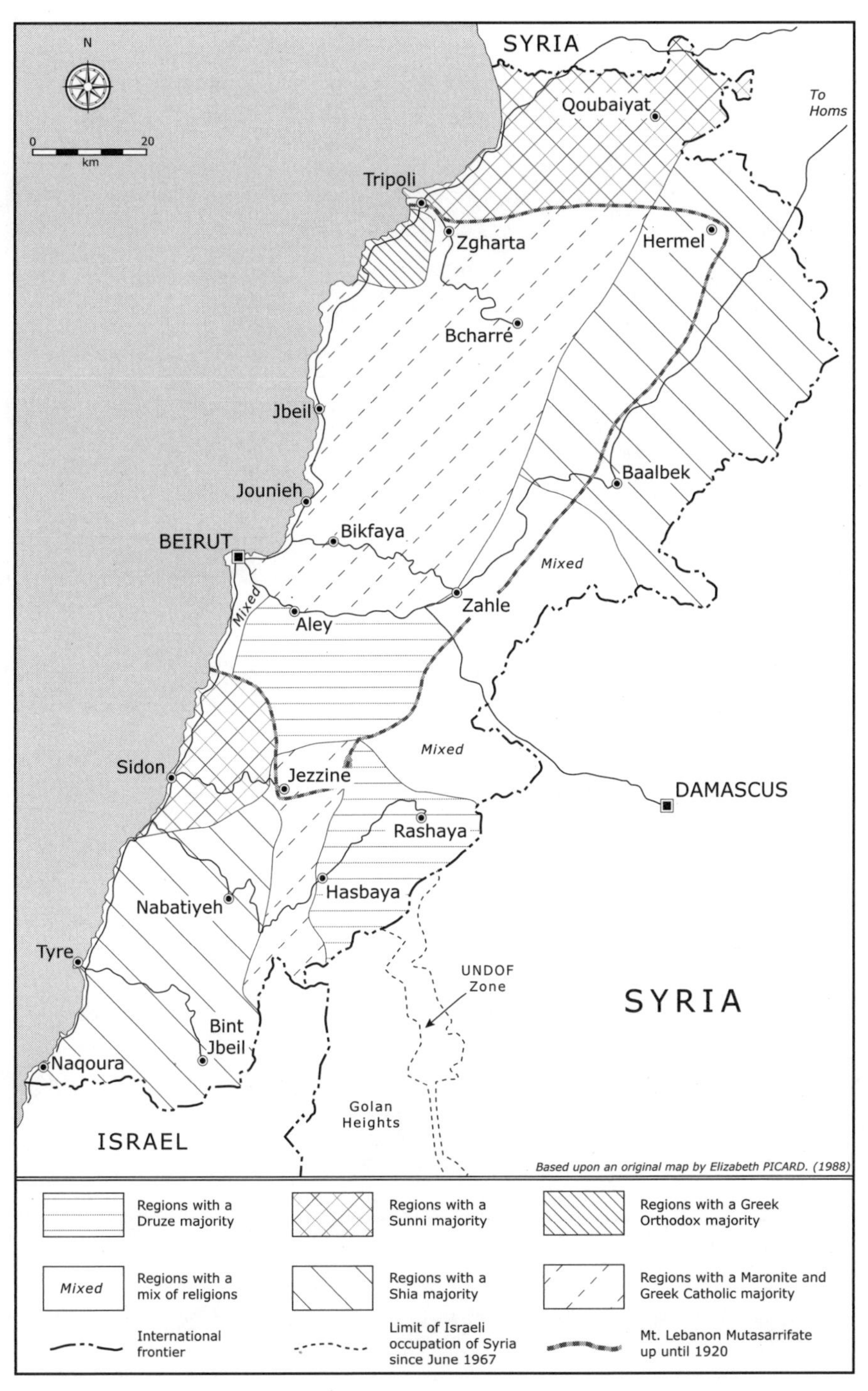

Geographic repartition of sectarian communities in Lebanon

INTRODUCTION

The assassination of Wissam al-Hassan, the head of Lebanon's police intelligence services, in October 2012, once again presented an occasion for the Country of Cedars to externalize its internal contradictions and persistently deadlocked political life. The reactions that the drama aroused were too acute to mask a socio-political tension that was blatantly tempted to express itself through violence. To contain the risk of systemic collapse, local actors had only relatively limited room for manoeuvre. Hezbollah, the premier Shiite group and the country's leading political party, appears to have been at the heart of the security equation. Viewed by some as the number one threat to civil peace, and by others as its sole guarantor, it was nonetheless unanimously recognized as the key player in Lebanon's stability. Its sometimes organic regional alliances with an Iranian regime hard hit by sanctions from the international community and a Syrian leadership fighting relentlessly for survival warranted the increasingly numerous and pessimistic questions as to the party's ability to stay secure and sustain itself in its own country. Depending on political preferences, the ensuing conclusions concerning Lebanon's prospects promised either salutary deliverance or unbridled chaos.

A look at Hezbollah's history, however, reminds us that this is not the first time that its decline—if not disappearance—had been prophesied. Its participation in the first post-war parliamentary elections in 1992; the liberation of South Lebanon in 2000; the American war against Iraq in 2003; the vote on Resolution 1559 by the Security Council of the United Nations in the autumn of 2004; the Cedar Revolution and Syria's withdrawal in 2005; the Israeli offensive in the summer of 2006; the clashes of May 2008; the indictment brought by the Special Tribunal for Lebanon; and the bloody events tearing at neighbouring Syria since 2011 all offered occasions for many observers to predict a significant weakening of Hezbollah, if not its outright dissolution. Yet it is clear that this succession of adverse contexts and events has not diminished the organization's strength, and was even accompanied by an increase in popularity with its public. It is true that eight years after its last military face-off with Israel and six years after the armed confrontation with March 14, Hezbollah found itself in uncharted waters. The Syrian regime, which has been instrumental in the emergence and maintenance of Hezbollah's regional power, particularly in facilitating its supply of weapons over the years, and in the party's dominance on the domestic political scene by helping, to some extent and for a certain period of time, to keep its local competitors in check, was in danger of disappearing. The different groups and actors that were likely candidates to succeed it shared a common animosity towards the party, seen as complicit in the crimes committed by the Syrian authorities against their people. Prospects for close cooperation between the future masters in Damascus and Hezbollah's leadership looked uncertain. A return to power of the anti-Assad March 14 coalition that Hezbollah and its political allies seemed to have permanently neutralized in January 2011, and also the annihilation of Lebanese armed resistance against Israel, could be envisaged. Were such a reversal to take place on the political chessboard, the distinctive features of Lebanese politics, the traditional rules of the game, and the profound changes it has undergone during the past fifteen years nevertheless indicate that a change in power relations will not come easily. The spirits that drive the day-to-day political rivalry of the pro- and anti-Syrian groups and actors in Lebanon cannot be altered by the mere flux of current events and of regional and international support. The stakes transcend the simple alternation of power, and instead involve the very structure of the country's socio-political life and identity.

This book aims to provide some answers to these questions about the future of Hezbollah—and, by extension, of Lebanon. The approach chosen here is a study that is both empirical and analytical, and has as its point of entry the mobilization of the party in the country where it originated. Were it to lose certain of its regional assets, Hezbollah must be able to retain sufficient local support in order to preserve its position and strength. More than weaponry, it is the leverage provided by popular mobilization in its home country that will ensure its continued existence. The central issue that frames this book hence is discovering the nature of the relationship between Hezbollah and its public, and identifying both the structural and contextual elements that drive it. This interrogatory cannot find answers by limiting itself to a mere reflection on contextual considerations; it requires a retrospective that is both historical and sociological. In other words, the aim here is not to examine mobilization at a particular time, but to trace the trajectory of the support that an organization derives from a part of society. This is done by identifying that trajectory's stages and the factors in each that explain the ever-tighter bonds between mobilizer and the mobilized.

Hezbollah's mobilization and Lebanese politics

At the conclusion of the First World War, the freshly defeated Ottoman Empire was dismembered by the victors. In the autumn of 1918, French and British troops marched into the Levant, ending 400 years of Ottoman rule. The territory of what was soon to become Lebanon fell under French influence. A few months later the Versailles Conference opened, to debate, among other issues, the fate of the fallen empire's Arab provinces. A tug of war ensued between the Emir Faisal, son of Emir Hussein ibn Ali, the Sharif of Mecca, allied with the French and British during the war, and the French government: the former hoped to establish an expanded Syria under his authority while the latter wanted to appropriate the Syrian coast. A considerable number of indigenous representatives succeeded one another to press for the Arab option defended by Faisal. But three delegations from Mount Lebanon, most notably the one presided over by the Maronite Patriarch Monsignor Hoayek, in November 1919 succeeded in persuading the French prime minister, Georges Clemenceau, to commit to the creation of a Lebanese state.

Greater Lebanon was born on 1 September 1920. The initial plan was to confine it to Mount Lebanon, the intent being to endow it with as homogeneous a population as possible, in this case Maronite. However, economic considerations quickly pointed up the non-viability of a state comprising a few square kilometres of mountainous terrain, poorly suited for agriculture, deprived of all access to the coastal ports and far from the great Syrian and Palestinian trading cities. Future Lebanon's borders were therefore expanded to encompass Mount Lebanon, Mount ʿĀmil, which extends them to the south, the coastal strip flanking them, the Bekaa Valley in the north-east, and the rises on the western flanks of the Anti-Lebanon Mountains and Mount Hermon.

This expansion of the borders had wide-ranging consequences for the country's sectarian make-up. Lebanese society consisted of seventeen different religious communities.[1] In the early 1930s Christians of all faiths slightly outnumbered their Muslim compatriots, comprising 51.2 per cent of the population. The Maronites were the leading Christian community (28.8 per cent of the population), followed by the Greek Orthodox (barely 10 per cent). Among the Muslim communities, the Sunnis predominated (22.4 per cent of the population), followed closely by the Shiites (19.6 per cent), and the Druze (6.8 per cent). Faced with this religious mosaic, the French mandatory authorities opted to make Lebanon a republic organized according to a special political system called "confessionalism", summed up as a division of powers between communities. Enshrined in today's Constitution, especially in Article 95, it was initially specified by the National Pact of 1943, a verbal agreement between representatives of the Maronites and the Sunnis, the two major communities at the time. Under it, the position of president of the Republic was reserved to the former, that of prime minister to the latter. The speaker of the parliament was to come from the Shia community. Seats in parliament were distributed by a ratio of six Christians for every five Muslims. The seats were then reallocated by community within each of these two major groupings, and by district.

Until the 1980s, the political history of Lebanon was summed up by two (redundant) struggles. The first pitted the Maronites, much favoured by the sectarian distribution of political resources, against the Sunnis, who, supported by the Druze, some Shiites and Christians, were increasingly insistent on sharing these resources more equitably. A second embroiled the Maronite leaders in a fierce intra-sectarian race for the community's top leadership position.

The challenge brought by the Muslim groups was energized all the more by demographic changes that by all indications were trending to their advantage.[2] Fifteen years of fratricidal war (1975–90) led to a redistribution of power in favour of the country's Muslim communities, particularly the Sunnis. If the Taef Agreement, ratified by Parliament in August 1990, sealed the end of the civil war, it also recast the political system. Parliamentary seats were thenceforth equally distributed between Christians and Muslims, and executive power devolved mainly to the Council of Ministers. The prime minister, constitutionally required to be a Sunni, is now the country's de facto main political leader.

Table 1: Sectarian composition of the Lebanese population (1922, 1932, and 1984)

	Official census 1922		*Official census 1932*		*Private estimate 1984*	
	Count	*%*	*Count*	*%*	*Count*	*%*
Maronites	199 182	32.7%	226 378	28.8%	900 000	25.2%
Greek Orthodox	18 409	13.3%	76 522	9.7%	250 000	7.0%
Greek Catholics	42 426	7.0	46 000	5.9%	150 0004.2	4.2%
Other	12 651	2.1%	53 463	6.8%	225 000	6.3%
Christian Total	335 668	55.1%	402 363	51.2%	1 525 000	7.0%
Sunnis	124 786	20.5%	175 925	22.4%	750 000	21.0%
Shiites	104 947	17.2%	154 208	19.6	1 100 000	30.7%
Druzes	43 633	7.2%	53 047	6.8%	200 000	5.6%
Muslim Total	273 366	44.9%	383 180	48.8%	2 050 000	57.3%
Grand Total	609 034	100%	785 543	100%	3 575 000	100%

Source: Michael Johnson, *Class and Client in Beirut*, New Jersey, Ithaca Press, 1986, p. 226.

But the demographic changes that Lebanon's population has been undergoing since then, which favour the Shiite community, for a long time ranked third among the denominations in terms of political power and precedence, put into question the power-sharing system entrenched under the Taef Agreement, a system that has become increasingly less representative of the society's confessional composition. The distribution of seats in parliament grants thirty-four seats to the Maronites, twenty-seven to the Sunnis, and twenty-seven to the Shiites. In percentage terms, this means that 26.5 per cent of parliamentary representation accrues to the first and 21 per cent each to the second and third. Yet some private studies estimate that Shiites make up a minimum of 40 per cent of the Lebanese population.[3] In a country whose political system gives priority to the majority community at the expense of the majority opinion, the numerical growth of the Shiites cannot continue without eventually causing a profound change in the rules of the game. Sooner or later, the distribution of power currently in force will be seriously questioned. The formulations, proposals, and practices put forward by some political actors already suggest that a large portion of them is well aware, either with enthusiasm or regret, of the ineluctability of such a reform. Whether the transition to a new distribution of power is achieved by peaceful and fruitful negotiations between the various protagonists, or whether it will result from several years of violence as in 1975, the Shiite community will undoubtedly be central to the process.

This is all the more so since, for over thirty-five years, it has been the natural breeding ground for Hezbollah, an organization that differs significantly from the traditional political structures and that, for the past twenty years, has served as catalyst for a profound change of identity in its community of origin. To understand the future of Lebanon requires understanding both Hezbollah's nature and the foundations of its relationship with the community. From this perspective, a first observation imposes itself. The mobilization orchestrated by Hezbollah pertains to three categories. The first is military. As will be amplified shortly, Hezbollah is a socio-political apparatus dedicated to defending the interests of an armed organization, al-Muqāwama al-Islāmiyya fī Lubnān (the Islamic Resistance in Lebanon (IRL)). Mobilizing in the Hezbollah sense primarily means enlisting recruits for armed combat against the Israeli occupier. But this mobilization effort is also designed to convince the Lebanese people to support the Resistance, morally and practically, whenever necessary; in this sense, it is a political mobilization. Finally, in seeking to forge a new culture that would constitute the identity of what the party refers to as *mujtamaʿ al-muqāwama* (resistance society), Hezbollah seeks to secure the maintenance of this support and its durability through a socialization effort. This brings with it deep-going changes in Lebanese society that exceed the party's original political mobilization aims: the mobilization is therefore also social in nature.

According to Hezbollah, with the established term of *taʿbiʾa* the party's official language picked up the Persian *bassidj*, literally meaning mobilization. The Iranian Islamic Revolutionary Guards, better known as the Revolutionary Guards or Pasdaran, in fact played a key role in the creation of the IRL and the former's structural organization served the IRL as a partial model. Terms specific to the Iranian Revolution, such as *mustakbir* (arrogant, as applied to the imperialist regimes), *mustadʿaf* (disinherited, referring to unfree or impoverished people), *al-Shaytān al-akbar* (the Great Satan, that is, the United States), and *al-Shaytān al-asghar* (the Little Satan, or Israel) were at one time and, on occasion, are still noticeable in Hezbollah rhetoric. But rather than argue about the meaning that the Iranian revolutionaries gave the concept in the late 1970s or early 1980s, it is more pertinent to focus on the meaning given to *taʿbiʾa* by the members of Hezbollah, who are Lebanese and who, for the most part, are unaware of the Iranian revolutionary origins of the vocabulary they use.

In Arabic, the term *taʿbiʾa* has both the meaning of military mobilization—i.e. conscription—and political or social mobilization. It refers simultaneously to recruitment and the militant state. It defines men ready to do battle, but also the party base or the active members of an association or organization. Hezbollah militants use the concept to describe both the process of recruiting fighters and the civilian grass-roots members. They expand it by a third dimension: by *taʿbiʾa* they also mean the call on society to support the Resistance. The most frequently used explanatory terms are *tahdīr* and *istiʿdād*, translatable respectively as preparation and availability (for). Thus, the party, using the first concept, says that it works to conscientize the public and, with the second, that it expects that public to react positively to this "raised consciousness", to include standing ready to answer the call. To summarize: mobilization, within Hezbollah's meaning of the word, covers the recruiting of both fighters and members, attracting sympathizers to itself, and the seducing of minds. It relates to time in a dual fashion: it seeks to encourage involvement in immediate and concrete action shoulder to shoulder with the organization and its cause, while it also pursues socialization of the public in anticipation of a potential, future availability for action. Logically, the term implies persistence through time: the goal is to be able to count on a general investment in action alongside the Resistance whenever the party requires it. As a corollary, anyone who is active in the ranks of Hezbollah (or IRL) or who is in the right frame of mind to answer the call becomes the mobilized. This includes party members, cadres, and grass-roots activists, as well as followers, whether active regularly or occasionally.

A fresh look at Hezbollah and its mobilization

A *sine qua non* condition for grasping the significance of a relationship based on mobilization and a correct appreciation for the sources from which the agreement between mobilizer and mobilized springs requires a deep knowledge of both. The literature on Hezbollah extant today suffers from undeniable shortcomings. Chronologically, the party was the subject of study by (Western) intelligence services before it became one for sociology. In defence of the researchers who took it on in the 1980s, it must be said that the organization was essentially clandestine at the time, and balked at being approached by observers. Two types of texts were the result, both problematic. One type chose to democratize data obtained primarily from the intelligence services; the other, preferring to limit itself to a strictly academic examination of the subject, contented itself with flawed information which most often had been passed through the distorting prism of the studied object itself. In all cases, the reading derived from them is incomplete and less than reliable. This is all the more so because the intelligence agents, like the researchers, did their basic research in the capital when the process that should have been observed at that time was taking place in the rural north-east. The 1990s and the opening of the party to outside observers at that time unfortunately were not seized as occasions for revisiting the previous work in order to provide a more solid picture of Hezbollah. When research did address new aspects of the party, it was built on the extant versions. It was not until the mid-2000s that a new generation of junior scholars, the vast majority emerging from the French academic system, started revisionist work—in the positive sense of the word—on a Hezbollah whose discourse, developments, and practices increasingly challenged the earlier analyses that had been elevated, for want of anything better, into time-honoured classic and immutable versions. Unfortunately, for reasons to be clarified shortly, from 2006 on, the party chose to shut its doors to external observation and study, making it no easy task once again to gain an appreciation of it.

The presentation of Hezbollah in this book is part of this new effort to question the original study of an organization that has always been viewed as enigmatic. Undeniably, I have had the privilege of being able to cast a dual look at Hezbollah, from both inside and out, thanks to a family history that has allowed me to live in the North Bekaa region, which is key for the history and identity of my subject, although I was not born there. By having been fully integrated into the local society in which I spent part of my childhood and my teenage years in the 1980s and 1990s, by returning to it regularly during a succession of long university vacations, and by residing there between 2006 and 2010, I had a unique and precious opportunity to closely observe first the early stages, then the consolidation, and finally the rise to power of an organization that is today the major actor on the Lebanese political stage and a protagonist of the Middle East game that cannot be ignored. If I began my thesis work with an exhaustive reading of the extant literature, I placed greater reliance for my assertions on years of participant observation, hundreds of interviews with highly placed as well as ordinary members of Hezbollah, with followers of various confessions and from diverse ideological and militant backgrounds, and various critics with differing motivations and grievances. Finally, I benefited from the support that my work received from other witnesses to Hezbollah's rise, who had the useful and generous idea of supplying me with historical documents—tracts, militant writings, and posters—or who simply shared memories with me whose contents are not common knowledge. These comprise all the elements that made possible for the picture of Hezbollah that I present here to coalesce, but above all from which originate any solidity, richness, and originality to which this work may eventually lay claim. I am infinitely grateful to all these acquaintances, these friends, these actors, and these observers.

What is Hezbollah?

Is the Islamic Resistance Hezbollah's military arm?

Used by analysts, political scientists, and observers of the Middle Eastern scene, the term *Hezbollah* frequently reflects an encompassing approach, covering both the military apparatus and the totality of the civilian, social, or political institutions linked to the party. When the effort is made to differentiate these components, the Resistance (*al-Muqāwama*) unambiguously denotes the military apparatus, but, remarkably, the term *Hezbollah* is then used again to refer to the party's civilian organization: the noun *Hezbollah* is therefore used to designate both the non-military part of the organization and the organization in its global dimension (civilian and military). This confusion between an entire organization and parts of it reveals how observers understand the hierarchical and organizational relationships within Hezbollah, a misunderstanding betrayed by now commonplace formulas that present the Islamic Resistance as "the military arm of Hezbollah" or "the armed wing of Hezbollah".

This representation of Hezbollah as an Islamist party possessed of a subordinate militarized appendage collides with the reality of an organization of a totally different nature. The socio-historical reality of the Hezbollah complex requires an inverse reading of the organizational and functional relationships between the Resistance and Hezbollah. The Islamic Resistance in Lebanon is not Hezbollah's military arm: Hezbollah is the socio-political arm of a military organization, the IRL. Indeed, the latter is not a paramilitary structure ready to intervene on the Lebanese scene to implement decisions emanating from the civilian leadership of the organization. Actually, the secretary-general of Hezbollah is fundamentally a military leader who supervises the work of a civilian[4] leadership team dedicated to ensuring, on the social and political level, all of the support and the popular base that the IRL needs to sustain itself.

Definition of an "Islam of resistance"

Hezbollah is generally defined as an Islamist organization. The establishment of political Islam in Lebanon would be the original template for its paradigms, and resistance against the Israeli occupation would constitute one of its practical applications. Yet it appears that while the Hezbollah ego is not lacking the religious dimension, this dimension did not assume meaning, and to this day has had no effect other than as a vector for a different original value: that of resistance. Hezbollah brings together a collection of people mobilized primarily around the idea of refusing the Israeli occupation (and any form of "oppression"—*dhulm*—in general). For this group, Islam, among other referents, acts as a guarantor of the legitimacy of the principal cause.

If we define Islamism as an effort directed towards Islamizing a political system, we need to note that Hezbollah's political practice has never aimed at such outcome, even a partial one. Since the late 1980s, the party has during its demonstrations ceased to evoke the notion of an Islamic regime, a theme moreover that the party's parliamentary members have never sounded in either their public or parliamentary activities. If the mobilization discourse of the party and its social practice actually employ religious referents, does that by itself make Hezbollah an Islamist party? This choice of the party to take no action towards an Islamization of the Lebanese political system, or of part of it, therefore leads to a bias in favour of concepts such as militant

Islam, Islamic militancy, and Islamic currents/movements at the expense of those of Islamism or Islamist. Admittedly, Lebanon's multi-sectarian socio-political context, in which the Shiite community has only made its voice heard effectively for a few decades, goes a long way towards explaining Hezbollah's difficulty in practising activism of an Islamist nature. It is no less true that an internal sociology of the party confirms this suggested division of roles between Islam and military *jihād*, that is, between Islam and the resort to arms. In the eyes of Hezbollah's leadership, Islam seems not to be an ultimate goal that could be achieved by means of armed struggle, but inversely is a means in the service of armed struggle for a thoroughly temporal cause. In this way, Hezbollah embodies what I will call an "Islam of resistance". Whereas, for certain Islamist groups, weapons are in the service of an Islamization of society or of a political regime, Hezbollah's practices and religious referents are in the service of its arms.

How does it sustain its mobilization?

A mobilization of the clientelist type?

Though extremely popular, the argument that the support provided by the Syrian and Iranian regimes is the true driver of Hezbollah's success deserves to be qualified and relativized. Two dominant ways of conceiving of this support must be rejected. The first makes Hezbollah into a satellite of its regional mentors, stripped of room for manoeuvre or its own priorities, that will be consistently armed and financed in exchange for obeying the orders of its two sponsors. The second does not bother to qualify the nature and importance of this support by period. Proponents of the regional support argument too often neglect to draw the distinction between the nature of the aid provided by Damascus and that provided by Tehran, only rarely differentiating the types of relations existing between Hezbollah and each of its two allies. In the Iranian case, the analysis requires making an additional effort of qualification by differentiating the sources or poles of authority at their origin (religious power, political centres). In particular, the linkage between Iranian financial aid and Hezbollah's mobilizing power, which, in practice, involves social action by Iranian parent institutions attached to the party (the Islamic Charitable Relief Association, Foundation of the Martyr, Foundation of the Wounded, and Foundation for the Construction Effort), is often cited as the main reason for the success of its mobilization. Unquestionably, this argument is overblown. Without denying that Hezbollah's social welfare apparatus plays a role in sustaining its mobilization, clientelism is not its source. The virtue of this network of social institutions resides in producing a benevolent public image of the party: objectively rather ineffective in its financial support to the needy, this social action apparatus presents a front, a showcase, and serves the mobilization less by assuring it of self-interested allegiances than by playing on the ethical referents of the society to which it addresses itself.

Thwarting external destabilization

In this connection, the relationship between Hezbollah and its public is strongly influenced or reinforced by the positions as well as social and political practices of the Other, an actor external to the mobilization under examination here. In Hezbollah's case, we can distinguish between three Others: the national Other, embodied since 2005 in the March 14 movement; the regional Other, represented by the state of Israel; and the international Other, epitomized by the international community. The Other's discourse, schemes, and, especially, "errors" as perceived by Hezbollah's public do play a not inconsiderable role in sustaining Hezbollah's mobilization over time. In bipolarized settings such as the political chessboard that is Lebanon and the regional arena as perceived in Lebanon, the game is zero-sum: each gain by one side is a loss for the adversary and vice versa. One camp's accumulated difficulties and defeats comfort the other with the notion that it finds itself "on the good side of the barricade". Dwelling on rival mobilizations therefore will also have its uses for the present analysis, since they illustrate how certain obstacles that they cannot surmount play a role in reinforcing Hezbollah's popularity.

Mobilization over time: a new society

Independent of what Hezbollah's leaders have been able to devise or plan, groups of militants active inside the party's various institutions, just like followers who are ready to approve its action or position-taking, impart a meaning to their support that they themselves define. Thus, mobilization—in part—gets away from Hezbollah to become the property of its public. Set up as clients free to take or leave what makes sense to them in the party's discourse, the public discards one part and reprocesses another. It is a piece of luck for Hezbollah that its public has not only integrated certain representations that the leadership wanted to convey to its followers, but that this public has appropriated some of this meaning in the form of enduring identity markers, in turn infusing the mobilization with a new general significance that works in the party's favour.

More than any other factor, this reworked meaning of the mobilization is today the principal guarantor of Hezbollah's popularity. It is much more interesting that the Shiite partisans and followers, inserted into a society that is subject to influences other than just Hezbollah's, have hybridized the referents of identity and belonging and unwittingly become vectors for change in their community. With the Shiites expected to represent an increasingly substantial part of the Lebanese population, Hezbollah's mobilization has, without prior planning, set in motion profound, widespread social change that is nothing less than the prime mover in a makeover of the whole society—and of its national identity.

Mobilization over time

Studying mobilization and reception

With these empirical hypotheses posited, the choice of a theoretical framework becomes easier to make. Social science offers a rich corpus of theories and methods dedicated to the study of mobilizations, under the heading of "social movement theory" (SMT). It usually treats mobilization as a moment of collective expression or action that requires identifying the prior conditions, mechanisms, and resources used in structuring it and in making it happen, as well as identifying the contexts and opportunities that allowed its action to be staged. Mobilization is therefore conceived of as a phenomenon at the end of a chain where various processes geared to concretizing a collective action come to a head. The key question is how the structures necessary for its existence are set up and activated. Most often, the argument retraces the history of the deployment of resources and the launching of action, and how they are articulated. The time line is short or limited, shrunk to the juncture of the moment before the mobilization crystallizes and the moment when it goes into action. The question of how it maintains itself over time, however, is ignored in the vast majority of cases.

In a quasi-systematic manner, observers who try to account for Hezbollah's mobilization dwell on the contents of its discursive production (speech, prose, and events) or its media, pointing a finger especially at al-Manār as the engine that aligns the minds of the Shiite community to the party's modes of representation. Without denying that the public is not insensitive to Hezbollah's discourse, three points need to be stressed in this regard. First, the party's followers, just like the rest of the Lebanese population, have other sources of representation than this single discourse. Next, sustaining Hezbollah's mobilization does not preclude parallel allegiances and cross-affiliations. Hezbollah is not the sum total of the Shiite community, which had a prior history and has experienced other political, ideological, and spiritual adventures than this one alone—and it continues to do so. The community has at its disposal other referents, other sources of values, representations, and perspectives than simply those that the party tries to instil. Finally, it needs to be said that a mobilization is not a one-way top–down relationship running from mobilizer to mobilized. Hezbollah's public is not a docile receptacle for what the party would like to inculcate: it is itself a vital actor in the mobilization's evolution. Admittedly, the public carries it but also reshapes, reorients, redefines, and transforms it, giving mobilization an intensity that the party never planned, or even expected. Mobilization is also a bottom-down process.

An approach that focuses on the moment of onset of Hezbollah's mobilization and on the process of attraction towards the mobilizer that it culminates in is therefore inadequate. To begin with, the examination of this mobilization consists less of understanding isolated moments of action than of grasping the underpinnings of a collective loyalty that remains intact despite adverse circumstances. Rather than determining the reasons for grouping together for a demonstration, for instance, what should be sought out are the reasons accounting for an enduring loyalty over time. The factors that explain a gathering at a moment in time may turn out to have limited effect when it is a long-term relationship that should be decoded instead. Furthermore, an approach focused on identifying the resources intentionally used by the mobilizer is also too limited. Compensation with resources—of whatever nature—of the mobilized by the mobilizer is not what links Hezbollah and its public. Things become that much more complicated when, as mentioned earlier, the mobilized is never the perfectly malleable object of the mobilizer.

These two points represent a first set of reasons that argue for a "cultural" approach, i.e. one favouring sense and meaning (a meaning-making approach) over one simply identifying resources rationally injected by the mobilizing actor to gain the attention of the mobilized group (resource mobilization theory (RMT)). The real objective here is to identify and expose not issuance but reception.

Recognizing the role of "unforeseen" elements

In addition, a major advantage that the meaning-making approach provides but that the RMT approach lacks is that it fully accounts for the power of the environment to shape and sustain the mobilization. Admittedly, RMT does not ignore the environment or context-linked political opportunities, but they are employed as explanatory elements only if in the form of a resource identified as such by the mobilizing actor, which he uses consciously and deliberately. RMT falls short by not acknowledging everything the environment injects into the mobilization whose effect the mobilizing actor has neither the chance to evoke nor to prevent. A meaning-making approach, by contrast, permits factoring in the environment's power to affect the mobilization either in a positive or negative manner independent of the mobilizing actor's will. This effect impacts the mobilization by the unconscious intermediation of the mobilized, because, just like the mobilizing actor, the environment also moulds the representations and values of the mobilized group, creating the risk of disharmony between them and the representations disseminated by the mobilizing actor. The mental constructs championed by the mobilizing actor and those promulgated by the environment can therefore rival each other at any moment in the minds of the mobilized group. These minds are thus perpetually a site where these occasionally antagonistic representations may clash with each other. Explaining how a mobilization succeeds in sustaining itself over time thus necessitates observing what transpires in this competitive space in order to identify how, over time, potentially destabilizing representations are dismantled by being confronted by representations redounding to the benefit of the mobilizing actor. This only a meaning-making approach is able to accomplish.

Favouring "sources of perception"

If the identification of resources injected into a mobilization by the mobilizing actor is not a foolproof method, conversely a simple description of the mobilized public's representations will not suffice. This does not mean simply ignoring the mobilizing actor as other studies have done with the mobilized group; it calls for studying their interconnection. The method applied here is conceived as having three stages. The mobilizing actor will be presented in a descriptive manner, i.e. as what he is, what he says, and what he does. Next to be captured is the universe of meaning of the mobilized group where it touches on the mobilizing actor, so that then we can retrieve from among the objective elements emanating from the latter what has had or not had a grouping effect. Finally, and of most interest, we will observe how elements put at the public's disposal by the mobilizing actor were reprocessed syncretically by this public in a framework where other elements issuing from the environment—but also from the group's passing or internalized experiences, its code of ethics, and its identity—are employed, and generate new mobilizing elements that even the public is not conscious of.

Rather than seeking the resources that went into the mobilization, the question throughout this work will therefore be what sources of perception permitted it to exist, and especially to sustain itself. They offer the advantage of dispensing with the rational intentionality of resources without removing the objective dimension of the elements issuing from the mobilizing actor. They thus reference substance that is emitted consciously or unconsciously, intentionally or not, by the mobilizing actor and which has a positive impact on mobilization—whether it is in its "rough" form as emitted or in a form reprocessed by the public. Sources of perception also preserve an advantage over the resources concept by acknowledging the positive elements emitted by the mobilizing actor and identified as such not by him but by the public.

Structure of the argument

This work is articulated in two epochs. The first section presents both a history and sociology of the Islamic Resistance in Lebanon and of Hezbollah, from their creation to the liberation of the southern part of the country in 2000. It was indeed in 2000 that the original mission was accomplished and the problem arose of how to sustain a mobilization whose *raison d'être* no longer seemed to exist. The first section therefore provides a description of the IRL and of Hezbollah, but also exposes the original wellsprings of their mobilization. Four types of elements play a part in its crystallization and maintenance between the 1980s and 2000 whose effects persist in subsequent years regardless of the evolving contexts. The first consists of the successes and accomplishments of the IRL's tug-of-war with the Israeli army (Chapters 1, 2, and 3). The network of Hezbollah's social and welfare organizations constitutes the second type (Chapter 4). Next comes Hezbollah's organizational structure, designed to guarantee the soundness of the internal edifice (Chapter 5), and, last, there is the charisma of the third secretary-general, Hassan Nasrallah, which progressively became one of the mainstays of the party's mobilization (Chapter 6).

The book's second, more chronological, section places the relationship tying Hezbollah to its public into an evolutionary framework in order to show how the relationship resists adverse contexts over time. Subdivided into four periods marking out the great reorientations of the Lebanese political context on the one hand and the major inflection points spotted in the development of the representations and state of mind of Hezbollah's public on the other, it explicates a Lebanese and regional current state of affairs centred on the IRL and the party: from the time of the Syrian tutelage and the Syrian withdrawal of 2005 (Chapter 7) to the summer 2006 war (Chapter 8), passing through the implosion of the internal scene in May 2008 (Chapter 9) to Hezbollah's assuming power directly in January 2011 and its positioning in the face of the Syrian crisis (Chapter 10). The section is capped by a final chapter (Chapter 11) focusing on the party's public, particularly the Shiite community. Dedicated to examining the development, in parallel with Hezbollah's, of both the politically and identity-oriented representations of its followers, it describes what they have retained of the sources of perception to which they were exposed over the years and how they appropriated them.

PART I

WHAT IS HEZBOLLAH?

PRESENTING AN ORGANIZATION AND THE FIRST WELLSPRINGS OF ITS MOBILIZATION

1

ON THE ORIGINS OF HEZBOLLAH

A SOCIAL AND POLITICAL HISTORY OF PROTO-HEZBOLLAH MILITANCIES

During the 1960s and 1970s various militant currents made themselves felt in Lebanon's Shiite community, from which Hezbollah's founders would soon emerge. This pre-Hezbollah Shiite history is richly instructive on the party's deep nature. By identifying the environment in which some of its cadres and members took their first militant steps, their objectives and modes of action back then, the rivalries that pitted them against the members of other groups, the relationships they maintained—or did not—among themselves, and the conditions that led them to abandon their original groups for Hezbollah and the IRL, it becomes possible to better discern what Hezbollah is, what it is not, and what drove the mobilization of its first generation.

The extant versions of the history of the Shiite "political awakening" and the creation of Hezbollah that followed in its wake are in agreement.[1] The Shiite presence in Lebanon is said to have remained "mute and ignored"[2] until 1959 when Mūsā al-Sadr, an Iranian cleric with family roots in South Lebanon, established himself in Lebanon. He set about raising the awareness of the community and prevailed on the Lebanese authorities to recognize his movement. He then gave it a militant civilian structure, Harakat al-Mahrūmīn (the Movement of the Dispossessed), soon accompanied by a military wing, Afwāj al-Muqāwama al-Lubnāniyya (the Brigades of the Lebanese Resistance), better known by the acronym AMAL. The story is that Hezbollah began taking shape in 1982 around pro-Iranian Islamist networks preached to by Muhammad Husayn Fadlallāh, a cleric installed in Beirut's southern suburbs and for many years put forward as the organization's head, or at least its spiritual guide. Hezbollah's mobilization would have reaped the benefits of al-Sadr's activism: supposedly it was thanks to a massive influx of AMAL defectors into its ranks that the new organization could be built "on the ruins" of the former.[3] As Hezbollah's story is usually built up solely around the activism of two main figures, Mūsā al-Sadr and Hassan Nasrallah, the moment when the proto-Hezbollah networks crystallized into Hezbollah tends to be glossed over.

In reality, the party's genesis is much more complex than this. The groups from which Hezbollah's first members emerged are more varied than is generally asserted, their interconnecting points and decision centres are embodied in persons other than the actors cited in the official versions. Hezbollah's appearance in the early 1980s was in fact the result of the merging of two militant Islamic networks that had developed in different regions of the country. Subhī al-Tufaylī, leader of al-Daʿwa in Lebanon, and ʿAbbās al-Mūsawī, distinguished student of the Iraqi Ayatollah Muhammad Bāqir al-Sadr, represent the two heads of the Bekaa network. In the Beirut region, the Lebanese Union of Muslim Students, AMAL, and other, smaller groups were in essence the circles in which the people who would be among the first members of Hezbollah surfaced. For several years, most Shiite militant activity took place in the capital; militancy in the Bekaa did not really start up until 1978, after the return of al-Tufaylī from Iran and al-Mūsawī from Iraq. As for the South, it only joined in the Hezbollah adventure's second phase. The proto-Hezbollah militancies of the capital and the Bekaa during the early times remained distinct from one another in their choice of priorities, their nature, and their attitude to action. In Beirut, they were quietist; their effort consisted essentially of setting in motion a religious renewal of society, focused on current events in the Lebanese—but also the national or global—world of the Shiite clerics. In the Bekaa, the action already consisted of mobilization favouring armed resistance, with reliance at all times on Islamic values. Here they did not preach Islam as an end in itself, or to increase the number of believers; they opted instead for a discourse with military overtones, and recruited young people who were encouraged to learn how to handle weapons. It follows that these two types of Shiite Islamic militancy, one cultural, the other inspiring resistance, would react in different ways to the events that shook Lebanon during the transitions of the 1970s and 1980s.

Shiite and Lebanese

Shiism and politics

The Shiites, who today represent just over 10 per cent of world Islam, differ from their Sunni co-religionists on certain points of dogma, including political ones. For one thing, they favour having the community's affairs managed by *imāms* descended in a direct line from ʿAlī, cousin and son-in-law of the Prophet Muhammad, ʿAlī being the first *imām*. The second and third, respectively, are Hassan, his eldest son, and his younger son Hussein. The latter's martyrdom at the hands of Umayyad troops in Karbala in Iraq is commemorated every year by Shiite communities worldwide as ʿĀshūrāʾ, or the "Ten Days", in reference to how long the siege lasted before the final fall. Next came Hussein's descendants; the last and twelfth in the line,[4] with the first name of Muhammad like the Prophet's, disappeared in a mysterious fashion at the age of eight, in 873 CE. Shiite tradition holds that he is not dead, but "in occultation", present but invisible. At first he continued to communicate with the faithful through four intermediary delegates until the last of them died in 941 CE. The period between 873 CE and 941 CE is known as the Minor Occultation (*al-Ghayba al-sughrā*), and the time since then is called the Major Occultation (*al-Ghayba al-kubrā*). This new period is fated to last until the end of time, when the twelfth *imām*, henceforth known as *al-Mahdī al-muntadhar* ("the Guided Awaited One") will reappear shortly before the Resurrection and Judgement Day to establish a reign of justice and truth.

Ever since the *imām* Muhammad al-Mahdī lost his last mediator, the conduct of the social, religious, and especially political affairs of the world's Shiite communities has been debated. The *marjaʿiyya* (principle of "reference"), established in the course of the nineteenth century, holds that the ordinary believer should practise "imitation", *al-taqlīd*, that is, apply the religious edicts (*fatwās*) issued by a small number of ulema (religious scholars) designated as *marjaʿ al-taqlīd* (source of emulation). Every believer is free to accept the *marjaʿ* of his choice, whose *fatwās*[5] he is morally obliged to obey. The principle of *marjaʿiyya* is transnational, with a Lebanese Shiite free to choose an Iraqi or Iranian *marjaʿ*. The Shiite faithful pay a tithe—unknown to the Sunni faithful—to the chosen *marjaʿ* or his official representative (*wakīl*). Called the *khums* or "fifth", it is to equal 20 per cent of the net profits from a business or the annual amount saved from a salary.[6]

Competing with the concept of *marjaʿiyya* is *wilāyat al-faqīh* (government by legal expert).[7] Contrary to what is often claimed, *wilāyat al-faqīh* was not invented by Ayatollah Khomeini, but he adopted it, commented on it and, especially, applied it, in the process making himself the foremost incarnation of this legal expert, the *al-waliy al-faqīh*. According to Khomeini,

> The Islamic government is fully the government by divine law. As for the official responsible for applying this divine law, he is the legal adviser (*faqīh*), the possessor of knowledge and of justice, who assumes *all of the Prophet's prerogatives, all the prerogatives of the twelve infallible imāms of the Imamite Shia, all their prerogatives without exception whatsoever*, without, however, possessing any of their personal qualities or their privileged place by the side of God.[8]

This attribution to a human being of the prerogatives traditionally reserved for the *imāms*[9] would be hotly disputed, and considered blasphemous by some. As for *marjaʿiyya*, it is careful to accord to the religious men only the power to regulate the private and public (social) affairs of the community without any right to govern politically, a privilege that is reserved strictly for the Prophet and his descendants. *Wilāyat al-faqīh* is also regularly attacked as Khomeini's ill-disguised ambition to declare himself head of Shiism worldwide:

> If a legal adviser, bearer of knowledge and justice, comes to form a government, the holders of power in the society will have the same duties toward him that they have toward the Prophet, and the people will be required to listen to him and obey him.[10]

Incorporated into the Iranian Constitution in 1979 as one of the political system's structural tenets, the *wilāya* made the Guide of the Revolution the supreme authority in the state and by extrapolation appeared to provide the means for placing the various Shiite communities solely under Iranian political direction, in the first instance under Khomeini from 1979 to 1989 and Khamenei ever since. It follows that *wilāyat al-faqīh* and *marjaʿiyya* represent rival conceptions of Shiite religious and political sovereignty, with *wilāya* referring to the idea of a communitarian power anchored in Tehran,[11] while *marjaʿiyya* represents free choice and independence from the Iranian power centres.

Being Shiite and being Lebanese

There is no unanimity on the date the first Shiites arrived on the lands that would be formed into the nation of Greater Lebanon in the twentieth century. Besides the real difficulty of finding precise, reliable historical data, political considerations have consistently hindered their acceptance and diffusion. Christian conservatives have always claimed that they were the first community to settle on Mount Lebanon, seen as the heart of the Country of Cedars, as one of the arguments legitimizing their claims to the pre-eminence of their community in the area. Lebanese historiography, traditionally following their narratives, makes it axiomatic that the faithful of Saint Maron were the first of the future Lebanese to establish themselves in the Mountain. If, in fact, the Maronites did settle there in two waves, during the seventh and eleventh centuries, the Shiites seem to have arrived in the region early on as well.[12] Historians agree that the latter were forced to emigrate *en masse* towards Jabal ʿĀmil, the part corresponding approximately to South Lebanon, and toward the northern Bekaa, around Baalbek–al-Hermel, at two tragic moments of their history. Between 1298 and 1305, the Mamluks, accusing the Shiites of "plotting with the Crusaders and the Mongols and to reject Islam and the Muslims",[13] led several military campaigns against them. The bloodiest is said to have taken place in the month of Muharram of the Christian year 1303[14] with the straightforward objective of eradicating the Shiite community of Mount Lebanon. The ensuing massacre is known as the "ʿĀshūrāʾ of Kesruan",[15] and the expelled Shiites were replaced by Maronite settlers and Sunni of Turkmen origins.[16] The second wave of immigration took place in the middle of the eighteenth century, when the Shiites of the Mountain were attacked by the Shehab, local rulers, and their vassals.[17] That caused the Shiites to vacate the Lebanese coast all the way to Sidon and retreat to the interior lands in the South and the northern Bekaa.

Faced with the creation of Greater Lebanon by France in 1920, not all Shiites reacted the same way. Some versions have it that those in Mount Lebanon supported the creation of the new state and chose a delegate for the commission of six notables, which, presided over by the (Maronite) Patriarch Hoayek, went to Paris in 1919 to petition the victors of the First World War to create Lebanon. In contrast, those in the Bekaa and the South called for attachment to Syria, thus supporting their pan-Arab Sunni co-religionists. Their resistance was finally overcome in 1936 under increasing pressure brought to bear by the mandatory power.

As Lebanese citizens, the Shiites basically became a community on the peripheries, in the geographical as well as figurative senses of the word. A huge majority settled in the underdeveloped rural zones of the country, removed from the centres of political power and the country's economic heart. They were dominated by a handful of great families that made clients of the community and monopolized what little political power it enjoyed. Feudalistic in the South, clan-based in the Bekaa, the local dynasties represented the Shiites in the political spheres of the new Lebanese state only fitfully, and badly even then.[18] In theory, the sectarian system reserved the presidency of the Chamber and 20 per cent of the seats in Parliament to them. Nevertheless, as Elizabeth Picard noted, the Pact of 1943 accorded the community only secondary positions and, before 1974, none of the higher offices.[19] The Shiites were also the last of the three categories of Muslims to gain their own community institutions: the Sunni had theirs from 1955, the Druze from 1962. The Shiites would wait until 1967 for Mūsā al-Sadr to take up the fight to obtain their own institutions and the right to manage their own community's affairs; until then, they remained under the implicit tutelage of the Sunni community, with the Supreme Islamic Council and the mufti assuming responsibility for representing them and speaking for them.

This political isolation was exacerbated by a lacklustre socio-economic situation. An IRFED[20] report published in 1958 points out that 4 per cent of the Lebanese population monopolized 33 per cent of the national income while 50 per cent had to make do with 18 per cent.[21] The South leads the list of most disadvantaged areas, crowned "champion of underdevelopment" with an income that is five times less than that in Beirut.[22] During the 1960s Mūsā al-Sadr remarked that "until just a few years ago, all of Beirut's newspaper vendors, shoe shiners, porters, doormen, elevator operators and café waiters [were] Shiite."[23] Augustus R. Norton confirms:

> Using 1971 data ... the average Shiʿi family's income was 4,532 Lebanese pounds (L£3 = $1 in 1971), in comparison with the national average of 6,247 L£; the Shiʿa constituted the highest percentage of families earning less than 1,500 L£; they were the most poorly educated (50 percent with no schooling vs. 30 percent state-wide); and the Shiʿa were the *least* likely, in comparison with their cohorts from other recognized sects, to list their occupation as professional/technical, business/managerial, clerical or crafts/operatives, and the *most* likely to list it as farming, peddling, or labor. ... In al-Biqaʿ and al-Janub [the South], the percentage of students in the population (about 13 percent) lagged by as much as 5 percentage points behind Lebanon's other three regions. ... In 1971, only 6.6 percent of the Shiʿa had at least a secondary education, compared to at least 15 percent and 17 percent for the Sunnis and the Christians, respectively. ... For 1974 ... while the South had about 20 percent of the national population, it received less than 0.7 percent of the state budget.

> … The south has the fewest paved roads per person and per acre. Running water is still missing in all villages and towns although water pipes were extended to many areas in the early sixties. Electricity networks were erected at about the same time, but they are inoperative most of the time. Sewage facilities are available only in large towns and cities. Outside the larger centers telephone service is completely absent except for a single manual cabin which is usually out of order. Doctors visit the villages once a week and sometimes only once a month. Clinics are maintained only in large villages and do not function regularly. Hospitals and pharmacies are found only in the larger population centers. Elementary school is usually run in an old unhealthy house provided by the village. Intermediate schools were introduced to the large towns in the mid-sixties.[24]

This situation, according to Norton, had changed little during the 1980s.[25]

Finally, along with these socio-economic and political difficulties, Shiites were relegated to the lowest status within the national community. Indeed, in the Lebanese mentality, a strict hierarchy of collective sectarian representations accompanies the sectarian distribution of power. If the Shiites are generally treated with condescension by Christians for being Muslims, they are also ranked lowest among Muhammad's followers, simply assigned to last place. The term *metwālī* was applied to the Shiites, and was often used to mean "boorish", "illiterate", "fatalistic", "dirty", "backward", and "barbaric"; the term, as Yann Richard notes, "is associated with derogatory japes, with humiliation".[26]

This general state of the Shiite community is no less worthy of attention because it rapidly grew to be the largest numerically, essentially because of a birth rate that for decades was significantly higher than of any other group.[27] Thus, while the Shiites made up slightly more than 17 per cent of the population when Greater Lebanon was created in 1920, by the 1980s some private estimates put the percentage at 27 per cent, with the Sunnis a close second at 26 per cent, followed by the Maronites at 23 per cent and trailed by the other communities, each representing at most 7 per cent of the population.[28] A non-official survey published by the *Financial Times* in 1984 even estimated that the Shiites then represented 30 per cent of the population, the Maronites 25 per cent and the Sunnis 21 per cent.[29]

Inexplicably, for a long time the Lebanese political class of all faiths chose to ignore this steady growth by the Shiite part of the population, and, until the arrival of Mūsā al-Sadr, it disregarded the political challenge posed by the community's mobilization. The traditional Shiite leaders did not really seek to exploit this numerical potential, preferring to hold on to their traditional power bases rather than conducting new political experiments.[30] However, there were some early attempts at activism from the community's base. With its primary aspirations being improvement of its social and economic status, while remaining hostile towards a communitarianism that penalized it, the community showed a preference for the Communist Party (LCP), providing it with a base and some cadres. It also turned to the Lebanese National Movement

(LNM) of the Druze socialist and officially anti-confessionalist leader Kamal Jumblatt.[31] However, in truth, it was not until the 1970s that the first purely Shiite political mobilization got off the ground, when Mūsā al-Sadr gained institutional independence for the Shiite community vis-à-vis the other Muslim groups and set up Harakat al-Mahrūmīn as the first Shiite militant structure.

The Shiite politico-religious scene 1960–1970

Mūsā al-Sadr: official recognition for the community

1959–1973: portrait of a reformer

Sayyid Mūsā al-Sadr was born in 1928 in Qom in Iran into a family originally from South Lebanon and known for having produced a number of renowned ulema.[32] Illustrating this distinction, his father, Sadreddīn al-Sadr, was a *marja*ʿ teaching in Qom. His cousin and future brother-in-law, Sayyid Muhammad Bāqir al-Sadr, himself a *marja*ʿ and great teacher in the very prestigious *hawza* (religious school) of Najaf in Iraq, was also the leader of al-Daʿwa, the Islamic renewal party opposed to the regime. Mūsā al-Sadr began his secular and religious studies at Qom, and then studied economics in Tehran. In 1954 he pursued religious studies in Najaf, taught by, among others, Muhsin al-Hakīm and Abū al-Qāsim al-Khūʾī, two great *marja*ʿs of the time. Four years later, his studies completed, he returned to Qom to take up teaching.

In December 1957 his Lebanese cousin ʿAbdul-Husayn Sharafeddīn died in Tyre. Mūsā al-Sadr was invited by the city notables to succeed his cousin since there was no one in Lebanon qualified for the post at that time. The young candidate for the position had already visited Lebanon, first in 1955 and a second time in 1957, just prior to Sharafeddīn's death. He accepted what he viewed at the time as a challenge and an adventure, and put his suitcase down for good in the Country of Cedars in 1959. Quickly realizing the socio-political backwardness that characterized the country's Shiites at the time, he made improving the community's situation his priority. As an anti-Communist, he aimed to free it of the influence of leftist organizations. In 1961 he revived Sharafeddīn's social welfare activities, adding his own institutions in the process: an orphanage, a nursing school, a language school, a technical school, and a *hawza*. Financed by parts of the Shiite diaspora in Africa, and by four great *marja*ʿs whose *wakīl* he was, he managed to gain independence from his community's feudal notables.

Mūsā al-Sadr also sought to maintain good relations with the Lebanese state. Unlike the dissent stirred up by the leftist parties calling for an end to the sectarian political system, his actions registered as respect for existing institutions, recognition of the ruling class, and an evident willingness to cooperate with it.[33] In his relations with the other communities he advocated religious coexistence, and supported the view that Lebanese multi-sectarianism, far from being a handicap, was a source of richness. He did not shrink from speaking in churches, and just as openly frequented the Maronite shops in the Muslim quarters at a time when the tension and mutual distrust between Christian "Libanists" (essentially Maronites) and leftist Muslims (Sunni, Shiite, and Druze) were escalating dangerously. Al-Sadr quickly gained a popular following, and not just within his own community. He was perceived as dynamic and open, and also credited with having great charisma. His Shiite co-religionists appreciated him all the more when his activism finally bore fruit: in 1967 the Lebanese Parliament endorsed the creation of a Supreme Shiite Council (SSC), which began functioning two years later, presided over by none other than al-Sadr. In other words, the emancipation of the Shiites was fully recognized by the Lebanese authorities and the community thenceforth got to manage its own affairs.

1973–1978: the time of rifts, before the "disappearance"

Although al-Sadr sided with the Palestinian Resistance upon arrival in Lebanon, his relations with it gradually deteriorated. In 1969 the signing of the Cairo accords authorized the Palestinian factions to attack Israel from Lebanese territory. Yasser Arafat moved to Lebanon. The pace of operations by the PLO fighters from the south of the country was stepped up, particularly from 1970, with the arrival of thousands of Palestinian combatants driven out of Jordan after Black September.[34] The step-up in Palestinian attacks was accompanied by a similar acceleration in Israeli reprisals, to which the inhabitants of South Lebanon, basically Shiites, fell victim first. In May 1970 al-Sadr called a general strike to protest at the authorities' indifference to their plight. While this led the government to create the Council of the South, with funds for financing the region's reconstruction and development, al-Sadr pushed for more. In 1974 the tobacco farmers in the South, mainly Shiites, rallied against the government. The cleric supported them, and called on the entire country to strike and engage in civil disobedience. Over a span of six weeks, he gave a series of speeches that gave the impression that he had broken with his earlier legalist positions. Tackling head-on one of the community's taboos by exhorting it to stop living with an inferiority complex, he called his co-religionists to action. In mid-March, at Baalbek, he uttered the following, now-famous phrase: 'Al-silāh zīnat al-rijāl' (in essence, "Guns make the man"),[35] and announced the formation of Harakat al-Mahrūmīn. A protest movement, it conceived of itself as a pressure group for defending the rights of the very poorest and those neglected by the state. Multi-denominational in theory, it grouped together militants from diverse political bodies: Baath, the Lebanese Communist Party (LCP) and the Communist Action Organization in Lebanon (CAOL), etc.; it nevertheless remained essentially Shiite.

In January 1975 al-Sadr called on the Lebanese to raise an armed resistance force to respond to the multiple attacks that were then being launched by the Israelis against Kfarshuba[36] in the south, and neighbouring villages. In early July an explosion shook ʿAyn al-Bnayyeh, a hamlet in the Bekaa Valley, several kilometres south-east of Baalbek: a landmine had exploded accidentally in a military training camp that the public and *a priori* the authorities were unaware of. Several people were killed or injured. The press, catching wind of the incident, revealed that Harakat al-Mahrūmīn militants were receiving weapons training. Mūsā al-Sadr, faced with a *fait accompli*, had to explain. The next day he acknowledged the existence of Afwāj al-Muqāwama al-Lubnāniyya, soon to be known by the acronym AMAL, which also, fortuitously, means "hope". The organization had been created in May 1973, but al-Sadr is said to have wanted it stay a secret until it was fully operational. Its weapons as well as the cadres in charge of training were Palestinian, and AMAL and Palestinian units conducted their first joint operations in the Kfarshuba area from 1975 on.

However, these good relations with the armed Palestinian groups did not last. In May 1976 the situation of the Christian militias was judged to be so precarious that the president of the Republic, Sleiman Frangieh, officially requested Syrian military intervention to forestall a victory by the "progressives" (essentially Muslims). On 1 June several thousand Syrian soldiers crossed into Lebanon to save the Christians from what seemed certain defeat by the Lebanese left. Al-Sadr sided with Damascus[37] and, logically, AMAL withdrew from the LNM. Within the Shiite community, for the most part aligned with the progressives, the turnabout was all the more controversial because six months earlier, during the slaughter of "Black Saturday" carried out by Christian militias,[38] many of the victims had been Shiites, and, two months after the Syrian troop incursions, the Christian conservative Kataeb militia emptied Nabʿa (a southern suburb of Beirut) of its Shiite inhabitants after the quarter surrendered.[39] This, plus the fall of Nabʿa, accelerated the fall of the Palestinian camp at Tall al-Zaʿtar.[40] It turned out that the capitulation of Nabʿa had been negotiated by al-Sadr. To a large part of the community, the *imām*'s legalism seemed like compromise, and as a result, the cleric's popularity plummeted.[41] His image regained some of its previous lustre after Kamal Jumblatt was assassinated in 1977, putting an end to the LNM's genuinely multi-sectarian spirit: Walid Jumblatt, Kamal's son, adopted a more communitarian posture and Mūsā al-Sadr became de facto the sole referent for the Shiites.[42]

In late August 1978 al-Sadr went on an official visit to Libya. He would never return. The last time he was seen was on 31 August, when leaving his hotel to meet with President Muammar Qaddafi. According to the Libyans, the cleric and his two companions took a plane to Italy; but the Italian authorities, after inquiries, asserted that the three men had never boarded. The Libyan authorities were soon suspected of having acted on behalf of Palestinian groups. Al-Sadr's disappearance traumatized the Shiite community. They refused to contemplate his death, choosing to speak of an "occultation" instead. His absence would set in motion far-reaching changes in the community's socio-political trajectory. In particular, it allowed the emergence of Shiite personalities who until then had been eclipsed by him and who were to have a paramount role in the creation of Hezbollah.

A disruptive outsider: the Shiite opposition to Mūsā al-Sadr

Despite his great popularity, al-Sadr's initiatives and successes antagonized more than one notable and religious personage in his community. To start with, he alienated the feudal lords in the South by trying to free the Shiites of Jabal ʿĀmil from their control. After that, he upset a great number of the militant clerics, beginning with Muhammad Jawād Mughniyyeh, like him installed in the Tyre region.[43] Born in 1904, into a family of ulema in the South but orphaned at the age of twelve, Mughniyyeh "had known misery".[44] He arrived in Najaf in 1925 to study under the ayatollah Sayyid Abū al-Qāsim al-Khūʾī. In Iraq he discovered politics, a subject for which he would propose a series of polemical theories several years later. Returning to Lebanon in 1936, he became *imām* in a village near Tyre, a ministry previously filled by his recently deceased brother. He soon abandoned his religious discourse, realizing that it was ineffective for communicating with the peasants in the area and instead threw himself into a vigorous social activism. While he did build mosques, he was just as active in helping the poor. His reputation as a dynamic cleric with integrity got him appointed to a judgeship on the Jaafari (Shiite) tribunal in Beirut in 1948. However, his political views backfired on him. Patently progressive, he supported Gamal Abdel Nasser and the Algerian independence movement until asked to change his political position or resign. Although he shared an interest with al-Sadr in intersectarian dialogue, he did not like him; "the success [of the latter] must have upset him", according to some.[45] More to the point, this hostility related to the fact that Mughniyyeh saw al-Sadr as a politico. While al-Sadr, like Mughniyyeh, aimed to improve conditions for the Shiites, he did it by exploiting the sectarian system when, in Mughniyyeh's eyes, he should have been fighting it. For this rebellious cleric, the tradition of the Shiite *imāms* justified revolt against all despotisms. In his view it was essential to preach against corruption and tyranny; submitting to them amounted to renouncing Islam.

Another prominent cleric who did not view al-Sadr's actions kindly was Sayyid Muhammad Husayn Fadlallāh.[46] Coming from a family of ulema originally from the village of ʿAynātā in South Lebanon near Bint Jbeil, he was born in 1935 in Najaf. Following in his father's footsteps, he enrolled in the *hawza* and after graduating taught religion there. An intimate and protégé of *marja*ʿ Muhsin al-Hakīm, he became close to the al-Daʿwa party. Judged promising, he became a party intellectual and published numerous articles in its journal, *al-Adwāʾ al-islāmiyya* (The Islamic Lights), edited by Muhammad Bāqir al-Sadr. He entered Lebanon in 1966 and took up residence in Nabʿa, where he set up a clinic, a religious cultural centre (*husayniyya*), and a religious school, al-Maʿhad al-Sharʿī al-Islāmī (Islamic Law Institute). His discourse clashed with that of Mūsā al-Sadr, who had arrived in Lebanon seven years before him: while al-Sadr construed a Shiism that called for acceptance of the system and for quietism, Fadlallāh was more combative and espoused a hybrid "Islam, nationalism and anti-imperialism".[47] Where al-Sadr promoted a Shiism that conformed to the traditional conception of the political game as played in Lebanon and was an integral part of it, Fadlallāh preached a reformism by the community for the community, notably through education and conscientization. Bettering the Shiite condition through the intervention of the Lebanese state did not form part of his systems of argumentation. In 1976, when the civil war was raging and Lebanese Forces militia attacked Nabʿa where he lived, Fadlallāh wrote *al-Islām wa mantiq al-quwwa* (Islam and the logic of force), destined to remain one of his best-known works, notable for its exhortation of Muslims to take action against the "imperialist danger". After the quarter fell, he fled to his village of ʿAynātā, but soon after returned to settle permanently in Bīr al-ʿAbed, in Beirut's southern suburbs.

Officially, relations between Muhammad Husayn Fadlallāh and Mūsā al-Sadr were never bad.[48] But diplomatic formulations also never quite obscured the fact that they were, in reality, far from good. By way of example, the creation of the SSC proved contentious, and when the institution was inaugurated Fadlallāh failed to present his congratulations, an explicit act of rudeness under the rules of Middle Eastern politeness. A review of contemporary Lebanese archives and old statements by Fadlallāh himself helps us to better understand the situation: the quarrel between the two men did not stem from "a few differences on specific political points",[49] but mainly from two distinct causes. The first was the inevitable rivalry between two great clerics, Mūsā al-Sadr, whose charisma and successes garnered him a dazzling popularity (even if a bit tarnished after 1976), and Muhammad Husayn Fadlallāh, whose driving ambition to achieve nothing short of the *marjaʿiyya*, was never a secret. The second put Mūsā al-Sadr at loggerheads not only with Fadlallāh but also a large part of the community's clerical class: the very problematic impact of the SSC's creation in 1967. Certainly, for the majority of Shiites, the addition of the Council to the Muslim communitarian institutions was highly satisfying as it signalled recognition by the Lebanese government of their separate status. But in Sunni as well as Shiite clerical circles, the creation of the SSC was interpreted differently. With the gulf widening between a part of the political class that was essentially Christian, confessionalist, conservative, right wing, and scarcely inclined to feel animosity towards Zionism or sympathy for the Palestinian cause and, on the other side, a mostly Muslim class demanding a more equitable sharing of socio-economic resources and power, the SSC represented a dishonourable compromise. At that time, the majority of Shiites sided politically with their Sunni co-religionists. To them, the creation of the SSC appeared to be the price paid by the state to buy the allegiance of the Shiite community and so detach it from the Sunnis, back then still the tip of the opposition's spear. In short, they viewed it as a stratagem to draw the Shiites to the side of the Maronites.

al-Ittihād: cultural re-Islamization of the community

In parallel with Mūsā al-Sadr's actions, which were more social and political than spiritual, another kind of militancy developed among the Shiites from the early 1960s, especially in Beirut's southern suburbs. Religious, essentially student based, quietist and legalistic in nature, even if it was critical of what it saw as government inaction, this movement aimed at setting in motion a cultural dynamic of re-Islamizing the community. It was driven by an ensemble of small neighbourhood associations, mosque committees (*lijān masājid*), small groups of religious men organized around a few sheikhs, and a few student associations. They included al-Shabāb al-Muʾmin (the Believing Youth), active at the American University of Beirut, the Lebanese University, and the Arab University; Rābitat al-Tullāb al-Muslimīn (the League of Muslim Students), mostly centred at the Arab University; and, most important and dynamic, al-Ittihād al-Lubnānī lil-Talaba al-Muslimīn (the Lebanese Union of Muslim Students).

Al-Ittihād was started in 1974.[50] Its headquarters were at al-Ghubayrī, one of the main communities in Beirut's southern suburbs. Grouping together practising Shiite students, it aimed to take part in the Islamic renewal that had started, according to one of its founders, "with the return from Najaf of a certain number of religious figures, like Muhammad Husayn Fadlallāh or Muhammad Mahdī Shamseddīn and the arrival in Lebanon of Mūsā al-Sadr".[51] With less than a dozen members initially, it worked to "spread the Islamic culture" in university circles, and also in high schools. It gradually attracted young regulars from religious centres and mosques. Its activities were purely cultural, centred on the study and discussion of religious texts:

> The thoughts of certain ulema—*marja*ʿs, like Bāqir al-Sadr—were taught from their books. Each person in turn was assigned to read up on a subject, prepare it, and summarize a book.[52]

Next came the creation of cultural committees (*lijān thaqāfiyya*), which were attached to mosques and "taught *fiqh* (Islamic jurisprudence), called the people from the neighbourhood to come listen to a lecture by a sheikh on certain days, offered courses in *tajwīd* (reading psalms from the Qur'an) and learning the Qur'an".[53]

In 1976 al-Ittihād acquired a magazine, *al-Muntalaq* (the Starting Point), which described itself as an "independent Islamic magazine" of "meagre resources."[54] It carried useful information on questions of interest to the association at the time. Between 1976 and the 1982 Israeli invasion it remained purely religious in nature; its commentary was reserved for subjects touching on dogmatic debate and current Shiite clerical events, starting with the assassinations of the religious in Lebanon and the Middle East and, more sparsely, the rest of the world. It dealt extensively with the Iranian Revolution, the disappearance of Mūsā al-Sadr, and the execution of Muhammad Bāqir al-Sadr.[55] It reported on the celebrations organized for Shiite religious holidays and the discourses of men of religion. Finally, it chronicled the regular activities of al-Ittihād and the various neighbourhood Islamic, student, and women's associations: religious ceremonies, tutoring courses, welcoming of clerical delegations, and the dispatch of representatives to international conferences.

On the political level, al-Ittihād was one of the action vehicles of al-Daʿwa. After the return of Shamseddīn and Fadlallāh to Lebanon, it had actually developed a branch in the country that operated clandestinely, essentially to protect itself from the Iraqi Baath, which was by then also established in the Country of Cedars.[56] In practice, al-Ittihād was close to Mūsā al-Sadr and Harakat al-Mahrūmīn; some of its members actively participated in the movement's activities and took part in its constitutional congress. The Iranian Revolution caused great enthusiasm in the association, which adhered closely to Mūsā al-Sadr's philosophy, and then Shamseddīn's (i.e. generally to AMAL's), before the 1982 Israeli invasion led some of its members to make other, more revolutionary choices.

A year of three major events: 1978

Three events in 1978 set off a profound change in the militant Lebanese Shiite scene. In March, Tel Aviv launched Operation Litani, and Israeli tanks invaded Lebanon for the first time. At the end of August, Mūsā al-Sadr "disappeared". In December the Shah of Iran gave up power to his council, presided over by the liberal opposition's Shapur Bakhtiar.

The fallout from al-Sadr's disappearance

Following the disappearance of Mūsā al-Sadr, the management of SSC's affairs devolved to Sheikh Muhammad Mahdī Shamseddīn.[57] A Lebanese born in Najaf in 1936, he studied religion under Muhammad Husayn Fadlallāh and Muhammad Bāqir al-Sadr.[58] He returned to Lebanon in 1969, three years after Fadlallāh. Close to al-Daʿwa, he attempted to distance the Shiite community from leftist circles and militant communism. He then founded his own cultural association, al-Jamʿiyya al-Khayriyya al-Thaqāfiyya (the Cultural and Charitable Association), with its first seat in Nabʿa. In 1975 he was nominated as delegate to the SSC. He joined AMAL before al-Sadr's disappearance, but left the movement in 1983, after a disagreement with its leadership about the Shiite position on the Israeli presence in Lebanon.[59] His perspective on the Lebanese political system and the regime would remain faithful to that of al-Sadr. He became an advocate for intercommunitarian coexistence and refrained from attacking sectarianism, preferring to reform the sectarian quotas rather than calling for their abolition. In his view, a complete overhaul of the system was a long-term goal. Between 1979 and the mid-1980s he supported the Iranian Revolution and was keen on maintaining good relations with the new regime in Tehran. However, even while defending Islamist regimes, he insisted that they should only exist in countries with very large Muslim majorities. He stressed that the Shiites of his country were Lebanese, and must not consider themselves as holding any other nationality. He also called on

> all Twelver Shiites of all countries and of all societies to assimilate with their respective countries and societies and not to keep apart from others, for the essential principle is that of Islam and the unity of the *ummah*.[60]

In other words, he rejected the notion of the Shiites as a "minority"; he insisted that they must not lay claim to anything as uniquely due them, even when subjected to certain injustices. It follows that the SSC under his leadership featured a pronounced legalism and represented a Shiite position hostile to any hint of revolution, holding the view that the problem of the Israeli occupation of South Lebanon was strictly for the Lebanese authorities to solve.

With Mūsā al-Sadr gone and Shamseddīn turning his back on protest Shiism, Muhammad Husayn Fadlallāh became the de facto leading Shiite cleric in Beirut. In the South, no one could overshadow him; Mughniyyeh, his only potential rival, had died in 1979. In the Bekaa, the clerical circles, insignificant until 1978, experienced a strong militant renewal at the end of the decade with the return of ʿAbbās al-Mūsawī from Iraq and Subhī al-Tufaylī from Iran; but al-Tufaylī was discreet in his activities and al-Mūsawī, younger than Fadlallāh, had no intention of rivalling the "master", preferring to concentrate his efforts on the Bekaa countryside. Thus, Fadlallāh appeared to head up the Shiite protest movements in Beirut. He and Shamseddīn appeared as the authors of most of the articles in the religious magazines. His were the most sought after for their policy soundness and their action-oriented vision. His mosque at Bīr al-ʿAbed became the place most visited for prayers by the capital's Shiite Islamic militants. His visibility was enhanced by his aspirations for the *marjaʿiyya*, which motivated him to multiply his interventions, conferences, and public appearances. This high degree of visibility certainly explains why many have seen in him the "head of Hezbollah", or at least its spiritual guide. Indeed, some of the Beirut militants who would later join the party or the IRL gathered around him, starting with those who came out of the neighbourhood religious associations or al-Ittihād.[61] However, despite his contact with the Iraqi branch of al-Daʿwa and his public support of the Iranian Revolution until the mid-1980s in the service of ambitions that reached beyond the limits of Lebanon's Shiite community, he would steadfastly refuse to let himself be locked in a partisan straitjacket and never took part in Hezbollah.

The Iranian Revolution and the Israeli invasion

The fall of the Shah's regime and the proclamation of the Islamic Republic two months after Ayatollah Khomeini's return to Iran in 1979 gave rise in Lebanon to several Shiite currents favourably inclined towards the new Iranian regime. Two different major tendencies crystallized around different readings of the events. The first interpreted the Revolution's success above all as an anti-imperialist, anti-American one, as a liberation that finally allowed an oppressed people to take its destiny into its own hands again. This was all the more exciting for having been achieved by Shiites, and it put a symbolic end to the "curse" that, until then, had tainted the Shiite relationship to power with oppression and illegitimacy. Nevertheless, even as it saluted the virtues of an Islamic regime, this initial tendency was always circumspect with regard to the question of importing it to Lebanon. The second reading, more religious, more Islamist, and more revolutionary, chalked up the success of the rebellion against the Shah as a victory of Islam over a regime allied to the West and to Israel. This grouping therefore was to make the establishment of an Islamic republic in Lebanon its top priority.

Al-Ittihād: patience rather than resistance

When the news of the Shah's fall reached Beirut, the capital's Shiite religious militants celebrated the event by organizing a great demonstration:

> In 1978 the mosque committees and al-Ittihād held a meeting and afterwards organized a great demonstration to acclaim the Revolution, even before its final victory. The committees took the occasion to rename themselves al-Lijān al-Musānida lil-Thawra al-Islāmiyya (Committees in Support of the Islamic Revolution). Among the militants was Sheikh Ahmad al-Zayn—a Sunni *qādī* from Sidon—Sheikh Rāghib Harb, and Sheikh Zuhayr Kanj from al-Shiyyāh.[62] There was also no shortage of participants from al-Ghubayrī, [and] from al-Shiyyāh. AMAL and al-Ittihād also took part.[63]

Nevertheless, al-Ittihād refrained from calling for the installation in Lebanon of a regime like that taking over Tehran. Over the next few years the association remained loyal to Shamseddīn and Fadlallāh, and kept to the AMAL line, as it had always done before.[64] In a telling sign, *al-Muntalaq* seemed little concerned with the questions of *jihād* against Israel. Until 1982 the Palestinian cause and the fight against Tel Aviv had rarely been invoked, and then only in passing. The 1978 Israeli incursion was only mentioned in the August–September issue (the incursion ended in June), and then merely by reference to another religious publication that dealt with the subject. In this issue, *al-Muntalaq* mused that it would be desirable to achieve "a little of what is owed to this Islamic land"; the images, however, that it published did not illustrate the Israeli depredations in South Lebanon, but the "Muslim tragedy" in Burma. There was no mention of any potential duty to resist, no commentary on Zionism to be found anywhere. Israel was barely reproached for "spreading the *fitna* (dissension) among the Palestinian Muslims and Muslims of Jabal ʿĀmil":[65] 'Jabal ʿĀmil, qadruhu an yasbur' (Jabal ʿĀmil has to grit its teeth and bear it), the editor-in-chief contented himself with writing.[66] Eventual allusions to *jihād* related to the Iranian Revolution or support of the Afghan resistance, and, in the summer of 1981, the month of Ramadan was declared the "month of *sumūd*", that is, of passive resistance. When it did evoke the Israeli shelling of South Lebanon, *al-Muntalaq* put the stress on quoting ʿAbdel-Amīr Qabalān, a respected member of the SSC, calling for "everyone to abide by the ceasefires", and Shamseddīn, who placed the onus for declaring war against Israel on a "union of Arab countries".[67] It is thus impossible to say that al-Ittihād was following a logic of active resistance before 1982.

The "Islamic Movement": standard-bearer for Shiite Islamism in Lebanon

Sādiq al-Mūsawī, grandson of the Ayatollah Sayyid ʿAbdallāh al-Shirāzī,[68] was among the Iranian clerics fleeing persecution by the Shah's regime who took refuge in Lebanon from the second half of the 1970s. His first sojourn in the Land of Cedars, however, dated from 1970.[69] Before the victory of the Revolution he had published some writings that already featured a vocabulary originating in dissident Iranian circles.[70] He took a leading role in a small network of ulema that issued its communiques under the name ʿUlamāʾ al-Dīn al-Munādilūn fī Lubnān (the Ulema Fighting in Lebanon),[71] modelled, by all appearances, on Jamʿiyyat al-ʿUlamāʾ al-Munādilīn al-Irāniyyīn fī Lubnān (Association of Iranian Ulema Fighting in Lebanon). In 1983 the movement changed its name permanently to al-Haraka al-Islāmiyya (the Islamic Movement).[72]

There are indications that, rather than being a disciple of Khomeini, Sādiq al-Mūsawī was an adept of Ayatollah Hussein Ali Montazeri. His activism was distinct from that of the al-Ittihād circle:[73] his hostility towards the Maronite regime and lack of reservations about establishing an Islamic regime in Lebanon showed his position to be clearly revolutionary. In this, he found fellow travellers in Muhammad ʿAlī al-Jūzū, the mufti of Mount Lebanon,[74] and, in particular, Saʿīd Shaʿbān, leader of Harakat al-Tawhīd al-Islāmiyya (Movement for Islamic Unity) in Tripoli. The two men, despite being Sunnis, were also stirred by the Revolution, and called for an Islamic regime in Lebanon. In al-Mūsawī's eyes the Iranian Revolution constituted a political victory for Islam. The linkages between the old Iranian regime and Western countries (led by the United States and Israel) were naturally pointed up in sharp relief, but his satisfaction with the advent of an Islamic regime in Iran resulted above all from relief at seeing a Muslim population liberated from living under a non-Muslim authority.

Communications from al-Haraka al-Islāmiyya rapidly became routinized until the (quasi-) disappearance of Sādiq al-Mūsawī from the Lebanese politico-religious scene at the close of the 1980s. They included tracts, posters and news commentary reacting to current events, interventions by the political class or articles appearing in daily newspapers. The formulas employed in these communication vehicles were rapidly honed to the point where they became a signature. The movement remained limited in scope and lacked in-house publications or a media apparatus, but was well-known enough on the Lebanese socio-political scene to see its communiqués published regularly and simultaneously in *al-Nahār* and *al-Safir*, the country's two leading daily newspapers.[75]

While the circles in which Hezbollah and al-Haraka al-Islāmiyya would soon develop did share a hostile attitude to political confessionalism and adopted an ideological perspective that an Islamic regime was the best of all worlds, they did not share the same priorities. Until the Israeli invasion of 1982, the proto-Hezbollah circles in Beirut were content to work for a grass-roots Islamic renewal, seeking to revive a sensibility and religious practice in society, far from even a hint of rebellion against the Lebanese regime. Their mobilization had a spiritual essence, and their activities were mainly cultural. In the Bekaa, ʿAbbās al-Mūsawī and his disciples preached a military mobilization of their audiences against the Israeli occupation starting in 1978. In contrast, the problem of active resistance to the Israeli army was secondary among al-Haraka al-Islāmiyya's preoccupations. Instead, it focused on mobilizing Lebanon's Muslims, Shiites as well as Sunni, for an eventual overthrow of "the Zionist and Crusader Maronite regime".[76] The "crimes" recited in its communiqués were not those committed by Tel Aviv's troops in the South, but rather those perpetrated by the Christian Kataeb and Lebanese Forces against "Muslims" (Lebanese or Palestinian). It was not about getting rid of the Israeli occupier, but about disposing of all those who committed the massacres at "Nabʿa, Sinn el-Fīl, Dekwāneh, and Tall al-Zaʿtar" against the "sons of Islam". Consequently, the "beasts to be slain" were not Yitzhak Shamir or Ariel Sharon but Camille Chamoun and Amin Gemayel.[77] The communiqués routinely closed their assertions or commentaries with an appeal to "let the banner of Islam fly over the cherished Lebanese soil".[78] The slogan was "No to the regime of the Maronite minority, yes to the Islamic Republic".[79] The flyers and posters frequently contained quotes from Ayatollah Khomeini, the selection revealing al-Haraka's priorities: "The Lebanese regime is illegitimate and criminal"[80] and "Whosoever follows Islam must demand [the establishment of] the Islamic Republic". Also prominently featured, almost routinely, were quotes from Hussein Ali Montazeri, once again calling for battle, not against Israel but against the Lebanese regime. While the proto-Hezbollah circles (notably around Muhammad Husayn Fadlallāh) insisted, as Hezbollah later would also, that they "would never impose an Islamic regime on the Lebanese by force", al-Haraka al-Islāmiyya did not shrink from explicitly threatening the "Maronite regime".[81] Al-Mūsawī hence spoke of imposing an Islamic republic on everyone in Lebanon, including the Christians. This question of how to relate to the political system that al-Haraka al-Islāmiyya refused categorically to recognize as legitimate and with which it refused to negotiate appears to be one of the reasons why al-Haraka would not join Hezbollah on its creation, just as it explains Sādiq al-Mūsawī's animus towards the party in 1992, when it agreed to participate in the first post-war parliamentary elections.[82]

First storms in AMAL

Following al-Sadr's disappearance, AMAL chose a new president in the person of Hussein al-Husseini, an MP from the Bekaa who only remained in his post for a short time. When he resigned in 1980 he was replaced by Nabih Berri, originally from the South and a lawyer by profession. The Movement then passed through a difficult phase. The loss of a guiding light such as al-Sadr cleared the way for a competition between two currents, one religious and the other secular. The former, excited by the Iranian Revolution, hoped that AMAL would choose an explicitly Islamic direction, adopting a *marjaʿiyya* who would continue in al-Sadr's footsteps. The latter essentially wanted a communitarian movement, one that, while not averse to adopting a certain religious veneer to keep the believers in the organization, did not want to surrender decision making to the clerics.[83]

With these internal undercurrents swirling, the Movement held its fourth congress in 1981. The religious faction decided to demand that AMAL pledge its allegiance to the principle of *wilāyat al-faqīh* on the spot, and to threaten a defection en masse if this met with a refusal. More precisely, the project would involve sending a delegation to Tehran to ask Khomeini to designate his representative to AMAL, thus giving legitimacy to the Movement's decisions and directions. In the face of a potential schism, a compromise was found just ahead of the session. The religious faction refrained from raising its demands during the meetings, but a consultative mission was given permission to travel to Iran after the new leadership's election.[84] In addition, if Nabih Berri were to retain the top post, the vice presidency would go to someone representing the religious side, namely, Husayn al-Mūsawī.[85] The split was avoided, but not for long.

In Baalbek: the return of Hezbollah's future founders

In fact, 1978 turned out to be a pivotal year in Lebanese Shiite history because it saw the return to Lebanon of two clerics who would soon be instrumental in founding the IRL and Hezbollah. The first, Subhī al-Tufaylī, was born in 1948 in Brītāl, a village situated a few kilometres south-east of the town of Baalbek in the northern Bekaa.[86] His father, ʿAlī al-Tufaylī, had intended him to join the military. The youngest of eleven children (three girls and eight boys), the young Subhī nursed other ambitions. In 1965, at just seventeen years of age, he left the Bekaa to study religion at the Najaf *hawza*, where he was taught by Muhammad Bāqir al-Sadr. His years in Iraq gave him his start in politics when he joined al-Daʿwa. His fervour earned him a death sentence from the Iraqi regime in 1974, leading to his precipitate return to Lebanon. He took an interest in elections for the SSC organized in 1975, and he drew up a slate of candidates to oppose the faction led by Mūsā al-Sadr. When the vote went against him, he resumed his religious studies the following year, this time at the *hawza* in Qom in Iran, where he studied the *Khārij*[87] with Sayyid Kādhim al-Hā'irī. During his studies, he became involved in politics again; joining the ranks of the Iranian opposition, he participated in demonstrations against the Shah's regime and on several occasions escaped counter-attacks by the security forces.

In March 1978 the Israeli army launched Operation Litani, an invasion of South Lebanon. Subhī al-Tufaylī would later say that the news "affected him deeply".[88] He asked himself what means of action were within his reach and, given his wealth of contacts in Iranian clerical circles, supported by a small group of Lebanese ulema, he solicited the support of several *marja*ʿs, including al-Kalabīkānī, al-Najafī, and Sharīʿatmadārī. His efforts are said to have borne fruit in that one of the three *marja*ʿs agreed to issue a *fatwā* for killing Jews in Tehran in reprisal if the Israeli occupation was expanded.[89]

During 1978 al-Tufaylī made several trips to Lebanon to rouse the Shiite community there in support of the Revolution. Following a revamping of the Lebanese branch of al-Daʿwa, he is said to have become its president.[90] He returned to the country for good in 1979, and that year participated in the creation of Tajammuʿ al-ʿUlamā' al-Muslimīn fīl-Biqāʿ (Association of Muslim Ulema of the Bekaa), a group of Shiite ulema with roots in the Baalbek–al-Hermel region. Corresponding groups were then set up in the two other big Shiite areas in Lebanon: in the South, Hay'at ʿUlamā' Jabal ʿĀmil (Committee of Ulema of Jabal ʿĀmil),[91] presided over by Sheikh ʿAfīf al-Nābulsī; and al-Liqā' al-ʿUlamā'ī—Hay'at ʿUlamā' Bayrūt (Meeting of Clerics—the Committee of Beirut Ulema) in the capital. The Tajammuʿ al-ʿUlamā' al-Muslimīn fīl-Biqāʿ, presided over by al-Tufaylī, placed itself under the authority of *wilāyat al-faqīh*. Its clerics launched a conscientization campaign aimed at the Shiite public at large by preaching (*tablīgh*) and directing (*irshād*), with the goal of bringing about an "Islamic awakening of society".[92] Ultimately, the movement would have at least seventy members, spread across the entire Baalbek–al-Hermel area.[93] Initially close to the SSC, it distanced itself from that body to continue endorsing the Iranian Revolution, which the SSC's leadership refrained from doing.

In the late 1970s al-Tufaylī joined a small committee tasked with forging links between the different Lebanese Shiite Islamic currents of the time.[94] Operating under Iranian supervision, this working group had three members: Subhī al-Tufaylī, Husayn al-Mūsawī, number 2 in AMAL's leadership, and the Iranian ambassador to Syria. They set about monitoring the general affairs of the Islamic movements throughout Lebanon. Al-Tufaylī participated in the formation of Islamic committees (*lijān islāmiyya*) based in Beirut and placed under the influence of al-Daʿwa-Lebanon. Their mission, among other aims, was ensuring media and cultural support for the ulema in Lebanon under threat from the Iraqi regime.[95] At this time he organized a series of demonstrations in support of the victory of Khomeini's Revolution, with the first one taking place at the end of 1978 in the southern suburbs of Beirut. It was thus al-Tufaylī, not Fadlallāh, who headed up the pro-Iranian Lebanese networks from which the members of Hezbollah would soon emerge.

The second founding father of the future IRL was Sayyid ʿAbbās al-Mūsawī, born in 1952 in the village of al-Nabī Shīt, about a dozen kilometres south-east of Baalbek.[96] According to Sheikh Muhammad Khātūn, his long-time friend and biographer, his birth was marked by a heavenly sign: the youngest daughter of the *imām* Hussein supposedly visited al-Mūsawī's mother in a dream while she was carrying him to announce that she would bear a boy whom she was to name ʿAbbās.[97]

Young al-Mūsawī spent his first years in al-Nabī Shīt. His parents were not well off; there were few jobs to be had in the village and the Mūsawīs had no land to farm. The father, Abū Husayn, had worked in construction since his teens; finding that his earnings were not enough to raise his children, he left for Kuwait in search of more lucrative work. At first, his wife and children remained in the village. In 1958 they joined him in Kuwait, but a year later the family returned to Lebanon permanently, settling in the southern suburbs of the capital, in the al-Shiyyāh quarter.

During his Beirut years ʿAbbās al-Mūsawī attended al-Sāhil school, where, good student that he was, he earned his certificate. As a teenager he developed an interest in the Palestinian question, and the defeat of the Arabs in 1967 is said to have affected him profoundly. At the same time, Palestinian military operations multiplied; Khalīl ʿIzzeddīn, a Lebanese fighter, was killed at the battle of Tallat al-Arbaʿīn (South Lebanon) in 1968. ʿAbbās al-Mūsawī, still a teenager, attended the public funeral organized to mark the occasion, and then embarked on a militant course focused on the fight against Israel. He decided to undergo military training, which, at the time, was available in Damascus. He set out, with a friend, for the Syrian capital, but the two youths had no papers, and were turned back at the border. They returned to Beirut, but, undeterred, al-Mūsawī decided to find another way through. Without telling his parents, he set out for Damascus on foot, crossing the border in a sparsely populated area, and hitch-hiking through Syria to a training camp in the capital. But, injured during training, he was soon repatriated by his parents, who had come looking for him.

Khātūn reports that "during his convalescence, ʿAbbās al-Mūsawī prayed a great deal". Barely recovered, the teenager asked his father to help him go to the mosque of al-Shiyyāh, so that he could pray behind Sheikh Muhammad al-Qubaysī with whom "he would have many discussions". At that time, Mūsā al-Sadr used to frequent the al-Shiyyāh quarter on regular visits to one of Abū Husayn al-Mūsawī's close relatives. Via his father, the teen let al-Sadr know that he wished to meet him and take some courses in religion with him. Mūsā al-Sadr agreed to have the young man take an entrance examination. He passed, and al-Mūsawī left to take a place by his master's side in Tyre. However, his stay there would not be long. It was al-Sadr in fact who advised him to leave for Najaf, "Tyre not being suitable for the final stage of a religious education worthy of the name". The cleric wrote to his Iraqi cousin and brother-in-law, Ayatollah Muhammad Bāqir al-Sadr, recommending his young protégé.

ʿAbbās al-Mūsawī therefore left for Iraq in 1969, at the age of seventeen. There he became acquainted with, among others, Rāghib Harb, a compatriot with whom he would work several years later in the struggle against the Israeli occupation. He became close to Bāqir al-Sadr, and remained in Najaf for three years without re-entering Lebanon, "preferring to use his vacations for getting through his course of study faster". In 1973 he returned to the country for the first time, and immediately began preaching to the young people of al-Nabī Shīt, and then in neighbouring villages. His vision was clear: create a group of ulema who would share a "posture of resistance against the oppressors". To accomplish this, his strategy would be to continue his studies in Najaf, while passing the month of Muharram in Lebanon every year, preaching to his young followers.

This "posture of resistance" at that time related to the occupation of Palestine and then, starting from 1978, to the Israeli invasion of Lebanon. But it also meant standing up to the authoritarian political regimes into which the young al-Mūsawī gained insight during the Najaf years, and which affected him directly and personally. For example, the Iraqi regime executed several Najaf ulema in 1974, and some clerics of Iranian origin were expelled without warning. Late 1977 was very difficult for the students at the *hawza*, starting with the Lebanese, many of whom were arrested and interrogated, variously suspected of being members of al-Daʿwa, AMAL, or a pro-Syrian Baath party. While al-Mūsawī was back in Lebanon for a time he learnt that the situation in Najaf was deteriorating, and that his name was on a list of people wanted by Baghdad. He immediately planned to leave for Iraq to support Bāqir al-Sadr, but the master ordered him to stay in Lebanon "as long as the situation does not improve". Far from improving, however, the situation deteriorated yet further, and all the Lebanese students still in Iraq returned home in the course of 1978. Five or six of them clustered around al-Mūsawī in Baalbek and resumed their religious studies under his direction. In keeping with the practice of Shiite religious education, al-Mūsawī, at the end of his third and last round of studies, was allowed, in conformity with Shiite religious tradition, to instruct less-advanced students in courses in the lower rounds. Lacking the funds to establish a *hawza*, al-Mūsawī and his students rented a two-room apartment in town on a two-month basis. This school, soon known as al-Mahdī al-Muntadhar school, moved several times before finally settling into an apartment building next to the Imām ʿAlī Mosque in the centre of town. Muhammad Husayn Fadlallāh, based in Beirut, would cover part of the school's expenses and grant some scholarships to students.[98]

Between 1978 and 1982 al-Mūsawī concentrated his energies on religious teaching. He trained his disciples in both religious matters and in oratorical arts and, beginning in 1980, sent them into local villages, "especially to those that have never seen a man of religion". The training he imparted to his students conformed to his particular concept of the role of the *ʿālim* (the cleric). According to him,

> since the forces of Arrogance were preparing to attack, we need to be ready to repel them; the [Iranian] Revolution has re-established the balance and created a solid base

> from which [it became possible to] fight the worldwide Arrogance and its local imitator, Israel.[99]

In other words, the Islam that he preached was above all an Islam of resistance; he was preparing the young ulema that he trained to be "soldiers on all fronts", a vanguard, role models on all levels—including the military. For this reason, al-Mūsawī required his students to go through military training in the Bekaa training camps. The training was modest in scope, certainly, but even if most of these youths ultimately never saw battle against Israeli forces, it created a new type of Shiite cleric with a great mobilizing impact: *al-ʿālim al-mujāhid* (the cleric–fighter).

By criss-crossing the Bekaa from north to south with impassioned calls to armed resistance, between 1978 and 1982 al-Mūsawī and his students unknowingly put in place a fledgling network of the mobilized that would soon constitute the first manpower of the IRL.

2

HEZBOLLAH, CARRYING ON THE ISLAMIC RESISTANCE IN LEBANON

CRYSTALLIZATION OF A NEW MILITANT STRUCTURE

On the eve of the Israeli invasion of June 1982, the world of militant Shiism was thus splintered into diverse groups with Communist ties, nationalist Arab parties, AMAL, al-Daʿwa and its satellite groups, and neighbourhood religious associations generally centred on a cleric or a mosque (al-Ittihād, al-Shabāb al-Mu'min, and Islamic committees). Many of these affiliations, moreover, intersected, with AMAL and Harakat al-Mahrūmīn welcoming militants from all backgrounds and orientations. Until then, the principal line of differentiation between the different groups had been between the supporters of the secular and religious options. But the 1982 Israeli invasion provoked a redistribution of militant affiliations by inserting a new line of separation, with activists henceforward having to choose between resisting the occupier and accepting a *modus vivendi* with it. Once again, things would develop in different ways in the capital and the Baalbek region—but also in the South.

The 1982 invasion: linking of resistance elements and networks

June 1982: Tel Aviv's troops enter Beirut[1]

On 11 March 1978 a PLO commando infiltrated Israel from Lebanon and hijacked a bus near Tel Aviv, killing thirty-seven Israelis. Three days later the Menachem Begin government launched Operation Litani, with the objective of occupying a part of Lebanon's border region to stop Palestinian attacks staged from there. The Israeli army that entered the Lebanese side therefore set up a "security zone" extending from 10 to 25 kilometres into the southern part of the country and covering approximately 10 per cent of Lebanon's territory, home to nearly 200,000 people at the time.[2] The operation resulted in more than a thousand, mostly civilian, dead[3] and displaced 250,000 people, the great majority of whom were Shiites. On 19 March the United Nations Security Council (UNSC) passed Resolution 425 calling on Israel to withdraw and creating the United Nations Interim Force in Lebanon (UNIFIL), an international force with a mandate to "help restore the Lebanese government's authority in this part of the country". Tel Aviv's forces did not withdraw until 13 June, a full three months later. Defying the UNSC, they did not turn the "security zone" over to UNIFIL, but rather to a militia of Lebanese collaborators paid and equipped by Israel. At the time, it was named the Army of Saad Haddad after its leader, a former commander of the Lebanese army who had defected.

Four years later Menachem Begin decided to break the Palestinian Resistance operating from South Lebanon once and for all, which, in his view, called for a military operation ranging as far as Beirut. Also gaining ground within the Israeli General Staff was the idea of establishing a Christian state in the Country of Cedars to be headed by the chief of the Lebanese Forces, Bashir Gemayel, with whom they would sign a peace treaty. On 10 May the Israeli government made it official by approving military action in principle against the Palestinian bases in Lebanon. Alexander Haig, the American secretary of state, gave his backing on 25 May, declaring that an invasion would be accepted by world public opinion if there was "undisputable aggression". On 3 June three fighters from the Palestinian Abu Nidal[4] group attempted to assassinate Shlomo Argov, the Israeli ambassador in London; the Israeli government immediately invoked the attack as a *casus belli* for launching the offensive. Designated Operation Snowball, but better known in the media as "Peace in Galilee", it kicked off on 6 June 1982. The Israeli troops, 60,000 strong, fanned out across Lebanon, with artillery and naval support. Locales in the South were massively bombarded. Starting the next day, Beaufort, the stronghold of the Palestinian fighters, as well as Tyre, Nabatiyeh, and Hasbaya, fell into Israeli hands. The same day, the Druze Shuf in Mount Lebanon also surrendered.

On 9 and 10 June Israeli troops arrived in Beirut. They reached the outskirts of the airport in Khaldeh (the southern gateway to the city) and bombarded the capital's southern suburbs. On the 13th they reached Baabda, the presidential seat, and stationed themselves in East Beirut, the stronghold of the Christian militias. Together, they completely encircled (mostly Muslim) West Beirut. However, they failed to overcome the resistance put up there by Palestinian fighters and their Lebanese allies, and a siege commenced. The Israeli army subjected the area to intensive bombardments from land, air, and sea. At the start of July water and electricity to West Beirut were shut off; the Lebanese Forces supported the Israelis in imposing a complete food blockade that cut off all resupply. On 29 July the PLO gave up and announced its readiness to evacuate Beirut without military or political *quid quo pro*. The Israeli forces responded by continuing their assault, and made several attempts to land on the city's waterfront. When they were repeatedly repulsed by the besieged, they launched a general offensive on 4 August under a hail of shells. On 7 August the Palestinian forces signed the Israeli–American agreement submitted to them by Washington's envoy, Philip Habib, providing for the evacuation of their fighters. But even then the Israeli attacks did not cease: on 10 August a second general offensive was attempted, but once again did not succeed. On 17 August 500 civilians were killed. President Ronald Reagan increased the pressure on the Israelis, and they finally accepted the Habib Plan two days later. The Palestinian combatants evacuated to various Arab countries, including Tunisia and Syria between 21 August and 3 September under the protection of an international peacekeeping force made up of American, French, and Italian troop contingents. More than 12,500 Palestinians and 2,000 Syrian soldiers pulled out of Lebanon.[5]

Despite the departure of the PLO combatants and of their leader, Yasser Arafat, the Israeli troops stayed in position in the South, around Beirut, and in Mount Lebanon. On 23 August the Kataeb, arrogating the Israeli victory to themselves, tracked down the members of the Lebanese parliament and spirited them off to the Fayyadiyeh military base under military escort. There, surrounded by Tel Aviv's tanks, the relocated parliament elected Bashir Gemayel as president of the Republic. He never had a chance to assume his post, however: he was assassinated on 14 September, a mere three weeks later, in an attack that destroyed the apartment building in which he was meeting with leaders of his party.[6] The Israeli army then invaded West Beirut,[7] and turned over control of the Palestinian camps there to the Kataeb. A group led by Elie Hobeika, the intelligence chief of the Lebanese Forces, avenged Gemayel's assassination by carrying out a three-day massacre on 16, 17, and 18 September in the refugee camps of Sabra and Shatila, with Israel's complicity.[8] This caused a great stir in Tel Aviv afterwards. Amin Gemayel, Bashir's older brother, was elected president a week after the assassination, ushering in a truce among the Lebanese parties. In the ensuing days the Israeli army pulled out of West Beirut, Khaldeh airport and the port, but continued to occupy a large part of Lebanon.

The toll exacted by the invasion has been difficult to establish with any certainty. The UN would estimate later that the invasion and siege of Beirut resulted in 6,775 deaths and nearly 30,000 injured on the Lebanese side, with 80 per cent of the victims being civilians.[9] Lebanese authorities, after adding up numbers from the Red Cross, the police and the hospitals, gave the number of Lebanese, Palestinian, and Syrian dead as 17,825, and confirmed the number of injured at 30,000.[10] Of the 17,825, nearly 10,000 were non-Lebanese combatants (Palestinian and Syrian); of the nearly 7,825 dead civilians, 5,515 died in the Beirut area. With time, these figures were revised, however: *The Christian Science Monitor*, in October 1982, gave a total of 48,000 victims, both dead and wounded, but estimated the number of dead in Beirut at 2,000.[11] The Associated Press, in 1991, cited the largest and generally accepted number of 20,000 Lebanese and Palestinian dead, with the majority being civilians.[12] On the Israeli side, the Defence Ministry gave figures of 349 killed and 2,127 wounded, but, according to the Israeli press, the numbers were more likely to be 600 dead and 3,500 wounded, of whom a reported 2,000 were disabled.[13]

The Lebanese Council for Development and Reconstruction (CDR) estimated the losses in key sectors of the economy at $1.9 billion. The housing sector alone accounted for 45 per cent of the total damages (12,000 dwelling units were severely damaged or demolished). Industrial production dropped to 70 per cent of its 1981 level, and a third of the sector's wage earners lost their jobs. Agricultural losses amounted to $50 million, South Lebanon suffering the most, losing more than 75 per cent of average production.[14] The losses in the education sector reached $85 million, in the health sector $72 million; the electricity grid sustained damages of $75 million and the communications sector $62 million.[15] To sum up, the second invasion of Lebanon by its neighbour from the south did a great deal to worsen the socio-economic dysfunction that confronted the country as its internal political life continued to deteriorate.

In Beirut: splits in AMAL and ad hoc resistance

On 22 and 23 May 1982, Iran, at war with Iraq for the previous two years, succeeded in retaking Khorramshahr, the major Iranian port that had been in enemy hands since the beginning of the conflict. In the light of this victory, Mahdī Hāshimī, a close friend of Muhammad Montazeri and head of the Pasdaran's Unit of Liberation Movements,[16] organized an international congress in the Iranian capital for early June.[17] When Israeli troops crossed into Lebanon on 6 June, a large number of prominent Lebanese Shiites were therefore in Tehran, among them Subhī al-Tufaylī and ʿAbbās al-Mūsawī. When the invasion was announced, both wanted to return immediately, and they compiled a list of their countrymen also desiring to return home as soon as possible.[18] While their Iranian hosts assured them of support, they also cautioned against giving in to defeatism. An emergency meeting was arranged with Ali Shamkhani, the vice-commander of Pasdaran, who urged resistance and discouraged any idea of betting on a negotiated solution, especially one under American auspices.[19]

When the Lebanese delegates to the congress finally returned to their country, they were plunged into a situation made all the more chaotic because the capital, and especially the Muslim quarters, were still under enemy bombardment. The invasion had serious repercussions for AMAL's internal affairs. The organization was crumbling, with some militants and cadres discreetly having headed south, where there was no action to speak of at the time. Some of the cadres even discussed the possibility of getting the "yellow card" that the occupier issued to collaborators and their relatives to facilitate passage through Israeli checkpoints.[20] The more the noose tightened around Beirut, the more fractious the mood within the Movement became. In June, Elias Sarkis, the Lebanese president, formed a Committee of National Salvation, composed of the five leaders of the country's major denominations, to negotiate with Philip Habib, the American emissary, and the Israeli government. Bashir Gemayel represented the Maronites and Walid Jumblatt the Druze. Nabih Berri triggered an outcry in Shiite circles when he agreed to represent their community on the committee.[21] This is how an old-time cadre of the Movement described what happened:

> An all-Shiite meeting was held in the home of ʿAbdel-Amīr Qabalān in Burj al-Barajneh [a southern suburb of Beirut] during the siege, bringing together Berri, Muhammad Mahdī Shamseddīn … ʿAbdel-Amīr Qabalān and some other AMAL cadres and members … The announced purpose of the meeting was to discuss the Shiite position in light of the latest events, particularly with regard to participating in the Committee of Salvation organized by Philip Habib with Amin Gemayel[22] as its president. President Berri presented Philip Habib's initiative … as a golden opportunity that offered the Shiites the possibility to insert themselves into the heart of the Lebanese equation that until now had rested solely on the two Maronite and Sunni pillars. Henceforth, there could be four pillars: Maronite, Sunni, Shiite, and Druze. Berri encouraged those present to serve on the Committee. Shamseddīn accepted, but with reservations. In the end, fewer than 20 percent were in favor. The others refused because it meant recognizing the Amin Gemayel regime and endorsing cohabitation with the occupier.[23]

Ignoring these reservations, Berri went on to participate in the Committee of National Salvation, causing AMAL to implode that July.[24] There was a dual split, ideological and geographical. Indeed, the discord was accompanied by a worsening of the traditional rivalry between Shiites of the Bekaa and those from the South. A first group, gathering around Husayn al-Mūsawī, the number two in the party, dissented and left both AMAL and Beirut. Moving back to the Bekaa, he set up AMAL al-Islāmiyya (Islamic AMAL). A second group, consisting mostly of cadres from Beirut, also split from AMAL, but, averse to exile in the back country with the old comrades, remained in the capital to start the "Committee of Beirut Cadres."

Abū Hishām: restoring the "true AMAL" in the Bekaa

Husayn al-Mūsawī, going by the name Abū Hishām[25] in Hezbollah circles and in the Baalbek region, was born in 1943 in the Bekaa village of al-Nabī Shīt, like his cousin ʿAbbās al-Mūsawī.[26] After finishing at the local primary school he entered middle school and then the Lyceum al-Kulliyya al-ʿĀmiliyya in West Beirut. Bachelor's degree in hand, he next enrolled at Beirut Arab University to study Arab literature. After graduating, he returned to Baalbek to teach Arabic in one of the town's public secondary schools. Discovering an interest in politics, he became an activist for AMAL, gradually moving up in its ranks, eventually heading up the executive committee and acting as party spokesman. His political career took an important turn in 1978, when he became head of the faction sympathizing with the Iranian Revolution, and decided to set AMAL on a more religious path after Mūsā al-Sadr's disappearance. With the situation of the leadership team presided over by Nabih Berri becoming more fragile, he was elected as the Movement's vice president in 1981.[27]

Following the Israeli invasion and Berri's participation in the Committee of National Salvation, Abū Hishām split officially from AMAL and moved to the Bekaa with his followers. On 16 August he announced the creation of AMAL al-Islāmiyya, from the Imām ʿAlī Mosque, which stands in the very centre of Baalbek. The new organization described itself not as a splinter group of AMAL, but as denouncing AMAL's members and instead seeking to embody a return to the original values that made up the AMAL ethos during the Mūsā al-Sadr years. In other words, AMAL al-Islāmiyya intended to be the "true" AMAL. Its charter reiterated that AMAL was originally set up as an "Islamic movement". AMAL al-Islāmiyya represented a return to this original path, presenting itself as "an Islamic ideological movement that adopts Islam as dogma, as principle, as perspective, and as criterion".[28] Its leadership declared collaboration with Israel "illegal", and, on that basis, condemned the leaders of AMAL who "have adopted the Israeli, American and Kataeb positions as theirs, who have participated in the Committee of Salvation", asserting that "what [Berri] has done is to betray the Movement, the *imām* al-Sadr, and the *ummah*". AMAL al-Islāmiyya also chose "to take the path of *wilāyat al-faqīh* and follow the directions of the Islamic Revolution's leadership", conceiving of itself as "a part of the Great Islamic World Revolution", and hence establishing a relationship with the Revolution "as part of the whole, or from the particular to the general". On the domestic stage, AMAL al-Islāmiyya was "neither sectarian nor localist" and its leadership described itself as "devoted to the unity of the Lebanese people, to cooperation between its communities and constituencies, and to the establishment of good relations between them based on respect and justice". In line with these ideas, it "rejects completely the candidacy of Bashir Gemayel for president of the Republic, for that would put Lebanon's destiny in the hands of an Israeli butcher with a Lebanese face". Three points therefore distinguished AMAL al-Islāmiyya from AMAL: its leadership intended to embody a movement of believers and practicants; it recognized the authority of *wilāyat al-faqīh*; and it chose the road of resistance to the occupation.

The Committee of Beirut Cadres and the battle of Khaldeh

In actuality, AMAL al-Islāmiyya remained handicapped by the regional origin of its leader. In spite of his ambition to attract members from all areas to his cause, the movement remained highly localized. AMAL's Beirut cadres, who also chose to walk out in 1982, started up a different entity, the Committee of Beirut Cadres. When Tel Aviv's forces reached the capital, it committed itself to the battle, supporting and receiving support from the Palestinian factions and the Lebanese National Resistance Front (LNRF), an ad hoc coalition of small resistance units mainly from communist circles.[29] The AMAL centre at Bīr al-ʿAbed, which the Committee managed to get possession of, the al-Imām al-Ridā Mosque, and the homes of several dissident cadres served as the primary venues for coordination meetings. There was also the AMAL headquarters at Hayy al-Sullum,[30] retaken with support rendered by militants from Laylakeh,[31] al-Ouzai,[32] Bīr al-ʿAbed, and Burj al-Barajneh. Among the Committee's comrades in arms who distinguished themselves in the fighting were several militants from Shiite circles in the capital: al-Ittihād, mosque committees, and the committee of the Muttaharī Library.[33] Their principal marshalling places were al-Ghubayrī, where al-Ittihād had its headquarters; al-Bastā,[34] with just over sixty young people, most of them under the age of twenty; Musaytbeh,[35] where at the local mosque Naʿīm Qāsim, then a chemistry professor who would later become Hezbollah's deputy secretary, encouraged men who were eager to join the fight. Among these Beirut resisters were Muhammad Raad, Muhammad Fneish, Muhammad al-Burjāwī, ʿAlī Daʿūn, ʿAbdallāh Qasīr, ʿAlī ʿAmmār, and many others who would rise to leadership positions in Hezbollah or represent it in the state apparatus years later.[36]

The battle of Khaldeh, at the southern approaches to Beirut, became the rallying point for Shiite resisters from various quarters of the capital. When the Israeli army reached this nerve centre of the city the fighters from Islamic circles split along two fronts, "Khaldeh/al-Laylakeh" and "Faculty of Sciences/Khaldeh triangle" where they fought alongside the LNRF, the Palestinian forces, and remnants of the Syrian army.[37] According to one fighter:

> The units at that time were not really organized properly; each group consisted of three or four individuals and carried out operations based mostly on personal initiative. ... The link between all these groups from the start was ideological, without any structure [for tying them together] or any special organization. These took shape after the invasion and the battle of Khaldeh. ... They also stationed night sentries, and everyone gave body and soul to the fight.[38]

In Baalbek: the birth of the IRL

The role of Iran

The 1960s and 1970s saw a great influx of Iranian opponents of the Shah's regime into Lebanon. They lived to the rhythm of the opposition's advances in Iran, but also of what was happening in their host country. When the Palestinian raids from South Lebanon into northern Israel began, they thus found themselves split between supporting Mūsā al-Sadr and AMAL on the one hand and the Palestinians on the other. Mustafā Shamrān and Ibrāhīm Yazdī, who would later occupy key posts in the Iranian Islamic regime, were friends with al-Sadr.[39] Yazdī had met al-Sadr while they were students at the university in Tehran. When al-Sadr happened to mention to Yazdī that he was looking for a director for his technical school in Tyre, Yazdī suggested Shamrān, who then moved to Lebanon in 1971. In parallel with his professional obligations, Shamrān once more took the path of ideological mobilization. He enrolled almost 150 "believing professors" from several South Lebanon villages, who came once a week to the school in Tyre to be taught "Islamic ideology" by Shamrān. Serving as the model for this effort were Muslim student associations whose development he had supervised in other countries.[40] He would have been active in similar fashion in Beirut, but the obstacles were "too great". Mūsā al-Sadr, Muhammad Husayn Fadlallāh, and Muhammad Mahdī Shamseddīn supported him in his efforts by holding several conferences at the school. A not-so-trivial fact: among the faithful attendees at these weekly meetings was a young AMAL cadre named Hassan Nasrallah.[41]

On the other hand, Ali-Akbar Mohtashami-Pur, a former student of Khomeini's, who arrived in Lebanon in 1972 from Najaf, was unhappy with al-Sadr's activities. His reservations dated back to 1970, when, on the death of Muhsin al-Hakīm, al-Sadr chose Abū al-Qāsim al-Khū'ī as *marja*ʿ instead of Khomeini. Shortly after arriving in Tyre in July, Mohtashami-Pur witnessed an Israeli attack on the town; he was shocked to realize that the local clerics blamed the Palestinian fighters. Unhappy with al-Sadr's quietist, legalist politics, he returned to Iraq and communicated his fears to Khomeini that South Lebanon's ulema were turning the population against the Palestinians. Two others in the Iranian opposition shared Mohtashami's sympathies for the Palestinian *fedayeen*: Muhammad Montazeri, son of the ayatollah Hussein Ali Montazeri, and Jalāleddīn Fārsī, who was close to Yasser Arafat.[42] These rivalries among pro- or anti-Palestinian, pro- or anti-AMAL Iranian revolutionaries were transferred to Tehran when the Revolution swept away the Shah's regime and the former exiles became senior officials in the new government. Yazdī became deputy prime minister in charge of revolutionary affairs and minister of foreign affairs; Shamrān had a role in setting up the Pasdaran[43] and then became minister of defence. At that stage the Revolution favoured AMAL; nearly 500 of its fighters signed up as volunteers in early 1979 to fight alongside the revolutionaries.[44] However, 1981 marked a turning point in Tehran's Lebanon policy. In quick succession, AMAL's principal sponsors inside the regime lost their positions: Shamrān died in June 1981 under mysterious circumstances and Montazeri was assassinated; Yazdī went over to the opposition. Relations with the PLO had already started to go downhill as a result of Arafat's refusal to condemn the 1980 Iraqi attack against Iran. Until then, Khomeini had adopted an ambivalent policy towards AMAL and al-Sadr: in 1972, when Mohtashami-Pur made his report on the Lebanese situation, the ayatollah called on Muslims to support the Palestinian fighters in the countries where they were active;[45] in 1978, a short time after al-Sadr's disappearance, he expressed the hope of seeing him return as soon as possible "to finish his work". He clarified his remark two weeks later, saying that by "his work" he did not mean leading Lebanon's Shiites out of their misery but rather fighting Israel.[46] However, in 1981 he named Mohtashami-Pur ambassador to Syria; some versions have it that he tasked the latter's disciple and Lebanese friend Subhī al-Tufaylī with restructuring al-Daʿwa-Lebanon. From that time on Mohtashami and al-Tufaylī felt secure enough to begin monitoring the first Lebanese networks sympathetic to the Revolution, and to lay the groundwork for the IRL the following year.

Dispatch of the Pasdaran to the north Bekaa

When the Israeli invasion happened in 1982, the Bekaa, following Beirut's example, supported the national Resistance, even though the local hostilities there can be summed up as a series of lethal Israeli hit-and-run raids. As soon as the clerics from the area who were in Tehran in early June returned home, particularly Subhī al-Tufaylī and ʿAbbās al-Mūsawī, they prepared to welcome the Revolutionary Guard battalions. Indeed, following the meeting that preceded their Lebanese guests' quick departure, the Iranian authorities rushed a senior delegation to Damascus, comprising the minister of defence, the commandant of the Pasdaran, and the commander of ground troops, to discuss the modalities of Iranian assistance to the Lebanese Resistance. At the time Iran and Syria maintained cordial relations,[47] and the Syrian regime gave its blessing to the stationing of Iranian troops in Lebanon. The 27th brigade, which had distinguished itself at Khorramshahr and was considered the best in the Iranian army, set out for the Country of Cedars, reinforced by the 58th elite division.[48] They were in Damascus by 11 June. But it appears that right from the time they arrived at Zabadani in the border area adjoining the Bekaa, Damascus actually had no intention of letting the Pasdaran cross into Lebanese territory. A furious Ahmad Motevasselian, the brigade commander, hurried to Tehran on 24 June to get orders from the hierarchy; but when he met Ali-Akbar Rafsanjani, then the parliament spokesman, and Ahmad Khomeini, the ayatollah's son, they both judged the Israeli victory too complete for an Iranian intervention to have any chance of changing the outcome. Khomeini himself stated that the invasion was only a "plot to divert Iranian attention from the war in Iraq" and that "the road to Jerusalem runs through Karbala".[49] The Iranian troops were therefore ordered to turn around immediately. However, not all Pasdaran would be repatriated. It seems that it was on Mohtashami's insistence that a small contingent (between 500 and 2,000, according to various sources)[50] was authorized to enter Lebanese territory, strictly and explicitly conditional on their not engaging in combat. Their mission was to be limited to providing logistical support and combat training for local recruits. The former ambassador to Syria explained:

> After the Israeli invasion ... the imam Khomeini changed his mind about sending massive forces to Lebanon and Syria. In other words, when the fifth plane transporting Pasdaran, Bassij[51] and the elite Dhū al-Fuqār brigade landed in Damascus, imam Khomeini refused to send any reinforcements. I was the ambassador to Damascus at the time and had serious concerns about the situation in Lebanon and Syria. I therefore left for Tehran and met with imam Khomeini. ... [In response to my insistence on sending troops to Lebanon] the imam calmed me and told me: "The forces you want to send there will require a great deal of logistical support, and the problem is that there are only two ways to ship that support, either through Iraq or Turkey. We are in a difficult war with the former, and the latter is a member of NATO and allied with the United States. The only possible solution therefore is to train the young Shiites over there."[52]

Birth of an 'Islam of resistance'

The Pasdaran who entered Lebanese territory set up camp in the Bekaa in July 1982.[53] Their camp was near Jantā, a hamlet in the Baalbek region, and it was here that a new paramilitary structure, al-Muqāwama al-Islāmiyya fī Lubnān (the Islamic Resistance in Lebanon, or IRL), was born. Consistent with the resistance Islam that he had been preaching for several years, ʿAbbās al-Mūsawī urged his students as well as the public to whom he preached to undergo training there. Leading by example, he and Hassan Nasrallah joined the first class. According to Subhī al-Tufaylī, more than a thousand young people were trained this way in the summer of 1982,[54] then formed into clandestine groups and sent south to carry out the first operations against the occupation there.[55]

The Pasdaran did not stop at just training and arming the future IRL's combatants. Something even more valuable that they were able to provide to the Lebanese was know-how. The internal organization and operating mode of Hezbollah, in particular, in no small part derive from what the Iranian emissaries in Lebanon taught the party's founding fathers.[56] The Pasdaran also taught ideological conscientization to the future Hezbollah cadres. Clerics from the Pasdaran detachment's Cultural Unit[57] made it their task to disseminate what would become known, especially in the 2000s,[58] as "a culture of resistance". The term describes a complete reciprocal social system, within which the militant, instead of limiting himself to simply preaching solidarity with the Resistance, will practise reciprocal solidarity, meaning in this case that if the IRL was to expect support from society, it must help society. During the first half of the 1980s the Pasdaran were thus seen working on the land alongside the peasants and field workers of the north Bekaa, sowing, reaping, and helping farmers raise cattle and sheep. Based on numerous accounts gathered in the region, it was not so much that revolutionary Islam was broadcast in the mosques but rather that it demonstrated in the fields, by fighters with rolled-up sleeves and scythes in hand, illustrating the theory with hands-on practice. In this way the Pasdaran gained popularity among a population used to being overlooked by the Lebanese government, which was then even less capable than ever of responding to their needs because it was mired in a civil war. In the eyes of the locals, the Pasdaran, although armed, did not "in the least act like the militias". People appreciated their discretion as much as their helpfulness: the Revolutionary Guards seldom let themselves be seen in the streets of the area's towns and villages. According to several members from Hezbollah's earliest days, these interpersonal relationships forged between the Pasdaran and the local population constituted one of the principal factors in people's allegiance to the party.

A resistance fed by defectors?

It is generally argued that the ranks of the IRL were initially inflated by AMAL veterans and Communists. Several years of fieldwork carried out in the Baalbek area and the southern Beirut suburbs with the goal of reconstructing the sociology of the first battalions of the Resistance and the first generation of Hezbollah members suggests that this proposition needs qualification. While many AMAL cadres actually did quit the ranks of their original organization to fight the invader as part of the Committee of Beirut Cadres, the original core of IRL comprised mainly young people from the Bekaa who lacked political, much less militant, pasts. Some AMAL fighters and Communists did subsequently join up from the Pasdaran training camps, but they did not flock into the Bekaa until a second epoch, after the lifting of the Beirut blockade—hence, not before September 1982.

Moreover, it should be noted that not all fighters trained by the Pasdaran joined the IRL. Among those who did, two categories must be differentiated: defectors from AMAL were mainly cadres, for the most part originally from Beirut. The presumed Communist defectors seem to have come mostly from the South and from the ranks of the Communist Action Organization in Lebanon (CAOL)[59] and not the Lebanese Communist Party (LCP).[60] Furthermore, no one from a Communist background was part of Hezbollah's decision-making apparatus; the rare members integrated into the party who had a previous political past were "Palestinians", that is, Lebanese fighters who were active in Fateh or were trained in its camps. The former Communists or CAOL members were in all likelihood integrated into the ranks of the IRL rather than Hezbollah. The notion of a massive influx into Hezbollah's ranks from AMAL and the LCP is therefore largely inaccurate.

In addition, a statistical calculation using the list of IRL martyrs who fell between 1982 and 2000 reveals that if we rank the towns and villages that furnished fighters to the IRL by the number of martyrs per inhabitant, the Bekaa, Baalbek, Brītāl (the birthplace of al-Tufaylī), and al-Nabī Shīt (the birthplace of al-Mūsawī) are at the top of the list. This primacy of the Baalbek–al-Hermel region is corroborated by the fact that the South is home to nearly 60 per cent of Lebanon's Shiites, while the north Bekaa only has 25 per cent.[61] Adjusted for the number of Shiite inhabitants, these statistics fully justify Hezbollah's traditional designation of the Baalbek–al-Hermel region as *khazzān al-Muqāwama*, "the reservoir of the Resistance".

Linking the resistance networks

As noted earlier, while the siege of the capital persisted the combatant networks in Beirut could not benefit from the military training dispensed by the Pasdaran in the Bekaa. The resisters in West Beirut and the South had to fall back on what they had learned in previous training with AMAL or Palestinian groups. However, some initial help furnished by the Iranians did make it through the blockade to the besieged in Beirut:

> With the noose tightening around Beirut and the suburbs, with the relationship with Berri's command suspended for five months straight during which all material and logis-

> tical support to the fighters was cancelled, and taking into account the arrival of the Pasdaran in the Bekaa and their setting up training camps to help those trying to resist, it was decided to send an emissary into the Bekaa to contact the Iranians and tap their resources. One of the [Beirut fighters] hence took off, circumventing the Israeli checkpoints. He returned successfully after three days, with just L£25,000 (16.5 USD), but it was the first aid they had obtained since the blockade imposed by the AMAL command.[62] The atmosphere at the time being that of the Fitr celebration [Ramadan], the fighters were overjoyed by this support. The relationship with the Pasdaran would develop steadily after this, and they eventually reliably supplied us with requisite materiel and military gear.[63]

Once the siege was lifted, the fighters from the battle of Khaldeh and the militants coming from the ranks of the Beirut Resistance organized an initial series of recruit groups to send to the training camps in the Bekaa. Thus the Bekaa and the capital came to be formally linked.

The creation of Hezbollah

"In the beginning was the *Muqāwama*": Hezbollah, a Lebanese idea

Nevertheless, beyond fielding a flexible military unit for all who wanted to bear arms against Israel, most of the Shiite resistance networks were after something more: they wanted to set up an institutionalized structure for action. The creation of the IRL and Hezbollah was prompted much less by an attempt to export the Revolution—a notion that Tehran by then already regarded as obsolete—than the response to a Lebanese imperative. A short time after the invasion, with military training already under way, the representatives of the Shiite Islamic networks from the Bekaa and Beirut thus met for the purpose of jointly outlining a new organization in bold strokes. With the basic principles in place, a nine-member committee called the Lijnat al-Tisʿa (Committee of the Nine) was formed, bringing together three delegates from each of what will be the main constituent elements of the future structure, specifically AMAL al-Islāmiyya, al-Ittihād, and the Association of Muslim Ulema in the Bekaa.[64]

In an interview graned to the historian Amīn Mustafā at the start of the 2000s, Hassan Nasrallah recounted the manner in which this first committee was set up and enumerated the founding principles adopted by the new organization then being gestated. Just weeks into the invasion, the nine delegates met in Baalbek at the al-Mahdī al-Muntadhar school of ʿAbbās al-Mūsawī.[65] Here they decided on (i) the unicity of the movement, in which the constituent organizations must dissolve and whose leadership would operate on a collegial basis, without anyone at the top; (ii) the Islamic nature of the movement, with Islam its first and foremost inspiration; (iii) allegiance to the principle of *wilāyat al-faqīh* and, as a corollary, respect for

Khomeini's recommendations, these having the force of obligations. But above all, they decided (iv) that the principal mission of the movement would remain "a fighting mission" (*muhimma jihādiyya*): "in other words", said Nasrallah, "*we wanted a Resistance, we did not come to form a political party*, for we had no choice but resistance for putting an end to the occupation".[66]

They then debated the type of action:

> The brothers then reviewed all the options available for fighting the occupation, in light of the experience of the Palestinians and Israeli occupations of other Arab countries. They discussed international resolutions and the manner in which the international organizations treated this issue, be it the UNSC or the Arab League. They concluded that armed struggle was the only solution for fighting the occupation, for keeping it from being consolidated. ... It was decided that this Resistance would operate in guerilla mode (*harb ʿisābāt*), that it would wage a war of attrition, for the long term.

With the new organization plotted in outline, the Committee of the Nine left for Tehran to ask for the revolutionary regime's support. ʿAbbās al-Mūsawī was chosen to act as its president and spokesman. Naʿīm Qāsim, today deputy secretary-general of Hezbollah, describes the trip:

> The delegation presented its project of forming a Lebanese organization. Khomeini approved. He blessed the initiative and insisted on the necessity of making the fight against Israel its top priority, a religious concern and duty not only for Lebanon's Muslims but for Muslims throughout the world. This is how the first cell was formed. Summary action plans then fleshed out the basic principles previously decided on.[67]

Before bidding his guests farewell, Khomeini is said to have imparted a final piece of advice—"al-Muhimm huwa al-ʿamal" (What matters is to work)[68]—and to have warned them that theirs would be a long struggle and they should not "expect to reap the fruits of their action in their lifetimes".[69]

The Council of Lebanon (early 1983) and Hezbollah (May 1984)

With the Committee of the Nine back in Lebanon, a first civilian structure tasked with protecting the interests of the IRL was set up: Shūrā Lubnān, the Council of Lebanon. With Tehran's backing,[70] it was composed of five people, three Lebanese and two Iranians: Subhī al-Tufaylī, representing al-Daʿwa, ʿAbbās al-Mūsawī, for the Association of Muslim Ulema in the Bekaa, Muhammad Raad, for al-Ittihād, plus ʿAli-Akbar Mohtashami-Pur, then Iran's ambassador to Syria, and Ahmad Kanʿānī, the Pasdaran commander in Lebanon.[71] The link-up between the Beirut and Baalbek networks was thus institutionalized under Iranian supervision, and the subsequent linking of the combatant networks was effected in the same manner as for the civilian leaderships.

The new team, "responsible for setting up the organization, drawing up a hierarchy, establishing rules, systems and programmes, forming the working groups and specialized committees",[72] held its first meeting early in 1983.[73] In May 1984 the network of institutions attached to it permanently adopted the name *Hizbullāh* (Party of God), which was endorsed from then on as the sole and unique name to appear on all its flyers and communiqués.[74]

With Hezbollah in business, the new members were asked to leave their original organizations for the new one. Contrary to Nasrallah's intimation, this does not mean that these organizations disappeared entirely. Al-Daʿwa-Lebanon was dissolved,[75] but al-Ittihād continued with members who did not join the resistance networks.[76] As for AMAL al-Islāmiyya, it managed to preserve a distinct existence alongside Hezbollah, on occasion even publishing its own communiqués[77] despite the fact that Husayn al-Mūsawī would occupy leadership posts in the latter.

Name, flag, slogan

The party leadership acknowledges that it adopted the name Hezbollah in reference to two suras of the Qur'an: the sura *al-Mujādala*, which states that "it is the party of God that will know bliss"[78] and the *al-Mā'ida* sura, which proclaims "it is the party of God that will be the victor."[79]

By party, its founders did not mean a political collective along modern Western lines but what the Qur'an describes as a group of partisans, of followers, of allies: *hizb Allāh* is therefore a group of believers, those close to God, the faithful of God, as opposed to *hizb al-Shaytān*, the party of the devil that gathers together the evil people, the miscreants.

The new organization adopted a bright yellow flag, with unmistakeable similarities to the Pasdaran's flag: a raised fist clutching a Kalashnikov, the globe, and the Qur'an can be seen on both banners. But instead of quoting the sura *al-Anfāl* ('Wa aʿiddū lahum mā istataʿtum min quwwa' (Raise against [the enemies of God] all the forces that you can)),[80] as the Pasdaran does on its flag, Hezbollah prefers one of the verses from which it drew its name ('Fa-inna Hizballāh hum al-ghālibūn' (It is the party of God that will be the victor)). In addition, it initially emblazoned its flag with the slogan *al-Thawra al-islāmiyya fī Lubnān* (The Islamic Revolution in Lebanon), but switched a few years later to *al-Muqāwama al-islāmiyya fī Lubnān* (The Islamic Resistance in Lebanon). With that, it made official a new terminology largely cleansed of Iranian revolutionary sloganeering and refocused on its true, more Lebanese priorities.

The Open Letter of 1985

During its first few months the new organization stayed hidden to avoid attracting the occupier's attention.[81] An exhaustive search of the Arab-language national daily

Figure 1

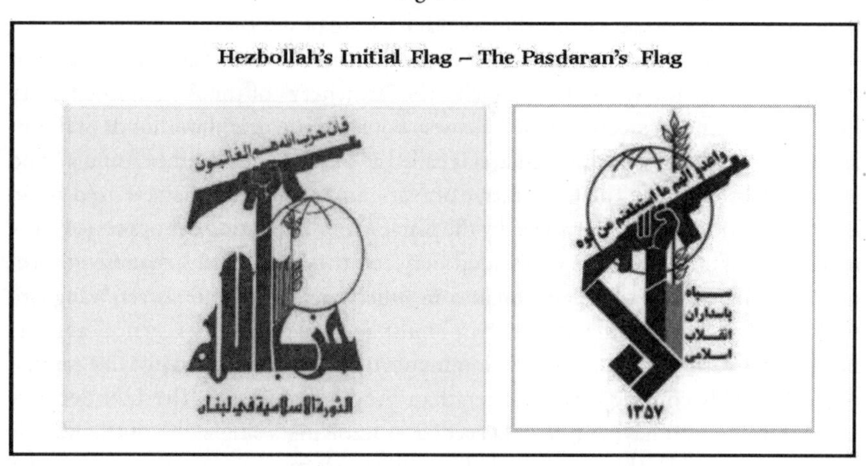

Hezbollah's Initial Flag – The Pasdaran's Flag

newspaper archives shows that the very first communiqué signed by Hezbollah and bearing its logo (its flag in black and white) was published on the second anniversary of the Sabra and Shatila massacres, in September 1984. Before this date marches and parades organized by the party already carried its name on giant posters or banners, but it was not used as the exclusive appellation or in signing official communiqués. Hezbollah officially announced its existence to the world on 16 February 1985, commemorating the first anniversary of Rāghib Harb's assassination; he was a cleric from the South eliminated by the Israelis for having incited rebellion in the village of Jibshīt against the occupation. During a great demonstration organized in Beirut's southern suburbs, Sayyid Ibrāhīm Amīn al-Sayyid, a cleric from the village of al-Nabī Aylā in the Bekaa and a former AMAL representative in Tehran who had joined the ranks of AMAL al-Islāmiyya before finally moving over to Hezbollah and becoming its spokesman, read an "Open Letter to the World's Oppressed". It was a kind of charter in which Hezbollah identified its enemies and allies and laid out its paradigms and objectives.

Calling itself "the sons of the *ummah* of the party of God", that is, an association of faithful believers in the Creator's injunctions, it declared at the outset its allegiance to the principle of *wilāyat al-faqīh*. It stated that it did not conceive of itself as a party in the literal sense of the term, which would reduce it to a "narrow scope" but as "an *ummah* linked to Muslims throughout the world". Continuing in this vein, it affirmed its commitment to "Islamic unity", in other words, to closeness and cooperation between Sunnis and Shiites. It accused the "oppressors" of being in league against the Muslim world. The anti-imperialist paradigms are easily discernible. The United States in particular is "the source of all evil", with NATO and Israel acting as its proxies. They are accused of having "invaded [the Muslim] countries, where they have destroyed villages, slaughtered children, violated sanctuaries and installed in positions of power individuals who have committed the worst massacres against the *ummah*" with the goal of keeping the Muslim world in a state of subjection.

The text is highly contextualized. It evokes the massacres of Sabra and Shatila at the hands of the Kataeb and the Israelis, the "treachery" of the American emissary Philip Habib, the massacres by the Lebanese Forces in the neighbourhoods of Beirut and on its peripheries. Bashir Gemayel is called a "butcher", his brother Amin a "paid agent of Washington". The Committee of National Salvation is characterized as "an Israeli–American bridge borrowed by the Kataeb for dominating the oppressed". The agreement of 17 May 1983 concluded between the Israeli and Lebanese governments[82] would seek to turn Lebanon into an American protectorate; Israel, "vanguard of the United States in the Middle East", must be "wiped out of existence" and any negotiation with it is unthinkable. Communism is also condemned just like capitalism, the USSR coming off no better than the United States. The UN Security Council is suspect, having never succeeded in resolving a single one of the Middle East's problems; UNIFIL is accused of having transformed the South into a "buffer zone for Israel". The Arab regimes are also castigated, vilified for their "defeatism". Hezbollah's friends, by contrast, are "all those oppressed peoples of the world", "all those who fight" the same enemies that it fights.

The party's declared objectives were (i) "once and for all chase the Americans, the French and their allies out of Lebanon"; (ii) "bring the Kataeb before a just tribunal for the crimes they have perpetrated against Muslims and Christians"; and (iii) allow all Lebanese "to control their fate and to freely choose the form of government they desire". On this point, Hezbollah stated its "Islamic commitment", affirming its perspective that the best of all possible regimes is an Islamic one, but that, "contrary to political Maronitism", it did not intend to "impose it on the Lebanese by force", because the Qur'an commands that "there can be no coercion in religion".[83] The party further affirmed that it wanted to achieve its objectives in a "legal" manner in the hope of "preserving Lebanon from all dependence on East or West" and putting an end to Israel's occupation of the country. In domestic politics, Hezbollah condemned sectarianism and declared itself "unconcerned" by the political life of the day, as it emanated from a system that the party judged to be "invalid down to the roots". Finally, it had a special word for Lebanon's Christians: it "does not wish them any ill". They were encouraged to embrace Islam, but the statement stresses that there is no intention of converting them forcibly. It exhorts them above all to cut their ties to the Kataeb and the Lebanese Forces, which "are incapable of guaranteeing peace and tranquility to Lebanon's Christians" due to their "communitarian particularism, their [attachment] to their sectarian privileges, and their alliance with colonialism and Israel". It goes on to insist that "the Lebanese crisis proves that sectarian privileges are one of the principal causes of the great upheaval ravaging the country" but "if [the Christians] think that Hezbollah wants to take revenge on them, their fears are not justified; any who live in peace can continue to live in [Hezbollah's] areas without fear of anyone whatsoever planning to interfere with them".

Shiite reactions to the emergence of Hezbollah

Not all Shiite Islamic networks joined Hezbollah. Sādiq al-Mūsawī and al-Haraka al-Islāmiyya, for instance, remained outside the project. Fusing al-Haraka and Hezbollah might have been an option,[84] but their reasons for not joining forces are unclear. It is not unreasonable to think, however, that because al-Haraka's priority was overthrowing the Lebanese regime rather than resistance against the occupation, and Montazeri and the proponents of exporting the Iranian revolution were already losing influence in Tehran when Hezbollah was born, al-Haraka refused to join the new organization.

Even within resistance circles, many clerics also chose to distance themselves from Hezbollah's party structures. According to Sheikh Hānī Fahs, Rāghib Harb may, in a meeting in the winter of 1983, have received an offer from Subhī al-Tufaylī to become part of the new structure for resistance action.[85] Harb would have declined such an invitation, probably because he was close to the apolitical *marja*ʿ al-Khūʾī, Khomeini's Iraqi rival.[86] The same was true of another cleric close to Harb, ʿAbdel-Muhsin Fadlallāh, who, while taking an active part in IRL activities, remained outside Hezbollah. So did Muhammad Husayn Fadlallāh, whom numerous authors and analysts for many years tagged as the head of the party, or at least its spiritual guide, even though he was never actually a member of Hezbollah.

In attempting to present a sociology of the first Hezbollah networks, a few authors have advanced the hypothesis of a 'Najaf connection',[87] suggesting that the party formed around a network of students of religion who first met in Najaf. First of all, it needs to be kept in mind that the majority of Arabic-speaking clerics, circumstances permitting, did their studies, or at least part of them, in Iraq, regardless of their ideological and political preferences. Conversely, of the clerics who did graduate from Najaf, most either played no role in the party's formation or refused to take part in the project. In addition to Rāghib Harb, whom ʿAbbās al-Mūsawī actually did meet in Najaf, these included Muhammad Husayn Fadlallāh, Muhammad Mahdī Shamseddīn, ʿAbdel-Amīr Qabalān, Hānī Fahs, ʿAlī al-ʿAfī, and ʿAlī al-Amīn—all of whom were or still are influential clerics on the Lebanese Shiite religious scene. Some of Hezbollah's founders did indeed embark on a course of study in Iraq but, after 1978, they left to live in Iran for some time, including ʿAbdel-Karīm ʿUbayd and Subhī al-Tufaylī himself.[88] Others, such as Muhammad Yazbek,[89] did join the party, but they played no significant role in founding it. More to the point, many of the party's founding clerics never set foot in Iraq, such as Naʿīm Qāsim, who did his entire religious studies in Lebanese *hawzas*.[90] Finally, a large number of the Hezbollah founding cadres were not clerics, beginning with Husayn al-Mūsawī and Muhammad Raad. In truth, IRL and Hezbollah crystallized around a team of clerics and lay people who met in Lebanon. Coming from a variety of backgrounds, they united around two principles: giving priority to creating an armed resistance organization and pledging allegiance to *al-waliy al-faqīh*. Rather than a Najaf connection, there was a Lebanese Resistance under *wilāyat al-faqīh* connection.

The Association of Muslim Ulema: attracting Sunni clerics

Concurrent with a Hezbollah gradually taking shape there was an Association of Muslim Ulema in Lebanon, a group that, in contrast to the exclusively Shiite Association of Muslim Ulema in the Bekaa, had since 1982 brought Shiite and Sunni clerics together. A grouping of Lebanese ulema who supported Iran's revolutionary government, it counts among its membership such figures as the Sunni clerics Ahmad al-Zayn, the *qādī* of Sidon, and Saʿīd Shaʿbān, emir of the al-Tawhīd movement in Tripoli.[91] Founded in Tehran at the time of the Israeli invasion, it received Khomeini's blessing, for he saw it as a counterweight to "disunity in Muslim ranks".[92] A small group of twenty or so clerics,[93] some coming from Dār al-Fatwā (Sunni) or the SSC (Shiite), it declared its solidarity with "all sincere Islamic liberation movements" and as such was responsible in theory for supporting the Lebanese groups intending to take up arms against the occupation. At first, its actions mainly consisted of coordinating the activities of the Islamic committees (*lijān islāmiyya*), a collection of neighbourhood associations active in the Beirut area.[94] In 1983 it vociferously opposed the signing of the 17 May Agreement, which earned it a lethal confrontation with the authorities and a vehement reprimand from the SSC.[95] Anxious to avoid accusations of wanting to destabilize the powers that be, it published a communiqué to clear itself of any intention to challenge the Lebanese government.[96] At the end of that same month it pushed through a new charter which, while giving due consideration to "the leader of the Islamic Republic of Iran as leader of the entire *ummah*", reaffirmed the organization's commitment to Lebanon and respect for its institutions.

Beyond its support for the cause of the resistance, the Association's record for the past thirty years indicates that its role ultimately remained one of working to resolve disputes between Sunni and Shiite communities (the War of the Camps, clashes between AMAL and Hezbollah, etc.)[97] Since the 1990s its activities have been pared back significantly, its leadership remaining content to express itself sporadically, whenever it comes to displaying solidarity with the Iranian regime or the Palestinian cause, or to express Sunni support for Hezbollah when polemics with its opponents threaten to take a sectarian turn.

The special case of South Lebanon: the resistance of Rāghib Harb

Hezbollah and the Association of Muslim Ulema in Lebanon thus came into existence as support structures that were at once social and political, mobilizing for the IRL, a military organization created by linking up resistance networks originating in the Bekaa and Beirut. South Lebanon was the last of Lebanon's Shiite areas to see

Hezbollah move into its territory. As long as the Israeli occupation persisted north of the Litani river, the IRL did not set up any headquarters or bases there. Only in the second half of the 1980s, after the Israeli army had fallen back to the border "security zone", did the IRL and Hezbollah develop their structures in the South.

In 1982, when Israeli tanks crossed the border, heading north, they encountered little resistance. As they rolled through villages of the South, flowers and rice were even thrown at "those who came to rid the region of Palestinians". But this passivity did not last. If 1982 remained generally calm in the South, 1983 saw a marked deterioration in relations between occupied and occupier. The protests began in March, when Israeli forces arrested Rāghib Harb, *imām* of the village of Jibshīt near Nabatiyeh, who had been agitating for mobilization against Tel Aviv's troops for several months, just as ʿAbbās al-Mūsawī was doing in the Bekaa.

Harb, oldest of five brothers and three sisters, was born on 25 October 1952 in Jibshīt,[98] whose inhabitants "lived by cultivating tobacco, grains, olives, oranges, and roses". His father, Hājj Ahmad Abū Rāghib, a farmer who raised sheep, is depicted as "a believer of great righteousness". The family was poor, the home modest. The father paid his *zakat* (religious tax) "at a time when few people were religious". His brother, Hājj Abū Mālik Harb, Rāghib's uncle and future father-in-law, occasionally preached (*tablīgh*), and gave the call to prayer in the village.

The boy's first few years of education were at Jibshīt's modest school; he would rise at dawn with his parents to help them cultivate tobacco. At a very early age he sympathized with the Palestinian cause: by the age of thirteen he had already received his first military training, and bore arms with the Palestinian *fedayeen*. Around the age of fourteen or fifteen he left his school in Nabatiyeh, but, before leaving, promised to "meet with his friends at the mosque in the near future" to teach them "*jihād* against the enemy". At seventeen he told his parents he wanted to drop out of school for good to undertake religious studies, a project that had his mother's support. He therefore left for Beirut in 1969. However, like all Shiite theology students, he dreamed of Najaf, and that is where he finally headed in 1971. In 1974, after three years in Iraq, where he took courses from Muhammad Bāqir al-Sadr, Harb returned to Lebanon for good. He taught religion in Jibshīt; he also led the Friday prayer, which had just been reinstituted in Lebanon under a *fatwā* issued by al-Khūʾī making it "obligatory—barring hindrances—for all people living within at least 5.5 km of where it is said". In the beginning he had an audience of fewer than twenty, but gradually the crowds grew to the point where the Jibshīt mosque came to be called "the Qom of Jabal ʿĀmil". In 1976, Harb, having trained enough emulators in Jibshīt, handed over the village's religious leadership. He then settled in neighbouring Sharqiyyeh, where he strove to counter the influence of the Iraqi Baath, which was strong at the time. But what the people of Sharqiyyeh wanted most was a school. Harb responded constructively, calling for a collective effort and pitching in to dig the foundation on a piece of property that was a religious endowment (*waqf*); thanks to donations collected locally, a two-storey school was eventually constructed. In the wake of increasingly lethal Israeli attacks, Harb also cared for the area's orphan population, numbering nearly eighty girls and boys. Finding no place to house them, he transformed his own home for a time into a refuge for girls, leaving his family with an adjacent room and kitchen to share. Boys were settled in an old building attached to the village's *husayniyya* (Shiite religio-cultural centres) that had formerly housed the municipality's school. Harb wasted no time in starting a charity (*mabarra*), to which his charges were eventually transferred in 1978.

When the 1982 invasion happened, Harb was in Tehran with other Lebanese clerics. While some departed as soon as they heard the news, Harb extended his stay in Iran by two months.[99] Back in Lebanon, he found Jibshīt under Israeli control. He immediately threw himself into a mobilization against Tel Aviv's forces, warning against the temptation to collaborate, and shouting from the rooftops, as it were, that Israel, far from being an army of liberation that had rid the South of Palestinian fighters, had come as an invader. With slogans such as "Boycott Israeli goods", "Collaboration with Israel is proscribed (*harām*)", "Opposing the Israelis is a duty", and, especially, the widely hailed "Al-Mawqif silāh wal-musāfaha iʿtirāf" (the stance[itself] is a weapon; shaking the [enemy's] hand is to acknowledge [him]),[100] he strove ceaselessly to set the population against the occupier.

His opposition to Israel's presence was not confined to words. Like al-Mūsawī in the Bekaa, he intended to be a *ʿālim–mujāhid*, a cleric–fighter. He regularly changed from his *ʿabāya* (cloak) and turban into a military uniform and joined a group of young people assigned the duty of guarding the entrance to the village.[101] The Israeli army arrested him in March 1983, but, given the scale of the multiple protest demonstrations and sit-ins that followed, the Israelis released him a few weeks later but forbade him to set foot in Jibshīt. He not only disregarded this, he again began inciting people to take up arms, and personally coordinated the activities of the fighters. The Israelis, exasperated, had him killed by local agents on 16 February 1984, provoking a general rebellion in the South. But that rebellion had only been biding its time: the break between occupied and occupier had actually taken place in October 1983. That year, as every year, a procession was held on 16 October in Nabatiyeh for the ʿĀshūrāʾ annual march. Fifty thousand people gathered for the traditional march.[102] The procession was in full swing when an Israeli convoy tried to drive through the city, the commander insisting that the convoy pass through the middle of the marchers. The jeeps, trying to create a passage, jostled and knocked down some of those present. In the face of this apparent provocation, the crowd hurled insults and then stones at the military. In the scuffle, one of the jeeps was overturned. The Israelis retaliated by opening fire, killing two people and wounding fifteen.[103] This led to Nabatiyeh being besieged for three days; houses were raided and many people arrested. In response, there was protest rally after protest rally and, on 25 October, a general strike was declared throughout the South. When he learnt of the Nabatiyeh incidents, Shamseddīn, forsaking his usual quietism, issued a *fatwā* declaring "civil resistance against Israel":

> (i) All collaboration in any form whatsoever with Israel is religiously prohibited and rises to the level of high treason; (ii) those who collaborate with Israel must be shunned by the community; (iii) the inhabitants of the South [must] not budge from their land; (iv) [it is necessary to wage] war to secure the unity of Lebanon, its land, its people and its institutions.[104]

By late autumn 1983 the revolt was in full swing. The South was in rebellion and, apart from the (Christian) villages under Kataeb control, sit-ins and demonstrations were staged one after the other throughout the region. The ranks of the resistance swelled with new members. The day after Harb's assassination, the general strike was called, and was observed throughout the country (except in the Kataeb and Lebanese Forces zones.) Confrontations took place between Israeli soldiers and Lebanese civilians in the villages of Kfār Sīr (Nabatiyeh) and Maarakeh (Tyre); the latter was occupied and put under blockade by the Israelis. The protests spread to Tyre and adjoining villages. In late March 1984 the confrontations reach a crescendo in the village of Jibshīt: 150 Israeli armoured cars and half a dozen helicopters attacked the village, followed by a ground assault that resulted in dead and wounded civilians. Protest movements, repression, sit-ins, strikes, and blockades continued. At the end of October, conflict erupted in the Ansār prison camp near Nabatiyeh when the prisoners rose up in support of the regional general strike, and the guards opened fire, killing or wounding some.

At this time the IRL, active since 1982 under the banner of the Lebanese National Resistance Front (LNRF), began conducting operations under its own name. The following year it set up its first bases and headquarters in the South. The path of an Islam of resistance thus began with the goal of liberating South Lebanon totally and finally from any Israeli presence.

3

TRAJECTORY OF AN ISLAM OF RESISTANCE

FROM FOUNDING TO LIBERATION

In June 1982, when Israeli tanks crossed the border and headed towards Beirut, Tel Aviv's troops had already been occupying a portion of Lebanon's territory that the Israelis called the "security zone" and the Lebanese "the occupied strip" (*al-sharīt al-muhtall*). The inter-Lebanese truce concluded around the time of Amin Gemayel's election, after the blockade of the capital and Bashir's assassination, and the evacuation of Palestinian forces from Beirut, were not followed by a complete withdrawal of the Israeli army. The increasingly frequent attacks by the Lebanese National Resistance Front (LNRF), under whose banner the IRL had fought in the early stages, nonetheless convinced the Israeli leadership that a limited response was called for. In January 1985 Tel Aviv adopted a plan of withdrawal in three phases; after the end of the third one, which occurred on 1 June that year, a 1,500-strong Israeli ground force[1] remained to occupy the "security zone" only, whose boundaries it had, however, extended beyond those of the area it had controlled in 1978. It follows that this 850-square-kilometre slice of South Lebanon, covering about 10 per cent of the country, would become the IRL's preferred field of action.

The realities of Israeli occupation

Arrests, raids, blockades, and expulsions

The Israeli authority in the occupied South translated into a number of repressive measures designed to stifle or punish any protest against the foreign presence. Since taking up its position in southern Lebanon, the Israeli army largely blocked off "rebel" and, soon after, "potentially dangerous" areas. After being targeted by several attacks, it set up numerous checkpoints and extensive curfews. Some roads in the South were only open to foot traffic. A system of passes with frequent searches controlled the comings and goings of everyone living there. From the summer of 1984, the area under Israeli control was severed permanently from the rest of Lebanon. Sectarian routes of travel were set up: Christians went by boat from Jounieh to Jiyeh and then to Sidon; Muslims had to pass through the checkpoints at Bātir (Jezzin) and Jeb Jennīn (Bekaa). From the autumn of 1984, the Bātir route could only be negotiated on foot.[2] Furthermore, massive expulsions took place; by 2000, more than half of the 200,000 people who had lived in the occupied zone of 1978 had fled or been forcibly dislodged from the area.[3]

Backing up the Israeli army on the ground was a Lebanese militia paid and armed by Tel Aviv.[4] While the officers of this auxiliary force were mostly Christian militiamen, soldiers, or officers formerly with the regular army, the enlisted ranks consisted of 70 per cent Shiites, 17 per cent Druze, 10 per cent Christians, and a smattering of Sunnis. Depending on the time frame, the militia would have numbered between 2,400 and 3,500 men armed and trained in Israel. There was also an administrative staff of 500 attached to it at the headquarters located in Marjayoun, a mostly Christian town in the South, while its intelligence services were based at the infamous Khyām prison.[5] The militia force was originally named the Army of Saad Haddad, after the senior ex-Lebanese army officer who commanded it. In April 1979 he proclaimed the (ephemeral) "State of Free Lebanon" in the area he controlled, at which time the militia took the name Army of Free Lebanon (AFL). In April 1984, after Haddad's death in December 1983, General Antoine Lahd, a former director of military intelligence in the Lebanese army, took command.[6] Following the Israeli withdrawal from Tyre in April 1985, General Lahd merged the various militia units into what became known as the South Lebanon Army (SLA).[7]

On the ground, the SLA's mission was to provide backup to the Israeli forces—and sometimes to replace them. Its men were often the interface between the population and the Israelis: they manned the occupation checkpoints, and collected taxes and percentage fees on economic flows, through the ports, shops, and roads on the occupier's behalf. They were in charge of recruitment, most often through threats: nearly 40 per cent of the population of the "security zone" was forced to collaborate.[8] The SLA was also in the forefront of sweeps and expulsion operations, during which Muslims in particular were forced to leave the zone.[9] The militia also participated in Israeli offensives in a division of labour that generally had the Israeli army standing back while the militia did the "dirty work".[10] Finally, it was responsible for managing the detention centres that Israel established in the occupied zone.

The prisons of the occupation[11]

Between 1984 and 2000 11,000 Lebanese, or more than 15 per cent of the population still living in the "security zone", passed through the prisons of the occupation in Lebanon or Israel.[12] Arrests and imprisonment were most often based on mere suspicion of collaboration with the Resistance or followed refusal to cooperate with the SLA or the Israeli army. These arrests were resented all the more by the local population because they were often made randomly during arbitrary raids, with women, children, adolescents, and the elderly just as likely to be targeted as men. During the early days detention centres were opened more or less throughout the areas under control of the Israelis or the Lebanese Forces, in Ashrafiyeh (East Beirut), Beirut, and Nabatiyeh. With the number of inmates increasing significantly, Israel opened the first dedicated centre, covering more than 50,000 square metres, at Ansār, a village near Nabatiyeh. Consisting of tents surrounded by walls, electric fences, and guard towers, it would have accommodated between 8,000 and 9,000 persons, incarcerated without any form of lawful arrest or trial. When the various Lebanese resistance groups made life difficult for the Israeli army in 1983, both in Beirut and Sidon, the occupier, believing the camp to be vulnerable, transferred just over a thousand prisoners to ʿAltlīt in Israel. ʿAltlīt only housed these prisoners for a few months. That same year, the Israeli army took over Khyām, a village near Nabatiyeh. The French Mandatory power had a barracks for its stables there during the 1930s; Israel converted the structure into a prison, to which, in 1984, it transferred the Ansār prisoners who had been sent to ʿAltlīt. They closed Ansār in 1985,[13] and sent the prisoners still there to the Khyām camp as well.

It became the "centre from hell".[14] Officially, the SLA was in charge, but it was just as often used by the Israeli army to conduct what were reputed to be strong-arm interrogations.[15] The numerous testimonies of torture suffered there by inmates tell of beatings, threats, humiliation and abuse in the presence of families, protracted exposure to cold or to the full sun, rape, attacks by dogs, electric shocks, and use of prisoners as guinea pigs by the Israeli pharmaceutical industry. Amnesty International called the centre "the prison of shame" and the Lebanese said 'Ellī bifūt mafqūd, ellī byetlaʿ mawlūd' (Whoever enters there is given up as lost, and whoever emerges has been resurrected). The length of incarcerations at Khyām varied from two months to more than fifteen years. Some of those released were let go because of severe health problems.[16] It would emerge that no treatment was ever given to the wounded;[17] more than a dozen died in Khyām because of maltreatment.[18] Inmates would have no access to a lawyer: until 1995, when ICRC was allowed for the first time to make a few rare visits,[19] Tel Aviv denied that it had any prisoners at Khyām, and the centre was in fact never legally constituted.[20]

Integration of the South with Israel's economy[21]

Along with these typical occupation practices, Israel worked to integrate the economy of South Lebanon with its own. Israel's economic penetration into Lebanon had begun in 1976 with the principle of the "good frontier". This euphemistically referred to several points of entry that were open despite the state of war existing between the two countries and through which goods had started to flood from Israel into the South. But normalization did not start until 1978: Ra's al-Nāqūra and the passage at

Metulla were declared international crossing points. However, this was a one-way integration. Israeli products and services (banks, travel agencies, and export companies) were widely available in the South Lebanese market, and at prices immune to competition because of dumping,[22] but Lebanese products faced rigorous protectionism. Lebanese production moreover was hampered by the policy of destroying irrigation channels and the shutting down of agricultural and industrial buildings. The value of these Israeli flows into Lebanon amounted to $7 million in September 1982 and passed $20 million in December, compared with the volume of Israeli exports to Egypt (a country with which Israel had been at peace for three years), which never exceeded $10 million during this time. Moreover, the waters of the Hasbani and Wazzani rivers came under the occupier's control. Pumps were installed at their headwaters and along their channels to supply residential communities in northern Israel.[23] The impact of this on the South's economy was severe; 50 per cent of the workforce lost their jobs and eventually left the region.

The first years: IRL amateurish but activated, Hezbollah hesitant

Gradual takeover of the resistance landscape (1984–1985)

On 16 September 1982, as West Beirut was being invaded by Israeli tanks following the assassination of Bashir Gemayel, and with the Kataeb just having entered the Palestinian camps at Sabra and Shatila, George Haoui, secretary-general of the Communist Party (LCP) and Muhsin Ibrahim, secretary-general of Communist Action Organization in Lebanon (CAOL), announced the establishment of a national defence structure against the occupying force called the Lebanese National Resistance Front (LNRF). Its members, drawn mainly from the ranks of the LCP and CAOL, were soon joined by Lebanese militants from various backgrounds—notably from the Baath and the Syrian Social Nationalist Party (SSNP)[24]—and by Palestinian fighters from the refugee camps. At first the skirmishes were concentrated in the capital, and the volunteers from Shiite Islamic ranks did not fight under any particular banner (al-Ittihād, Believing Youth, Committee of Beirut Cadres, etc.). In the South, the first operations involving Islamic fighters from the Bekaa were conducted in October. A year later, with operations in the capital ended, actions by the Resistance focused mainly on the South, and secondarily in the West Bekaa. For about a year and a half the IRL, fighting alongside the LNRF, did not conduct any operations under its own name, but rather under the latter's or that of small groups that would soon fuse into it, and so it was in their names that the IRL scored its first successes.

Between late 1983 and 1985 the LNRF had numerous restrictions imposed on it in favour of the IRL. According to Georges Haoui, there was a "regional and international drive" to limit the resistance solely to the Shiite community, in particular the IRL.[25] This gradual pushing aside by external pressure of the pluripartite and plurisectarian resistance in favour of the Islamic Resistance led to increasingly serious clashes between the two groups. Some intellectuals and LCP members were assassinated, by militant Shiite groups or by Hezbollah, according to some versions.[26] But the advantage shifted permanently to the IRL, and the first communiqué signed by it wherein it took sole responsibility for an operation against the occupier appeared in May 1984.[27] From the second half of the year it was responsible for carrying out most acts of resistance.

The IRL moves into Jabal ʿĀmil

Before 1985, opposition to the Israeli presence in Lebanon was mostly grassroots and spontaneous. As mentioned previously, neither the IRL nor Hezbollah moved into the occupied zone until after the last stage of the Israeli withdrawal had been completed, on 1 June. ʿAbbās al-Mūsawī, who had already distinguished himself by his ability to mobilize young people in the Bekaa, and been toughened by his basic training in the Pasdaran camps, was tasked with setting up the IRL infrastructures in the South. He stopped running the *hawza* in Baalbek and moved to the village of Tayr Dabbā near Tyre. He commenced by working with a senior cadre living in that city, but this was interrupted when the Israeli army arrested his contact in the spring of 1985 and imprisoned him in Israel. It was only upon his release at the beginning of July that year that "the work of coordinating and implementing IRL in the South will start in earnest"[28]—which would make it the summer of 1985.

An IRL military leader described how the organization started out in the area:

> Before the withdrawal, we used the walkie-talkie in a very rudimentary way, but still, that's how we were able to raise effective mobilization groups and patrol the villages. Sayyid ʿAbbās al-Mūsawī went to the village of Dayr Qānūn al-Nahr [southern Lebanon] and organized training for inhabitants between the ages of 10 to 60. Like the rest of us, he carried the weapons, wore the military uniform and walked down the street like anyone else. We finally got a training camp in addition to the one in Bekaa ... and we started to launch attacks against the [Israeli] positions inside the occupied zone.[29]

In the field, ʿAbbās al-Mūsawī was assisted by several ulema. One of them was ʿAbdel-Karīm ʿUbayd, who would take charge of the region after al-Mūsawī. A native of Jibshīt, he became active in turn in the resistance networks, this time in Hezbollah's ranks.[30] ʿAfīf al-Nābulsī, from the village of Bissariyeh (Sidon), joined the party for a few years but, while remaining close to it, nonetheless chose to leave it;[31] today he still chairs the Committee of Jabal ʿĀmil Ulema, which he had a hand in organizing, and issues some of the *fatwā*s required by Hezbollah. By far the most active cleric at al-Mūsawī's side in the South, however, was ʿAbdel-Muhsin Fadlallāh, born in Najaf[32] to the Fadlallāh family of ʿAynātā,[33] from which Muhammad Husayn Fadlallāh also came. Following respected family custom from father to son, he took the path of religious studies in Iraq, leaving when he was just fourteen years old. After studying for twenty-three years he returned to Lebanon and settled in the village of Kherbet Selem, near Bint Jbeil. There he opened a *hawza* and assumed teaching duties. Jolted by what was happening in the South and the repeated clashes between Palestinian militants and the Israeli army, he, like Rāghib Harb, conceived a militant hostility towards the occupier. But unlike Harb, whose activity was essentially mobilization by discourse, ʿAbdel-Muhsin chose clandestine work, and transformed his village into a staging area for anti-occupation action. His own home became a veritable headquarters, from which several uprisings in the area were planned, and a venue for meetings and discussions by local ulema looking for action. He also distinguished himself at the time by issuing the *fatwā*s necessary for religious justification of martyr operations, a role that Israeli and Western intelligence services subsequently attributed to his brother-in-law Muhammad Husayn Fadlallāh.[34] He also did not hesitate to take part in some combat operations, such as the operation at Kūnīn in 1986, when he used his own car to spirit away two Israeli soldiers that the IRL had just abducted. Naturally, he maintained excellent relations with the IRL, but, while he participated in founding the Committee of Jabal ʿĀmil Ulema, like many others he refused to join Hezbollah, preferring to act from outside a partisan structure.[35]

The first notable successes

The IRL started out amateurishly. Most of its operations were modest, its resources limited. As even the fighters admitted, their first successes were small scale. The first obstacle was a psychological one that impeded recruitment, as Naʿīm Qāsim, the party's deputy secretary-general, recalled:

> When the Resistance began, most Lebanese people were not convinced of [the effectiveness] of resistance against the Israeli occupation because the missions pursued by the Palestinian groups had not been encouraging. ... People were not willing to pay the price. ... It was not in the natural order of things to help restart the resistance, the idea prevailing at the time rather being that the resistance would end.[36]

There were also logistical barriers impacting the means available to the fighters as well as their skills. This is how one IRL military official described them:

> At the outset, we faced many difficulties: there were few of us, the South was vast, and our means were modest. We hid some weapons like Kalashnikovs and B-7s, but they saw limited use. Our experience was minimal, we worked like beginners. While we could rig an explosive charge using wire, filling a crate with some explosives such as TNT, crimping a detonator to it and running wire 100 or 200 meters long, but to set it off we used a 50, 60 or 70 amps car battery. All this was a far cry from military methods, [even] basic ones, but we wanted to do something, even if it was with such devices and these very modest means. ... We were fairly well able to start carrying out some operations, easy ones: two resisters would approach an Israeli checkpoint, open

> fire and then escape; we also targeted a truck in the Nāqūra area and another at Sarafand. ... In 1982, we viewed them as good hits.[37]

A few months later, however, the IRL had already achieved improved outcomes. Its attacks against Israeli positions and convoys were more decisive. It also carried out several significant strikes using what Hezbollah termed "martyrdom operations" (*'amaliyya istishhādiyya*), known as suicide bombings in the West. Like the other organizations (the leftists) that were fighting the occupation, the Islamic Resistance did in fact organize a series of such attacks, with the most spectacular one carried out on 11 November 1982 by Ahmad Qasīr, aged nineteen. The target was the HQ of the Israeli troop commander in Tyre; the building was completely demolished, killing 76 Israelis and wounding 118. Let it be noted here that in Hezbollah idiom, *istishhād*—the act of dying as a martyr—does not equate to suicide. According to the concept's theorists, suicide involves an act of resignation, a rejection of life whose only objective is to provide relief for the individuals who choose to end their own lives.[38] *Istishhād*, on the other hand, is seen as a military act—solely military—carried out by a person who does not seek death as an end in itself but as an instrumentality. The converse of what is attributed to the act of suicide holds true for *istishhād*, in that it becomes the supreme incarnation of sacrifice, an act of courage, made for others and not for the self.[39] Starting with a utilitarian understanding of the planned death, conditions for *istishhād* were very strict, and the number of candidates chosen for its implementation very low: during twenty-two years of occupation, the IRL had officially planned only twelve martyr operations. With Islam condemning suicide just as Christianity does, the IRL's leadership would not have decided to send a young person to their death unless the operation's outcome had an acceptable degree of certainty: "If the harm caused to the enemy or the heavy losses in their ranks or even victory depend on the death and martyrdom of a few fighters, then the act is considered to be legitimate."[40] A potential *istishhādī* in any case may not carry out his operation unless he has first obtained the agreement, by *fatwā*, of a cleric of high eminence.

The Israelis have admitted that these operations had the effect intended by their instigators. They are first and foremost about instilling a siege mentality and a sense of fear in the occupier. After the Qasīr operation the Israelis moved their barracks to higher ground at a remove from residential zones, and Tel Aviv relied more heavily on the SLA as a buffer between its troops and the local populations. The IRL's other goal was to have Israel re-evaluate the merits of its presence in Lebanon:

> Launching military operations against the occupation forces was very tempting at the time, because the officers and Israeli soldiers were in a cocky mood; they were using public transport and private vehicles, they hitchhiked by the roadsides. ...
>
> This operation [by Qasīr] was an enormous slap at the security, policies, and psychology of the occupation forces. The defence minister at the time, Ariel Sharon, described

it as a "massacre". Others spoke of "major disaster"; they put the blame on Sharon and called for his resignation for having overcommitted Israel in Lebanon.[41]

Indeed, in January 1985 it was these operations, along with regular attacks by the LNRF, and in particular the significantly more frequent ones by the IRL, that persuaded the Israeli General Staff of the need to retreat much of the territory where the army was still deployed, and they forced an Israeli army tactical withdrawal to the "security zone" starting in June that year.

The war with AMAL (1988–1990)

With the Israeli withdrawal from part of the South and the emergence of the IRL into the limelight, friction soon froze the IRL's relations with AMAL. The latter undoubtedly saw the IRL as a rival, and a Shiite one at that, on "its" main territory. But other, serious, disagreements also put the two groups at odds. First, Syria was trying once and for all to bring the Palestinian factions under its control after most of the PLO cadres had evacuated in 1982, relying on AMAL to proceed with a siege of several refugee camps in Beirut and the South starting in June 1985. This would become known as the War of the Camps, and ended only in March 1988. Hezbollah, without actively participating, sided with the Palestinians and severely criticized AMAL. Then there was AMAL's legalistic take on the problem of the Israeli occupation: it accepted Resolution 425 and proposed settling the issue through diplomatic channels, via the Lebanese authorities. Meanwhile, some of its fighters were quick to sympathize with Israeli soldiers on the ground in a shared antipathy towards the Palestinian *fedayeen*. All these issues put distance between AMAL and Hezbollah, which categorically refused any rapprochement with the occupier and flouted international resolutions as well as diplomatic channels, taking their ineffectiveness for granted.

In the spring of 1988, sporadic clashes occurring since 1985 escalated into a real war for control of the country's three major Shiite areas (the South, the Bekaa Valley, and the southern suburbs of Beirut). Life in the three regions proceeded to the rhythm of these clashes for nearly two-and-a-half years. A first suspension of hostilities was signed in February 1989. By this point, AMAL had been expelled from the Bekaa and the southern suburbs of Beirut, where Hezbollah was from then on in sole control. The South was divided, with part of the area called the Iqlīm al-Tuffāh, as well as Jabal al-Sāfi and the village of Luwayzeh (Jezzin) dominated by Hezbollah; the rest of the region (not occupied by Israel) was under AMAL's authority.[42] However, clashes resumed in July 1990 in Iqlīm al-Tuffāh, where Hezbollah was surrounded for more than three months. The siege ended only with changes in the regional context, when the power of the Syrian regime in Lebanon was strengthened by the provisions of the Taef Agreement. The peace, co-sponsored by Damascus and Tehran, was signed between the two factions on 9 November 1990. The reconciliation was of crucial importance for the IRL: besides the fratricidal dimensions of these struggles (former minister Georges Corm estimated lives lost on both sides at 2,000 just from 1988 to 1989),[43] the main consequence of this war was a sharp slowdown in action by the IRL; with its fighters occupied with battling AMAL, and also prevented from accessing areas occupied by the Israeli army and the SLA, IRL operational performance reached its ebb between 1985 and 1988. The 1990 reconciliation cleared the way for a return of Hezbollah and the IRL to the areas in the South from which they had been expelled and to intensify the fight against Israel's troops once more.

Hezbollah support for IRL: the first mobilizations

Along with its original mission of developing a civilian organization dedicated to defending the interests of the IRL, Hezbollah worked to swell the latter's ranks. To this end, *al-ʿAhd* (The Commitment),[44] a weekly that appeared for the first time in June 1984, and Sawt al-Mustadʿafin (the Voice of the Oppressed), a radio station that went on the air in 1985, were started up. But both had limited scope: the broadcasts of Sawt al-Mustadʿafin covered an area not much greater than Baalbek–al-Hermel, and very few people, even within the party, read *al-ʿAhd*. The bulk of Hezbollah's mobilization efforts were practical, and catered more directly to people. To attract the largest possible number of young people to the IRL, Hezbollah clerics and their students increased their interventions and speeches at religious ceremonies (ʿĀshūrāʾ, Ramadan) or social events (weddings, funerals of fighters), which they attended in person.[45] They harangued potential recruits during demonstrations or marches organized in response to political events related to the Israeli occupation or heinous acts of the Lebanese government (Harb's assassination in 1984, signature of the Agreement of 17 May in 1983).[46] Although occupied daily by military training or fighting against the occupation in the South, the Resistance fighters were also called on to take on preaching duties in both public and private spheres when not busy with military activities. In the beginning, military and civil functions were not differentiated.

> At the time, there was no distinction between fighter and militant; the militant was both *taʿbiʾa* [mobilized] because he was a *mujāhid* [fighter] and *taʿbiʾa* because he had the task of mobilizing the entire population around the spirit of resistance.[47]

The fighters were also active in their own families, and called on personal experience to convince people closest to them to join the Resistance. They spent many hours in the fields helping farmers during the harvest, emulating the Pasdaran in this respect. Leveraging their own militant commitment, they initiated discussions in chance encounters on street corners and in cafés.[48] Field investigations in the Baalbek–al-Hermel area indicate that these interpersonal exchanges, rather than sermons delivered in the mosques, were what attracted most of the first combatants to the IRL's training camps.

The years of uncertainty

Much of the extant literature on Hezbollah in the 1980s associates it with violence, summed up in a series of bombings and hostage takings routinely assumed to be sponsored by the Iranian regime.[49] Few works show an interest in the party's existence, let alone its everyday life. The 1980s have more to tell us than that. A confused decade for Hezbollah, including in its relations with the Islamic revolutionary ideology, it nevertheless remains a gestation period and an extremely rich first coming of age.

Hezbollah and terrorism

On 18 April 1983 a car bomb exploded outside the American embassy in Beirut where a meeting of CIA officials and other members of the organization was taking place, leaving sixty-three people dead. On 23 October a double suicide attack, simultaneously carried out against the barracks of the American forces and French paratroopers in Beirut, resulted in 243 dead among the former and 58 among the latter. This shocked the American government into recalling its troops from the Multinational Force in February 1984, and the French troops were repatriated at the end of March. A previously unknown organization, Islamic Jihād, claimed responsibility for the "double exploit". The group was nevertheless tagged by Western intelligence services as a cover for Hezbollah. In fact, a relationship with Islamic Jihād—and other groups that would gain notoriety by hostage taking—was difficult to establish. The principal suspect was Imad Mughniyeh, a former bodyguard of Muhammad Husayn Fadlallāh; after belonging to a group of Palestinian fighters, he is said to have moved to an Islamic Jihād steered by Tehran.[50] Mystery shrouds the career of this person until his assassination in Damascus in February 2008, at which time Hezbollah hailed him as a great military strategist who was active in IRL ranks. The problem of his hierarchical ties to the Iranian government, visibly stronger than those he maintained with the party, and the fact that Hezbollah did not exist as such at the time of the acts attributed to him, complicate an assessment of the degree to which the party was implicated in the terrorist initiatives attributed to Mughniyeh. For their part, the party's leaders have regularly and consistently denied these accusations—however, not without some among them not hesitating to salute the work of "brothers" for carrying out certain attacks that have been rationalized as a "just" punishment meted out by the "oppressed" to their "oppressors".[51]

The way the Western—and especially the American—intelligence services read the Lebanese Shiite scene at the time, especially in the capital, moved the CIA to mount an assassination of Muhammad Husayn Fadlallāh, whom it suspected of instigating the attack against the Marines in 1983 and of supporting martyr operations. On 8 March 1985 a car bomb exploded outside the Fadlallāh home in Bīr al-'Abed, causing 80 deaths and wounding 256.[52] The main target escaped unharmed, saved by chance when an old woman detained him a few moments by the front door for a chat. Hezbollah conducted its own investigation, and found the local agents responsible for the operation. Eleven of them confessed that the attack was instigated by the American services, advised by Israel's Mossad and financed by Saudi authorities. On the ground, the operation was staged in collaboration with the Lebanese army intelligence affiliated with the Lebanese Forces militia. An investigation by the *Washington Post* concluded that the CIA was duped by the Lebanese Forces, which in all likelihood fingered Fadlallāh to settle their own score with the cleric.[53]

The 1982 and 1983 attacks were not the only terrorist acts blamed on Hezbollah by the West. Between 1982 and 1992 nearly 105 were kidnapped in Lebanon, mostly Westerners and mainly in Beirut.[54] The first was the Dean of the American University of Beirut (AUB), David Dodge, abducted shortly after the second Israeli invasion.[55] Nearly a dozen died in captivity, presumably either for lack of adequate medical care or they were killed. The last of the hostages were released in June 1992. For some of these operations no one took responsibility, and for others mostly obscure groups did so, such as the Organization of Islamic Jihād for the Liberation of Palestine, Organization for Revolutionary Justice, the Fajr Organization, the Khaybar Brigade, the Organization of the World's Oppressed, etc.[56] The name surfacing most often remained Islamic Jihād. Hezbollah was once more accused of using these as cover names on behalf of Tehran, which at the time was in a standoff with Washington, and Paris in particular, over the Eurodif affair.[57] Imad Mughniyeh moreover would be directly implicated in the kidnapping and detention of the French sociologist Michel Seurat.[58] The leadership of Hezbollah denied any involvement in this case also. The works of several researchers[59] conclude that hostage takers of various stripes in reality acted for different sets of reasons, sometimes related simply to fishing for ransom or for family reasons.[60] However that may be, while the Iranian regime officially claimed that its ability to influence the decisions of kidnappers was limited,[61] it exploited the hostage crisis to its advantage. Many releases were effected by its mediation with the kidnappers, allowing it to smooth over differences especially with the French government.

A quest to establish an Islamic state?

Hezbollah's philosophy of the State

Contrary to what many studies tend to suggest, Hezbollah's discourse on power and its relation to the state has been relatively constant through the years. The party has always acknowledged its "Islamic commitment" (*iltizām islāmī*) to the idea of an Islamic government as the ideal. However, two points need emphasizing. To this day, no theorization or official texts stemming from Hezbollah circles exist that would offer a definition of what the party means by "Islamic government". Nor is there any statement of how such a regime would manifest itself or what its constitution would be. An institutionalized version of the Islamic state, such as the one developed by

Egyptian Islamist thinker Tāriq al-Bishrī,[62] for example, does not exist.[63] As much as the concept of resistance has been pushed as a subject in party circles[64] since the second half of the 2000s, by the same token, the question of the Islamization of power seems not to have been a subject worth developing. Beyond that, the party's senior leaders as much as its cadres have always voiced their wish to see the emergence of a "strong and just" state—the terms used here being anything but trivial. In other words, Hezbollah intellectuals have developed less a philosophy of an Islamic state than expressed pragmatic, commonly held aspirations for a state that is strong (one that, unlike the contemporaneous Lebanese state, would be capable of protecting what is essentially a Shiite population in the South against Israeli aggressions) and just (one that, unlike the sectarian system, would be capable of meeting the socio-economic needs of the least privileged communities, foremost those of the Shiite community). In this, Hezbollah's political discourse is closer to the Lebanese communitarian tradition than to Islamist paradigms.

The second point is that the party leadership has set two conditions necessary for the establishment of an Islamic government in Lebanon. The first, mainly heard during the 1980s, is that the entire Middle East must have adopted an Islamic regime before Lebanon can. For Hezbollah it would be "unthinkable" to have an Islamic regime if they don't exist in the other parts of the region, thus refusing to conceive of Lebanon as an "isolated" Islamic state.[65] The second condition, based on a verse from the Qur'an that asserts that "there can be no compulsion in religion" (*lā ikrāh fil-dīn*),[66] states that an Islamic regime should not be imposed by force but chosen democratically by referendum or by parliamentary vote. Hezbollah insists, moreover, that this government must receive a true mandate by plebiscite. As early as 1986, Subhī al-Tufaylī claimed to favour an Islamic state on the condition that it is "demanded by a majority";[67] ten years later, it was Hassan Nasrallah who said:

> I do not deny that Hezbollah wants to see an Islamic Republic establish itself [in Lebanon] someday. ... However, the establishment of an Islamic Republic cannot be done by force or imposition. This requires a national referendum. And a positive 51 per cent referendum vote would not be an acceptable outcome. It would require a positive 90 per cent referendum. From that standpoint, and given the current context, the establishment of an Islamic Republic in Lebanon is not possible at the present time.[68]

The odds of setting up a Hezbollah Islamic state

The party's wish to see an Islamic regime established in Lebanon in a democratic manner is compromised even more because the distribution of seats in parliament is well defined in the Constitution. Under a first amendment to the Constitution in 1990 that followed the signing of the Taef Agreement, and then under a second one passed in 1992, 128 seats are allocated equally between Christians and Muslims. Of the 64 seats reserved for the latter, Hezbollah, as a Shiite party, is entitled to a maximum of 27 seats, which it competes for with other political groups of the same denomination, mainly AMAL, which insists on getting its fair share of the seats. In other words, the party can only initiate regime change, either by a parliamentary vote or referendum, with broad support from allied parties favouring an Islamization of power. However, apart from one or two Islamist (Sunni) factions, no Lebanese party is likely to be interested in the project. The party has always recognized this structural blockage, and even admitted on several occasions that the religious composition of society, above anything else, made it impossible to bring about an Islamic government in Lebanon. Unable to change the rules of the game in this regard, and despite its principled opposition to political sectarianism, once the party became resigned, like the other Muslim groups, such as AMAL and the PSP, to having to live with the Taef Agreement, it has consistently suggested that it is willing to settle for the system currently in place as a temporary situation, thus conceding that Lebanon was "not yet ready" in fact to move to a democracy of the one man, one vote kind.

Barring change in the rules of the institutional game, the party has only two options available: to establish an Islamic regime by force, by a coup, and so contradict its official stance; or to establish it on the local level in areas it controls, such as the northern Bekaa, southern Lebanon, and the southern suburbs of Beirut. To this day, the party has never tried to realize either of these possibilities. In point of fact, while it is true that Hezbollah during the early years (1982–7/8) tried to subject the people then under its dominance to some form of social control by imposing, for example, conservative restrictions on dress and liquor sales, it never worked to overthrow the regime or to establish institutions paralleling those of the Lebanese state. The party was not even tempted to imitate the PLO which, in the 1970s, was building what would later be referred to as a "state within the state", imposing its authority over large parts of Lebanese territory, in which it distributed identification cards, licence plates, and passes published by its own institutions. No "Hezbollah emirate" or "Hezbollah caliphate"[69] has ever been proclaimed, and the party has consistently scotched any rumours to that effect. In short, Hezbollah has never been revolutionary in the Western sense.

Hezbollah and the Lebanese state

This theoretical and practical respect for the existing system in no way signifies that the party has always had harmonious relationships with the Lebanese authorities. During the 1980s Hezbollah faced off with the army on a few occasions. Examination of these clashes indicates that their thrust is not so much to eradicate the political system as to rebuff the state, to keep it at a distance—in conformity with the interests of the IRL. First, there is the matter of finding infrastructure that it needed for its development. Between 1982 and 1983, after a first failed attempt, a procession of militants led by Hezbollah officials took possession of the so-called Barracks of

Sheikh ʿAbdallāh[70] south of the city of Baalbek, by all accounts without any shots being fired. Evacuated by the army, the barracks were turned into the Pasdaran's area HQ. That takeover was all the more strategic because these were the largest and best-equipped barracks in the Bekaa. In the same way, Hezbollah occupied the Baalbek École Normale, at one time transformed into the Khomeini Hospital. With the Pasdaran camped in the Baalbek suburbs, Hezbollah's leaders were careful to keep the IRL beyond the reach of the necessarily opposing authority from Beirut. By way of example, in March 1983, while Amin Gemayel intended "to subdue the terrorists"[71] and to re-establish the authority of the government over its territory, the Lebanese army, moving to its firing range at Taybeh, close to Brītāl, was stopped just short of the village by an ambush set by al-Tufaylī followers. Both sides sustained casualties, but the objective was achieved: the regime was pushed far back from the IRL training camps established in the area. To put it differently, the collisions between Hezbollah and the Lebanese state in the 1980s were not part of an attempt at establishing an Islamic regime in Beirut, but answered to the mission vested in the party at its creation.

The end of the 1980s in Iran and Lebanon

The late 1980s were a pivotal period in the history of the Islamic Resistance and of Hezbollah. The open war with AMAL distracted many of the activists who now found themselves forced to loosen their conservative grip over society. When the clashes started, Hezbollah's conservative rigour eased even more significantly[72] because it was unpopular in the society over which they exercised it. Regional and national contexts both worked in favour of this softening in the relationship between the party and society on the one hand and between the party and the Lebanese government on the other. Khomeini having died in early June 1989, Khamenei, of a conservative bent,[73] succeeded him. The same year, Rafsanjani became president of the Iranian Republic; a practitioner of realpolitik who planned to lead Iran out of its isolation, he worked on improving its relations with Washington. These two trends, conservative and pragmatic, would combine against the third current coursing through the Iranian political landscape at the time, that of the radicals.[74] This was represented by Ayatollah Hussein Ali Montazeri and Ali-Akbar Mohtashami-Pur. Montazeri fell out of favour in 1989, a few months before Khomeini's death.[75] By August that year, Mohtashami-Pur was no longer Minister of the Interior. With the revolutionary tendency sidelined in Tehran, Hezbollah in Lebanon was ordered by Rafsanjani to become "a party like the others". The Pasdaran had been pulling out of the country since August 1988.[76] Grants awarded up to Hezbollah by the Iranian regime dwindled, old ties began to loosen. Tehran announced that it would from that time maintain the same level of relations with the different actors on the Lebanese political scene and deal more with the Lebanese government. Only the Revolutionary

Guards—who would also lose some of their pre-eminence during the period just beginning then—and the Office of the Supreme Leader remained Hezbollah's "true" friends in Iran. Finally, the end of the civil war in the Country of Cedars began a (relative) revival of the state and its institutions. The militias were disarmed, as required by the Taef Agreement. For Hezbollah, this raised the question of what kind of rapport to establish with a Lebanese government trying to re-establish its authority on its territory, a question made even more complicated by Damascus officially having the upper hand in Beirut's affairs from then on.

Lebanon comes under Syrian tutelage

With the end of the civil war, the Lebanese internal situation experienced a relative return to normalcy. Some targeted attacks and several Israeli raids reminded the Lebanese that the security situation in the country was not yet fully stabilized, but the renewal of institutional life, interrupted by fifteen years of war, proceeded apace. Parliamentary elections, last held in 1972, were held once again in 1992; and municipal elections, which had not occurred since 1963, took place in 1998. The 1990s were also years of reconstruction, begun in the aftermath of the civil war by the government of Omar Karameh but actually taken over by his successor, Rafic Hariri. Following the collapse of the Soviet Bloc, with which it had been allied, Damascus moved to improve relations with Washington. When Operation Desert Storm was launched in January 1991, its troops took part in the Western military coalition led by the United States. A few months later, in October, Syria participated in the Madrid summit where peace talks were initiated between Arab countries and Israel. In return, the Hafez al-Assad regime received significant financial support from the Gulf states, and Europe lifted the economic sanctions it had imposed in 1986 for Syria's involvement in terrorist operations. More importantly, Damascus obtained wide latitude from Washington in managing Lebanese affairs.[77] In so many words, the Land of Cedars came under Syrian tutelage.

Prior to this time, relations between the Syrian regime and Hezbollah had been anything but amicable. During the 1980s serious clashes had pitted the Syrian army or the SSNP against the party. The bloodiest episode of Syria–Hezbollah relations was undoubtedly the killings in February 1987 when a trivial dispute between Hezbollah militants stationed at the Fathallāh barracks, then in the hands of the IRL, escalated into a face-off with Syrian troops that had just rolled into West Beirut. A Syrian officer lined up twenty-three party members, and then put a bullet in the head of each.[78] At the time, the cartography of Lebanese regional alliances, particularly on the Shiite political landscape, had AMAL as the protégé of Syria's regime, while Hezbollah's protector was the Iranian government. When it subsequently came to resolving the disputes between Hezbollah and AMAL, Ali Akbar Rafsanjani would represent the former's interests and Hafez al-Assad those of the latter.

In 1989 new relations between Damascus and Hezbollah were inaugurated. That year the party, like most Lebanese political actors,[79] initially opposed the Taef Agreement. It provided for the disarmament of militias, but the IRL had no intention of surrendering its weapons or ceasing to struggle against the Israeli occupation. In addition, in Hezbollah's view, the agreement did much too little to abolish the system of privileges granted to the (Maronite) Christian community, and it appeared to enshrine the sectarian government.[80] Tehran intervened, and a compromise was reached. The Taef Agreement was revised to allow the IRL—and only the IRL—to keep its weapons for the sake of fighting the occupation forces in the South. With the interests of the Resistance safeguarded, Hezbollah made the best of a bad situation. Although it did not accept the provisions of Taef as quickly as AMAL or the PSP, ultimately it did so, contenting itself with merely describing the new system as "temporarily acceptable", a formulation to which it has adhered ever since.

This recognition of Syrian tutelage over Lebanon, plus the reshuffling of political cards in Iran, configured the relationships between Hezbollah and Damascus on the one hand and Iran and Hezbollah on the other in new ways. From the very start the nature of the links between the party and the Syrian and Iranian regimes differed greatly. In Iran, political power is dually configured. The presidency of the Republic is secular, as is the government; it is religious in the person of the Supreme Guide of the Revolution. Hezbollah's allegiance to the principle of *wilāyat al-faqīh* places it in a subordinate relationship with the Guide, not the president.[81] Moreover, running counter to the idea that *wilāyat al-faqīh* makes Hezbollah a remote-controlled satellite of Tehran, the link with the Guide actually only comes into play in special cases. Even then, allegiance to *wilāyat al-faqīh* translates into (i) a stamp of approval delivered *a posteriori* by a Guide who, by all indications, to date has never countermanded a decision taken by the party leadership; and (ii) refereeing in a way that always seems to second the majority view in the Council (*Shūrā*). In practice, this allows Hezbollah more room for manoeuvre, including in its decision making, management, and implementation of decisions, as long as the two men who held or hold the position of *waliy*—Khomeini followed by Khamenei—have been or are mentors who intrude relatively little into the affairs of the party. In the case of the former, it was for lack of interest (he was much more concerned about what was happening in Iraq than in Lebanon) and as for the latter, it was because he obviously has confidence in Hezbollah's leadership being able to make the right choices for sustaining the party. Not counting the Office of the Guide, it was during the 1990s that the Iranian government first distanced itself from Hezbollah. Under mandates by Rafsanjani (1989–97) and Khatami (1997–2005) the party lost the support of the "presidential link"[82] embodied during Khomeini's time by Ali Khamenei. Rafsanjani had already put out the word after his election that Hezbollah must become "a party like the others". Under Muhammad Khatami, Iran's interest in reaching out to other political tendencies in Lebanon and in respecting the country's sovereignty explains the relative weakening of the party's privileged status. In October 1997 Hariri was officially invited to Iran, noted by Houchang Chehabi as the first visit by a Lebanese prime minister since the Revolution, and one that would go on for five days;[83] during his visit to Beirut in 2003 the Iranian president met key local political figures without giving preferential treatment to Hezbollah.

Actually, Hezbollah did not suffer from this relative cooling of relations with the Iranian state. It remained sensitive to advice received from Iranian officials and dispensed in accompaniment to their decisions. In the early 1990s, consequent to agreements reached between Tehran and several Western capitals, the last remaining hostages in Lebanon were released,[84] with notable cooperation by Hezbollah. In 1997 Khatami recommended that the party open the resistance to participation by other Lebanese groups. This recommendation spoke to a need already felt by some Lebanese,[85] and it led to the formation of al-Sarāyā al-Lubnāniyya li-Muqāwamat al-Ihtilāl al-Isrā'īlī (Lebanese Brigades to Resist the Israeli Occupation (LBRIO)), a multi-sectarian regiment placed under IRL command. In lieu of the Iranian government largesse that the party had enjoyed during Khomeini's time, it compensated for the suspension of government subsidies under Rafsanjani and Khatami by developing a policy of self-financing.[86] Its bank balances and those of the IRL suffered even less because, following the death in 1994 of Muhammad ʿAlī Arākī, the last great *marjaʿ* of the time, the Hezbollah leadership chose Ali Khamenei as its *marjaʿ*. In return, the Guide appointed Hassan Nasrallah and Muhammad Yazbek as his two *wakīl*s in Lebanon, allowing them to collect religious taxes in the country and in the diaspora from Lebanese believers who chose Khamenei as their *marjaʿ*.

Although the link between Hezbollah and the Guide was vertical, for the time being it therefore remained rather flexible. This was much less the case with the Syrian regime—particularly during its tutelage over Lebanon—even though in this case it was horizontal. Damascus, responsible for Lebanese affairs, took a direct hand in managing them. To maintain local forces in equilibrium, Assad, father and then son, repeatedly imposed binding directives on the various Lebanese actors, Hezbollah included. The party, needing the good will of the Syrian regime to continue the resistance in the South and to get weapons deliveries from Iran shipped through Syrian territory, had to walk a fine line in this relationship of hierarchizing dependency as best it could. In so doing, it took advantage of the fact that the party's actions also had utility for the Assad dynasty. By supporting the resistance, the regime at least bought itself an image as a "resistant Arab" power that helped it maintain political legitimacy in its own country. Hezbollah, just as it did with the Lebanese government, practised non-confrontation in its relations with the Syrian regime to keep from compromising the IRL's interests. However, whenever it could, it ignored Damascus *desiderata*. For the municipal elections of 1998 and 2004, AMAL lobbied Hezbollah to run joint slates in hopes of profiting from the latter's popularity, but the party, sure of extensive victories, rejected this. The Syrian authorities in Lebanon intervened by pressuring the party on AMAL's behalf, but Hezbollah stood firm and ran its own slates in each of the two electoral contests.[87] Once more, in the spring of 2000, with the Syrian regime concerned over the possibility of Israel resigning itself to a unilateral and unnegotiated withdrawal from Lebanon—even appearing to hope that there would be no Israeli retreat—the IRL did not hesitate to ignore Syrian concerns by increasing the pace of attacks against the occupying forces. The IRL was indeed determined to keep the Israeli General Staff and the Tel Aviv government from backpedalling on an unconditional withdrawal.

In summary, while affinity and an ideological engagement connect Hezbollah to the Guide, a more or less balanced, implicit contract is all that links the party and Damascus. In neither case is Hezbollah a docile arm of one or the other regime. It has its own set of priorities and a great deal of room for manoeuvre.

Hezbollah under al-Mūsawī then Nasrallah

Internal changes

In 1989 Hezbollah for the first time built a formal political structure. It set up a Consultative Council (Shūrā), with nine members, all Lebanese,[88] with an Executive Council (Majlis Tanfīdhī) and a Political Office (Maktab Siyāsī) responsible for relations with the public. It also created executive positions for justice and a head of the military council[89] and, most importantly, that of secretary-general, with Subhī al-Tufaylī in the post. This first reorganization had no impact on Hezbollah's political activities, which remained limited to relatively low-key communications at that time. The step up to the next level came two years later, in May 1991, at the second party congress, at which ʿAbbās al-Mūsawī succeeded al-Tufaylī, blamed by some for the continued tensions with AMAL.[90] The leadership intended, in fact, to refocus Hezbollah and the IRL's activities, hampered by the years of battling AMAL, on the fight against the occupation. Without being officially rewritten, the party's basic political document, untouched since the Open Letter of 1985, was modified to give priority to the following five objectives: (i) liberate the South from occupation; (ii) repeal political sectarianism and build a system based on the popular vote;[91] (iii) establish relations with all Lebanese parties except those that collaborate with the occupier; (iv) attempt to strengthen Muslim unity; and (v) work to ensure unity in the Shiite ranks.[92] Items (i), (ii), and (iv) repeated the party's already familiar concerns and (v), contextual, was nothing more than official confirmation of the intent to finally end the war with AMAL. The real novelty lay in (iii) by launching a practice that was unprecedented for Hezbollah: building cooperative relations and coordinating with other Lebanese political groups, particularly Christians.[93]

Ultimately, the credit for the turnabout of the early 1990s went to the third secretary-general of Hezbollah, Hassan Nasrallah; al-Mūsawī did not live to enjoy the results of the adjustments to the party's general guidelines carried out under his direction.[94] On 16 February 1992 Hezbollah organized a large rally in Jibshīt to commemorate the assassination of Rāghib Harb. The party's Information Unit had announced the event, its time, and place three days beforehand.[95] Some biographies of al-Mūsawī treat as fact the story that he had a presentiment he would be assassinated that day.[96] An early version has it that he had spoken to several cadres a few days earlier about his impending death, and that at the last council meeting he is said to have advised his colleagues "not to abandon their responsibilities with regard to preserving the heritage [that is, the struggle against the occupation]".[97] Another version has Harb appearing to him in a dream and telling him: "You will come to me, I am waiting."[98] At the end of that day, al-Mūsawī, after delivering the keynote speech, is supposed to have hugged young Ahmad Harb, son of the deceased, and asked him if there was "something he wanted to ask his father",[99] "as if he knew he was going to find his friend soon after".[100] Indeed, he visited Harb's grave, and, after a lunch with the family of his former comrade in arms, left for Sharqiyyeh,[101] then for Kawthariyyat al-Sayyād,[102] where he visited the families of martyrs. During all these comings and goings, three Israeli planes constantly shadowed the convoy. As they approached Teffāhtā,[103] on the road back to al-Nabī Shīt, a rocket fired by an Israeli helicopter hit the vehicle of the secretary-general. Al-Mūsawī, his wife, and little boy sitting in the back seat were killed in the resulting blaze. Spokesmen for the Israeli military and government repeatedly affirmed subsequently that they had sought to destabilize the IRL by assassinating its head. Cognizant of this, the Hezbollah leadership chose his successor even before the funeral procession carrying his remains set out for his final resting place in the Bekaa Valley. The council elected his companion and disciple, Hassan Nasrallah, to lead the party.

Defending the IRL's interests, avoiding confrontations with the authorities

The question of Hezbollah's relationship to Lebanese institutional life really only began to occur in 1991–2. The issue was twofold: the party had to decide whether it was prepared to accommodate the state in areas where it had a presence; and it had to consider possibly taking part in the political game with institutions, including parliamentary and governmental ones. In each case, Hezbollah's leadership answered in the affirmative, and the "Nasrallah years" began by committing to political participation.[104]

Much has been made of the party's entering parliament in 1992, and its concern to bring its activities within the law. Many observers at the time were shocked by the integration of an Islamist party seen as hostile to state authority with the national institutional apparatus. Even today, the "mystery" persists, and is usually explained as a "shift" in the party's course.[105] It is said to have abandoned its regional priorities in favour of a "Lebanization", defined as the rejection of all outside influence and a nepotistic, communitarian understanding of power. However, for the Hezbollah of 1992 this is not what it was about. In reality, there was much more continuity in the logic of the party's action from the time of its creation to participation in national politics than is generally believed. In absolute terms, it does not prevent an organization from also keeping a regionalist focus. However, in Hezbollah's case, it appears that in practice its priorities have always been Lebanese-centric. In fact, the party has never considered a territorial or administrative affiliation with any country in the region (Syria, Iran), and never intended to register its primary affiliation anywhere but in Lebanon. As noted by James Piscatori, transnational relationships forged in the name of Islam do not prevent attachment or loyalty to countries of origin.[106] The party's choice to participate in the parliamentary elections of 1992 was precisely with the objective of "making the voice of the Resistance heard in Parliament" ('La-nwassel sawt al-Muqāwama lal-Barlamēn').[107] For Hezbollah it was not about de-ideologizing or becoming a (clientelist) party like all the others, but sitting in the chamber of parliament in order to fulfil, then and always, the task for which it was created: defending the interests of the IRL. This harmonizes perfectly with what the party has always been. Aside from this tactical choice, there can be no question of an abandonment of principle by Hezbollah, of a great reversal and metamorphosis. Participation in politics and concern for legality are for Hezbollah the possibilities offered by a flexible *répertoire d'action*, but it only wields its tools on behalf of the same enduring concern. Its primordial goal remains unaltered. The Taef Agreement, Lebanon's coming under Syrian tutelage, the distancing by the Iranian regime, and the war with 'AMAL first and foremost illustrate the threat posed by an unpredictable environment that could force the IRL to fight an armed foe other than the Israeli army. Participation in national politics must be placed in the context of the party's general strategy and not just studied in isolation. From the late 1980s the party was committed to work to minimize the threats potentially emerging on the domestic scene. It is vital for the IRL not to alienate society, to keep a home front from opening up as a potential second front that, together with the Israeli army, might clamp the Resistance in a vice. In the calculations of the party leadership, a fundamental tenet is to avoid rousing the Lebanese and the government against the IRL.

Consequently, the issues addressed by Hezbollah members from the benches of parliament dovetailed with their function as appendages of the Resistance. Specifically, its deputies demanded aid for the populations bombarded by the Israeli army, and a system of compensation. They pleaded the cause of prisoners held in Israel or Khyām, whom they accused the government of having abandoned and whose cause the party wanted to have declared a matter of national interest. Hezbollah *inter alia* sought to have the media publicize the IRL by supporting its political rallies and international meetings, summits and conferences: "The State should support the Resistance by transforming all government institutions into institutions of resistance"[108]—in other words, emulate what the party does through its own institutions. During each military crisis with Israel, the party expected the state to complement its work by providing political support for the cause of the Resistance domestically, and to support it diplomatically in the face of Israeli and Western pressures. Using this logic, the party attacked the excessive fiscal deficit policy practised by Hariri. The party feared that the existing debt burden would not only be impossible to repay but could potentially imperil Lebanon's sovereignty, since its inevitable rescheduling or forgiveness by Western governments and international organizations would probably come with political conditions at the party's expense. As part of its deficit policy, the party also attacked Hariri's predictions of an imminent peace agreement in the Middle East, categorically rejecting any normalization of relations with the state of Israel.

At the same time as it defended the interests of the *Muqāwama*, Hezbollah criticized economic and social inequalities. Once more, it took on the policy of reconstruction, criticizing the gap between the large sums budgeted for the capital and the minimal ones authorized for the outlying regions—mainly the South and the Bekaa—when, as the party recalled, these two regions had been waiting for decades for the state to provide them with basic services such as a power grid, running water, and schools. Party members called for regional development with budgets based on need, not split down the middle. Similarly, they complained of inequality in the treatment of the displaced from the Mountain[109] and those from regions such as Dekwaneh, Tall al-Zaʿtar, and Nabʿa.[110]

Unlike Islamist parties of the region that had also chosen parliamentary participation, Hezbollah, in more than twenty-five years of representation in parliament, has never used the chamber to call for even a partial Islamization of power. In the political horse-trading that it engages in with other Lebanese and regional political parties, the Islamization of laws, institutions, or even of society never enters the negotiations, never constitutes a benefit or a payoff. The party's speeches also very rarely fall back on Islamic references to gain legitimacy. Hence, when the party condemned the Hariri government's income-tax policy, it did so not by invoking the Islamic prohibition on *ribā* (usury or charging interest, forbidden in Islam), as the Sunni Islamist party al-Jamāʿa al-Islāmiyya did, but because, according to Hezbollah, this tax hit the poor the hardest. The sociologist Dalal al-Bizri also noted that Hezbollah members do not use the *basmala*,[111] and they have no objection to a Saturday holiday, which the representatives of al-Jamāʿa al-Islāmiyya had stigmatized and proposed to switch with Friday instead, a proposal that garnered no support from Hezbollah, unlike what might have been expected from another Islamic party.[112] "Neither Islamization, nor the concept of the "Islamic state" or the question of the application of *sharīʿa* seem to figure among their major concerns. Even when the debates are conducive to the issue, they do not necessarily reference it."[113]

"All but the *fitna*"

Once it had joined the political game, Hezbollah positioned itself as an opposition party. Its critiques of the Hariri governments were manifold. An initial squabble pitted them against each other from the start: in November 1992, although Hezbollah was the most important party in parliament,[114] its candidate to head the government, Ibrāhīm Bayyān, was rejected in favour of Hariri. As already mentioned, the latter's ultra-liberalism and reckless deficit policy were other bones of contention, as well as some vaguely anti-IRL policies and Hariri's support for a Middle East reconciled with Israel. Nevertheless, Hezbollah did not conceive of itself as a splinter group—it criticized the political system while continuing to recognize it. As previously stated, jettisoning the existing system was not in question for the party. An unmistakeable case in point is that, from the second half of the 1980s, nearly all of its institutions filed applications for registration with the Ministry of the Interior. Political contacts between Hezbollah's leadership and the Lebanese government took place even before the party chose to participate in the elections. It would have been approached by Lebanese authorities from the winter of 1990, while the government was being formed, with an offer to participate in it.[115] As a token of good will, after its acceptance of the Taef Accords, the party returned to the army and state institutions all the locations and buildings it had appropriated from them in the early 1980s.[116] Thus, in order to safeguard IRL interests, Hezbollah during the 1990s opted for political consensus and a low profile to forestall any domestic quarrels. The basic principle on which its relationship to the state rested was clear: as long as the government did not harm the interests of the IRL, the party would not hinder the government's work and would not take any steps to undermine its power. As discussed earlier, this relationship was conceived as a complementary partnership expressed in a division of labour. The implicit deal was that the IRL would defend the national territory on the ground militarily while the government was to support the Resistance domestically and abroad, both politically and through diplomacy.

As long as this agreement held, the party did its part by not shattering the civil peace at any time. Hezbollah's interest in maintaining this understanding was such during this period that the party even refused to be provoked into reprisals against the authorities, or in the context of clashes with other social and political actors. The most telling example of this determination is the "Massacre of 13 September" 1993. On this date the agreements reached during secret negotiations between representatives of the Israeli and Palestinian sides, later designated as the Oslo Accords, were signed. In response, Hezbollah and other Lebanese parties called for protest demonstrations. The government banned the gathering under the pretext of safety concerns. The organizers persisted, while remaining open to a compromise with the authorities. One that was offered involved modifying the route slightly, to which Hezbollah agreed. The march started in the direction of the airport, as planned, when the army suddenly opened fire on the demonstrators. Nine people were killed, including two women, and dozens injured. Alerted immediately, Hezbollah's leaders forbade the protesters from retaliating, ordering them to return to their homes immediately. Between protecting the IRL and defending the community, the party's priorities were clear.

This mutually rendered support for a *pax civilis* and the IRL's interests also translates into a marked rapprochement with Christian actors and leaders. The allusion to Lebanese parties that "collaborate with the occupier" presented under point (iii) of the new priorities promulgated by the second congress set the stage for Hezbollah to come to terms with a party such as Kataeb, still a despised enemy in the Open Letter of 1985, because its leadership in the war's aftermath moved closer to Syrian policy, at Israel's expense. The Political Bureau established a channel for exchanges, communication, and coordination with various political and religious groups,[117] efforts that led, among other things, to drawing up joint electoral slates with Christian parties during legislative elections.

In the thinking of the party leadership, it was no longer about keeping the state or other political formations at arm's length. But instead of following the traditional practices, in which positions of power are primarily baskets of resources for community or local leaders to redistribute to sectarian clienteles mobilized mainly for electoral purposes, Hezbollah introduced a new element to the domestic scene by treating the various players as potential partners for helping to advance the cause. In this respect, the essence of Hezbollah's political strategy was not to shrink from inclusivity. Instead, its goal was to gather a maximum of national players around the Resistance. Inasmuch as Damascus controlled the Lebanese chessboard, the job was facilitated because the obstructive nuisance value of opponents was neutralized in advance by the Syrian censor. As presented in the second part, the end of Syrian tutelage would to some extent change the nature of this *modus vivendi* governing relations between the various Lebanese parties up to that point.

Shattering the image of "extremism" (*tatarruf*)

With Hezbollah disposed to take into account the new context of the late 1980s, it also set the stage for an evolution in the attitudes and behaviours of its militants towards those outside it—starting with the other components of Lebanese society. The party worked assiduously to counter the perception that it was an extremist organization. This concern led it to make twin choices: (i) the abandonment of practices perceived as backward, reactionary and intolerant, in favour of new ones judged more conducive to "gentlemanizing" its image prevalent both in the community at large and outside it, as well as in the eyes of party members themselves; and (ii) having recourse to intensive and multifaceted communications.

It is no coincidence that Hezbollah modified its flag during the 1990s. Its logo no longer read "The Islamic Revolution in Lebanon" (*al-Thawra al-islāmiyya fī Lubnān*) but "The Islamic Resistance in Lebanon" (*al-Muqāwama al-islāmiyya fī Lubnān*). The name change reaffirmed a priority—the resistance—and indicated that it was modifying the Iranian-inspired revolutionary idiom. With regard to its co-religionists, the social pressure the party exerted during the first half of the 1980s was relaxed significantly by the end of the decade. In predominantly Shiite cities, drinking establishments were able to resume their trade unmolested as long as they did so with relative discretion that respected the morals that are usually prevalent in all Muslim cities (whether Shiite or Sunni). Provocative clothes were visible again in the streets and public places, the wearing of the chador declined quickly to an ultra-minority. Concerts of popular or foreign music were tolerated, as were artistic and leisure activities once regarded with severity, starting with dancing.[118] With regard to Lebanese of other communities, the party practised détente: at Christmas and Easter, it sends delegations to present holiday greetings to their notables, both, local representatives and top government leaders. It liberalized its media, frequently featuring people from outside the community as well as from other political tendencies; women without veils are present on the sets of al-Manār, and Christians work in several of the party's institutions. Foreigners, meanwhile, are objects of special care, including a marked hospitality geared to convincing them of the falsity of received ideas about the party (accusations of terrorism, fundamentalism, irrational violence, or anti-Semitism). From the late 1990s Hezbollah even developed a Jewish policy, under which it invited, in its own name, rabbis, personalities, and activists from non-Zionist Jewish organizations to Lebanon. This is done mostly in a framework of discussions for promoting interfaith peace to highlight whenever possible the non-anti-Semitic character of the party, and the political and ideological—that is, non-religious—nature of its aversion to the state of Israel. American academics Noam Chomsky and Norman Finkelstein, the former travelling in the Country of Cedars in 2006 and 2010, and the latter in 2008, were received with honour by party cadres—by Nasrallah himself in Chomsky's case. In 2010 Fareed Zakaria, star host of the American television channel CNN, did a segment of his show on the support provided by Hezbollah for the renovation of the Magen Abraham Synagogue in Beirut, the last remaining one in the capital. In other words, the message that the party wants to convey is clear: Hezbollah is a national party, it is moderate, and it is a champion of civil peace that is open to the world; it is far removed from judging the religious preferences of others or condemning national allegiances, and only takes into account political and ideological convictions—leaving only sympathy for Zionism as the one point of view that it does not intend to accommodate.

On to liberation

In parallel with these course corrections made by Hezbollah to its socio-political praxis, the 1990s saw the resumption of fighting between the IRL and the Israeli army in South Lebanon. With the war against AMAL over, and especially the election of Hassan Nasrallah as secretary-general, the pace of IRL attacks against the occupier accelerated.

The IRL improves its methods—and its performance

Without retracing the entire history of the IRL or providing a comprehensive chronology of all operations it carried out leading up to the spring of 2000, it remains for us to point out the most significant of them—those that influenced Hezbollah's public at the time, but also the Israeli army and society, those that illuminated the retreat in May 2000 and that went into the gradually building perception of *ustūrat al-Muqāwama*, "the legend of the Resistance".

Despite the cessation of hostilities with AMAL, ratified in 1990, the grand return of the IRL actually only took place with the accession of Hassan Nasrallah as head of the party in 1992. He wasted no time. No sooner was he elected than he pledged to "make the Israelis pay" for his predecessor's assassination.[119] As it happened, the Israelis were bringing up reinforcements to the border, starting on the night of 17 February. Hezbollah called for a general mobilization, to which the villages in the border region responded immediately, and the IRL fired sixty rockets into northern Galilee settlements. Prime Minister Yitzhak Shamir initially announced a large-scale operation, but the General Staff would ultimately launch only a limited operation. The attack came on 20 February. The villages in the South were pounded with covering fire for the reinforcements being brought up to the Kafrā–Sarbīn–Hārīs (Bint Jbeil) triangle, where the IRL immediately hurled itself at them. That day the Israeli army would announce the loss of a top officer and three soldiers.[120]

From that time on, the Islamic Resistance harassed the Israeli and SLA forces, firing on their positions and attacking their convoys. The number of operations increased spectacularly, rising from 378 in 1994 to 660 in 1995, to 763 in 1996, 786 in 1997, 1,164 in 1998, and 1,528 in 1999.[121] Several martyr operations were conducted. The most spectacular were those carried out in August 1992 and in April 1995, each one costing the Israeli army between twenty and thirty dead or wounded. On 28 February 1999 Erez Gerstein, the highest-ranking Israeli officer in Lebanon, was killed in an IRL operation, and on 30 January 2000 the number two in the SLA, ʿAql Hāshim, suffered the same fate. The ratio of IRL losses to Israeli army losses dropped from 10:1 in the early 1990s to nearly 1:1 by the end of the decade.[122]

According to some IRL leaders, the quality of its operations at this time is explained by the development of counter-espionage capability. The SLA itself was infiltrated.[123] To better protect its officers, "having drawn many lessons from the mistakes of Palestinians and LNM",[124] but also remembering the assassination of ʿAbbās al-Mūsawī, the Resistance shrouded its movements and actions in absolute secrecy. It set up its own surveillance and intelligence-gathering apparatus, and coordinated with the official Lebanese security organs and their counterparts in Syria. In this way, it managed to set several ambushes for the occupier and its militia. The most famous was at al-Ansāriyyeh in September 1997. On the night of 5 September an Israeli elite commando unit from the Shitat Marine Brigade landed on the

Lebanese coast to mine an IRL trail into the village of Ansāriyyeh near Sidon, outside the "security zone".[125] The commandos walked into an ambush set by the Resistance, a unit of which, informed in advance of the Israeli operation, was lying in wait. After a firefight lasting more than three hours, seventeen Israeli soldiers had been killed or injured.[126]

Despite the arrival of reinforcements in the form of Israeli air force planes, which bombed the battlefield, the IRL fighters managed to carry off the bodies of the dead Israeli soldiers, precious currency for its prisoner exchanges with Tel Aviv. A previous such exchange had taken place following the so-called operation of Kūnīn in March 1986, during which the Resistance had captured two Israeli soldiers.[127] The first part of the exchange, in 1991, had secured the release of ninety-one prisoners from Israeli jails and allowed the IRL to recover the remains of nine of its fighters; in the second, in 1996, Hezbollah returned the bodies of the two soldiers in exchange for the release of forty-five prisoners from Khyām and the return of the bodies of 123 fighters. The Ansāriyyeh operation in 1997 allowed the party to negotiate a new exchange in June 1998, in which fifty prisoners were released from Khyām and ten from Israel, and the bodies of forty fighters were turned over.[128]

Operations Accountability (1993) and Grapes of Wrath (1996)[129]

Along with attacks that they launched or fended off daily in the war zone, Tel Aviv's troops staged several large-scale offensives, like so many shock-and-awe operations intended to demoralize the IRL. Two among these stand out by their size and their politico-military consequences: Operation Accountability in 1993 and Operation Grapes of Wrath in 1996.

On 25 July 1993 the Israeli army launched the first one. Acting Prime Minister Shimon Peres stated at the time:

> The strikes have two goals: to answer those who attack us directly, especially Hezbollah, and to draw [the] attention of the Lebanese people and government concerned to the need for pressuring Hezbollah to stop its activity.[130]

Ehud Barak, then chief of staff, was more explicit, warning the Lebanese government that it "must disarm Hezbollah, otherwise Israel will do it".[131] For seven days its planes, supported by the fleet, bombed the South, the western and northern Bekaa, Beirut, and the northern part of the country, targeting infrastructure (water and electricity networks, bridges, and roads), residential areas, private or public institutions (schools, shops), and the Palestinian refugee camp of Nahr al-Bared (near Tripoli). The attacks resulted in 140 Lebanese civilians killed, 500 injured, and 200,000 displaced; 13 IRL fighters were killed, 120 locales were affected, and 10,000 dwellings were destroyed. According to UNIFIL, the Israelis flew 1,200 air sorties and fired more than 28,000 shells during the first five days alone. The IRL responded by intermittently firing Katyusha rockets, 500 by an Israeli count, and it also carried out thirty operations on Lebanese territory against the Israeli army and SLA. Offensive operations ceased on the evening of 31 July, upon American mediation requested by the Israeli authorities. The operation ended formally with a verbal agreement between the Israeli government and the IRL, known as the July Agreement, which committed the Resistance to stop firing rockets into northern Israel, while the Israeli army was to refrain from targeting civilians or localities outside the occupied zone. In effect, the two sides agreed to confine hostilities to the "security zone" and refrain from harming third parties in attacks.

Three years later, in April 1996, facing the IRL's continuing attacks on its troops stationed in Lebanon, Israel staged a second major operation. Two months earlier *istishhādī* ʿAlī Ashmar had killed two soldiers in an Israeli convoy near Marjayoun. The situation at the time seemed particularly propitious for a severe response, because in mid-March the summit of Sharm al-Sheikh in Egypt had affirmed international commitment to fighting terrorism. Two weeks later the Israeli army went on the attack by shelling civilians at Yātir (Bint Jbeil); the July Agreement now breached, IRL Katyushas began falling on northern Israel. Opting for escalation, on 11 April the Israeli army launched Operation Grapes of Wrath. Lebanese civilians were targeted even more than in 1993; on the 18th the Israeli air force hit a UN headquarters in the village of Qānā, where more than a hundred women, children, and elderly had sought refuge under the protection of Fijian peacekeepers. Emergency responders counted 118 civilian dead and 127 wounded. The offensive lasted 18 days and resulted in 250 civilian deaths, 5 dead Lebanese army soldiers, and 14 IRL fighters. The Israeli army initially suffered no dead and 127 wounded in its ranks.[132]

The political, military, and diplomatic consequences of the 1996 offensive far exceeded those of 1993. The IRL surprised the Lebanese public, the Israeli army, and the international community with how well it was able to sustain its attacks. The rate at which Katyushas were fired daily never slackened despite the sustained bombardment of the IRL positions by the Israeli army. In Israel, the debate on the efficacy of keeping troops in southern Lebanon intensified, given their seeming inability to protect the north from enemy rocket fire. It reinforced a sense of insecurity and disquiet that was already strong within an Israeli population targeted for years by the Palestinian Hamas, which had carried out several suicide attacks in Israel between 1992 and 1996.[133] Shimon Peres, the Labour Party candidate in the general elections slated for May, who, having built his campaign on pledges to ensure the country's security, had therefore authorized the operation against Lebanon, lost the election to the Likud candidate, Benjamin Netanyahu. In Lebanon, the IRL experienced its great moment of glory. The ceasefire, proclaimed at 6 p.m. on 27 April 1996, this time was documented in what is known as the April Agreement. It emulated the provisions of the July Agreement, but compliance was now monitored by a commission comprising Lebanon, Israel, France, the United States, and the UN. On the diplomatic, and especially the symbolic, level the agreement officially recognized the IRL's right to fight against the Israeli army as a right of self-defence. This meant that it had evolved, in terms of image, from a terrorist organization into a resistance force whose struggle the international community had legitimized.

The IRL develops its communications

The Resistance achieved its successes in part thanks to a first-of-its-kind initiative, namely a media policy with a military dimension that simultaneously aimed to captivate large numbers of Lebanese and to demoralize the occupier and Israeli society. The IRL very early on made it standard operating procedure to film some of its operations. Initially, the goal was to archive the clips for use in training combatants.[134] Very soon, the General Staff opted to utilize these videos not only within a psychological warfare framework against the Israeli armed forces, but also for promoting its cause in Lebanese society. To accomplish this, the IRL used a specialized team, al-Jihād al-Iʿlāmī (Combat media [unit]), which attacks through the camera lens with the strategic goals of:

1. Recording, in sound and images, the realities of confronting the occupier on the ground, revealing the enemy's incompetence, showing him as he flees the battlefield, and exposing the actual number of his losses; ...
2. Demoralizing Israeli soldiers and collaborators barricaded in frontline positions, spreading terror among them to make it easier to defeat them on the battlefield;
3. Luring the occupier into broadcast ambushes, as in the case of the al-Dabsheh operation[135] ... by the Resistance unveiling what had really happened using the clips it had shot, the occupier was forced to retract earlier statements, causing a storm of criticism and mutual recriminations among Israeli officials;
4. Encouraging some soldiers to refuse to perform their military service in the Lebanese quagmire, by showing them first hand the tragic fates of their comrades ...;[136]
5. Encouraging protests by parents of soldiers against the Israeli presence in Lebanon.[137]

Starting in the 1990s, Hezbollah therefore posted many IRL video clips on the internet. The wild popularity of its sites among many Lebanese at the time is well attested. They also attracted a great deal of traffic from Israelis, spurring the authorities into hacking some of them and shutting them down.[138] For their part, Israeli media showed these videos repeatedly,[139] not shrinking from broadcasting the IRL's propaganda to the army and the society.[140] The results of this strategy met the expectations of the Resistance: in the late 1990s, finding a way out of Lebanon became one of the top political issues in Israel. In May 1999 it was the election issue that got Ehud Barak elected as prime minister. In effect, Israel recognized the inevitable and imminent need to end the stationing of its troops in Lebanon.

Victory: May 2000

The Israeli government makes its move

From the early years of the occupation, worries about the level of commitment of its national army in Lebanon were expressed in Israel. Nevertheless, it seems that it was only after Operation Accountability in 1993 that the Israeli army's presence in the Country of Cedars became a real issue.[141] It was only then that the usefulness of keeping troops there who not only struggled to control the situation on the ground but often found themselves under siege began to be criticized more publicly. The military class was divided, with some generals unhappy about seeing IRL rockets set up along the border, fearing that, should they retreat, even more of Israel's cities would be within their range.[142] But the state of generalized poor morale among the troops serving in Lebanon was gaining increased traction in the media, and the public was being won over to the idea of redeployment. The debate gained momentum with each general election. In 1996, shortly before Operation Grapes of Wrath, Peres campaigned on the idea of a phased withdrawal in exchange for security guarantees, provided that the Lebanese authorities first showed themselves capable of ensuring the security of the evacuated areas. If so, the withdrawal would be expanded to other areas until all of the occupied territory was completely evacuated. Netanyahu, the winner at the polls, offered the "Lebanon First" plan, under which he proposed making peace with the neighbour to the north and thus detaching the Lebanese dossier from the Syrian one.

Neither proposal was followed up, the Lebanese putting an end to them by calling them dead on arrival. Relying on UNSC Resolution 425, they demanded instead an unconditional withdrawal and claimed that Israel "wants security, not peace". The thinking in Beirut was that calm on the border could only be guaranteed by a comprehensive peace agreement, and that they would not want to negotiate it on their own, but jointly with Damascus. From the Syrian point of view, an Israeli retreat from Lebanon was scarcely to be desired. The Syrian regime's thinking was that, with the Israeli army beyond the IRL's reach, they would lose leverage in negotiations that they themselves were holding with Israel's government at the time. Equally vexing, a departure of the Israeli troops from Lebanon necessarily raised the pressure for a withdrawal of the Syrian army from Lebanon.

In March 1998, under increasingly insistent public pressure for a withdrawal,[143] Tel Aviv offered a new, conditional pull-out, subject to security arrangements negotiated beforehand. On 1 April the Israeli government accepted UNSC Resolution 425 adopted sixteen years before, and, in early March 1999, as part of their respective campaigns for the elections in May, Netanyahu, the Likud candidate, and the Labour Party's Barak both talked of bringing the troops home within a year. Netanyahu was the first to mention the idea of a unilateral withdrawal, on 3 May 1999. His rival, who won the election on 18 May, did not yet contemplate such a withdrawal, but on the day he declared victory he reiterated his pledge of a withdrawal slated for "a year from now". In July he insisted that the withdrawal would take place only as part of an agreement with the Syrian regime. In September the withdrawal was announced for 7 July 2000 at the latest, but only under a framework agreement. In the face of the continuing refusal by the Lebanese government, and after the failure of an Israeli–Syrian summit organized by Washington in January 2000, the Israeli argument changed: Tel Aviv finally resigned itself to a unilateral withdrawal, with or without agreement. However, brandishing its acceptance of Resolution 425, the government continued to urge the international community to "assume its responsibilities" as it called for the deployment of a sufficient number of peacekeepers in the soon-to-be-evacuated areas. In other words, Tel Aviv intended to assign the responsibility for preserving the "stability of South Lebanon"—that is, the security of northern Israel—to the UN.

Lahdist and Christian fears

The Israeli government was not alone in worrying about the withdrawal arrangements and their consequences. In Lebanon, the SLA was frantically seeking guarantees from the Lebanese government. Hezbollah, having promised at the beginning of March 2000 to spare any Lahdists who gave themselves up to the IRL before the official redeployment announcement,[144] withdrew its offer two weeks later.[145] This unsettled the SLA even more, since at the same time Tel Aviv was temporizing on what safety arrangements and compensation it intended to provide. In January 2001 the deputy minister of defence, Ephraim Sneh, had guaranteed the protection of the militia in case of a withdrawal;[146] however, two months later the government made known its refusal to give them refuge in Israel[147] and promised them compensation of $175 million. In April it finally agreed to welcome 800 SLA members and their families.[148] Early in May Antoine Lahd, worried that a majority of his men would not be able to take refuge on the other side of the border, demanded amnesty for members of his organization—a demand immediately rejected by Beirut.

Conservative Christians, a segment of whose political class had maintained close relations with the occupier, especially during the civil war years, and many of whom had been cadres or worked in Israel as part of integrationist projects, were the second group fearful of the consequences of an Israeli departure. The memory of the reprisals of September 1983 was still fresh,[149] and the fear of revenge attacks by the IRL weighed on their minds.[150] Throughout the spring, senior Christian leaders lobbied the government and the president of the Republic for guarantees for their co-religionists in the South and assurances of protection for them.[151] Monsignor Nasrallah Boutros Sfeir, the Maronite Patriarch, pronounced himself in favour of a general amnesty for the SLA.[152]

Hezbollah: a forced retreat "without glory and without honour for Israel"

Hezbollah had a wholly different view of the eventual Israeli redeployment. In the eyes of the leadership, the evacuation of Israeli troops would be "more honorable for Lebanon if done without agreement".[153] Not only must the Israeli army depart the South as quickly as possible, but it must do so without glory and without compensation. A week after the Israeli elections of May 1999 rumours were already rife about a withdrawal by the SLA from the Jezzin area. The militia, harried by the IRL, which had multiplied its attacks against the Lahdists that year, was in an untenable situation.[154] Despite this, the Israeli military command was reluctant to send troops into the area. On 28 May the Israeli government finally agreed to evacuate the district. Five days later Jezzin became the first liberated area in the South since 1985.

This first Israeli retreat whetted the IRL's appetite. As previously discussed, it now accelerated the pace of its attacks, and carried out a number of audacious operations. Recall that General Erez Gerstein and his staff were killed during this period, in February 1999. In December an *istishhādī* killed seven Israeli soldiers and wounded eight; a month later the IRL assassinated ʿAql Hāshim, the SLA's number two. In retaliation, Israeli warplanes flew a series of murderous sorties, especially against civilians. Brandishing the terms of the April Agreement, the IRL threatened to start firing Katyushas into northern Israel again. After a failed assassination attempt against a Hezbollah leader, in the course of which six civilians were killed, the IRL killed an Israeli soldier and wounded seven, all on the same day, 6 February. In response, Lebanese infrastructure was bombarded: the three power stations at Jamhour (Baabda), Baalbek, and Dayr-Nbūh (Denniyeh) were levelled.[155] As March began, the Lebanese civilian areas were targeted once more. For the next two months, attacks, counter-attacks, and reprisals continued. Israeli shelling of residential areas, schools, mosques, and even the ICRC headquarters was followed by the launching of Katyushas into northern Israel. Nevertheless, on 5 March the Israeli Council of Ministers signed off on Barak's proposed withdrawal plan and reconfirmed a full repatriation before the end of July, with or without any agreements with the Syrian and Lebanese governments. At the beginning of May it seemed that the IRL's retaliation was getting the better of the Israeli General Staff, which officially announced that it would de-escalate.

The withdrawal under way

In fact, in the meantime the withdrawal manoeuvres had already begun. From the end of March the SLA began reorganizing in anticipation of Israel's departure, and desertions from its ranks were growing. The Israeli army dismantled its positions from the second half of April in a so-called crawling retreat, gradually turning over its outposts and bunkers to the SLA. At the end of the month it went into overdrive. Against all expectations, it withdrew without notice during the third week of May, from 21st onwards, in four days, under dozens of covering raids.[156] On 21st May five villages were liberated: Qantara (Marjayoun), ʿAdshīt al-Qusayr (Nabatiyeh), ʿAlmān (Marjayoun), Dayr Siryān (Marjayoun), and Taybeh (Marjayoun). On 22nd May the SLA dissolved, and IRL fighters were already at the border. On the 23rd Khyām prison was stormed by locals, who broke down the doors with rocks and poles, releasing the remaining prisoners. On 24th May at 6.42 a.m. Beirut time, the last Israeli soldier passed through the Fatima Gate, the main gate on the southern border, and the remaining occupied villages were liberated.

For most of the Lebanese population these four days were a veritable appointment with History. The national television channels for several days carried emotion-laden images, news stories, and reports. As the Israeli army gradually withdrew and the IRL fighters advanced towards the border, they reported on the military manoeuvres on both sides, the withdrawal of Israeli tanks and gear, the shelling by which the IRL kept the pressure on them to accelerate their departure and the protective covering fire the Israelis returned; the cameras lingered on the towns and villages liberated by the Lebanese as the people who had been driven out by the occupier gradually returned. They showed enthusiasts from every corner of the country not wanting to miss any of the general excitement wasting no time to rush to the South by car. The images are of hurried returns to villages just evacuated, and unbelieving faces, triumphant insults aimed at the occupier, reunions, embraces, ululations, the throwing of rice and flower petals, collective outbursts, tears, songs and dances. And then there are the Lebanese and Hezbollah flags hoisted on the occupiers' and their militia's former checkpoints and buildings, and all the gear abandoned by Israeli soldiers and the Lahdists (tanks, weapons, uniforms, chairs, tables, and office supplies).

One of the most moving moments was the liberation of Khyām prison. Villagers are shown running towards the camp, breaking down doors, yelling names or words of comfort, prisoners calling for help, barely visible through narrow slots in their cell doors. There are doors crashing down, daylight flooding into dark holes, the prisoners blinded by the light, embraces, the prisoners staggering out of jail, clutching the shoulders of their liberators. The weakest among them are carried outside, disoriented, looking for their families, who are running in all directions looking for them; and then come the reunions between husbands and wives, parents and children, brothers and sisters, in a cacophony of laughter and tears.[157]

On the other side of the border, the Israeli repatriation was also full of emotion. The soldiers fell into each other's arms once they were through the Fatima Gate, kissed each other, and cried at "having come through it unharmed". They shouted, they whistled, they pulled out their phones to call family and cry out in a quavering laugh of relief, "Yes, yes, that's right, Mom, I'm back. I'm fine."[158]

If anything, the joy was heightened when the IRL did something unexpected when confronted with its local enemies, the SLA and the collaborators. The IRL General Staff forbade all reprisals against civilians and Lahdists, an order that was obeyed impeccably.[159] The withdrawal took place under perfect discipline. Contrary to what some had feared, the IRL did not attack Christians. It even refrained from entering villages reputed to be bastions of collaboration.[160] Christian villages were placed under the authority of the ISF (internal security forces, equivalent to the police) and gendarmes. The Resistance also conducted itself in a discreet fashion in the towns and villages of the Sunnis and the Druze, the inhabitants obviously not afraid of any potential aggression from the IRL.[161] This did not prevent some 6,000 Lebanese from hastening across the border to seek refuge in Israel;[162] a large number of them would, however, return to Lebanon in the ensuing months.[163] With the last soldier withdrawn, Israeli and IRL patrols passed each other on their respective sides of the border without incident.[164] Terje Rød-Larsen, the UN envoy, said that the Liberation proceeded in an "exemplary manner".[165]

In the following days Lebanon thoroughly immersed itself in the great moment. There was a mad rush to the South, Lebanese from across the country flocking to the liberated areas to participate in the collective celebration, causing monstrous traffic jams. The Fatima Gate became a place of pilgrimage,[166] and those present ceremonially toured the occupiers' and their allies' old checkpoints and headquarters. A few days after the victory Hezbollah organized a huge rally in Bint Jbeil, where Nasrallah delivered a speech that has since become a fixture in Hezbollah discourse. In it, he offered the Liberation to "all Lebanese". At the start of the following month the party organized a travelling exhibition of its spoils of war: a huge IRL convoy toured Lebanon displaying equipment abandoned by the occupier and the militia.

The Lebanese authorities declared 25 May a national holiday. Hezbollah received praise and compliments from (most of) the political class, as well as from the leaders of Arab countries, who spoke of "Arab pride restored". Ali-Akbar Mohtashami-Pur, the IRL's Iranian sponsor, and Mahdī Karūbī,[167] former head of the Iranian *Shūrā* and then presiding over the Iranian parliament, sent congratulatory telegrams;[168] the foreign minister, Kamal Kharrazi, went immediately to Beirut, and from the airport directly to the South, "to celebrate the victory".[169]

Thus ended on 24 May 2000 a chapter in the conflict narrative between Lebanon and its southern neighbour. The cost was considerable. Once again, the numbers are not hard and fast. The number of Lebanese civilians killed in the Israeli wars in Lebanon before 1999 have been estimated at 23,507 dead and 46,885 injured.[170] Between 1982 and 2000, 1,373 IRL fighters died on the field of honour.[171] Over the same time span, the Israeli army lost 1,580 men[172] and recorded 6,485 wounded.[173] Finally, the SLA incurred 824 dead and 1,439 wounded.[174]

But if Israel had turned the page on its twenty-two-year occupation of Lebanon, Hezbollah and the Lebanese government had not. A last area of a few square kilometres where the Israeli border meets those of Lebanon and Syria, in which the hamlet of Shebaa and the Kfarshuba heights are situated, was not returned by Israel. Tel Aviv considers it Syrian territory, but Beirut, Damascus, and Hezbollah insist that it is

Lebanese. The IRL therefore did not yet lay down its weapons. It also had another reason for not doing so: it still had to free the last Lebanese captives languishing in Israeli jails. Citing a lack of interest by the Lebanese authorities and the international community in their plight, the Resistance made it its mission for the 2000s to end their confinement. It was a commitment that would soon turn out to be the genesis of Operation Truthful Pledge, and the starting point of the war that Israel would wage against Lebanon in the summer of 2006.

4

HEZBOLLAH, A SOCIAL ENTREPRENEUR?

SOCIAL ACTION AND MOBILIZATION, OR BUILDING THE "RESISTANCE SOCIETY"

It seems to be a universally accepted thesis that Hezbollah's mobilization derives its strength from the party's vast clientelist network of social and welfare institutions that are woven through the Shiite community.[1] However, calling Hezbollah an employer and welfare organization, or even a "state within the state", overstates the case. There is no question that the party to some extent performs the functions of a state that for all intents and purposes is largely missing from the Shiite areas of the country. But the same could also be said of any social institution or NGO active in Lebanon, particularly in these areas. When the government fails to deliver, any actor originating social service, however modest, in such vital fields as health, education or even infrastructure maintenance in effect becomes a substitute for the state. Hezbollah does not have exclusive pride of place in this regard, since most Lebanese political parties, starting with the Future Current (FC), the Lebanese Forces, and AMAL, as well as many prominent political figures, for a long time have operated networks of social welfare associations, and continue to do so, quite dynamically in some cases. It is true that among all Lebanese extra-governmental institutions active in Shiite areas Hezbollah ranks near the top, when it is not ranked first, but a careful reading of its performance relative to the community's size proves that the party cannot boast of being its welfare institution.

This chapter is first and foremost dedicated to a deconstruction, or, more precisely, a demythification, before it proceeds to a reconstruction. For even if the theory that Hezbollah's social apparatus gains a clientele's loyalty by wrapping its beneficiaries in a material interest in the end is refuted, nonetheless it is true that this network of institutions does impact mobilization. What is really involved is meaning making, with Hezbollah's social action primarily pushing the public's symbolic reference buttons—most notably the ethical ones. The network does indeed support mobilization through the image that it projects of the party and the message that it is geared up to convey well before it comes to handing out money. Hence, this chapter is not content only to describe Hezbollah's social welfare institutions, for these are just one subset in an array that comprises a vastly larger universe of social action. All the subsets have the same function: to sustain the Resistance and diffuse its values. What we will therefore address here is the party's total social action apparatus, defined as the ensemble of its social welfare institutions and its structures for social control.

Sustaining the Resistance

Hezbollah's most numerous, and most important, institutions are those dedicated to directly supporting the Resistance. This includes providing aid to the families of combatants, the families of detainees in the prisons of the Israeli occupation, and people injured in the bombardments. The party also rebuilds houses and buildings damaged or demolished in the attacks and solicits political and financial support for the IRL from the public.

Supporting the families of martyrs[2]

Jamʿiyyat Muʾassasat al-Shahīd al-Khayriyya al-Ijtimāʿiyya,[3] better known as Muʾassasat al-Shahīd, the Foundation of the Martyr, is without question one of the most important Hezbollah associations. Together with Jamʿiyyat Muʾassasat Jihād al-Bināʾ al-Inmāʾiyya, or Jihād al-Bināʾ (the Developmental Association for the Construction Effort),[4] it represents the party's priorities when it comes to social action. The Foundation was set up on 1 August 1982, a few weeks after the Israeli invasion. As the Lebanese branch of the eponymous Iranian Bonyad-e Shahid Foundation it delivered services at the time to three categories of people: martyrs, the wounded, and prisoners.[5] Services provided to the wounded and prisoners gained autonomy over the years, eventually leading to ad hoc associations being set up for them.

Muʾassasat al-Shahīd today has a twofold mission: supporting the families of martyrs and honouring their memory. In the lead-up to the war of summer 2006, the Foundation was supporting 1,440 families of dead combatants, 276 families of prisoners liberated by the party and 965 children of fighters. It guaranteed each family a decent monthly stipend, adequate housing, and coverage of medical expenses. The tributes to dead fighters and tending to their memories are provided by two programmes, Takrīm al-Shahīd (Tribute to the Martyr) and Āthār al-Shuhadāʾ (Relics of the Martyr). Under the first, the Foundation renders all necessary honours when a death is confirmed, and assists the family for the duration. It also acts as executor for the deceased's last wishes and maintains their grave. The second programme refers to the activities of the centre bearing the same name. Opened in 2004[6], it has the official mission "of highlighting resistance action by gathering and preserving the heritage of the Resistance, in particular by preserving the legacy of the martyrs".[7] It collects the fighters' personal effects, their wills, letters, and writings (prose and poetry), as well as testimonials and memories that the families are willing to share. The centre intends to produce posthumous biographies of combatants and encourages families and researchers to do the same, with the ultimate objective of publishing an encyclopaedia of resistance martyrs. A central museum (in Beirut) is also in preparation for exhibiting clothing worn by fighters at the time of death, plus a variety of their personal effects. Along these lines, the centre organizes annual exhibitions, particularly during ʿĀshūrāʾ. Lastly, Āthār al-Shuhadāʾ takes care of maintaining and beautifying graves and mausoleums, the placing of commemorative plaques at places where fighters died, and it lobbies local authorities to rename streets or buildings in their honour.[8]

The Foundation has several funding sources. It basically relies on four *takafful* programmes, a support system of benefactors from among the public supportive of the Resistance:[9] (i) The "Support the Children of Martyrs" programme pays for food, clothing, schooling, and medical expenses through monthly subscriptions; (ii) "Specialization and Higher Education" pays for the education of martyrs' children at university, technical or professional institutes; (iii) "Monthly Subscription" accepts donations in any amount from all who wish to support the families of martyrs; and (iv) "Health Care" provides complete medical coverage (for office visits, medications, treatments, surgery, and preventative care).

The Foundation of the Martyr owns institutions and establishments for the benefit of its wards. Profits reaped from opening their doors to the general public help fund the Foundation's support programmes. Its flagship institution is al-Rasūl al-Aʿdham (Supreme Prophet) Hospital in Beirut's southern suburbs. Founded in 1988 as a field hospital for war wounded, it now occupies six floors, has the most modern equipment, and enjoys a solid reputation. It has been classed in the A category (five stars) by the Ministry of Health, and is ranked first in Mount Lebanon and second in all of Lebanon. Mustashfā al-Shahīd Rāghib Harb (the Martyr Rāghib Harb Hospital) is the Foundation's second medical centre. Construction began in 1993 in the village of Tūl near Nabatiyeh (in the South), and by 2002 it was a 5,000-square-metre medical complex financed by benefactors from the Lebanese public and equipped by the Iranian Red Crescent.

The Foundation also owns schools and technical training institutes. In the autumn of 1987–8, it opened the Mujammaʿ Shāhid al-Tarbawī school (Shāhid Teaching Campus) for (among others) the children of martyrs and prisoners. In 2004 this facility was integrated into the network of the al-Mahdī schools.[10] Starting with 1,850 students, it has now grown to nearly 2,400.[11] Still on the education front, in 1989 the Foundation inaugurated the al-Rasūl al-Aʿdham Training Institute for Paramedical Sciences associated with the hospital of the same name.[12] From the time it opened its doors through 2005 6,000 students graduated.

Lastly, the Foundation has acquired a number of petrol stations,[13] probably following the example of al-Mabarrāt, Muhammad Husayn Fadlallāh's charity, which has long invested in this sector.

Caring for the wounded, reintegrating the disabled

Al-Jamʿiyya al-Khayriyya li-Musāʿadat al-Jarhā wa Maʿūqī al-Harb fī Lubnān (the Charitable Association for War Wounded and Disabled in Lebanon), better known as Muʾassasat al-Jarhā (Foundation for the War Wounded), started its work in 1982[14] as a simple department in the Foundation of the Martyr. Its mission was to provide treatment and hospital care for fighters and civilians injured in Israeli attacks and see them through to complete recovery. Patients received wheelchairs, prostheses, and other equipment. As it gained autonomy, Muʾassasat al-Jarhā founded two medical centres in the southern Beirut suburbs, the al-ʿAbbās Centre for Physical Therapy in 1992 and the al-ʿAbbās Prosthetics Centre in 1998. By 2001 the latter had helped nearly 600 wounded and disabled.[15] In addition, it maintains a number of campuses and Houses of the Wounded (Bayt al-Jarīh) (one in Beirut, two in the South, and one in the Bekaa), with therapy and medical centres, gyms, physiotherapy halls, libraries—and classrooms. Indeed, the Foundation aims to assist the injured and disabled in their reintegration by also providing educational opportunities (computers, handicrafts, higher education), or by helping them to find and finance them. As part of this effort, it offers micro-credit, primarily to aid the victims of mines, while it also provides ongoing financial support to the permanently disabled and their families. In the latter case especially, the Foundation ensures that the disabled have housing that is adequate to their needs. If necessary, it pays for specially adapted living quarters or relevant upgrades to existing residences.

Supporting the families of prisoners, aiding former detainees[16]

Like the previous two institutions, al-Jamʿiyya al-Lubnāniyya lil-Asrā wal-Muharrarīn (the Lebanese Association for Prisoners and the Liberated, LAPL) came into being in 1982, as the Committee for Prisoners and Detainees (Lijnat al-Asrā wal-Muʿtaqalīn), an offshoot of the Foundation of the Martyr. Some years later it also split off from the parent institution and began to operate independently, with a minimal staff of four or five Hezbollah members. Today the team has a twenty-member board of directors and nearly 150 volunteers spread throughout Lebanon. Its general assembly brings together nearly 4,000 ex-prisoners.

LAPL action targets prisoners held in South Lebanon and in Israel as well as ex-detainees and their families. More than 11,000 Lebanese have done time in Israeli jails in Lebanon or Israel. Hezbollah and IRL members make up 60–65 per cent of the total. However, the LAPL keeps files on all Lebanese prisoners, regardless of denomination and political affiliation. Its role is to maintain the list, constantly update it, try to keep informed on what prison people are in, the conditions of their incarceration, and the state of their health. It participates in international efforts by other human rights groups that defend the rights of prisoners, organizes sit-ins and protests, and addresses its own memorandums to the Economic and Social Commission for West Asia (ESCWA) and the UN. It is also present at prisoner exchanges between Hezbollah and the Israeli authorities, coordinating its actions with those of the party on these occasions.

When prisoners are released, LAPL works to reintegrate them in the following manner:

> Reintegration takes at least three years, especially when the prisoner has spent ten years or more behind bars. The reintegration process has three stages: psychological reintegration, healthwise rehabilitation, and re-entry into society. We start by bringing doctors into the picture to re-establish the detainee's mental balance upset by years in prison. Some former detainees dream constantly of being struck, or they start screaming at night. Others have become claustrophobic and need to be outside all the time or see greenery constantly. That calls for therapy. Upon release, the prisoner is examined by a general practitioner, who refers him to the appropriate specialists. We provide thorough medical check ups. If an operation is indicated, we schedule it. All of this is done at our expense. Finally, we work on the ex-prisoner's re-entry into the social and professional world. Some want to study English or computers or go back to school. Others choose to return to the Resistance. Some who come back from Palestine are now bilingual in Hebrew and teach it to the fighters or do translation work for TV, radio, or the newspapers. Still others want to learn a craft. Our mission is to find them training that suits them or helps them get a job.[17]

However, aid to former detainees does not come in one size for all. The Association draws no distinctions between prisoners while they are imprisoned. Even though Hezbollah will work to free members of the LCP and the SSNP as well as Christians, Druze, Sunni and Shia, Lebanese and non-Lebanese, along with IRL fighters, once they are released, ex-prisoners who are members of the IRL and of the party become the LAPL's priority. LAPL will attempt to find training for all who request it, but it will only find jobs for Hezbollah or IRL militants. The others are told to turn to their own political group. This distinction also applies in providing family assistance. Members of parties other than Hezbollah never receive subsidies at 100 per cent from the Association; this privilege is reserved for families of party or IRL members (wives, children, and parents of prisoners). For the latter, medical and children's education expenses are covered, as well as a monthly stipend and help with housing.

The moral and psychological support afforded to former detainees is also provided to their families. Association representatives visit them regularly, once a week in most cases, but at least once a month:

> We arrange excursions. We stay in contact with the school, we keep track of the children, in situations where the father would be summoned if he were around. We support the mother. If she wants to file a complaint, make herself heard, we represent her and will defend her. We regularly arrange meetings with His Excellency, Secretary General [Hassan Nasrallah], who personally follows their cases and who the families get a chance to speak with. And then we also see to it that letters are delivered to the prisoners.[18]

Finally, families are the guests of honour at various events organized by the LAPL. Some ceremonies are relatively private, such as those observing the anniversary of the family member's date of imprisonment. But most are open and publicized, such as those organized for the Day of the Lebanese Prisoner (23 May), Day of the Fight against Torture (14 February), Freedom Day (29 January), Mother's Day for all prisoners (21 March), and the Day of Palestinian and Arab Prisoners (17 April).

Evacuating, treating, and vaccinating[19]

Jamʿiyyat al-Hayʾa al-Sahhiyya al-Islāmiyya (the Islamic Health Committee Association (IHC)), commonly known as al-Hayʾa al-Sahhiyya, has since its inception provided emergency services, notably through its Civil Defence offshoot. Later it set up clinics, medical centres, and hospitals in different parts of Lebanon.

Civil Defence

Al-Difāʿ al-Madanī (Civil Defence) is the primary IHC institution.[20] Its first headquarters officially opened in April 1984, but a previous, smaller team had already been active between 1982 and 1984.[21] Created to support the Resistance's fight against the Israeli occupation, it works closely with the IRL in multiple capacities. Its teams work at the scene of accidents or disasters, providing resuscitation, first aid, ambulance transport, blood transfusions, and evacuations. With its mobile medical clinics, IHC provides medical care in outlying areas of the large cities. It is assigned a fire-fighting role, putting out fires caused by bombardments of residential districts, and participates in landmine awareness campaigns organized by the National De-mining Office. Finally, it takes on environmental and public health missions, including taking care of household waste collection in some of the southern suburbs of Beirut, rodent control and insect eradication on rubbish dumps, and more.

Today, IHC's Civil Defence covers the three principal Shiite areas of Lebanon from a dozen centres. Its manpower complement of roughly 350 people is divided into management cadres, trainers, and paramedics. They are supplemented by two groups: the first one is composed of volunteers, trained in first aid, and first responders for fighting fires and conducting a variety of rescue operations; while the second one comprises seasonal workers mobilized during times of war or in the summer.

IHC services and programmes

IHC provides an array of medical services, from office consultations to hospitalization, free or at a nominal fee. It organizes vaccination campaigns and education workshops (pregnancy, immunization, oral hygiene, chronic diseases, immune system, anti-smoking, cardiovascular disease, early diabetes, AIDS), some of which it puts on in conjunction with the Ministry of Health, UNICEF, or WHO.

School health programmes get high priority. IHC specifically targets primary school students in certain private schools in its operational areas, but also services ninety public schools scattered throughout Beirut and its suburbs, the Bekaa region, South and North Lebanon with almost 16,000 students from kindergarten to sixth grade. Delivered by a dozen doctors and specialists assisted by nurses (three nurses per doctor) and volunteers (totalling 154 in 2002–3), these interventions primarily include screening,[22] referrals to the appropriate doctors, certain types of on-site care, and education campaigns.

Institutions and establishments attached to IHC

Beside Civil Defence, IHC operates fifteen medical centres, as many clinics, and twenty dental clinics. It owns three hospitals: the Hospital of the South, in Nabatiyeh, the Martyr Salāh Ghandūr Hospital[23] in Bint Jbeil, and al-Batūl Hospital in al-Hermel. The latter two, the most important, treated a total of 156,476 patients in 2005. Al-Batūl Hospital would receive nearly 1,150 patients a month, in a region that had only one poorly equipped public hospital and al-Yatīm Hospital, which could not meet local needs. Before May 2000 the hospital at Bint Jbeil, set up by the Israeli occupation forces, treated SLA members and the occasional Israeli soldier. Sacked by Lahdist militia in the days preceding the Israeli withdrawal, the hospital was at first supported by the Lebanese Ministry of Health. After liberation, IHC took it over, with the agreement of the authorities, and renamed it the Martyr Salāh Ghandūr Hospital because of its proximity to where this martyr carried out his operation in 1995.[24] The new management called on volunteer doctors from Nabatiyeh, Beirut, and the Bekaa region and solicited donations from individuals. In 2001 the Iranian authorities donated new equipment and helped refurbish old equipment, allowing the hospital to reopen in late May 2002.

A history closely linked to the IRL

IHC differs from Hezbollah's other social institutions because it is the only one that ventures into the field with the Resistance fighters, at the risk of also losing personnel and volunteers in the fighting.[25] It must be noted that from its inception Civil Defence has been especially active during major Israeli offensives.[26] Its history is closely linked to that of the IRL. For example, during the July 1993 offensive, fifty

Civil Defence vehicles, more than 100 medics, and 130 volunteers were mobilized. Under fire, ambulances evacuated more than 200 wounded and carried out sixty corpses, taking the dead back to their home towns or villages and helping with the funerals. With the support of Mu'assasat al-Shahīd, al-Rasūl al-A'dham Hospital, the Association of Muslim Doctors, the Association for Care of the Wounded, and other Muslim health associations, IHC kept its twelve medical centres open around the clock for the duration of the week-long offensive. Twenty teams of doctors (about eighty) provided free consultations and care, and looked after 400–700 casualties per day. IHC provided over 200 units of blood to hospitals, organized distribution of medication worth L£50 million (33,000 USD) to more than 5,000 families, and distributed milk and baby supplies (nappies, etc.) to more than 1,500 families in the various refugee areas. After the staff of Nabatiyeh public hospital abandoned it, IHC sent in eleven doctors and nursing teams to keep it open.

In 1996, during Operation Grapes of Wrath, IHC mobilized 72 ambulances and 217 medics. Their first mission was the speedy removal of civilians from the areas under artillery fire. At the height of the bombardment, 400 wounded and 90 dead were transferred to various hospitals, which once more were supplied with 500 units of blood. Twenty-five mobile clinics were sent to refugee camps throughout Lebanon. In the 103 camps visited, 17,051 sick people were treated and 34,000 medications distributed. In the end, as in 1993, some fifty of the dead were transported to their home towns or villages.

In May 2000 the withdrawal of the Israeli army from the South was IHC's chance to enter the liberated area in the wake of the IRL fighters. The liberated area at the time had only a few scattered clinics and two hospitals. Gradually, as the Israeli forces and the SLA fell back, IHC entered the newly liberated towns and villages. Nine mobile clinics brought treatment and medication to the needy populations of some fifty villages. Between May 2000 and May 2002 180 doctors, 140 nurses, 190 medics and 173 assistants treated 35,078 patients and distributed 38,405 medication units. The amount of aid provided by the IHC clinics exceeded L£200 million (132,000 USD).

Building, rebuilding, and developing[27]

Hezbollah's leadership believed that healing in its struggle against the Israeli occupation was not enough, but that reconstruction was also required. Jam'iyyat Mu'assasat Jihād al-Binā' al-Inmā'iyya or Jihād al-Binā' (Developmental Association for the Construction Effort), which was set up in October 1987 as a branch of the Iranian association Jahad-e Sazandegi,[28] is both Hezbollah's large construction firm and its instrument for urban and rural development.

Its construction missions are twofold. First, it builds the party's own facilities (al-Mahdī schools, mosques, cultural centres, *husayniyyas*, and IHC clinics and hospitals) as well as houses and apartments for the families of martyrs, and handles their

Figure 2

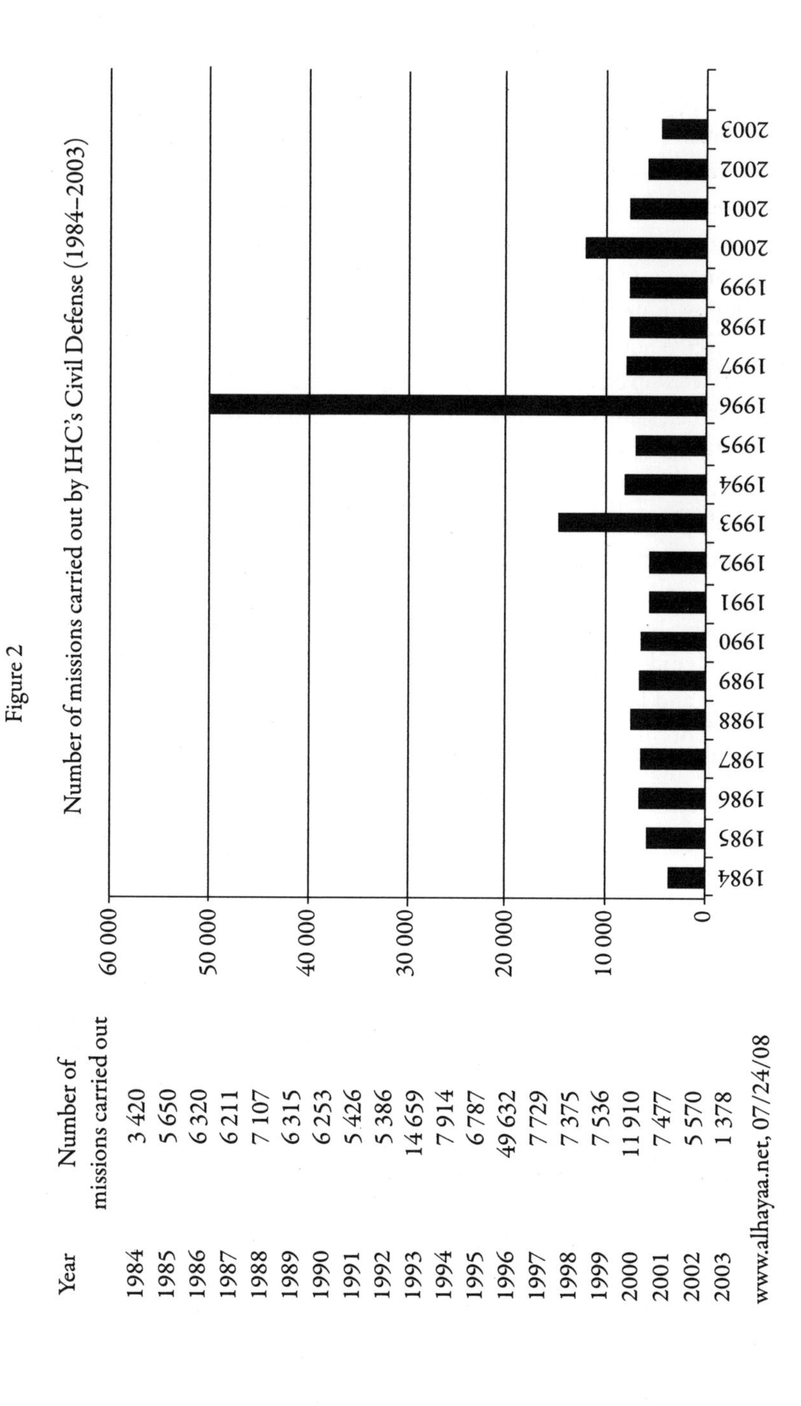

Year	Number of missions carried out
1984	3 420
1985	5 650
1986	6 320
1987	6 211
1988	7 107
1989	6 315
1990	6 253
1991	5 426
1992	5 386
1993	14 659
1994	7 914
1995	6 787
1996	49 632
1997	7 729
1998	7 375
1999	7 536
2000	11 910
2001	7 477
2002	5 570
2003	1 378

www.alhayaa.net, 07/24/08

expansion and maintenance. Second, they really excel at repairing and rebuilding the party's facilities and those of its institutions in the aftermath of Israeli bombardments. But the Association also works on private houses with no connection to Hezbollah and belonging to people of all denominations, as well as to damaged or destroyed shopping malls, premises, and infrastructure—all at the Association's expense.

In the urban environment, Jihād al-Binā' maintain thoroughfares and pave roads. At the request of the party it builds sports centres and holiday resorts. Its Committee on the environment (*Lijnat al-bī'a*) is responsible for dealing with the problems of public sanitation in Shiite areas neglected by government services. The Committee also performs public services, for instance in Beirut's southern suburbs, where its trucks collected household rubbish daily for almost five years. The Committee equally organizes clean-up campaigns with the help of municipalities and al-Mahdī scouts,[29] conducts urban sanitation education campaigns, and teaches domestic pest control.

Jihād al-Binā' is also active in rural areas, especially in the Bekaa, where it operates in support of local farmers. Its technical institutes teach the cultivation of olives, tobacco, almond and apple trees, mulberry trees and silkworms, grapes, citrus fruits and grains, and livestock raising. It provides training in how to prune and vaccinate fruit trees, keep bees, farm fish, modern irrigation techniques, and how to choose and use fertilizers. The lectures are supplemented by hands-on training and on-site support. It lends or leases agricultural equipment—harvesters, mowers, and tractors—to small farms and farmers experiencing difficulties. Seedlings and cuttings, fertilizers and treatments are provided on credit with repayment deferred until harvest time. The institution's veterinarians render services on request by farmers. More broadly, sizeable investments are made in projects for installing running water, with Jihād al-Binā' digging wells and installing pumping stations, just as the Association works to alleviate the government's shortfalls in electricity distribution by installing generators in a large number of neighbourhoods.

Financing the IRL

Determining the date on which the Committee for Islamic Resistance Support (CIRS, Hay'at Da'm al-Muqāwama al-Islāmiyya) made its debut presents a challenge. Interviews with Hezbollah cadres have the Committee's activities beginning "with those of the Resistance", which would make it some time in the first half of the 1980s. However, its existence was not announced until the decade's end;[30] and the rare texts that do venture a founding year give it as 1990.[31]

Today, CIRS has nearly 2,000 representatives—mostly volunteers—spread over the entire Lebanese territory.[32] Its main objective, unsurprisingly, is "to provide material and psychological support to the Resistance".[33] To do this, it collects donations from the Lebanese public and the diaspora, and organizes public events for communicating and promoting the IRL cause. Its fundraising campaign is carried

Number of projects completed
by Jihād al-Binā' (1988–2008)

Nature of project	*Construction*	*Rebuilding*
Housing for martyr and needy families	59	147
Hospitals	2	4
Medical centres	6	15
Clinics	13	15
Mosques	66	73
Husayniyyas	20	75
Mausoleums and *hawzas*	3	–
Schools	13	68
Institutes	4	5

Professional training provided
by Jihād al-Binā' (2000–2008)

Profession/Domain	*Number of sessions*	*Number of participants*
Paramedic	8	52
Electrician	5	40
Carpenter	3	42
Mechanic	4	28
Iron worker	3	15
Concrete layer	2	30
Painter	4	23

Reconstruction, compensation, and aid
provided by Jihād al-Binā' (1988-August 2007)

Type	*Number of cases*	*Amount ($ millions)*
Housing	28,300	133.5
Repair of damaged housing	(unavailable)	190.7
Economic and commercial facilities	12,500	30
Direct losses (farming)	1,300	2
Direct losses (livestock)	2,000	3
Public transport	2,300	4
Aid to damaged villages	(most affected)	3
Aid to fisheries	3,500	0.7
Wa'd project	–	14[1]
Total expenditures	–	$380.9 million

[1] This amount is cumulative through 14 August 2007; it is not the total amount invested in the project.

on through several programmes:[34] (i) Monthly Subscription—contributors pay a fixed monthly amount of their choice; (ii) the Resistance Money Box for Children and Houses—donations are deposited in a money box in the shape of Jerusalem's Dome of the Rock that CIRS places in individuals' homes with their approval, letting families "participate easily in supporting the Resistance" by putting in small sums as and when they can; (iii) the Jerusalem Dome in stores, hospitals, schools, factories, and associations—same as for (ii), but with contributions by the public in these locations; (iv) Support for the Fighter—to cover the costs of combatants' clothing;[35] (v) Equipment for the Fighter—to finance their combat gear; (vi) Buy a Rocket—to finance a piece of a rocket; (vii) Buy a Bullet—to finance ammunition purchases; (viii) In-Kind Donations—to collect food, household items, clothing, shoes, etc.; and (ix) Cash Gifts.

The only stable revenue stream that CIRS can count on is the *huqūq sharʿiyya*, the Shiite *khums* religious tax. The Committee has in the past benefited from occasional partial transfers of those taxes by several *marjaʿ*s,[36] but since Nasrallah began collecting them in Khamenei's name as the latter's *wakīl* these transfers have become standard practice. Authorized to direct these incoming cashflows, the secretary-general would in fact make CIRS their primary beneficiary.[37] Other sources of funding, particularly gifts from benefactors, are much less reliable. The Committee's public relations officer admits that they fluctuate in accordance with the situation. After a period of decline following the Liberation, giving rose once again in the aftermath of the summer 2006 war. In an effort to smooth out these dips in revenue, the CIRS developed a lively business in party memorabilia: party flags, photos, and posters; CDs of IRL hymns, DVD tributes proclaiming the valour of resistance heroes, calendars,[38] pins, trinkets, bracelets, phone cords, T-shirts, headbands, caps, lighters, key chains, wallets, moneyboxes, even a "Resistance perfume", and atomizers for car interiors are all for sale, as are children's toys.

CIRS also resorts to fundraising drives, sponsoring and organizing public events. Mobile roadblocks commemorating significant dates in the history of the IRL and celebrating its valorous deeds are regularly set up at crossroads of major highways in the Shiite areas, with lots of military music, Lebanese and party flags, while volunteers manning them solicit the generosity of motorists moving through them. The Committee organizes conferences (with the resistance as their recurrent theme), exhibitions, and *iftārs* during the month of Ramadan, with invited personalities from the world of politics and economics[39] as well as the staging of literary competitions and plays. All are designed to make the invited audience into stakeholders and encourage them to give generously. In recent years, CIRS has also put on contests of *zajal*, forms of poetry and folk songs highly popular with the Lebanese public, that draw several thousand people at a time.[40]

Rendering help to the poor

Along with these groups, set up in direct support of the IRL, Hezbollah has an affiliated association for assisting the most deprived populations, as well as a financial arm that attempts to foster improvements for socio-professional categories facing hardships.

Aiding the poor and orphans[41]

Between 1985 and 1986 a group of fifty—mostly Shiite—merchants and professionals applied to various international organizations for funding to start up a new welfare organization. Only the Iranian Mission for Education responded positively. A delegation from the group was invited to Iran to study the model of the national association Komite Emdad Imam Khomeini. In 1987 its Lebanese subsidiary, Lijnat al-Imdād al-Khayriyya al-Islāmiyya[42] (the Imdad Islamic Association Committee for Charity), better known as Jamʿiyyat al-Imdād or simply al-Imdād, was founded to become part of the Hezbollah network.

Al-Imdād is therefore the party's charitable foundation. Unlike the previously profiled associations, the beneficiaries of its largesse are the destitute in Lebanese society in general, and the Shiite community in particular, rather than the IRL. The new institution's leaders started by taking a census of the population in need, carried out in coordination with the predecessor of the ACSD[43] and a group of 500 volunteer students from the Faculty of Arts and Sciences at the Lebanese University. While Jbeil and Kesruan, under control of the Lebanese Forces, were excluded from the survey, the volunteer teams succeeded with the census of families in the "security zone" in the South.

Of the 152,000 families contacted, 57,000—of all denominations—received an initial aid package consisting of scholarship support between $100 and $300 per family and a food ration costing $40, containing mostly dairy products and bags of grain (rice and lentils). The census was then sorted for the 5,000 families with "no income, no property, and no financial support". Al-Imdād provided them with some financial support, although, as management acknowledged, "this support [was] modest". The goal was to ensure a minimum daily ration of bread in the amount of L£40,000 (26 USD) for one person, L£75,000 (46 USD) for two, with the upper limit set at L£150,000 (92 USD). Each family also received a complete set of clothes ("from pants to shirt, to footwear, to underwear and coat") two to four times a year (twice on a schedule, twice more as and if needed), and food aid, consisting of a portion of lentils, oil, or other commodity with a long shelf life, three times a year. The funding source for this aid was the Blue Money Boxes, familiar for years to Lebanese society. In 1995 there were in fact 60,000 large metal money boxes placed just about everywhere in the Lebanese public sphere and at some major intersections.

In the late 2000s they made it possible to collect $2 million annually, "100% of the aid provided to the 5,000 families" aided by al-Imdād.

Another of the Association's aid categories consists of service offerings. Most often, this comprises measures to enrol indigent children in school, make it possible for people who otherwise could not afford it to visit a doctor or even be hospitalized. In each case, al-Imdād makes contact with the school, the doctor, or the hospital to negotiate affordable rates that it then partially or fully covers. Also, it works with municipalities and local associations on all kinds of home improvements (repairing doors, installing toilets, etc.). In these specific cases, it pays nothing but instead negotiates with municipalities, craftsmen, and merchants of good will to donate the materials necessary for the installation or repair (leftover paint cans, unsold utensils, etc.) which the Association's volunteers then use to do the actual work.

In 1989 al-Imdād set up its first training programme for labour-market integration, Iktifā' Dhātī (Self-Sufficiency), which continues to operate to this day. The programme's goal is to place persons from needy families into the labour market—usually the mother or a son. The Association first trains the individual, often someone lacking a degree or training of any kind at the start. Once trained, he or she is then placed in a job in a hairdressing salon, a bakery, a deli, or a small shop, in restaurants (peeling vegetables, doing dishes, etc.), in house cleaning or as household help.

The Kafālat al-Yatīm fī Usratihi programme (Supporting an Orphan in his Family) concentrates on helping "orphaned" children. These are not necessarily children whose parents are both gone, but children who have lost their *muʿīl* (the person taking care of the family), ensuring the financial sustainability of the home. The programme started modestly in 1992, and became truly effective "from 1994 to 1995". The Association recruits benefactors (*kafīls*) among the Lebanese public or in the diaspora as sponsors for the orphans. The programme is flexible, the amount of support being subject to negotiation between the Association and the *kafīl*. The amount of support is theoretically set at $1,000 per year, but many *kafīls* do not cover all of the child's expenses. The money is not directly disbursed to the families; instead, the Association manages how it is spent. According to al-Imdād, the benefit for the family resides in the Association's bargaining power *vis à vis* other economic and social parties with concomitant savings. For its average 3,800 orphans al-Imdād has a pool of nearly 8,000 *kafīls* among the Lebanese public or the diaspora. Monitoring stops on the day beneficiaries start their studies, sometimes before they turn eighteen. At that time they are discharged from the Kafālat al-Yatīm and added to the list of beneficiaries under another programme called al-Tabannī al-Jāmiʿī (University Adoption). This one works like Kafālat al-Yatīm, but the *kafīl* commits to cover the cost of studies, partially or fully. When the orphan gets a job, the mission of al-Imdād is finished, "because then the orphan is able to take care of himself".

According to the public relations manager of the Beirut branch, funding for schooling and education is of particular importance for the Association. A total

4,000–5,000 families benefit from its work with schools. Al-Imdād negotiates reduced tuition with the schools attended by their children, sometimes even paying it out of the Association's own pocket. It also operates its own network of five schools and a technical institute—not to be confused with the Hezbollah al-Mahdī schools, which are separate from those of al-Imdād. The first al-Imdād school opened in West Bekaa in 1992. Next came a school in the Kesruan in 1993,[44] and then another one in the Batroun region in 2001, areas where most establishments are private and upscale and thus out of reach of the local Shiite populations. Realizing that it was not getting enough in scholarships for its charges from existing schools, al-Imdād leadership approved two schools in Beirut's southern suburbs, first in 1996 and then in 2004. They became self-supporting and helped cover the expenses of attending the Association's other schools. In 2001–2, once again in the southern suburbs, it opened a technical training centre that so far has trained nearly 6,000 students of both sexes. Although a majority of children that these schools serve are not from poor families (these represent only 20 per cent of the student body), the tuition fees are still attractive, averaging £L600,000 (370 USD) per student per year. By comparison, at one private Catholic institution in a mid-sized city (Zahleh) where the rates are lower than those of upscale schools in Beirut and Mount Lebanon but higher than those of private schools in Shiite areas: the 2009–10 tuition amounted to £L2,400,000 (1,482 USD) for pre-school, £L2,625,000 (1,605 USD) for the primary grades, £L2,750,000 (1,698 USD) for middle school, and £L3,025,000 (1,852 USD) for high school.

Finally, along with these schools, in 1999 al-Imdād opened a centre for children with Down syndrome, the first of its kind, al-Markaz li-Riʿāyat al-Tifl al-Muʿāq (Centre for the Care of Handicapped Children), in 2002 renamed al-Markaz lil-Riʿāya wal-Taʾhīl (Centre for Assistance and Training). It started with a small centre, consisting of a large outfitted room with space initially for just a few children. This type of establishment is very rare in Lebanon, so success came quickly, and a few years later al-Imdād opened a large centre that now cares for 250 children of both sexes between the ages of one and 25, divided among four locations: Beirut (45 children), Nabatiyeh (27 children),[45] al-Hermel (35 children), and Baalbek (150 children).[46]

Financing small vocational projects

Last but not least, Hezbollah aids the poorest through a micro-finance institution, al-Qard al-Hasan (the Good Credit). Founded in 1983 to keep the Lebanese victims of the Israeli occupation from "becoming refugees in their own land",[47] today it offers loans of up to 5,000 USD, repayable over a maximum of thirty months. While at its debut this initiative participated in fostering a—limited—class of small craftsmen and merchants, the economic slumps in the 1990s and the 2000s expanded the spectrum of what these loans were used for: 50 per cent went to meet daily subsistence needs; 27 per cent to repay previous loans; 6 per cent for housing; 5 per cent for hospitalization, school, or university costs; and 3 per cent for household needs.

The Association enjoys a good reputation. A status report on NGOs providing micro-credit in the Country of Cedars issued in 2001 by the Lebanese Ministry of Social Affairs in cooperation with UNDP and the EU, reported that of the forty Lebanese NGOs then on the list, Hezbollah led with 7,500 loans per year, while Caritas, a Catholic charity very active in Lebanon, was second with 1,500. At the time, total credits extended by al-Qard al-Hasan amounted to $4.5 million, or 25 per cent of the total funds provided by all NGOs.[48] By 2009 this total had increased to $117 million for the benefit of more than 72,000 individuals.[49]

Educating and guiding the next generations

School and university

School: up to high school

Al-Muʾassasa al-Islāmiyya lil-Tarbiya wal-Taʿlīm (the Islamic Institution for Education and Teaching (IIET)), was set up in 1993. It is "a pedagogical association, whose aim is to serve the new generations, to build an aware, educated generation that carries a message, and that does so by establishing schools and institutes and by training teachers".[50] It also has responsibility for managing and planning curricula for the Hezbollah schools, known as the Madāris al-Mahdī. These al-Mahdī schools offer all grades through high school. In practice, IIET coordinates and supervises implementation of Hezbollah's education policy, which is first discussed and then decided on in the central decision-making Consultative Council.[51]

Today there are fourteen al-Mahdī schools in Lebanon, seven in South Lebanon, three in the Beirut area, and four in the Bekaa, with places for 19,500 students in all.[52] They were initially considered to be low-quality schools, but it took them just a few years to gain widespread respect in the Shiite areas. Despite their slow start, the schools have always stood out from other institutions by their strict discipline and the high work ethic demanded of both students and teachers. This allowed them to quickly position themselves as quality institutions of learning whose graduates today have a 100 per cent pass rate in the state examinations, with more and more honours.[53]

Mobilizing academia

Hezbollah ensures that it has a presence among both students and teachers at Lebanese universities. They animate campus networks in support of the IRL cause, in coordination with the students and teachers of allied political groups (AMAL, and the Aounists from 2006). Among the students, militants designated as 'masʾūl al-ʿamal al-jāmiʿī' (in charge of university action) organize the mobilization of their fellow students, primarily through interpersonal communication and managing activities planned by the party.[54] At the faculty level there is Hayʾat al-Taʿlīm al-ʿĀlī (the Committee on Higher Education), established around 2002, which brings together university professors who sympathize with the Resistance.[55] They number about 400 in total, distributed among different universities, with the most members at the Lebanese University (70 per cent). The Committee is composed of 70 per cent Shiite, 15 per cent Sunni, and 15 per cent Druze or Christian members.

Finally, Hezbollah is active in various committees and groups of academics whose activist positions meet those of the Resistance. The most important is al-Hamla al-Shabābiyya li-Munāhadat al-Wisāya al-Amīrikiyya (Youth Campaign against American Tutelage). While not being at the origin of this group, Hezbollah regularly asks its own students to join demonstrations with it, since this campaign has, especially post-2005, organized several rallies and sit-ins to protest against American policy in the Middle East.

Civics and resistance

Jamʿiyyat Kashshāfat al-Mahdī (the Association of al-Mahdī Scouts) was formed in 1985 in Beirut's southern suburbs.[56] After licensing by the Ministry of Education and the Arts in 1992, it joined the Lebanese Scouting Federation in 1997.[57]

In 2005 the Association's ranks had grown to number more than 45,000 girls and boys, between the ages of six and eighteen,[58] and by 2010 they were at 70,000.[59] Its activities dovetail with those to be expected from an association of scouts, except that resistance is one of the key values instilled in the Wolves and Cubs. They are also taught values that accompany resistance: courage, patriotism, and respect for the martyrs. These values are reinforced in practice when al-Mahdī scouts routinely participate in the "resistance" activities of other institutions. For example, they attend party events, or march in the Jerusalem Day parade, and are sometimes mobilized to work alongside Jihād al Binā' in clearing and backfilling operations after a bombing.[60]

The female militant

Membership in Hezbollah is officially reserved for men. Naʿīm Qāsim, the party's deputy secretary, justified this on the grounds that women do not have to take part in combat[61]—a roundabout reminder of the organization's true military nature. On the other hand, nothing stops women from volunteering. Al-Hay'āt al-Nisā'iyya (the Women's Committees) constitute the organizational framework conceived by Hezbollah for its female militants. The party inculcates them with the culture of resistance through an array of year-round conferences and cultural activities. Distributed at all levels of the social action apparatus—in schools, hospitals, the Foundation of the Martyr, the Foundation for the Wounded, the LAPL, the ACSD—where they do the same jobs as men, female militants provide a concrete image of women's engagement with the Resistance. They regularly host women from the cultural, political, and non-profit scene as guests at breakfasts organized to promote the values of the Resistance. They set up workshops and handicraft groups; proceeds from the sale of their products go into the CIRS coffers. Some women take on the task of sewing or knitting winter clothing that the fighters sometimes need.[62] Very active at election time, they assist their male fellow militants in managing the mobilization of Hezbollah supporters. But above all, they are highly valued for mediating between the party and women outside it. With regard to families that the party aids financially or psychologically (families of martyrs, of the wounded, of prisoners, etc.), they are highly regarded for functioning as dedicated and effective social workers. As a cadre himself admitted:

> When mothers or wives of martyrs and prisoners have tricky problems at home, they sometimes have trouble speaking openly with us male representatives. In that case, we send someone from one of our women's committees, to make it easier for them to talk and unburden themselves. Then, our sisters [colleagues] pass the problem along to us, and we handle it. When there is a martyrdom, our sisters help us break the news to families without being too brusque—I mean, let's face it—women are more gifted when it comes to psychology than us! (*laughs*) And they are a massive presence at funerals and receptions for condolences, to hold hands and help the family members cope.[63]

The managers of Hezbollah's social institutions are not alone in their regard for this complementarity of men and women in militant action. The party's top leadership is equally cognizant of it. Far from simple tokenism, it consistently supports this participatory conception of women's role in the resistance effort. It lauds the logistic and material support that female militants can provide in war time, the support they render by accepting the need for their loved ones to sacrifice themselves, and their role in mobilizing young people (men) to enter on "the path of resistance",[64] be they husbands, brothers, or sons.[65] It is therefore not surprising that the Women's Committees[66] became a fully fledged Unit in Hezbollah's internal organization of the early 2000s, and, in 2005, the head of this Unit, already a member of the party's Executive Council, officially joined its Political Council.[67]

Sports

Al-Taʿbiʾa al-Riyādiyya (Sports Mobilization) is one of the subdivisions of Hezbollah's Executive Council that are usually referred to as Central Units (Wahadāt Markaziyya).[68] Open to males of all ages and faiths, the Unit mainly teaches "popular sports": football, basketball, volleyball, handball, table tennis, karate, taekwondo, and running.[69] The Unit also offers sessions for amateurs and professionals, with a specialty in training referees and coaches "in coordination with professional guest instructors from the Asian or regional level".[70] The Unit also organizes national and pan-Arab championships. In this context, its showcase and pride is unquestionably the football team, al-ʿAhd,[71] one of the foremost standard bearers of the party's image:

> The club was established in al-Msaytbeh quarter in what was called West Beirut, in 1964. So, it's an old club. It was officially licensed in 1969 and played in a number of

> championships until the outbreak of that cursed civil war in 1975. It was dormant until 1984, when the managing authority chose to disband it because of the war and the Israeli invasion. At the time, we were a group of young people who had set up a small private, ordinary football team. And it was to us young people, at the time scarcely eighteen-year-olds, that the club administration turned over the licence. Obviously, the team that played on the stadium field and the administrative team were one and the same (*smiling*). We start to move up from 1985 to 1986, 1987 and 1988, becoming one of the top clubs in terms of dynamism and motivation. That year, in 1988, newspapers voted us top dynamic club, *Farīq nijmat al-ʿahd al-jadīd* [Star team of the new era]—that's what we called ourselves then. ... We made it to the semi-finals of the Lebanon Championship. Well, we lost 2–0 to the al-Tadāmun team from Beirut. ... But we were the first team from the second division to reach this level in a competition that usually involved roughly a hundred teams![72]

Al-ʿAhd thus sprang into life as "the club of the Hezb guys who play soccer".[73] In 1992 it changed its name to Nādī al-ʿAhd al-Riyādī (al-ʿAhd Sports Club).[74] That year the club "took off", but its ascendancy was soon hampered by the Lebanese Football Association (LFA), using the pretext of its links to Hezbollah. The confrontation between the club and the LFA burst out into the open. The club's vice president, at the time also head of the LFA's Beirut region, turned in his resignation. The stalemate continued until 1996–7, when Amīn Sharrī, who would later become an MP for the party, took over the team. Thanks to his network of acquaintances, relations with the LFA resumed "after a break of about a year", and "things soon [fell] into place". In 1996–7, with the team now allowed to re-enter the competition, the new management was determined to move the team up to a more intensive level. That same year it moved up into the first division. During the ensuing years, al-ʿAhd applied itself. The culmination came in 2004 when it won the Lebanon Cup for the 2003–4 season. It won it again in 2004–5, in a competition involving 100 teams. The club won all its matches, starting with those that it played against the champion, al-Nejmeh.[75] Finishing the season in style, it beat al-Nejmeh a second time during the Super Cup in 2005. That year al-ʿAhd won five of the six tournaments held that season. In 2006 it finished third over all, but in the following years moved up again easily.

al-ʿAhd trophies won since 2008

Winner, Lebanon Football Championship	2008	2010	2011
Winner, Lebanon Cup	2009	2011	–
Winner, Lebanon Super Cup	2008	2010	2011

www.alahed.com, 12 June 2013.

Counting all ages, the club roster has 120 names on it. Along with the official members, there are hundreds of players in training (up to 600) attending the sports schools that the club organizes in July. Al-ʿAhd enjoys comfortable, modern, expansive and fully equipped facilities. The complex bears the evocative name Mujammaʿ al-Shahīd al-Sayyid ʿAbbās al-Mūsawī al-Riyādī (the Martyr Sayyid ʿAbbās al-Mūsawī Sports Complex). After playing on sand for twenty-five years, the team has had a grass pitch since 2000. Outside the 2,000-seat stadium, players can enjoy a semi-Olympic-sized swimming pool, large changing rooms, and a second hard field. During boom years, the club can afford foreign players, mainly Arabs and Asians. As for trainers, they come in various nationalities. The team has been trained by "an Armenian, an Iraqi, a Syrian, a Ukrainian, an Egyptian, and a Lebanese". In 2007, a German, Robert Jasper, was its head trainer.

Al-ʿAhd has an annual budget of $400,000–500,000. The general shareholder assembly of some 500 individuals is not remunerated, and finances the club through annual membership dues of $100. The total take from this source being modest, most of the budget is covered by gifts from the twenty members of the administrative council and, especially, by sponsors: al-ʿAhd has more sponsors than any other Lebanese team, with five logos emblazoned on its strip. The rest of its requirements are met with money from the LFA, TV revenues, and stadium box-office receipts.

Communicating with the community and beyond

Media apparatus

During its existence, Hezbollah has equipped itself with several media outlets, some of which by now have fallen by the wayside. Currently, the organization owns three major media outlets: al-Nūr radio station, *al-Intiqād* weekly, and al-Manār television channel.

While al-Nūr is widely listened to in the Shiite areas, and competes with major national radio stations such as Sawt Lubnān (Voice of Lebanon), *al-Intiqād* remains a media vehicle with a very limited reach, and it has never managed to become Hezbollah's equivalent of the *Daily Worker*. It has only a small readership among the militants as well as the cadres, who turn instead to national newspapers such as *al-Safīr* (left-leaning) and even *al-Nahār* (liberal, now pro-March 14), but especially to *al-Akhbār*. Without any institutional links to Hezbollah, this daily defender of the IRL[76] supports March 8, and has since 2006 become the primary printed source of information for militants and for followers of the party. In any event, in May 2008 the paper edition of *al-Intiqād* disappeared, and today only an electronic version survives.[77]

al-Nūr	*al-ʿAhd/al-Intiqād*
Al-Nūr (The Light) first went on the air on 9 May 1988. It was first licensed as a national radio station first class in September 1999. It broadcasts 24/24 on FM. Its programming includes: news bulletins; political, economic, social, sports, educational, cultural, religious, historical, scientific, developmental (health, agriculture, nutrition, public health) programmes, not forgetting entertainment programmes for youth and children; 95% of its broadcasts are produced in house. Since May 1999 it has put podcasts on the internet, and since February 2006 has offered continuous satellite radio transmission. It has been a member of the Arab States Broadcasting Union since 2000.	The weekly *al-ʿAhd* (The Commitment) is the first media property established by Hezbollah: its debut issue was published on 29 Ramadan1404 (June 1984). Since then it has dedicated its pages to following the IRL's action, the Israeli responses, and to reporting news of Hezbollah and the "resistant society". It changed its name to *al-Intiqād* in the early 2000s when it obtained the Lebanese government licence. Since 30 May 2008, the date of its last printed issue (no. 1269), only an electronic version in Arabic, English, French, and Spanish survives on the internet, available at www.alintiqad.com/www.alahednews.com.lb.

www.alnour.com.lb, 23 August 2009. Archives of al-ʿAhd/al-Intiqād.

Al-Manār (The Beacon) is regarded as the most popular Hezbollah media outlet, both by the community and outside it, and even beyond Lebanon's borders. Initially conceived by a group of people not linked to Hezbollah, who intended it to be Qanāt al-Muqāwama (the Resistance Channel),[78] it went on the air for the first time on 4 June 1991 from a small apartment in the southern suburbs of Beirut. Its management team's ambition then was still modest. It was on for six hours a day on a trial basis, and the signal did not reach beyond the southern suburbs. The new channel at the time contented itself with broadcasting brief news items on abuses committed by the occupier and on operations by the IRL.

According to one of al-Manār's founders, today a Hezbollah MP, Hezbollah struggled to convince itself of the desirability of a new television channel dedicated to publicizing the prowess of the Resistance, given its own policy at the time for promoting it itself. As already mentioned, the IRL has been making videos of its operations since 1983, al-Lijna al-Fanniyya lil-Iʿlām al-Islāmī (the Artistic Committee for Islamic Media Communications) being responsible for their archiving. At the time, these videos were primarily used to train fighters, but the party decided to show them to the public from 1986. It sent some to Tele Liban, but most screenings took place in mosques, cultural centres, *husayniyyas* and Islamic bookstores. Media coverage of IRL operations had thus existed before al-Manār came into being, so, rather than creating its own channel from the ground up, Hezbollah saw al-Manār, created outside its organization, join it *a posteriori*.[79]

Al-Manār launched its first TV news broadcast in October 1991 on the occasion of the Madrid Conference on the Middle East. In order to avoid going head to head with the other channels, it was decided to limit the broadcast to twenty minutes and start it at 7.45 p.m.[80] The transmission time soon lasted from 5 p.m. to midnight, and its broadcast area, at first limited to Beirut, soon expanded to all of Lebanon. The channel's popularity really took off in the spring of 1996, with its thorough reporting of the Israeli April offensive. It used the opportunity for broadcasting messages for the first time, urging Lahdists to desert.[81] It also encouraged Israeli soldiers to rebel against their superiors and to refuse to serve in Lebanon, at the same time urging their mothers to keep them from dying on the other side of the border. Paradoxically, its first recognition came from Israeli channels that picked up its messages and reused its images.

That same year the Lebanese government decided to impose a licensing system on the media landscape. Out of a plethora of channels, only four were granted legal status. Al-Manār was denied a licence because of its "Muslim" character, while the owners of multi-sectarian channels were given precedence. Also held against al-Manār was its narrow nature, reflected in its self-identification as "the resistance channel". Exceptionally, however, it was allowed to operate temporarily without a licence "as long as the occupation continues". Management, aware that a change in the political context could mean the end for the channel, corrected the disqualifying defects in the ensuing year. It formed al-Majmūʿa al-Lubnāniyya lil-Iʿlām (the Lebanese Communication Group), to which it transferred ownership of the channel after stacking the board with some Christian supporters from leftist circles. Then, after changing its programme line-up, it filed a new licence application as a "general" channel. With the Iranian ambassador to Syria, Muhammad Hasan Akhtarī,[82] intervening on its behalf with the Syrian authorities,[83] the station received its licence in July 1997.[84]

In 1999, cutting-edge equipment made its appearance in the channel's brand-new building. With the licensing battle behind it, management launched a major drive for modernization and improvement in production values. Several million dollars would be spent with international companies, with a first contract signed with Thomson for turnkey installation of the al-Manār digital broadcast studio. The French engineers spent two weeks on site to train the technicians on the new equipment, then the production staff spent a week in France to learn how to operate the studio. At the same time, management signed a contract with Sony to supply still cameras, digital video cameras, and editing equipment. Al-Manār personnel went through intensive training sessions in France, the UK, Holland, Tunisia, Egypt, and Syria.

Management also worked to diversify and improve the quality of programmes. With the new equipment, al-Manār produced its own news reporting, documentaries, and political broadcasts. In October 1998 the station had made a deal with al-Jazeera that allowed al-Manār to carry the former's political talk shows for a year. In late 2000 discussions were held with TF1, France's premier TV broadcaster, to set up a comprehensive training plan for its staff, but the Jospin government in the end vetoed the project. Meanwhile, the chain diversified its programmes further by switching to social topics and sports. A great moment of glory arrived in May 2000, when it provided the best coverage among all Lebanese channels of the Israeli withdrawal from the South. It was thus the first channel to broadcast live from the village square of al-Taybeh on the evening of 22 May, when it was liberated. On this occasion it was on the air for twenty-four hours non-stop. Hezbollah's leadership said later: "Without al-Manār, we would have lost the victory."

The Liberation was also the occasion on which the station broadcast outside Lebanon for the first time. With the inauguration in 2000 of Arabsat (for the Middle East and Europe) and Nilesat (for Africa) satellites, new opportunities presented themselves to al-Manār. In March 2000 it obtained a satellite broadcast licence from the government. Management chose 25 May, the symbolic date celebrating the end of the occupation, for its inaugural broadcast beyond Lebanon's borders. It "borrowed" the transmitter of the Lebanese Broadcasting Company (LBC)[85] for four hours a day, appearing for the first time on Arabsat with images of a newly liberated South Lebanon. Management realized that this choice meant it must keep the wider Arab and international audience distinct from the Lebanese one, and thus it provided two types of programming: the news broadcasts to the Lebanese public retained their national-centred concerns, and news broadcasts by satellite gave priority to Arab news. Renamed the "Channel of the Resistance and of Liberation" in May 2000, it became the "Channel of the Intifada" in September, with the inauguration of its satellite programme.

Once more, in order to better cover the events just then roiling the Palestinian territories, the station stepped up its broadcasting hours outside Lebanon from four to eighteen a day, and soon thereafter to twenty-four. The events of 11 September 2001 finally allowed the chain to expand its coverage even further afield: Palestine remained the priority, but the satellite programme also covered the war in Afghanistan and then the American invasion of Iraq. The station opened additional offices and increased the number of its correspondents. Throughout these years it strengthened its position in the Lebanese media landscape. Its resources grew, its production values became progressively more professional. In 2001 it launched an

English-language newscast, and in 2002 it added one in French. It was proud to welcome politicians of all stripes and of all faiths as guests. The station quickly climbed to third place in the rankings of the seven national channels. Although recognized with several dozen awards at contests and competitions organized in Lebanon, abroad (Cairo, Tunis, Manama, and Paris), and by the United Nations, it experienced a relative setback outside its borders, when, from 2004 on, it was denied permission to broadcast to a certain number of Western countries.[86]

Celebrations, events, and exhibitions

Several times a year Hezbollah organizes ceremonies, festivals, rallies, contests, and competitions. Some occasions are systematically commemorated by the central apparatus as Muslim religious holidays (primarily the birthday of the Prophet and 'Āshūrā'), but also a number of secular holidays, the great majority of which celebrate famous events or topics related to the Israeli–Palestinian (Jerusalem Day) and Israeli–Lebanese (Liberation Day) conflicts. These occasions are celebrated in all Shiite areas of Lebanon, with lots of parades, decorations and speeches. One detail that all these events have in common, along with sports tournaments or singing contests, is that the accompanying speeches do not boost Islam and its injunctions, but rather the Resistance and its associated values. Once again, Hezbollah shows itself less as an Islamist organization seeking to attract audiences to the mosque than as a supporting apparatus for the secular armed struggle.

Table 2: Principal celebrations observed by Hezbollah

Day of Liberty	January 29
Anniversary of the Iranian Revolution	February 11
Start of the week of the Islamic Resistance/anniversaries of the Harb and al-Mūsawī assassinations	February 16
Earth Day	March 30
Day of the Palestinian Prisoner	April 17
Day of the Lebanese Prisoner	May 23
Liberation Day	May 25
Victory Day	August 14
Day of the Martyr	November 11
Khomeini Memorial Day	June 4
Jerusalem Day	Last Friday of the month of Ramadan
Day of the Wounded	4th of the month of Shaaban
Day of the dispossessed/Birthday of *imām* al-Mahdī	15th of the month of Shaaban
Anniversary of the capture of every Lebanese prisoner still imprisoned in Israel	–

In addition to these official celebrations, each of the party's social institutions have tended increasingly to organize its own celebrations, fitting its activity or mission. Thus, the Foundation of the Martyr invests itself to a much greater degree in the Day of the Martyr, the CIRS is more visible and more active during the week of the Islamic Resistance, and LAPL every year organizes as many rallies as there are prisoners to be remembered.

For several years now, Hezbollah has also organized permanent or temporary exhibitions. Every summer since the early 2000s the Department of Information for the Bekaa region sets up Maʿrad al-Muqāwama, the month-long Exposition of the Resistance, at the entrance to Baalbek's Roman citadel, a popular tourist destination. Over a space of several hundred square metres they exhibit photos, spoils of war, weapons (unloaded and defused) in recreated thematic scenes, with militants standing by to provide explanations and comments for visitors. Originally thought up by the Baalbek team,[87] the idea was picked up in autumn 2007 by the Central Information Unit, which went on to organize Bayt al-ʿAnkabūt (the Spider's Web)[88] on a half-acre in Beirut's southern suburbs. It invites the visitor on a journey of discovery through the IRL's tunnel labyrinth in the South and some of its war booty of Israeli radios, binoculars, weapons, boots, helmets, etc., with everything marked off by panels with explanatory texts enhanced by graphics and highly professional design.[89] In May 2010 this type of exhibition reached its zenith with the opening of the Mlita complex, better known as Mathaf al-Muqāwama (the Museum of the Resistance). On 60,000 square metres of a decommissioned IRL military base in the South, the party put on an expanded and enriched tour of resistance fighter action scenes, with militants on hand to provide explanations, accounts of battles and invitations to any and all to support the Resistance, regardless of denomination or political tendencies. The circuit, which would attract over 380,000 visitors during its first three months, is today a theme park that is on the must-see list of what to visit in the South fully as much as the area's traditional tourist venues.[90]

Hezbollah, a Shiite welfare state?

With the description of Hezbollah's means for social and media action now complete, what are we to make of this collection of networks and institutions? Observation on the ground of their functioning over the years leads to the conclusion that the improvement of living conditions in Lebanese society, to wit those of the Shiites, is not their *raison d'être*. With the exception of al-Imdād, these institutions only modestly contribute to better living conditions for the community, and cannot claim to be a financial redistribution network whose purpose or effect is to clientilize the community around Hezbollah. Most of the cadres and volunteers are without doubt sincerely motivated to help their society, suffer to see their compatriots in misery, and try everything within their power and at their level to improve their lives.

Nevertheless, the agenda of Hezbollah's social institutions, and especially their budget allocations, reveal a different priority.

Associations and networks in the service of the IRL

Al-Imdād aside, Hezbollah's social welfare institutions share this characteristic: their actions are directed towards supporting the struggle against the occupation. Janine Clark, an academic who has extensively studied the social apparatus of several Islamic parties and movements in the Arab world, groups their action structures under the term "Islamic social institutions" (ISIs).[91] An analogy respectful of Hezbollah's uniqueness in the militant world would allow one to classify its institutions as "resistance social institutions" (RSIs).

There are two types of RSI. Those I will classify as "active support RSI" take part in IRL combat, even if only as a rearguard picking up the pieces. They support the fighters' families (Foundation of the Martyr), take care of the wounded (Foundation for the War Wounded), rebuild homes demolished during the bombardments (Jihād al-Binā'), and encourage the public to help fund the resistance effort (CIRS). That done, they seek to defuse any protests that could break out on the domestic scene and threaten the Resistance. Those that I will now call the "RSI of communication and social control" (media, celebrations, women's committees, educational and sports facilities) do not so much heal wounds as immunize. By disseminating the values of the Resistance and promoting its exploits, they spread the "culture of resistance" (*thaqāfat al-muqāwama*) and forge the "resistance society" (*mujtamaʿ al-muqāwama*). This is recognized by Hezbollah's leaders, as the party's deputy secretary-general made plain during a conference held in 2002:

> The Resistance needs a rear support base, behind the front lines. ... It is unreasonable to think that a Resistance formed of armed groups can succeed if cut off from its society. ... The front is only the front window on the confrontation. It is the rear where all forms of support, cultural, social, educational, and political support combine. ... This is what made victory possible. ... The enemy believed that his problem was limited just to fighting armed men, only to discover that his problem was a whole society with its diverse components.
>
> We cannot conceive of a Resistance being victorious without a social safety net [assured to] fighters, families of martyrs and the wounded, without them being assured of getting what they need in terms of education and health care. ... The Resistance did not ignore the everyday needs of families of fighters and martyrs; as a result, these needs have not proved to be a handicap for the rear base that might have compromised the struggle.[92]

The function of these institutions is thus to ensure that society suffers the least amount not of misery per se, but of the specific miseries that IRL actions might cause. The principal aim of the Hezbollah social apparatus is not to set in motion a wholesale social development of the Shiite areas, but to defuse any rancour, resentment, or discontent that could jeopardize the support of the Lebanese public—particularly that of the Shiites—for the Resistance. Above all else, it is designed to keep a potentially dangerous home front from emerging.

That said, what about the effect of these institutions in strengthening and maintaining the mobilization of the party? More to the point, can we detect in this social action apparatus the armature of a clientilized community?

Hezbollah, a welfare organization?

Contrary to widely held theory, the Hezbollah social apparatus cannot lay claim to having constructed a clientilized community network around the party that could guarantee continuity of its mobilization. In reality, these institutions only have very relative capabilities and success.

Let us start with the finances. Of all the social, educational, and media institutions linked to Hezbollah, only four are branches of Iranian associations: the Foundation of the Martyr, the Foundation for the War Wounded, al-Imdād, and Jihād al-Binā'. The supposedly astronomical amounts disbursed to the party's social apparatus by Iran go to just these groups—out of about fifteen. Moreover, these four institutions all have the same financial relationship with their respective parent companies. While the parent covers the salaries of employees in Lebanon, the office rent and supplies, all projects and programmes must be fully funded by the Lebanese branch—implying that Iranian budget amounts flowing to the Lebanese subsidiaries are more modest than is usually supposed.

This does not mean that Iranian money does not flow to the Hezbollah institutions, but what matters is understanding where it originates and where it ends up. The real financial support from Tehran comes not from the political/government authorities, but from the centre of religious power, embodied by the Guide.[93] Moreover, the support provided by the Guide comes less from his office's funds and those of his institutions, as previously noted, than from religious taxes directly collected by Hezbollah on the Guide's behalf from the community in Lebanon and the diaspora. Currently, Nasrallah directs them mostly to CIRS—in other words, to the IRL—not to the party's social action institutions, which are required to self-finance. As discussed earlier, the Foundation of the Martyr supports its recipients with donations from benefactors among the Lebanese public and revenues from some of the establishments it runs (the hospital and petrol stations). The Foundation for the War Wounded relies on two medical centres that also finance their operations by offering their services to the larger Lebanese public. Al-Imdād uses the Blue Money Boxes and sponsors for supporting its orphans. The only help provided by the Iranian parent for this empowerment strategy has been to supply 60,000 (empty) money boxes. Al-Imdād's head of public relations also acknowledges that donation collections fluctuate from year to year. Liberation was followed by several lean years. Sponsoring of orphans in addition suffered from the Western environment after 9/11 due to restrictions on international bank transfers to the Middle East. While al-Imdād does benefit to some degree from religious taxes donated by certain *marja*ʿs, their contribution to its budget is of secondary importance: Nasrallah, Khomeini's *wakīl*, favours IRL, and Muhammad Husayn Fadlallāh, the only rival *marja*ʿ of Khameini in Lebanon, oversaw his own network of welfare associations, al-Mabarrāt.[94]

While the al-Imdād school network is self-sufficient, the system of consolidated accounts allowing the more prosperous schools to cover the needs of the less well off,[95] many al-Imdād social projects are only partially self-sustaining, the rest being financed by a few meagre subsidies pried loose from municipalities, international organizations, and (impoverished) Lebanese government ministries:

> The Ministry of Social Affairs is also a partner, especially for our disabled: the Ministry is supposed to pay us a grant for each of the 150 cases it agrees to subsidize—out of the 525 disabled people we have in our care overall. For a time, we managed to collect $3.50 each per day. When March 14 came to power, the amounts were cut in half. ... There is also the problem of health. We have 15,000 people per year who need hospital care. But we cannot support all those who need a gallbladder operation costing L£2 million (€1,000), for example. In this case, I personally negotiate with the Ministry of Health to try to get this person in at the Ministry's expense. We contribute L£100,000 (€50), the ministry pays 80 per cent, the hospital gives L£100,000 and the patient puts in a little of his own.[96]

Other Hezbollah associations finance themselves in the same way. In short, they live on (i) donations collected within the Shiite community and from circles supportive of the Resistance; (ii) revenues from their own activities or the activities of institutions attached to them; (iii) donations and religious taxes; (iv) support by committees of friends; (v) some government subsidies and aid from international organizations; (vi) advertising; and (vii) volunteer services provided by outside experts and specialists who agree to provide their time to party institutions free of charge or for token amounts.[97]

After the question of financing comes that of payouts. If the aid dispensed by Hezbollah's social action institutions succeeds in being ranked among the top tier in Lebanon, it must be related to the size of the Shiite community and the extent of its needs. Today, the Shiite community represents roughly 40 per cent of Lebanon's population, amounting to about 1.5 million people. However, the numbers (prior to 2006) show that only 1,440 families of martyrs and 276 families of prisoners are fully taken care of by the party's social apparatus. Conceding that these are on average six- or seven-person families, they still only represent a total of 10,300 to 12,000 individuals. There are also 965 children of martyrs, 3,800 orphans, and some thousands of the wounded, which brings us to a rough total of 20,000 people. Five thousand deprived families receive their daily bread, a few bags of grain as well as some clothes from al-Imdād, hence 30,000 to 35,000 people.[98] For all of Lebanon, there are nineteen schools and training institutes (al-Imdād and al-Mahdī), four hospitals, and fifteen or so medical centres affiliated with the party. Compared to the community's size, these numbers look very modest. Very few people in fact benefit from Hezbollah's financial generosity.

Finally, Jihād al-Binā', the party's star institution, justly esteemed for its outstanding work in erasing the traces of the destruction wreaked by Israeli air and artillery strikes, scarcely measures up as the development vehicle that the Shiite areas have such dire need of. In the aftermath of the 1993 and 1996 Israeli offensives in particular, the enterprise was able to chalk up some proud reconstruction successes. So too, after 2006, its Waʿd project,[99] "to raise the southern suburbs [of Beirut] from the ashes,"[100] was a tour de force. Yet, despite this, it is not its function to pave all roads in the Shiite areas, to build homes and retrofit existing buildings up to standard. Its agricultural and urban programmes are largely confined to providing services and, on the whole, do not encompass distribution of money or equipment. The number of projects and their dimensions are insufficient and impact only a limited area and number of farmers. The vocational training it has provided for just under twenty years remains very modest, and the amounts invested in development projects, objectively speaking, are minor. This is a far cry from the depiction of the party as a welfare state within the Lebanese Shiite community.

Hezbollah, the employer?

Another assumption that must be called into question is that of a redistributionist Hezbollah setting aside jobs for its protégés, either in state institutions or its own. Unlike most political groups, which tap government resources for decades by taking over certain development funds or ministerial portofolios,[101] Hezbollah has hardly any access to this kind of resource and, by corollary, is not able to place job seekers in jobs that it would otherwise monopolize. The community knows this, and usually turns to AMAL for this kind of service. The daily *L'Orient–Le Jour* in 2006 stated that Hezbollah, as an employer, had registered nearly 17,000 people with the National Social Security Fund (NSSF). However, this figure is thought to be inflated in all likelihood; "other sources insist that Hezbollah institutions have some 2,000 employees."[102] The figure of 17,000 employees is no doubt overstated. Observation of the party's social and internal institutions reveals a circumstance that also casts doubt on the high number: the small number of people that each of them employs. Leaving aside Jihād al-Binā' perhaps, the party's institutions in all of Lebanon function with at most some dozens of salaried employees.[103] These are, moreover, not paid by Hezbollah but by the Iranian parent organization or, as it were, by the institution's management, which takes the salary payments into its own revenues. The largest section of the social institution staff in fact consists of volunteer activists. For example, al-Imdād counts 90 full-time salaried employees, 10 contractors (part time), and 730 volunteers.[104] As for the Hezbollah members who manage the party's internal affairs, only the cadres are paid; the ordinary members work "for God and the Cause".[105] The number of cadres is also relatively low, mainly because some have more than one role in the central decision-making apparatus and are responsible for several functions in multiple institutions at the same time.

Building a unique image, weaving close ties

Even if Hezbollah has not succeeded in turning its social institutions into an engine for clientilizing the Shiite community, this does not keep these institutions from playing a part in sustaining the mobilization. At the same time as they garner practical support for the Resistance, they also convey a certain image of the party to the public. Academics such as Iman Farag and Janine Clark have proposed relevant analyses of how Islamic movements practise ethics.[106] Their studies of several Islamic social institutions in Egypt, Jordan, and Yemen led them to contradict many authors who hold that these institutions weave clientelist links between the Islamic groups and potential members and supporters. They go on to argue that these institutions above all embody a particular ethical image of the groups they belong to. In other words, these institutions in a sense act as vehicles dedicated to better the party's image. This holds true for Hezbollah's social action apparatus as well. Al-Imdād, the RSI, party media, and various associations that operate in coordination with its institutions form a complete communications ensemble designed to both embody and disseminate the values that the party wishes to instil in the public. The social welfare apparatus therefore must not be understood as a cash machine, nor as a lever detached from the rest of the party's social action arsenal, but only as a permanent subset of it.

Social action, resistance, and patriotism

The main values, championed in all their possible permutations, are resistance and its first cousin, patriotism. IHC in particular is the perfect embodiment of social action shoulder to shoulder with the Resistance, even under fire. The Foundations of the Martyr and for the War Wounded, the LAPL, and Jihād al-Binā' form a rear support base tasked with healing the wounds caused during the Israeli attacks. This story told by the vice president of the al-ʿAhd football club illustrates how these institutions try to carry the values of the Resistance over into daily life:

> In 1997–8 Lebanon was in the playoffs for the World Cup. At the time, I was the club secretary and I suggested to the board of directors to have all representatives of the Lebanese supporters' clubs join us at our club, under one slogan in a single league that would be called "the All-Lebanon League of Supporters" (Rābitat Jumhūr Kull Lubnān).

> We held a press conference, where Hājj Amīn Sharrī announced the creation of the League, and the media played our idea up big. The All-Lebanon League was launched, and it placed ads in all Lebanese newspapers: "Support the Lebanese National Team—signed the All-Lebanon League of Supporters [Idʿam muntakhab Lubnān—Rābitat Jumhūr Kull Lubnān]'. And it was us—the Hezbollah—that funded this campaign on behalf of the whole of Lebanon. So much so that one of our brothers, a member of the Orthodox community, called me and said, "You folks, you not only teach people how to defend their country, but you also teach them sportsmanship and good values!"[107]

Solidarity, sacrifice, selflessness, and closeness

The fact that most of the aid dispensed by Hezbollah institutions comes in the form of services, and the bulk of their workforce consists of volunteers, inevitably helps to convey the idea of a disinterested party that is available, close to the population, even inserted in it; in short, a party people can count on when the going gets rough. Thanks to its vast network of volunteers, the party manages to establish close, that is, direct and personalized, contact with a human face that, over time, becomes familiar to the people it is courting:

> People ask us, "How do you do take care of so many people? Why do people like you so much?" We work with people as if they are family. People who donate money, who help us, but also our volunteers belong to the same society as the needy—and we also belong to it. Just as Hezbollah, by resisting, defends a country that belongs to all its inhabitants, so al-Imdād works through members of the public to help other people in that same public. As an example, our volunteers visit people with the idea of keeping them in a certain circle of social relations. When there is a death, we will visit them; when there is an illness, we try to get them a doctor. This is the spirit in which all of Hezbollah works.[108]

Credibility and professionalism

The functioning of the Hezbollah social apparatus also embodies the party's declared commitment to legality, as part of its quest for credibility. This same concern, combined with a barely disguised need for recognition, explains why the institutions' representatives like to constantly point out, with some pride, that their associations operate under government licence. For the same reason, given any opportunity they will also point out that their institutions have joint projects with foreign entities—preferably Western ones. The Foundation of the Martyr emphasizes agreements with European hospitals to make its cardiology centre a certified research clinic,[109] and LAPL sometimes coordinates with the UNDP or the EU to find training for former prisoners. All institutions are encouraged to play up their professionalism, be it al-Manār, al-Rasūl al-Aʿdham Hospital, or the al-Mahdī schools. Awards, decorations, and signs of national and international recognition earned by these institutions are always on display for the general public.[110] Last but not least, all party institutions that rely on the generosity of the general public make it a point to provide receipts for the sake of accounting transparency. This is not a trivial gesture—in a country where diversions of political and social funds are commonplace, it tends to be appreciated all the more.

Tolerance, anti-confessionalism

Finally, these institutions are bearers of the party's claim for openness towards the other faiths; they aim to give a substantive expression of its principled stand against confessionalism. Care and services are dispensed to applicants regardless of their denomination, a point that representatives of Hezbollah institutions also never forget to mention. To cite one example among many, the director of an al-Mahdī school encountered during a field survey pointed out that his school has many non-Shiite students, including Christians. In another instance, the treasurer and vice president of the al-ʿAhd club was very proud that the team had a Sunni player from the Future Current (what's more, one with "long hair"),[111] that the trainer is a German who could "not get over how nice and *civilized* [Hezbollah members] were to him".[112] Party media boast of the presence of unveiled women on their sets, of some of their broadcasts being hosted by non-Shiite presenters, and the fact that many of their guests are senior Christian leaders. And whenever the IHC assists the IRL during exchanges of prisoners and of the bodies of fighters with Tel Aviv, not only does it prepare the Lebanese bodies recovered in accordance with their faith, and does not deliver the coffins to the families "until after saying the appropriate prayers for the repose of their souls",[113] it also shrouds the remains of Israeli soldiers in accordance with the Jewish religious tradition before turning them over.[114]

In other words, serve and promote the IRL—again and again. Therein lies the true *raison d'être* for Hezbollah's social action apparatus viewed in its entirety. Despite the spread of the institutional network attached to it, the party can hardly be described as a state within a state. Its charity only touches a limited part of the Shiite community, and the party cannot afford to guarantee that which the community has the right to expect from Lebanon's government. It is certainly better than nothing, but the gulf between its support and the needs of the community in terms of health, sanitation, infrastructure, and schools remains immense. As a corollary, it is not possible, in studying the wellsprings of Hezbollah's mobilization, to suggest that the reasons for its strength and persistence reside in a clientilizing social action apparatus. It is not without its effect, but the positive effect arises less out of gratitude for parallel cash flows than psychological factors related to the image that these associations project for the organization. This makes meaning making rather than reasoning along material utilitarianism lines all the more fitting as the approach of choice.

5

HEZBOLLAH'S INTERNAL ORGANIZATION

STRUCTURE, MEMBERSHIP, INTERNAL OPERATIONS

It is impossible to define what kind of legal entity Hezbollah is. It may seem odd, but Lebanon does not have a law governing parties. The legislature has not seen fit to impose any restrictive conditions, either on how they are to be set up or financed. While the Lebanese use the term "party" (*hizb*) as a practical category for referring to the country's various political groups, in public law the only collective action structure, political or otherwise, is that of the "association" (*jamʿiyya*). However, despite its concern for acting within the law, Hezbollah is not listed with the Ministry of Interior under this rubric. The reason is simple: as already stated, Hezbollah does not present itself as an association, but as a group of networked institutions. The party's institutional oddity is heightened by the hybrid nature of the ideological and cultural roots of its institutions as well as of its organizational functioning. Hezbollah is usually understood as an Islamist group, but its structure is nothing like that of the Muslim Brotherhood or al-Qāʿida (Sunni).[1] Admittedly, an Islamic version of the decision-making process is to some extent reflected by the collegial command structure (*shūrā*). But the organization at heart is not Islamic. Indeed, Hezbollah's structure and its internal operations owe a good deal to communist and socialist models.

Organizational setup

Settling the question of whether the founders of Hezbollah were consciously inspired by leftist models remains fraught with difficulty. Historically, given both their sectarian origin and their geographical roots, the evidence points to its members having more interactions with the militants of the LCP than those of the Kataeb, for instance. According to some, Hezbollah at its origin was joined by numerous communist defectors; the thesis of the "communizing" of Hezbollah's apparatus by association therefore seems *a priori* plausible. Nevertheless, a study of the party's central apparatus as well as Hezbollah's institutions in the Bekaa where the party came into being gives grounds for asserting that, in fact, there were very few defectors from the CAOL and almost none from the LCP. The likelihood that Hezbollah's general structure was inspired by the communist model is the result of two influences. The first was exerted by the IRL mentor, the Pasdaran, which helped set up the IRL, and whose own organization displays strong similarities with communist structures.[2] The second is that of a transfer of ideas not from the LCP but from AMAL, hence an indirect one. The AMAL structure is indeed closer to the LCP's than Hezbollah's, and Hezbollah's structure differs from aspects of the LCP that can already be discerned in the structure of AMAL.[3] This makes Hezbollah's resemble a reworked version of an "amalized" communist structure. From a historical and sociological perspective, moreover, the influence of AMAL on Hezbollah was more substantial than that of the LCP. This is reflected in the greater number of transfers from AMAL to Hezbollah and the more intertwined geographical and familial connections of the two. Finally, it should be recalled that when Hezbollah began to take shape in 1980s, the key leader of the organizing effort was Hassan Nasrallah—an ex-AMAL cadre.[4]

Hezbollah adopts categories used by socialist parties to group the lowest levels of its militants.[5] Like the French Socialist Party,[6] for example, it aggregates its militants in "groups"[7] (*majmūʿa*, pl. *majmūʿāt*), which correspond to the LCP's *firʿ*s. These groups of between thirty and thirty-five individuals are in effect neighbourhood groups, sorted by place of residence.[8] Four or five of these groups at a time aggregate into "factions" (*fasīl*, pl. *fasāʾil*) representative of a (small) town or cluster of villages, depending on size. As in the case of the FSP, factions in turn group into "sections" (*shuʿba*, pl. *shuʿab*). In Hezbollah's case, each of these also represents one village or one town, but in this case with more sharply delineated administrative boundaries. For the next level, the party employs a category not utilized by other Lebanese parties, the "sector" (*qitāʿ*, pl. *qitāʿāt*).[9] Comprising several sections, a sector usually covers an area equivalent in size to the Lebanese administrative *caza* (roughly equivalent to a city and surrounding suburbs and villages). Finally, agglomerated sectors form "organizational areas" or "regions" (*mintaqa tandhīmiyya*, pl. *manātiq*) corresponding to the concept of a region as defined by the Lebanese authorities (roughly equivalent to the British county).

Sections, sectors, and regions each have leaders. Each sector has a council (*shūrā qitāʿ*) as does each region (*shūrā mintaqa*). In their composition, functions, and hierarchical links to the party's other institutions, these councils correspond fully to the communist regional or sectional committees.

The central apparatus

Parallels can also be drawn at the central apparatus level between communist parties and Hezbollah.

Figure 3

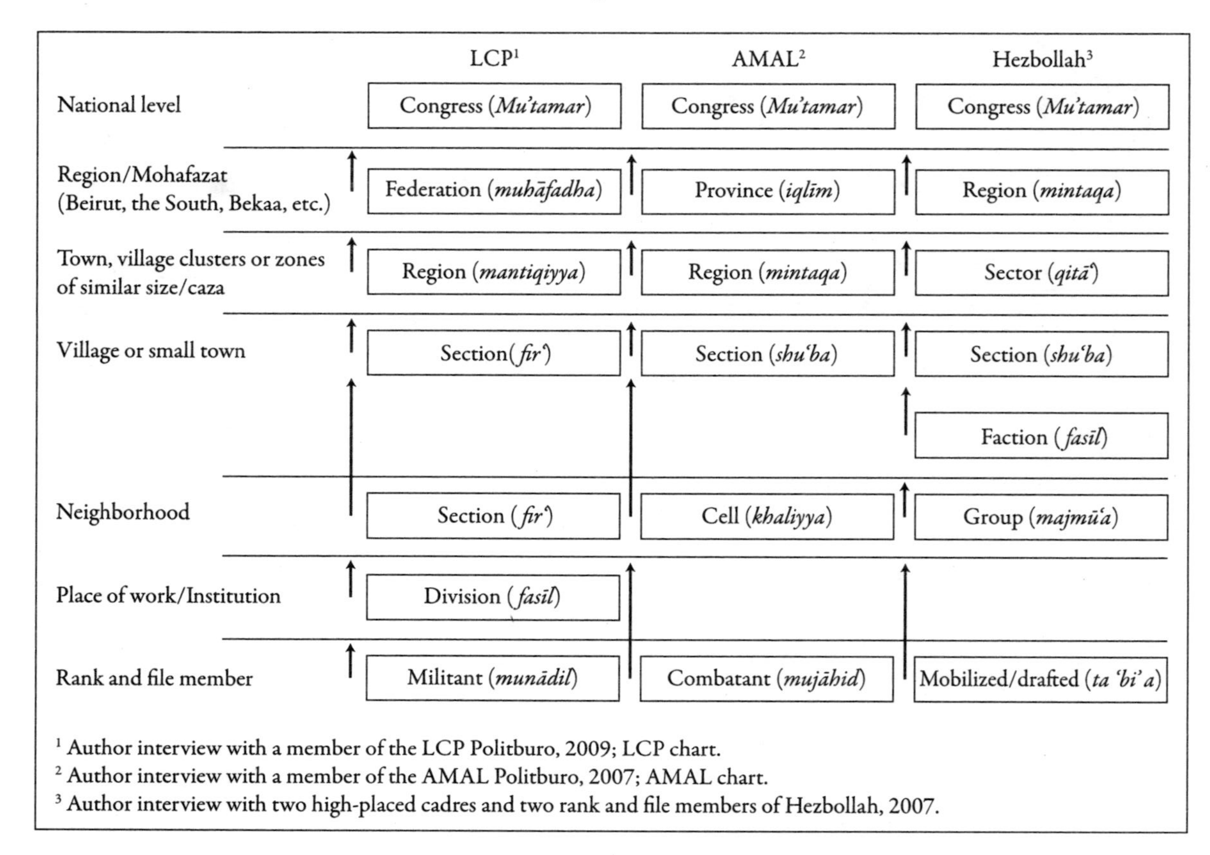
LCP[1]
AMAL[2]
Hezbollah[3]
National level
Congress (*Mu'tamar*)
Congress (*Mu'tamar*)
Congress (*Mu'tamar*)
Region/Mohafazat
(Beirut, the South, Bekaa, etc.)
Federation (*muhāfadha*)
Province (*iqlīm*)
Region (*mintaqa*)
Town, village clusters or zones
of similar size/caza
Region (*mantiqiyya*)
Region (*mintaqa*)
Sector (*qitā'*)
Village or small town
Section(*fir'*)
Section (*shu'ba*)
Section (*shu'ba*)
Faction (*fasīl*)
Neighborhood
Section (*fir'*)
Cell (*khaliyya*)
Group (*majmū'a*)
Place of work/Institution
Division (*fasīl*)
Rank and file member
Militant (*munādil*)
Combatant (*mujāhid*)
Mobilized/drafted (*ta 'bi' a*)
[1] Author interview with a member of the LCP Politburo, 2009; LCP chart.
[2] Author interview with a member of the AMAL Politburo, 2007; AMAL chart.
[3] Author interview with two high-placed cadres and two rank and file members of Hezbollah, 2007.

The central councils

Majlis Shūrā al-Qarār (the Collegial Consultative Council), known as the Shūrā al-Qarār (Decision-Making Consultative Council) is Hezbollah's decision-making body. It consists of seven members and, since 1989, has been chaired by the secretary-general, backed up by a deputy secretary since 1991.[10] Elected every three years by the General Congress, the majority of Council members are clergy, while the lay members are individuals who have distinguished themselves in the struggle against the Israeli occupation. The Council prepares a three-year action plan in accordance with the broad strategic political, and social parameters mandated for it by the Congress.

Hassan Nasrallah has been the party's secretary-general since February 1992. He has been re-elected by the Consultative Council at every congress held since. He is assisted by the deputy secretary-general, a position occupied by Naʿīm Qāsim since 1991, and by the Political Advisory Office (al-Muʿāwiniyya al-Siyāsiyya) chaired by Hussein Khalil, the secretary-general's political right-hand man.

The organization chart has the Consultative Council overseeing the work of a series of central institutions who handle the party's day-to-day operations. These include the Office of Organization (al-Maktab al-Tandhīmī) functioning as a disciplinary office, and the security apparatus (*al-itar al-amniyya*), charged with surveillance of the party members and preventing any infiltration by foreign intelligence services. Most importantly, the Consultative Council sits hierarchically atop five central councils, *al-majālis al-markaziyya*, which form the core of the central apparatus.[11]

Executive Council (al-Majlis al-Tanfidhī)

This is responsible for implementing the Consultative Council's action plan. This makes it equivalent to the communist Secretariat. Chaired by a member of the Shūrā, it brings together the region heads and heads of the Central Units (CU), bodies that implement the party's policy in specific areas (media, health, social, education, etc.).[12]

Political Council (al-Majlis al-Siyāsī)[13]

Although it took the place in the early 2000s of the former Politburo, which was mainly responsible for the party's relatively low-key external communications during the 1990s, the Political Council, unlike the Communist Party Politburo, is not a decision-making body. Assigned responsibility for three functions—advisory, communications, and coordination with other actors on the Lebanese political and social scene—it studies the general political situation and provides the Consultative Council with decision analysis and recommendations regarding recurring issues or those of the moment. As the need arises, some of this council's members make up an ad hoc study committee, the Lijnat al-Tahlīl al-Siyāsī (Policy Analysis Commission). Alongside them, others are responsible full-time for following "dossiers" (*malaff*, pl.

malaffāt), one for each of as many individual actors as Hezbollah plans to work with, or at least have contacts with. There are, for example, dossiers on relationships with Christian parties, with Palestinian groups, with Arab groups, with international entities, with public associations, on women's activities, etc.

Parliamentary Action Council (Majlis al-ʿAmal al-Niyābī (PAC))

This comprises the party's current and former MPs.[14] Since 1992 its presence in parliament has been manifested by Kutlat al-Wafāʾ lil-Muqāwama (the Loyalty to the Resistance Bloc (LRB)), encompassing Hezbollah members and its supporters elected on party slates. The role of the PAC is to monitor LRB actions and interventions and to discuss official positions and strategies for communicating them. LRB MPs who are not Hezbollah members may attend PAC meetings if an agenda item touches on their interests. Even though Hezbollah has not yet added a government action council to its structure—despite being part of the government since 2005—there is a government action dossier (*malaff al-ʿamal al-hukūmī*). The team in charge, consisting of the party members who head government ministries and assisted by a number of special advisers, is led by the deputy secretary-general.

Judicial Council (al-Majlis al-Qadāʾī)

This council brings together the regional heads of the judiciary as a religious court with jurisdiction over disputes between persons who wish to obtain a *sharīʿa*-compliant ruling. Most of the cases that come before it involve individuals who are members of Hezbollah or are in its orbit.

Military Council (al-Majlis al-Jihādī)

This oversees the IRL and its attached security organ (*jihāz al-amn*). It is responsible for ensuring the safety of Resistance members and armaments, including by surveillance of known or suspected collaborators. A few sources affirm that the Military Council is required to be chaired by Hassan Nasrallah.[15] If this is indeed the case, it would mean that the positions of primary responsibility for IRL and of the Hezbollah secretary-general overlap. The rule says that when the triennial party congress meets, the dividing up of the Consultative Council chairs on the five central councils takes place before the election of the secretary-general. Thus, the identity of the secretary becomes obvious as soon as that of the Military Council's chairman is announced. In other words, the one given primary responsibility for IRL and its security apparatus is necessarily going to be the one to lead Hezbollah, providing further proof that Hezbollah as an organization serves the IRL—and not vice versa. Clearly, whoever heads the military organization outranks the leadership on the civilian side.

The General Congress and central–local/local–central links

When in session, the General Congress (al-Mu'tamar al-Markazī), is the highest authority of the party. It is an organ of decision and control, and at the same time an electoral college. It works in all respects like communist and socialist congresses. Made up of the sector chairmen and those of the CUs, it can bring at least 300 people together. Since 1995[16] it has been held every three years (1995, 1998, 2001, 2004, and, exceptionally, in 2008/9).[17]

The Congress has two main missions. It discusses general party policy "at all levels without exception".[18] Sitting above the Consultative Council in the hierarchy, the Congress reviews the Council's past work, and criticizes or endorses the policy implemented by each CU during the previous three years and their plans for the next three. It also performs a major electoral duty: like a communist congress, it elects the Decision-Making Consultative Council. It does so by choosing seven people, including five who are willing to serve as leaders of the Central Councils and two who must "possess the qualities required of a secretary-general". Having previously lost a head of the organization, in 1992, Hezbollah now takes the precaution of electing two individuals to be part of the Council so one of them could immediately replace the secretary-general should he disappear.

The first order of business for the seven members as soon as they have been elected by Congress is to select five of their number to become chairmen of the Central Councils.[19] No one is forced to chair a council if not interested in serving in the post. The two selected to replace the secretary-general may be among the five.[20] With these individual posts filled, the Consultative Council as a whole elects the secretary-general, who in turn designates a deputy secretary.[21]

Once appointed, the new chairman of the Executive Council goes on to appoint the heads of the CUs. Following a procedure that once again recalls communist party practice, it polls the regional and sector councils for a list of possible candidates. The Consultative Council endorses or rejects the final list. At these triennial elections, the sector cadres that compose the respective sector councils nominate a chief for each of them subject to approval by the Executive Council. The chosen sector chiefs meet and then submit a list of names to the Executive Council for appointment of the regional councils; once more, the Executive Council approves the proposed lists as presented or as revised at its direction.

The Central Units

Reporting to Hezbollah's Executive Council is a series of Central Units (al-Wahadāt al-Markaziyya) that are the party's operating units par excellence. In this, Hezbollah's structure mimics the Pasdaran, whose CUs are a characteristic structure of that institution.[22]

Each CU has a manager. Collectively, they make up the Executive Council, which is chaired by a member of the Consultative Council. Units are specialized by subject matter and have their analogues in each region (Beirut, Bekaa, and the South). These decentralized versions are called departments (*qism*), whose heads then report to the head of the Central Unit.[23]

Social and professional mobilization

The importance of the Social Unit (al-Wahda al-Ijtimāʿiyya) in Hezbollah relates above all to the fact that it manages the IRL's primary support institutions, some of which are nothing other than the Iranian subsidiaries linked to the organization. It manages the Foundation of the Martyr, the Foundation for the War Wounded, al-Imdād, Jihād al-Bināʾ, LAPL, and CIRS. In the socio-medical realm, the Unit is assisted by the Health Unit (al-Wahda al-Sahhiyya), particularly by IHC, its flagship institution.

Hezbollah is active in professional circles through the Professions Unit (Wahdat al-Mihan al-Hurra) and the Unions and Workers Unit (Wahdat al-Naqābāt wal-ʿUmmāl). The first is relatively dynamic, and handles coordination between Hezbollah and allied groups in professional circles. It acts as a device for communication and negotiation with political parties that are also active in professional circles. The second, however, is quasi-active, sponsoring only one union, the Confederation of the Loyalty,[24] which withdrew from the Confédération Générale du Travail—Liban (CGTL), the Lebanese national trade union organization, in 2004.

As already mentioned, the Women's Committees Unit reflects the fact that Hezbollah, in its internal workings, does not neglect women. From its inception, the party dedicated a good part of its social activities to mobilizing this public. Beyond its role in mobilizing women, the Unit is responsible for information and education on issues that affect women's daily lives. The Unit regularly organizes conferences, lunches, and theatre performances designed to bring to life and promote women's role in sustaining the Resistance, and also runs professional training workshops (reading and writing, arts and crafts, sewing, etc.) and puts on lectures (advice on "how to live well and manage your pregnancy", balanced nutrition for children, safeguarding against everyday dangers in the home, steps to take in case of accident, etc.)[25]

Mobilizing high school and university students and teachers

Hezbollah's social and media activities made their debut in 1984[26] in the General Activities Unit (GAU, Wahdat al-Anshita al-ʿĀmma), also simply known as al-Anshita (the Activities). It was active in only three spheres at the start: media and communications, students, and women. Two years later the GAU went through its first split. The dynamism of party cadres who were formerly with al-Ittihād, known for committed activism in university circles,[27] led to hypergrowth in student activities, and soon required a separate unit. Consequently, in 1985–6 Student Mobilization (al-Taʿbiʾa al-Tullābiyya) was set up,[28] separate from the other social activities. Initially, it targeted only academia. Gradually, however, Taʿbiʾa developed an interest in schooling. In 1993 it set up the Islamic Insitution for Education and Teaching (IIET, al-Muʾassasa al-Islāmiyya lil-Tarbiya wal-Taʿlīm) to oversee the al-Mahdī schools, also established that year. At the same time, al-Taʿbiʾa al-Tullābiyya took its current name, Mobilization Unit for Education (MUE, Wahdat al-Taʿbiʾa al-Tarbawiyya), and in addition to mobilization in student circles was given the task of developing mobilization activities for secondary schools. This unit also breathed life into associations in the professorial ranks that supported the Resistance, of which the Committee for Higher Education (Hayʾat al-Taʿlīm al-ʿĀlī) is the principal one.[29]

Media and communications

Hezbollah's media and public communications activities, universally acknowledged as a strength of the organization, started modestly indeed. Before the party deployed its current media apparatus in the late 1980s, its communications almost exclusively targeted mobilization and were mainly done by the Cultural Unit and members of the Consultative Council. Clerics for the most part, they would harangue the public on social or religious occasions. A radio station first appeared in 1985 in the Baalbek region. Called The Radio of Islam—The Voice of the Oppressed (Idhāʿat al-Islām—Sawt al-Mustadʿafin),[30] it was initially supervised by the Iranian Cultural Centre of Damascus.[31] In June 1984 the weekly *al-ʿAhd* put out its first issue.[32] Once it obtained its Lebanese government licence, it was renamed *al-Intiqād* (The Critique), in reference to Hezbollah having moved into the political opposition.[33]

The audiences for these early media ventures were quite limited. Sawt al-Mustadʿafin, which soon preferred to call itself Sawt al-Muqāwama (the Voice of the Resistance), found competition from within the organization by Idhāʿat al-Nūr (the Station of Light), which began broadcasting from the capital in May 1988.[34] After a law was passed in September 1996 putting a cap on new radio and television licences, al-Nūr was permitted to continue broadcasting, while Sawt al-Mustadʿafin had to go off the air in July 2002,[35] leaving to al-Nūr the distinction of being the party's only radio station.

In the early years, Hezbollah's televised communications consisted of merely a few hours of retransmitted Iranian TV news bulletins in time slots sub-leased from the broadcaster Baalbek Television (Talfizyūn Bʿalbak). Over several years the party sought to develop a channel of its own, but was frustrated by the Lebanese authorities' refusal to grant a licence.[36] The Iranian ambassador to Syria had to intervene before al-Manār could go on the air in June 1991, with a first broadcast from the southern suburbs of Beirut.

Today, Hezbollah manages its public relations and media activities through the Information Unit (al-Wahda al-Iʿlāmiyya) and Media Activities Unit (Wahdat al-

Anshita al-Iʿlāmiyya). The former handles the party's external communications, including links with the press and the research community. It deals with interview requests and sets up meetings for them (or not), and it is to this unit that the party's media outlets, including al-Manār and al-Nūr, are attached. The Media Activities Unit is occupied with staging events, organizing festivals in support of the Resistance, and setting up exhibitions extolling the exploits and lives of the martyrs. Its strategic importance has grown over the years, the Unit also being responsible for producing political and mobilization-oriented graphics (posters, images, paintings, and suitable slogans).

Internal operations

The Cultural Unit (al-Wahda al-Thaqāfiyya) is responsible for religious and doctrinal mobilization. Staffed mainly by clerics, it disseminates the mobilization discourse within the organization's ranks. Unlike the units handling information and media activities, which cater to the general public, this unit orchestrates internal cultural training (*al-tathqīf al-dākhilī*).[37] It focuses on mosques, *hawza*s (religious schools), and *husayniyya*s. It mostly organizes conferences and the publication of educational material and books, such as biographies of the martyrs, many of which result from writing competitions.[38]

The equivalent of a personnel department within Hezbollah is the Human Resources Unit (al-Ahwāl), reminiscent of the Communist Party cadre section. It manages the membership records and party careers. This is where job-placement requests in the organization's various institutions are handled.

Finally, the party's daily financial management is in the hands of the Financial Unit (al-Wahda al-Māliyya), a very strategic unit with an unsurprisingly low profile.

Managing government relations, communicating with Western delegations

The Liaison and Coordination Unit (Wahdat al-Irtibāt wal-Tansīq) is responsible for coordination between the party and some of the Lebanese state's institutions. Specifically, it handles contacts with the Ministry of Justice, the Department of the Interior, and the Lebanese army.[39]

Despite what its name might imply, the Unit for External Relations (Wahdat al-ʿIlāqāt al-Khārijiyya) is not Hezbollah's Ministry of Foreign Affairs. Party foreign policy is segmented by region and compartmentalized by dossiers (portfolios). Relations with Arab countries are managed by a member of the Political Council, while policy towards Western countries and international organizations (the UN in particular) falls to the External Relations Desk, which the secretary-general himself manages.[40] In this regard, it resembles the foreign policy section of a communist party. The Unit for External Relations supports the secretary-general with this dossier. The staff follows Western writings about the party in the American and European press and receives foreign political, media, and student delegations.

The unique case of sports mobilization

Sports Mobilization (al-Taʿbiʾa al-Riyādiyya) provides training in diverse sports such as football, track and field, table tennis, and martial arts to athletes of all ages and faiths. As mentioned previously, in Beirut it is best known for its al-ʿAhd football club. Organizationally, Sports Mobilization is the only institution of the party that exists strictly in a regional version, although it functions under the authority of the Executive Council just like a CU. The regional Sports Mobilizations do not report to what would be a central sports unit or sports mobilization unit. Instead, the Sports Mobilization manager in the capital coordinates directly with the head of the Beirut region.[41]

The financially and administratively independent institutions (FAIIs)

Grafted on to the Hezbollah Executive Council and the CUs is a series of special bodies, officially described as "financially and administratively independent institutions but working in coordination with Hezbollah" (muʾassasāt mustaqilla māliyyan wa idāriyyan wa lākin taʿmal bi-tansīq maʿ Hizbillāh). Again, they are linked to Hezbollah in the same kind of institutional relationship that exists between a communist party and its "front organizations" ("organismes annexes"). While the bodies previously described are staffed only by party members, this is not necessarily true for FAII cadres and employees. Hezbollah members can even be in the minority in these institutions, with most of the workforce consisting of supporters of all faiths. The board of directors too does not consist only of Hezbollah members. The board chairman, who does have to be a member of the party, represents the sole link to the party's organization. That means that an FAII is not free to choose its board chairman as it sees fit. Instead, the board proposes a name to the Hezbollah Executive Council. If the candidate is approved, the nomination goes to the Consultative Council for endorsement. It then either approves the name, sends the proposal back for revision, or suggests a candidate of its own to the board.[42]

Historically, FAIIs were created ad hoc, grafted onto the Hezbollah organization in response to needs arising at specific times as it grew. However, not all of them were FAIIs. Some began as institutions of the party, but the connection was eventually cut when they achieved critical size and became too difficult to manage internally.[43] Transforming Hezbollah bodies into FAIIs offers two benefits. It allows the party to hire technically skilled specialists not found in its pool of militants. This is the case with al-Manār, al-Nūr, or in-house graphics design for some of its communications campaigns. Also, on the financial plane, the party avoids having to compensate mem-

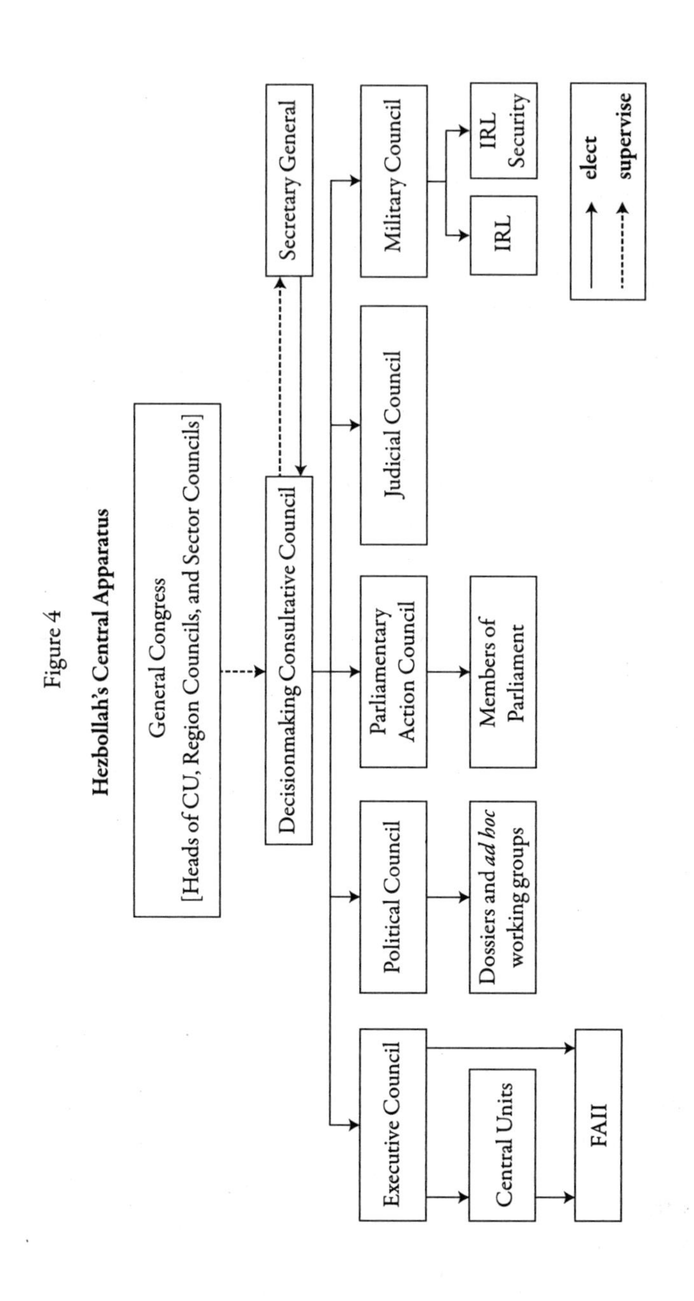

Figure 4
Hezbollah's Central Apparatus

bers that it moves into different jobs. The FAIIs therefore function not as a partisan but as a free-market business structure. They include al-Imdād, the Foundation of the Martyr, the Foundation for the War Wounded, the LALP and CIRS (linked to the Social Unit); al-Manār, al-Nūr (Information Unit); al-Mahdī schools (Unit of Mobilization for Education); and al-ʿAhd (Sports Mobilization).

The Advisory Centre for Studies and Documentation (ACSD, al-Markaz al-Istishārī lil-Dirāsāt wal-Tawthīq) constitutes a special case within this complement of FAIIs. It performs a dual function. A multilingual[44] social science library, it archives (among others) the party's communications trove. But it also produces studies on a variety of topics—political, economic, social, and environmental. It reports not to a CU manager but directly to the deputy secretary-general, who appoints its director after having proposed a candidate to be endorsed by ACSD's board of directors. The ACSD's director reports both to the CU managers (*ergo* the Executive Council) and the members of the Decision-Making Consultative Council. The Centre acts as a think tank here, furnishing studies upon request on topics of the CU's choosing. Should the research requested be on subject matter that the Centre is not working on, it is allowed to turn down the CU's request. On the other hand, if the study is commissioned by the Consultative Council, the ACSD is obligated to give it priority over any other project.

Joining Hezbollah

Adherents, militants, and supporters

When is a person said to be "in Hezbollah" (*bil-Hizb*)? As is true for all the other parties, not every Hezbollah member enjoys the same status. Political science usually defines an adherent as an official member upon the signing of a membership form and paying of dues at initiation.[45] This does not necessarily mean that the individual is active within the organization's ranks; his support for the cause may stop with this payment. Moreover, he is not inducted, and does not necessarily engage actively with the party. In this respect he differs from the militant, who is an active member, who manages, so to speak, the life of the party on a daily basis.

If we stay with this ranking by degree of solidarity, we discover that, in Hezbollah's case, there is no such thing as an inactive member. All members are politically supervised and active, be they cadres or rank-and-file members. Adherent, member, and militant are synonymous terms. Around the party, defined here as the group of active members, there are two categories of supporters. The ones that I call "passive supporters" are content with voting for its slates periodically, and with giving moral support to the Hezbollah cause. They may even step up their support by contributing to party social action with donations to related institutions (al-Imdād, the Foundation of the Martyr, CIRS, etc.). "Active supporters" do more by turning over the *khums* to Hassan

Nasrallah or Muhammad Yazbek. In times of conflict they may support the IRL at their level and within their means, hiding fighters in their homes or getting food, medicines, or basic necessities to them. Some may even be called "crypto-Hezbollah", participating in the party's daily routine and its political activities but without being party members. They may not hesitate on occasion to change their way of life or specific social habits to better fit in with the party culture. For its part, the party has sufficient confidence in them to give them responsibility. A perfect example of this kind of sympathizer is a category of parliamentary deputy elected on a Hezbollah slate, whose loyalty the party had a chance to test in the past, in the context of social or political activities in which the candidate already had a track record. Their status is not quite up to that of party member deputies (the crypto-Hezbollah types are not members of the Parliamentary Action Council and only may attend its meetings upon invitation by the council's chair). Nonetheless, once they have been elected, their political activism is indistinguishable from that of the party's deputies.

Who can join Hezbollah and how?[46]

Membership in the party is only open to men. There are no women "members of Hezbollah" (*ʿunsur*). The party leadership explains this state of affairs by reference to the fact that women are not obligated to take part in armed combat.[47] There is only one way of becoming a member of Hezbollah,[48] and it involves a two-step process. It begins with a training session for the membership candidate, the *taʿbiʾa dīniyya* (religious mobilization). Courses are given in mosques and religious cultural centres (*husayniyyas*) during the day or after work. The duration of this first stage of cultural training depends on how fast the candidate can complete the mandatory hours. However, a majority of candidates study or work, which often forces them to opt for evening classes. Far from being solely devoted to religion, these classes are also political conferences where religion is only the vector for another, secular value, that of resistance. According to one Hezbollah member:

> They do not give us courses on Islam as such, like about the Prophet's life, etc. Anyway, that's all common knowledge already. No. The first lesson we were given, for example, was the fact that Islam orders us to fight anyone who attacks us, that it is forbidden to stay idle and watch an enemy demolish our homes, kill our families, occupy our country. The next lesson was on the Israeli occupation army and all the evil it was doing in Lebanon, and all the disasters awaiting us if we let them do it. ... Well, and then, obviously, they remind us what [the Imam] Hussein did, how he was brave before the enemy, that sort of thing.[49]

In other words, the universe of meaning that Hezbollah inculcates in its future members has the *muqāwama* as its matrix rather than Islam. Islam is not absent—these are after all religious classes—but Islam is used as a system of justification. It is called on to help a higher cause, even though this cause may be profane. The *jihād* here serves less for implanting Islam than Islam is used to advance the cause of *jihād*.

Once successfully through this stage, the candidate joins the *taʿbiʾaʿ askariyya* (military mobilization). He receives general weapons training (pistol, Kalashnikov, etc.) and specialized training according to "his tastes and abilities" (to use a party member's words). The training completed, candidates are assigned to one of a number of specialties: infantry, artillery, mine-laying, the Russian machine gun, rockets, etc. At the end of this second training session, the trainers do triage. The recruits with most military aptitude join the IRL as *mujāhids* or fighters. Others become members of Hezbollah, with the rank of *taʿbiʾa*, a designation translatable both as "mobilized" and "conscripted".

A necessary precondition of this two-step membership qualification is for the candidate to present an impeccable personal history. The entry process is rigorous, often made more so by requiring a sponsor who is already a member—once again a practice that socialist and communist parties also follow.[50] Cadres as well as rank-and-file militants recognize that Hezbollah "does not let just anyone join" and that exhaustive background information is gathered on each applicant. Most members start out being sympathizers (*munāsir*), then they become aspirants (*tahdīrī*) before being finally accepted as "members of the mobilization" (*ʿunsur taʿbiʾa*). In principle, only candidates who currently have or previously had contact with the Israeli authorities and/or whose "behaviour is incompatible with Hezbollah morals" are rejected. The effectiveness of this mode of recruitment in eliminating potential "dangerous elements" seems proven in practice, for several reasons. For one, the division of rank-and-file members in groups based on where they live makes getting the necessary information on a postulant easy. All the party cadre has to do to find out everything he needs to know about the candidate is to inquire among the *taʿbiʾa*s in his neighbourhood. The local leaders will be that much less inclined to give an easy pass to the applicant's candidacy because, if it is approved, it is their group that the new member would join. Members who can be persuaded to sponsor a candidate and to testify as to his probity are well aware that the party's internal discipline will not deal lightly with them if the sponsored candidate turns out to be a harmful element.

Membership categories

The candidate who succeeds in joining Hezbollah does not get a document certifying his membership. Hezbollah, in fact, does without a card system entirely, unlike other Lebanese parties such as the Kataeb or AMAL. Party officials most often rationalize this peculiarity by arguing that Hezbollah does not see itself as just a political party, but as a support organization for the Resistance cause, thus putting its existence and action into a much wider context.[51] The proof of identity of a person joining Hezbollah is the affiliation with a group (*majmūʿa*), which is not conditioned on the payment of membership dues. Instead, he will make occasional additional payments not into the party's but into his group's coffers to help pay for the operating costs of the *majmūʿa*.

Each *majmūʿa* adopts the name of a martyr of the IRL or of an *imām*, allowing it to both differentiate itself from and to recognize others. Although the members of the same group know each other, they do not necessarily know names in other groups, but are *a priori* able to make the connection between the name of a group and the neighbourhood in which it is based.

A *majmūʿa* can number up to thirty people. Weekly, usually hour-long, meetings are mandatory, and have two dimensions: cultural and informative. The first half-hour is devoted to religious culture, the second addresses the "political point", with the group leaders explaining the latest decisions and strategies from the Central Consultative Council and passing on the latest directives and word of the moment. With these meetings, they are once again mimicking the ways of the socialist and communist organizations.[52] They are also the occasions when Human Resources announces the latest training courses slated for the militants, starting off with military training courses.

Along with this first type of meeting, all members of Hezbollah regardless of their level must take religious classes that are provided most often by the Cultural Unit, but also courses in policy, management, and party administration. Every member's progress is monitored by Human Resources. Based on the number of courses in religion that the militant managed to take in-house, and based on his first (military) specialty, it puts together a personalized training programme for him. While participation in the programmes (*burnāmaj*, pl. *barāmij*) is in principle mandatory, the dates, duration, and exact format are negotiable. According to one militant, "it depends on whether we have time, if our professional or personal circumstances allow it."

Immersed as they are in various social circles, members of the base serve Hezbollah in variety of ways. Contrary to what may prevail in other Islamist organizations, they are not preachers, nor do they perform official recruitment duties. This would mean they would have to out themselves, revealing their membership to the public. The fact is that the members are fairly unobtrusive in daily life. While some cadres are easily recognized, their duties often having a public component, the rank-and-file members are nearly impossible to identify. They lead daily lives like everyone else and rarely wear articles of clothing that would make them stand out. In the vast majority of cases, no one knows if a person is in Hezbollah unless they spend time with him or find it out by word of mouth.

A primary function of the rank-and-file members is to act as sources of information for their own hierarchy. In its determination to keep a finger on the pulse of the fickle public and to identify threats that may loom for the party, the Hezbollah leadership relies on the *taʿbiʾa*s to relay striking facts, unusual changes, trends and rumours, which they are likely to come across day by day. This information is of crucial importance. For one thing, it helps IRL security services track down pro-Israeli spy networks. In this regard, the base has the role of watchdog. For another, it gives the leadership a sense of what its public or community may think about what it does or says. This lets it know whether Hezbollah's public is on board with the party's choices. The base therefore also functions as a barometer. Lastly, some data reported back by members in the base give them a social worker role, especially when they report problems in their quarters. Indeed, many families now supported by al-Imdād have been identified by members of Hezbollah in their neighbourhood,[53] or Jihād al-Binā' is regularly kept informed about areas needing rubbish collection.[54]

As well as roles where information flows from bottom up, there are roles where information goes top down. Hezbollah members, integrated with the society through family, social, and professional circles, also function as disseminators of specific ideas that the party leadership wants to spread. These may range from its version of specific events to spreading false information about itself. For example, after the summer 2006 war, when the Israeli intelligence services began a major drive to gather information on IRL's military capabilities, Hezbollah circulated a very different (and therefore useless) set of numbers through the base. A favourite channel for circulating false rumours about the party's internal affairs, the base helps to protect the sensitive parts of the organization by shuffling the cards.

A last function of the base is organizing celebrations for Hezbollah and the electoral framework. It does most of the leg-work. According to a militant, these occasions are sensitive because the rank-and-file members will be out in public (although mingled in with supporters, they may be able to preserve some anonymity). Though they may also help boost the number of participants, their primary role lies elsewhere: they install the infrastructure, equipment, decorations, check that spotlights, microphones, and speakers are working, and are sometimes called on to bolster security. During election time they go into action around voting centres in their own quarters, distributing hats, T-shirts, drinks, and lunch boxes to voters. They provide transport to polling stations for voters who need it and step up in support of the party's information and communication apparatus.

Most rank-and-file members' sole reward for these valuable services to the party is the consolation that they are working "for God and the Cause".[55] The non-employees among them do not get paid, nor can they access services offered by the party's social institutions (al-Imdād, the IHC, etc.) without charge, a privilege reserved for the cadres. This is how one militant rationalizes it:

> We get charged just like normal people. Not only don't we get paid, we actually wind up giving money to the party. Sure, we are not obligated to do it, but it's clear that we're expected to put in some money. It makes sense: if we don't do it, who will?[56]

In practice, unpaid members do get some compensation, but only up to a point. Preferential mutual-aid networks operate between merchants and service providers who are members. For example, vouchers distributed by al-Imdād to the needy are good primarily in shops owned by party members. Hezbollah's good reputation for honesty and ethics also pays dividends for non-salaried members. Customers who know (or believe) that a business owner or manager is a party member will tend to take their business to him rather than someone else. But the monetary rewards of a non-remunerated belonging to Hezbollah only seldom go beyond this type of benefit.

After joining the party's ranks, the *taʿbiʾa* can choose to remain a non-employee member of the party, that is, remain in the status of what I call "stripped-down membership" (*al-intimāʾ al-mujarrad*), or become a salaried member, full or part time, with a chance of becoming a cadre. This is another analogy with communist organizations, in that Hezbollah's salaried employees can be compared to paid CP cadres, and the unpaid *taʿbiʾa*s to communist militants who are classed as volunteers.

Hezbollah has two categories of salaried members: the *mutafarrigh* and the *mutaʿāqid*. The first, as the name suggests, has a full-time job. He devotes all of his working time—and sometimes his time off—to professional work for the party. As for the second, he is contractually obligated to work only part time for the party. In addition, the *mutafarrigh* is privileged to enjoy, free of charge or for very little money, the services of the party's social institutions such as the IHC or Jihād al-Bināʾ. During winters the party also provides him with heating oil and covers the cost of the *hajj* (the pilgrimage to Mecca).

Employees may be moved into one of two career tracks: the political; or management and administration. The first leads to decision making, consulting, and communication provided by the very small number of members on the Consultative Council, the Political Council and the personal advisers of the Shūrā, the party's parliamentary deputies, and the units and departments of information. Most employees enter the second track. Here they staff the various positions in the different party institutions: director of a CU or a regional department, member of an administrative team, an engineer with Jihād al-Bināʾ, a graphic designer in the CU for Media Activities, principal of an al-Mahdī school, etc.

There are very few employees. A field observation of the functioning of CUs as well as of departments reveals that party institutions are each run with less than a dozen employees. The number of applicants in any case would be significantly higher than the available slots. This is far from being a party that draws its strength from a large number of cadres. By corollary, Hezbollah's staff budget is relatively small. In reality, the IRL's fighters appear to be the true beneficiaries of the organization's largesse. It covers all their expenses, from rent to cars, daily living expenses, and their children's education. As mentioned earlier, the Foundation of the Martyr subsidizes the needs of the families of martyrs and pays their children's university fees. Compared to the IRL, Hezbollah is ultimately a relatively poor party—further evidence that the first gets priority over the second.

Organizational effectiveness and sustained mobilization

Although incomplete, this general description of Hezbollah's internal organization helps identify some of the party's strong points that ensure the effectiveness of its militant action while sustaining its internal mobilization.

Advantages of the communist structure

In his typology of political parties, the sociologist Maurice Duverger established a clear difference between the structures with vertical links connecting two parts of an organization, with one subordinate to the other, and those linked horizontally, which attach parts of the same organization to each other on an equal footing.[57] In the former category, into which Hezbollah fits, "we end up ... with a strict compartmentalization", where groups on the same level cannot communicate with each other except via mediation from those higher up.[58] Vertical linkages prevent schisms and internal opposition, since dissent arising in an institution does not contaminate others placed on the same level, while each higher level acts as a firewall that is "all the more powerful because the cadres are better trained and of tested reliability".[59] It strengthens internal cohesion, with the risk of contagion from dissent being attenuated by a centralization that also reinforces the vertical nature of the linkages. Indeed, the head of an organism is not accountable to the colleagues who have chosen him, but to the superior organism. One duty of the former is to apprise his superior of any dissension brewing in the group entrusted to him, "not in order to defend his point of view, but to provoke a saving intervention from the centre".[60]

The effectiveness of vertical linkages is further buttressed by the way information, remarks, and slogans travel both up and down. Duverger says:

> Think what you like about the Communist Party: the mechanisms it has forged must be recognized as being remarkably effective, and you cannot deny them a certain democratic character, because of this constant concern with keeping in touch with the base, with being "attentive to the masses". ... More profoundly still, the value of this method comes from the fact that it is not purely passive, it does not stop at merely registering the reactions of the masses, but it allows acting on them, channelling them carefully, prudently, but profoundly.[61]

For Hezbollah, this mode of organizational operation has an additional advantage: it is a better arrangement for warding off harmful actions brought against it from outside. The communist structure is ideal for secret action, particularly because of its "watertight compartments" that limit the extent of any infiltration by hostile agents.[62] As already mentioned, members of one group rarely know those in others. In the realm of security, this protective impermeability of the communist structure serves Hezbollah in that no one inside a social, artistic, or media institution of the party really knows what is going on in the others.

Wilāyat al-faqīh and *al-taklīf al-sharʿī*: bedrock principles of internal discipline

Among Hezbollah organizational traits, the strength of internal discipline is far from being the least important. In addition, it is regularly commented on by observers. This is one character trait that does not derive from the crypto-communist nature of the party, but arises from its Shiite culture—starting with its decision to swear allegiance to *wilāyat al-faqīh*.

Wilāyat al-faqīh in practice

Wilāyat al-faqīh is a principle that Hezbollah has consistently and officially adhered to. In response, the party's opponents have continuously denounced this assumed obedience to Iranian authority as clear proof of Hezbollah's non-Lebanese character. They accuse the party of being under foreign tutelage in its decision making and its priorities. They conceive Hezbollah as nothing more than a subcontractor for Iranian policy in Lebanon, since its first allegiance is to the head of the Islamic Republic (the Guide of the Revolution), which puts it ahead of the Lebanese authorities.

The reality is not quite so schematic. The *wilāyat al-faqīh*, of religious origin and legitimation, in essence is a principle of political governance. Khomeini himself said: "The *wilāya* means the government, administration and political management of a country."[63] In practice, Hezbollah's adherence to the *wilāyat* of Khomeini and Khamenei is reflected not in the Iranian regime setting the party's priorities and strategies, but by the party's requests to the Guide of the Revolution for endorsements or authorizations. Such requests are only made for specific types of decisions: (i) those that can threaten the national interest of the Islamic Republic (military action against the Israeli army, for example); (ii) those that call into question a basic principle of the party's *modus operandi*; or (iii) those whose religious legitimacy (*al-sharʿiyya*) requires clarification (participation in national politics, for example).[64]

Naʿīm Qāsim, deputy secretary-general of Hezbollah, succinctly describes the nature of the hierarchical relationship between the Iranian regime and the party leadership under *wilāyat al-faqīh*[65] as allegiance to the *waliy*, that is, as Guide of the Revolution but not to the Iranian government:

> There is no link between the manner in which the Iranian Islamic state conducts its affairs and how Hezbollah manages its own. These are two separate things. The Iranian government and Hezbollah move in different directions, although they can sometimes encounter each other on the road of their commitment to the recommendations and guidelines of the *waliy al-faqīh*.[66]

As far as the Hezbollah leadership is concerned, the *waliy al-faqīh* is "the guarantor of the application of Islamic law ... and outlines the broad political guidelines that touch on the interests of the *ummah*". In that capacity, "he is the one who decides on war and peace, who is responsible for the security of the people, their property and their honour". Hezbollah acknowledges having asked the *waliy* for his endorsement on several occasions. The very founding of the organization received Khomeini's blessing.[67] In 1992, when the party considered entering Lebanese politics, its leadership first took a vote internally and then had the result confirmed by Khamenei.[68] On the occasion of every General Congress, the *waliy* is asked to accept the membership of the Consultative Council voted in by the cadres.[69] The same applies to military operations against the Israeli army: the concept and planning fall to the party[70] but some initiatives with particularly important strategic implications require a green light from the *waliy*.[71]

That said, Qāsim concedes nonetheless that the *waliy al-faqīh* alone in fulfilling these responsibilities is not able to keep up with every detail of their implementation. Hence there is an implied "delegation of its powers to individuals or groups" locally. The authority of the *waliy* would be subject to limits, starting with "the objective environment and particularities of each group or country". In Hezbollah's case,

> the administrative follow-up on details and features, appropriate decision making, day-to-day political action, cultural and social activism, and the tactics of the fight against Israel are the responsibility of the command structure [of the party]. This command structure is elected in accordance with the internal rules [of the party]; in effect, it is represented by the Consultative Council and chaired by the secretary-general; its legitimacy is consecrated by the *waliy al-faqīh*.[72]

The legitimacy accorded to Hezbollah's command by the *waliy* would thus assure the party "great autonomy" in setting its priorities, in planning, and in strategizing. The party would turn to the *waliy* only in cases where "a clarification or authorization is necessary to vouchsafe the legality of decisions adopted". In other words, Hezbollah decides, the *waliy* endorses—or doesn't. According to a senior official, the room for manoeuvre enjoyed by the party leadership

> has been significant, particularly in everything that touches on political decisions without giving rise to questions of a religious nature, such as questions of confidence in the government or lack thereof, the approval or rejection of a law, or the adoption of policies or practical programmes needed to achieve fairly precise objectives.[73]

Hezbollah regularly emphasizes its freedom to make decisions, plan, and act in order to highlight that there is no contradiction between its allegiance to the *waliy* and loyalty to its home country and the interests of its home country:

> Experience shows ... there is no contradiction between being Lebanese and being Hezbollah—as far as national identity is concerned—and the fact that the party defers to the *waliy al-faqīh* regarding its political line, strategic decisions and policies. ... Hezbollah's national vision has not clashed with the interests of the Lebanese because of any guidelines and *fatwā*s issued by the *waliy al-faqīh*. ... Although he wields unlimited political power throughout the *ummah*, the *waliy al-faqīh* tacitly recognizes the

> existence of borders between peoples and national groups, which subdivide the *ummah* and impose specificities on each group in its particular national environment. ... This allowed Hezbollah and its leadership to harmonize their ideational and religious loyalty with the principle of the *wilāya*, their desire to serve the national interest of the Lebanese people, and their participation in Lebanon's state institutions.[74]

Wilāya and internal cohesion

Wilāyat al-faqīh, through its practical retranslations into Hezbollah's general operations, in large part explains the party's cohesion and internal discipline. At the command level, allegiance to the *waliy al-faqīh* minimizes disagreements thanks to his role as arbiter. The *waliy* recommends political and military strategies that let the party leadership avoid having to deal with serious differences over the ordering of priorities,[75] and settles dissension between currents or individuals that bear on crucial questions of the life of the organization. The party members, whose adherence to the organization is conditioned by their allegiance to the *waliy*, have no choice but to obey or leave (voluntarily or by being expelled). In 1991 Khamenei's support for the Consultative Council's decision to elect al-Mūsawī to take over as the new secretary-general to the detriment of al-Tufaylī prevented a war between leaders that would have been fatal for Hezbollah. In 1992 discord between al-Tufaylī and a majority on the Consultative Council over the question of the party taking part in the parliamentary elections was contained thanks to a Khamenei *fatwā* that supported the Council's choice. This caused a senior cadre to acknowledge that "the *wilāya* played a very positive role in attaining organizational discipline that was born of religious respect for this principle, ensuring unity in the internal ranks".[76]

For the base and the mid-level cadre, respect for the *wilāyat al-faqīh* goes hand in hand with obedience to the decisions of the leadership—obedience manifested in an exemplary discipline recognized by observers and envied by other Lebanese political groups. The link between this iron discipline and allegiance to the *wilāya* is, however, not direct, as the recommendations by the *waliy* do not reach down to the daily world of the militants. The relationship exists, but through the concept of *taklīf sharʿī* (religious obligation).[77] A senior official defines the concept as follows:

> For those who adopt [*wilāyat al-faqīh*] it translates into what is called religious obligation (*taklīf sharʿī*) which assures a sense of innocence and absence of guilt on the religious plane to the person obligated to carry it out (*al-mukallaf*). ... It keeps the rationalization and personalizing of interests from turning into so many reasons for dissension, splits or distancing, thanks to the existence of a respected referent who settles these disputes and strips out any negative consequences from them. It does not mean, however, closing the door on criticism and blocking the freedom of thought or expression.[78]

Originally, there was no link between *taklīf sharʿī* and the concept of *wilāyat al-faqīh*. The *taklīf sharʿī* is inherent in Shiite dogma and refers to the obligation, born of respect for religious precepts, to implement a directive that would be presented as *taklīf sharʿī*. This standard phrase, accompanying a directive from the leadership, indicates that it is expected to be strictly obeyed. But it has also been used by other Shiite organizations—starting with AMAL. The notion is particularly effective in Hezbollah's case since it does not appeal only to the individual's militant devotion to the cause, but just as much to his belief in God. The leadership must be obeyed all the more because it consists of both political and religious leaders. In addition, the *waliy al-faqīh*, supreme source of political authority, reposes his confidence in them. Since Hassan Nasrallah acknowledged Khamenei as *marjaʿ* in 1994, the Guide of the Iranian Revolution had played the dual role of religious authority in Hezbollah, as *waliy* and as *marjaʿ*.

Guaranteed by both the member's militant commitment and his faith, the *taklīf sharʿī* thus ensures that the members will obey the leadership. However, contrary to what some commentators have seen fit to suggest, the *taklīf sharʿī* is not used routinely. The Hezbollah leadership falls back on it almost exclusively in situations where a general lack of buy-in to its decisions would seriously harm the party. For example, in January 1998, allegiance to the *wilāya* and the principle of *taklīf sharʿī* checked a mass defection of cadres from the Bekaa that the al-Tufaylī expulsion from Hezbollah had threatened to set off.[79] Liberation without any acts of reprisal in 2000 and the Shiite vote in favour of mixed slates supported by the party in 2005 were made possible thanks to *taklīf sharʿī*.[80] During the bloody clashes between March 14 and March 8 militants in January 2007, and during Hezbollah's armed intervention in the streets of Beirut in May 2008, the party leadership kept the situation within bounds by declaring both the ban on retaliatory fire in the first case and on attacking civilians in the second as *taklīf sharʿī*.[81]

Discipline and external communication

Iron discipline guaranteed by the members' voluntary allegiance to the principle of *taklīf sharʿī* has another useful effect, in this case on external communications. This is not everybody's business. As an organization with large sections that are secret, Hezbollah does not empower just any member to express himself in public. The content of political discourse is determined by the command apparatus, as are its major lines of argument. Members and cadres of the Information Unit and departments are responsible for disseminating it, as are some political leaders in the regions. But they make (almost) no personal revisions to it. Other party members, cadres or rank-and-file militants are compelled to seek permission from their superiors before speaking out. The result is a system of authorizations managed by the Central Information Unit, under which any researcher or journalist has to present him/herself and put in a request before having a chance to meet with an appropriate contact. In terms of mobilization, the party puts up a united discourse and stakes out coherent positions that boost its credibility. From the security perspective, this allows identification of individuals who try to approach it and helps prevent leaks of Information.

I could not bring my project of uncovering the sources of Hezbollah's internal cohesion and the strength of its mobilization effort to a close without turning to one last element: the personality of the third secretary-general and his militant path. They indeed combine into a major element in the attraction the party holds for militants as well as supporters. This dimension of Hezbollah's mobilization is too important to be addressed in a sub-part, much less in just a paragraph. It deserves a chapter all its own.

6

THE HASSAN NASRALLAH PHENOMENON

LEADERSHIP AND MOBILIZATION

In 2011 the American weekly news magazine *Time* for the first time included Hassan Nasrallah, Hezbollah's third secretary-general, in its annual ranking of the "100 most influential people in the world". Without question, Nasrallah has, over the past several years, earned a place among the top leaders of the Arab world. *The Muslim 500* has ranked him among the top thirty in the Muslim world dating back to 2009. Several Western commentators have described him for some time as a "second Che Guevara". Whether he arouses admiration and enthusiasm or insult and rejection, there is no denying that his career is now an integral part of the history of the Middle East.

In *The Spellbinders*[1] Ann Willner dwells on Sukarno's charisma, which she then compares with a dozen other historical exemplars from around the world. From this, she proposes a list of elements without which no person can rightly claim to have charisma. According to Willner, very few individuals can actually be described as being or having been charismatic. As Max Weber had suggested before her, she deems charisma as not identifiable by the qualities possessed by the person judged as charismatic, but by their effect, meaning that charisma is born of reception. Interestingly, she does not consider charisma to be solely the doing of the public. Like most authors, she inquires into that which, upstream, has led to the existence of a certain image. In the process, she restores some role to the charismatic person themelves in how they are perceived. This role is not a theatrical artifice in the sense of a deliberately projected image; the charismatic person is, according to Willner, responsible for the perception the public has of them: by saying what they say, doing what they do, carrying on the way they do, they suggest, most often unwittingly, elements that the public then uses as support for building an image of them. It hardly matters if this suggestion is premeditated or not: the perception builds less around what can be objectively observed in the leader than around ideas sometimes only insinuated by what he emanates. As a corollary, Willner refuses to see "causes" of charisma in what a person is, says, or does, preferring instead to identify "sources of perception". The notion of cause would mean that the public is incapable of projecting an image on the leader other than one that is explicitly conveyed by the cause, assuming the public perceives exactly what is objectively emitted. However, using the concept of the source of perception instead amounts to recognizing that what emanates from the leader gives free rein to the imagination of the public. This does not necessarily give the public the objective meaning that it must see there, but the meaning that its culture, representations, values, and subjective reading of context inspire.[2] Willner therefore remains squarely within a logic of meaning-making centred on the public. She hence interrogates the public, not the leader, on what ought to be the qualities of the charismatic person. Four categories of factors to be found in the public's representations would thus allow identification of the charismatic. First is the assimilation of the leader likely to be described as charismatic with one or more dominant myths of their society and culture, so that the public conflates them with a hero of the past.[3] The second is the accomplishment of what seems to be an extraordinary or heroic feat; the third, projection of special qualities on the leader and the feeling that they have a mysterious or powerful aura; and, lastly, exceptional rhetorical talent.

Based on these conclusions, the following pages will try to reconstruct the rise of Hassan Nasrallah's mature yet still evolving charisma. Setting the stage for this effort will be as rigorous and detailed a biography of the man as possible, from his childhood until his accession to the post of secretary-general. This section therefore will be mainly informative. Charisma not being of essence during those years, what matters is knowing his social background, his past experiences, and the beginnings of his rise inside the organization. From this indeed emerge sources of perception which then will lend themselves to an analysis of his charisma per se, starting from his appointment as secretary-general. From that point on, instead of charting a factual biographical course, the focus shifts to a change of perception that occurred among some of the public between 1992 and 2000. The account's milestones will no longer necessarily coincide with the important stages in Nasrallah's life but with moments that were transformative for his image. Progressively, the repercussions from this dynamic perception of the relationship between the organization that Nasrallah leads and its public will become apparent.

An attempt at a biography

Writing a complete and definitive biography of Hassan Nasrallah presents a challenge. Although the man by now is a key figure on the Middle Eastern scene, there is an inexplicable poverty of biographical data about him. Naturally, capsule bios about him abound on the internet, with information about him that is brief, often inaccurate, and sometimes absurd. For example, the English-language website NNDB[4]—a database dedicated to presenting "a who's who from around the world"—posts this presentation of Nasrallah next to his portrait: "Date of birth: 31-Aug-1960—Religion: Shiite Muslim—Race or ethnicity: Middle Eastern—Sexual orientations: Straight—Profession: Terrorist."[5] Besides these documents of questionable worth there are certainly a few usable texts, but most biographical accounts only repeat each other, often literally. For those that provide a minimum amount of material, the content is often unreliable and replete with blatant contradictions. As of today, an autobiography of a few pages, two interviews and a scant half-dozen papers are all an inquiring mind can draw on to learn about the life and militant career of Hezbollah's leader.[6]

Childhood and adolescence between Beirut and al-Bāzūriyyeh

Hassan Nasrallah was born on 31 August 1960, in the Sharshabūk quarter of Beirut's eastern suburbs, near the area called La Quarantaine (al-Karantīnā),[7] a multi-confessional neighbourhood of Arabs, Kurds, and Armenians.[8] Before the civil war erupted in 1975, many of the poor neighbourhoods on the outskirts of the capital were inhabited mainly by Shiites of humble means, the Nasrallah family among them. Originally from the village of al-Bāzūriyyeh near Tyre, Hassan's father ʿAbdel-Karīm settled in Beirut, as did many Shiites whom unemployment drove out of the South. Young Hassan grew up in Nabʿa, where his father sold fruit and vegetables. The family's situation improved somewhat with time, and ʿAbdel-Karīm opened his own grocery shop, which enabled him eventually to eke out a living for his wife and nine children. Hassan, the eldest of the siblings, worked at his side when his school work allowed.

As a child he went to the neighbourhood primary school, and then attended the public high school in Sinn al-Fīl, a Christian neighbourhood east of Nabʿa. He became interested in religion as a teen—an odd interest as far as those around him were concerned, his family not being especially devout and not having much contact with religious men.[9] Nasrallah himself referred to this precocious attraction to the religious in an anecdote:

> When I was ten or eleven years old, my grandmother had a big long, black scarf. I would wind it around my head and tell everyone that I was a sheikh, so they had to pray behind me.[10]

During this time he began to frequent the mosques in Sinn al-Fīl, Burj Hammud, and, especially, Usrat al-Taʾākhī in Nabʿa directed by Muhammad Husayn Fadlallāh, with whom he took some classes.[11] It was also at this time that he came to admire Mūsā al-Sadr, whose imposing picture dominated the family shop. Nasrallah would say later that as a teenager he would spend long hours meditating in front of this portrait and praying to God to "make him like Sayyid Mūsā some day". In a logical consequence of this admiration, Nasrallah would sign up a few years later with AMAL.[12]

Studies and encounters in Najaf

After a first few militia-related incidents of a security nature, foreshadowing the civil war that broke out the following year, the Nasrallahs fled Nabʿa in 1974[13] and settled temporarily at Sinn al-Fīl, with the father commuting daily to Nabʿa to run the family shop.[14] The respite was short-lived: between 1975 and 1976, Christian militia emptied the neighbourhood of its Muslim inhabitants. The Nasrallahs were expelled in 1975. The family retreated to al-Bāzūriyyeh, where, soon afterwards, the young Hassan befriended a village cleric, Sheikh ʿAlī Shamseddīn. Together, they set up a library in the town's Islamic centre, where young Hassan was given formal responsibility for teaching simplified religious lessons to the young people frequenting the place. Nasrallah fulfilled his mission all the more zealously because he nurtured an ambition to form a cell of religious militants as a counterpart to the pan-Arab nationalists and leftist supporters who were the only active political forces in the village at the time.[15]

Before Hassan's family was forced into exile "he had never been interested in politics,"[16] and no one in his family had ever belonged to any party.[17] But 1975 was a pivotal year for him; it saw him start attending a public high school in Tyre, and most especially marked his militant beginnings when he and his younger brother Hussein joined AMAL and "despite [his] youth"[18] he was appointed party head for al-Bāzūriyyeh.

His political activities, however, did not diminish his desire to study religion, which he says gnawed at him from the time he was "thirteen or fourteen years of age".[19] The fervour of his political efforts at al-Bāzūriyyeh having waned due to the ever more marked inroads of the Marxist intellectuals and communist militants, he dropped out of college as well as ceasing his political activities: in December 1976 he departed for Najaf, having managed to gather from his father and some family friends the modest sum necessary to cover the cost of his travels.[20] At the time, he was encouraged in his initiative by Sheikh Muhammad Mansūr al-Gharawī, a cleric whom he had met in the mosque at Tyre and who taught courses on behalf of Mūsā al-Sadr. A close friend of Muhammad Bāqir al-Sadr, al-Gharawī sent a letter of recommendation for the attention of the Grand Ayatollah, in order to solicit the latter's protection for the young man as well as a stipend.

Arriving penniless in Najaf, Nasrallah went to the home of the only person he knew there, Sheikh ʿAlī Karīm, one of the family's acquaintances in Nabʿa. He asked him how best to get his letter of recommendation to Bāqir al-Sadr. Karīm thereupon presented him to one of al-Sadr's students, a certain "sayyid ʿAbbās al-Mūsawī". According to an anecdote that regularly surfaces in biographies of Nasrallah, the young novice at first mistook his fellow countryman for an Iraqi, finding him to be "very dark haired and swarthy". Hoping to be introduced to his contact's teacher, Nasrallah then supposedly tried addressing him in classical Arabic.[21] A stony-faced al-Mūsawī apparently let Nasrallah struggle for several minutes before reassuring him with a laugh: "That's all right, don't bother! I'm Lebanese like you, I come from al-Nabī Shīt, a village in the Bekaa." Nasrallah himself describes this first meeting, characterized as harmless teasing, as the starting point for what would eventually become a great friendship between the two men that was enlivened by a great complicity and harmony of viewpoints. Al-Mūsawī then and there took young Nasrallah under his protection and brought him to his ayatollah, who extended a benevolent welcome to the applicant and officially made al-Mūsawī his mentor. After the interview, al-Mūsawī moved his protégé into a room on the *hawza* campus. Nasrallah now began a hard regimen of studies under his compatriot, who taught him the *Muqaddimāt*, the first of the three cycles of Shiite religious teachings. Al-Mūsawī's methods turned out to be inflexibly rigorous: all students had to put in double effort and "cram" for their courses without cease; the official two days off (Thursday and Friday) every week from the *hawza*, as well as the Ramadan and pilgrimage vacations, were used to accelerate the programme of study. As a result, Nasrallah finished his first cycle in 1978, or after two years of study "instead of five".[22]

A vignette oft-repeated in Nasrallah biographies tells how the future leader of Hezbollah succeeded in attracting the attention of Muhammad Bāqir al-Sadr during his sojourn in Najaf, a fact that party supporters like to recall as an early sign of their idol's exceptional character. On a date cited with qualifications in some biographies as 30 November 1977, Hassan Nasrallah, along with many classmates, took the turban;[23] but,

> before approaching Sayyid Muhammad Bāqir al-Sadr, he gave a small speech that sparked the sayyid's admiration. When al-Sadr placed the turban on Nasrallah's head, he said [to him]: "You are a great person. I smell the perfume of leadership on you. If Allah wills it, you will join the companions of the Mahdī."[24]

Return to Lebanon, last years with AMAL

Nasrallah's studies at Najaf were cut short by the developing local political situation. In June 1978 Iraqi security forces once again harassed the *hawza* students, including the foreigners. The Lebanese in particular were accused of being members or sympathizers of al-Daʿwa, of AMAL, or of the pro-Syrian Baath. In the wake of the February 1977 uprising,[25] Muhammad Bāqir al-Sadr was imprisoned, and the non-Iraqi students were harrassed. Arrests by the year of arrival[26] in the country were planned. The targets of the first roundup would be students who had arrived in 1978; those who had arrived in 1977 would be caught up in the second one. Hassan Nasrallah would later stress that he barely escaped the latter, since he had arrived in Iraq "on 15 December 1976".

Back from an errand that had taken him away from Najaf, Nasrallah found out that there had been an Iraqi police crackdown that very day, in which a number of his fellow students who had arrived in 1976 had been arrested. Fortunate to have been off campus at the fateful moment, he took advantage of the fact that his name had not yet been communicated to the border authorities to quietly re-enter Lebanon. His companion ʿAbbās al-Mūsawī was already in Lebanon when the police rounded up the students in Najaf; his compatriots returning from Iraq urged him not to go back. It proved to be sage counsel: less than two years later, Bāqir al-Sadr was hanged by the Iraqi regime.

When Hassan Nasrallah returned to Lebanon in the summer of 1978, the South was in the grip of the Israeli army's Operation Litani, launched in March. Preferring not to settle in al-Bāzūriyyeh, he joined al-Mūsawī in Baalbek. Realizing the impossibility of a return to Najaf in the near term, the latter had just founded the al-Imām al-Muntadhar (the Awaited *Imām*)[27] religious school, where Nasrallah was able to resume his interrupted studies. After completing his first cycle under the direction of al-Mūsawī, once again his teacher and mentor, he completed the second cycle, the *Sutūh*, in 1982.[28]

At Baalbek, Nasrallah also resumed his political activity within AMAL. He was appointed head of administration (*mas'ūl tandhīmī*) for the Bekaa region, and then named chairman of the party's organizational court. Promoted to member of the Politburo and political head for the Bekaa, he remained active in AMAL until the 1982 Israeli invasion. Like many others, he left the party in June in protest against the formation of the Committee of National Salvation and Nabih Berri's participation. Joined by a handful of former AMAL members and elements from the Shiite Islamic movements, he laid the first groundwork for the IRL.

First duties with Hezbollah

Hassan Nasrallah's political career in Hezbollah until his election as secretary-general in 1992 remains poorly documented. In particular, his role in the party's early years is hardly ever mentioned. From his autobiography we learn that he was twenty-two years old when Hezbollah was formed and that he was a member of the Bāsiq Force[29] within the Resistance[30] at the time. A biography put out by the Lebanese Cultural Centre (though without citing any sources) ventures that "when the [proto-] Hezbollah forms in 1982, Nasrallah does not have a seat on the Consultative Council [*al-Shūrā*]".[31] Still, he is bound to have played a significant role in the early structuring of the party due to his involvement in creating several key positions within the organization. The same document also stresses that he was "very active during this era in the recruitment and mobilization of fighters".[32]

For his part, Nasrallah, without citing specific dates, merely states that he was made head of the Baalbek region shortly after the party's formation, and then was put in charge of the entire Bekaa.[33] In 1985 he became personal assistant to Ibrāhīm Amīn al-Sayyid, at the time head of the Beirut area, before being promoted to deputy head of that region. When the party decided to separate political activities from organizational functions, al-Sayyid chose the political path and Nasrallah took over as head of the Beirut area. Most of the texts suggest that Nasrallah next joined the Consultative Council in 1987 when he became chair of the Executive Council.

An early version has it that he spent some time—between 1985 and 1986—at Qom in Iran, with the party's permission, to resume his studies there. He himself states that he intended to stay there "for at least five years".[34] However, he was obliged to return in haste to Lebanon a few months later, in 1986, following the first clashes between AMAL and Hezbollah.[35] While the versions agree on this attempt to resume his religious studies in Iran, Nasrallah himself, in a 1997 interview and in his autobiography, dates his departure for Qom and the return somewhat later, to 1989.[36] Rumours would circulate at the time attributing Nasrallah's departure to dissension within the party leadership, but he himself has rejected this version on several occasions, insisting, on the contrary, that the leadership wanted him to defer the trip, and that it finally acquiesced only when he insisted.[37] During his absence, his responsibilities as head of the Executive Council fell to his deputy, Naʿīm Qāsim. Upon returning, he resumed his activities within the leadership, but without holding any particular office.[38]

In May 1991, Hezbollah held its then-biennial congress to elect the party's principal bodies. According to some authors, Nasrallah, at just thirty-one years of age, stood for the post of secretary-general.[39] But it was his mentor, ʿAbbās al-Mūsawī, who became secretary-general. While some accounts suggest that Nasrallah was only in charge of the party's ideological mobilization, a duty that he performed until his election as secretary-general in 1992, he himself contradicts them by recounting that "when Sayyid ʿAbbās al-Mūsawī was chosen secretary-general, Naʿīm Qāsim was appointed deputy secretary-general; and [thus] I resumed my former function [as head of the Executive]".[40]

On 16 February 1992, when ʿAbbās al-Mūsawī was assassinated by the Israeli army, his student and long-time friend Hassan Nasrallah was immediately designated to complete his term, and so became the third secretary-general in the party's history. The chosen one would hesitate before accepting:

> The Consultative Council held a meeting to choose a successor [to al-Mūsawī]. They chose me. That day, I was very apprehensive, greatly concerned, because I was much younger [than the others] at the time. Until then, I had only had internal management missions and lacked experience in the party's external affairs. But the Council insisted that I take the job. I initially refused, but then, when the [party's] experts stepped in, I ended up accepting.[41]

Hassan Nasrallah would be re-elected head of Hezbollah at every subsequent General Congress, held in 1993, 1995, 1998, 2001, 2004, and 2008–9. Many analysts denounce this as happening on Iran's orders, more specifically that the choice was imposed by Ayatollah Khamenei himself.[42] But the leadership of Hezbollah has always denied this, justifying this repeat election by pointing to the secretary-general's "exceptional" qualities, with special emphasis on his effective leadership of the Military Council.[43]

From party leader to national hero

February 1992: A new leader "who seems impressively young"

Apart from members of Hezbollah and some assiduous followers of its rallies, few people had heard of Hassan Nasrallah before his election to head the party. When ʿAbbās al-Mūsawī was assassinated in February 1992, the Lebanese countryside was trying to cope with an unusually harsh winter. It snowed for weeks on end, the schools, already closed for two weeks, stayed shut for nearly a month because of impassable roads. On the afternoon of 16 February the news came that the secretary-general of Hezbollah had been murdered, incinerated in his car along with his wife and six-year-old son by Israeli rockets. That evening, in Shiite areas everywhere, families and friends braved the weather to meet and discuss the event.[44] All segments of the political spectrum condemned the assassination. Even in circles hostile to the party it was said: "Had he died of natural causes, well, good riddance, but the Israelis killing him, that is unacceptable." Sympathizers openly called for revenge.

Anxious to avoid letting Tel Aviv think it had succeeded in destabilizing the organization, the leadership hastened to choose a successor, and appointed Hassan Nasrallah. The new secretary-general issued a statement, voicing determination to "make the Israelis pay". Beyond this promise, perceived at the time as just what the occasion called for, a more serious concern was raised for the Lebanese when the new Hezbollah leader appeared on their television screens: the new secretary-general looked "damn young".

It is true that at this time Hassan Nasrallah was only thirty-one years, five months and two weeks old. His youth concerned even his supporters a little, and they desperately hoped that he would be up to the tasks ahead of him. There were two competing schools of thought. The first gave him little chance of success. The assumption was that the Hezbollah leadership was in a hurry to elect him to spite the Israelis, but that he would probably soon be replaced, or would front for the leadership. Another school of thought tended—although in lukewarm fashion—to buy into what the party leadership saw in the new secretary-general: he may have been young, but he was experienced, having already held positions of high responsibility within the party. He would therefore "manage without (too many) problem(s)".[45]

These general impressions, shot through with generally low expectations, were quickly replaced by general astonishment when, a few days after al-Mūsawī's assassination, IRL Katyushas fell on Israel.[46] Nasrallah immediately announced that this heralded a new military strategy representing Hezbollah's response "as promised" to his predecessor's assassination. The first impressions were quickly revised, and public places and sympathetic publications reverberated with his praise: "He is young, but ... looks like he is motivated!"

The public takes notice: 1992–1997

This equating of the new secretary-general's "motivation" with that of the IRL attracted increasing notice in party circles between 1992 and 1997, as Nasrallah's public profile grew. The pace as well as the strength and quality of IRL operations steadily improved during his first two terms. It is true that the end of the clashes between AMAL and Hezbollah undoubtedly let the IRL refocus on its fight against the Israeli occupation and thus improve the results of its efforts. With his emphasis on giving absolute priority to battling the occupier, Nasrallah's image benefited from the success of the Resistance. To what extent Hezbollah political strategies, positions, and initiatives since 1992 can be attributed to Nasrallah is, of course, difficult to determine, given the party's collegial decision making. However, it cannot be denied that Hassan Nasrallah has regularly received the credit for the "exploits" chalked up by the party and the IRL in various fields since 1992.

Thus, the retaliatory capability of the Resistance during the 1993 Israeli offensive "pleasantly surprised"[47] the supporters and was considered a token of credibility for both the IRL and its leader. The fact that the Israeli General Staff named its operation "Accountability" was seen as an acknowledgement by the enemy of the opponent's effectiveness in action. An important milestone in the evolution of Nasrallah's image occurred in 1996, and not only in the eyes of his supporters. During the crisis of April that year, the Israeli army's brutality, peaking in the Qānā massacre, resulted in a great outpouring of sympathy for the Resistance throughout the general Lebanese population.[48] Given the context, Nasrallah, logically, could not do wrong. In particular, the way this offensive ended gave an additional boost to the already positive image he enjoyed at the time. The signing of the April Agreement marked the international community's official legitimization of the IRL's actions. Many Lebanese at the time perceived it as a long-overdue recognition of injustice. Under Nasrallah's leadership the organization had moved the semantics of the fight against Israel from terrorism into a battle for freedom. Similarly, the IRL's right to fire Katyushas into Israeli territory, having been carried out in retaliation, was also recognized at this time. It seemed to prove that the strategic choice Nasrallah had made in the wake of the al-Mūsawī assassination was sound, and it earned him the image of a competent military strategist. On another level, the IRL's effectiveness during the offensive was interpreted in Lebanon as directly responsible for the defeat of Shimon Peres in the Israeli elections held shortly after the crisis.[49] Nasrallah was seen as the leader of an organization capable of destabilizing the opponent's political class by having it rejected in its own country. Without question, 1996 was the year that the image of the Islamic Resistance in Lebanon began to form as the only Arab armed force capable of standing up to the Israeli army for the first time since the 1967 defeat, whose ability to do damage had punched through the enemy's armour hard enough to impact its domestic politics.

In tandem with these episodes of military glory, the Nasrallah image was burnished on the domestic scene by a different kind of success. As already mentioned, the Hezbollah leadership had opted at the end of the 1980s to change the way it related both to government institutions and Lebanese society in favour of a policy of cooperation, moderation, and openness. This choice was embodied by the accession of al-Mūsawī as head of the party; with the latter's assassination just a few months after his election, the dividends from this choice eventually accrued to his successor. The cooperative attitude towards the state and the opening to various components of Lebanese society were ultimately also considered to be the third secretary-general's work. From 1992 on, a mental dividing line was gradually drawn between the Tufaylī years and those of Nasrallah.

Between taking over as head of Hezbollah and 1996, Nasrallah therefore gained a reputation as a pugnacious, bold military leader, capable of inflicting severe blows on the enemy. At the same time, on the domestic front, he seemed to be the personification of Hezbollah's pivot to legality and cooperation.

In September 1997, another facet of the man's character was suddenly revealed when Hādī, his eldest son, was killed in action on the Southern front. This event expanded Nasrallah's image: alongside the now-familiar one of the leader appeared that of the man and father—and it impressed. His reaction and attitude, as well as that of the rest of his family, to the event are, without question, the main, or the real, foundations for the living legend of Nasrallah.

September 1997: disappearance of the son, tribute to the father

On 12 September 1997, one week after the Ansāriyyeh operation,[50] IRL fighters prepared to attack an Israeli patrol in the South in the vicinity of Jabal al-Rafīʿ, between the villages of ʿArab Sālīm and Sujud. Among them was eighteen-year-old Hādī Nasrallah, the secretary-general's oldest son, who had recently joined the IRL. They launched their attack, and succeeded in killing several Israelis, but Hādī Nasrallah and two of his comrades were also killed and their bodies carried off by Israeli soldiers.

The Lebanese media of all stripes immediately pounced on the incident. In particular, the manner in which the Nasrallah family grieved for their son and brother in private, but in public displayed a remarkable stoicism, was the subject of countless write-ups.[51] Here is an example of what people read in the press:

> On the morning of 13 September 1997, a Saturday, while Hajjeh Umm Hādī[52] did some shopping, a series of news flashes was broadcast on al-Nūr about the latest developments in the situation at Iqlīm al-Tuffāh [South]. Returning home, she had a strange,

inexplicable feeling and began to pray fervently to God to save them from misfortune. Shortly thereafter, Sayyid [Hassan Nasrallah] himself came home to tell her that the IRL had lost contact with four young fighters during the previous day's attacks, Sayyid Hādī among them. ... She said: "Call, find out about him, he's your son!' He replied: "It's precisely because he is my son that I will not allow myself to call. When the brothers [fighters] have more news, they will call me immediately." ...

The brother [fighter] tasked with bringing the news to the Sayyid [Hassan Nasrallah] did not know how to begin. ... He exchanged a few words with the Sayyid, but confusion overwhelmed his remarks. The Sayyid made it easy for him: "Was Hādī among the brothers who fell as martyrs?" He replied [simply]: "Yes."[53]

The encounter between the Nasrallah couple after the announcement of their son's death became the stuff of legend. Before breaking the news to his wife, Hassan Nasrallah spent some time weeping quietly alone in one of the rooms in their house. He then joined his wife, saying to her: "Congratulations. Your son is a martyr." The mother, thus presented with the fait accompli, was stoic:

Umm Hādī thanked God for His generosity and lifted her hands toward heaven: "Lord, accept this offering (*qirbān*) from our hands. O Hādī, may God find you worthy of Him as you made me worthy of al-Sayyida al-Zahrā'. And do not worry [about me], because what you have just done for me is to bring me close to the Prophet's family."[54]

Also published is a testimonial by Zaynab, Hādī's sister, emphasizing maternal courage:

At dawn on a September day, we learned that four IRL members were in a firefight at Jabal al-Rafīʿ, that contact with them had been lost, and no one knew if they had died or returned victorious. That morning, I woke up as usual and went into the kitchen. There I found my mother sitting and crying hot hears. Astonished, I asked her [the reasons for her state] but she did not answer me. ...

Some time later, there was a knock on the door. My mother opened it and let three women in who had come to comfort her in her distress. I went into the living room to serve them coffee where they sat. ... I heard one of them tell my mother: "If he is wounded, they will take care of him and he will return safe and sound, God willing." I wondered who the wounded person in question was and asked my mother. "It is your brother Hādī," she answered me. I right away felt a strong pain in my stomach, and I kept quiet for hours.

Suddenly, the phone rang. One of the women answered it, and then hung up. ... Another of the women called me into the kitchen. I asked her what had happened. After a brief introduction, she told me "Your brother has fallen as a martyr." I started crying without a sound. She said to me: "Above all, don't say anything to your mother for now and don't let her find out." However, while knowing that hiding anything

> whatsoever from my mother would be difficult, I went back to the living room, pretending to be very busy.
>
> My mother was told in the course of the afternoon. What struck me and everyone else is that she did not cry then, but contented herself with raising her eyes to heaven and saying: "Am I worthy of thee, O Zahrā'?"[55]

Three days after the announcement of Hādī's death, the daily *al-Safir* reported on the condolence ceremony organized by women of the family.[56] The reporter covering it wrote that the secretary-general's wife had received the condolences in the women's *husayniyya* of Haret Hreik, with her daughter Zaynab (twelve years old) and her son's fiancée, Batūl (sixteen years old) by her side. Also present were both of the young man's grandmothers. All of them would react the same way and display the same attitude, refusing condolences and asking for congratulations instead. The mother of the martyr in particular would cheer up the women who came in crying, counselling patience. Throughout the receptions, she remained dry eyed. When asked about her courage, she replied: "It is the gift of patience; I pray that God will never take it away from me."[57]

In an interview granted to the daily *al-Nahār*, his young fiancée described Hādī as a caring and affectionate boy, concerned about the well-being of his betrothed, who was also a childhood friend. She spoke of him as a young man who was "religious, lived modestly like other poor young people, hated swagger and vanity".[58] She said that his last words to her had been "Take care of yourself," and that her mother-in-law had given her this advice: "My dear, I want you to be strong and patient, as I know you can be because you are pious." In the end, she confessed to being proud of her fiancé's martyrdom, but acknowledged that she suffered and cried a great deal. She concluded by adding, "but our way is that of sacrifice, if we want to liberate our land from the occupier".

Of all the tableaux and testimonials reported by the media, the speech by Hassan Nasrallah broadcast live on television twenty-four hours after the death of his son definitely made the strongest impression. Hezbollah's leadership had decided to celebrate the day after the clash, 13 September, as the fourth anniversary of a 1993 demonstration during which security forces had killed several civilians.[59] A ceremony was planned in Haret Hreik, in Beirut's southern suburbs, at which the secretary-general was to speak. Na'īm Qāsim, the deputy secretary-general, contacted Hassan Nasrallah that very day, "around noon", to suggest that he deliver the speech instead: "It was a very heavy loss and the father's affect absolutely has to be impacted[by] it." But Nasrallah rejected the offer with "firmness and determination", both so as to "not show the enemy any sign of weakness" and because he "did not see what would prevent him from speaking himself".[60] Qāsim continued to insist, ending with an assurance he would stand by in case Nasrallah changed his mind. But Nasrallah went ahead, and delivered his own speech. After he paid tribute to the victims of the peaceful demonstration of 13 September 1993, he turned to his son's martyrdom:

On this occasion, I extend to my brothers, my relatives, to the families of the IRL martyrs and to the families of martyrs of the Lebanese army my sincere congratulations for this divine, human, and national award that they earned on the occasion of past battles. I would like to make some improvised remarks—it was not planned as part of the speech [that I had prepared] on 13 September, but the event naturally requires me to talk about it. My martyr son chose this path of his own free will, and I would like to say this both to the [Israeli] enemy and to our friends:

Let no one think that because this young man's father is none other than the secretary-general [of Hezbollah] that he was pressured by his father and thus sent into battle by him. ... This young man has taken this path no differently than any other resistance fighter who fell as a martyr or is still fighting at the front. ... These noble men of integrity have taken this path in all lucidity, voluntarily, by their own choice. If we, I, his mother and my father, have today a distinguished martyr [in our family], it is because we did not object, we did not block his way, we let the young man go where he was destined to go, where he chose to go, there where he thought he should go. This is the first thing I wanted to clarify.

The second relates [to the fact] that the Israelis may think they have won a victory by killing the son of the secretary-general [of Hezbollah]. They have not killed the son of the secretary-general. That is because the son of the secretary-general was not taking a stroll in the middle of Haret Hreik when they killed him. This is not a covert operation or a covert-type strike [that they pulled off]. ... This fighter, like his comrades, was at the front line. It was he who charged at the enemy, not the enemy who charged at him. He went at the enemy on his own legs, weapons in hand and of his own free will. There is the difference, and that is why it is not a victory for the enemy and why it is unthinkable that it would be.

This is a victory for Hezbollah, an honour for Hezbollah. This is a victory for the logic of the resistance in Lebanon. ... Today, this is what we would say to the enemy: we are not a movement or a resistance whose leaders wish to live their private lives [quietly] and fight you through the children of brave, loyal and faithful people. The death of the martyr Hādī is an illustration of the fact that we, the leadership of Hezbollah, do not jealously guard our children for our personal future. We are proud of our children when they march to the front and we are proud of them when they fall as martyrs. In this resides the value of the Islamic resistance of Hezbollah. ... And I say to the families of martyrs whose bodies are still kept by the enemy: here is one more thing that we share.[61]

Willner already had detected it:

There are some circumstances in which the specific situation of the leader in relation to the type of act can magnify the perception of heroism. If the act is one that appears to involve personal sacrifice on the part of the leader or reflects a stance least expected from someone of his background, it gains an added dimension of valor.[62]

Ineluctably, the death of Hādī Nasrallah added a positive element to his father's image, it being so uncommon to see a political leader sacrifice his son on the altar of the cause, and face the loss with such stoicism. Internally, Hādī's martyrdom cemented the credibility of his father's leadership. It is not unreasonable to think that his death played a role in Nasrallah's re-election as head of the party in 1998. This required an amendment to the bylaws lifting the prohibition against a secretary-general running for more than two terms in succession. Qāsim stresses that

> the martyrdom of Sayyid Hādī pinned a new decoration on the secretary-general's chest, symbolizing his pugnacity and steadfastness in the face of challenges and hazards, in total conformity with his commitment to the Hezbollah line.[63]

In this way, Hādī's death had important consequences for the party's mobilization. Qāsim states that

> the martyrdom of Sayyid Hādī would give the party's progress a significant boost. [Hādī] was the son of the secretary-general who had dedicated his entire life to this path. ... This event not only contributed to this progress ... but it also reflected the perfect consistency of the leadership with itself and with its theories in a practical application of the ideas it stands for.[64]

Qāsim nonetheless did not see—or at least did not mention—the profound changes triggered by the event at the level of the bond between the public, Nasrallah, and the party. For with Hādī's martyrdom in September 1997, this connection entered clearly and lastingly into the realm of the affective and emotional. Before 1997 it had been possible to be sympathetic to the leader of an organization whose struggle appeared genuine. In 1997, however, a veritable love affair began, in two phases. With the death of the son, the character of the secretary-general was split in two. From behind the military leader suddenly appeared a man, the father for whose grief it is possible to feel compassion, as well as respect and admiration for his courage. This is the first time that Nasrallah was clearly distinguishable as an individual. This was true even in circles that were hostile to the party, where, for the first time, a real curiosity grew about this man who, until then, on the whole had seemed of little importance.[65] Hassan Nasrallah was no longer perceived as just the leader of Hezbollah, but henceforth as *Hassan Nasrallah*. He became distinct from the organization he heads; it is for him, the man, that a sense of very strong personal attachment developed. People felt sadness for him before they experienced any for the party, and it is the appearance of this human dimension that gave him a connection with his admirers. In the second phase, he was made great as a political leader by stoicism perceived as a sign of integrity. He became a military leader who did not shy away from the supreme sacrifice in waging his war when fate imposed it on him. This shared perception is illustrated by a survey taken in Beirut in late 1997 which showed that only 39 per cent of people of all faiths in the capital considered Nasrallah as a "fundamentalist", while 70 per cent stated that they "support the Resistance he heads", and 73 per cent considered him "charismatic".[66]

June 1998, or September 1997—Act II

Less than a year later the emotion and respect that the death of the Hezbollah secretary-general's son had aroused among the public were revived by an exchange of prisoners and fighters' remains between Israel and the party on 25 and 26 June 1998. From the standpoint of numbers of prisoners released (60) and mortal remains turned over (approximately 40 IRL fighters), this exchange was similar to the preceding one in July 1996 (45 prisoners freed, more than 130 bodies turned over by Israel), but the public paid special attention to the 1998 exchange, because among the bodies was that of Hādī Nasrallah.

In September 1997 speculation was rife, starting on the Israeli side, that the death of the Hezbollah secretary-general's son presaged an accelerated exchange of bodies between the Israeli government and the party. The betting then was on Nasrallah's paternal feelings and predictions that Hezbollah would be more flexible in its conditions in order to speed up the exchange and recover Hādī's body as rapidly as possible.[67] The party, however, did not give Hādī's remains any priority over those already in Israeli hands, and so they were not turned over until June 1998.

A posteriori, this only made the attitude that Nasrallah displayed in 1997, when he refused to have his son treated differently from other martyrs, seem that much more sincere. His bearing on receiving the coffins and the welcome he paid to that of his son once again were impressive. As he had in September 1997, Nasrallah acted with total dignity. Accompanied by his second son, Muhammad-Jawād, and standing together with him in front of each coffin in turn, he read the *Fātiha*[68] for the repose of the soul of the fighter resting in it, and paused in reflection before each body. He and Jawād paused very little longer before the one holding Hādī's remains. For no more than an instant or two, the father's emotion briefly pierced the leader's stoicism. But his courage in containing his undoubtedly strong emotion was noted. Once again, what was perceived as a marker of courage and integrity was widely hailed by the public and press alike.

May 2000: the "charismatic anointing"

Two years later, with the "incredible but true" liberation of South Lebanon, Hassan Nasrallah's image soared even higher. He was not only promoted to national hero; in Lebanon and the Arab—actually, to a certain degree, the Muslim—world, Hezbollah's secretary-general officially entered history to take his place among the greats, and ever since has belonged to the exclusive pantheon of men viewed as charismatic.[69] The adjective had been applied to him since September 1997 by the press and among a large segment of the public, but it is actually only from 2000 that he qualified to be labelled charismatic according to the scientific criteria that Willner enumerated. She argues that four sets of factors must be detectable in a public's representations as sufficient for identifying a leader as charismatic: (i) an "extraordinary or heroic" deed; (ii) "likening of the leader to one of the dominant myths of the culture"; (iii) projection of a series of qualities onto the leader and eyes "of a certain kind"; and (iv) a big talent for rhetoric.

(i) The accomplishment of an "extraordinary or heroic" deed was fully satisfied by the Liberation. Willner advances three factors that serve to make an action remarkable: low probability of success, the attendant riskiness, and its importance for all concerned. Nasrallah, and the organization that acts on his orders, had expelled an occupier from Lebanon that armed action had never before managed to take down, in Lebanon or anywhere else. Before the success of the IRL, Middle Eastern armed groups that had dared to try and drive Tel Aviv's troops out of their country unconditionally had all failed. Further, the Liberation of 2000 was the outcome of a struggle that the international community had only recognized as legitimate in 1996, and that had from the beginning turned out to be extremely dangerous.[70] The risky and unique elements of the "feat" of Liberation are easily detectable here.

(ii) From 2000 on, comparisons between Nasrallah and the great heroes of the Arab cause, and also of the great conflicts in world history, multiplied. Nasrallah was called the "New (Abdel-) Nasser" and, in leftist circles, the "Che Guevara of the Arabs".[71] He thus became explicitly likened to mythical heroes with a cause.

(iii) Hezbollah's followers—and not just they—had detected exceptional qualities and virtues in Nasrallah even before the spring of 2000, but the victory that year multiplied the phenomenon by an order of magnitude, leading to a whole new series of positive projections. The secretary-general's name *Nasrallāh*, or "Victory of God", appeared predestined. Newspaper articles dwelt on his eyes, "shining behind his glasses".[72] Moreover, according to his admirers, the man's charm was not confined to his glance. His voice seemed to leave very few people unmoved; some described it as "reassuring" or "soothing". His entire face supposedly radiated a "Muhammadan light" (*nūr muhammadiy*).[73] It was also usually said that "Nasrallah is handsome", in every way. These good looks were regularly advanced, even if in jest, in response to anyone maintaining that "if Nasrallah bears a very apt family name, the same cannot be said of his first name".[74] The immediate retort by Nasrallah's admirers to this is "in fact, the Sayyid has a very apt first name because he really is *hasan* [handsome]".[75] Supporting this perception, women increasingly and openly confessed a weakness for him.

(iv) Finally, from 2000 on, Nasrallah's talent for oratory, always recognized, has increased. The Sayyid "knows how to talk" (*byaʿrif yehke*): this is certainly one quality that even the critics have granted him more than willingly. The connection between audience and speaker is unmistakeable, easy to detect. People listen to his speeches with the same respect with which the true faithful listen to sermons in a mosque. They also laugh at his pleasantries, loudly and strongly cheer every flight of poetry—his audience does not "tune out". Better yet, they cite and recite key phrases from his speeches, learn passages by heart, and reproduce them on walls, posters, T-shirts, and key chains. Some formulations, having turned into true slogans after 2000, became battle cries during the summer 2006 war.

The Other in forming the image of the charismatic man

Alongside these criteria inventoried by Willner and identifiable in the case of Nasrallah, another category of factors appear to have influenced—and continues to influence—the process of forming his image: the Other. The role of the Other manifests itself in two ways. First of all, it constitutes an element of comparison. The Nasrallah image is not only constructed by the public's view of him, but also by the way that the public perceives the Other. To put it another way, the Other is an element of comparison which, like the theory of colour in painting, makes certain traits stand out in the observed object.[76] Nasrallah's qualities are that much more strongly perceived to the extent they are qualities that the Other lacks. Second, the Other acts as a mirror. This time it is how the public perceives the gaze that the Other turns on Nasrallah. The Other is no longer the element of comparison; its perception is. The process of forming the Nasrallah image revolves around what the Other says about him, what it sees in him.

The Other as element of comparison

The positive image that Nasrallah is able to enjoy is reinforced by a series of comparisons, conscious or unconscious, that his admirers make with his peers on the Lebanese political scene. Years of civil war and Syrian tutelage created and kept in power a leadership class composed mostly of militiamen, people of dubious integrity, and straw men. For most of these politicians, the rise to power primarily represents access to clientilizing resources. It also goes hand in hand with a visible improvement in their personal financial situation, which most put on ostentatious display. Nepotism is widespread. When someone takes over a position of responsibility, it is almost always to the benefit of his close relatives and, in most cases, the father makes sure that his son or nephew succeeds him.

In comparison with this trend, to which only very few of Lebanon's leaders do not conform, Nasrallah appears as a contrast that is all the more appreciated by his admirers. A questionnaire I circulated among 300 supporters in late 2008 showed that the qualities routinely attributed to Nasrallah are: great intelligence; sincerity; integrity and incorruptibility; sobriety; rejection of favouritism; and also courage; love of justice and equity; tolerance; faith and piety; and a sense of humour. In fact, reference is often made to how modestly the man lives, how sparingly he eats, how hard he works, and that he only sleeps a few hours every day. His personal accessories consist of a pair of ordinary spectacles that he appears to have exchanged only once in ten years for an equally ordinary pair. But, above all, it is said that he cannot be bought. He gained this reputation in 1996, when the news circulated that the American government had offered $500 million, juicy economic partnerships, and guarantees for IRL combatants, in exchange for the weapons of the Resistance—an offer that was rejected.[77] This image of the incorruptible Nasrallah, honest and devoted to his cause, was reinforced by the death of Hādī, and again during the last months of the occupation, when the Israeli authorities multiplied their offers for a negotiated withdrawal, which Nasrallah rejected without exception. It was difficult, in any event, to accuse a leader of nepotism who stoically loses his son to the cause. Even before Hādī's death, it was not expected that he would take his father's place. And this applies even more clearly to the second son. There are stories that Nasrallah supposedly even refused to pull strings for a loan application by his father to one of the party's financial institutions. Lastly, in a society rent by confessionalism, directed by a political class adept at bribery of its constituents and prone to speaking on occasion in explicitly sectarian tones, Nasrallah's anti-sectarian creed attracts notice. The rumour that has him wearing an amulet of the Virgin around his neck is not to be taken lightly. And many Armenians say with pride that during the years of his youth spent in the vicinity of Burj Hammud, Nasrallah learned a few words of their language that he is pleased to use whenever he receives representatives of that community.

In other words, Nasrallah's courage and heroism would appear less striking had persons of similar stature existed among the Lebanese political class. People would not sing paeans to his modest lifestyle, his forgoing of materialism and luxury, his discourse on tolerance, his incorruptibility, and other virtues traditionally ascribed to him were he not seen as unique in possessing these qualities.

The Other as element of confirmation

Recognition by the critics

Lastly, the Shiite community's pride in having someone of Nasrallah's calibre head up their community is nourished by the respect that the party's opponents, even the most virulent ones, have grudgingly accorded him. As one example among many, an article commented on the death of the secretary-general's son by saying:

> On that day, a pundit who routinely attacked Nasrallah and Hezbollah wrote in a commentary: "Whatever our disagreements are with you, we can only bow before you, so uncommon is it in our times that the leader of a political party will allow his son to go and fight against Israel alongside the other fighters."[78]

Naturally, the praises or even tributes that his adversaries pay to Nasrallah are perceived by his admirers as further evidence of their idol's exceptional character. Seen as proof of how well-founded their admiration for him is, this image of him, even held by his critics, encourages them. Thus shared (even if less intensely), this recognition makes the Nasrallah image, in their eyes, move from subjective perception to the certainty of proven reality.

Worshipped by some ... hated by others: the Israeli factor

This effect of independent confirmation of Nasrallah's image by his critics is multiplied by an order of magnitude when it is of Israeli origin. Willner had noticed that charismatic men are unique in never being regarded with indifference or neutrally. Those who do not share the enthusiasm of the public for a charismatic person often nurture a strong animosity, if not tenacious hatred, towards them.[79]

Venerated by the Resistance and its supporters and respected by many outside the party's orbit, Nasrallah quickly became enemy number one in Israel, and also in the United States, particularly during the presidency of George W. Bush. The Israeli leadership has compared him to Hitler more than once, and the Mossad has tried for more than twenty-five years to assassinate him. In October 1992, only months after al-Mūsawī's assassination, a commando operation led by Ehud Barak was mounted to assassinate Nasrallah and his family in their Bīr al-'Abed home, guided by Muhammad Hammūdī, a local informer recruited by the Israeli services.[80] After the operation failed, having been uncovered by the Hezbollah security apparatus some hours before it was to be executed, the Mossad tried again to kill Nasrallah—in vain—by placing an explosive charge in a bunch of flowers in front of the podium where the secretary-general was to speak at a ceremony organized by the party. In May 2004 the Lebanese security services put behind bars the members of a network run by Jamāl Zaʿrūra, a Palestinian woman recruited and trained in Tunisia by Israel. Her mission was to assassinate Palestinian cadres in Lebanon and Hezbollah leaders—including Nasrallah. In April 2006 the Lebanese army's intelligence branch dismantled a cell operated by a Sunni, Ghassān Slaybī, who for a long time kept the headquarters of Hezbollah's General Secretariat in the Beirut suburbs under surveillance with the intention of assassinating Nasrallah, or at least Naʿīm Qāsim. During the summer of 2006 the Israeli Air Force dropped more than 20 tons of bombs on the apartment building that was supposedly the secretary-general's home in the capital's southern suburb. They destroyed the entire quarter without, however, succeeding in killing Hassan Nasrallah.

This Israeli campaign to liquidate Nasrallah had the psychological effect of strengthening the bonds of the IRL's partisans with him in two ways. From a reactive and emotional standpoint, the more his life is threatened—especially by a despised enemy—the more they hold him in affection. On the rational level, in the Arab anti-

Zionist mentality, Tel Aviv only wages war against freedom fighters. In the logic of "the enemy of my enemy is my friend", individuals pursued by the various Israeli governments automatically garner sympathy. The Israeli leadership's grudge being seen as proportional to the damage that the person targeted with such hostility is able to inflict, a Nasrallah demonized by Israel can only gain more respect from the critics of Tel Aviv's policies. Interestingly, Hezbollah mines the Israeli antipathy to the secretary-general for his personal glory, systematically skewering its expressions on the party's internet site for promotional ends like so many badges of honour.

Charismatic leadership and mobilization

Nasrallah's image is a major asset for mobilizing Hezbollah. Even before 1997 it was apparent that he had succeeded in reassuring large swaths of Lebanese society previously distrustful of the party. His speeches on the impossibility of establishing an Islamic state in Lebanon, tirelessly repeated, had a positive effect on many people opposed to the idea of Islamic rule in the country, making Hezbollah seem less disagreeable and less threatening. As the leader of an organization that he seemed to control well, Nasrallah was seen as a bulwark against Hezbollah reverting to intolerant practices, or any future abuses. In 1997, the death of Hādī contributed to this gradual betterment of the party's image as a consequence of a growing regard for Nasrallah. This moment of compassion gave both Nasrallah and his organization a different status. Before his son's demise, the exploits of the party, and especially of the IRL, had redounded to the benefit of Nasrallah's image, and praise for the IRL's exploits spilled over on its leader. After the death of his son, his virtues as a father benefited the organization he presided over. It may be stretching the point a bit, but we can say that, prior to 1997, Nasrallah was the leader of Hezbollah, but that after 1997 Hezbollah was sometimes called "Nasrallah's organization." This subconscious inversion of the relationship favoured the party's mobilization, as Nasrallah's virtues ended up being projected on all who belonged to Hezbollah and the IRL. This rediscovery of Hezbollah through the revelation of its chief explains why fighting under the orders and leadership of such a man seen as such a hero has had growing appeal. It was considered respectable to be a fighter in the Resistance ranks before 1997, but it became heroic to do it under Nasrallah's orders. A non-trivial act illustrates this enthusiasm for the Resistance precipitated by Hādī's death: at the condolence ceremony, Nasrallah received a large number of people from all parts of the country, including a group of youth from various confessional backgrounds, who formally told him of their wish to fight alongside the IRL. For all their ideological differences, especially on the religious plane, they nevertheless insisted on wanting to fight under IRL command.[81]

Liberation in 2000 finally facilitated the emergence as a grand strategic thinker of someone that some people at first viewed, more or less openly, either as a besotted dreamer or a madman in pursuit of an objective deemed to be unrealistic. In the face of all those who had called for abandoning the military option in the early 1990s in favour of diplomatic negotiations with Israel, Nasrallah was seen as the "only one who understood", and this "from the beginning", that negotiation with Tel Aviv would come to nothing, and that only armed struggle could achieve results. The IRL thus became the first to benefit from the renewal of the resistant spirit preached by Nasrallah. Its cause appeared to be more just, its members found themselves admired as members of a heroic caste that many young men fantasized about joining.

Despite the significant impetus given to Hezbollah's mobilization by the rise of Nasrallah's image, in the early 2000s its charismatic potential for maintaining the party's popularity had not yet been fully realized. As will soon be detailed in Part II, between 2000 and 2006 Nasrallah played a leading role in consolidating the gains made by the IRL. But in 2006, when the IRL once again met the Israeli army in combat, the image of Nasrallah assumed such powerful dimensions that it made him a guarantor—if not the principal one—of the strength of his organization's mobilization.

PART II

MOBILIZATION AND POWER OR HOW TO SURVIVE IN A PERILOUS ENVIRONMENT (2000–2015)

7

"NEW MIDDLE EAST", "CEDAR REVOLUTION"

IMPERILLED GAINS (2000–2006)

What next for a Resistance that has liberated its national territory?

The Israeli withdrawal completed, a number of voices in Lebanon and the international community rose to demand the deployment of the Lebanese army in the formerly occupied South, both to ensure the safety of those living in a region that had not seen any national defence forces since the late 1960s and to guarantee peace on the border. Hezbollah and the Lebanese government opposed the idea, intent on keeping the army out of an area that the IRL leadership thought it still needed. Indeed, according to them, the Resistance had not completed its work. First, was still a final strip of border territory to liberate around the Shebaa Farms, the Kfarshuba heights, and the village of Ghajar. Hezbollah, along with the Lebanese and Syrian governments, consider them part of Lebanon, but Israel regards them as Syrian, and thus not covered under Resolution 425 but rather under 242, *ergo* not needing to be evacuated.[1] For Hezbollah, the struggle for the liberation of the last southern territories held under occupation thus did not end with the Israeli withdrawal. The IRL was also less inclined to lay down arms as long as it was committed to a second mission: obtaining the release of the last Lebanese still held in Israeli prisons. These included ʿAbdel-Karīm ʿUbayd, a cleric affiliated with the party and taken from his home in Jibshīt (Nabatiyeh) by Israeli commandos in July 1989, and Mustafā al-Dīrānī, AMAL's former head of security and defector to Hezbollah, who also was kidnapped by an Israeli commando team from his home in Qsar Nabā (Baalbek) in May 1994.[2]

The IRL therefore carried out several attacks against Israeli military positions around the Shebaa Farms and the Kfarshuba hills between autumn 2000 and summer 2006. The Israeli army regularly responded or took the initiative, mostly in localized fashion confined to the same area. It also made a point of overflying Lebanese territory constantly, daily in South Lebanon. In April 2001 the Israeli army announced "new rules of engagement": it would no longer target just the Lebanese, but also

Syrian positions when carrying out reprisals. However, the two sides managed to avoid escalation, and none of the clashes degenerated into open warfare.

Coinciding with these sporadic, limited attacks, during October 2000 the IRL conducted two snatch operations with the intent of orchestrating a prisoner exchange with Tel Aviv. In the first, just four-and-a-half months after Liberation, on 7 October, a group of Resistance fighters set up an ambush on an Israeli patrol in the vicinity of Shebaa; simultaneously, another group launched an assault against an Israeli position in the same area.[3] In retaliation, the Israeli army bombed the villages of Kfar Hama and Habariyeh and the road connecting Shebaa to Kfarshuba, while also firing on first responders and members of the Indian UNIFIL contingent as they evacuated the wounded.[4]

A mere one week later, on 15 October, Hezbollah organized a conference in Beirut in support of the Palestinian cause under the second Intifada. While Nasrallah was speaking, a party cadre approached to whisper in his ear. The secretary-general, suddenly beaming, announced to the audience that the party's security unit had apprehended a colonel in the Israeli intelligence. Tel Aviv first denied, then later confirmed the arrest, but claimed that he was merely a businessman working for a consulting firm linked to Israeli electronic and armament companies, a fifty-four-year-old air force reserve officer who had allegedly disappeared in Switzerland ten days earlier.[5] The incident caused concern in the Lebanese government, which feared that if the kidnapping had indeed taken place in Switzerland, that is, if Hezbollah had acted in a third country, it meant a violation of Swiss sovereignty. The next day Nasrallah clarified that it was not an abduction, but the capture of an Israeli agent on Lebanese territory. His real name was Elhanan Tennenbaum, "he lives in Tel Aviv" and "belonged to an artillery unit that shelled Beirut in 1982".[6] Having travelled to Belgium on an Israeli passport, and then to Lebanon on an admittedly fake foreign passport, he fell into a trap set by Hezbollah security after making contact with a party cadre he was trying to recruit. The contact told Tennenbaum that he wanted to meet him face to face without any intermediaries, not abroad but in Beirut, before he could put him in touch with a senior member of the party.[7]

Two months later Israel put out feelers to Hezbollah, with Germany acting as go-between. On 25 August 2003 the bodies of two Resistance fighters were repatriated; in exchange, the Israeli government received information on Tennenbaum. The main exchange did not take place until 29 January 2004.[8] The event received widespread media attention in Lebanon; but even without the communication campaign orchestrated around it by the national media and the party, it was an impressive exchange. It was indeed unprecedented: Hezbollah secured the release of nearly 450 detainees—23 Lebanese, 400 Palestinians, 5 Syrians, 3 Moroccans, 1 Libyan and 1 German; the remains of 59 fighters were repatriated, information on 24 missing Lebanese and maps of minefields laid by the Israeli army in South Lebanon were provided in return for Tennenbaum, the remains of the 3 soldiers kidnapped in October 2000, and information on the pilot, Ron Arad.[9] On the day, the event went national: the entire political class, from the president of the Republic and prime minister down to government officials and a host of MPs and law-enforcement representatives were on the tarmac of Beirut airport to welcome the former prisoners, with large celebrations staged afterwards.

The party took advantage of the occasion to present itself as a lenient jailer.[10] On the eve of the great day al-Manār broadcast an interview with Tennenbaum that Israeli television hurried to rebroadcast with the title "al-Manār Exclusive",[11] during which he could be seen getting dressed, putting on aftershave, and getting ready to leave. He acknowledged having been "well treated" and freely admitted having discovered "a human side of Hezbollah that he had not suspected", saying that his guards had supplied all the medicines he needed, for he was a seriously ill man.

Three Lebanese remained incarcerated: Samir Quntar, a former member of the Popular Front for the Liberation of Palestine (PFLP),[12] sentenced to a 542-year prison term for killing an Israeli civilian, his little girl, and a police officer in 1979; Nasīm Nisr, a native of al-Bāzūriyyeh (Tyre), accused of spying for Hezbollah;[13] and Yahyā Skāff, from Akkar (North Lebanon), imprisoned for his part in a March 1978 commando raid.[14] In his speech welcoming the former prisoners, Nasrallah made a commitment to secure the others' release in the near future. Referring to the Israeli soldiers kidnapped in 2000, he said:

> Our fighters were a bit aggressive and brought the soldiers back dead. But next time, I promise you, we will capture the [Israeli] soldiers alive. Israel made a mistake in not releasing Samir Quntar that it will regret, for we now make it our priority.[15]

And so, the tone was set: the IRL reserved the right to carry out further kidnappings of Israeli soldiers. The "Truthful Pledge" would be redeemed on 12 July 2006.[16]

An evolving domestic scene

The conservative Christian comeback

After the end of the 1975–90 civil war Lebanon came under Syrian tutelage, and the Taef Agreement chipped away at some of the political privileges of the Christians. The prerogatives of the president, a Maronite, were reduced in favour of the prime minister, a Sunni. The ratio of seats in Parliament was no longer 6:5 (Christians:Muslims), but became 50–50. For conservative Christians, the war's major protagonists, the *pax Syriana* years were years of depression, of "dejection" (*ihbāt*). The first half of the decade was particularly difficult: the principal leaders of the Maronite community had been either disgraced or murdered. Faced with determined attempts by the Lebanese Forces to take control of the Kataeb party, even by force of arms,[17] Amin Gemayel, a former president (1982–8) and supreme commander of the Kataeb, went into voluntary exile in France at the end of his term in office. Michel Aoun, former chief of staff of the Lebanese army, followed him two years later: after the failure of his 'War of Liberation' (1989), Syrian bayonets chased him from the presidential palace in Baabda, where he had taken refuge, and he was rescued *in extremis* by the French authorities, who organized his evacuation (1991).[18] On 21 October 1990 Dany Chamoun, leader of the National Liberal Party, his wife Ingrid and their two little boys, seven-year-old Tarek and five-year-old Julian, were assassinated in their home.[19] The remaining conservative Christian forces went through a period of alienation. The Maronite patriarchate, which, however, had supported Aoun's War of Liberation, accepted the Taef Agreement as soon as it was signed. The Kataeb took their chances with Damascus, with the leadership of Georges Saadeh (1989–98), Mounir al-Hajj (1999–2000) and especially Karim Pakradouni (from 2001 on). The result was a split between Pakradouni's supporters and those of Gemayel. The latter founded the Kataeb Reform Movement, its direction falling to his son Pierre, elected MP for the Metn region in 2000, but while the Syrian domination continued, this cell of supporters united around the family leadership kept a low profile. The leaders of the Lebanese Forces did likewise. Elie Hobeika, the former head of intelligence, had joined the political game in 1985 on the side of the Syrian regime. In April 1994 Samir Geagea, leader of the Lebanese Forces, was arrested after being accused of instigating a bombing in a church in Zouk Mosbeh in Jounieh in February that year in which nine people were killed and fifty-five injured. After five sensational trials, Geagea went to prison for war crimes, with three life sentences, for the murder of Dany Chamoun and his family; the murder of Elias Zayeck, a Lebanese Forces cadre killed in 1990; and an assassination attempt against Michel Murr, the deputy prime minister, in 1991. In 1999 Geagea was sentenced to another life term for the murder of former prime minister Rashid Karameh, assassinated in 1987. In March 1994, a month after the attack in Zouk Mosbeh, the Lebanese Forces was declared illegal and dissolved by the Council of Ministers.

Christian protest action therefore essentially remained the prerogative of the Aounists. Their actions, initially involving sit-ins and relatively small demonstrations, precipitated the first, occasionally violent, clashes with the security forces, and arrests beginning in 1998. It was not until June 2000 that the Christian conservative opposition actually resurfaced, when the Maronite Patriarch Monsignor Nasrallah Sfeir, who had previously acquiesced in the Syrian presence, had a change of heart and sided with the Aounist current and those in its wake who, with increasing intensity, demanded that Syria redeploy its troops. At the same time, he supported a Conservative Christian re-entry into the country's political life, lobbied for an end to the election boycott[20] and for adoption of an election law that was "more equitable"—that is, one that better represented Christians close to the Kataeb Reform Movement and the Lebanese Forces. The opposition felt even more motivated by the return of President Amin Gemayel at the end of July, from his French exile. At the start of September they called for the release of Samir Geagea and the return of

Michel Aoun. The movement took off: Patriarch Sfeir, the Assembly of Maronite Bishops, the Free Patriotic Movement (FPM, Aounist), the National Liberal Party (NLP), and the Lebanese Forces (LF) spoke with one voice. They were joined by Walid Jumblatt, head of the Progressive Socialist Party (PSP) and principal non-Maronite neighbour of the anti-Syrian Christians of Mount Lebanon. At the beginning of August 2000 a grand Druze–Maronite "reconciliation" organized in the Mountain made official the new linkage between the two formerly hostile camps. The visibility of the anti-Damascus camp reached its apogee in late April 2001, with the meeting of Kornet Shehwan, a small Christian village in Metn. It brought together several prominent Christians who, for the first time in years, adopted a common position, proposing an action plan for reviving a Christian political class and envisioned taking over Sfeir's campaign for the "recovery of Lebanon's sovereignty", that is, a complete Syrian withdrawal.[21]

As for the other two great Lebanese communitarian elements, they kept their distance from the protests. The Sunnis, most grouped around Rafic Hariri, had no real complaints about a tutelage that guaranteed their political precedence. As for the Shiites, they focused even less on the Syrian presence in Lebanon as they became increasingly preoccupied with embarking on a different national story that was then taking shape around the accomplishments of the IRL.

Hezbollah and Rafic Hariri: bittersweet relations

Although they were both aligned with Syria, the Future Current (FC) of Prime Minister Rafic Hariri and Hezbollah had never enjoyed completely friction-free dealings. The first designation of Rafic Hariri as prime minister in 1992 came at the expense of the party's candidate, Ibrāhīm Bayyān. The neo-liberal Haririan policy, moreover, imposed burdens on vulnerable social groups, among which the Shiites figured prominently. One other, more important, bone of contention was the prime

Figure 5

Growth of the Lebanese gross national debt (1993–2010)

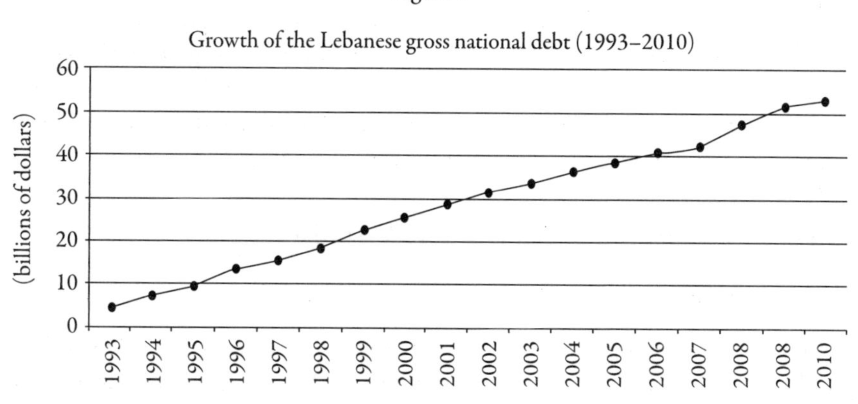

minister's policy of financing the government with exponentially growing debt. Total government indebtedness, which had already registered a marked increase from 1992, grew yet more onerous as another $15 billion was added between 2000 and 2005.

Hariri, in fact, was betting on the Middle East peace process to have (part of) Lebanon's debt forgiven as quid pro quo for a reconciliation with its southern neighbour. Hezbollah, however, was dead set against any normalization with Israel. The party leadership was also concerned with preventing the international campaign against the Resistance from making its neutralization the price demanded for discharging Lebanon's debts. This fear grew over time, stoked by the continual pressure on the Lebanese government by the international community to disarm the IRL, especially after the attacks of 11 September 2001 and the pivoting of American policy in the Middle East. Under another rubric, the relationship between Hezbollah and the Hariri government, already tainted by blood in the past, notably in September 1993, when nine unarmed people taking part in a party-organized protest march against the Oslo Accords had been killed by the army, succumbed to renewed tensions in the spring of 2004 with the repeat of a similar scenario. On 27 May a demonstration by the Lebanese trade union federation, the Confédération Générale du Travail—Liban (CGTL), in the southern suburbs of the capital turned into a riot following clashes between protesters and security forces. The Ministry of Labour was looted and burned; seven people were reported killed and fifty wounded.[22] The Resistance initiatives in the South were a final point of contention, providing another reason for the government and Hezbollah to engage in polemics. Anxious to consolidate the gains of reconstruction and attract FDI, Hariri wanted the front in the South to remain as peaceful as possible, and several times, for example in January, February, and April 2001, he escalated his criticism of certain IRL initiatives.

Nevertheless, these disagreements and frictions never led to a rupture. Despite the warning shots, the president of the cabinet refrained from threatening the interests of the IRL—a *sine qua non* for maintaining good relations with Hezbollah. In tune with the recommendations coming out of Damascus, he made no move to deploy the army to the South. Better yet, when the United States launched an international campaign against the IRL, starting in the autumn of 2001, he showed solidarity with the Resistance and blocked any initiative aimed against it. For its part, Hezbollah did nothing to destabilize the political set-up. In the aftermath of the 2004 demonstration, its leadership, as in 1993, immediately called for calm and forbade any reprisals.[23] Despite differences, the Hezbollah–Hariri pairing remained intact.

"September 11", "The New Middle East", and "the Cedar Revolution"

"A-list terrorism"

Arguing that "Hezbollah's violent acts threaten American interests", the United States put the party on its list of terrorist organizations in October 1997. From then on, its policy initiatives aimed against the party multiplied, especially in the form of serial pressures on the Lebanese government. For example, throughout 2001 and 2002, Washington attempted to set preconditions for the convention of the French sponsored Paris II international conference on the economic development of Lebanon. Washington wanted the Lebanese government to agree to deploy their army to the liberated South and place restrictions on the Resistance as a prerequisite for the assembly. The French, however, overlooked the American demands, and the conference was convened under French leadership.

The attacks of 11 September 2001 and the American neo-conservative administration opting for a muscular policy in the hope of fostering the emergence of a democratic "New Middle East" free of the Islamist jihadi dimension, quickly made it clear to Hezbollah that it would soon have more concerns than usual. As the news of the attacks broke, the Lebanese authorities were quick to condemn al-Qāʿida's initiative and to express their support to the American authorities and people. On 16 September, Hezbollah's leadership also deplored the deaths of innocent people, but cautioned against succumbing to the "panic that the United States wants to create worldwide to free its hands ... by invoking an anti-terrorist struggle".[24] Besides being concerned that the situation "would obscure the Israeli aggression against the Palestinian people who pay a high price for aspiring to have a state of their own", Hezbollah also stated that "the question is whether the true American policy is to punish those responsible for the attacks or to take advantage of the situation to increase its grip on the world". There was palpable fear in pro-Resistance circles that the American government would wage an organized war against Hezbollah, using the attacks as a pretext.

These fears turned out to be justified: the new American policy in the Middle East did indeed target the party. The American ambassador to Lebanon, Vincent Battle, began in mid-September with the accusation that "Lebanon *shelters* terrorist organizations", but stopped short of saying that the country was among those that "*support* terrorism".[25] Nonetheless, he strongly urged Beirut to sign up for Washington's anti-terrorist coalition.[26] The Lebanese government showed its reluctance, as the American terms affected its policy of support for the Resistance. The United States insisted, and on 10 October declared open season on Hezbollah when the FBI published the names of its twenty-two most wanted terrorists on its website. Listed among them were three suspected of being Hezbollah members: Imad Mughniyeh, Ali Atweh, and Hassan Ezzedine, accused of hijacking a TWA aircraft in 1985.[27] During the third week of October the American authorities went further, demanding that the Lebanese government ratify all UN agreements bearing on the war against terrorism. But when Washington published a new list of terrorist organizations in November, with the Islamic Jihād, Hamas, PFLP General Command, and Hezbollah on it, Lebanon officially declared itself "unconcerned", refusing to classify Hezbollah as a terrorist group. Supported by the parliamentary committees, Hariri himself announced that he opposed freezing the party's assets.[28] The American presidency declared this support of Hezbollah "unacceptable", announcing that "[the Lebanese government] cannot on the one hand condemn al-Qāʿida and on the other hand embrace Hezbollah or Hamas".[29] The pressure on Beirut intensified in mid-December: the national security adviser, Condoleezza Rice, called on Lebanon to "stop the terrorist activities of Hezbollah". At the same time, the assistant secretary of state for Near Eastern affairs, William Burns, stated that the American struggle against international terrorism "applies in a specific manner to the case of Hezbollah".[30] In early January 2002 the situation became more complex when the Israelis intercepted the *Karine A*, a vessel carrying a full cargo of weapons through the Red Sea. In Tel Aviv's view, one that was shared by Washington, the ship had been chartered by Hezbollah and Tehran and was bound for Palestinian armed groups in Gaza and the West Bank. Beirut and the party leadership issued firm denials.[31] A few days later an American delegation visiting Lebanon insisted that the government "turn over members of Hezbollah who have carried out terrorist actions against the United States".[32] The American UN ambassador, John Negroponte, described the party as a "terrorist organization with an international dimension",[33] and, in August, Senator Bob Graham, referring to Hezbollah, told the NBC network that Washington "must deal with training camps that have sprung up in Lebanon and Syria ... where the next generation of terrorists"[34] was being trained. This American obsession with the party reached a climax the following month, when Assistant Secretary of State Richard Armitage went so far as to call it more dangerous than al-Qāʿida itself: "Hezbollah maybe the "A team" of terrorists, maybe al-Qāʿida is actually the "B team". ... They're on the list, their time will come, there is no question about it... We're going to take them down one at a time."[35]

A few days later, Ambassador Battle made it crystal clear: "Hezbollah is central to our campaign against terrorism,"[36] and as a sanction for the Beirut government's perceived lack of cooperation, Congress suspended an aid package of $10 million earmarked for Lebanon.[37]

The American focus on Hezbollah from the outset appeared suspect to both the party leadership and the Lebanese government. Not only did Hezbollah not threaten American interests in the Middle East or in the United States, but the American government did not seem interested in the idea of hunting down al-Qāʿida in Lebanon. In July, following a meeting with the speaker of the parliament, Nabih Berri, Ambassador Battle even stated that "the American administration is satisfied with the substantial assistance provided by the Lebanese government in the fight against the al-Qāʿida network"—before once again reverting more emphatically to the Hezbollah theme.[38] In Lebanon, this war against the party thus appeared to be waged on behalf of Tel Aviv, especially after the *Karine A*. affair.[39] There was no doubt that in June 2002 the Israeli government was running a full-press diplomatic and media campaign against Beirut, accusing it of harbouring al-Qāʿida networks and suggesting that the country might be targeted for strikes.[40] Asserting that "the greatest terrorist threat comes from [Lebanon] and Hezbollah",[41] it argued that the latter was preparing a large-scale operation against Israel. This caused the Lebanese government to implement a diplomatic strategy aimed at countering these allegations.[42] At year's end, rumours were flying about joint military planning by the United States and Israel to hit "terrorist targets", some of them in Lebanon. In November 2003 the al-Manār affair began in France when Prime Minister Jean-Pierre Raffarin called the channel "anti-Semitic", and in December 2004 banned its broadcasts in France, followed by similar bans in the United States, the Netherlands, and Spain.[43] Various accounts of what was behind this affair circulated in Lebanon at the time, blaming it on the "Zionist lobby", "especially one in the French parliament" that "followed [Ariel] Sharon's orders."[44]

The situation was all the more strained because the preparations for the American war against Iraq were well under way. The Lebanese government feared both repercussions from the invasion and an eventual attack against Lebanon. In the end, it was an international resolution that hit Beirut—and Damascus.

Adoption of Resolution 1559 and the Hariri assassination

Along with its involvement in Iraq, starting in March 2003, the United States escalated its pressure on Syrian–Lebanese relations. The idea of collaborating with France gained traction in Washington. In June 2003 Jacques Chirac demanded a road map for Lebanon and Syria, and, four months later, in October, the American House of Representatives passed the Syria Accountability and Lebanese Sovereignty Restoration Act (SALSA), which authorized the imposition of sanctions against the Syrian regime should it continue to "support international terrorism and [to be] suspected of manufacturing weapons of mass destruction".[45] In May 2004 the threat was acted on. France and the United States stepped up their collaboration significantly during August that year. The former sought a Syrian withdrawal from Lebanon and the latter wanted to put the IRL out of action. After the marked discord concerning the Iraq problem, a joint response was finally possible in the Lebanese case, as the Syrians began to try and extend the term in office of the Lebanese president, Émile Lahoud, before it expired in the autumn. On 27 August Paris, Washington, London, and Berlin reacted to the interventions announced by Bashar al-Assad concerning this issue, declaring their opposition to Syrian interference in Lebanese affairs. Damascus and Beirut turned a deaf ear: the next day, in less than ten minutes, a three-year extension of Lahoud's term was approved by the Lebanese Council of Ministers. In response, the UNSC adopted Resolution 1559 on 2 September. It called for (i) the withdrawal of all foreign forces from Lebanon; (ii) a presidential election devoid of any interference; and (iii) disarming of all militias, Lebanese or not, present on Lebanese territory[46]—in other words, the IRL and the Palestinian groups. 24 hours later, the Resolution ignored, Lahoud's term was extended by the Lebanese parliament. Three Jumblattist ministers, Ghazi Aridi, Marwan Hamadeh, and Abdallah Farhat, as well as another minister, Farès Boueiz, all opposing the extension, resigned from the cabinet. Hariri for his part refused to take up his old post. The new ministerial team at the time was chaired by Omar Karameh, a pro-Syrian whom Hariri had succeeded in 1992. Neither the just-extended president nor the new head of the government were inclined to satisfy the international community with respect to either the Syrian withdrawal or the disarming of the IRL. By way of a response, they conditioned both actions on the conclusion of a regional peace agreement. Late 2004 and early 2005 thus turned into a stand-off between a Beirut backed by the Syrian regime and the international community.

One month after the passage of Resolution 1559, Marwan Hamadeh escaped an attack targeting him in the vicinity of the American University of Beirut, in the western Ras-Beirut neighbourhood. The Lebanese opposition assumed that it was a message from Damascus, which might equally have been addressed to the international community, Mr Hamadeh having a French mother. At first the opposition avoided arousing Syrian fury by not reacting too vehemently, and focused its efforts instead on looking ahead to winning the parliamentary elections in May and June 2005. Discussions revolving around a possible Syrian withdrawal then seemed to suggest that it would be negotiated between Damascus and the government that would emerge from the elections. The train of events suddenly accelerated on Monday, 14 February 2005, when, at 12.50, a huge explosion shook the upscale "Hotels" district in the heart of sea-front Beirut. The remarkably powerful explosion set off in front of the Saint-George Hotel damaged neighbouring buildings and shredded vehicles parked in the street for several hundred metres.[47] The Lebanese had barely received the news when they had an even greater shock: its target was none other than Rafic Hariri. Seriously injured, he died in the ambulance rushing him to the American University Hospital.

As the news of the assassination spread, masses of people took to the streets immediately to voice their pain—and anger. The demonstrators were unanimous in assigning blame to the Syrian regime for carrying out the assassination, or at least ordering it. The anti-Syrian slogans burst out loud and clear. That evening, the Baath Party headquarters in Beirut was attacked, and a portrait of President Bashar al-Assad torched.[48] Two days later the dead prime minister's funeral brought more than a million people to Martyrs' Square[49] in downtown Beirut. In the weeks that followed, tens of thousands of Lebanese—several hundred thousand on some days—regularly returned to the square to set up camps that they vowed not to abandon unless the government resigned. Their assemblies were dynamic and creative, with concerts, candlelight vigils, and torch parades. The protesters used their bodies in collective exercises in creating living graphics, forming great words such as "independence" or "truth", the Lebanese flag, or even the face of Hariri on a large scale. Across the country, events linked up and multiplied; statues of Hafez al-Assad and his sons Bassel and Bashar were toppled, public parks named after them were renamed, and some Syrian workers randomly attacked. In the political arena, the opposition declared war on both the Lebanese government and the Syrian regime. It called for a boycott of the state funeral planned by the government, calling on it to resign and calling for the resignations of the intelligence service heads and for an international investigation. The Hariri family went over to the opposition, joining the protests hitherto carried out by the Druze and Maronite communities. "The Intifada for independence", also called the "Cedar Revolution", began. The opposition's response to Nabih Berri when he called for dialogue was "First the truth, then the dialogue", and they called for the formation of a non-partisan government to organize the parliamentary elections. The international community took advantage of the situation to step up its pressure on the Syrian regime. Several leading American figures also called for an international inquiry. The Syrian ambassador to the United States was declared *persona non grata*, Condoleezza Rice no longer ruled out the use of force, and the American Joint Chiefs of Staff even contemplated taking action against Syria. A week after the assassination, the United States, France, and the European Union demanded the immediate implementation of Resolution 1559, and the European parliament rejected any association with the Syrian regime until it withdrew from Lebanon. Saudi Arabia, Jordan, and Egypt also threw their support behind a withdrawal from Lebanon. Under this cumulative international pressure, Damascus caved. On 26 April the last Syrian military transport crossed the border.

Meanwhile, there were several new developments on the Lebanese political scene. Under pressure from the street, the Karameh government fell on 28 February amid jubilation by the demonstrators. Though he was reappointed to form a government, he was unable to do so. Najib Mikati, an MP from Tripoli and former minister of public works and transport, who was a moderate despite a personal friendship with Bashar al-Assad,[50] was named prime minister in mid-April. Hezbollah, after having condemned the assassination from the moment it was announced, took up an unequivocal position on the political chessboard only two weeks after the attack, when it called a larger gathering for 8 March "in support of Syria" and "against foreign interference and Resolution 1559".[51] Hundreds of thousands of supporters and sympathizers[52] gathered in Riyad Solh Square in Beirut, a few hundred metres from Martyrs' Square, where the opposition was still demonstrating. In the speech he delivered on the occasion, Hassan Nasrallah rejected all Western interference, warned the Israeli government that it "will not win with politics what it has failed to win militarily" (that is, disarming the IRL via Resolution 1559). Interestingly, he said that he did not oppose a Syrian withdrawal "in principle", but preferred to achieve it under the Taef Agreement, a "Lebanese" framework, rather than a Resolution 1559 "imposed by the West". He also called the anti-Syrian politicians to a dialogue to "jointly" find a solution to the crisis, one "that respects civil peace and harmony". The opposition responded by calling for a big rally for the 14th. A record number of people—more than a million by some estimates[53]—gathered on Martyrs' Square, renamed "Liberty Square" for the occasion. The speeches differed somewhat depending on the denomination. The Sunnis, through the Hariri family, emphasized the new national unity, treated the loyalists gently, acknowledged the results achieved by the IRL, and emphasized the commonalities between the authorities and the opposition despite the crisis.[54] The Maronite and Druze parties were more virulent; in their speeches they focused on and inveighed against the links to the Syrians, and demanded the resignation of the head of state and heads of the services. The truth about the assassination and withdrawal by the Syrians, however, were at the top of everyone's lists.[55]

After the two great demonstrations the opposition renamed itself the Alliance of March 14, while the groups remaining aligned with the Syrian regime were called the Forces of March 8. These two gatherings would assume great importance, less for the speeches that were made there than for the special significance that they subsequently took on. During the 1990s the Christian camp had fallen into a period of *ihbāt* (demoralization), and the Sunnis had benefited from the recalibration of power accorded to them under the Taef Agreement—within limits set by Damascus. While the takeover of the streets and squares of the capital's downtown district by the protesters in February and March 2005 had put Lebanese of all confessions and all regions side by side, it had still mostly been carried out by residents of Beirut, primarily Christians and Sunnis. A very strongly symbolic dimension emerged on the spot: the Christians, revolted by the excesses perpetrated by a foreign power whose presence they had vehemently rejected for years, found common cause with their Sunni compatriots in mourning the loss of their standard bearer. Hariri's assassination would therefore be portrayed as the great moment of inter-Lebanese unity and "national reconciliation". Most Sunnis gratefully perceived the Christian mobilization as a sign of solidarity. The Christians, for their part, interpreted the Sunnis move into the opposition as a belated but welcome recognition of the "just cause" fought for by the Maronites since the 1980s, which had made Syria into the arch-enemy. An understanding was therefore sealed between the two communities that had been most involved in the civil war. The notion of a "spirit of March 14" materialized to designate a peace between "Christians" and "(Sunni) Muslims" without calling it that. The Syrian withdrawal was celebrated in a shared anger that marked the true end point to fifteen years of civil war.

The new grouping was, in effect, competition for Hezbollah. Despite some (tentative) references (by the Sunnis) to the achievements of the Resistance in 2000, the great narratives that gradually grew up around the tragedy that had just struck the country and the "happy ending" to an unhappy slice of Lebanese history did not include the Liberation. While March 14 lauded the section of Resolution 1559 that required immediate Syrian withdrawal, it did not call into question the clause calling for the IRL to disarm. It historicized the victory over Israel, and emphasized that over Syria. More importantly, the story in March 14 narratives tended to jump directly from the end of the civil war—in the late 1980s—to 2005, the intervening period being reduced to fifteen blacked-out years during which the national life was placed on hold. Nothing was considered to have happened between these two points in time that merited being called a great event. This message was clearly reflected in the name that the mobilization gave itself: 2005, al-Istiqlāl al-Thānī (2005, the Second Independence)—the first being the independence of 1943 that saw the end of the French Mandate. But Hezbollah had already categorized the Liberation of 2000 as "Second Independence". Thus, for Hezbollah and the Shia, the mobilization of spring 2005 (which should have been the "Third Independence") sought to relegate the importance of the end of the Israeli occupation in 2000, making it clear that the IRL's achievements did not matter.

This downplaying of Hezbollah's cause was equally evident in the identification by the protesters between being anti-Syrian and being Lebanese. The opposition political class did not hesitate to treat loyalists and those who did not support the protests as "Syrian clients", as "agents of Syria" or of "the Syro-Lebanese intelligence services".[56] Equating Lebanese identity and anti-Syrianism thus directly competed with the linkage established in 2000 by Hezbollah between being Lebanese and being hostile towards Israel. From then on, the Shiites as a group were implicitly kept at arm's length by the radicals of the Cedar Revolution. The latter's refusal to include the end of the Israeli occupation in the list of national events would, in itself, be seen by many Lebanese as a non-recognition of the suffering endured for over twenty years by the country's South. But the comments made by some opposition figures were explicit. In January 2005 Pierre Gemayel, the son of former President Amin Gemayel, then a Kataeb MP, had attracted attention when, on being asked by reporters about the fact that the opposition of the day obviously underestimated the huge number of people (Shiites) who did not share its views, he replied: "They are quantity, we are quality."[57] One obviously displeased activist after the March 8 demonstration had this to say: "We let [the Shiites] celebrate when they made *their* liberation [in 2000]; now let them let us make *ours*."[58] In mid-March the journalist Gebran Tueni, publisher of the daily *al-Nahār*, regarded as the living icon of March 14, evoked the loyalist rally in these terms: "The Shiites are brainless sheep who follow their leaders without thinking."[59] Comments such as this would remind many Lebanese of the discriminatory sectarian talk of the war years. The Shiite community got the message loud and clear, as a young March 8 demonstrator testified:

> I went down into the street because I wanted to express my opinion. Supporters of the opposition occupied the street for days and weeks as if they were the sole representatives of the Lebanese people. I think it is time to admit that there are two political visions in Lebanon. This is not a sectarian division. It is true that I am Shiite, but that is not why I took part in the event. I just wanted to show that I do not share the views of the opposition and that I am as Lebanese as the others.[60]

The organizers of the protests in spring 2005, coming from civil society as well as the political scene, also launched the first appeals to what would soon constitute the grand policy outlines of March 14 when it came to power. Once again, many of these positions largely reflected Maronite radical creeds of the 1960s and 1970s, leaving many Lebanese feeling that the Cedar Revolution at best had the profile of a conservative movement and at worst represented a backward leap. The opponents went so far as to say that "spring will come to Damascus", in a clear allusion to their hope that the Syrian regime would fall; some observers in Lebanon saw this stand as unhelpful provocation against the latter.[61] They also favoured an alliance with the West, more particularly with the (neo-conservative) United States and France, and peace with Israel, in the context of the Iraq war and the war against terrorism. All this frightened large segments of the population. With regard to domestic policy, the opposition talked about making permanent what the Taef Agreement wanted to be temporary: the egalitarian allocation of parliamentary seats between Christians and Muslims. March 14 hence clearly refused to deconfessionalize the political system. Finally, some called for the disarming of the IRL—one of many points that put the opposition at odds with Hezbollah's paradigms.

Many Lebanese, non-Shiites among them, were also concerned that the Cedar Revolution, far from putting up a new class of politicians whose past actions and philosophies were in harmony with the cause being promoted, merely contented itself with once more putting former warlords in charge of internal affairs who, ironically, had entered politics under Syrian mentorship. Their profiles, as much as their political records, marked by years of plundering the Lebanese state and diverting its resources for clientelist purposes of patronage and militias, did not seem to make them the ideal candidates for performing the tasks that March 14 had officially made its own—the restoration of institutional functions and the return to the rule of law. In the eyes of many Lebanese, Samir Geagea remained above all a war criminal and an ex-Israeli agent, and there were many families still mourning members killed by the Lebanese Forces.[62] The Gemayel family was also associated with a federalist, confessionalist Maronitism and years of collaboration with Tel Aviv. The Druze leader Walid Jumblatt, who refused to fire on the Israeli army while it was taking the Shuf in the summer of 1982, but whose fighters not only massacred dozens of Christian civilians during the war years but fought against the Lebanese army itself, did not fit the profile of a humanist or a defender of law. Finally, Saad Hariri himself, although not handicapped by a bloody past and inter-communitarian depredations, was at the time considered by many to be "too young for the job" and, having spent most of his youth either in the United States or Saudi Arabia, too unfamiliar with Lebanese socio-political issues. While genuine enthusiasm poured into the streets and public squares of Beirut in the spring of 2005, an alternative mobilization, though ignored at the time, was already gathering momentum.

The anti-Syrian coalition takes power

With the Syrian withdrawal completed, the opposition entered the parliamentary elections of 29 May and 5, 12, and 19 June optimistically. Michel Aoun, in exile since 1991, announced that he would return on 7 May, and there were discussions with loyalists on a possible amnesty law that would free Samir Geagea. Thus, the former top Christian leaders seemed to have made their comeback, boosting the community's morale and marking the end of the *iḥbāṭ*. Saad Hariri, son of the former prime minister and designated by the family as his father's political heir, announced in early May that his faction would abide by the decisions of the opposition's coordinating committee.[63]

Despite this ideological rapprochement giving rise to the hope of unity in the ranks of March 14 during the elections, the old confessional reflexes along with traditional power-sharing arrangements between the communitarian leaders quickly reasserted themselves. Less than three months after the February tragedy and the hopeful momentum of March, the parliamentary elections in the spring were like a cold shower. The first to turn his back on his comrades-in-arms was none other than Walid Jumblatt, who had struck a tone that was the most radical and revolutionary. In early April, even before the completion of the Syrian withdrawal, he cultivated contacts in the government and with the speaker of the parliament, without keeping his allies informed. They were boycotting the loyalists at the time. When the electoral alliances were finally set, Jumblatt's PSP presented its candidates alongside those of AMAL and Hezbollah, which by then had also succeeded in attracting the candidates of the FC. Opportunistic politics carried the day, and the elections proceeded on the basis of lists on which loyalists and members of the opposition faced off against candidates from their own side.

Despite these inconsistencies, March 14 saw its way clear to victory in the elections, with 72 out of 128 seats. Fouad Siniora, a member of the FC and former minister in two of the governments headed by Rafic Hariri (2000–4), became president of the first post-tutelage Council. He immediately showed himself in favour of a national unity government in which all political forces would be represented. While Hezbollah surprised everyone by announcing its willingness to participate—for the first time in its history—it was Michel Aoun, with his increasingly explicit anti-Haririan and anti-Sunni policy, who categorically refused to do likewise. The distribution of portfolios did not proceed easily. The maintenance of confessional balance was partly to blame for this, but weighing just as much on it was the fact that, in the context of the time, some portfolios had become too strategic to be relinquished to the new opposition. Hezbollah and AMAL, with an eye to blocking a future implementation of Resolution 1559, wanted Foreign Affairs assigned to a Shiite individual allied with them. The majority was intent on wresting the security apparatus, that is, the Interior Ministry, from the former loyalists, and, by preventing them from taking over the Justice Ministry, keeping them from hampering the work of the Commission of Inquiry that had been set up to look into the assassination of Rafic Hariri. The new government took office on 19 July, with twenty-four members. It seemed fairly well balanced, reflecting the FC's wish to not frustrate the new opposition: Fawzi

Salloukh, who was close to the Supreme Shiite Council, got Foreign Affairs, Muhammad Fneish, a Hezbollah cadre, got Water and Power. Justice went to Charles Rizk, a close associate of Samir Geagea, and Defence to Elias Murr, a former staunch pro-Syrian who had recently joined the opposition. The majority also managed to take Interior and Telecommunications.[64]

The tasks facing the new government were Herculean. The Syrian army was gone, but much remained to be done. The state, in its capacity as supra-partisan, has never been a strong player in Lebanese politics, nor on its institutional or administrative sides. During fifteen years of civil war the militias dismantled it, redistributing the resources of its agencies, and fifteen years under Syrian tutelage did not revive it. By that spring of 2005 the Lebanese state, in the widest sense, needed to be built new from the ground up. To do this, the *sine qua non*s posited by both March 14 and the international community were the restoration of state sovereignty over the entire country, and the monopoly on legitimate violence. This meant disarming the IRL and the Palestinian camps, and also sending the army to South Lebanon, a region from which it had largely been absent since the late 1960s. There was also a need to establish an effective administration, and hence a budget. However, Lebanon's national debt was in 2005 estimated at over $40 billion, giving little hope of quickly restoring the institutions. The country's financial difficulties left no means of putting a policy in place for the kind of economic and social development desperately needed in the peripheral regions (Akkar, Bekaa, the South, and the suburbs of the capital).

Moreover, Beirut wished to restore friendly relations with Damascus. It was an ambitious goal. After the withdrawal, the Syrian regime took a series of steps aimed at humiliating Lebanon, backed by a Syrian press that railed against the leaders of March 14.[65] An improvement in relations became even more uncertain because, in the large enthusiasm triggered by the withdrawal, a number of individuals in March 14—beginning with Walid Jumblatt—had urged the spread of the protest movement to Damascus. In often highly undiplomatic language, they sought the removal of Assad from power, sometimes explicitly encouraging a coup. Their motivation was increased by the results of the International Commission of Inquiry which was soon to take over the Lebanese authorities' investigation into the Rafic Hariri assassination. On 31 October after a Syrian refusal to cooperate in the Commission's work, the UNSC passed Resolution 1636, calling on Damascus to cooperate and stop interfering in Lebanon. Some days earlier, the Security Council had called on Syria to establish previously non-existent diplomatic relations with Lebanon, and to define the border between the two countries, particularly in view of a possible settlement of the issue of the Shebaa Farms. Finally, on 15 December, the UNSC passed Resolution 1644, which reiterated Syria's obligation to respond to the requirements of the Commission of Inquiry. In other words, the Lebanese dossier garnered three Resolutions affecting the Syrian regime in less than ten months.

This encouraged Damascus to dig in its heels. During this time, Lebanon experienced renewed security breakdowns. Several attacks targeted Christian areas of Beirut and its suburbs, and several political or media personalities belonging to the new majority current were murdered. For example, on 2 June, Samir Kassir, a columnist for the daily *al-Nahār* and an outspoken critic of the Syrian regime, died in a car bomb. The day before delivery of the International Commission of Inquiry's second report, said to furnish new evidence of the involvement of Syrian leaders, Gebran Tueni, *al-Nahār*'s publisher, was killed. This cluster of dramas occurring about the same time, just before or after deadlines related to the investigation, suggests that they were either warnings or punitive acts that Damascus was aiming at its Lebanese critics and their Western allies. The new government's conciliatory approach, well intended as it was, was thus sabotaged by the Syrian regime and part of the Lebanese political class that had gone into defensive mode.

Relations with Hezbollah

A new start: concessions by both sides

The spring of 2005 saw one demonstration after another in the capital as the end of the Syrian military presence in Lebanon loomed ever closer. Hezbollah adopted its typical position for times of crisis: keeping in the background, it refrained from commenting on events unless absolutely necessary. Nevertheless, while discreet, it was not silent. It is no coincidence that the rare but regular statements issuing from its leadership always contained the same message: "No to the disarmament of the Resistance." Far from being formulated at innocuous moments, they appeared whenever the opposition or the international community expressed too insistent a commitment to implementing Resolution 1559. In the general cacophony of the political class, Hezbollah, without joining the roiling debates of the times, beyond sending warnings, sought above all to explicitly reiterate its main priority. It is noteworthy that, contrary to the stance taken then by other loyalist parties such as the Kataeb of Pakradouni or AMAL, Hezbollah's leadership at no time opposed the ending of Syrian tutelage over Lebanon. It did attend or was represented at pro-Syrian meetings, but refrained from calling for the Syrian army to remain. It even offered to focus on organizing elections and instructing the resulting parliament to handle the Syrian withdrawal. In its discourse at the great demonstration of 8 March 2005, the party focused on warning against implemention of Resolution 1559 while contenting itself with a mere expression of "heartfelt thanks" to the Syrian regime for supporting the Resistance, and promising to keep "loyal" relations with it.[66] But at no time did it in any way call for the Syrian army or Rustom Ghazaleh, the head of Syrian intelligence in Lebanon and its de facto representative in the country, to remain. Obviously, "friendly and faithful relations" could be maintained from opposite sides of the border. The party's position on the Beirut Spring is therefore easy to understand, even if it shows through only in filigree. It remained consistent to the attitude with which it has always approached politics, indicating its readiness to accommodate the new situation as long as those in power—now the March 14 Alliance—did not try to disarm the IRL. In other words, March 14 was free to carry out whatever policy it wanted as long as it did not conflict with the interests of the Resistance.

Initially, the deal offered by Hezbollah to the new majority looked as if it might work, especially as the Siniora government signalled its readiness to make several concessions to March 8, particularly to the Hezbollah–AMAL duo. In June Nabih Berri was re-elected as speaker of the parliament, a post he had occupied without interruption since 1992. As already mentioned, the Foreign Affairs portfolio went to a close associate of the SSC. Despite Washington's insistent objections, Hezbollah joined the government, for the first time ever. In his first press conference, Ghazi Aridi, minister of information and a member of the PSP, commented on the American government's choice to boycott the Hezbollah minister by declaring that "great powers cannot ask Hezbollah to enter politics but then complain when one of its members joins the government, which is the natural fulfillment of this demand".[67] Finally, to the delight of the party, the Ministerial Statement ignored Resolution 1559, in favour of the following formulation:

> The government considers that the Lebanese Resistance is the sincere and natural expression of the national right of the Lebanese people to defend its land and dignity against Israeli aggression, threats and ambitions, to work towards completing the liberation of Lebanese lands, and to persevere in repelling Palestinian naturalization.[68]

Hezbollah was not ungrateful. Its thanks took the form of approving all other points of the Ministerial Statement, beginning with administrative decentralization and a revision of the electoral law to favour the small constituency option (though unfavourable *a priori* to the new opposition to which it now belonged), two favourite projects of the conservative Christian camp. Although it expressed some reservations about how the government intended to go about implementation, it did not oppose the proposed de-Syrianization of the state apparatus, beginning with the restructuring of the ISF (internal security forces, equivalent to the police). Consequent on a formal promise by the government that the international investigation would not be politicized—hence not used against Hezbollah—the party did not hamper the work of the International Commission of Inquiry. It even accepted the idea of a financial aid conference under Western sponsorship, provided that such aid would not be subject to political conditions (that is, the implementation of Resolution 1559). In early September, it went so far as to refrain from protesting against the decision by the government to strike 25 May—the official anniversary of the 2000 Liberation—from the list of official holidays.[69]

The inexorable march towards a break

A great victory for the opposition after the assassination of Rafic Hariri came in early April 2005 with the passing of Resolution 1595 by the UNSC. It resulted in the formation of an International Commission of Inquiry to shed light on the former prime minister's assassination. Wary of an easily influenced Lebanese commission, March 14 made an international investigation the spearhead in its fight against the Syrian regime. The reasoning was that if the foreign commission was to succeed in pinning sponsorship of the assassination on Damascus, Lebanon would not only be immunized against further assassinations, but also against any chance of the Syrians once again gaining the upper hand over Beirut's domestic politics. Another mainly loyalist part of the political class, however, expressed its mistrust of an investigation that, under the guise of impartiality and professionalism, could be exploited by the new majority as a means of getting rid of its political rivals. There was particular concern that the findings of an external investigation should not be tailored by the international community and Israel to get rid of Hezbollah. Taking note, the government reiterated that the Commission was expected to remain under the authority of the Lebanese Justice Ministry. It was simply to present its reports, and the Lebanese authorities would then decide what action to take, especially with regard to arresting any suspects. Based on this arrangement, the sceptical parties agreed first to give the Commission a chance.

It got to work in mid-June 2005, presided over by a German judge, Detlev Mehlis. His methods quickly proved problematic. He was accused of letting himself be unduly influenced by the political figures with whom he associated, and who appeared to compromise the impartiality of the research. The opposition in particular was convinced that his proclivity for cronyism, especially with radical elements of the March 14 Alliance, not only influenced his words but also how he steered the investigation. A second criticism concerned the judge's repeated breaches of the investigation's confidentiality. Again very early, Mehlis displayed a penchant for press conferences and interviews in which he exposed several aspects of his research and, even while conceding a lack of hard evidence, proceeded to make accusations. Even though some of them were indirect, they created turmoil on the Lebanese political scene. In particular, his work disrupted the relationship between Hezbollah and the government. In an interview in July with the French *Le Figaro*, the judge admitted that the Commission "approached the Israeli intelligence services, which have provided [it] with good information".[70] The statement hit the opposition like a bombshell. As they saw it, the judge had just confirmed what they had suspected about the Commission all along: that this was a highly politicized investigation. The next day the UN spokesman in Beirut hastened to deny that the Commission had used the services of Mossad, and said that *Le Figaro* had not been authorized by Mehlis to publish the item. The correction came too late: the credibility and impartiality of the

Commission, already suspect in the eyes of the opposition, were severely shaken by this early setback. Therefore, in late August, when the Commission's work led to the arrest of Generals Jamil al-Sayyid, Mustafa Hamdan, Raymond Azar, and Ali al-Hajj, at the time the heads of General Security, the Republican Guard, Military Intelligence, and the ISF respectively, the opposition protested. When rumours circulated during this same period about an alleged involvement of Hezbollah in the assassination, as a secret report issued by Mehlis to the UNSC supposedly indicated, circles close to the party cried foul, claiming that the judge had issued a report ordered by Israel.[71] As for Hezbollah's leadership, it chose not to respond to the accusations other than to call them "idiotic".[72] The insinuations made by Mehlis were all the more problematic in that they indirectly laid blame on the Shiite community for the assassination of a Sunni leader and played a role in the mounting animosity between the two communities. The tension around the work of the Commission increased even more when its credibility took another hit in the autumn with the start of the affair of the "false witnesses". Several people deposed by Mehlis, who used their depositions as the basis for his main arguments, recanted and accused specific individuals in March 14—Saad Hariri, Walid Jumblatt, and Marwan Hamadeh—of prompting them to make false statements, or paying them to lie.

Hezbollah reacted to the resulting political intrigues by going into defensive mode. After responding with disdain to the first rumours about its involvement in the murder, it raised the stakes in early October. It began by expressing its disapproval of the government routinely calling on the services of the American FBI for every inquiry following an explosion or assassination. At the time, Washington was issuing repeated statements hostile to Hezbollah, making it difficult for the latter to believe that the investigations conducted by the American law enforcement agency were not unbiased. As the release date for Mehlis's initial report approached (20 October), politicians engaged in a frenzy of speculation that led some March 14 cadres to renege on the government's assurances regarding the IRL's interests, and to call more or less openly it to be disarmed. Two days before the report was to be submitted, Hezbollah's leadership insisted that the parties reach terms "once for all" on the question of the Resistance. It reiterated its reservations about the investigations conducted "by using foreign security experts", called into question their reliability, and expressed concern about giving Western intelligence services access to the Lebanese security apparatus.[73] Nasrallah repeated that "all Lebanese want the truth [about the Hariri assassination]" but demanded "incontrovertible proof and clear conclusions".[74] In late October the government acknowledged the need for a frank discussion with the party, following the filing of the report by Terje Rød-Larsen, special UN envoy for monitoring the implementation of Resolution 1559. In effect, he condemned all actions by the Resistance as illegitimate, reaffirming that "as far as the UN is concerned, Resolution 425 has been completely complied with since the Shebaa region is not Lebanese". The previous week, Hezbollah had shown solidarity with the March 14 ministers by formally accepting the findings of the Mehlis report, despite its misgivings. The day after the Rød-Larsen report was made public, it was the government's turn to support Hezbollah. Agreement was reached on initiating an internal dialogue—with emphasis on the word internal—dealing with Resolution 1559. In the course of the press conference following the cabinet meeting, the information minister, Ghazi Aridi, insisted that it would be dangerous to link progress of the inquiry into the Hariri assassination (stemming from Resolution 1595) to the dismantling of the Resistance's arsenal (called for under Resolution 1559).[75]

The entente was short-lived. Ten days later, on 10 November, President Bashar al-Assad addressed the nation, and attacked Fouad Siniora and Saad Hariri. The Lebanese government met the same day, hoping to express unanimous solidarity with its leader. Protesting against a move that they called premature, the AMAL and Hezbollah ministers left the meeting before the vote, unwilling to adopt an immediate position which "could have serious consequences for Syrian–Lebanese relations"[76] and needing to conduct preliminary discussions with their party leaders. The excuse proffered by the Shiite ministers quickly revealed itself as a mere pretext. That week was indeed the starting point of a real crisis between Hezbollah and the Council. The real reason for the withdrawal of the Shiite ministers became evident a few days later, when Nasrallah said that the prime minister had given the party "reasons for concern" because of the stance on 1559 attributed to Prime Minister Siniora in the Rød-Larsen report.[77] A week after the report's delivery, Terje Rød-Larsen had indeed given an interview to the daily *L'Orient–Le Jour* in which he gave to understand that the prime minister had promised him that he would enforce the Resolution, and that was why Lebanon had been granted more time.[78] Hezbollah therefore feared that the head of government would backtrack on the assurances contained in the Ministerial Statement. Wishing to ascertain the true intentions of the Council head, the leader of the Hezbollah parliamentary bloc, Muhammad Raad, addressed the following question to him in parliament in mid-November:

> Is it true that you stressed before [Rød-]Larsen your government's commitment to implementing all the provisions of Resolution 1559, and that you requested additional time for doing so? Is it also true that you informed Mr Larsen of the start of an internal dialogue whose success you guaranteed in the context of disarming the militias (that is to say the Resistance) and dismantling them? [We asked this question] so that the confusions and fears would no longer generate divisions among the Lebanese on a national issue of such sensitivity.[79]

But Fouad Siniora refused to answer. Hezbollah responded by opting for a less diplomatic tone. On 25 November 2005, during a major public rally organized by the party to celebrate the recovery of the bodies of three of its fighters, returned the same day by Israel, Hassan Nasrallah delivered a resounding warning in which courtesy was replaced by a rising anger, expressed in a harsher tone:

> In all candour, we are for debate and dialogue in Lebanon, but we reject the charges. We will no longer remain silent from now on before those who accuse us. To those who want to debate, we will respond that having a different point of view is their most natural right. As for the one who will accuse us, even before answering, we will say to him: *Enta mīn*?! Just who are you?! Before 1982, what were you doing? In 1982, what did you do? Where were you? With whom? Allied with whom? What was your position? You, what did you give to this country? What have you sacrificed for this country? Let's talk about your relationship with the [Western] embassies, your relationship with the Americans, with the Israelis, with the West! So before you come seeking a quarrel, we will ask you ... (more firmly and more threatening) before you come to quarrel with us, we will ask you (shouting): *Enta mīn*?![80]

Simultaneously, an implicit showdown took place in the Council of Ministers between the Shiite and March 14 ministers. On 25 November, when Marwan Hamadeh and Ghazi Aridi floated the idea of an international criminal tribunal (ICT) to try the perpetrators of the 14 February attack, the Shiite ministers prevaricated, arguing that this move was premature since the results of the Commission's investigation were still "subject to discussion."[81] Soon, several politicians—and the press as well—began talking about how March 14 was weary of and annoyed with the repeated blocking of the government by the Shiite ministers.[82] As far as the ruling majority was concerned, Hezbollah and AMAL were merely carrying out directives dictated by Damascus. Both parties were accused of trying to protect the Syrian regime with their attempts to block an ICT. Yet, regardless of the latter's likely wishes, Hezbollah had its own reasons for opposing such a tribunal. As previously mentioned, the findings of the Mehlis Commission had failed to convince the entire Lebanese political class; moreover, the at times overenthusiastic engagement by the international community against Hezbollah had discredited the assurances of the non-politicization of the investigation. As far as Hezbollah and its allies were concerned, the investigation was merely an instrument in the hands of an international community whose primary objective was not so much weakening or toppling the Syrian regime but dismantling Hezbollah itself. One thing that Hezbollah feared in particular, and came to fear all the more over time, was that an eventual ICT would be placed under Anglo-American, not French, jurisdiction, because of the comparative ease with which Anglo-American law allows the arrest of suspects without evidence. In the eyes of Hezbollah's leadership, an ICT under Anglo-American jurisdiction could become the means by which not only the international community but also March 14 could get rid of the party by sending its chief cadres to languish indefinitely without trial in Guantanamo on the suppositions of a biased judge, manipulated by Israeli intelligence.

On 12 December, Gebran Tueni was assassinated. The government took the opportunity to officially request an ICT that day. The Shiite ministers left the room before the vote, thus suspending their participation in the Council—without resigning from it. They let it be known that they would rejoin the Council only when the government "once for all" disavowed Resolution 1559. For the first time, Hezbollah's leadership directly and severely criticized the prime minister, and Sheikh ʿAfīf al-Nābulsī[83] published a *fatwā* prohibiting Shiites who were neither AMAL nor Hezbollah from accepting nominations as ministers.[84] At the end of December the party threatened a walk-out of parliament. The crisis continued unabated until the beginning of February. Shiite ministers finally rejoined the government after Fouad Siniora officially and formally agreed to declare that "the Resistance has not and will not be called by any name other than *the National Resistance*".[85] The hatchet had been buried—but not for long.

Late 2005–early 2006: a turning point

Jumblatt turns against his electoral ally

When Resolution 1559 was passed in September 2004, Walid Jumblatt had pronounced himself in favour of a Syrian withdrawal from Lebanon, but drew a distinction with regard to two aspects—the Syrian withdrawal and the disarmament of armed factions—to protect the IRL's arsenal. Following the assassination of Rafic Hariri in mid-February 2005, Jumblatt changed his tone and attacked Hezbollah. Not mincing his words, he called the party "an instrument of Syrian pressure" and "a factor for disunion among the Lebanese".[86] In early summer, under pressure because of the elections and the need to form joint lists with Hezbollah in PSP areas (especially in the West Bekaa) to assure his party's victory, Jumblatt toned down his rhetoric and did a U-turn. Accusing the West of working on behalf of Israel, he rejected the idea of international aid conditioned on disarming the Resistance, which he praised as the "very symbol of dignity and pride", the "bulwark of our unity, our real independence and our sovereignty".[87] He also moderated his rhetoric towards the Syrian regime at the same time, defending it against Washington and Tel Aviv.[88] The Mehlis report and the speculation that grew around it, both on the Lebanese political scene and in the Western diplomatic circles, encouraged new corrections: on 15 December, the day that the vote on Resolution 1644 extended the life of the International Commission by six months and foreshadowed the formation of an ICT, Jumblatt did a third about-face and threw himself into a frenetic campaign against Hezbollah and the Syrian regime. The alliance formed for the parliamentary elections in the summer shattered, which led the March 14 circles to fear for the survival of the government.[89] Radical to begin with, the Druze leader's new position became provocative when he decided to lend credence to rumours about a presumptive involvement by Hezbollah in Hariri's assassination, picking up information put forward by Judge Mehlis concerning the truck used in the assassination. The judge had actually posited that the vehicle had left from Beirut's southern suburbs, information passed on to the Commission of Inquiry by Mossad.[90] Taking his latest hostility towards IRL's cause to an extreme, Jumblatt belittled it and played down the impact of the Liberation in 2000, characterizing the weapons of the Resistance in January 2006 as "weapons of treachery".[91] A few months later he refused to apply the label "Resistance" to the IRL and slapped the seal of "illegality" on it, affirming that "the State cannot coexist with the militia".[92] He accused Hezbollah of being a "puppet organization" acting on orders of the Syrian and Iranian regimes,[93] and, employing sectarian locutions, called on the party and the IRL fighters "to be Lebanese first".[94] In so doing, he started a practice that would become widespread in March 14 circles during the year ahead: national excommunication, used by the majority to arrogate to itself the right to determine who is Lebanese and who is not.[95]

Michel Aoun's choice

In view of the PSP leader's vexing fickleness, Hezbollah found itself in the position of needing to look for more steadfast allies. In the spring of 2005, a section of the public sympathetic to the opposition chose to interpret Michel Aoun's return from his years of exile in France as an impending strengthening of their position on the political stage. He returned on 7 May, but immediately adopted an attitude and discourse that confirmed the sense already felt by some that the old hero of Lebanese anti-Syrianism was not disposed to cooperate with March 14. His behaviour upon arrival in Beirut immediately ruffled some feathers.[96] But he really antagonized the opposition with his manifest intent of being seen as its top leader. His words concerning the presidential election scheduled for 2007, for which he had already declared his candidacy, reflected his certainty that he represented the political preferences of a majority of Lebanese. He criticized Saad Hariri, sometimes with insulting innuendos pierced by the resentment of a community stripped of part of its privileges by the Taef Agreement to the advantage of a rival community. In other words, Michel Aoun did not adhere to "the spirit of (Sunni–Maronite reconciliation) of March 14". He likewise irritated the anti-Assad people by not hesitating to appropriate the achievements of the opposition in obtaining the Syrian retreat, declaring: "March 14, that's me; as to them, they're February 14."[97] In allusion to the war that he had waged against the Syrian army in 1989 and his role in the American vote for SALSA consequent to his testimony to Congress in 2003, he nominated himself as the true leader of the league united in hostility towards the Syrian regime. At the same time, he called those representing themselves as belonging to March 14 "subservient to the Hariri family"—hence to Sunnism. In speeches that became more and more sectarian, he asserted a desire to defend "the independence of the Christian decision", positioning himself as the head of a Christian camp subject "neither to Koraytem, nor Mukhtara".[98] He also did not seem reconciled to the differences that during the late 1980s had put him at loggerheads with the Patriarch of the Maronite community, Monsignor Nasrallah Boutros Sfeir. Rejecting the attachment to the confessional system revived by March

14 Christians united around the Monsignor (Lebanese Forces and Kataeb), he played the laity card, advocating a reformism at once anti-confessional and modernizing. In this way, he gave notice of his determination to question Sfeir's stature as "head of all Maronites", considering that the latter's legitimacy was more of a religious nature.

His increasingly explicit refusal to lose himself in the Christianism of March 14 plus the popularity that he enjoyed at this time in late 2005 made him into a political object that both political camps eagerly sought to seduce. The new majority did so out of fear of seeing him join the opposing camp, and the new opposition wanted to assure itself of a heavyweight ally in parliament.[99] Finally, in February 2006, he put an end to the suspense by announcing the signature of a "Document of Understanding" between his party, the Free Patriotic Movement, and Hezbollah. On 6 February Aoun and Nasrallah together presented the contents of the agreement during a conference organized in the church of Mar Mikhael in Haret Hreik. The choice of location was fraught with symbolic meanings: Aoun himself was born in this mostly Shiite suburban quarter of the capital. The church had been damaged during the civil war and rebuilt to show the determination of the Christians to remain in a neighbourhood that had been hostile at one time. As for Hezbollah, it reiterated on this occasion the party's attachment to a good understanding with the Christians. On the domestic scene, the accord was above all a victory for Hezbollah: profiting from the inter-Christian rivalries, it had succeeded in attracting a significant part of a community which *a priori* had no reasons to be favourably inclined towards the party. In the context of March 14's progressively stepped up campaign against IRL's weapons, and international pressures aimed against the party itself and the Syrian regime increasing, Hezbollah faced the urgent need of assuring itself allies in parliament, in particular for blocking any law that could harm the Resistance.

8

THE THIRTY-THREE-DAY WAR

THE RESISTANCE PUT TO THE TEST (12 JULY–14 AUGUST 2006)

In January 2004, an exchange of prisoners between Hezbollah and Tel Aviv freed 430 Lebanese and Arab detainees from Israeli prisons. In the course of the ceremony organized by Hezbollah to mark the occasion, Hassan Nasrallah formally committed to doing his utmost to liberate the last Lebanese still languishing in the southern neighbour's prisons. During the next two years, the IRL therefore tried several times to kidnap Israeli soldiers in the border zone to use them as currency in exchanges.[1] It finally succeeded at 09.05 Beirut time on 12 July 2006, when one of its commando units attacked an Israeli patrol, killing six soldiers and capturing two others, losing one of its own fighters as it withdrew.

Nasrallah immediately announced the success of the operation, which he called al-Waʿd al-Sādiq, or Truthful Pledge.[2] Insisting that his organization did not want an escalation, he invited the Israeli government to engage in indirect negotiations. The Israelis turned a deaf ear. Although Hezbollah's leader had explicitly absolved Fouad Siniora's cabinet of all responsibility, admitting that the government was not kept informed of IRL's plans, Ehud Olmert's government saw that the Lebanese authorities were to blame along with the party. Affirming that the kidnapping had involved a violation of Israeli sovereignty,[3] he set out as the primary objectives recovery of the two kidnapped NCOs; "break Hezbollah";[4] and force the Lebanese government to implement Resolution 1559.[5] Promising to "set Lebanon back 50 years"[6] he ordered Operation Change of Direction,[7] a series of air and ground attacks that observers and the public at large would soon call the Thirty-Three-Day War.[8]

A conflict of thirty-three days and nights[9]

Israel: Strike from the air, avoid ground combat

While Israeli warships patrolling in Lebanon's territorial waters imposed a naval blockade from the outset and shelled coastal areas non-stop during the entire conflict, the offensive was mainly conducted from the air. Beirut International Airport, the country's only civilian airport, was the first to be hit with repeated attacks and burned. Sustained bombing of the national highways linking Lebanon with Syria soon made them impassable. Ten days after the start of hostilities, Lebanon was completely isolated from the rest of the world. Inside the country, bridges and main roads were systematically destroyed, and within a few days the South was isolated from the centre and the capital, then the capital from the Mountain, and the Bekaa Valley from the rest of the country. Progressively, the routes linking the cities in the same region, then the smaller roads linking villages and small towns to the larger cities suffered the same fate, Israeli shellfire pockmarking the roads with impassable craters and its pilots attacking any vehicles still trying to negotiate them. Refugees, mostly on foot, moved across the country and into Syria. Israel frankly avowed that this progressive fragmenting and sealing off of the regions was designed to prevent the IRL's forces from regrouping, and to prevent any logistical back-up, food resupply, and equipment from reaching them. With the same aim, the Israeli army destroyed trucks and transport vans and pounded petrol stations, greatly reducing vehicular traffic.

It also demolished Hezbollah facilities (buildings, offices, hospitals, clinics, pharmacies, schools, charities) and the residences of its leaders. Seeking to capture party cadres, it staged a series of helicopter-borne commando raids in a number of areas. And in the last days, with the frequency of IRL rocket attacks on northern Israel continuing, the Israeli General Staff decided to order a sweeping ground offensive intended to "cleanse the South to a 5 to 30 km" depth of any IRL presence.[10] In addition to the 15,000–20,000 Israeli troops[11] already engaged on Lebanese territory against a handful of villages close to the border, nearly 20,000 additional troops were sent in as reinforcements in an attempt to locate and destroy the adversary's rocket launchers.

A war "solely against Hezbollah"?

Throughout the conflict the Israeli authorities were at pains to present the offensive as directed "against Hezbollah, not against the Lebanese government or people". Yet, as they would eventually acknowledge in a semi-public way, Lebanon's government facilities and civilians were also targeted deliberately, as a means of both collective punishment and putting pressure on Hezbollah.[12] From the start, the military airports at Qleiat (North) and Rayak (Bekaa) were bombed.[13] On 18 July the Jamhour base in the Beirut hills in a majority Christian area[14] was also hit and, two days later, a police station near the village of Rmeish (South) met the same fate.[15] The Baalbek Hall of Justice was damaged on 20 July, and a Lebanese army base at Aytanit (Bekaa) was bombed on 29 July.[16]

UNIFIL and its peacekeepers were either collateral or direct damage victims of the Israeli attacks, as on 15 and 26 July (a member of UNIFIL wounded, four UN observers killed)[17] and 6 August (three peacekeepers injured).[18]

Of all the Israeli army's targets, the civilian population unquestionably had the worst of it. Many perished in bombardment of buildings, offices, and houses belonging to Hezbollah cadres, or even petrol stations mostly situated in densely populated residential areas. Houses and buildings collapsed on top of their occupants. In the southern suburbs of Beirut, in Tyre, Nabatiyeh, and Baalbek, entire areas, sometimes inhabited by tens of thousands of people, were flattened.[19] In the southern suburbs of Beirut, Israeli aircraft attempting to assassinate Hassan Nasrallah dropped at least "22 tons of bombs"[20] on the apartment building housing the General Secretariat, demolishing the entire neighbourhood. Many civilians also fell victim to the war waged against tankers and transport vehicles, their drivers burned alive at the wheel. This systematic destruction of lorries, delivery trucks, vans, and buses quickly created panic in the population, forcing their owners to find covered hiding places for them. These attacks had another effect, all the more devastating for coming on top of the blockade imposed on the country and the unusable roads and highways: large parts of the population soon suffered from hunger, the effect being multiplied by bombing of the country's food infrastructure. On 24 July the Israeli air force destroyed Liban Lait, the principal dairy in the Bekaa, and the Nahas poultry farm, whose still-smouldering remains were looted by families in search of food. On 4 August Israeli bombardments killed thirty-three and injured twelve in a raid on the village of al-Qāʿ, near al-Hermel. All the victims were destitute labourers harvesting vegetables from fields that soon became engulfed in flames. On 10 August Israeli warplanes launched three successive raids against a fish farm in West Bekaa. In South Lebanon, entire families trapped in their villages were reduced to eating rats and leaves fried in oil leftovers.[21]

But the majority of civilian casualties of the Thirty-Three-Day War resulted from bombardments that targeted neither Hezbollah nor its logistics structures. The homes of tens of thousands of Lebanese who had nothing to do with the party came into the cross-hairs along with those of the organization's cadres. Even funerals came under fire. Two tragedies in particular left their mark. One was the "second massacre of Qānā". In April 1996, during Operation Grapes of Wrath, this village in the South came to embody the quintessential martyr village when Israeli warplanes bombed a UNIFIL headquarters there, in which over a hundred people, the majority of them women, children, and the elderly, had sought refuge. Paramedics counted 118 civilian dead and 127 wounded. Ten years later, on the night of 29–30 July, the village once again became a target. About sixty people, mostly women and children, of whom nearly half were physically or mentally disabled, crowded, panic-stricken, into a basement. At around 1 A.M. the building, hit by several Israeli rockets, collapsed on the refugees. Rescuers rushing in at dawn pulled the bodies of fifty-eight people, mostly children,[22] out of the rubble. The second tragedy was the "Marjayoun convoy". This happened on 10 August. Acccording to an initial version, a unit of Israeli soldiers occupied the base at Marjayoun (South), operated since the Liberation by a joint ISF and Lebanese army force.[23] Taken hostage and refusing to accept cohabitation with the Israelis, the Lebanese force demanded to be evacuated. The acting minister of the interior, Ahmad Fatfat (Sunni FC) managed to negotiate an evacuation via French and UN mediation. Abandoning the base to the Israelis the next day, 350 gendarmes and soldiers formed up in a convoy escorted by UN forces, to whom they handed their weapons, as demanded by the Israelis. They were joined by nearly 3,500 civilians also ready to flee the area. With permission from the Israelis and UN, nearly 500 cars followed the army and ISF jeeps. The convoy started out, escorted by two UNIFIL armoured cars. At Kefraya in the Bekaa, halfway between Marjayoun and Zahleh, the convoy suddenly came under attack from Israeli drones. Eight people, including Lebanese soldiers, were killed and forty wounded.

A Resistance underestimated

Katyusha attacks on northern Israel

Incapable, back in 2006, of fielding military aircraft, drones, or anti-aircraft defences, the Islamic Resistance confined itself to ground-to-ground action from South Lebanon. The destructive capacity of its Katyusha rockets was limited to northern Israel within a radius of 75 kilometres from the border, with Safed, Haifa, and environs bearing the brunt. Although Nasrallah once threatened to hit Tel Aviv if Beirut was attacked, the Israeli capital in the end was spared.

Despite a lack of precision and a limited range, the rockets launched by the Resistance were effective. First, they were frequent. Despite intensive and continuous bombardment of southern Lebanon, the Israeli army never managed to diminish the attacks: at the start of the conflict the Resistance fired between 120 and 140 rockets per day on average,[24] but achieved a record 250 by the beginning of the second week of August.[25] This proved that the Israeli strategy of fragmenting Lebanon and its destruction of roads and means of transport did nothing to prevent the flow of weapons to the South. Finally, the IRL barrages led the Israelis (and outside observers) to question the validity of their intelligence: before 12 July the Israeli army had estimated the Resistance's rocket inventory at some 15,000, after a statement by Nasrallah himself that gave the number as 12,000.[26] In any event, on the twenty-sixth day of its offensive Israel was forced to admit that Hezbollah's military ballistic and combat capabilities seemed to have survived intact. The military experts believed that Hezbollah could sustain this level of bombardment for at least two more months using medium-range missiles and its rockets, knowing that it had so far refrained from using its Zelzal I (150 kilometres) and Zelzal II (250 kilometres) long-range rockets, capable of reaching Tel Aviv.[27]

An agile Resistance

Moreover, the IRL's responses and attacks relied on mobility. Its fighters followed a simple but obviously effective rule: the rockets were launched from ramps that were systematically moved after each salvo, transported on trucks when they were not carried on the fighters' own backs. They were also fired from entrances to tunnels of whose existence the Israeli army apparently was not aware and that its planes could not reach.[28] This great flexibility of movement and action proved both a liability and an asset: these random launches degraded their accuracy, so the damage caused by IRL rockets in northern Israel remained well inferior to that caused by the Israeli army in Lebanon. The advantage was that they could not be taken out from the air and could keep up the rate of fire.

An unexpected aggressiveness in ground combat

For most of the conflict, Israel rejected the idea of a ground offensive. The memory of the "Lebanese quagmire" from which the army had extricated itself only six years earlier was still fresh. The prompt destruction by the IRL of an Israeli tank that entered Lebanon following the capture of the two soldiers on 12 July was regularly cited as a deterrent.[29] Rather than embarking on a large-scale ground operation, the Israeli army carried out limited incursions to "remove the threat of firing by Hezbollah into [the] territory [of Israel]".[30] The first tanks to drive into the Alma al-Shaab/Ra's al-Nāqūra sector a few days after the start of the conflict turned back immediately under heavy IRL fire.[31] Other probes around Mārūn al-Rās,[32] ʿAytā al-Shaʿb, and Bint Jbeil, where localized battle fronts had developed,[33] resulted in several pitched battles. The Resistance's ability to block each of the adversary's offensives stunned the Lebanese, as well as the Israeli military staff, government, and public. Not only did the Israeli army fail to get the better of the IRL, it also suffered some painful setbacks, daily losing more than a dozen Merkava tanks—a first in its history—and suffering a veritable trauma in terms of casualties. Very frugal with the lives of its soldiers, it had for years favoured battle tactics that avoided face-to-face fatalities, but now it was sometimes losing up to ten soldiers or officers in action a day. For example, 26 July, two days before the Israeli army abandoned Bint Jbeil, was particularly brutal:

> The battle raged yesterday at Bint Jbeil, in South Lebanon. The Israeli elite force and Hezbollah fighters clashed throughout the day in what was, according to the Israeli army, "the fiercest battle in years". Tel Aviv on Tuesday nevertheless announced it controlled the town, but this was contradicted by yesterday's action, since fighting of exceptional violence continued in the region and even in the town's centre. The elite Israeli troops suffered what could only be termed heavy losses: thirteen or fourteen soldiers dead according to some Arab media and a large number of wounded. ... That prepared the way for the final tally announced in the evening, when the Israeli army acknowledged the death of eight of its elite soldiers in clashes at Bint Jbeil.[34]

On 6 August IRL Katyushas killed twelve soldiers at a military base near Kiryat Shmona in Israel; three days later fifteen Israeli soldiers were killed in Lebanon and thirty-eight wounded, the heaviest losses in a single day by the Israeli army's own admission since the conflict began.[35]

Unable to prevent rockets from being fired into the northern part of the country, and despite its acceptance of Resolution 1701, which, on 11 August, recommended an end to hostilities, the Israeli government tried a final ground operation. In doing so, it exploited the fact that the UN Resolution had set no time frame for the ceasefire. The major ground attack commenced on 12 August. From the day that the Israeli ground forces moved into the South, the Hujayr valley became a "cemetery for Merkavas".[36] Under the dumbfounded gaze of Lebanese following the attacks live on al-Manār, a line of Israeli tanks advancing in single file was stopped in its tracks. Although they had just entered Lebanese territory, tanks exploded one after the other with the regularity of a metronome, causing those at the back to turn in hasty retreat. Easier targets than pilots, the infantry were immediately targeted by the IRL. Since its fighters were masters of a terrain that the enemy no longer knew, they inflicted heavy losses on the opponent while themselves being well protected by systems of tunnels and bunkers. On just the first day of the expanded ground offensive, the Israeli army lost thirty-nine tanks and tracked vehicles and registered twenty-four dead and ninety-six wounded.[37] The results for the IRL were even more astounding, given that the balance of forces was *a priori* against it: 40,000 Israeli soldiers mobilized for the offensive[38] against an estimated 2,500[39] to 5,000[40] IRL fighters, of whom only a portion were fighting in the South.[41] The psychological and symbolic impact of this was striking on both sides of the border.[42]

The psychological warfare tool

Both sides resorted to psychological warfare techniques. Just as during the occupation, for the IRL it was a matter of working on the nerves of Israeli soldiers and officers. Aware that Tel Aviv was seeking to deprive it of the ability to hit Galilee by destroying its rocket launchers, the IRL time and again followed a bombardment of one of its presumed firing positions with a launch from the same site, telling the enemy that his barrage had failed. For example, on 26 July,

> the Israeli planes hammered Hezbollah positions at Rashaya from which some thirty rockets were immediately fired toward northern Israel. ... Israeli fighter bombers carried out a dozen raids in quick succession against three Hezbollah positions in the Arqub. Within three minutes of the last strikes, a salvo of thirty rockets was launched from one of these Arqub positions toward Israel.[43]

Beyond being a thumb in the eye of the Israeli air force, these tactics were also intended as morale boosters for the Lebanese. On this level, Nasrallah's speeches played a key role. Regularly delivered, in a calm, confident tone, they would take stock of the day's operations, foreshadow future attacks, promise victory, and try to strengthen the population's spirit of *sumūd* (perseverance, patience). The press published a message of support by Resistance fighters addressed to the secretary-general of Hezbollah and the Lebanese, side by side with Nasrallah's response. After the war this correspondence was included in the anthology of the party discourse, and the famous Lebanese Christian singer Julia Boutros turned it into verse and song. Nasrallah himself was tempted into dramatizing the situation. In his speech of 14 July, delivered live, he announced at one point:

> Now, in the open sea off Beirut, an Israeli warship that has been bombarding our infrastructure, shelled people's houses and civilians, look, it is on fire, and it will sink with its Zionist crew of dozens on board. And this is only the beginning.

As he spoke these words, an Israeli warship stationed in Lebanese waters appeared on the screen, and the mesmerized television viewers could see a live rocket launched from Lebanese territory score a direct hit. In the ensuing minutes, news flash after news flash on all TV and radio channels announced that an Israeli patrol vessel had just been hit by an IRL rocket and that the Israeli forces on high alert were scrambling to save the crew.

For its part, the Israeli army also deployed a series of initiatives to destabilize the enemy psychologically. Its target was not so much Hezbollah as the Lebanese public, which it tried to mobilize against the Resistance to stage an armed uprising, after which the party presumably would be rendered harmless. Massive leaflet drops on several Shiite locales contained a series of appeals designed to distance them from Hezbollah. The party and, more specifically, Nasrallah—caricatured in some leaflets as a snake swallowing Lebanon—were described as responsible for the Israeli attack and intent on destroying the country.[44] In addition, the Israeli army hacked Lebanese telephone landlines and wireless networks: automated messages recorded on discs threatened attacks and bombardments of telephone users' towns and villages. Someone answering the telephone would hear a voice with a strong Israeli accent asking, "Are you Christian or Muslim?"; if the answer was "Christian", the machine would hang up, but if "Muslim", the recorded threats would start. Mobile phones were also flooded with text messages containing threats or crowing about victories, especially after commando operations.[45]

There were also radio messages addressed by the "state of Israel to Lebanese citizens". From the second week of the conflict, indeed, the frequency of the Voice of the People (Sawt al-Sha'b), the Lebanese Communist Party's radio station, was hacked daily and messages broadcast that left no doubt that the strikes against civilians were intentional.

Israeli army radio messages, summer 2006

To the citizens of Lebanon,

Hezbollah's terrorist activities against the territories of the state of Israel are responsible for the situation you find yourself in at this time. Be aware that the state of Israel will continue to act with force and determination to put an end to terrorist actions launched against it from Lebanese territory. Remember that Israel has the means to deal painful blows to Lebanese terrorist elements, as it has shown these past days.

Where did Hassan Nasrallah disappear to? He ran away to his cave, just as those of his ilk, the terrorists, who took to their heels from [the battlefield] the moment [that they heard] the first shot fired.

[Signed:] The State of Israel

Message broadcast for the first time 21 July 2006.

To the citizens of Lebanon,

The Israeli army struck with courage and strength at Baalbek, the operations centre of the terrorist Hezbollah gang (*ʿiṣābat Ḥizballāh al-irhābiyya*), as part of defending the citizens of the state of Israel and recovering abducted soldiers of the Israeli Defence Army (*Jaysh al-difāʿ al-isrāʾīlī*).

Be aware that the Israeli Defence Army will continue to send [***46] to all locations where Hezbollah terrorists are found, striking with force and determination to destroy their ability to implement their criminal gang ideology against the citizens of the state of Israel.

Citizens of Lebanon, the forces of the Israeli Defence Army do not act against the Lebanese people but against the Hezbollah terrorist elements and will continue to do so for as long it is deemed necessary. Do not allow the Hezbollah gang to take you hostage and use you as a human shield on behalf of foreign interests.

[Signed:] The State of Israel

Message broadcast for the first time 2 August 2006.

Come on, Hassan, come if you are brave and face the facts!

Come on, if you're a leader, shout, and face democracy!

Come on, if you're a man, submit to the laws of humanity!

Come if you are a son of Adam, elevate your spirit with the conscience of humanity!

Come on, come out of your lair; surrender, your end is near!

The day the Lebanese put their festive clothes on for the passage through Masnaʿ,[47] get up Hassan, pack your bags and head for the passage! For you, all Lebanese will eagerly fill in all the holes that will have been made in the Beirut–Damascus highway![48] They'll be happy to see you on your way and will raise the flags of freedom, light and progress!

Get out of here, get out to far away places! There, hackneyed ideas don't go out of style, for they are always fighting the last war!

You're an expert, clear-sighted and subtle, you know perfectly the secrets of the opposition, and there is no doubt that you will find new places to devastate, in your capacity as emissary and servant of your masters who spare no effort to try to create chaos in the Country of Cedars! Go, Hassan, go join the Syrians, look for new enemies, and dig up old causes for generating disagreements, conflicts and hatred! Go join the Iranians, support them, come to their assistance, and together, close your doors on the new world!

Release the Lebanese people and government from your stifling, deadly grip! Crawl away from this country, you disgusting viper! Silence your lips, pull in your fangs, stop doing whatever pleases you! Pass through the passage at Masnaʿ and never return to the mountains of Lebanon!

Message broadcast for the first time 26 July 2006.

Citizens of Lebanon,

Summer, 2006. Calm prevails in Lebanon, the economy prospers, foreign investment and growth rates are high. Restaurants and cafés are full, it is high season for tourism, festivals, foreign exhibitions, and crowded beaches—and suddenly, the dream goes up in smoke.

Blood, fire, columns of smoke, courtesy of the party leader who has usurped the right to control your destiny and your future. ... In fact, Hassan is a docile instrument of the Syro-Iranian plot for exploiting Lebanon. He is ready to demolish Lebanon and sell it cheap to his masters.

Why do you keep sending Lebanon's sons to their death, Hassan? Why do you continue to lie to them, to hide their coffins and the tears of mothers for a meaningless death? Why do you change your stories and entangle yourself in obvious and simplistic lies? Enough already of acting like the hack political analyst, crawling from your cave into the cellars of al-Manār to try and sell crap discourse to the public. We say to you: Come out and join your people, stand before the court of the Lebanese people! But you're not a leader, you're the boss of a gang of thieves and rapists of the Land of Cedars.

He sits alone in the darkness of his hideaway bereft of the support of his people, isolated in the Arab world, and shunned on the international scene. Even Arafat, in 1982, enjoyed broader Arab support. [Lebanese], is this the leadership you want? Should a drug lord decide your fate?

Message broadcast for the first time 29 July 2006.

To the members of Hezbollah,

Do you really believe that the battlefields are like what you are shown in the propaganda films of the al-Manār channel? Are you really able to run to the top of a hill in the blink of an eye? Did you believe your leaders when they said that those confronting you were no more than a cobweb that would tear before your eyes?

They lied to you all these years and lie to you still today. You know very well that you are sent like sheep to the slaughter when you are lacking military equipment, ammunition and training. You know very well that the [***] of your leaders are not up to dealing firmly with fully trained soldiers who defend their country, their people and their homes. You are only mercenaries, and the Lebanese people do not support you. Run far away, as far as possible, and save your lives. Hassan and his gang have promised you surprises. In fact, they themselves have admitted that the state of Israel surprised them with its power and ability to resist.

We will let you in on a secret, Hassan. We have prepared some painful strikes for you. The iron fist of the Israeli Defence Army strikes hard and nobody can imagine what surprises it holds in store. The long arm of the state of Israel is strong and has shocking power, and it can hit you where you least expect it.

O, protectors of Lebanon, who are these people who launch rockets from inside your homes against your will and put your life at risk? Who are these people who scurry to hide in your houses like mice? Who are these people, citizens of Lebanon, who use you as human shields? The answer is clear to everyone. The gang will eventually fall now that the rats have fled. It is far from an honour to stay in its ranks.

Members of the Hassan gang, do not hide behind the Lebanese people. Enough of subjecting the sons of your people to danger and slaughter. We will pursue you and find you in every basement, every cave, every house of innocent citizens where you take refuge. We will come to the weapons caches that every hour of every day threaten those who have nothing to do with this war. Release the sons of your people, let go of this human shield.

Message first broadcast 21 July 2006.

> Citizens of Lebanon,
>
> Do not let Hassan trick you. What can the Resistance really achieve? It can only undo Lebanon, destroy your aspirations for sovereignty and a free Lebanon, trample your future, and devastate your economy. Decide your future yourselves; do not allow Hassan to destroy Lebanon.
>
> Hassan says: It is perfectly legal and my right to take refuge in the homes of innocent citizens, far from the violence of Israel's fist of steel. It is perfectly legal and my right to store hazardous explosives in the basements of houses in villages and hamlets and put people's lives at risk. It is perfectly legal and my right to send elements from my gang to fire rockets from the houses and streets of villages and hamlets. It is entirely my right to expose you, citizens of Lebanon, to danger, when I myself hide in a safe place.
>
> Message first broadcast on 7 August 2006.

Israeli objectives ratcheted down one by one

When it launched Operation Change of Direction, although the Israeli cabinet announced its intention to push Hezbollah as far from the northern border as possible and recover the two captured soldiers, it admitted seeking first of all to pressure the Beirut government into disarming the IRL.[49] On 14 July Ehud Olmert said that he was willing to suspend the Israeli action on three conditions: Hezbollah must release the two soldiers; it must stop firing rockets; and the Lebanese government must commit to implement UNSC Resolution 1559.[50] For some members of the Israeli ruling elite it was also a matter of correcting the negative image the retreat from Lebanon in 2000 had created for its army, with damage to its reputation as an "invincible" fighting force. What was at stake was thus also symbolic and psychological in nature, with the army having to "back up Israel's deterrent power in the region, its security resting on deterrence".[51]

At first, Tel Aviv appeared sure of victory. Recourse to diplomatic channels and negotiations with Hezbollah were totally out of the question. During the second week Israel's ambassador to the United States had this to say:

> We have delivered a severe blow to Hezbollah, with hundreds of Hezbollah terrorists killed. ... A large part of its arsenal no longer exists, mainly the long-range weapons. Israel has made progress and in a few days you will see a completely different situation.[52]

Yet, at the same time, some Israeli officials for the first time raised doubt about the army's ability to recover its abducted soldiers or destroy Hezbollah by force. On 23 July Eytan Cabel, minister and secretary-general of the Labour Party, took note of the unsatisfactory results in the field and admitted that it was "unrealistic" to try to "completely eliminate Hezbollah as a military force in Lebanon".[53] The minister of justice, Haim Ramon, also did an about-face: rather than breaking the adversary, he pinned his hopes on "a situation where there will no longer be an armed Hezbollah member within 20 kilometres of our border".[54]

At the end of the second week Israel also had to deal with the first international calls for a ceasefire. Pushing the IRL back from the border seemed increasingly chimerical, and the idea of an interposition force in southern Lebanon gained ground. On 23 July Ehud Olmert informed Western diplomats that his government supported the deployment in Lebanon of an international military force, *a priori* sourced from NATO, with the task of controlling the Syro-Lebanese borders and disarming the IRL.[55] Shimon Peres, the deputy prime minister, however, said: "But I want a serious mission, not like UNIFIL, the UN observers who do not disarm terrorists."[56] Similarly, while the government insisted officially on the unconditional liberation of the two soldiers through the offensive, behind the scenes it began to accept the idea of a prisoner swap with Hezbollah.[57] At the end of the month, Olmert acknowledged that Israel was heading for "difficult days". He declared a desire for a safe zone "of one to two kilometres in [southern Lebanon], instead of the twenty to thirty of just a few days earlier",[58] without in any way occupying Lebanon again; the goal would be simply to keep Hezbollah from "reinfiltrating Israel". On 10 August, faced with the military's failure to prevent rocket launches and the party's refusal to release prisoners except under a formal exchange, the Israeli authorities finally saw no other way but a settlement through diplomatic channels. They approached the UN to obtain (i) the immediate and unconditional return of the abducted soldiers; (ii) immediate cessation of all hostilities from Lebanon against Israel and Israeli targets; (iii) full implementation of Resolution 1559; (iv) deployment in southern Lebanon of an effective international force together with the Lebanese army along the Blue Line; and (v) for Hezbollah to be prevented from replenishing its operational capabilities, mainly by halting the shipment of arms and military equipment from Syria and Iran into Lebanon.[59]

Resolution 1701 was passed on 11 August. Tzipi Livni, the minister of foreign affairs, declared:

> From the beginning of the war, we realized that all the goals we set would not be attained, but this Resolution addresses most of the goals we set for ourselves.

She added:

> We want effective forces. We want either NATO forces or other forces *capable of fighting*. We asked that this not be a part of UNIFIL. [Going forward], it will not come to a UNIFIL that we know as weak observers, but a strengthened UNIFIL, with a broader mandate that gives it *the possibility and the duty to exercise force*.[60]

In other words, by the Israelis' own admission, Tel Aviv henceforth would count on the international community to take over where the offensive had failed, that is, not only to disarm Hezbollah but also to dismantle it.[61]

To show or not to show solidarity

The Lebanese government and March 14 confront the war

With the announcement of the Israeli soldiers' capture and an attack on Lebanon imminent, the first reaction of the Fouad Siniora cabinet was to dissociate itself from Hezbollah: "The Lebanese government was not aware of the operation, it is not responsible for and has nothing to do with it."[62] In the same vein, the prime minister reminded the party that the government alone would decide when it comes to peace or war.[63] Condemning the Israeli offensive, which he called "immoral collective punishment", he called for an urgent meeting of the Security Council and expressed willingness to cooperate with the United Nations and friendly countries. On 24 July he unveiled a proposed solution, which he presented, even before getting his government's endorsement, to an international conference convening in Rome two days later under EU auspices. Bringing together the representatives of some fifteen countries and three international organizations, it was a systematic effort to find a solution to the crisis. Siniora proposed an immediate ceasefire and presented a draft plan containing seven points, of which sending the Lebanese army to the South was one of the most important.[64] The next day, upon Siniora's return from Rome, March 14 succeeded in pressuring Hezbollah so that his proposal was accepted unanimously by the government.

This first agreement between the country's two great political tendencies was followed by a second rapprochement on the 30th, on the occasion of the Qānā massacre. Symbolic national mourning was proclaimed, the prime minister changed his tone and dug in. The decision was made to pursue Israel for war crimes, and, after a visit to Lebanon by the American secretary of state, Condoleezza Rice, on 24 July, she was asked to cancel a second visit planned for a few days later. The government, and particularly the prime minister, however, were (almost) alone in softening their stance towards Hezbollah. The leaders of March 14 remained united in their stand against the party. Hezbollah's argument that the IRL had launched Operation Truthful Pledge to free the last remaining Lebanese prisoners from Israeli jails was not considered convincing. For most of them, all that the IRL's initiative did was simply respond to a Syrian and/or Iranian directive.[65]

France tries to stand out

It was an interpretation widely shared by Western governments. When the conflict broke out on 12 July the international community unanimously criticized the IRL initiative and repeated the need to disarm the "militias in Lebanon". Syrian and/or Iranian responsibility for triggering the crisis was taken for granted. In the ensuing week, President Jacques Chirac stated that Hezbollah did not make this decision on its own;[66] George W. Bush accused Syria of trying, through these events, to "return to Lebanon".[67] The same day Tony Blair attacked the Syrian and Iranian regimes.[68] Differences emerged, however, concerning the Israeli response: the offensive was considered legitimate by Washington, Berlin, and London, and disproportionately so by Paris. These differentiated analyses were reflected in the Security Council when, on 12 July, Kofi Annan put both adversaries in their place, demanding the immediate and unconditional release of the two abducted soldiers and calling on Israel to show restraint. However, two days later the UNSC failed to agree on how the Israeli attack ought to be categorized, and ended its meeting without demanding a ceasefire. The result was that the diplomatic option was blocked for several weeks, during which France insisted that discussions be held within the UN framework and a ceasefire be agreed as soon as possible. Meanwhile, the United States, supported by the UK, tried to buy time for Israel to complete its mission, rejecting any initiative that would impede its action in Lebanon. Throughout the conflict Washington even continued to provide fuel for the Israeli Air Force, and replenished its cruise missile arsenal.[69]

During the second week, however, a disagreement emerged inside the American government: while George W. Bush wanted to let Tel Aviv have a free hand, Condoleezza Rice, noting the progressively difficult position in which the Israeli army seemed to have become mired in, came around to the idea of obtaining a ceasefire as soon as possible. She therefore made a lightning visit to Beirut on the 24th, but returned home without making any progress. On the 26th, the Rome international conference logged another failure after an American manoeuvre favouring Israel. The Israeli government interpreted this as an international blank cheque for its offensive.[70]

A few days later, France, blocked by the United States up to that point, floated a new diplomatic initiative that took advantage of the shock of the Qānā tragedy. Paris rejected the US–British proposal for sending a strengthened multinational force to South Lebanon before obtaining a ceasefire, and, on 30 July, circulated a draft UN Resolution calling for an immediate cessation of hostilities. Despite the differences within the American government, opposition to the French proposal was united on this issue. President Bush still refused to call for an immediate ceasefire, saying that "this crisis began with the unprovoked terrorist attacks against Israel by Hezbollah" and that Israel has "the right to defend itself".[71] Condoleezza Rice spoke of the need for a ceasefire "as soon as possible", but then qualified it as not having to be "immediate"[72] upon receiving a formal request by Israel to give its army another ten days to two weeks.[73] A joint French–US text was finally discussed in the UNSC beginning on 5 August. While Tel Aviv declared itself satisfied,[74] Beirut believed that the text ignored Lebanese demands listed in its seven-point plan, and so it demanded: (i) the addition of the issue of Lebanese prisoners in Israel; (ii) a reference to an immediate withdrawal of Israeli forces from occupied areas on Lebanese territory;[75] (iii) the addition of a demand for immediate Israeli withdrawal from the Shebaa Farms;[76] and (iv) the striking of any reference to Chapter VII in the paragraph dealing with the presence of international forces in South Lebanon.[77] To strengthen the hand of the Arab delegation representing Lebanon at the UN during the discussions, the Council of Ministers, meeting at the same time, again twisted Hezbollah's arm to arrive at a unanimous decision to send 15,000 army troops to South Lebanon.[78] This signalled the return of regular forces to a region from which they had been absent since the late 1960s. The decision made a positive impression on the UN secretary-general, and also on the French, American, and even Israeli representatives. On 11 August Resolution 1701 was passed; the next day the Israeli and Lebanese governments accepted it. However, since it omitted a date for the cessation of hostilities, the conflict did not officially end until the morning of 14 August.[79]

The toll exacted by the war

An initial assessment established the number of casualties on the Israeli side at 119 soldiers and some 40 civilians killed, plus 300,000–500,000 people displaced[80] (4–6.5 per cent of the population).[81] The losses on the Lebanese side were much heavier: 1,191 civilians killed, 4,054 wounded,[82] and over 900,000 people displaced (more than a quarter of the Lebanese population).[83] According to the Israeli army, Hezbollah lost 530 fighters.[84] As for the party, it initially estimated the number of Resistance members killed in combat at "just over a hundred *shahīds* (martyrs)",[85] later revised to 250.[86] An initial estimate also established material damages of $5.7 billion for Israel[87] and between $6 billion[88] and $12 billion[89] for Lebanon, but for the latter these amounts were soon revised upward.

On the Israeli side...

For the Israeli government the offensive was a mixed bag. Despite the intensity of thirty-three days and nights of uninterrupted bombing, and ongoing efforts to locate and destroy the enemy's rocket launchers, the army never succeeded in reducing the frequency of Katyushas fired into northern Israel. The war caused the death of 1,200 civilians in Lebanon, but not a single high-ranking Hezbollah cadre figure among them. Contrary to claims by the Israeli General Staff (especially after dropping 22 tons of bombs on the Secretariat General) no Hezbollah leader was missing from the line-up the day after hostilities ended. The press repeatedly mocked the number of kills in the ranks of IRL fighters. For example, an article in *Maariv* in late December, picked up by *Haaretz* three days later, reported comments by retired general Danny Reshef that each IRL fighter killed cost the Israeli national budget 12.5 million shekels ($3 million);[90] other calculations subsequently raised that figure to $10 million.[91]

In addition to a performance critiqued as lacklustre, the number of Israeli soldiers killed in combat provoked a real malaise in an army that up to then could boast of having only suffered minor losses over several decades of confrontations with Arab enemies. The figure of 120 soldiers killed could be considered honourable for a month-long war waged in the field with 40,000 men, but it was a heavy psychological and symbolic burden for an army traditionally very solicitious of its soldiers' lives.

Eventually the Israeli government's hopes for Resolution 1701, and particularly the strengthened UNIFIL, came up against a reality that was much more limited than expected. As previously mentioned, when during the first week of August 2006 the Israeli cabinet resigned itself to making use of diplomatic channels, it did not abandon its primary objective. Foreign Affairs Minister Tzipi Livni formulated it very clearly: Israel was counting on the international community not only to disarm Hezbollah, but to dismantle it.[92] Resolution 1701, passed on 11 August, should in theory have met these expectations, by providing an enhanced UNIFIL presence in South Lebanon. However, questions about its mission and prerogatives posed problems from the start. The Resolution provided for the exclusion of any sales or supply of arms and related materiel to Lebanon, apart from those authorized by the Lebanese government, but it failed to specify the means or the practical methods available to UNIFIL for accomplishing this mission. Similarly, the question of whether the Interim Force itself should disarm the IRL or whether it was an internal Lebanese affair was left unsettled. The countries willing to contribute the core of this revamped force, notably France, Italy, and Germany,[93] conditioned their participation on obtaining firm, explicit guarantees from Hezbollah and Iran regarding the security of their forces in the field. The October 1983 assaults were still fresh in their memory.[94] To speed up the guarantees, France also made an additional gesture for Hezbollah's benefit. With the American government on two occasions having threatened the Lebanese authorities with a new Resolution or a joint intervention if they did not succeed in disarming the party,[95] the Quai d'Orsay declared that a "second Resolution on Lebanon is unnecessary", and did this on the day that the Israeli minister of foreign affairs was in Paris on an official visit.[96] Hezbollah acknowledged the French attitude to be cooperative, and the next day at the UN provided the security guarantees covering the French UNIFIL troops. Hassan Nasrallah confirmed: "There will be no problem with UNIFIL in so far as its mission is not to disarm the Resistance."[97] The rules of the game were now set. Not only could UNIFIL not interfere with the IRL's existence in any way, but it was entrenched as a Western presence that Hezbollah—or the Syrian and/or Iran regimes—could thereafter put pressure on. The fact is that, in the ensuing years, without themselves directly acting against UNIFIL, they turned a blind eye to operations instigated against it by other groups.[98]

... and on the Lebanese side

On the other side of the border, Israeli bombardments had done much more damage. Entire parts of Lebanon were flattened. The average daily IRL rockets launched on Galilee, estimated at between 150 and 250, need to be compared with, for example, 2,000 shells fired in a single day by Israel just on the village of ʿAytarūn.[99] The Israeli army fired a total of 40,000 to 100,000 shells, launched 2,000 missiles, and flew 15,000 air sorties.[100] The IRL, limited to ground operations, fired just under 4,000 rockets[101] into a zone less than 100 kilometres deep.[102] The economic and social consequences for Lebanon were heavy, and not likely to be remedied quickly. The war had destroyed much of the fifteen-year reconstruction effort that had followed the end of the civil war. The national debt, then estimated at over $40 billion, underlined the Lebanese government's inability to tackle the challenge of rebuilding imposed on it by the Israeli army. This did not include the massive and urgent task of mine clearing in the South. On the morning of 14 August 2006, more than a million cluster munitions that the Israeli army had scattered over residential areas and entire villages were lying ready to explode.[103]

Report prepared by the UNDP on the Thirty-Three-Day War in Lebanon

- Over 1,200 dead; one-third children under twelve years of age.
- More than 4,400 injured; 15% suffered permanent disabilities.
- Over 200,000 people lost their homes.
- The unemployment rate doubled to 20%.
- Over 100,000 people, mostly highly skilled, left Lebanon permanently.
- 612 public schools, 80 private schools, 16 hospitals, and 65 clinics were damaged.
- 97 bridges and 151 roads were destroyed and three runways and reservoirs at Beirut airport were damaged.
- 15 million tons of fuel oil were spilled into the Mediterranean sea.
- The country must clean up more than 2.5 million cubic metres of debris.
- Losses in the agricultural sector amounted to $280 million.
- 850 companies and factories were hit by bombardments.
- The tourism sector lost more than $1 billion.
- Losses in the transport sector amounted to $120 million, in the electric power sector to $160 million, and in telecommunications to $135 million.

L'Orient–Le Jour, 17 January 2007.

With the conflict over, a time of reckoning between the Lebanese government and Hezbollah had arrived. The war's aftermath opened a new phase in Lebanese socio-political life, in which grudges, polarization, and obstacles would have their share, only to culminate in the bloody events of May 2008.

9

ESCALATION, COLLAPSE, AND TEMPORARY STATUS QUO

AUGUST 2006—JANUARY 2011

On 22 September, a month and a week after the war ended, Hezbollah with great fanfare celebrated *al-Nasr al-ilāhī* (the Divine Victory).[1] In the heart of Beirut's southern suburbs, on an expanse of ground flattened by the Israeli army and cleared by Jihād al-Binā' services, a million people of all confessions from throughout Lebanon responded to Nasrallah's invitation to celebrate the failure of the Israeli offensive.

However, even with the armed confrontation suspended, the war continued apace, only by other means. In the months and years that followed the Thirty-Three-Day War, the Israeli factor continued to impact Lebanese politics and Hezbollah's mobilization in two ways. A number of news accounts emerging from Israel soon "confirmed" that Tel Aviv had in effect lost the war—hence, that the IRL had won it.[2] This reinforced the satisfaction and admiration of the party's base for the Resistance and pride in supporting it.[3] For all that, the Israeli government's menacing statements and moves against its northern neighbour would keep Lebanon in a state of anxiety about a possible new war. This to some extent helped supporters close ranks around an IRL that, more than ever, was perceived as the only armed force capable of defending the country and its people.

The end of hostilities with Israel ... war goes on

Reverberations from Israeli news

Barely two days after the war ended, the Israeli press revealed that Dan Halutz, chief of the Israeli General Staff, had sold his stocks at noon on 12 July on the day the war started, just three hours after the two soldiers were abducted and a few hours before actual hostilities broke out—and before the Tel Aviv stock market crashed. The ensuing large-scale political scandal[4] evoked general hilarity in Lebanon for weeks, and when

Halutz resigned in mid-January 2007, the Lebanese opposition, gathered in Riyad al-Solh Square in Beirut, celebrated the event with a great fireworks display.[5]

Surveys conducted in Israel of public dissatisfaction with the army and government's performance during the war were one more aspect of the news transmitted from south of the border. On 16 August an initial tally reported that only 3 per cent of Israelis surveyed believed that the operation helped their country achieve most of its objectives, against 33 per cent in a poll conducted eleven days earlier; 58 per cent believed that the objectives were only partially achieved, against 16 per cent in a prior poll.[6] The next day another survey suggested that 84 per cent of Israelis were unhappy with their government.[7] As winter ended, the opinion polls did not become kinder: a scant 2 per cent of Israelis at the time expressed satisfaction with Ehud Olmert.[8]

But of all post-war news out of Israel, it was certainly the evolving work of the Winograd Commission that was of most interest to the Lebanese. Of particular interest were its revelations about what had been behind the war preparations, and what these implied for the Lebanese political scene. The decision to create the Commission was made on the day that hostilities ceased. Chaired by Judge Eliyahu Winograd, its brief was to investigate the Israeli "failures" in the July War. Its final conclusions were presented to the public in January 2008. An early scandal had already erupted during the conflict when media and diplomatic sources suggested that some among the Lebanese political class supported the Israeli action, and had urged Tel Aviv to "not stop the offensive until you have finished Hezbollah".[9] The Commission's interim report confirmed that individual March 14 leaders had collaborated during the war. Cognizant of the negative impact that such a revelation would have for Hezbollah's Lebanese adversaries, the Commission chose not to name the implicated individuals in the final report.[10] In Lebanon, speculation was rife as to their identities. Going by their radical positioning and previous behaviour, Jumblatt, Hamadeh, Fatfat, and Geagea stood out among the suspects, the PSP leader in particular because in late August 2006 he had had to explain his contact in France with an Israeli MP.[11] The Winograd report had yet another, highly telling, consequence for the Lebanese domestic debate. Accused of negligence in waging war without a prior plan, the Israeli prime minister was forced in early March 2007 to confess that the plans for the Lebanese war had been drawn up four months before the conflict.[12] Olmert's admission was a bombshell in circles close to Hezbollah, who needed to hear no more to realize that the Israeli prime minister had just swept away the accusations levelled at the party as responsible for the tragedy in the summer of 2006.

Israel's other wars

While some news out of Tel Aviv gave Hezbollah and its public cause to congratulate themselves and feel vindicated in their political and strategic choices, others had a more dangerous effect, keeping tensions high between the protagonists of the Thirty-

Three-Day War. The twenty-two-day Israeli offensive against the Gaza Strip between late December 2008 and mid-January 2009, which left 1,300 Palestinians dead, revived memories of the 2006 war among the Lebanese.[13] But even more than the events that shook the Palestinian territories, Israel's actions on Lebanese soil gave the Lebanese reason to fear a war of revenge.

Repeated violations of Lebanese sovereignty

The first violation of Resolution 1701 occurred on the night of 18 August, four days after the ceasefire. That evening, an Israeli commando unit consisting of an officer and two soldiers was dropped by helicopter near the village of Būdāy in the western outskirts of Baalbek. Wearing uniforms and driving vehicles made to resemble those of the Lebanese army, the group is supposed to have started patrolling the village in the vicinity of the school belonging to Sheikh Muhammad Yazbek, a member of the Hezbollah Shūrā. It did not take the IRL security service long to grasp the real identity of the group[14] and go on the attack. The officer was killed and both soldiers wounded, one seriously.[15] The next day the Israeli government justified the action by claiming that it was "to prevent the flow of weapons to Hezbollah and in Israel's view it is not a violation of Resolution 1701".[16] The party, for its part, recalling how the Israeli patrol very precisely penetrated into the heart of Būdāy and lingered around Yazbek's school, argued that the purpose of the action was either to kidnap or murder the dignitary. The UN took note but did not react.

In Lebanon the incident provoked outrage, all the more so because Israel's air and sea blockade of the country that had begun with the war had still not been lifted. Beirut tried all manner of diplomatic leverage to end it, but Tel Aviv turned a deaf ear. As the conflict wound down, the Israeli government conditioned lifting the blockade on deployment of a multinational force on the Lebanese–Syrian frontier and at Beirut's airport. France and the UN were opposed, but Israel had American support.[17] In the same vein, until the end of September, all civilian flights originating in Lebanon were diverted to Jordan, where Israeli intelligence were given permission to search baggage and check the identities of all Lebanese passengers before allowing a plane to take off for its original destination. The Lebanese government filed a complaint in the UNSC, but to no avail. The naval blockade was eventually lifted on 9 September, thanks to Qatar Airways, which, ignoring Israeli warnings, had challenged the ban a few days earlier by landing in Beirut and reinaugurating air traffic.

A second battle that Lebanon had to wage against Israel regarded the reoccupation of part of its territory. The Israeli army did not withdraw all units on 14 August. Lebanese lobbying of Western governments and the UN to get the last Israeli soldiers out turned into a veritable soap opera, punctuated by Israeli promises, constantly renewed, for a withdrawal that was constantly postponed. The redeployment finally took place in early October, but remained incomplete, since the Israeli troops continued to occupy part of the border village of Ghajar[18] (South)—still under Israeli authority in the summer of 2015.

Finally, claiming continued arms traffic by Hezbollah, the Israeli air force continues to fly almost daily sorties over Lebanese territory.[19] This has overlapped with many initiatives interpreted in Lebanon as pure harassment: mock sorties over some localities, cracking the sound barrier, harassing shots, the sending of toxic balloons, threats against the movements of the commander of the Lebanese army, tapping phone lines, serious and persistent speculation about a new war against Lebanon, and the detention of Lebanese civilians at the border. Beirut lodged several formal complaints with the United Nations and friendly Western governments—to no avail.

The assassination of Imad Mughniyeh

On Tuesday, 12 February 2008, about 11 p.m. (local time), a car exploded in the Kfar Susseh neighbourhood of the Syrian capital; its only passenger was killed instantly. He was none other than Imad Mughniyeh, wanted since the 1980s by Israel and the United States. He had been living shrouded in secrecy, and wildly contradictory versions had circulated of what he was doing and places where he was sighted. Hezbollah was content at first to describe him as a top party cadre; a few days after the murder, however, it revealed that he was one of the IRL's ground operations coordinators. Mughniyeh, who had reportedly planned some of the battlefield manoeuvres that would lead to the Liberation of 2000 and who had been the brains behind IRL operations during the 2006 war, was given the formal title of *Qā'id al-intisārayn* (Commander of the Two Victories). The party leadership immediately accused the Mossad, which denied responsibillity but did not hide its satisfaction. The assassination increased tension between Hezbollah and Israel; the latter, fearing retaliatory action, strengthened its security measures. As a corollary, Lebanon settled a little deeper into worry about an impending escalation, if not a new war.

Threats and psychological warfare

This fear grew substantially from the summer of 2008, when the Israeli government openly and insistently threatened its northern neighbour. Defence Minister Ehud Barak reiterated *ad nauseam* that 1701 was not being complied with, that it had "failed".[20] UNIFIL was strongly criticized, and the Lebanese government was accused of having "yielded to Hezbollah's exigencies".[21] The warnings came one after the other, and they were explicit: when the next attack comes, "the Lebanese government itself [will] not be spared".[22] In July, the threats came with increasing frequency and stridency. The following month, the Israeli intelligence services asserted that Hezbollah was seeking to equip itself with ground-to-air missiles[23] so that the IRL would be capable of shooting at the Israeli air force in case of attack. The strident tone went up another notch when Olmert threatened to put all of Lebanon to fire and the sword.[24]

Apocalyptic attack scenarios filtered through to the press.[25] These threats were serious, to the point where, in February 2009, Michael Williams, the UN secretary-general's emissary, presented Beirut with a formal warning from Tel Aviv.[26]

These threats did not target Hezbollah and the Lebanese government alone. Resorting to procedures used during the 2006 war, the Israeli army conducted a veritable psychological war against the Lebanese population by repeatedly hacking into the telecommunication networks. In mid-July 2008, it left voicemail messages on the landline and mobile phones of thousands of subscribers in Beirut, in the Bekaa and the South: "Here is the State of Israel. We will hit back firmly against any aggression by Hezbollah. The Lebanese people and the government must stop supporting terrorism."[27] For several weeks in the autumn the entire telephone system in southern Lebanon was jammed, and the lines in the rest of the country were hacked again for more than a month: hiding its calls behind a British number, the Israeli army offered $10 million for any useful information on Hezbollah.[28] In November faxes were sent to post offices in many Southern cities, again promising the sum of $10 million for information on Israeli soldiers still missing from the 2006 war.[29] Finally, in January 2009, during the Israeli offensive against Gaza and rocket attacks on Israel from the South—responsibility for which Hezbollah strongly denied[30]—the Israeli calls started again: "Tell your friends in Hezbollah to stop attacking us or you will regret it."[31]

Spy networks

This harassment of the Lebanese population by Israel reached a new level in the autumn of 2008, and especially in the spring of 2009 with the discovery of a significant number of spy cells working for Tel Aviv. In early November 2008 two individuals suspected of having gathered information on "a party office" (the party remains unnamed) and of having "monitored the movement of party members on behalf of the enemy"[32] were arrested. In February 2009, Marwan Faqih, a car dealer and the owner of a petrol station from a village near Nabatiyeh, was the next to be arrested for spying for Israel. Exploiting the confidence of several Hezbollah members and cadres, he would plant tracking devices in cars he sold to them, giving the Mossad the capability of tracing their itineraries.[33]

In mid-April 2009 it turned into a free-for-all. It began with the arrest of Adib Allam, a retired ISF general from the village of Rmeish (South), and of his wife and nephew.[34] The former officer was suspected of passing information on Hezbollah and the Lebanese security forces to Israel. It soon became clear that dismantling the networks of Israeli agents had barely begun. In the course of their confession to the police, the Allams surrendered parts of their address book,[35] leading to the uncovering of dozens of cells throughout May.

The profile of some people put under arrest created a serious malaise. The status of Allam as a former high-ranking ISF officer was already a source of consternation.

Equally embarrassing, however, was the case of Ziad Homsi, former president of the city council of Saadnayel (Central Bekaa)[36] and deputy mayor at the time. Homsi belonged to the Future Current (FC) and was also a veteran of the resistance against Israel. The discovery of his defection thus caused embarrassment in Sunni circles, illustrating the extremes to which the change in environment, which now fostered animosity between Sunnis and Shiites in the context of the FC–Hezbollah rivalry, could lead.[37]

By mid-May more than thirty networks had been broken up.[38] Their members were Lebanese of all faiths, mostly recruited in the 1980s and 1990s. Their mission was to gather information on Hezbollah and IRL, as well as on the Lebanese army and Palestinian groups.[39] Most of the spies were recidivist former members of the SLA who had been given light sentences under the great pardon granted by the Lebanese government in 2000. In the context of the discord between Hezbollah and conservative Christians, who had always advocated a general amnesty for collaborators, these profiles vindicated Hezbollah's position. Nasrallah set the tone on 22 May, when he recommended their execution. This was a setback for March 14, which was allegedly "protecting communitarian balance even when it comes to hangings".[40] Nasrallah stated, without hesitation:

> On behalf of all the martyrs, I call for the death sentence for spies. Enough of the joke [prison sentences] of a month, two months or a few years [meted out to former SLA]. ... Let us not play games with justice or security to find a so-called confessional balance in the ranks of collaborators with the enemy: start by executing the Shiite spies![41]

Showdown with the government and March 14

Along with these effects from the regional scene impacting the national chessboard, changing inter-Lebanese political relations during the period contributed, largely through a process of escalation and polarization, to turning Hezbollah and the Shiite community against March 14, and vice versa.

Not surprisingly, the end of the conflict brought with it the start of a reckoning between Hezbollah and March 14. While the latter's moderate current, which included the prime minister, did not—at first—intend to discuss the IRL's weapons, the radicals accused the Resistance not only of having started the war that had just devastated the country, but of having started it on the orders of Syria and/or Iran. They attacked Hezbollah as what they called a "mini-state" or a "state within a state"; they called for an end to the "duplication of political authority" and for the extension of state sovereignty throughout Lebanon. They insisted that there was an irreconcilable dichotomy between the concept of the state itself and Hezbollah, with the latter's weapons repeatedly cited as "the last obstacle to erecting a state of laws".[42] The idea of a Lebanese victory over Israel was also discredited. Rather, they said that the war had just illustrated "the incorrectness of the logic of resistance as propounded by

Hezbollah",[43] and that the army alone should be responsible for defending the national territory. Hezbollah responded by rejecting these accusations, reckoning instead that the conflict proved that the IRL "must defend Lebanon as long as the army lacks the capacity for doing so".[44] It dismissed out of hand any invitation to disarm, and criticized the government for having mismanaged the crisis, including by its refusal to back the IRL.[45]

On 11 September the tension went up another notch with Tony Blair's official visit to Lebanon. The media buzz was in full swing for weeks around the fact that the British prime minister, a constant supporter of Israel during the war, had been briefed on preparations for it even before it was launched.[46] His coming to Lebanon less than a month after the end of hostilities thus triggered Hezbollah's ire and shocked much of the public. The government was castigated for its "unconditional alignment with the West", ranging from the hug Fouad Siniora gave Condoleezza Rice on her lightning visit to Beirut in the middle of the war to the handshake between the Lebanese prime minister and his British counterpart. Nasrallah delivered a fiery speech for the occasion in which he accused the English leader of having 1,200 deaths on his conscience.[47] A week later the German chancellor, Angela Merkel, announced that the German UNIFIL contingent was sent to Lebanon "to defend Israel's right to exist", causing an uproar in the circles close to Hezbollah.[48] And when the news coming out of Israel confirmed the collaboration between its government and some March 14 officials during the war, the infuriated party leadership rained charges of treason on its adversaries.

The battle over reconstruction

Overlaid on this war of the words was an intense competition regarding the issue of reconstruction. To the government it seemed too much of a lever for mobilization to be abandoned to Hezbollah, and so it became a major political issue. Indeed, the losses to the Lebanese economy caused by the month-long war were initially assessed at $9.5 billion.[49] In a preliminary report dated 17 August, the Lebanese parliament's Committee on Public Works, Energy, and Water estimated the damage wrought by Israeli bombardments at over $3.6 billion.[50] The cost of rebuilding damaged homes, offices, and shops, a total of 30,000 units, was estimated at $3.4 billion, not counting the cost of rebuilding the country's infrastructure (bridges, road networks).[51] The Lebanese government, indebted to the tune of $40 billion even before that summer, was unable to meet the challenge. To get around the problem, the prime minister announced in late August that the government's reconstruction programme would be structured as an international collaborative effort, divided among sponsor countries generously willing to finance the various areas slated for reconstruction.

From the first day of the Israeli offensive, the Iranian regime, probably to tamp down accusations that it had instigated a war that would prove devastating for

Lebanon, announced its willingness to rebuild "everything that the Israeli army destroys".[52] In this way, it also lent its support to Hezbollah, which, without assistance, would in all likelihood have had difficulty taking on all of the reconstruction needed. Nasrallah followed suit, and on behalf of Hezbollah also offered to rebuild all the houses and private residences damaged or destroyed during the conflict just getting under way.[53] This dual proposal instantly raised the concern of both the Lebanese government and the Israeli General Staff, the latter openly urging the world not to allow Iran to rebuild Lebanon because "it would solidify the presence of Hezbollah even more, especially in South Lebanon".[54] A pugnacious Mahmud Ahmadinejad, Iran's president, reiterated his country's commitment on 15 August, exactly one day after the suspension of hostilities, announcing that Iran was ready to boost its aid to the tune of several hundred million dollars.[55] Aware of the Lebanese prime minister's distrust of any potential Iranian meddling in the affairs of the Country of Cedars, especially to Hezbollah's advantage, the Iranian ambassador, Muhammad Rida Shibani, tried to reassure by specifying that this aid must be subject to an agreement between the two governments. Two days later, a top-level Iranian delegation arrived in Beirut. Chaired by Ali Saeed Loo, the Islamic Republic's vice president, it also comprised the ministers of housing and urban construction, roads, and transport, the vice-minister of energy and water, plus the president of Tehran's city council and several other senior officials. Illustrating determination, the following week the Iranian authorities bypassed the Lebanese National Electric Company; taking advantage of the fact the repairs by the Company were still pending, Tehran took the initiative to send several power generators to the South at its own expense.[56]

Initially, Fouad Siniora refused to oblige Tehran. For more than a month after their visit the Iranians waited for official permission to get involved, while expert teams from countries approved by the Lebanese government (Saudi Arabia, Qatar, the United Arab Emirates, Canada, and Belgium) were already active on the ground. The American government, receptive to Israel's warnings but not wanting to directly and significantly commit given its close alliance with Tel Aviv, actively lobbied its wealthy Arab allies, particularly Saudi Arabia and the Gulf states. The repeated, increasingly strident approaches to Beirut by Iran set the US on edge and led it to openly criticize Riyadh's commitment in Lebanon as "too limited" and to call for "more cooperation, from a political point of view but also financially".[57] In early September, Washington also lent its support to the Lebanese warding off Iran by accusing the Sadirat Iran government bank of financing Hezbollah, Hamas, and Islamic Jihād.[58] Three weeks later the United States Treasury prohibited any links between the US financial system and the Iranian bank.[59]

Conscious of being excluded from the reconstruction, the Iranian authorities were by no means ready to concede. In late September, Hay'at Iʿādat al-Iʿmār (the Reconstruction Committee), in partnership with the Iranian Red Crescent, Hay'at Imdād al-Imām al-Khumaynī (the Procurement Committee of the Imam Khomeini) and other government social agencies, finalized a comprehensive assistance programme.[60] It was intended to cover repairs of hospitals, schools, roads, and power grids damaged or destroyed by the Israeli army, and provide more direct assistance to affected populations.[61] In early October ambassador Shibani, supported by a new delegation from Tehran, again met Siniora and announced that Iran was ready to do even more.[62] For ten days the prime minister expressed some remaining objections, but, wearied by the Iranians' insistence, he finally agreed to sign a memorandum of understanding on condition that Iranian participation was confined to rebuilding a bridge and part of the road network.[63]

Encouraged by this initial breakthrough, Tehran tried to outmanoeuvre Washington by echoing a suggestion originally floated by George W. Bush in late August, namely for providing technical support to the Lebanese army.[64] The Iranian regime was therefore offering not only to arm it but especially to modernize it, by providing it with military equipment "more appropriate to the nature of threats facing Lebanon". Recalling that the weak point in Lebanon's defences during the summer had been its inability to counter Israeli air attacks, Shibani offered to equip the Lebanese army with anti-aircraft defences[65]—an offer that the Lebanese government turned down categorically.

The government outdone

Circumscribed and channelled by the Lebanese government, Iranian aid nonetheless made itself felt through Hezbollah's reconstruction work. While the ministerial-level reconstruction programme did not take off until the first week of October, the party began its programme on 14 August, the day on which hostilities ended.[66] The party leadership officially gave itself a year to rebuild demolished homes and apartments to the tune of $100,000 per dwelling, and while this was pending it agreed to disburse between $10,000 and $20,000 per qualifying family to pay a year's rent on a furnished apartment.[67] A project titled Waʿd (Promise), tailored to the southern suburbs of Beirut, was supposed to rebuild them "even more beautifully than before".[68] Compensation payments began to flow the first day that calm was restored, and Lebanese TV stations showed Hezbollah militants with jute sacks stuffed full of money handing out thousands of American dollars to the heads of families waiting in long queues in the capital's suburbs. The same assistance was distributed in Baalbek to qualifying families who had not been rehoused for free in one of the apartments of the ʿAyn Būrdāy *hawza* reopened for this purpose.[69] Fifteen days later the party paid indemnities to the Palestinian refugee camps affected by the bombing, beginning with Ain al-Heloueh[70] in the suburbs of Sidon; it also compensated Lebanese fishermen deprived of their livelihood at the time of the Israeli naval blockade.[71]

Along with these reactive distributions, Jihād al-Bināʾ cleared rubble throughout Lebanon. The very day that hostilities ended, a detailed map of the affected areas, colour-coded according to the severity of their damage, was pinned up in the Association's offices showing sites to be rebuilt or repaired.[72] Two weeks later Hassan Nasrallah announced the start of reconstruction by the party's specialized units.[73] The next day they set to work, starting on their first projects in the Akkar area in the country's north-west[74] and in the South.[75]

By comparison, the Lebanese government was slow in getting its compensation programme off the ground, partly because of a real lack of resources. Ten days into the war several countries had talked about their intention to disburse multiple emergency funds to support the Lebanese government: Saudi Arabia said it was prepared to advance $50 million and, a few days later, $500 million.[76] Kuwait pledged to contribute $20 million, the United Arab Emirates $5 million, Morocco $5 million, and the European Union €12.6 million.[77] At the international conference convened in Stockholm in late August to assist Lebanon's reconstruction effort, Beirut received a formal pledge of gifts amounting to over $940 million. Adding the previous financial commitments, this increased the total pledged to $1.2 billion.[78] However, by the third week of September the Lebanese Treasury had only received $124 million of the total aid promised[79] and, by the end of December, Saudi Arabia was the only country to have paid the full amount promised during the war. This delay by the donor countries naturally affected the launch dates for compensation and reconstruction by the Lebanese state. The government only presented the mechanism and modalities during the first week of October for the areas outside the capital[80] and in early November for Beirut's southern suburbs.[81] The first assistance only reached the South at the end of October,[82] and the capital's suburbs not until late December.[83] Meanwhile, nothing had yet been paid to families in the Bekaa. Compounding the delay was the sparse amount of compensation paid. Whereas it took at least $50,000 to rebuild an apartment in Beirut or a house in the Bekaa or the South, the assistance provided by the government not only reached too few families but compensated them in amounts ranging from $500 to $40,000 for anything and everything, including reconstruction.[84]

As for the results of the international assistance, at the end of December 2006 it was rather mixed picture. As already mentioned, Saudi Arabia had already advanced $50 million to the Lebanese government during the war to cover urgent needs; in late July it offered $500 million to finance reconstruction, and it deposited $1 billion in the Bank of Lebanon to bolster the Lebanese economy and the Lebanese pound.[85] In response to Siniora's October appeal the Kingdom promised to sponsor twenty-nine villages, on whose repair and reconstruction it would spend another $232 million.[86] Kuwait also deposited $500 million in the Bank of Lebanon, offered to donate $300 million, and sponsored twenty-one damaged cities and villages.[87] The United Arab Emirates committed to rebuilding eighteen more. Other countries were also involved in the effort, although at a more modest level, such as Qatar (rebuilding four towns and villages), Jordan (seven villages), and Egypt (seven villages). Wealthy Lebanese individuals and various associations paid for the reconstruction of sixty-four of the ninety-seven bridges that Israel had destroyed. According to government estimates, these commitments should cover about 75 per cent of the costs of reconstruction.[88] By the autumn most schools sponsored by the Gulf states—particularly Qatar and the UAE—had been made ready for the start of term. However, at the end of December the reconstruction projects promised by these countries, and especially Saudi Arabia, turned out to consist of prefabricated housing, of limited size and comfort. Estimates of the reconstruction needs were ultimately revised upward when it was discovered that international donations would not cover most of the costs, which, in all probability, had been greatly underestimated. As early as mid-October the prime minister made known his intention to seek a grant for $3.2 billion in supplementary gifts from the third Paris conference, slated for late January 2007.[89]

Slowness by the donor countries was not the only reason for the limited success of the government's reconstruction policy. The cabinet's own stance was problematic and, starting in late August, precipitated unease even in the ranks of March 14. Indeed, the day the prime minister first raised the idea of reconstruction sponsorships, the president of the Council for Development and Reconstruction (CDR),[90] Fadl Chalaq, resigned. He maintained that he and his team had developed several alternative plans some weeks before and submitted them to the prime minister without "ever receiving a response". He protested against the shunting aside of the CDR by the government, which he accused of never having commissioned any study of what it would take to reconstruct the country, or even a survey of the damage's extent, "when these are the agency's primary functions". Chalaq accused the cabinet of having taken the path of least resistance.[91]

At the same time, the position of the ministerial team on this issue became even more tenuous when clashes erupted between the population and security forces. With the approach of winter, some of the distressed families had already started to rebuild their homes, ignoring the government directive to wait for a comprehensive urban reconstruction plan to be put in place. In October, at Raml al-Aali, a neighbourhood in the capital's southern suburbs, ISF personnel opened fire on some of these people and two boys aged eleven and fifteen were killed. The tragedy was immediately politicized,[92] and was interpreted as the government becoming radicalized in its competition with Hezbollah for control of the reconstruction effort. On the Shiite side, the incident reverberated even more because the interior minister at the time was Ahmad Fatfat, suspected of collaborating with Israel during the summer war.[93] The victims' parents clamoured for his resignation.[94]

Tribunal, presidential election, unity government: stalemate time

The end of the Thirty-Three-Day War also meant that the political agendas were resumed at the point where they had been frozen on 12 July. For March 14 it was time to refocus on the issue of the tribunal charged with trying the killers of Rafic Hariri. A Belgian judge, Serge Brammertz, who succeeded Detlev Mehlis at the head of the International Commission, made a series of interim reports to the UNSC between September 2006 and November 2007. These caused fewer tensions than those of his predecessor, thanks to the discretion with which he conducted his work and his refusal to "disclose any name whatsoever" before the investigation concluded. Still, the issue of the court continued to create stalemates.[95] On 11 November 2006, two days before the Council of Ministers met to consider, and eventually approve, the status of an international tribunal, Shiite ministers withdrew from the cabinet and tendered their resignations on the pretext that the majority had refused to vote for a national unity government. March 14 accused Hezbollah and AMAL of having ordered their ministers to withdraw because of the tribunal, which they both denied. Hezbollah resurrected the argument that it had already raised before the war, namely its suspicion that the United States, after trying to disarm the IRL by means of Resolution 1559, and, beginning in the summer of 2006, through Resolution 1701 and the strengthening of UNIFIL power, was trying to disable Hezbollah on Israel's behalf by having its leaders imprisoned by an international tribunal.

The government, shorn of its Shiite ministers, did not back down. On 13 November it officially approved the text creating the tribunal. AMAL and Hezbollah used the Shiite resignations to impugn the legitimacy of the decision taken by the rump cabinet, quoting a passage from the preamble to the Constitution that "any power that violates the coexistence pact is illegitimate".[96] For his part, the prime minister defended the legality of decisions by the diminished cabinet, retorting that the resignations had not been accepted. The UNSC sided with the majority and recognized the constitutionality of the document signed by the truncated government, and, on 21 November, voted unanimously for the text. The opposition did not admit defeat. After the UN vote the tribunal draft was sent to the Lebanese government, which approved it on 25 November. It then sent it on to President Lahoud, who vetoed it. Three days later the Council of Ministers voted a second time on the text and sent it for debate and ratification to parliament. Speaker Nabih Berri, however, did not call parliament into session for this purpose. Between the end of 2006 and October 2007, the parliament was not summoned once.

The doggedness of the speaker in thus preventing the tribunal statute from being ratified progressively raised the tension between majority and opposition. In the spring of 2007 the March 14 MPs protested one morning every week on Nejmeh Square[97]—but to no avail. The majority and the international community warned the opposition repeatedly that in case of failure by the Lebanese authorities to move the process forward, the UNSC would be obliged to ratify the creation of the tribunal, but without having to take into account the views of the various other Lebanese parties. The threat of registering the tribunal statutes under Chapter VII of the UN Charter, which provides for the use of armed force, was drummed home constantly.

Faced with Berri's stonewalling, in early April the majority members sent a memorandum to the UNSC asking it to take "alternative" measures.[98] They received satisfaction with the passing of Resolution 1757 on 30 May, establishing a tribunal of an international character under Chapter VII to try Rafic Hariri's assassins.

The tension escalated further on the domestic scene when the issue of the tribunal became entwined with two other front-page political debates: the national unity government and the presidential election. Upon the cessation of hostilities with Israel, the stakes were raised and the situation became more complicated. On 22 September 2006, during his speech at the "Victory celebration", Nasrallah had announced that the party supported the formation of a unity government, a proposal originally formulated before the war by Michel Aoun's Free Patriotic Movement. The united opposition therefore demanded that Fouad Siniora's entire cabinet, judged illegitimate since the resignation of the Shiite ministers, be replaced by a new cabinet that "reflects the realities on the ground and not a fictional majority".[99] For the opposition, a guaranteed "real participation in historic decisions" was vital, with the existing government seen as being "unfit to protect the Resistance".[100] With the downsized government initially opposing any adjustment to its make-up, in early November Nasrallah called for demonstrations to make it yield. Berri, raising the spectre of a resort to the street by the opposition, organized two weeks of meetings in an attempt to achieve a compromise, during which insults flew. The opposition, whose tone was characterized as "putschist"[101] by the majority, received warnings from the majority that the opposition labelled "bellicose".[102] While March 14 in the end proposed a cabinet reshuffle that would see the FPM join it, it categorically rejected the idea of a blocking third called for by Hezbollah, suspecting that the party wanted to use it to prevent convening of the tribunal.[103] The opposition for its part declared itself ready to accept arbitration by an international court, affirming that it was not hostile to the institution itself. But it insisted that this should take place only after a unity government had been achieved.[104] The deadlock continuing, in late November 2006 Nasrallah began mobilizing for a large protest slated to start on 1 December. AMAL, the Baath, the FPM, the Marada,[105] and the Lebanese Democratic Party called for a massive turnout.[106] On the appointed day, Riyad al-Solh Square in downtown Beirut filled with hundreds of thousands of demonstrators. The gathering started out like a street fair, with balloons and refreshment and food stands. Two days later, however, a descent into wholesale violence seemed imminent: on 3 December a young Shiite AMAL supporter, Ahmad Mahmoud, was killed by a sniper in Kaskas, a Sunni neighbourhood of Beirut. Berri and Nasrallah immediately appealed for restraint, urging no reprisals. The crowd gathered on Riyad al-Solh Square simply paid tribute to the victim, whose body was brought to the place of assembly.[107] It soon became clear that the protest would continue there for the duration. Outfitted tents were set up on the site, and the protesters took shifts, both day and night. Christmas and New Year were celebrated there, in an atmosphere openly declared transconfessional.[108] Faced with the majority's inflexibility, the opposition considered more drastic measures. It therefore suggested that it might resort to civil disobedience and paralyse the port and the airport,[109] but ultimately it never acted on the threat. However, it organized a series of supplementary demonstrations. One of these, on Tuesday, 23 January, precipitated dramatic events when a strike turned into a riot, resulting in four deaths and a hundred wounded in Beirut,[110] and two days later there were three more dead and more than 150 injured.[111] Many commentators saw it as the start of a civil war, but this was narrowly avoided thanks to speedy interventions by Nasrallah, Berri, Hariri, and Jumblatt, who called on their supporters to clear the streets on the spot.[112]

The bloody events of late January 2007 to some degree altered the course of political events. In early February Naʿīm Qāsim reiterated the party's refusal to threaten the civil peace and called for a discussion on a government formula that would have "no winner or loser". The majority expressed a willingness to negotiate. That was the beginning of a veritable soap opera about possible political and confessional combinations for a distribution of portfolios that would satisfy both camps. Put on the table would be 19 + 10 + 1, 18 + 9 + 3, 12 + 8 + 4, 19 + 11, 3 × 10, etc.,[113] but none of this would ever get anywhere because of the opposition's determination to obtain a blocking minority and the majority's refusal to grant it one.

From spring 2007, a second problem related to arrangements for the presidential election relegated the matter of the unity government to the back burner and created another standoff. Émile Lahoud's term in office was to expire in November 2007, and there was friction concerning the quorum[114] and his successor.[115] For a time, the tension grew around the clear and obstinate desire of Michel Aoun to take over the top office and March 14's categorical refusal to let him have it. It seemed as if an agreement could be reached in the spring of 2007, centring on the army's commander, Michel Sleiman, but it came to nothing.[116] Things got so out of hand that when Lahoud left the presidential palace in Baabda the night of 23 November, his successor had not been chosen and the country would have to manage its political life for several months without a president.[117]

"War starts with words"[118]

> "You're a traitor!" "No, you are!"

If these stalemates over management of the country's institutional life fed the tension between March 8 and March 14, the verbal exchanges, sometimes of a personal nature, between leaders on both sides played an equal part in sharpening mutual animosities in the political sphere as well as among society. The Hezbollah camp favoured accusations of treason and collaboration, vilifying the majority as trying to transform Lebanon into a satellite of the USA and Israel, selling out national sovereignty, and taking orders from Washington, Tel Aviv, or even Riyadh. Michel Aoun lent a hand by giving speeches and press conferences rife with name-calling and what were in essence anti-Sunni sectarian insults. From its side, March 14 accused its opponents of being in the pay of the Syrian and Iranian regimes and hostile to the recovery of Lebanese sovereignty. Hezbollah in particular came in for virulent criticism. It was pelted with calls to "Lebanize", to stop putting Syrian and Iranian interests before those of its country, and to urgently shed its arsenal, which made it "antithetical to the state and legality". Depicted as "dedicated to the destruction of Lebanon",[119] it was accused of plotting to overthrow the regime and change the system.[120] Epithets fired at it included "mafia",[121] "bandit",[122] "fascist",[123] "assassin",[124] "terrorist",[125] and "enemy of civilization".[126] Anticipating and speculating about the results of the international inquiry, the March 14 radicals claimed that Hezbollah was behind all the political assassinations that had plagued Lebanon for the previous three years—starting with the one that almost killed Marwan Hamadeh in 2004 and the one that carried Rafic Hariri away in 2005.[127] Walid Jumblatt was the first to voice the accusation explicitly, in December 2006; the reaction in Hezbollah circles was so heated that a resumption of the civil war seemed possible, to the point where Saad Hariri personally and publicly stepped in, saying that he did not think the party was implicated in his father's death.[128]

Heightened communitarianism

The stalemate that developed over the threefold problem of the tribunal, a new government, and the presidential election, amid accusations of treachery and allegiance to foreign governments, was all the more dangerous because it was accompanied by a progressive sharpening of communitarian logic. March 14's discourse in particular repeatedly took the form of well-organized campaigns directed against two communities whose majorities belong to the opposition: the Shiites, who found themselves portrayed as without any vestige of Lebanese identity, and the Armenians, who were categorized as second-class Lebanese. This then set up a reactionary dialogue between two types of narratives that, as much on one side as the other, added to the meaning-making process already under way from 2005, refining and strengthening the paradigms already assimilated by each camp regarding both the self and the Other.

The "I love life" campaign

In the autumn of 2006, March 14 added two concepts to its mobilization vocabulary: "culture of life" and "culture of death" (*thaqāfat al-hayāt, thaqāfat al-mawt*), originally used to describe two supposedly antinomian attitudes involved in the need to detoxify the national political climate.[129] They were quickly reworked to provide support for a certain political discourse whose vexing sectarian undertones were undeniable. Indeed, with the approach of Christmas that year billboards appeared throughout Lebanon covered with red posters bearing the phrase "*I love life*" in English, French, and Arabic. The verb "*love*" in each phrase was replaced by the picture of a heart (*I ♥ life, J' ♥ la vie,* الحياة ♥).[130] At first, the phrase intrigued. Soon, TV spots picked up the formulation and the logo; against that backdrop, personalities associated with the majority explained what the slogan meant to them. In the course of the following year it would become the principal March 14 slogan. Reinforcing the message, new posters appeared splashed with a simple "We want to live". The whole thing was crowned with a gigantic New Year's party held in Beirut at the Biel.[131] The new uses for "I love life" and "We want to live" now began in earnest. More and more explicitly, journalists, political personalities, and ordinary citizen sympathizers of March 14 employed the term "culture of death" to designate Hezbollah's supposed love of war and martyrdom, and "culture of life" to describe March 14's existential issues, presented as articulated around a "normal" life. Simultaneously, a leap was made from the political to a communitarian register, by implictly characterizing the Shiite dogma as a culture of death, due to the centrality that ʿĀshūrā' occupies in it, and hence as essentially sad, tragic, and valuing death.

At first, the opposition mocked the campaign and produced its own series of posters, in this case an altered reprise of the March 14 posters. The slogans and typography (white text on a red background) were purposely retained but contained supplementary phrases recalling the values championed by the opposition and which, executed in graffiti-like lettering, alluded to the popular, protesting side. "I love life" became "I love life in all its colours", a dual allusion to the anti-communitarianism that the opposition claimed to promote and to the national unity government that it called for.[132] In the same way, "We want to live" became "We want to live in dignity/ in Lebanon/in security", allusions to the accusations levelled by the parliamentary minority against the majority as injuring national dignity, forcing the labour force into exile, and making Lebanon live to the rhythm of assassinations.

Driving home the point, the opposition produced its own poster campaign towards the end of winter 2006–7, this time using posters on a dark-green background and with a rainbow, yet again in reference to uniting the diverse components of the Lebanese political scene. Countering the majority's slogan, judged "puerile" (*waldaneh*) and "operatic" (*wujdānī*), the messages were decommunitarized and refocused on issues of a political nature. The posters, under the heading of *bil-arqām* ("the proof is in the numbers"), highlighted the policy mistakes that the opposition laid at the feet of the majority: 61 per cent of the population voted for the minority;[133] $45 billion in debt; 15 per cent VAT; a L£300,000[134] minimum wage; 42 per cent of young people have left the country; 83 per cent of emigrants have not returned to the country. One poster in particular attacked the policy of indebtedness, already criticized during Rafic Hariri's time: under three Eiffel Towers lined up by increasing size could be read: *Paris I = $26 billion in debt; Paris II = $32 billion in debt; Paris III = $45 billion in debt.*[135]

That spring the majority responded with two new poster campaigns. The first emphasized the benefits of Paris III by promising electricity for all and pay commensurate with effort. The second showed the red background of "I love life" and, with the same typography, ran down the list of supposed main concerns of the majority's followers, stressing: "I go to work; I'm going out tonight;" and "I stay in Lebanon". Once again, the slogans attracted the opposition's ridicule and were slyly reworded, after which the poster wars eventually subsided.

The "Persians" are "colonizing the Mountain"

The effect of the culturalist criticisms levelled against the opposition by March 14—and specifically against the Shiites, who, in addition to being portrayed as tending to be morbid, found themselves implicitly shown as not liking "to go out at night" or "to go to work" during the day—was multiplied by another anti-Shiite sectarian campaign paralleling 'I love life". This time it was orchestrated by Walid Jumblatt.

The first component of the discourse was to deny that the Shiites shared in Lebanese national identity. The IRL was first to be targeted by the attacks: judged as being subservient to Tehran, it was invited to "Lebanize". Gradually, the comments came to apply just as much to the Shiite community as a whole. Derogatory attributes—such as those labelling them "backward" and "uncivilized"—which had been applied to the community for decades, were dusted off again. Formulations emphasized the "danger that threatens the very Lebanese identity" of which the Shiites do not seem to be part. The excommunicatory dimension of this campaign had the support of the Assembly of Maronite Bishops, and of Patriarch Sfeir himself: those "who do not support the tribunal" were declared "non-Lebanese".[136] Increasingly sophisticated and pointed campaigns gradually chipped away at the Shiites' Lebanese and Arab identities while associating them with the "Persians". This idea was especially developed by Marwan Hamadeh, Walid Jumblatt's right-hand man, who repeatedly pointed a warning finger at his Shiite compatriots as "vanguards of Persian colonization of the Middle East". This idea of ascribing "Persianness" to Lebanon's Shiites also appealed to some Sunni personalities, starting with the mufti of Mount Lebanon, Sheikh Muhammad Ali Jouzou, a fervent supporter of the Iranian Revolution in the 1980s but a convert to an extreme brand of Sunnism in 2005.

The second component correlated with the first one to reveal March 14's fear of the Shiite community's demographic trends. The fact is that the Shiites always had a higher birth rate than any of the other communities. The gradual gentrification of certain sections of the community during the last decades had led to an increase in the number of (young) Shiite cadres in the capital. Unable to settle in Beirut itself, more and more of them had by that time been settling for several years on the peripheries bordering the Mountain, in areas such as Hazmiyeh or towns like Aley. Walid Jumblatt, between January and April 2007, chose to interpret this natural development of an offshoot of the Shiite community as a strategy conceived by Hezbollah for carrying out a "colonization" of Lebanon's non-Shiite areas. The Druze leader began by "revealing" that the party had purchased land in the Aley area, located in the foothills of the Mountain joining it to Beirut. A few months later, in April, he argued that the same process was under way in the Sunni and Druze regions of the South.[137] For the rest of the year Jumblatt expanded on Hezbollah's "colonizing" aims, accusing it of "attacking the demographic structure of the country" and seeking to force the non-Shiite populations to leave "their" lands, if not Lebanon, at the cost of "ethnic cleansing" if necessary, and for the benefit of a community guilty of working for "Iran's expansion to the East's Mediterranean shore". Hezbollah denied buying any land in Aley. It also made the point that "even if it were true", all Lebanese, of any faith, are "still free to buy land wherever they please", and reiterated that the party had never opposed the settlement by non-Shiites in its areas.[138] But the Jumblatt narratives did make converts,[139] and throughout 2007 Hezbollah's "illegitimate territorial ambitions" remained controversial.

Excerpts from Walid Jumblatt's speeches on Hezbollah's "colonization programme" for Lebanon's non-Shiite regions

It seems that certain suspect parties, using aliases like Ali Tajeddine, are buying up vast tracts of land, primarily in the areas of Jezzin, Aley, Souk el-Gharb and other sectors, with the aim of completing the setting up of the (Persian) state in Lebanon. ... [This is being done] by the route of forming colonies, ghettos, military bases and security perimeters encircling national areas of Lebanon. They are thus surrounding them with human and military cordons ready to attack these regions, probably within a framework of preparations for the second phase of surprises held in store for us by the forces of darkness.

The direct and indirect plans aiming for the benefit of the "divine" political project to modify the face of Lebanon by changing its structure based on coexistence and wipe out its demographic and social givens by a programme of infiltration of well-defined areas will not succeed in changing reality, nor in overturning the national equilibriums on which Lebanon has historically been based and that will remain this country's solid foundation.

These parties that wrap themselves in purity and religiosity and who pursue a project of a state within a state are setting up local entities by way of a colonization programme, financed by "clean money" disbursed in millions of dollars and perhaps soon in millions of euros, as soon as the currency will have been changed in that great metropolis, Tehran.

L'Orient–Le Jour, 4 January 2007.

In the Shuf, specifically, there has not been this kind of buying yet. The area around Aley, the village of Souk el-Gharb is almost swallowed up, with half of it bought up. The aim is to link up Souk el-Gharb, the surrounding villages of Kayfun and Qomatiyeh and the southern suburbs [of Beirut]. In other words, a junction with the 'state of the southern suburbs'—and I purposely speak in these terms—that will cut the Aley region in two.

In the Jezzin area, huge tracts have been sold. The last date land that risks being sold belongs to the Nassif family, a Christian family living somewhere in America. We are talking about 20 million square metres between Kfarhuna and Jezzin. Twenty million square metres, in other words, this is not a person who wants to buy land to build a house for his family. What we have here is a colony [and there are other purchases] on the hills overlooking the coast, specifically Sidon.

This is how the junction of the South with Jezzin and with Mashgharah in the Bekaa is accomplished. This is all about expansion of the Hezbollah state in the South, which de facto already exists. Between Hermel, Baalbek, and southern Lebanon, setting such a space up is more difficult because the region is more complex and varied. But, in the long term, this does not prevent "them" [Hezbollah] from doing it. ... Each village or Shiite concentration has now become a military bastion. ...

Hezbollah is pursuing a hegemonic project of buying land, setting up colonies, and later on maybe even some villages, of positioning its rockets. ... And if anyone refuses, they contemplate one day sweeping him aside by military means. This project began in Lebanon, continues on through the Syrian Shiite–Alawite country—that is completely under Iranian tutelage because the Alawite regime favours its Alawism over its Arabism—and through an Iraq that is in pieces. They themselves say that Baghdad may become Shiitized. The ethnic cleansing going on in Baghdad is frightening. We are talking about 4,000 or 5,000 deaths per month. Thus, the physical Lebano-Syro-Iraqo-Iranian axis is becoming a reality on the ground. Before, in Saddam Hussein's day, there was an Arab bastion against the Persians. But this is no longer the case now. Iraq has ceased to exist. ...

This is the overall state of things, and we are caught in a vicious cycle, because all of Lebanon as a multiconfessional, pluralistic entity risks disappearing under the weight of Hezbollah's military and cultural totalitarianism. Of course, there are always Shiites who reject this state of things, wanting to be Lebanese and not Persian, and who reject the *wilāyat al-faqīh*. It reminds me of Hitler when he invaded Austria, because a part of the Austrian people of German origin had called for the *Anschluss*. Hitler used the presence of Germans everywhere as a pretext for sending the rest there. Let us remember Czechoslovakia, the Sudeten Germans and the Volga Germans.

L'Orient–Le Jour, 10 January 2007.

> Are we also to abolish the Taef state, the consensual democracy, and the compromise on which the participatory formula is based and that takes no account of demographic development? Or to abolish Lebanon's independence and its Arabness and attach it to the Syro-Iranian axis?
>
> Does that also mean that we seek to bury the coexistence formula by the organized buying up of land by institutions related directly or indirectly to Hezbollah and, beyond that, to Iran, transactions that pave the road for a political and then a demographic exodus of certain areas of South Lebanon and perhaps even of Beirut?
>
> Is the goal to eliminate what is practically the only democracy in all the Arab and Islamic Middle East [that is, Lebanon] and install in its place a state that does not meet the aspirations of the Lebanese people, who have opted for a secular and not a religious political system, in which the freedom of individuals and groups is sacred? ... And beyond that, is the goal to abolish the culture of life and of joy in exchange for the culture of death and darkness?
>
> We are facing an existential threat to the [Lebanese] entity, the coexistence formula, Taef, democracy, freedoms, variety, pluralism, and participation.
>
> *L'Orient–Le Jour*, 27 April 2007.

Violence on the ground

Between early 2007 and the spring of 2008 the ultra-polarization on the political stage led partisans of the two sides to clash repeatedly on the ground. Four incidents in particular raised fear of a general conflagration. Although they were political in origin, they were perceived as confessional in nature and so only added to the intercommunitarian grievances. The first, previously mentioned, was the dual clash of January 2007 in the streets of Beirut between supporters of March 14 and March 8. The second was the murders of a young boy and a young man in April 2007, both with the first name Ziad, aged twelve and twenty-four, at the hands of clan members from the Baalbek–al-Hermel region in the Bekaa. The tragedy seemed at first to have stemmed from a family feud, but quickly took on both a political and communitarian cast. Both victims were Druze and their parents were members of the PSP; the perpetrators were Shiite and sought to avenge their brother, who had been killed earlier in the year. In January 2008 a demonstration against prolonged power outages in the (Shiite) al-Shiyyāh quarter in Beirut's southern suburbs degenerated into an altercation between police and demonstrators when the former opened fire. Eight people were killed and fifty wounded.[140] Lastly, three months later, in April, two Kataeb cadres were murdered in Zahleh (Bekaa) and three others injured when a close associate of Elie Skaff, an MP allied with Michel Aoun, opened fire on the Kataeb party headquarters. Although it was an inter-Christian incident, the tragedy once again had communitarian echoes (Maronites vs. Catholics), and representatives of the two churches had to intervene to calm partisans of both sides and their supporters.

The Hezbollah "coup d'état" and the "invasion" of Beirut

In the spring of 2008 the political situation was thus a complete stalemate. The opposition, keeping parliament closed and refusing to have the Shiite ministers rejoin the government, proved that it could thwart March 14 in the exercise of its power. The country had been without a president since November, the government had been incomplete for eighteen months. Interconfessional animosity dominated much of the political discourse, and incidents on the ground multiplied.

In early February Saad Hariri abandoned his habitual posture of moderation vis-à-vis the opposition to solemnly declare: "In kāna qadrunā al-muwājaha, fanahnū lahā!" (If our fate is to be confrontation, let's have it!)[141] The message was made all the more clear when Walid Jumblatt took it up three days later, addressing March 14's adversaries: "You want a war? Then bring it on!"[142] Less than three months later, on 2 May, al-Manār reported statements by senior Israeli officials claiming that the head of the PSP was implicated in the assassination of Imad Mughniyeh, its security unit having provided information to Mossad. On the same day Jumblatt held a press conference,[143] where he "revealed" that Hezbollah had runway 17 at Beirut international airport under surveillance, using hidden cameras. Tension escalated to new extremes on both sides of the political divide. The powder keg was full, and only needed a match to set it off. The explosion came four days later, at 4.30 a.m.

Jumblatt's press conferences and the cabinet's decision

On 2 May 2008, in observance of Labour Day and the fifty-ninth anniversary of the PSP, Walid Jumblatt summoned the press. Before a bevy of cameras he announced the existence of a document related to an important security matter concerning runway 17 of Beirut international airport, designated as an old runway used by private aircraft.[144] He reported that containers were positioned along a road next to the runway and that members of the airport security had spotted three people in civilian clothes, one of them holding a camera he had just removed from a container. Abruptly, Jumblatt then asserted that Hezbollah possessed a private telecommunications network in Lebanon linking the Shiite suburbs of Beirut to the country's South, the West Bekaa, and the Baalbek–al-Hermel area. He claimed that a branch of this network was being built on the western slope of Mount Lebanon between the Kesruan region and Jbeil. He suspended his narrative, completing it the following day during another press conference. Claiming to possess an exchange of official correspondence between the

Ministry of Defence and army intelligence, he reiterated his accusations that Hezbollah was implicated in the political assassinations that had been shaking the country since 2004. He did so by linking the assassinations and the airport runway surveillance mentioned the previous day, stating that: "With the help of the cameras, Hezbollah can abduct or kill anyone they want on the road to the airport and even on runway 17." He attacked the head of airport security, General Wafic Shuqair (a Shiite), accusing him of being in the pay of Hezbollah. He also called for the barring of Iranian aircraft, which he accused of flying in money and weapons, and demanded the expulsion of Iran's ambassador from Lebanon. Referring again to the party's parallel telecommunications network he added: "It is not by coincidence that the opposition's protest sit-ins take place in the centre city where the same telecommunications network is also run through." He suggested that the network was supposed to run "very close by the French embassy", but that Hezbollah "did not have the guts to go that far". Last, he commented on the general strike announced for 7 May by the CGTL, saying that Hezbollah had planned the strike with the aim of carrying out "a new occupation of Beirut, just as on 23 and 25 January 2007".[145]

Hezbollah's leadership responded immediately with a communiqué in which it accused Jumblatt of purveying "hallucinatory scenarios worthy of a spy thriller".[146] As for the containers, it explained that they belonged to and were used by Jihād al-Binā᾽ for storing material for reconstruction in the southern suburbs. They were located not on the airport but on adjacent land. To deter thieves they had been mounted with video cameras, "hardly sophisticated, visible from a distance and not hidden in any way". "If Hezbollah wanted to really set up a surveillance, it could have placed sophisticated cameras the size of a flea, nearly impossible to detect." The party's communiqué then points out Jumblatt's difficulty in posturing as defender of Lebanon's security, "he, whose security service may well have collaborated with Mossad in the assassination of Imad Mughniyeh". The party reprimanded its accuser for wanting to embroil the army and the security forces in domestic conflicts, and warned that such an attempt could have "disastrous results for everybody". Regarding the issue of the telephone network, Naʿīm Qāsim himself intervened to attest to the fact that it was needed for the IRL's security, and that the party therefore considered it part of its armaments and consequently subject to the same special regime as its weaponry.

Hezbollah's explanations did not deter March 14. Reprising Jumblatt's version as its own, the Alliance's general secretariat published a virulent communiqué in which it also asserted that Hezbollah was attempting to connect its regions "to the [Lebanese] capital and to Syria"[147] through its communications network. In this extremely tense climate the interior minister, Hassan Sabeh, and the minister of defence, Elias Murr, demanded that the attorney general open an investigation through the Court of Cassation. On the evening of Monday 5 May the cabinet, still consisting only of March 14 ministers, met to decide its stance in the case. This meeting, the longest in Lebanon's history, went on till 4.30 in the morning of 6 May. As soon as the meeting was over, information minister Ghazi Aridi read out the decisions adopted. With regard to the matter of runway 17, the government announced the following:

1. General Shuqair was relieved of all his duties.
2. Hezbollah's telecommunications network was declared "illegitimate and illegal" and as constituting an "infringement on the sovereignty of the state and public money"; Hezbollah's argument that it needed the network for security was rejected.
3. All those involved in the network would be prosecuted, "whether they are individuals, parties or committees, the responsible departments and law enforcement units having to address the issue, with the Lebanese state entitled to remove those lines".[148]

In other words, the decision was made to send in the army to dig up and dismantle the IRL telecommunications networks—by force, if necessary. In opening his speech of 8 May, Hassan Nasrallah declared that it was nothing less than a "declaration of war".[149]

Confrontation

On Monday 5 May several unions repeated their call for a general mobilization in the context of a strike scheduled for two days later on the 7th. The CGTL had demanded a raise in the minimum wage from L£300,000 at the time (about €150) to L£960,000. The cabinet during its marathon meeting on the night of 5–6 May had voted to raise it to L£500,000.[150] The same day, it was learned that the national debt had passed $43 billion, up $2 billion from the previous year. The CGTL announced that the call to strike remained in effect, and Hezbollah called for massive participation.

The demonstration was due to start at 11a.m. on Wednesday 7 May in Beirut.[151] However, it was hurriedly cancelled by the CGTL due to fears of a security debacle. Half an hour before the appointed time, the situation on the ground was indeed hardly reassuring. The protesters were not the only ones to have mobilized: dozens of armed AMAL and Hezbollah members had stationed themselves on the capital's major thoroughfares. Tyres and mattresses were burned on some downtown streets, making them impassable. Jihād al-Binā' trucks dumped tons of sand on the road to the airport, quickly making it unusable. In less than an hour, AMAL and Hezbollah had occupied central Beirut's nerve centres. Soon, armed clashes erupted between their fighters and those of the FC, turning the event into what looked like civil war between Sunnis and Shiites. In several neighbourhoods, at Mazraa, Nueyri, and Bastā, the two sides clashed intermittently throughout the day. At Nueyri an FC office was attacked with B7 rockets then taken by AMAL; in Wata al-Mosseitbeh, clashes erupted between AMAL and the PSP.

In fact, the Shiite opposition's decision to resort to the street had been made the night before, after a meeting between the leaders of AMAL and Hezbollah, the vice president of the SSC, 'Abdel-Amīr Qabalān, and Sayyid Muhammad Husayn

Fadlallāh. Qabalān himself declared that "to call into question the security of the airport is to doubt our patriotism, our honesty and our sincerity in defending the nation",[152] suggesting that an attack on General Shuqair could be construed as an attack on his community. While March 14 did not hesitate to talk of an "attempted coup d'état", the opposition's stated goals were in fact more modest: to get the government to retract its decisions of the night of the 5th, reinstate Shuqair and countermand the deactivation order for the IRL telephone network.

On Thursday night Hezbollah and AMAL continued to battle militants with machine guns and RPGs in the West Beirut neighbourhoods. AMAL and Hezbollah launched an assault on FC offices in Ras al-Nabeh, Clemenceau, Hamra, Beshara al-Khury, Mazraa, Mosseitbeh, Mar Elias, Zokak al-Blatt, Verdun, Rawsheh, and Ramlet al-Bayda. By Friday morning they were in control of their opponents' main strongholds. Around noon the shooting dwindled, and the army deployed to Ras al-Nabeh and Mazraa, and also Tarik Jdideh, where AMAL and Hezbollah had not yet taken up positions. The previous night the FC media had also been muzzled: Future TV and the daily *al-Mustaqbal* were forced to close. The fighters turned the evacuated staff over to the army to see them returned safely to their homes. In the wake of AMAL and Hezbollah, some militiamen, later identified as members of the SSNP and small groups of agitators, took advantage of the confusion reigning in some quarters to carry out acts of vandalism and violence. By late afternoon the SSNP had set fire to an old building of Future TV and ransacked the Hariri Foundation headquarters in Ramlet al-Bayda, replacing portraits of Hariri with those of Assad father and son. One floor of the *al-Mustaqbal* building was set on fire.[153] The headquarters of the daily *al-Liwā'*[154] came under fire, and those of the weekly *al-Shirā'*[155] were stormed and looted. The home of the director of the daily *al-Nahār*'s website and of its publishing house was also attacked. Premises owned by March 14 leaders were stormed by militia. Snipers positioned themselves on rooftops to terrorize pedestrians.

The confrontations spilled over beyond the capital's limits. There were skirmishes between FC and Hezbollah at Bshamun and Doha-Aramun (Mount Lebanon). In Bednayel (Bekaa) the FC confronted opposition groups, leaving one person dead and several wounded. The country's disarray resulted in the settling of intracommunitarian scores: in Khaldeh, militants from the PSP and partisans of Talal Arslan, leader of the fringe Druze opposition and a Syrian regime ally, went after each other, resulting in two killed and several wounded among Arslan's supporters. The headquarters of the Shiite mufti of Tyre and Jabal 'Āmil, 'Alī al-Amīn (close to March 14), was assaulted by AMAL and Hezbollah fighters. In the north, pro- and anti-FC Sunnis joined the fray, facing off in Tripoli and the Akkar region.

Faced with the parlous situation on the ground, the government did an about-face: on Saturday 10 May, Michel Sleiman, the head of the army was given authority to take any measures judged necessary for ending the crisis. That day he decided (i) to keep General Wafic Shucair in his position until the investigation into the runway 17 surveillance affair was finished; and (ii) to handle the issue of Hezbollah's telecommunications network "in conformity with the general interest and security of the Resistance".[156] Hariri immediately approved the communiqué personally, and Jumblatt did the same. Elated by this victory, AMAL broke camp that same evening and lowered its flags in the neighbourhoods that it had taken. Hezbollah did likewise, voluntarily turning over the neighbourhoods it has occupied to the army. By the evening of the 11th calm had been established in West Beirut and the residents felt safe enough to begin going out into the street again.

However, although they withdrew from Beirut, the Hezbollah fighters' route on the 11th took them through the Druze areas of the Mountain, obviously planning to shut down the transmitters of the majority's television channels. By the morning Jumblatt and Talal Arslan had established contact, despite the fact that their supporters had shot at each other in Beirut, to prevent fighting in the Mountain and secure the release of four employees of the town council of Aley abducted by Hezbollah the day before. In early afternoon the party's fighters took the Druze village of Aytat under fire from the Shiite village of Qomatiyeh. Jumblatt immediately delegated Arslan, his Druze rival allied with Damascus, to negotiate an end to the hostilities. A ceasefire to start at 6 p.m. that day was announced, but the belligerents carried on regardless, and Jumblatt had to appeal for calm again. The situation normalized in the vicinity of Aley, but the fighting continued into the night in Mresti and Tumat Niha, in the Shuf, as well as Shueifat. It appeared that the inhabitants of the area, having learned through the media that Hezbollah had taken a number of villages between Aley and Shueifat, had immediately organized a local resistance, armed only with personal weapons. In Mresti, while Hezbollah fighters were taking the transmitter stations of LBCI, Tele Liban, and MTV under fire, the residents left them with a dozen dead and wounded. Jumblatt, upon receiving a call from Nabih Berri, prevailed on the people to free their prisoners, which they did only once the army arrived.

Doha: Hezbollah scores

Starting on 11 May, Arab foreign ministers met with the secretary-general of the Arab League, who was presiding over a gathering that had been arranged to address the Lebanese situation. They aimed to end the fighting on the ground and to find a way out of the deadlocked issues. A delegation headed by Qatar's prime minister, Hamad ben Jassem, arrived in Beirut on 14th May and invited the Lebanese leaders to meet in Doha. Inter-Lebanese negotiations began on 16th May and ended on the 21st. The two sides agreed within twenty-four hours to make Michel Sleiman president. They also reached agreement on the composition of a national unity government of thirty members, with sixteen ministers representing the majority, eleven the opposition, and three the president of the Republic. The parties undertook not to resign from the government and not to interfere with its functioning. They also promised to refrain from resorting to violence to achieve political gains, to stop hurling accusations of betrayal, and not to launch any further campaigns that might exacerbate political and sectarian tensions. In return for some concessions to the majority, Hezbollah carried its most important point. While electing the president was first in the order of priorities, in conformity with the wishes of the majority, the blocking third was conceded to the opposition. Michel Sleiman was elected and the discussion of IRL's disarmament was shelved for the time being.

As soon as agreement was reached to suspend the 6 May cabinet decisions, order was quickly restored in the Lebanese capital as well as in the Mountain. On 13 May, even before the discussions in Doha started, Future TV and Future News resumed their broadcasts, and *al-Mustaqbal* began publishing again the following day. Beirut international airport reopened on 15 May, and so did all major traffic arteries in the capital. On 21 May the Doha agreement was signed, the opposition dismantled its camp on Riyad al-Solh Square after 538 days of sit-ins, and downtown Beirut was once again thronged by tourists and regulars in the neighbourhood cafés. The final casualty list of the conflict was drawn up, showing 65 deaths, nearly a dozen of them in Beirut, and 200 injured.[157]

On Sunday, 25 May, General Michel Sleiman was elected president of the Republic as agreed, ending the top post's six-month vacancy. At first, Saad Hariri topped the list of likely prime ministers, but in the end it fell to Fouad Siniora to again form a government. Assembling one was more difficult and took longer than expected. Hezbollah insisted that Foreign Affairs must go to a Shiite (pro-March 8) and that the minister of defence, Elias Murr, suspected of having passed documents about the airport runway 17 to Jumblatt, should not be reinstated. For its part, March 14 intended to hold on to Telecommunications to ensure the smooth functioning of the international tribunal. The cabinet was finally introduced on 11 July: Foreign Affairs reverted to Fawzi Sallukh, who was close to Hezbollah and AMAL, and Telecommunications went to Michel Aoun's son-in-law Gebran Bassil. However, Elias Murr retained his post. Hezbollah was easily consoled, the Ministerial Statement having given it full satisfaction, since it guaranteed

> the right of the people, army, and Resistance of Lebanon to liberate or recover the Shebaa Farms, the Kfarshuba hills, and the Lebanese sector of the occupied Ghajar village, and to defend the country against any aggression and to protect its rights to its water resources *by all means legitimate and available*.[158]

Hard knocks for March 14

For March 14, the explosion of 7 May 2008 and the losses it sustained were not the only destabilizing events that it had to face in the run-up to the 2009 parliamentary elections. During the period the coalition had three pieces of good news, which, in theory, represented as many victories. First, the Special Tribunal for Lebanon (STL) set up to try Rafic Hariri's assassins was officially inaugurated on 1 March 2009; two weeks later, Syria opened an embassy for the first time in Beirut;[159] finally, the June 2009 parliamentary elections again gave March 14 a majority. Successful realization of the two main objectives of the Cedar Revolution, like the return to power of its defenders, however, would remain a mixed blessing.

Paris and Washington distance themselves

After its relative setback in Doha, March 14's position was all the more fragile because it had to accommodate a change in the tenor of French and American support for its cause. On the French side, President Jacques Chirac and his ambassador in Beirut, Bernard Emié, had involved themselves personally in actively supporting the March 14 Alliance. The end of Chirac's term in May 2007, followed by that of Emié in July, portended a cooling of France's engagement with the Country of Cedars. The French ministry of foreign affairs continued initially to offer mediation for resolving the inter-Lebanese disputes, doing their best in the autumn of 2007 to try to cut through the presidential Gordian knot, but they were finally frustrated by the stalemates and withdrew. From that moment on, France's activity in Lebanon was poised for retreat. This shift was clearly perceptible during the events of May 2008, an issue on which Paris not only involved itself too little and too late, but gave up its role as a major mediator to the Arab side. After more than three years of taking a hardline position against both Syria and Hezbollah, French foreign policy under the presidency of Nicolas Sarkozy opted for opening up. The process, begun immediately after the Doha meetings, culminated in a formal reconciliation that was celebrated on 14 July in Paris with President Bashar al-Assad as the guest of honour. During this visit, which lasted several days, they did not even bring up the question of the international tribunal for Lebanon. Two months later Sarkozy was in Syria. The oil company Total signed three cooperation agreements with Damascus, and the French president declared: "Assad has kept his promises in the Lebanese matter."[160] At the same time, the minister of foreign affairs, Bernard Kouchner, was in Lebanon, where he encouraged the March 14 forces to soften their position towards the Syrian regime.[161] In March 2009 Sarkozy drove home the point: "A national reconciliation is above all the responsibility of the Lebanese themselves."[162] The message was made all the more clear by a change in France's policy towards Hezbollah. In early May 2009, while the government of Great Britain announced its refusal to open discussions with the party and the new American administration declared that it was 'not ready' to establish contact with it, Kouchner said: "I have some connections with Hezbollah. They are members of the government. I invited them to France. ... We do not have a problem with that."[163]

As for the Americans, the end of the neoconservative era also meant a less favourable development for March 14. Washington's support was beginning to fray even before President George W. Bush's term ended. In January 2008 Michelle Sison succeeded Jeffrey Feltman as ambassador, and declared shortly after assuming her post that "US support for Lebanon is bipartisan".[164] In contrast to her predecessor, whose moves were judged repeatedly as being close to interference, including his advice to March 14 on the attitude to be adopted towards Hezbollah, which some considered to be too prescriptive, Sison displayed restraint and discretion. More significantly, US support was lacking during the crisis of May 2008, when the government expected it most ardently, and was counting on US ground forces intervening. As for Barack Obama's team, it signalled during its first weeks in office that it was hoping to find common ground with the Iranian regime. Like the French government, it also chose a policy of relative détente with Bashar al-Assad, apparently with the aim of reviving peace talks between Israel and Syria.[165] At the end of February 2009 the Syrian ambassador to Washington was received by Jeffrey Feltman, now the assistant secretary of state for Near Eastern affairs. Secretary of State Hillary Clinton was in Damascus in early March, and in May Rød-Larsen himself remarked on a "positive development" in Syrian–American relations.[166]

An exchange of ambassadors and the STL

In mid-August 2008 the Syrian regime and the Lebanese government agreed in principle to exchange ambassadors. This was initially expected to happen by the end of 2008, but was regularly postponed due to Syrian procrastination in picking an ambassador. The embassies only opened in Beirut and Damascus in January and March 2009 respectively, and the head of the Syrian diplomatic mission in Lebanon did not arrive until May.

Despite the fact that this exchange was one of the first demands of the Cedar Revolution, in the end it produced only lukewarm enthusiasm in March 14 circles. Indeed, it only became feasible on the express condition imposed by the Syrian government of keeping the Syrian–Lebanese Higher Council in existence. This body, a legacy of the Taef Agreement created for the purpose of strengthening and overseeing the "privileged relationship" between the two countries, was a *bête noire* for the majority. Also of serious concern was that the Syrian embassy in Beirut would ultimately be nothing more than a repetition of the former headquarters of the chief of Syrian intelligence in Lebanon. Installed at Anjar (Bekaa) during tutelage times, he was the real wielder of power in Lebanon, dictating his instructions to Beirut from there.

On 1 March 2009 the STL, established pursuant to a UN Security Council Resolution in May 2007, officially got to work. In majority circles it was a cause for celebration, and especially for hope: the start of the tribunal's work was held up as "proof that the international community has not completely abandoned" March 14, and Saad Hariri ventured to predict that "the tribunal will reach all the way to Damascus".[167] Less than two months later hope had turned to worry. On 29 April the four generals—Sayyid, Hamdan, Hajj, and Azar—who had been arrested in August 2005 at the behest of the Mehlis commission, were released for lack of evidence on a pre-trial ruling by the STL's Judge Daniel Fransen.[168] Saad Hariri and Samir Geagea tried to downplay the importance of the news, saying that the decision illustrated that the STL was not politicized, "contrary to what the opposition maintains". However, the generals' release was nothing less than a serious political defeat. The opposition, which was not fooled, celebrated the event with great pomp, seeing it as an acknowledgement by the International Commission of Inquiry of the dubious credibility of the Mehlis investigation's findings.

The exchange between Israel and Hezbollah

On 13 August 2006, even before the end of fighting between Israel and the IRL that summer, the press reported that Tel Aviv would be willing to consider negotiations for a prisoner exchange. This was confirmed in early September when Hezbollah and the Israeli authorities accepted UN mediation. Amir Peretz, the Israeli minister of defence, even suggested that his country might release Samir Quntar—truly a first.[169] This news caused an explosion of joy among IRL supporters: Hezbollah had always conditioned the return of prisoners on such an exchange taking place, and the acceptance, even belated, of this condition was interpreted as a bonus victory. It meant so much more on the symbolic level because the Israeli army officially launched the July offensive precisely because it had rejected such a process and was determined to recover its soldiers by force.

In mid-October, in return for the recovery of the bodies of two IRL fighters, Hezbollah gave Israel information on the pilot Ron Arad and the body of an Israeli soldier who had died during clashes in the summer of 2006.[170] At the end of May 2008 Nasrallah promised the impending release of the last Lebanese prisoners still held in Israeli jails. Tel Aviv confirmed by announcing the release of five Lebanese prisoners and the return of the bodies of ten IRL fighters in exchange for the two Israeli soldiers abducted in July 2006.[171] In a manner of speaking, Hezbollah and the Israeli government here carried out the last act of the Thirty-Three-Day War. Nasīm Nisr was released on 1 June and his fellow prisoners on 16 July. On this occasion Israel also returned the remains of 199 Lebanese and Arab fighters, twelve of whom had belonged to Hezbollah. The exchange, named Operation Ridwān in memory of Imad Mughniyeh, was coordinated by the ICRC.[172] In an illustration of the new relations between majority and opposition, the government, which had not been seen at the festivities two years earlier when Hezbollah celebrated the end of the war, this time decreed:

> the closure of all government agencies and public and private companies, municipalities, and public and private educational institutions, on Wednesday, 16 July 2008, to celebrate the release of prisoners from the jails of the Israeli enemy and the return of remains of martyrs to the country's soil.[173]

The event was huge. Present at the gathering were the president, prime minister and speaker of parliament, as well as former presidents, former speakers of parliament, former prime ministers, religious leaders, the deputy speaker of parliament, the deputy prime minister, ministers, ambassadors of the Arab countries, Iran and Germany, representatives in Lebanon of the secretary-general of the United Nations. Also present were the ICRC president, MPs, the president of the Supreme Court, the president of the Council of State, the attorney general at the Court of Cassation, the interim supreme commander of the army, the presidents of the press and journalists associations, the heads of the general security forces, the internal security forces, army intelligence, the acting *mohafez* of Mount Lebanon, the commanding officer of UNIFIL, and the airport's chief of security. President Sleiman spoke bluntly:

> If I have often repeated that the joy of the liberation of the South will only be complete after the liberation of detainees by Israel, I say today that our joy will reach its peak when we recover the sovereignty of our land in Shebaa Farms and Kfarshuba. I assure you that Lebanon has the right to recover its land *by any means possible*.[174]

The operation was not just a defeat for Israel; it was a major one for March 14, whose top leaders were obliged to attend the ceremony celebrating the return of the prisoners, to display their joy, offer their congratulations—and to render tribute to the IRL. On the evening of 16 July it seemed as if the entire Republic was on the tarmac of Beirut airport. Fouad Siniora, alongside Sleiman and Berri, was among the first to receive the former detainees. All ministers in the new government and the leaders of the various parliamentary blocs—including Saad Hariri—saluted the heroes of the day. In one scene watched by most of those present and TV viewers of all political persuasions, Marwan Hamadeh and Nayla Moawad, March 14 hawks, approached to shake hands with the prisoners and wish them a happy return—an embarrassing image for the parliamentary majority, whose hardliners in the government were obliged to show satisfaction with the IRL's latest achievements, only two months after voting in favour of its destruction by force of arms.

A general election "with existential stakes" or "little will change"?

Preparations for the parliamentary elections of 2009 were punctuated by several controversies. The majority tried to favour the emergence of a "centrist" bloc, a pool of political leaders close to the president of the Republic that, based on some electoral calculations, would make it possible to defeat the Aounist candidates. For its part, the FPM advocated moving to a third republic described as "secular and modern" that, as a result of the abolition of confessionalism as provided for in the Taef Agreement, would base itself no longer on communitarian quotas but on the democracy of numbers. The majority's Christian circles denounced this as heresy. The Sunnis in March 14, starting with Saad Hariri and the mufti of the Republic, Muhammad Rashid Kabbani, supported them by repeating their commitment to a "permanent" Christian–Muslim parity.[175] Similarly, there was a war of dichotomies between the two camps around the definition of what really was at stake in the elections, presented by both March 8 and March 14 as a choice between two incompatible options. For Hezbollah it was about contrasting a Lebanon "subject to the US–Israeli domination" and a "free and sovereign" Lebanon. To the parliamentary majority it was about a "free and sovereign Lebanon" versus a Lebanon "led by Iran and Syria". Obviously still reeling from the shock of May 2008, the March 14 Sunnis also put stress on the need for security, with slogans such as *al-Amn awwalan* ('Security first'), at the same time as its Christian alter ego launched itself into an existential war whose primary target was not the FPM but Hezbollah. The party represented a political threat above all: the theme of *wilāyat al-faqīh* was used to prove that Hezbollah could not possibly have any allegiance to the nation, and how incompatible it was with "the State". But the threat was also to identity: the party, if it won, would "change the face of Lebanon". Thus, when Iranian president Mahmud Ahmadinejad suggested at the end of May that an opposition victory in the Lebanese elections would change the regional order,[176] a wave of real panic washed over the March 14 Christian circles. Patriarch Nasrallah Sfeir went so far as to sound the alarm that "Lebanon as an entity and its Arab identity are threatened."[177] Many in the majority also predicted a resort to arms by Hezbollah on election day, so that the closer the deadline loomed the more highly charged with emotion the tone became: some even envisaged exile as "unavoidable" in the event of an opposition victory.

Hezbollah responded by labelling this discourse alarmist. Party officials downplayed what was at stake from the election, suggesting that the results would ultimately change little. Anticipating a possible defeat, the leadership signalled its preference for a new unity government in which the party and its allies would have a blocking minority—an option immediately rejected by March 14. Despite the tension and fears of mishaps, the parliamentary elections took place on 7 June without major problems. March 14 was victorious once again, winning 71 seats out of 128.[178] Nasrallah conceded defeat as soon as the results were announced,[179] but circles close to the party drew attention to the fact that March 14 only won a parliamentary majority (*al-aktharriyya al-barlamāniyya*) while the opposition won a majority of the popular vote (*al-aktharriyya al-sha'biyya*, that is, by numbers), as in 2005.[180] In terms of popularity in its community, Hezbollah could consider itself satisfied, with 90 per cent of Shiite votes in the Bekaa Valley and the South.[181]

The party leadership had other reasons not to be disappointed by the election results. Sunni factions nominated Saad Hariri to head the new government. Other elements within March 14 approved. To get the opposition to go along, especially Hezbollah and AMAL, Hariri showed himself conciliatory. At the end of June Nabih Berri was re-elected by the majority as speaker of parliament. Despite Samir Geagea's refusal, the opposition got its blocking minority. The Ministerial Statement adopted at the end of the month once again citing Lebanon's right to defend itself "by all legitimate and authorized means"[182] legitimized the IRL's weapons. As a tribute to the Syrian regime for having just given "permission" for his nomination as prime minister, Hariri retracted his accusations against the Baathist regime in the murder of his father. Further, he not only backtracked on the repeated predictions by his political family of the previous four years that the Assad dynasty would fall at the hands of the STL, but at the end of December went to Damascus on an official visit. The year 2010 therefore seemed to begin with March 14 abandoning its overtly hostile positions towards the Syrian regime. Hope for a return to calm on the domestic scene seemed that much more justified when it began to look (once again) as if Walid Jumblatt was seriously tempted to defect.

Jumblatt's Nth reversal: fall of the Hariri government

In May 2008 there were rumours in opposition circles that, following the cabinet's famous decision, Walid Jumblatt had turned over the keys to the PSP offices in Beirut to the army command (by all appearances, in order to deprive the opposition of any grounds for attacking them) just as he supposedly orderered all cadres and militants of his party to fall back to the Druze Shuf. In other words, according to these rumours Jumblatt, in several accounts described as one of the hardliners in that exceptional cabinet night session,[183] was well aware of the impact the decisions made that night would have—and he had correctly gauged the reaction of March 14's adversaries. Whatever the case may have been, scarcely had the Hezbollah fighters penetrated into the Shuf than Walid Jumblatt, who had showered his Shiite compatriots with vexing comments and confessional insults between 2006 and 2008, changed his tone immediately and implored "the noble brothers of the respected Shiite community"[184] not to take it out on the area's populations.

This first about-face, articulating the Druze leader's sudden realization of the real balance of power on the ground, was immediately followed by a new political reversal. After more than two-and-a-half years of having strenuously opposed Hezbollah and the IRL, Jumblatt executed a notable return to "Arabness", to "the Palestinian cause"—and to a defence of the Resistance. This was announced officially some hours before his departure for Doha on 16 May. His new positions were confirmed the following July, at the end of the prisoner exchange between Israel and Hezbollah, when Samir Quntar, a Druze from the Shuf, was freed. The PSP called for massive participation in the celebrations, in honour of "an event of national scale that deserves general unity". The invitation went on to say that "the liberation of the last detainees from Israeli prisons is a historic victory resulting from a long fight against the Israeli enemy and his policy of aggression."[185] More radically still: "The road of resistance must be taken all the way to the liberation of Palestine."[186] It was no coincidence that, when Jumblatt welcomed Quntar in Abey, he was accompanied by his son and successor, Taymur, and, seated at his right during the ceremony, was none other than Muhammad Fneish, the Hezbollah minister. Shouting into the media's microphones,[187] the Druze leader declared in a virulent speech that "Israel only understands the language of force"[188] and, making nonsense of March 14 credos, ferociously defended the coexistence of Resistance and state. Two weeks later he claimed that "the state has the right to resort to *any means, military or diplomatic* to liberate the Shebaa Farms *as they are Lebanese*".[189] Moreover, he said that he was not really convinced that the Special Tribunal would ensure that the Syrian president would be found guilty, and trotted out a new *mea culpa*. In May 2009 he jumped to Hezbollah's defence when the German weekly *Der Spiegel* reported on the party's possible involvement in Rafic Hariri's assassination.

These reversals, framing a rehabilitation of the Resistance and of the Palestinian cause and the revival of Israel's role as enemy number one, were accompanied by a number of clashes between Jumblatt and his March 14 partners. Friction first arose in early July 2008 with the Lebanese Forces, in connection with the jockeying by the various parties to form the government after Doha. Jumblatt conveyed his wish to include in the government a Christian minister from his party, immediately calling into question the number of Lebanese Forces Christian ministers. A little over two weeks later Jumblatt incurred the wrath of Sunni circles around Hariri when, in criticizing the armed fighting then going on in Tripoli between Sunnis and Alawites (Shiites), he said:

> The wounds inflicted in Beirut [in May 2008] cannot be healed by acts of vengeance somewhere else, in this way serving the calculations of nations that negotiated and entered into conflict and which, in the end, compromised.[190]

In April 2009, in the midst of the electoral campaign, he called for the abolition of political confessionalism, causing an outcry in the Christian March 14.[191] His remarks were in a video filmed without his knowledge at a meeting with Druze religious leaders which was broadcast on New TV, a channel close to the opposition. In it, Jumblatt declares:

> [the Christians and Sunnis of March 14] want to draw us into a conflict with the Shiites so they can sit and watch us kill each other. ... We have seen the Sunnis in Beirut [in May 2008]. A thousand men arrived from Akkar could not hold out for 15 minutes![192]

Referring to the Christians, he adds:

> The election will proceed even though it will not change much. Walid Jumblatt is no longer able to form a list in the Shuf because the isolationist tendencies[193] have re-emerged. A bad seed will always remain bad.

His new positions set his allies in the majority on edge all the more. They feared, following his hints at a desire to reconcile with the Syrian regime, that he might defect to the ranks of March 8 at election time. In late March 2009 he indirectly but unmistakably sought forgiveness from the Syrian president: two months before the elections the Syrian foreign minister, Walid al-Moallem, said that "Walid Jumblatt must know what he wants".[194] The latter then answered, "provocative words against Damascus are not beneficial" for Lebanon, and that:

> it is up to the Syrian people to decide its fate. I am not its intermediary. Moreover, I cannot pass from one extreme to the other. It is up to the Syrian people to decide if this regime suits them or not. ... I levied some accusations against the Syrian regime during a period that was one of the most difficult in Lebanese history, during the time of assassinations. ... Lebanon cannot be in a situation of permanent hostility with Syria. ... Lebanon also cannot enter a neutrality phase. I am against neutrality.[195]

Bashar al-Assad took note. It was accepted that the PSP stayed on the rolls as a March 14 component, but the way remained open for a rapprochement with the Syrian regime. With support and mediation by Nasrallah, it was a done deal in the spring of 2010: the Druze leader was in Damascus at the end of March and, received by the Syrian president, delivered a paean of praise for "Syrian policy in Lebanon".[196]

In the months following the 2009 elections Hezbollah was therefore relatively at ease. With Jumblatt boxed in, the majority of MPs could not *a priori* legislate against IRL's interests; in any event, not when the speaker had been won over to its cause. The prime minister had no intention on returning to confrontation, and the executive could at every turn be constrained by the blocking third. The chief of the Lebanese army's General Staff, finally, was an ally of Michel Aoun. Only the conservative Christians and some Sunni radicals remained openly hostile, but they were too few and too dependent on a political class whose majority was keen to avoid a collision.

This superficial harmony was short-lived, however. From the second half of 2010 the issue of the STL returned with a vengeance to the domestic scene, with rumours rife of an impending indictment of Hezbollah members. For more than six months the party put pressure on the government to officially declare the forthcoming results of the tribunal null and void. The cabinet categorically refused to do so, and the party leadership in the end invoked the blocking third on 12 January 2011. Eleven of the thirty ministers resigned, causing the Hariri government to fall. After meeting with Nasrallah on 13 January, Jumblatt officially switched to the ranks of March 8 on the 21st. The eleven MPs in his bloc henceforth belonged to the opposition, which, with 68 seats out of 128, became the new majority and won the right to form a new cabinet. For the first time in its history, Hezbollah openly and directly took the reins of power.

10

THE SPECIAL TRIBUNAL FOR LEBANON AND THE SYRIAN CONFLICT

HEZBOLLAH TAKES THE REINS

At the news of Rafic Hariri's assassination in February 2005, the leaders of the future March 14, doubting the impartiality of Lebanese justice under the influence of a pro-Syrian government, immediately made their preference known for an international inquiry. The loyalists, on the other hand, advocated a mixed or Arab commission because they feared that a Western investigation would be used under the guise of impartiality to dispose of Israel's foremost enemy and ally of Damascus in Lebanon, that is, Hezbollah.

Initially, responsibility for the attack was claimed by a then-unknown Islamist group, al-Nusra wal-Jihād fī Bilād al-Shām (Loyalty and Jihad in Greater Syria). In a video broadcast by al-Jazeera shortly after the attack, a young Palestinian Islamist named Ahmad Abū ʿAdas took credit for the suicide operation, which was intended to punish the former prime minister for his "excessively" close relations with the Saudi royal family. According to the Lebanese authorities, it seems he disappeared during March of the previous year and his family claimed that he went to Iraq at the time. Although al-Qāʿida denied any involvement, the Lebanese government's investigation initially favoured the fundamentalist trail.

Toward an indictment of the Syrian regime

Spadework by the Fitzgerald fact-finding commission

Despite the Lebanese government's reservations, a commission of inquiry mandated by the UN and chaired by Peter Fitzgerald, a deputy commissioner of Irish police, arrived in Beirut ten days after the attack. Its report, presented to Secretary-General Kofi Annan a month later, emphasized the failures of the Syrian and Lebanese security services.[1] The Syrian services in particular were held responsible for the general political tension pervading Lebanon during the months preceding the assassination. They were also blamed, together with the Lebanese services, for shortfalls in Hariri's security before his death, which had mainly been left to his private bodyguards. The Lebanese investigation was singled out for having suffered from "serious and systematic" shortcomings: it took several days after the attack to recover bodies hidden under debris; in a decision complicating the collection of evidence, the six vehicles of Hariri's convoy were removed from the crime scene immediately, and other important items were removed from the site of the explosion without being inventoried. A nearby bank's surveillance camera having recorded the "suspicious" movements of a small white Mitsubishi truck, the Lebanese government had hypothesized a car bomb; but the Fitzgerald commission found that:

> parts of a truck were brought to the site of the explosion by a member of the security forces after the assassination and were placed in the crater and then photographed in the crater by members of the security forces, creating doubts and suspicions about the truck actually being implicated in this assassination and thus seriously eroding the credibility of the investigation's main lead.

The attack was in all likelihood carried out by exploding a one-ton surface charge of TNT. The motives appear to relate to the tensions that were said to characterize relations in prior months between the former prime minister and President Bashar al-Assad: the latter supposedly reneged on his promise that the term in office of President Émile Lahoud, with whom Rafic Hariri had a difficult relationship, would not be extended. Moreover, the Syrian president had blamed the Lebanese prime minister for the passage of Resolution 1559.

The Fitzgerald report therefore recommended an independent investigation by an international commission. The Lebanese government gave its endorsement, but insisted that the powers granted to such a commission should "respect Lebanese sovereignty". As such, the commission must remain under the authority of the Lebanese Justice Ministry. It would thus confine itself to presenting its reports, with the Lebanese authorities then deciding what actions to take, potentially including the arrest of suspects. Based on this agreement in principle, in April 2005 the UNSC passed Resolution 1595, formally appointing an international commission of inquiry to investigate the murder of Rafic Hariri.

Virtues and disgraces of the Mehlis Commission

The Commission began its work in mid-June, presided over by a German judge, Detlev Mehlis. He presented a preliminary report on 25 August.[2] For the first time, he complained about the lack of cooperation by Syrian authorities in the investigation. The report's initial findings prompted him to ask the Lebanese judicial authorities to place four generals under arrest: Mustafa Hamdan, head of the presidential guard; Jamil al-Sayyid, director of General Security; Ibrahim al-Hajj, chief of the ISF; and Raymond Azar, head of army intelligence. Questioned as suspects by the Commission, they were imprisoned on 30 August. Although March 14 very publicly expressed its suspicions of President Lahoud, he was ultimately exonerated.

The Commission then presented two more reports, dated 20 October and 12 December. They pointed to both Syrian and Lebanese involvement.[3] The motive for the murder was once again linked to the deterioration in relations between the former prime minister and the Syrian president. On 26 August 2004 the two men are said to have met privately, at which time the latter is said to have announced his decision to Hariri that President Lahoud's term would be extended and to have threatened to "break Lebanon over [Hariri's] head" if Hariri opposed it. Senior Syrian and Lebanese officials allegedly decided to assassinate Hariri two weeks after the passage of Resolution 1559. The day before the murder, a witness, whose testimony added him to the list of suspects, was to have reconnoitered the Saint-Georges quarter with Syrian officers. Abū ʿAdas was said to have been spirited to Syria and detained there, and the confession tape was allegedly passed on to Jamil al-Sayyid. Sayyid, Azar, and Hamdan supposedly participated in planning the assassination, while Hajj was simply kept informed about it. Another witness, Muhammad Zuheir al-Siddiq, whose name would be made public and who described himself initially as a senior official in the Syrian security services, was reported as stating that the assassination was suggested by Nasser Qandil, a former Lebanese MP aligned with Damascus. The final decision was then said to have been made in the Syrian hierarchy. Senior officials of both countries would have met between July and December 2004 in al-Siddiq's apartment in Khaldeh, and later in Beirut's southern suburbs, in order to set up the assassination.

Mehlis also indicated that Hariri was under phone surveillance. He pointed out that one of the first steps that Hajj took as head of the ISF in November 2004 was to cut the number of agents on the former prime minister's security detail from forty to eight. The general defended this step by invoking a Lebanese rule stipulating this number of agents when protecting political personalities in Hariri's category.[4] The Mitsubishi van used to transport the explosives was stolen in Japan. It entered Lebanon from Syria, driven by a Syrian army colonel. A first witness allegedly saw it in Hammana, a village in Mount Lebanon, three days before the murder. For his part, Siddiq allegedly also identified it in a camp in Zabadani, on the Syrian border, where he supposedly also saw Abū ʿAdas. The Commission's research into the latter also was said to have identified another key figure: Sheikh Ahmad Abdel-Aal, head of public relations and military intelligence for al-Ahbash, a Lebanese Islamic group with close ties to Damascus.[5] Abdel-Aal is supposed to have told the Commission that Abū ʿAdas was a Wahhabite encountered in the Ain al-Heloueh Palestinian camp near Sidon (South), where he was linked, again according to Abdel-Aal, to Islamist groups. The inquiry concluded that Abū ʿAdas was a decoy used by the Syrian regime to lead the investigation astray. There was allegedly no evidence that he actually belonged to the al-Nusra group, or that the group even existed. The report also argued that it was impossible for him to carry out the suicide attack: according to the latest information available on him, he did not know how to drive.

The Commission was also interested in the phone networks. It discovered that a dozen mobile phones were used to maintain surveillance on Hariri starting in January 2005. Six lines in particular, active that morning in the vicinity of the spot where the assassination occurred, stopped transmitting after the explosion at 12.56 p.m. It appears that the six pre-paid cards came from Tripoli, a Sunni city in the north, from a store owned by an active Ahbash member closely linked to Ahmad Abdel-Aal.

Finally, the Mehlis reports highlighted how the Syrian authorities dragged their feet when it came to cooperating. When the judge asked to question Syrian officials and witnesses, Damascus reportedly made it a condition that the interviews would take place in Syria and in the presence of Syrian officials. Two officials also were supposed to have testified that all of Syrian intelligence's documentation on Lebanon had been burned, so no documents bearing on Hariri's assassination were to be found in its archives. However, the Commission would also stress the fact that transcripts of Hariri's telephone conversations were sent daily to Syrian officials and to the generals Azar, Sayyid, and Rustom Ghazaleh. A highly placed Syrian official is also said to have furnished arms and ammunition to groups and individuals in Lebanon for the purpose of creating public disorder in response to accusations that the Syrian regime was implicated.

On 10 October Ghazi Kanaan, director of Syrian intelligence in Lebanon from 1982 until 2002, was found dead. Damascus declared it a suicide, but many in Lebanon sarcastically called it an "assisted suicide". At year's end, Abdel-Halim Khaddam, a former Syrian deputy president who became a dissident and was in charge of the Lebanese dossier during the time of the tutelage, stated during an interview with al-Arabiya that both presidents Assad and Lahoud were personally involved in the assassination.[6] He also suggested that Rustom Ghazaleh, Kanaan's successor as head of Syrian intelligence in Lebanon until the end of the tutelage, had not only threatened the former prime minister but also stole $35 million from the Lebanese al-Madina Bank. Its collapse in 2003 had caused a great deal of noise because of the political repercussions it set off implicating senior Lebanese—and Syrian—officials.

Nevertheless, concurrent with these news items along the lines of the International Commission of Inquiry's work, its position and its conclusions posed problems from the start, and many critical voices were raised. First of all, the methods Mehlis employed upset the pro-Syrian political class, even putting the anti-Syrians in an uncomfortable position. The judge was in fact suspected of letting himself be overly influenced by radical figures of March 14. He was also reproached for his repeated violations of the obligation to confidentiality during the investigation, and a penchant for press conferences and interviews, all the more so since his statements caused real uproar. As a case in point, in an interview given to *Le Figaro* in July he openly admitted that the Commission had approached the Israeli intelligence service. These revelations caused the Lebanese authorities great discomfort because, quite apart from the Commission president's lack of discretion, and beyond the fact that the Commission was only approved on condition that it operated under the authority of the Lebanese judicial system, any kind of collaboration with the Mossad seriously undermined the inquiry's impartiality.[7] However, the judge did not change his working methods or his style of communication. In an interview with the German Deutsche Welle TV channel, reprinted in the 5 September edition of the *Der Spiegel* weekly magazine, even before the publication of the first report, he talked about a Syrian connection to the murder and a "conspiracy at the highest levels of the Lebanese state". He publicly accused Maher al-Assad, President Bashar al-Assad's brother and head of the presidential guard, and Assef Shawkat, head of military intelligence and the president's brother-in-law, of having plotted the assassination with Lebanese officials starting in September 2004. The next day, Intelligence Online, a Paris-based website specializing in intelligence matters, asserted that Mehlis had reportedly managed to move the investigation forward thanks to a high-ranking defector from Syrian military intelligence. A few months earlier the Saudi and US intelligence services had indeed prevailed on the chief of staff of the head of Syrian military intelligence to defect. The officer would first of all been taken to Saudi Arabia for questioning by the intelligence services, then undergone similar interrogations in the United States before eventually winding up working with Mehlis.

The Commission's work was placed in an especially bad light in October when the case of the "false witnesses" surfaced, which would play out as a political drama with multiple twists in the ensuing years. The Mehlis theses in fact rested mainly on the testimony of two key witnesses: Muhammad Zuheir al-Siddiq and Hussam Hussam, a Syrian who worked with the Syrian and Lebanese services during the tutelage. Three days after submission of the first report, on 20 October, *Der Spiegel* reported that some UN officials doubted the credibility of al-Siddiq, said to have been convicted on several occasions of embezzlement and fraud, to have repeatedly lied during the hearings, and to have been paid to change his story.[8]

In late November, Hussam Hussam, referred to in the Mehlis report as the "masked witness", was unmasked, and recanted his testimony. He accused Saad Hariri and Interior Minister Hassan Sabeh of having offered him $1.3 million to finger Maher al-Assad and Assef Shawkat as instigators of the assassination and to certify to the Commission president that he had seen the Mitsubishi van on a Syrian military base.[9] He also accused Walid Jumblatt and Marwan Hamadeh of having pressured other witnesses into giving false testimony to the Mehlis team; further, that he met not just Jumblatt and Hamadeh at Commission headquarters, but also the journalists Gebran Tueni and May Chidiac.[10] In mid-January 2006 Ibrahim Michel Jarjura, another key Syrian witness, was arrested for perjury. Recanting, he argued that Hamadeh repeatedly offered him money to say that he had met the former (Lebanese pro-Syrian) MP

Sleiman Frangieh, as well as Assef Shawkat and Ali al-Hajj, at the Sheraton in Damascus in July 2004. He also admitted to having met Bahia Hariri, sister of Rafic and an MP, before being questioned by the Commission.

The lack of judicial discretion on the part of Mehlis, his questionable methods, and the discredit that the false witnesses would cast on the Commission's findings explained the UN Secretary-General's decision to have the judge step down at year's end. In early January 2006 he was replaced by a Belgian judge, Serge Brammertz, who not only exercised restraint and practiced discretion but also refrained from commenting publicly on any element of the investigation. Shrouding his comings and goings in Syria and his interviews in complete secrecy, and refusing to name potential suspects, he reviewed all the work done by Mehlis, even reviving hypotheses that the latter had discarded. His reports, delivered to the UNSC beginning in early February, satisfied all parties—Damascus included, whose press went so far as to praise them as reflecting of the judge's "professionalism and discretion".[11]

The Inquiry and Lebanese political life

Hezbollah goes on the offensive

If the appointment of Brammertz gave the Commission of Inquiry a chance to rebuild the credibility damaged by Mehlis, it did not save Lebanese political life from deadlock over the advisability of establishing an international tribunal. In particular, it affected the relationship between Hezbollah and the government. As mentioned earlier, the report of 25 August was rumoured to point to a possible involvement by the party in the Hariri assassination. After an initial disdainful reaction, in early October the Hezbollah leadership sharpened its tone, criticizing the government both for taking systematic recourse to the FBI to investigate the various attacks shaking the country at the time and for its increasingly strident exhortations to disarm the IRL. In the spring of 2006 the project of an international tribunal was at the heart of the political disputes, with March 8 threatening more or less overtly to withdraw from the government should it not officially and definitively abandon the idea. After being sidelined by the summer war, the subject rapidly returned to the forefront of the political scene.

In mid-October the UNSC agreed in principle on a criminal court, not international but mixed, thus putting the body under Lebanese rather than international law. The agreement was made feasible by deciding to amend Article 3 of the draft submitted by the UN, an amendment also called for by both Moscow and Beijing. The article did in fact classify the attacks in Lebanon as crimes against humanity, which would have meant that any immunity could be lifted and that any suspect could be extradited.[12] The Russian authorities, seeking to protect the Assad family, introduced a further amendment which preserved intact the immunity of heads of state and senior officials. March 14 circles, clearly disappointed by a clause that appeared to let Bashar al-Assad off the hook, chose nevertheless to remain hopeful. The pro-Syrian political class, on the other hand, had not let go of its fears, and fully intended to do everything in its power to prevent the court from being convened. On 11 November the Shiite ministers withdrew from the government. The rest of the cabinet carried on regardless and adopted the draft of the tribunal in absentia. Thus began a long period of stalemate, during which the opposition tried to convince the majority not to follow through. The international community attempted to induce a more moderate stance among the opposition by raising the spectre of adopting the tribunal statutes in the UNSC itself. With the situation still paralysed, it proceeded to do so on 30 May 2007 (Resolution 1757).

Meanwhile, between autumn 2006 and spring 2007 the opposition pursued a sustained political and media campaign against the court. Hezbollah found especially peculiar the international community's insistence on convening it, in addition to that by March 14. According to the party's leadership, the tribunal was just one more means to be used against it within the framework of the international campaign initiated with the passage of Resolution 1559 in 2004.[13] With the international community failing to disarm the IRL, the National Dialogue meetings, initiated in the summer of 2005 under the pretext of intra-Lebanese exchanges, were seen as designed instead to get the job done on behalf of the West and Israel. A negotiated solution between the Lebanese actors proving more difficult to achieve than expected, the summer 2006 war appeared to be a strong-arm tactic by Tel Aviv to more readily achieve its aims. The defeat of the Israeli army did not deter Hezbollah's detractors, who would then have seen the court as a way of succeeding where policy levers and military initiatives had failed. To a March 14 professing not to understand the party's fears and recalling that Saad Hariri himself had officially declared that Hezbollah was neither accused nor suspected, Hezbollah's leadership responded that the "war of axes" (the Syria–Iran axis against United States–Israel) being waged in the Middle East did not allow a body such as the court to be viewed innocently. The party's leadership assumed that March 14 lacked the means to keep its promise or guarantee its assurances, just as it regarded with suspicion the haste with which the cabinet, now reduced to March 14 ministers only, pressed ahead with signing the draft, without reading or debating it, and moreover without soliciting the opposition's comments on it.[14] Beyond that, Hezbollah admitted that it was afraid that the tribunal would be retroactive, and that it would find itself forced to answer for terrorist acts that it had been accused of during the 1980s. It therefore chose not to submit to judicial proceedings whose ins and outs could not be controlled. Consequently, when Resolution 1757 was passed in late May 2007, the opposition warned that it would never recognize the tribunal.[15]

As previously mentioned, March 8, after deadlocking the government by refusing to have the Shiite ministers rejoin, hobbled the parliamentary process: Nabih Berri refused to convene the Assembly and prevented the presidential election from being held. The situation deteriorated further with the anti-Shiite sectarian campaign orchestrated by March 14 throughout 2007, and imploded in May 2008 when the majority opted for a direct confrontation. The signing of the Doha agreement a few weeks later put an end to the paralysis of political life at the cost of a compromise favouring the opposition in general, and Hezbollah in particular. The 2009 parliamentary elections once more gave the advantage to March 14—but shakily and for a short time. Less than two months after the election, Walid Jumblatt, while keeping his MPs in the re-elected majority, deserted it ideologically and began advocating on behalf of March 8 positions. The official and motivated rapprochement between the Druze leader and the Syrian regime was followed by a dramatic turnabout by Saad Hariri himself. Seeking the post of prime minister, he acceded to opposition demands by granting it a blocking minority in the government. Moreover, Hezbollah's weapons were legitimized by the Ministerial Statement. While Rafic Hariri's son yet again declared in March 2009 that the "tribunal will go all the way to Damascus", discussions got under way in July to organize an official visit to Syria. Having made his *mea culpa*, he was received with full honours by Bashar al-Assad in December, the reconciliation also enjoying a double blessing by the West and Saudi Arabia. In late 2009, Hezbollah could therefore approach the following months with a degree of equanimity.

However, a number of distressing elements arising from the tribunal's ongoing work persisted for the party. In May 2009 *Der Spiegel* reported that the STL was working on a lead implicating members of Hezbollah in the Rafic Hariri assassination. The idea of the party's responsibility was not new, Mehlis having previously assigned it plausibility in his October 2005 report, and *Le Figaro* in August 2006 starting to hint that Hezbollah might be incriminated. The article in *Der Spiegel*, however, was more detailed. It alleged that it was not the Syrians but Hezbollah special forces that had planned and carried out the attack, that there were no indications of Bashar al-Assad having been briefed on the project, and that the suspects had been identified from analysis of phone calls in the vicinity on the day of the attack. When the article appeared, the Lebanese political class as a whole remained sceptical. Once again, the investigation was criticized for its failure to observe professional confidentiality. More importantly, in suggesting that a prominent Sunni leader had been killed by a Shiite political group, the allegation was viewed as dangerous. Sceptics noted that the redirection of the accusations from the Syrian regime to Hezbollah seemed to dovetail with the change in direction of the Western position towards favouring Damascus and Western determination to make short shrift of the party following the Israeli defeat in 2006. It was also noted that even if it cleared the Bashar al-Assad coterie, the absence of a motive weakened the charge against Hezbollah.

March 14, in any case, anxious not to inflame relations with the party at the time, refrained from polemics. Nevertheless, it appeared less and less willing to ignore the accusation as the Western media continued to circulate the rumour. Muhammad Zuheir al-Siddiq, who became known as the principal false witness during the Mehlis Commission inquiry, again became the topic of conversation in April 2010 when, after having pointed the finger at the Syrian regime five years earlier, he accused Hezbollah of murdering Hariri. In late July *The Jerusalem Post*, picking up on news broadcasts by an Israeli television station the day before,[16] announced that the main suspect in the Hariri murder was none other than Mustafa Badreddin, a cousin of Imad Mughniyeh. On 8 November the *Wall Street Journal* suggested that the STL was set to accuse "two to six Hezbollah members"; two days later the story was picked up by the Israeli daily *Yediot Aharonot*, which asserted that the tribunal would indict Mughniyeh, Shawkat, and Qassem Suleimani, a general in the Iranian Pasdaran. Two weeks later, Canadian CBC television broadcast a report accentuating what it described as "the difference between the two Wissams":[17] the first, Wissam Eid, was an official in the ISF intelligence services who prepared an analysis of the communication networks used in the Hariri assassination. He supposedly had discovered the link between the telephone lines of the alleged killers, later tagged as members of Hezbollah. As some would have it, this prompted the Syrian regime and/or Hezbollah to murder him in January 2008. The second, Wissam al-Hassan, headed the ISF intelligence office and was responsible for Rafic Hariri's security at the time of the assassination. The report portrayed him as a potential suspect because, as one who should have been by the former prime minister's side on the day of the attack, the alibi he furnished for not being there proved to be false when checked out by the Commission. Although the credibility of the report would by and large ultimately be put in question, undermined by a circumstantial logic lacking proof, and especially by the great friendship and confidence that always characterized the relationship between al-Hassan and Saad Hariri,[18] the uproar it caused convinced Hezbollah that it was time to react.

The ouster of the government

In July 2010 the party began a concerted public-relations campaign designed to once and for all discredit the STL. Persistent rumour at the time had it that an indictment was likely to be issued "within two months" that some said would contain charges against Hezbollah members. Hassan Nasrallah spoke three times within the space of ten days.[19] The first time he pre-emptively declared the results of the inquiry "null and void if they are based on an analysis of mobile communications", pointing out that the Lebanese intelligence services had arrested many people spying on telephone networks for Israel. He used the opportunity to blame the ISF—thus indirectly the FC—for being slow to detain managers of Alfa, the principal Lebanese mobile phone company, after discovering they worked for Tel Aviv.[20] Immediately afterwards, the Hezbollah secretary-general called for identification and indictment of false witnesses and of the individuals who helped or forced them to give false testimony. He also announced that he had information proving that the indictment had been drafted starting as early as 2008, even before members of the party testified as witnesses before the Commission in April 2010. Saad Hariri supposedly had personally relayed the contents of the indictment to Nasrallah well before its release and offered to portray the suspects as "infiltrators" not acting on the party's behalf—an offer that Nasrallah declined. Recalling that the accusations propagated in the press against Hezbollah originated mainly in Israeli newspapers and media sympathetic to Israel, and accusing the prosecutor, Daniel Bellemare, of receiving visits from senior Israeli officers, Nasrallah insisted that the Commission move to investigate possible involvement by Tel Aviv in the assassination. In this vein, he organized a big-screen presentation in early August of "evidence" that was supposed to back up the party's theses. Commenting on reconnaissance photos purloined from the Israeli air force, he contended that it took detailed photos of the assassination site and the former prime minister's route of travel shortly before the attack. To back up his accusations, he mentioned the case of two spies on Israel's payroll. He alleged that one of them, Ahmad Nasrallah, was supposed to have provided false information to Rafic Hariri's security services about a planned assassination by Hezbollah. The second, Ghassan al-Jidd, was in the vicinity of the Saint-Georges Hotel on the eve of the attack. Hezbollah supposedly warned Lebanese authorities about his activities but al-Jidd, it seems, fled Lebanon before the police could arrest him.

Along with these allegations, the party leadership once more pressed the Hariri government to reject the conclusions of the STL. The cabinet was roundly criticized for failing to tackle the issue of false witnesses; in October the opposition ministers threatened to withdraw from all council meetings unless the topic was dealt with immediately. A few weeks later Nasrallah went so far as to threaten to "cut the hand" of anyone attempting to arrest a Hezbollah member in connection with the investigation, and Na'īm Qāsim evoked the risk of an "explosion".[21] In late November Hezbollah's secretary-general reported that the Ministry of Telecommunications had uncovered a new intercept of the Lebanese telephone network by Israel:

> Thus, the Jewish state has succeeded in putting in place a system that lets it set wiretaps on the entire network, to examine the content of messages sent in writing [text messages], to obtain personal subscriber data, and to track their geolocation position and their movements. It has also managed to duplicate SIM cards and use them to mimic any phone number, replacing the subscriber in making calls and sending messages without the user's knowledge from locations where he is not physically present. The Jewish state is also able to [add] another number [to the phone] which can operate in parallel to the number originally assigned to the subscriber. It can also listen in on conversations taking place in the user's vicinity. In short, Israel can resort to many illegal manipulations.[22]

Citing recent Israeli avowals that Tel Aviv had cooperated with the inquiry, Nasrallah drew a connection to recent comments by Israeli deputy prime minister

Silvan Shalom, then on an official international anti-Hezbollah tour, during which he is said to have expressed his satisfaction with the thought that "the STL was soon to make application of Resolution 1559 possible"—and thus the disarming of the IRL. Hezbollah's secretary-general construed this as proving that the STL was indeed the "fifth act" of an Israeli–Western attempt to take the party down.[23] Finally, in December, Nasrallah tried one last media blow, alleging that the Commission's vice president, Gerhard Lehmann, who was also a former officer of German intelligence, had sold the documents of the investigation to Lebanese contacts and others for $70,000 per set. He is even said to have offered the entire package to Hezbollah's leadership for $1,000,000. An offer is said to have been floated for an eventual winding up of the entire dossier in exchange for the party surrendering two of its members. This suggested that the tribunal was less interested in the truth about Hariri's assassination than in trotting out Hezbollah before the public as the guilty party.

The party's protestations carried no weight with March 14, which refused to distance itself from the STL. Out of patience, the opposition, on 12 January 2011—five days before the handing down of the indictment—decided to use its blocking third, causing the government to fall. The next day, on 13 January, Jumblatt met with Nasrallah and, on 21 January, he announced a complete switch to the ranks of March 8. The former minority now had the majority of seats in parliament and with it the privilege of forming the new government. With the approval of Damascus, it invited Najib Mikati to become the prime minister once again. Despite a personal friendship with the Syrian president, he was a millionaire businessman from Tripoli who enjoyed a reputation as a moderate. His brief stint in the Serail in the spring of 2005, when he had been in charge of organizing the first legislative election following the fall of the Karameh government after the tutelage, had been unanimously hailed as meeting the expectations of the Lebanese and international community.

As for March 14, it came out in favour of reappointing Saad Hariri. But reinstating the outgoing prime minister quickly became difficult to defend, especially in light of the way in which he had confused a large part of his public during his two years in office. The uncharismatic personality of the head of the FC, some political setbacks—including that of May 2008—and the 2009 rapprochement with the Syrian regime gradually eroded the trust and credibility that Rafic Hariri's heir had enjoyed in 2005. In addition, at the start of 2011 March 14 as an entity was battered by revelations daily filling the media stemming from an extensive series of US diplomatic cables released by WikiLeaks. These documents brought to light collaborations during the 2006 war by the majority of the March 14 Christian political class, something that until then had only been rumoured. It also brought up another embarrassment for the former majority, which was the underside of the May 2008 events.[24] The *coup de grâce* was delivered on 15 January, three days after the fall of the government, when the Lebanese New TV broadcast audio interviews that had taken place in 2007 between Saad Hariri, Gerhard Lehmann, the number two on the International

Commission of Inquiry, Wissam al-Hassan, the head of ISF intelligence, and the Commission's former chief witness, Muhammad Zuheir al-Siddiq.[25] The embarrassing point was that al-Siddiq appeared to have been a familiar of the former prime minister; the witness seemed not only to be conducting the interview but also to impose conditions both on the FC leader and the police official.[26] As it happened, Hariri had assured the Commission that he knew nothing about al-Siddiq and had never met him. These conversations posed more problems than simple perjury, for they raised the question of Saad Hariri's involvement in the affair of the false witnesses. On 25 January Mikati was approved by parliament by sixty-eight votes, his predecessor receiving sixty. March 14 denounced it as a *coup d'état* and declared its categorical refusal to join the new ministerial team in spite of being invited to do so by the new majority.

Far from objecting to this, Hezbollah seized greater control of policy levers as a result, and was better able to control the domestic situation, especially when the indictment was handed down on 17 January, confirmed on 28 June, and finally published on 17 August. Indeed, charges were brought against four party members: Salim Ayyash, Mustafa Badreddin, Hussein Oneissi, and Assad Sabra. Badreddin was said to have provided overall supervision of the operation, with Ayyash alleged to have coordinated the operational team responsible for the "material commission". Oneissi and Sabra were accused of having prepared the false claims recorded by Abū ʿAdas. Nasrallah's first reaction, in late June, was to repeat the accusation that the tribunal's intent was to tarnish Hezbollah's image.[27] Events came to the rescue. Lebanese media had been reporting for the previous month that the French government wanted to furnish evidence to the Commission that it had in its possession for some time and which "could be of interest to the investigator." In circles close to Hezbollah, the news reinforced the sense of the tribunal's politicization. Paris was thus suspected of having kept back useful data in the light of its rapprochement with Damascus in 2007 that it no longer had to guard after the uprisings in Syria in 2011.

In his speech following the publication of the indictment in August, Nasrallah, Israeli customs documents in hand, also pointed to the shipment of ninety-seven of the Commission's computers to Israel.[28] He repeated that "for the sake of the investigation's credibility, the tribunal should have employed neutral investigators, for its experts, officers, and advisers have a lot of anti-Resistance history and a history of collaborating with the CIA". To buttress these contentions, al-Manār simultaneously showed slides in the background detailing the profiles of (i) Nick Kaldas, one of the investigators and an officer of the Australian police, portrayed as linked to US intelligence and as having worked for Washington in Iraq in 2004; (ii) Michael Taylor, chief investigator since 2010, a former head of British intelligence; (iii) Dureid Bushrawi, "a French-Lebanese known for his hostility toward Hezbollah and his role in the matter of false witnesses", the legal adviser to the STL; and (iv) Robert Baer, a CIA officer, an expert on Hezbollah, said to have participated in the 1985 assassination attempt on Muhammad Husayn Fadlallāh and assigned at one time to tracking down Imad Mughniyeh. Nasrallah also called into question the integrity of the investigators. With supporting video, he reiterated that Gerhard Lehmann, the Commission's vice president, had sold documents related to the investigation, while accusing Daniel Bellemare, the prosecutor, of having "personally intervened to end Interpol's pursuit of Zuheir al-Siddiq". Finally, he attacked the STL's president, the Italian judge Antonio Cassese, noting that he had repeatedly expressed his sympathy for the state of Israel and participated in events reserved for people close to it.[29]

When the detailed act was published in August, Nasrallah and the party cadres showed their satisfaction: prosecutor Bellemare's office acknowledged that there was no "proof" for the accusation against the Hezbollah members and that it was built on comparative, circumstantial inferences. Nasrallah resumed his discourse of justification, insisting that "without doubt" Israel had manipulated the phone data—but clearly the concern was no longer what it had been.

The fact was that Hezbollah was now the engine driving the parliamentary majority. The foreign minister was a member of AMAL, the Ministries of Justice, Telecommunications, and Defence were in the hands of two Aounist cadres and of a third one from Sleiman Frangieh's Marada (pro-Syrian) party. But, regardless of the favourable balance of power, still constantly subject to change, in practice the party had nothing to fear from the STL. The charges levelled against it may have further degraded its image in circles that were already hostile, mainly in the West and a part of March 14, but ultimately no political preferences had changed. While some of its detractors were more than ever convinced of its faults, its supporters still believed in its innocence.[30] The verdict in any case would only have limited effects on Hezbollah. There was nothing coercive to fear in fact. Hezbollah understood this so well that despite its vocal opposition to funding the STL, it did not block the prime minister's decision in late 2011 to disburse Lebanon's share.

Dealing with the Syrian threat

By directly taking the reins of power in Lebanon in early 2011, Hezbollah seemed to have succeeded in protecting itself against any deleterious effects of the STL. But when it brought down the Hariri cabinet and installed itself on the majority's seats in parliament, the party leadership did not yet know that the flipping of power relations within the chamber would also enable it to cope with a totally different kind of threat, much more severe than that posed by the tribunal: the revolt in Syria against the regime of Bashar al-Assad.

The government tries neutrality

From the beginning of the Syrian unrest the Mikati government chose to distance itself.[31] It clearly feared that taking an official stance for or against the uprising would provoke tensions or even a conflagration in Lebanon. This analysis was widely shared by the overwhelming majority of players on the domestic scene; apart from the Lebanese Forces and the FC,[32] the other parties approved. The cabinet also had support from religious leaders: the new Patriarch, the Maronite bishop Bishara al-Rai, elected in March 2011 to succeed Boutros Sfeir, was joined by the Assembly of Maronite Bishops in condemning the violence on both sides. They voiced their fear of the fundamentalist alternative and supported the idea of a solution in Syria through dialogue, an assessment of the situation and positioning that was shared unanimously by the Catholic clergy, Orthodox, Melkites, Dār al-Fatwā (Sunni), the SSC (Shiite), and the Druze council. The international community concurred: the United States, France, Germany, Italy, and the UN emphasized the need for maintaining a stable Lebanon and guarding against importing the Syrian chaos.

In theory, this official neutrality signified a refusal to take a position for or against the Syrian regime on the regional and international scene. Consequently, the government refused to expel the Syrian ambassador, Ali Abdel-Karim Ali, despite insistent calls from March 14 and counter to the example set by some Arab and Western countries.[33] At the beginning of August 2011 it also refused to sign the UNSC's presidential statement condemning the use of force by the Syrian authorities against civilians, refrained from participating in the conference held by the Friends of Syria group in Tunisia in late February 2012, but also stayed away from a conference held in support of the Iranian regime in mid-March of the same year.

By the same token, it signalled a desire to remain as neutral as possible on two other issues, just as sensitive and difficult: how to deal with the influx of Syrian refugees and maintain border control. The first problem posed by the swelling flows of refugees was one of logistics. Ways had to be found of housing, feeding, and providing them with material assistance. Many of them were temporarily put up in schools. With the school year approaching in the autumn of 2011, but especially in 2012 and 2013, when the number of refugees reached new highs (more than 80,000 recorded in October 2012, 336,000 in March 2013, and more than 600,000 in July that year)[34] the government faced the challenge of relocating them. It also needed to find ways for them to earn a living, as Lebanese laws are less than flexible with regard to foreign labour. The refugees usually found precarious jobs as seasonal or day labourers at black market wages well below the Lebanese minima. Just as in tutelage times, this massive availability of cheap labour worsened the economic situation of many Lebanese. The burgeoning numbers of Syrian nationals in the country also fed political polemics. They raised the fear of a "Palestinian scenario" replicating itself in which naturalization might be required if the refugees never returned to Syria. With a Lebanese population estimated at about 4 million, this potential increase of nearly 15 per cent of the population in favour of the Sunni community provoked virulent communitarian reactions, especially among the Christians of the FPM.[35]

Besides, the Lebanese authorities had no effective counter-measures for borders that were porous to begin with and were made irremediably so by the feelings that

Lebanese in the border areas harboured for or against the rebels or the regime. At first, anti-Assad refugees settled in the Sunni north (Akkar), the Christian north (al-Qāʿ), and the Sunni centre in the Bekaa (Ersal), while pro-regime refugees headed for the Shiite Bekaa (Baalbek) or friendly areas in the South. It quickly became apparent that armed members of the Free Syrian Army (FSA) were welcomed in areas won by the FC. If the government agreed in principle to welcome unarmed civilian refugees, it was in fact incapable of preventing Syrian combatants from moving into Lebanon. It was just as powerless against the proliferating arms sales that rapidly undermined security conditions in large areas along the border.[36] The army refrained from responding to the incursions of the Syrian army, and to its sporadic bombardments of some Lebanese border areas carried out in hopes of hitting the FSA. But the accelerating and expanding flow of rebels and traffic to and from Syria forced it to exchange fire repeatedly with groups allied with the rebels, even with the FSA itself. The desire of the Lebanese authorities to remain neutral in the face of its eastern neighbour's internal situation thus turned out to be difficult to achieve, and Mikati's cabinet was caught increasingly between the hammer and the anvil, since Damascus had no qualms about pressuring Beirut.

Syrian meddling in Lebanon

Right from the start, the Syrian regime resented the Lebanese accommodationist stance. Damascus called for clearer actions in its favour. Ambassador Ali Abdel-Karim Ali demanded the arrest and deportation of FSA men who had sought refuge in Lebanon. In May 2012 the Syrian government filed a complaint with the UN in which it challenged "the supplying of weapons to terrorist groups in Syria and the infiltration of terrorists across the Lebanese–Syrian border".[37] Faced with these reproofs, the Lebanese government found itself torn between its extradition obligations and humanitarian considerations. Kidnapping on Lebanese territory of members of the Syrian opposition and its Lebanese supporters by Syrian troops, the arrest in June 2012 by the Syrian army of the president of the Akkar city council, the killing of several Lebanese citizens by Syrian army bullets, and shells fired from the other side of the border called into question respect for Lebanon's national sovereignty. Mikati insisted that the refugee issue should not be treated at the expense of Lebanese security, but avoided the question of extradition of FSA members by responding that the matter had been referred to the Ministry of Justice and was no longer in the hands of the political class. In April 2012 Minister of Social Affairs Wael Abou Faour (PSP), finally announced that Lebanon would not turn over any Syrian citizens to Damascus.

The Syrian Baath's resolve not to hold Lebanon blameless from the turmoil shaking Syria became abundantly clear when, in early August, a Lebanese former minister, Michel Samaha, an Assad ally, was arrested by ISF intelligence. He admitted the charges levied against him, of having transported explosives in his personal vehicle on the orders of Ali Mamluk, chief of the Syrian National Security, with intent to distribute them to local groups tasked with creating public disorder, including a series of bombings in North Lebanon. When Wissam al-Hassan, head of the ISF intelligence services, a Hariri confidant who was said by many to be the brains behind Samaha's arrest, was assassinated in downtown Beirut on 19 October, the air was thick with political and media commentary denouncing it as an act of vengeance plotted in Damascus.

March 14 between revolutionarism and more-or-less explicit fears

Until 2013, March 14's way of reading events was very different from that of the Mikati government. When Arab protests began with the Tunisian uprising in December 2010, the anti-Syrian Lebanese coalition struggled to hide its antagonism. The disavowal of pro-Western regimes and the nationalist Arab, occasionally anti-Israel, slogans that were heard in Tunisia and Egypt made March 14 uncomfortable. The regional and international preferences of the group of Arab countries normally thought of as "moderate" (Egypt, Tunisia, Jordan, and Saudi Arabia), preferences which were also held by March 14, were unfavourably compared to policy options that were presented as more democratic and sovereignist. Illustrating this malaise, the only Lebanese party to send congratulations to the Tunisian people when Zin al-Abidin Ben Ali abdicated on 14 January 2011 was Hezbollah. On 11 February, the day after Hosni Mubarak fell from power, former prime minister Fouad Siniora's commentary on the news consisted of praise for the former Egyptian president. However, the spread of the rebellion, and the international enthusiasm it engendered, particularly in terms of democratic hopes, soon forced the former Lebanese majority to stop contradicting its official position in favour of freedom. Gradually, it began to support the revolts—within limits dictated by its regional alliances. It welcomed the fall of Muammar Qaddafi in Libya and Ali Abdullah Saleh in Yemen, but refrained from supporting the attempts at fomenting political unrest in Saudi Arabia or Bahrain and from condemning the Saudi and Emirati military interventions that helped Manama quell the protests.

The start of the unrest in Syria in March 2011 acted like a powerful catalyst on the new opposition's siding with the Arab revolutions. On the March 14 website, the slogan in vogue henceforth was "the Lebanese March 14 and the Syrian March 15". But above all, the former parliamentary majority emerged from its position of observer to present itself as an actor fully participating in the insurrectionist process, not just that in Syria but regionally, going as far as to claim that it inspired them. Claiming paternity for the uprisings, March 14 overtly redefined February 2005 as the starting point for the Arab Spring, arguing that the angry masses had been inspired in reality by the Lebanese precedent (*sic*). Regional current affairs were perceived ultimately as an unexpected opportunity coming just at the right time: the desired effects of an indictment of Hezbollah by the tribunal seemed at the time headed nowhere, and the mobilization discourse within March 14, weakened by years of contradictions and failures, was in search of new inspiration. The hijacking of the revolts, incorporated by March 14 into its national struggle, let it rejig the justifications for its cause and lay before its public the reasons why it should not yet abandon its political elite. However, it was possible to detect some nuances in the argumentation, depending on the community; in essence, the "Arab Spring" was reworked in a manner that made it meaningful to the confessional trajectories of different actors. Samir Geagea was undoubtedly the leader who pushed this reappropriation of the protests the furthest. Throughout the spring of 2011, he repeated that the neighbouring societies in foment were only imitating the initiative carried out by anti-Syrian Lebanese in 2005. In January 2012 he declared that "this year will see the end of the Syrian regime".[38] He announced that "serious dialogue about Hezbollah's weapons will take place after Assad's fall",[39] certain that his end would "strengthen March 14 at the expense of Hezbollah".[40] But above all, he posited the conservative Christian battle of the 1970s as the genuine initial stage of the process at work in shaking up the various countries of the region. All of it is said to have begun "at Ashrafiyeh",[41] thus connecting East Beirut to "Homs, via Tunis, Cairo and Benghazi" in a consistent sequence of revolts.[42] Saad Hariri also declared his support for the Syrian people, but above all tied the Arab Spring to a personal animus against Mikati, accusing him of "treason" for taking over the post of prime minister. With regional winds shifting against the Syrian regional option, in March 2011 Jumblatt again turned hostile towards Damascus. He grafted the certainty of an imminent end of the Assad regime some time in 2012 onto open calls for regime change in Syria. He called on Syrian soldiers to desert and Druzes not to serve, which earned him his first rebuff from his Syrian co-religionists when they criticized his "interference".[43] Confident of victory, he refused any formula that would make the current regime part of a solution in Syria. However, with the gradual deterioration of the situation, and with the Lebanese parliamentary elections originally scheduled for June 2013 approaching, he tried again to secure his position in the majority: in the autumn of 2012 he argued that, ultimately, there "is no solution in Syria without Assad,"[44] and after the assassination of Wissam al-Hassan he exchanged volleys of insults with Saad Hariri on Twitter.

The Mikati government's attempts to please everyone were also roundly criticized. The former majority condemned the policy of neutrality chosen by Hariri's successor.[45] He was reproached for failing to respond to the Syrian regime's provocations as well as for his reluctance to commit to actively supporting the revolution next door. On the eve of the 14 February celebrations in 2012, Saad Hariri was blunt: "If I were prime minister, I would not have stayed aloof from what is happening in Syria", he said, because "it is not in Lebanon's interest" to stay out of the Syrian upheaval.[46] Failing to win the cabinet to his views, and despite sharp dissent from its Western allies, March 14 anticipated what it believed to be Assad's imminent fall by launching its own Syrian policy. Contacts were established with the Syrian National Council (SNC). From the spring of 2011, suspected arms shipments to the Syrian uprising by Lebanese supporters were confirmed when the first arrests of traffickers were made at Ersal, a Sunni village on the Bekaa border in FC country. In March 2012 an "unidentified" warship loaded with a cargo of weapons in all likelihood destined for the Syrian opposition was boarded and searched off the Christian area of Jounieh, north of Beirut. In late April 2012 the Lebanese navy seized a second vessel off Tripoli, the *Loutfallah II*, in whose hold it found thousands of Kalashnikovs, M16s and rocket launchers, plus ammunition and explosives by the ton, also intended for the Syrian rebels. Three days later a third vessel carrying arms consigned to the insurgents, the *Grande Sicilia*, was seized outside the port of Beirut. March 14 denied any involvement and accused its opponents of trying to destabilize it. In early October 2012, *The New York Times*, however, mentioned the FC MP Okab Sakr as being responsible for deliveries via Turkey of weapons and money originating in Saudi Arabia to the Syrian rebels.[47] A few days earlier the FSA spokesman, Louay Mokdad, had published a photo of himself in the company of Sakr on his Facebook page. After initial denials, Hariri eventually, on 18 October, admitted to "helping" the Syrian opposition, introducing Sakr as his personal representative, but denied furnishing "military" aid.[48] In late November, however, a series of audio recording transcripts published by *al-Akhbār* documented multiple conversations between Sakr and leaders of Syrian armed opposition groups that left no doubt about Saad Hariri's actual material support for the rebellion. For several weeks the FC remained mired in embarrassed silence.

Despite this return by March 14's leaders to their rhetorical roots, and direct involvement by a few in the Syrian conflict, this revolutionarism was not unanimous within the old majority. Two concerns prevented harmony between the Hariri and Geagea positions and the whole of March 14. The first was an anxiety, mainly among Christians, about the impact of Islamists possibly taking power in Syria. There was fear of persecution and forced exile, as in Iraq. While the entire anti-Assad political class dismissed the Islamist threat out of hand whenever mention was made of it during the first weeks of the Arab protests, there was a discernible shift from the autumn of 2011, with the success of Islamists in elections for a constituent assembly in Tunisia,[49] declarations by the president of the Libyan National Congress about a new government based on *sharīʿa*, and the first excesses by Egyptian Islamist MPs.[50] Illustrative of this lack of confidence that the radical Islamists were well disposed toward Christians, the Kataeb distanced themselves from the positions taken by the Lebanese Forces. Following the line adopted by the government, the Gemayels preferred to put daylight between themselves and the Syrian problem, seemingly not convinced in any case that Assad's fall would necessarily entail a weakening of Hezbollah.

Fear grew even more as the Lebanese Sunni community itself seemed to fragment over the Syrian issue. The FC tried to reassure the Christians by presenting itself as a moderate current, an alternative to Islamic radicalism and protector of Islamo-Christian parity. But while several members of the March 14 political class, including former prime minister Fouad Siniora, still argued that "al-Qāʿida does not exist in Lebanon",[51] not everyone had forgotten the incidents at Nahr al-Bared in the summer of 2007.[52] Moreover, the violent clashes that had regularly shaken Tripoli since then routinely betrayed the existence of jihadist networks on Lebanese territory.[53] It turned out that they were positioning themselves in open competition with FC's efforts to hijack the Syrian revolution. For example, Omar Bakri, a Syrian-born preacher who had found refuge in Lebanon after being expelled from Britain in 2005,[54] and until then had kept quiet, declared in the summer of 2012 that "instability [in Syria] is conducive to the spread of Islamism; the sleeping Sunni giant is waking up". He spoke of "dreaming of an "Islamist Spring" that would sweep through Syria and Lebanon and see the Sunni Muslims take back the reins of power."[55] According to him, the "caliphate" would soon be re-established.[56] But even more than Bakri and the Salafists in the north, Sheikh Ahmad al-Assir of Sidon in 2012–13 reflected the image of a Sunni Islamism that was hardly accommodative. Spotlighted by the media during a virulently anti-Hezbollah sit-in lasting more than a month during the summer of 2012, he tried to pose, given Saad Hariri's fall from grace ending in self-exile in 2011, as the community's new leader. While his discourse was essentially and violently anti-Shiite and sectarian, he had difficulty convincing the Christians with his reassuring messages. The sheikh's efforts ended up discredited by his Wahhabist vocabulary and his group's appearance (long beard, slight moustache, white robes and sandals), both uncommon in Lebanon and usually identified with the religious set in the Arabian Peninsula. He aroused suspicion especially by his refusal to submit to the dictates of the state and his bellicose demonstrations where he and his supporters showed up dressed for combat and armed to the teeth, ready to fight a Hezbollah supposedly "besieging" them. In June 2013 he attacked an army post, which degenerated into more than twenty-four hours of fighting. In end the military, which had lost fifteen men, succeeded in overrunning the headquarters of the dissident cleric, who managed to escape. These radical groups comprised only a small number of individuals among the Sunni community, but the manifest inability of the government to channel their discourse, their actions, and their links with foreign fundamentalist networks (Syrian, Palestinian, and Saudi) fed the fears of many Lebanese.[57]

Warring fears thus prevailed between one section of the Christian March 14 political class, which exploited the threat of Hezbollah's weapons but seemed confident about the pacifism and religious tolerance of a possible Syrian regime led by Islamists, and the Aoun faction, which defended Hezbollah's arms and predicted harrassment and abuse of Christians should the Islamists take power in Damascus. Recurring problems in the north, mainly around Tripoli, where the clashes between Sunnis and Alawites had never really stopped since 2008 and which resumed with greater intensity between 2011 and 2012, framed by the events in Syria, made for a more pronounced dichotomy: March 8 now felt compelled to speak of "illegal March 14 arms", which it portrayed as "weapons of *fitna*" (civil discord), unlike the weapons of the Resistance, which "protect the country". The Sunni alternative, represented by the al-Assir tendency, appeared briefly likely to win, when various FC members, starting with some MPs (in view of Saad Hariri's prolonged absence and the impression that he had been overtaken by events) were soon openly supporting the cleric, including against the government. On the other side, the FPM and Hezbollah stoked the fear of Sunni radicalism by having their media assiduously report abuses against Christians and other minorities by a host of fundamentalist groups in Syria, Egypt, and Iraq. In this same logic of "conscientization" and alarmism, in 2013 the FPM added the "invasion of Ashrafiyeh" to the calendar of its annual celebrations, to remind Christians living in the capital of an Islamist Sunni demonstration in February 2006 that descended into vandalism and led to the burning of the Danish embassy located in that quarter.[58] The Hezbollah "Christian policy" was put forward. The FPM also made frequent mention of the reconciliation between the Maronite bishop Bishara al-Rai and the Hezbollah leadership. This rapprochement was extended to the Pope's visit to Lebanon in September 2012, when Hezbollah sent a welcome escort of hundreds of al-Mahdī scouts wearing caps adorned with the Vatican coat of arms to Beirut airport in honour of his arrival. It also recalled the work done by Jihād al-Binā' after 2006 to repair churches damaged during the Israeli bombing, beginning with the church of St Joseph in the Haret Hreik neighbourhood. Finally, in November 2012, the FPM welcomed the Maronite Patriarch's invitation to the Hezbollah leadership, when he insisted that a Hezbollah delegation accompany him to the Vatican on the occasion of his elevation to the rank of cardinal.[59]

Hezbollah under fire from three sides

The Syrian opposition vs. Hezbollah

While supporting the government's isolationist policy, and reiterating its determination to keep the chaos unfolding in Syria from being imported to Lebanon, Hezbollah also staked out its own position on the Syrian issue. When anti-Assad agitation began in March 2011, Nasrallah did not hesitate: he admitted the party's preference for the powers that be, qualified as the "regime of resistance against Israel", and called on the belligerents to abandon violence in favour of a negotiated solution. This statement shocked and disappointed a large segment of the Syrian population. The image as a pan-Arab hero that Nasrallah had enjoyed up to that point suffered considerably as a result.[60] The relations between the party and the Syrian National Council deteriorated progressively. The SNC president, Burhan Ghalioun, declared that "in the event of a fall of the Assad regime, the new government would revise relations with Iran and Hezbollah drastically",[61] and drew this response from Nasrallah: "The so-called Syrian National Council ... and its leader Burhan Ghalioun ... are outdoing themselves to present their credentials to the United States and Israel."[62] And so, the tone was set. Relations failed to improve as Hezbollah was accused as early as the spring 2011 of sending IRL combatants to fight in Syria alongside the regular Syrian army.[63] In January 2012 al-Arabiya channel, citing a high-ranking Pasdaran officer, alleged that Hezbollah exchanged fire with the FSA in the area of Zabadani on the Syrian border.[64] The party, having systematically rejected accusations of involvement in Syria, once again denied any intervention in Zabadani.[65] However, IRL militants do appear to have helped the Revolutionary Guard repel armed attacks by Syrian groups on its base in the area, in a localized isolated operation.[66] No proof was, however, advanced of the Islamic Resistance aiding the regime's forces. The Syrian opposition issued threats anyway. In late January the FSA openly menaced the Hezbollah leader: its spokesman, Colonel Ammar al-Wawi, called on Nasrallah to "stop killing the Syrian people who welcomed the Lebanese with open arms during the 2006 war by opening the doors to their homes to them", and warned him "that he will be held accountable for his acts before the revolutionary tribunals after the Syrian revolution's victory".[67] During the third week of May 2012 Syrian rebels claiming to be from the FSA abducted a dozen Lebanese Shiite pilgrims as a punitive act.[68]

The allegations of the IRL's military involvement faded from the headlines for a time, until September 2012, when Mohammad Ali Jaafari, the Pasdaran commander, admitted that "the Qods Force and Pasdaran have a number of men on the ground in Syria and Lebanon", but insisted that "compared with the level of the Arab countries' support for and military presence in the rebel groups, we have done next to nothing over there".[69] Stressing that the Pasdaran were only "advisers" who had merely shared "intellectual support, advice, and [some] experience", he touched on the alleged involvement of Hezbollah in the crackdown in Syria, saying that "the forces of the Resistance and of Hezbollah are independent; ... in the past, Syrian forces were stationed in Lebanon to provide help, and it is natural that if Syria should also need help, the Lebanese people would bring it". These statements caused all the more consternation, in Syria as well as Lebanon, because in late January Qassem Suleimani, a Pasdaran general, had said that the Revolutionary Guards were "present in South Lebanon and Iraq" and that "these two territories, one way or another, are subject to Tehran's will".[70] Hezbollah had then denounced the misleading use of Suleimani's words,[71] asserting that they had been fabricated by the al-Arabiya channel "well known for its tendencies and political affinities [Saudi and pro-American]". The remarks were also invalidated by the Iranian Foreign Ministry. When Jaafari appeared to agree with Qassem, the Iranian Foreign Ministry again rejected his statements, declaring that they were taken out of context and insisting that Iran "has no military presence in the region, in Syria in particular".[72]

The question of Hezbollah's military involvement in Syria reappeared in October. On the 5th al-Arabiya broadcast two memos obtained from Syrian rebels supposedly found in the files of the regime's intelligence services. The first document, dated 12 December 2005, referred to the "success" of "Operation 213", "with the help of Hezbollah units". As 12 December was the day of the murder of journalist Gebran

Tueni, a connection was immediately made in Lebanon.[73] The Tueni family immediately filed a formal complaint against the Syrian regime, and their lawyer, the MP Boutros Harb, warned Hezbollah that it would have to "lift all the suspicions weighing on it".[74] The other document mentioned the arrival in Syria on 23 May 2011 of "a first support group of 250 Hezbollah members", suggesting, without however profiling the members in question or their mission, that the party was involved in the Syrian conflict. Hezbollah's front office immediately branded the documents as forgeries, once again pointing to al-Arabiya's regional bias.[75] In fact, on 13 October, al-Arabiya's management backtracked: the editor-in-chief of the English-language website officially apologized, admitting that the memos were indeed bogus and that the channel had been taken in by "a group of Syrian rebels that, however, they had worked with as reliable in the past".

A few days before the publication of the forged documents an IRL fighter, Ali Hussein Nassif, alias Abu Abbas, was buried in his home village of Būdāy in the Bekaa.[76] Six days later, at Ansār, another village in the Bekaa, came the burial of another fighter named Hussein Abdel-Ghani al-Nimr.[77] If the FSA is to be believed, Nassif was the "leader of Hezbollah operations in Syria" and was killed by a roadside bomb in the Syrian village of Qusayr in the Homs countryside. Nimr supposedly also died in Syria, after walking into an ambush set for his battalion by the rebels. Hezbollah merely said that Nassif "died among Lebanese and in defending them", and described him as "a good man and a good fighter, who died a martyr in the service of his country and of his Muslim brothers".[78] The controversy originated with a phrase used by the cleric officiating at Nimr's funeral. He was reported to have said that the deceased died while "doing his duty of *jihād* (*wa huwa yu'addī wājibahu al-jihādī*)". The formula was immediately interpreted as an explicit acknowledgement by Hezbollah of its involvement in the Syria fighting. The party's cadres and clerics, criticizing the media's lack of accuracy in bandying the concept about, tried to explain that in Hezbollah idiom the "duty of *jihād*"[79] can connote all kinds of tasks without necessarily referring to military combat. Nasrallah personally substantiated this in greater detail on 11 October:

> From the outset ... Arab satellite channels have put forward—when the conflict had not even begun yet!—that Hezbollah had sent 3,000 combatants to Syria to fight alongside regime troops. We said it was lies, that it was not true. And I say to you today: it is still lies, it is still not true. Regularly, we hear [claims made] of 1,500 fighters, sometimes 2,000, 4,000 or 5,000 fighters. To these fighters, they add casualties; they talk about 100 martyrs, 200 martyrs, 300 martyrs. ... But where are they? ... In Lebanon, nothing can be hidden. Anyone who is buried in any village is identified, is known to his family, to residents of the village. In any event, we do not bury in secret, we always do it in public, and it even goes on television. Well, so where are these 50 martyrs, these 100 martyrs, these 200 martyrs? ... Until this very day, we have not fought alongside the regime. ...

> So then, what is the story on this martyr Abu Abbas? ... There are a certain number of border villages on Syrian territory, near al-Hermel—Syrian villages in Syrian territory. But these villages are inhabited by Lebanese.[80] There are twenty-three villages and twelve hamlets whose population is entirely or partially Lebanese. The list of their names is available. The people living in them are Lebanese of all confessions: Shiites, Sunnis, Christians, and Alawites. They total about 30,000. ... That is where they earn their livelihoods and they work near the towns of Qusayr and Homs. ... These Lebanese, holders of Lebanese citizenship, have lived over there for decades, if not centuries. ... Some young people from these families and these villages are members of Lebanese parties for dozens of years. Not just Hezbollah, but all parties. But it's not that Hezbollah, oh, hey, Hezbollah that has sent young men over there, to do what I have no idea, no!
>
> Some from the Resistance battalions in the Bekaa, full-time cadres of the Resistance, who fought in the South and West Bekaa over the course of the last thirty years, live in these villages. ... To begin with, and you can go and verify this, they did like the Lebanese in Lebanon, they chose to stay out of the way of brawls between the [Syrian] regime and armed groups. ... But armed groups attacked them and chased many away, burned their houses, killed, kidnapped, ransacked and looted, even went so far as to attack their daughters and women. All this is documented, and let any Lebanese who does not believe it go check it for himself. ... Some of them gathered up their things and returned to Lebanon ... but most chose to stay. ... They bought weapons, stockpiled arms, you know, the borders are open. ... It has nothing to do with fighting alongside the regime, it has to do with a respectable humanitarian purpose, that of defending their lives and their children, their wives, their property against armed groups, some of which are Syrian, others come from the four corners of the world. ... I cannot tell them: "Leave, and I will send Hezbollah fighters to defend you," this is not my role. I cannot therefore stop them from defending themselves, be they in Hezbollah or in another party. ... And afterwards they tell us: He died "doing his jihadist duty"; (*laughs*) it's all right to amuse yourself by picking up concepts from others and their vocabulary, but it would be better to try to understand them before using them in whatever way. ... There you have it, the whole story that they made into such a big deal. As for Abu Abbas ... there, among these young men who died in Syria under the daily bombings and attacks by armed groups, was Abu Abbas.[81]

In other words, Hezbollah defended itself against its accusers by countering with the idea that its interventions in Syria were not ordered by its leadership, but reflected private, legitimate, and highly localized self-defence initiatives that some of its members, whose homes were on Syrian territory and whose mostly Shiite villages had been targeted by radical Sunni groups, had been forced to undertake.

The Syrian opposition, however, was not about to let the party plead extenuating circumstances. Throughout the autumn and winter of 2012 and the spring of 2013, and thus well before the battle of Qusayr in late May 2013, during which the IRL's engagement at the side of the regular Syrian army was undeniable, bellicose statements and promises of retaliation continued. In September 2012 a leader of al-Qāʿida in Syria, Mājid al-Mājid, explicitly threatened the party and announced plans to attack tourist sites in Lebanon for as long as the Lebanese government continued to support Hezbollah.[82] In early October the FSA leadership in turn promised to bring the war right into Beirut's southern suburbs if the party did not "put an end to its support for the regime of Bashar al-Assad".[83] In March 2013 it went so far as to signal its intent to invade Baalbek. The situation had a particularly dangerous aspect because, very early on, the FSA, like the radical religious groups in the Syrian opposition, tinged their anti-Hezbollah discourse with an explicitly sectarian animosity that often seemed to take precedence over the ideological dispute. The party's Syrian opponents renamed it Hizb al-Shaytān, "The Devil's Party"[84] and, in October 2012, the FSA directly addressed the Lebanese Shiite community:

> We warn our parents and Lebanese brothers of a certain sectarian colouration [Shiite] who took the wrong path, who listened to and made their own the degeneracy and debauchery of the Devil, Khamenei's *wakīl* in Lebanon [Hassan Nasrallah], and to them we say: Come back to the path of righteousness and truth before it's too late.[85]

The battle of Qusayr as turning point

Eventually, Hezbollah did admit to a joint operation that took place in late May 2013 in Syria where IRL fighters participated alongside troops of the Bashar al-Assad regime. For three weeks, Syrian soldiers and members of the Islamic Resistance battled side by side at Qusayr, a city in north-west Syria where it borders the Lebanese (Shiite) area of Baalbek–al-Hermel. With some thirty villages, mainly inhabited by Lebanese Shiites, the area had been taken several months earlier by the Syrian opposition. The battle was ferocious, and the total of casualities on both sides were in the hundreds.[86] The exact number of fighters is difficult to establish, but the media reported between 3,000 and 6,000 rebels fighting Syrian army units, backed by 3,000–4,000 IRL men according to French authorities, but 1,000–1,500 according to Hezbollah,[87] and just a few hundred according to other Lebanese dailies.[88] The Syrian army and IRL ultimately emerged victorious in early June, with observers crediting the IRL's role as the factor that enabled the regime to prevail. Previously, the Syrian army had been mired for weeks in low-intensity combat with the rebels in the area without achieving any conclusive result. The rationale given by Hezbollah's leadership for this intervention, but also by the IRL fighters who took part in the battle, is as follows: in the face of advances by radical jihadists in the area, and taking into account their intensifying attacks against Shiite areas on Lebanese as well as Syrian territory, which raised fears that they might advance deeply into Lebanon, the Islamic Resistance "had no choice" but to launch a counter-attack that would drive the aggressor back a sufficient distance from the border and thus ensure a return to peace and security in the territory in question. The IRL thus presented its entry into the Syrian arena not as an offensive but a defensive move.[89] This argument seems consistent with the fact that the Resistance was intervening around Qusayr, Homs, and Damascus, all close to the Lebanese Shiite Bekaa. The fear of a massive presence of radical anti-Shiite fighters at the gates of what is a key region for Hezbollah—the area centred on Baalbeck–al-Hermel—seemed to justify the need for securing the border area perimeter. The fact that this account emerged frequently and rather authentically from the testimonials of IRL combatants who had participated in the fighting, makes it an acceptable explanation for the choice that the Islamic Resistance leadership effectively made—to go into battle for the first time in its history in a country other than its own. However, this is not the sole reason.

The most plausible explanation for the IRL's involvement in Syria remains one of dual converging interests. The Syrian regime's efforts to re-take the areas of Qusayr, Homs, and Aleppo with the help of the IRL "unblocked" the major transportation and travel routes linking Damascus and the north-west, including the coast. It also made rebel access more difficult to the Lebanese Sunni Bekaa, where they had created a rear base and a resupply and rearmament centre. But, in the spring of 2013, for the IRL fighting alongside the regime it was still not a question of helping the regime restore its authority throughout the country, as is shown by the fact that the Resistance committed no fighters in the country's south, centre, or east. When it eventually did so in the south in the spring of 2015, it was once again for the purpose of securing the major roads linking the region to the capital.

Indeed, the IRL's participation in the Syria conflict appears above all to suit the IRL's own interests, translating, at the time, less into an attempt to save the Syrian regime than an anticipation of possible adverse repercussions for its own cause from an eventual fall of Bashar al-Assad. Let it be recalled that the terms of the strategic alliance that has governed Hezbollah's relations with Damascus since the early 1990s relates mainly to facilitating the logistics of flows of weapons through Syrian territory to the Resistance. These arrangements, in all likelihood, would not have survived if the FSA and/or its jihadist allies had seized power in Syria. The opposition groups are unquestionably divided, but share a common aversion to the Iran–Hezbollah alliance, which therefore would have had no hope of preserving the state of fruitful cooperation it still enjoys today with the Assad regime. In all likelihood, the IRL and its Iranian mentor would have had to resign themselves to taking a few hits during a rejockeying of the internal balance of power in Syria. A well-thought-out approach to the new possible situation could, however, have allowed them to preserve their essential core assets. The fact is that they do not have to be welcome in the whole of Syria; a stable and protected sanctuary is sufficient as long as it has some logistical facilities. In the north-west—mostly Alawite and Christian, hence doubly favourable to the Baath's regional preferences—Syrian confessional geography seemed to present a ready-made area where Hezbollah and Tehran could have re-established a presence and functional organization. In other words, in the space between the coast and the Damascus–

(Qusayr–)Homs–Aleppo axis—space where the IRL was in fact going into action. Intervening by force in the region thus seemed to be as much a preventative self-defence reaction as one of securing ahead of time part of an area to which it might have had to pull back its logistical manoeuvres in Syria for an indeterminate time.

In Lebanon, the IRL's participation in the Syria conflict was immediately stigmatized by March 14—FC in particular—and by supporters of Lebanon's isolationist policy, beginning with the president, Michel Sleiman. When the Syrian opposition fired multiple rockets from Syrian and Lebanese territories into Shiite residential areas of the Bekaa and the southern suburbs of Beirut, Hezbollah was widely blamed for this destabilization of Lebanon's domestic situation. In particular, there was concern that a series of hostile exchanges between belligerents and their followers on both sides might threaten to escalate into open warfare between Sunnis and Shiites.

The Hezbollah leadership, for its part, was trying to contain the growing pressure from its critics. In the face of charges made by the Syrian opposition during the battle of Qusayr that IRL militants had massacred hundreds of Syrian civilians, the party leadership issued denials, emphasizing the need to keep from confessionnalizing the conflict. It demonstrated its "sincerity" in the aftermath of the battle by allowing Syrian opponents who had fought at Qusayr to be treated in the hospitals of the Bekaa region where Hezbollah was present. Hassan Nasrallah, in speeches addressing those of his compatriots who blamed him for the country's deteriorating security situation, accused "radicals among the Sunnis", and called for national unity. When a car bomb shook the centre of the capital's southern suburbs on 15 August 2013, killing 27 and injuring 300 in the Rueiss quarter, his first condolences went to the families of the "Sunni victims". And when, six days later, it was the turn of Tripoli, the capital of northern Lebanon and the country's premier Sunni city, to be rocked by a double attack that left 40 dead and 350 wounded, Nasrallah again condemned the attack and, once again, appealed for solidarity.[90] In parallel with these communication campaigns designed to calm spirits, the Hezbollah leadership extensively mobilized the party's security services on the ground. In conjunction with the state security organs they investigated every attack and every assassination. Checkpoints manned by party members multiplied at entrances to Shiite areas and cities (the Beirut suburbs, Bekaa and South), searching vehicles and verifying motorists' IDs.[91] Despite these efforts, the party could not keep all of Lebanon in the autumn of 2013 from living in a state of high alert.

Repercussions on relations with the Lebanese Sunnis

The consequences of the de facto war between the Syrian opposition and Hezbollah could not be ignored; they were not limited to violent military encounters between the two sides on Syrian territory or clashes that spilled over on Lebanese territory. Hezbollah also had to manage the fallout from the situation on its relations with the Lebanese Sunni community, which had not waited for the outbreak of the Syrian rebellion to let itself be seduced by the idea of going into action against Hezbollah, the group that it viewed as having robbed the community of the political dominance it had enjoyed during the Syrian tutelage. The events of 2008 clearly showed that the outbreak of the anti-Assad rebellion in Syria only served to widen the fault lines of that had been running through the community for years.

As mentioned previously, Lebanon's Sunnis in the early 2010s were split between an FC losing some popularity and politico-religious extremes that seemed to be gaining credit among the community's base; they even benefited from the open support of several highly placed members of the FC itself. Saad Hariri was criticized between 2005 and 2011 for what appeared to be a personality weakness, a lack of political experience, a tendency to indecision and to follow the herd, but also for fleeing the country every time there was a great national crisis. His inability to "cleanse the community's honour" after what it perceived as a defeat by Hezbollah in May 2008 also came in for bitter recriminations. The lack of resolution with which Rafic Hariri's heir faced the Syrian regime, from his explicit, repeated accusations against Bashar al-Assad for the murder of his father, to his about-face in 2009 when he exonerated Damascus in hopes of being named prime minister, further damaged the image of the community's top leader. His toppling by the former opposition in January 2011 only led to some relatively mild protest in the streets of Sunni Beirut. His departure from Lebanon following his fall; his extensive use and abuse of Twitter to get his political messages across, to the point where they were mocked repeatedly by the press; the gaffe he committed in January 2012 by corresponding in a friendly and public fashion with Israeli Ministry of Defence spokesman Avichay Adraee;[92] the New TV affair, which made him an active player in the false witnesses affair; the WikiLeaks cables—all were issues that worked against him. On top of all this, in early March 2012 there was the "case of the $11 billion" that had been spent off-budget by the Siniora and Hariri governments between 2006 and 2009.[93] This scandal caused such a shock in Lebanese society that the parliamentary minority, fearing that the news spreading among the public would impact its mobilizing capacity, cancelled the annual March 14 celebrations traditionally held on Martyrs' Square in Beirut, instead holding a closed-door meeting for 4,000 supporters.[94]

In 2012–13 the Assir phenomenon offered a showcase of the second Sunni option, a radicalism that was simultaneously political, communitarian, and religious. Politically, it eschewed any further accommodation with Hezbollah. On the religious level, its competition with the party went beyond the traditional Sunni–Shiite differences, and turned into a competition to be Lebanon's spiritual leaders. Thus, when the affair of the Islamophobic film *The Innocence of Muslims* exploded in September 2012, and Nasrallah called on Muslims to "protest" and "express their anger"[95] over the insult to the Prophet, Ahmad al-Assir objected, accusing him of wanting to "kidnap Muslim leadership and make the *wilāyat al-faqīh* dominant".[96]

Although it might have seemed in the spring of 2013 that the radical option was in gaining influence and credibility—even to the point of March 14 media opening their doors to it[97]—it nonetheless did not yet attract the majority of the community. Its base simply did not feel strongly attracted to the Arabian Peninsula's Sunni paradigms and, above all, the community opted to prevent the domestic security situation from degenerating. Nevertheless, the anti-Shiite and anti-Hezbollah animosity shared by the FC and the religious radicals had the implicit support of a great many people. There was no shortage of private initiatives on the part of the Sunni community for expressing its bitterness towards a Hezbollah blamed for the community's humiliation in the spring of 2008 and for having usurped its dominance over the political decision-making process. When the incidents in Syria started, Hezbollah and the Syrian regime became objects of the same struggle, the fall of one seen as holding the key to getting rid of the other. Hezbollah flags were burned at Sunni anti-Syrian demonstrations in northern Lebanon and in central Bekaa. Early in March 2012 the son of the mufti of the Republic, Muhammad Rashid Kabbani, who had formerly been close to March 14 but had shifted to Mikati and Hezbollah in 2011, was beaten up by persons unknown.[98] In mid-May the dismantling of a Salafist network inflamed Tripoli, and violent fighting engulfed Sunnis and Alawites. In Ersal, a Sunni village in the Bekaa, there were abductions and counter-abductions of Sunni and Shiites from 2012.

Beyond the public disorder sporadically erupting in Sunni areas, the over-excitement coursing through the community in the light of events in Syria showed the collective malaise ever more blatantly. Thus, there seemed to emerge within the community the conviction of being targeted by the Lebanese authorities, particularly the army, and all of it at Hezbollah's bidding. In late May 2012 army troops shot two Sunni sheikhs, Ahmad Abdel-Wahed and Muhammad al-Mereb, at a checkpoint in the Akkar region, when the two men were en route to attend a rally organized by a member of the FC. Differing versions of the incident circulated. One was that the driver refused to stop at the barrier; a second that Abdel-Wahed took the wheel to drive off without permission after an altercation with a soldier. When the cleric refused to comply, the army opened fire on the vehicle. The incident was immediately politicized, with the FC and northern Sunni politicians accusing the army of killing the two sheikhs on behalf of Syria and Hezbollah. As soon as the media reported the death of the two clerics, clashes broke out in the (Sunni) Tarik Jdideh quarter in Beirut between FC groups and members of a small pro-Syrian group, the Arab Movement Party, which ended with the latter's leader, Shaker Berjawi, a Hezbollah ally, expelled from his headquarters and the neighbourhood. Similarly, some Sunni groups in the north threatened to create a "Free Lebanese Army" in imitation of the FSA. The following February, in Ersal, a Lebanese armed group attacked an army patrol. The town's mayor tried to excuse the attackers, arguing that the army was operating as a proxy for Hezbollah. In June, Ahmad al-Assir, declaring an "answer" to a Hezbollah "provocation", in this case the presence of the office of a section (albeit Sunni) of the LBRIO in a quarter bordering al-Assir's headquarters in Sidon, launched an assault on an army post that resulted in fifteen dead and a hundred injured in the army ranks.[99] These incidents illustrated how some Sunni elements saw themselves under assault by a Hezbollah suspected of having outsourced its destructive capacity to sovereign institutions of the state. The FC narratives acquiescing in this idea of confessional persecution by Hezbollah along with the government and army were before long picked up by media of all stripes, including those of March 14, as a "Sunni sense of victimization", as an "*ihbāt*" of the community, comparable to the one that had afflicted the Maronites during the Syrian tutelage.[100] The phenomenon, explained by a vacuum in Sunni leadership and defined by anti-Shiite resentment blaming Hezbollah for all of the Sunni community's failures, appeared all the more dangerous as the FC and the radical groups made it their new political capital, complicating efforts in the short term to de-escalate the tensions between Sunnis and Shiites.

The European Union against "Hezbollah's Military Wing"

The battle of Qusayr was not only a turning point in the history of the Syrian revolt, or one more milestone in the deterioration of relations between Hezbollah and the Syrian opposition or between Shiites and Sunnis in Lebanon. The siding of the IRL with the regular armies of Damascus in July 2013 persuaded France and, in its wake, the previously reluctant European states, to place the "military wing" of the party on the EU's list of terrorist organizations.

As previously discussed, a series of attacks and kidnappings of foreign nationals in Lebanon in the 1980s was assumed at the time to be the work of Hezbollah, then seen as a subcontractor of a revolutionary Iran engaged in a standoff with the United States and, especially, France. While Hezbollah's ability to put pressure on the kidnappers as well as the existence of family links between terrorists and some party members could be established with certainty, producing evidence of direct involvement of Hezbollah's leadership in the acts laid at its door always appear to have been fraught with difficulty.[101]

From the end of the hostage era at the very start of the 1990s, Hezbollah attracted attention with regard to terrorism on three occasions: in 1992, 1994, and 2012. In March 1992 a bomb exploded at Israel's embassy in Argentina, leaving 29 dead and nearly 250 wounded. Islamic Jihād took credit for the attack, but the Israeli government, which sent a team of investigators to the site, accused Tehran and hinted at Imad Mughniyeh's participation, thus implying Hezbollah's involvement.

In July 1994, again in Buenos Aires, it was the building that housed the bulk of Jewish institutions in Argentina that was targeted. An explosion destroyed, among others, the Israelite Mutual Association, killing 85 and wounding nearly 300. More than twenty-five years later, although the West and Israel considered Iran and Hezbollah's guilt beyond any further doubt, the Argentine judicial system had still not rendered its opinion.[102] The investigation had begun under Judge Juan José

Galeano, but he was removed from his post in 2005 for "serious irregularities in the investigation". Among the acts blamed on the judge was that he personally paid the main suspects in order to sway their testimony. Judge Alberto Nisman was named to replace him in 2006; he soon accused Iran and Hezbollah outright of having instigated the attack. A practising Jew, he was accused of "overly close" ties with the Israeli and American governments, and the WikiLeaks revelations in 2010 cast doubt on the integrity of his investigation. In addition, it was said that evidence furnished by Mossad to aid the investigation was discredited. For example, Ibrahim Berro, named by Mossad as the perpetrator of the attack killed in the explosion, had actually been killed in South Lebanon well before the attack. Moreover, according to some Lebanese dailies, Daniel Ambrosini, an explosives expert consulted by the Nisman Commission, was accused of falsifying his reports. In January 2013 Tehran and Buenos Aires agreed to set up a "Truth Committee" with responsibility for starting the investigation again from the beginning. The first inquiries determined that one of the organizers of the attack had been paid $400,000 by Carlos Corach, a practising Jew and minister of the interior at the time, and had also received the explosives from him.[103] Nisman quickly put an end to the new investigation, on the grounds that with this new inquiry the Argentine Foreign Ministry was damaging Argentina's judicial system. Some months later, Israeli officials revealed to the press that for their part they had "all those responsible for the attack" assassinated.[104] Most recently, in January 2015, Nisman accused President Cristina Kirchner of having tried to obstruct the investigation in order to protect Iranian officials. The affair caused a scandal in Argentina because, even though the president was cleared of all suspicion the following month by the legal authorities, Alberto Nisman died under mysterious circumstances four days after having filed his prosecutor's brief, which led to a far-reaching reorganization of Argentina's intelligence services.

Unlike the United States, which had put Hezbollah on its list of terrorist organizations in 1997, most European countries—France in the lead—for a long time remained unreceptive to persistent pressure exerted by Washington and Tel Aviv in favour of a clear and formal condemnation of the party. Some governments were, among other reasons, chary of jeopardizing the security forces they had committed in Lebanon (as part of UNIFIL). As the statutes of the European Union also specified the need to obtain a unanimous vote by the members for placing a group on its list, any attempt to include Hezbollah on it had long been considered doomed to failure.

Since the 2006 war successive Israeli governments have pursued several international campaigns against the party, repeatedly sounding the alarm about the latter's "preparations" for "imminent attacks" against Israeli citizens in various countries friendly to Israel. In 2012 alone, Tel Aviv accused Iran and Hezbollah of planning to do harm in Georgia, Azerbaijan, Kenya, Thailand, Cyprus, and Bulgaria. A lack of evidence meant that no follow-up action was taken on these charges until July 2012, when a Lebanese detained in Cyprus was accused of monitoring the arrivals of a series of aircraft from Israel and admitted to being a member of Hezbollah. The suspect, however, steadfastly denied having any information about a potential attack against Israeli interests.[105] On 18 July, fifteen days after the arrest, a bus carrying Israeli tourists in Burgas in Bulgaria was hit by what appeared then to be a suicide attack: there were seven dead and about thirty injured. Tel Aviv and Washington immediately accused Tehran and Hezbollah of being behind the attack, which they denied.[106]

A veritable soap opera surrounding the investigation by Bulgarian justice began, with charges and counter-charges flying about the existence of evidence of Hezbollah's involvement. By August it seemed clear that the alleged bomber and his accomplice had been carrying fake American documents. The main suspect had reportedly told several tourists shortly before the attack that he had "a Dutch mother and Iranian father".[107] According to media reports, one of his accomplices had supposedly been identified by a witness, who said that the suspect was linked to groups "preaching a radical Islam". At the same time, some Israeli media reported that two months before the attack Mossad had allegedly intercepted several calls between Lebanon and Burgas, with the calls spiking on the eve of the attack.[108]

In early January 2013 the Bulgarian authorities admitted that they were not yet ready to assign blame for the attack. Finally, on 5 February, Sofia accused Hezbollah's "militant wing", later amended to "military wing". The bomber had two Lebanese accomplices, both with dual nationality.[109] One of the suspects had allegedly received the funds required to pay for the operation "directly from IRL accounts" (*sic*).[110] The false identity papers were produced in a Lebanese workshop "known" to Western intelligence services. The investigators were said to have a picture of one of the alleged members of the terrorist group standing with members of Hezbollah. The suicide attack was ultimately an "accident" resulting from improper handling of the detonator by one of the three suspects.

Theories about alternative scenarios then emerged. An investigative reporter at the time, a correspondent for *Le Monde* and RFI in Sofia, who conducted an in-depth inquiry into the attack, did note for instance the "frustration if not anger of the local police and judges at seeing "Israeli and American agents" parade through their offices".[111] In mid-February 2013, the American investigative journalist Gareth Porter argued that the Bulgarian investigation had actually achieved little and pointed out the impossibility of levelling a charge at Hezbollah given the state of the investigation.[112] Porter's conclusions were criticized however; some indeed pointed out that a number of those whom he interviewed, notably among the officials, were former communists still close to Moscow and therefore quick to contradict the accusations levelled by Israel and the West.

When Bulgaria announced the official indictment of Hezbollah, the Lebanese press as a whole was sceptical. The daily *al-Nahār*, hardly one to be accused of sympathy for the party, gave extensive coverage to the state of Bulgarian domestic politics, indicating that the issue was being debated in Sofia, where the opposition had publicly criticized the powers that be for having yielded to external pressures.[113] *L'Orient–Le Jour*, another daily close to March 14, reported along the same lines: the report by Bulgaria's interior minister to a meeting of the National Security Council in fact failed to convince the Socialist Party, whose president, Sergei Stanishev, reproached the authorities for having announced conclusions not backed up by irrefutable evidence.[114]

In early 2013, Hezbollah's inclusion on the European list of terrorist organizations seemed unlikely because of several European countries' long-standing opposition to the idea, France's in particular. On 18 January the European ministers of foreign affairs did in fact move to nominate Hezbollah for the list. However, the initiative, which required the unanimous consent of the twenty-eight members, foundered after opposition from Paris and Berlin. That seemed to be the end of the matter when, at the end of May 2013, the top French diplomat, Laurent Fabius, personally announced from Amman that France had decided to support the inclusion of Hezbollah's "military arm" on the Union's blacklist, because of "Hezbollah's involvement at Qusayr".[115] On 22 July the European foreign ministers assembled once more, this time to vote unanimously to place "Hezbollah's military wing" on the list.

In Lebanon, this was welcome news in March 14 circles despite some misgivings about possible military action against the country on the pretext of that decision. The authorities and the centrist circles, on the other hand, starting with President Michel Sleiman and Prime Minister Najib Mikati, "regretted" it, saying that they "wished the European Union countries did a better informed reading of the facts" and asking to have the resolution "reconsidered".[116] The Hezbollah leadership, for its part, suggested that it was an accommodation to the US and Israeli governments.[117] It criticized what it saw as the bias of the decision by saying that the investigation of the Burgas incident was not yet finished. Above all, it held the EU responsible for any future attack by Israel, the Union having given Tel Aviv "legal cover for any aggression against Lebanon, with Israel [able] now to assert that it is combating terrorism".[118] Once again denying any involvement in the Bulgarian attack, it denounced comments made by Netanyahu, who, in expressing his satisfaction with the European decision, portrayed it "as an achievement of Israeli diplomacy", as the party deplored the fact that no European leader "asked him not to meddle in this affair".[119]

The Lebanese press in general was harsh, for differing reasons. Editorials favourable to the party stressed the contradictions shown by France, which was critical of the IRL for fighting Jabhat al-Nusra, affiliated with al-Qāʿida in Syria, and forgetful of its own interventions against the same type of radical Islam in Mali. The press noted that, despite previous statements by Laurent Fabius, the EU had made no mention of the Islamic Resistance's involvement at Qusayr. Instead, the Burgas attack had officially been advanced as the basis for the European consensus, said to be motivated by a "firm rejection of any threat to the security of European territory".[120] They then cast doubt on the incentive effect of the Bulgarian factor, when the conviction in Cyprus of a suspected member of Hezbollah in January 2013 had not led to a decision by Europe at the time to punish the party, even though Cyprus belonged to the EU.

To further confuse things, there were speculative scenarios from all political orientations concerning an incitement to action issuing this time not from Tel Aviv but from Riyadh. Since the IRL's involvement on the side of the Syrian regime at Qusayr, there had been several calls for *jihād* against Hezbollah in the Gulf States, especially in Saudi Arabia. The latter's determination to take Middle East affairs in hand could then be detected in the change of regime in Qatar in late June, the overthrow by the Egyptian army of President Muhammad Morsi, and the replacement, starting in July, of the Syrian opposition's leadership by one considered close to Riyadh.[121] Meanwhile, in the light of the Syrian regime's victory at Qusayr, the Gulf Cooperation Council (Saudi Arabia, Bahrain, the UAE, Qatar, Oman, and Kuwait) openly chose to intensify its efforts to take punitive measures against Hezbollah,[122] and to this end increase the pressure on friendly Western governments.[123]

The Lebanese media focused especially on what they considered to be the "contradictions" in the EU's stance vis-à-vis Hezbollah, voicing doubts about the Union's belief in the party's culpability. The Union intended to maintain "positive" relations with the "political" wing of the party, limiting the punitive dimensions of the decision to the "military wing", which it defined as the combination of the "Council for Jihad" and "External Security Committee". This, according to *L'Orient–Le Jour*, "did not prevent" the EU representative in Lebanon, Angelina Eichhorst, from standing among Hezbollah officials a few days later, "escorted by paramilitary and security elements of the party; in other words, by the very same terrorists that the EU had just sanctioned". It was also observed that UNIFIL would continue to meet with representatives of the IRL in South Lebanon.[124] When asked whether Hassan Nasrallah would be considered a member of the "military Hezbollah" or of the "civilian Hezbollah", Eichhorst was supposedly "evasive", asserting that the sanction was aimed at the military wing perceived "as such, not as a collection of individuals" (*sic*).[125] Criticisms erupted in circles close to the party, especially concerning the fact that the decision to condemn the IRL had been made before the end of the investigation. In a similar vein, it was felt that the European ambassador "is fooling everyone" in telling Hezbollah minister Muhammad Fneish that the inclusion of the IRL on the list of terrorist organizations "does not change the EU's position in favour of Lebanon's right to defend itself against any attack by Israel", assuring him that "in that event, the EU would support Lebanon".[126]

In an attempt to reassure the sympathizers, pro-Hezbollah media argued that putting the IRL on the European list of terrorist organizations would have little practical consequence for the party's manoeuvring room. Freezing its assets in Europe would have a limited impact, the party *a priori* not having any property there and not having any investments at stake in the western Mediterranean. Refusing to grant visas to members of the Islamic Resistance would be largely blunted by their tendency to operate clandestinely, and members of the "civilian"/"political" Hezbollah had no reason to worry in any case.

Be that as it may, in the run-up to the middle of the decade, there remained serious sources of concern to the party: Israel, the new Syrian forces, and domestic Sunni radicalism.

11

HEZBOLLAH IN THE EYES OF ITS PUBLIC

MEANING-MAKING AND MOBILIZATION[1]

Throughout the preceding ten chapters the guiding principle has remained the same. At no time has my presentation of Hezbollah proceeded in an encyclopaedic spirit; it deals only with those aspects of Hezbollah's historical, sociological, and organizational reality that explain the strength of its mobilization. Priority has been on issuance, and only the elements that served to foster the formation of a specific perception of the party by its supporters have been addressed. The present chapter now turns to the evolution of a reception, how the public close to Hezbollah dwelled on, reworked, and integrated these elements into reasons for retaining its political leanings over the years.

Earning its first pre-Liberation stripes

The year 2000 marked a temporary halt in the history of Hezbollah's mobilization. It was stock-taking time. Supporters of the Resistance were happy about the end of the occupation, and proud of their combatant-compatriots, who had managed a feat that no Arab armed force had yet been able to add to its roster of victories. But the party's general image back then was actually the result of an evolution spanning several years, making it richer and more complete. Personal memories as well as private and group discussions with residents of Beirut's southern suburbs and North Bekaa, and many targeted interviews with various local stakeholders, brought to light a series of strong points underpinning Hezbollah's popularity at the turn of the century. After being portrayed as somewhat inflexible (*saʿb al-taʿāmul maʿho*) and coercive (*dāghit ʿal-ʿālam*) during the first half of the 1980s, the party's image had improved in the early 1990s because of two key events. The first was the end of the war with AMAL in 1989–90, which lifted the party out of a cycle of civil violence that had affected the people living in Shiite areas for a long time.[2] The other, Israel's 1993 offensive, showcased the first effective results from IRL's renewed focus on the occupying force.

Between this first moment of recognition and the Liberation, there were two core elements in addition to the Resistance's military efforts that account for Hezbollah's increasing popularity.

Hezbollah, a party "with clean hands"

Quite logically, the public image of Hezbollah was partly influenced by how the Lebanese as a whole and regardless of confession perceive their political class. To start with, Hezbollah has always been widely respected by its supporters for what it does not have in common with the majority of Lebanese politicians: it has been able to elude certain anomalies the ruling class was tainted with by the civil war, and it exemplifies values that people thought had been lost with the advent of militia regimes. The bulk of Hezbollah supporters are thus convinced that it is a respectable party (*hizb muhtaram*) with clean hands (*īdayh ndīfeh*). These credentials imply two ideas.

The first is that Hezbollah is not a corrupt party (*mish fāsid*). Unlike other Lebanese groups—especially AMAL in the case of the Shiites—it is perceived as not diverting government resources or participating in the traditional divvying up between political and communitarian groups of government offices and appropriations. The self-financing of the party's social apparatus, its rejection of clientelist practices, and the fact that neither its cadres nor its politicians had ever been tainted by financial scandals at that time reinforce its image as an "honest" party.[3] The American academic Judith Palmer Harik also noted this perception during years of field research, arguing that

> Hezbollah could never be viewed as having preyed on the disintegrating Lebanese State, a charge levelled against its major Shiite rival, AMAL, and other political parties in Lebanon. In essence, Hezbollah's 'free money' and the disciplined behaviour of its partisans in comparison with that of AMAL members encouraged the organization's 'Mr. Clean' image.[4]

The second idea is that the party did not participate in the civil war. The clashes with the LCP and Baath that took place toward the mid-1980s, and especially the war the party fought with AMAL until 1990, could be cited as refutation of this thesis, but it is important to understand correctly what is meant by "Hezbollah did not participate in the civil war". What the term "civil war" means for the Shiite community is intercommunitarian massacres: in this, they draw a clear distinction between the conduct of the Kataeb, the Lebanese Forces, the LNM,[5] and AMAL on the one hand and the conduct of Hezbollah and the IRL on the other, with the latter two perceived as never having used weapons against opposing Lebanese groups of other confessions.

The dual meaning of *tāʾifiyya*

In Lebanon, the term *tāʾifiyya* takes on two distinct meanings. The first is political confessionalism. To say someone supports *tāʾifiyya* means that the person supports a governmental system based on a communitarian distribution of powers. This confessional logic having been retranslated in society through everyday hierarchizing distinctions between communities, saying that someone is *tāʾifi* also amounts to accusing the individual of bigotry and racism.

In the eyes of its supporters Hezbollah is doubly anti-*tāʾifi*. It officially stands against the confessional political system, declaring itself instead as favouring democracy of the one man, one vote type and as opposing communitarian racism in everyday life. By doing so, it once more reigns in the imagination of its supporters as the antithesis of the rampaging militias of the civil war years—starting with the Kataeb and Lebanese Forces. These groups not only collaborated with Israel but tried to partition Lebanon along "federal" lines,[6] not shrinking from "cleansing" their areas or those they staked out as theirs. In circles close to Hezbollah, people like to point out that the party is solicitous of harmonious coexistence between the various communities living in "its" areas. The fact is that in the Bekaa, the South, and the Beirut suburbs, non-Shiites—the Christians foremost—are left undisturbed. The social institutions and services manned by party militants ignore confessional differences. In politics, appeals for calm that issue from the party leadership in crisis situations and refusals to retaliate when the Shiite community is attacked are also cited as telling illustrations of Hezbollah's devotion to civil peace. Consequently, and in contrast to the majority of political factions that are seen as communitarian interest groups or clients clustered around a handful of families, the Hezbollah of the 2000s stands out as *al-hizb al-wahīd ellī huwwe watanē*, "the only national party"—in other words, the only party whose leadership adopts a transconfessional logic.

The advantage of "righteousness" and the disadvantage of "Iranianized" Shiism

Hezbollah may win hands down in a comparison against the Lebanese parties as a whole, but on the Shiite political stage, where AMAL is the main element of comparison, it finds itself in a more complex situation. As previously noted, a perception well established in the community gives the advantage to Hezbollah in terms of morality and righteousness. The party's activists have a reputation for usually being honest, upright, and disciplined.[7] On the other hand, AMAL's are often referred to as *zuʿrān* (thugs). AMAL's misdeeds during the civil war, incidents that are sometimes attributed to its militants, whose relationship to religion is judged as rather loose, kept this party from gaining the same exemption from the militia label enjoyed by its Shiite competitor.

However, this political preference enjoyed by Hezbollah within the community is not echoed systematically on the socio-religious level. The very fact that the party comprises militants who present themselves as believers and religiously observant leads many Lebanese to think of it as austere, puritanical, *a priori* not focused on life's pleasures and, in particular, as socially conservative. The discipline of its members, admired and appreciated for its effectiveness in preventing excesses, sometimes translates into a tiresome rigidity in daily life. That said, it does not mean that there are two groups, one composed of those hostile to religion who would not like Hezbollah and the other made up of the religious that would form the bulk of its supporter manpower. Some analysts have seen fit to argue that the most religious Shiites follow the party while those who are not believers or practitioners prefer AMAL or, more apolitically, Muhammad Husayn Fadlallāh.[8] This perception is incorrect. The degree of religiosity does not explain the mobilization around Hezbollah: the party has numerous supporters in left-leaning circles, who are scarcely attracted by religion, while great numbers of sincere believers and/or observant Shiites choose to give the party a wide berth. The point of contention is not the presence or absence of faith or religious practice, but the version of Shiism adhered to: Hezbollah adopts several paradigms and practices that belong to an Iranian version of Shiism, while the Shiism of AMAL and Fadlallāh is an Arabo(–Lebano)-centric one. If Hezbollah wins the contest for respectability and credibility against AMAL, it loses in terms of religious leadership—and still more so to Fadlallāh. In fact, it turns out that there are many Shiites who support Hezbollah in elections or who contribute to CIRS, while simultaneously keeping their distance from the party in their approach to life and relationship to God, opting for a liberated lifestyle and/or choosing to pay their *khums* to Fadlallāh rather than Khamenei.[9] The demarcation between the political sphere and the social and private spheres is well established, and different spiritual preferences do not in any way affect the ideological mobilization around the Hezbollah cause.

On the effects of Liberation

The Israeli withdrawal in 2000 reinforced the already positive perceptions enjoyed by the party in two ways. Initially, the Liberation produced a feeling of shared well-being; it created a festive atmosphere. The humiliations, the suffering associated with the occupation could be relegated to the past. The scale of the effort invested in the struggle against the occupier naturally gave rise to gratitude, but also generated respect and admiration for the IRL fighters who, for the first time in the history of the Arab–Israeli conflict, had forced the Israeli army to leave Arab territory against its will—and unconditionally, at that. The feat was perceived as all the more extraordinary because it had not been accomplished by a national army, but by a popular resistance (*muqāwama shaʿbiyya*) composed of young men significantly fewer in number than the enemy soldiers and much less well armed. By the way it conducted itself in combat, and especially during the Israeli withdrawal, the IRL reinforced the idea of a disciplined Hezbollah and a secretary-general who had his men under perfect control. In addition, it provided "supporting evidence" that it was guided by a national and anti-confessionnal logic, having liberated the South regardless of the confessional colour of villages under occupation. It also refrained from punishing the towns and villages deemed to be the homes of collaborators.

The speech by the Hezbollah secretary-general to celebrate the Liberation also marked the start of the formation of new great narratives within the Shiite community whose development and continual rewriting would soon be taken over by the community itself. The speech quickly took on strong identity connotations as Nasrallah issued the call to break the chain of inferiority complexes—not only those harboured by the Shiites vis-à-vis other Lebanese, having just demonstrated that they were no less worthy than their compatriots, but also those that the Eastern world in general maintains versus the West, to which the East must no longer think of itself as irretrievably subjected. Emphasizing the call for a humane liberation, Nasrallah harked back to the behaviour of the French after the German retreat in 1945:

> When the Nazi army was defeated in France, the French "civilized" Resistance proceeded to execute thousands of French collaborators without a trial; the Resistance in Lebanon and Lebanon are [therefore] more civilized than France and all the rest of the world![10]

By drawing this parallel with a society considered the epitome of the "civilized world" in Lebanon, and stipulating the Resistance public's moral superiority over this society, the Hezbollah secretary-general smashed the stereotype of the "barbaric Shiite" and made the Resistance supporter into a man who "could not be more civilized". But Nasrallah did not stop there: far from treating the IRL's achievements as uniquely its own, he acknowledged the part played by the other resistance groups in the success of what he characterized as a joint project. In this way, he offered the victory "to all Lebanese", "to all who resisted", and to all supporters of the Arab cause in general, suggesting that the resistance action was the template for a new national identity, which he presented as somehow the "real" Lebanese identity. It was a resounding rebuke to the communitarian theses of the resistance's critics, that is, the Christian conservative circles who traditionally associated Lebanism, Maronitism, confessionalism, and accommodationism with Israel. In its abstract and absolute sense, resistance offered the Lebanese people the chance to come together and generate a "new Lebanon", which, in antithesis to the Lebanon of the years of fratricidal war, would make inclusion and integration its pre-eminent values and thus far removed from any kind of communitarianism. Liberation in this way became the end point of a dark period of Lebanese history that saw civil war and the violent settling of scores between sons of the same country. In effect, a pardon was offered to the former allies of Israel and an invitation addressed to them to turn away irrevocably from all alliances with the former occupier, to rejoin what I would categorize as a "neo-Lebanism" permeated by Hezbollah paradigms.

The party's public retained some points from this speech while discarding others, and developed its own interpretation of the occupation's end. At first, the Liberation was regarded with a vast sense of collective relief at the ending of a trauma that had lasted over twenty years, replaced by a nascent sense of security and of safety that, at the time, seemed destined to last. In the months following the Israeli withdrawal, the formula *Sār finā nnām* (Now we can sleep) was widely adopted, with Hezbollah members for their part emphasizing the fact that *'Uyūn al-Muqāwameh sahrāneh* (The eyes of the Resistance watch over the country). This certainty of being secure, that Israel "will no longer dare to attack", became well entrenched.[11] Consequently, the party was seen as reliable, a group that "keeps its word". The abduction of two Israeli soldiers by the Resistance on 12 July 2006 was not given the name "Truthful Pledge" by happenstance. On a second level, the surge of pride that came with victory, the IRL fighters' conduct towards their Lebanese adversaries, and Nasrallah's comparison with the French case, combined with his vision of a "new Lebanon" and a nation stabilized by the disappearance of confessional categories, brought about a veritable metamorphosis in the community's collective identity. Liberation thus became a great founding moment, making 2000 a year in which a complex, dynamic revamping of the Shiite identity occurred. On the level of meanings, Liberation was the token, the proof par excellence of the community's identity as Lebanese. With the Shiites always cognizant of their devalued image in the eyes of their countrymen, they saw May 2000 as a gift to the latter that must convince them that the Shiites, far from being members of an inferior group, had paid the price in blood and deserve to be regarded as equal in their Lebaneseness. Moreover, by refusing to engage in reprisals, they felt that they had proved that they did not value gratuitous violence and that their countrymen did not have to fear them. In other words, the Liberation was the "baptism" of Lebanon's Shiites who thus made a new entrance through the front door to national identity and history. The process went on subconsciously, but it was real—as proven by the reactions and positioning of the community's majority from 2005 on. A dynamic was set in motion by which a communitarian inferiority complex disappeared and a stigma was cleansed. It was not that the Shiites did not feel Lebanese before, as shown by their massive mobilization around the resistance cause, but they needed the approving regard of the Other. With the Liberation came the widespread feeling that this fervently awaited recognition had finally been given.[12]

The years following the Liberation saw the consolidation of the aftermath of May 2000 and the routinizing of Hezbollah charisma. Supporters of the Resistance let go of pressures they had felt for years to bask in the glow of victory. Some form of mental distancing from action, from *ta'bi'a* as a proclivity for intervention, occurred in favour of enjoying results finally achieved. Armed resistance action was set aside, and its public settled into a post-combat state for a few years. This new perception explained the three major political positionings by Resistance supporters during the period. For one, they continued to support IRL actions. They criticized the American policy of targeting the IRL, opposing any penalizing of the Resistance "that has given so much", rejecting any eventual disbandment—especially since, in the eyes of party supporters, the American government cared only about Israel's welfare, not that of Lebanon. The situation in Iraq, where civil war broke out and Shiites were targeted by jihadist groups whose operations had been made possible by the US intervention, confirmed what the Resistance's supporters already believed. It also worried them, given Washington's declared desire to "export democracy to Lebanon". Paris, usually viewed benevolently, disappointed by choosing the "wrong side": they disowned Jacques Chirac, considered Lebanon's great friend between 1995 and 2000, following the passage of Resolution 1559 and the al-Manār affair. Fears engendered by the evolving regional scene thus promoted the feeling that traditional alliances with Iran and Syria remained the only realistic protection against the chaos that the West was suspected of trying to foment in the region around Iraq. Finally, just when Hezbollah's mobilization went into stand-by mode, a rival suddenly materialized around a campaign against the Syrian tutelage, so that, at the end of the period, two major mobilizations were coexisting. Activated in full "come-back mode", the Maronite community mobilized a new resistance, joined by Walid Jumblatt's Druzes. As long as the tutelage continued, the new grouping would not worry Hezbollah or its supporters. The competition was rather less capable of flexing its muscle on a political stage largely dominated by Damascus because it in fact remained self-circumscribed by a confessional discourse that kept its struggle from scaling to the national level. Moreover, the Sunnis, as the community that was the least badly off under the Taef Agreement, showed no interest in letting themselves be seduced by the protests. Nevertheless, the series of events that followed Rafic Hariri's murder in February 2005 soon made it incumbent on Hezbollah to re-evaluate the situation and ramp up its mobilization, because the competition from what, going forward, would be designated as the "March 14 Alliance" turned out to be more damaging to the party's interests than it had suspected.

Hezbollah's followers and the "Cedar Revolution"

When the assassination of Rafic Hariri suddenly upset the Lebanese political chessboard, the majority of the Shiite community at first chose to keep its distance. Not only was it uncomfortable about the possible fallout from a Syrian withdrawal, but the big anti-Syrian mobilization itself raised a number of concerns.

A favoured alliance with the United States and France

Because of the close relations that bound it to certain Western governments, March 14 appeared to the IRL public above all as the heir of groups in the 1960s and 1970s classed as conservative and predominantly Christian that had chosen rapprochement and identity assimilation with the West at the time, to the detriment of their Arab environment. The first fear the new movement thus raised is that it embodied the vector by which the former mandatory power and its American ally would "again" attempt to interfere in the conduct of Lebanese affairs. It is no coincidence that charges of "enslavement to colonial forces" and references to Lebanon's "French nostalgia" multiplied in the March 8 camp, and that it revived the memory of the 1983 attacks that led to the departure of the Franco-American multinational force. The fears deepened during the year after March 14 took power, as many leading figures in the new majority adopted as part of their vocabulary a whole range of concepts issuing from neoconservative circles and their affiliates: "war against terrorism", "constructive chaos", "new Middle East", and "Shiite crescent". In the same vein, some leaders in the new majority overtly called for Washington to do in Syria "what it just did in Iraq".[13]

The door opened to a return of Western influence by the new group in power fed the opposition's fears all the more because this influence was perceived as having as its real objective the subcontracting of Israeli policy. Rising pressure by the international community to disarm the Resistance seemed to confirm those fears, especially since Israel was at the time pressuring the USA to make Lebanon the object of its next military intervention. For its part, March 14 spoke openly about making peace with Israel, at times in a manner viewed as provocative by the populations that had suffered under the occupation.[14] Not surprisingly, the old dichotomies (pro-Syrian vs. pro-Israeli) resurfaced, causing many Lebanese to sense a return to the situation that had prevailed at the beginning of the civil war. But this time it was the Shiites who embodied what was left of "progressive" forces, the "Maronitization" of the Sunnis having tipped them into the "conservative" camp.

In fact, when March 14 came to power, a not insignificant number of its leaders (essentially from the Sunni party) seemed prepared to compromise.[15] However, the new opposition was concerned with how much resilience the majority would demonstrate against the pressure exerted by an international community calling on it to disarm the IRL. Washington had made no secret of the fact that it would directly link its support—including financial—to the implementation of Resolution 1559,[16] and the FC, now in power, had always been heavily reliant on international aid. Not to mention that March 14, under counter-attack by the Syrian regime, had a critical need for Western political and diplomatic support. If it was to win the challenges it had set for itself (international tribunal, negotiating an exchange of embassies with Syria, a halt to assassinations, etc.), its condition of dependency meant that it was hardly in a position to antagonize its protectors.

Logically, March 14's conciliatory period was brief, with the majority's calls for disarmament, initially low key but then more and more insistently, multiplying and coming on top of Jumblatt's frontal attacks against Hezbollah. Distrust of March 14 grew in Shiite ranks, and was soon fed by the government turning to the FBI to investigate assassinations, the cabinet maintaining its support for the Mehlis Commission even after its contacts with Mossad become public knowledge, and the FC organizing festivities in honour of John Bolton, America's United Nations ambassador and a notorious pro-Israel hardliner.[17] On the eve of the summer 2006 war, March 14 therefore seemed, in the eyes of Hezbollah supporters, to be little more than a tractable instrument in the hands of the international community.

In its attempt to reassure the March 8 public and win it over, the March 14 leadership floated two arguments. First, it presented the International Criminal Court as a potential boon for all of Lebanese society. The reasoning was that, by identifying the killers, most probably linked to the Syrian regime in March 14's view, and the imposing of sanctions on Damascus by the international community as a consequence, the court would achieve two things—it would stop the series of assassinations that had shaken Lebanon since the autumn of 2004, and would also put an end to Syrian interference in Lebanese domestic affairs. Second, the majority tried to convince the opposition to shelter under the Western rather than the Syrian umbrella, arguing repeatedly that Lebanon could count on French and American support and protection. If Lebanon were aligned with the West, the reasoning went, the Resistance would become superfluous, since the West would take charge of protecting the country against the Israeli threat.[18] But not only did Hezbollah's public have a different take on the efficacy of an international inquiry and, especially, on the integrity of the committee conducting it, but it also doubted the ability of Western governments to keep Tel Aviv's *capacité de nuisance* in check. In addition, more than any other sect in Lebanon, the Shiite community was paying attention to the Iraqi situation. When the George W. Bush administration addressed the Lebanese problem in 2004, and again in 2005, Shiite circles were noticeably on edge about a presumed US attempt to "Iraqize" Lebanon. This lack of confidence in neoconservative America therefore explains the growing fear starting in 2005 that March 14 would become the gateway to "constructive chaos"[19] in Lebanon. Without necessarily being fans of the Assad dynasty, the Hezbollah public was nevertheless disinclined to see the Syrian regime fall or to help hasten its demise for America or Israel's benefit. Its default position was therefore to stay close to Damascus, which, despite obvious drawbacks, seemed a better strategy for ensuring stability and avoiding an Iraq-type option.

New era, old fault lines

March 14 did not upset supporters of the Resistance only because of its close relations with the US and European governments. If it felt to them like a return to the years when Lebanese had to choose sides between confessionalist conservatives and progressive leftists, it was because some segments of the new majority, mostly Christians, had also interpreted the Cedar Revolution as a belated but welcome rebirth of their old causes and former paradigms. As mentioned previously, a large number of Lebanese of all confessions viewed with disfavour the return to power of the former militia leaders and heads of the conservative current from the civil war years, starting with Samir Geagea, the Gemayels and Walid Jumblatt. Many people believed that the leaders of March 14 were not right for the task confronting them, that militiamen who for several years had battled each other to break up and destroy the Lebanese state were not the people to lay the foundations for it fifteen years later. Moreover, the wounds of war were not yet all healed, with entire families nourishing hatred towards the groups that had kidnapped and/or murdered their parents, children, brothers, and sisters.[20] There were also reminders that the leaders of the anti-Syrian movement did not really begin criticizing the Syrian regime until it had publicly announced the withdrawal arrangements for its troops. It was pointed out that these same leaders had been docile collaborators with the Syrians during the tutelage. The positioning of the Sunnis, under Saad Hariri's leadership, alongside the pro-Americans meanwhile blindsided the Islamic Resistance's supporters. Though they would consider the emotion aroused by the assassination of the former prime minister to be legitimate, they failed to comprehend why the Sunnis would shift in favour of a political line that they had fought ferociously in the 1970s and 1980s. Rafic Hariri's son was therefore blamed for dragging his community into making political choices that flew in the face of its historical positions.

Another reason for the distrust was a certain kind of insider discourse among March 14 peers that clashed with official pronouncements. Despite public calls for national unity, sectarian commentary resurfaced quickly. As noted before, the Shiites very early on had the feeling that the March 14 party was not for them. In the euphoria of the festivities organized on Martyrs' Square in the spring of 2005, the vast majority of the intercommunal reconciliation speeches delivered praised the reconciliation between the Maronite and Sunni communities, but made (almost) no mention of the Shiite community or the years of Israeli occupation. Sectarian comments by Pierre Gemayel and Gebran Tueni did not go unnoticed. For example, despite calls by Nasrallah not to react, a few days after Tueni's speech a demonstration was organized in the heart of the (Shiite) city of Nabatiyeh, at which protesters showed up leading sheep on leashes.[21] The day Tueni was assassinated in December 2005, and the November day the following year when Pierre Gemayel was killed, the sound of Kalashnikovs fired in the air as a sign of joy echoed in the southern suburbs of Beirut, the South, and in the Bekaa; in the streets, pastries were handed out to passers-by.

To the re-emergence of remarks openly belittling the Shiites were added what were viewed as reactionary political choices. Very early on, March 14 declared its commitment to making Islamo-Christian parity no longer the temporary provision provided for in the Taef Agreement, but a permanent political formula, regardless of the evolving communitarian demographics. Very quickly, therefore, far from being perceived as a forward-looking reformist movement, March 14 found itself likened to the confessionalists of the 1960s and 1970s, in both meanings of the term: sectarian in everyday life and conservative on the political stage. In February 2006 a young Shiite from the Bekaa summed up this feeling to me: "March 14 sent a very clear message [to us Shiites]: 'Shoe shiners you were, shoe shiners you will remain'". This perception of rejection gradually put the Resistance's public on the defensive. This is what motivated knee-jerk reactions, such as one in June 2006, when, in the middle of the night, hundreds of people took to the streets and burned tyres to protest at a satirical television programme poking fun at the Hezbollah secretary-general—and his Shiite accent—aired on a network close to the majority.[22]

In the heady days after Liberation, large numbers of Shiites had believed that their reading of the end of the occupation was shared by the vast majority of Lebanese and that the country's diverse communities had finally recognized the Shiite community as their equal. With March 14's downplaying of the Liberation and its discourse, they suddenly realized that the old paradigms retained their potency, that the sacrifices the Shiites had made in the South for years had in fact not improved their image or earned them credit with their countrymen. This powerful sense of disappointment would have serious implications for how the relationship of the Shiite community evolved, not only with the Resistance and Hezbollah but also with the other communities. Superimposed on this without any prior warning was the 2006 war, which would propel the Shiite community towards taking a novel, highly sophisticated look at its own situation and its relationships with others.

The Thirty-Three-Day War: Consecration

Of all Lebanese, members of the Shiite community undeniably suffered the most from the Thirty-Three-Day War and its consequences. Shiite areas, which were also Hezbollah's, were the primary and unvarying targets of the bombing, and most civilian casualties came from Shiite ranks. At the end of the conflict, after the moment of relief over the suspension of hostilities passed, the vast majority of Shiites, as well as Hezbollah sympathizers of other confessions, found themselves in the grip of two emotions: anger and resentment at the state of Israel and the West, on the one hand, and pride in the IRL, on the other.

Multidirectional anger

Predictably, the anger of Hezbollah supporters directed against Israel was a function of the extent of the damage and the number of victims. The loss of loved ones (ranging from family members and friends to neighbours and acquaintances), the expulsions, the demolition of houses and shops, the shredded bodies shown by the media, corpses abandoned on roadsides, all the scars left by the Israeli army revived their hatred for Lebanon's southern neighbour. The collective punishment inflicted on the

Lebanese population with the aim of turning it against Israel's enemy came to nothing. Contrary to the line put out by Tel Aviv, the international community and March 14, Hezbollah supporters overwhelmingly thought that Israel, not the IRL, must be held responsible for the tragedy that had befallen the country, and that Operation Truthful Pledge was only a pretext for a war that Israel was thought to have planned for all along. Even while the conflict was raging, speculation was rife that "it is impossible for an attack of this magnitude not to have been planned" and that "the operational mode and strategies point to a premeditated action". The Israeli army's excesses, including massacres of women and children, the population driven to famine, the use of bombs prohibited by international law (phosphorus bombs, chemical gases against Beirut's southern suburbs), the bombardment of UN positions, hospitals, orphanages, schools, Red Cross centres, refugee camps, funeral processions, and motorists reinforced an already negative image of the Israeli government as "arrogant", "racist", "immoral", "bloodthirsty", and placing itself "above human and divine laws". Some commentaries emanating from Israel's political class were judged as "devoid of all humanity"—even within the ranks of March 14.[23]

The Israeli army's psychological warfare, waged by distributing leaflets and broadcasting radio message loops that accused Hezbollah of being the cause of the Lebanese population's torments and calling for "[the] liquidating [of] the Nasrallah gang", had the opposite effect to the one intended. Party supporters mocked Tel Aviv's propaganda and many people "did not know whether to laugh or cry"; they "wondered if the Israelis really believe what they say", or said that it is "hard to believe the Israelis still do not understand anything about Lebanon". Indeed, most often the radio broadcasts were far removed from the real situation on the ground. Diatribes ridiculing the "false exploits" of the "Hezbollah mercenaries" and praising the "bravery" of the Israeli soldiers, broadcast while the IRL scored unexpected victories on the battlefield and TV channels were showing images of haggard Israeli soldiers crying and calling their mothers, forged the image of a military untethered from reality and deserving to be the butt of jokes. Some Israeli text messages provoked genuine laughter. For example, when five Lebanese were abducted on 1 August, after all-night fighting in the vicinity of the Dār al-Hekmeh Hospital in Baalbek, Israeli military radio announced at dawn: "Total victory! We captured five Hezbollah militants in the heart of Hezbollah territory and we returned without a scratch!" Texts such as this one appeared at 5 a.m. on Lebanese mobile phones: "Congratulations to the Israeli army. We managed at Baalbek to get back our two abducted soldiers and kidnapped three Hezbollah cadres." The operation had actually ended in complete failure, and news of the five people captured, all well known in Baalbek as having nothing to do with Hezbollah, had already provoked general hilarity.[24]

The stand taken by the government and March 14 personalities and their comments, all more or less hostile to Hezbollah, also created a backlash. The government was accused especially of bad crisis management. It was reproached for not having supported the IRL in a context where solidarity among the Lebanese parties was seen as imperative. As a result, certain gestures or initiatives were perceived as inopportune, starting with the visit by Condoleezza Rice to Beirut while the conflict raged. Giant posters bearing a photo of Fouad Siniora embracing the American secretary of state upon her arrival, kissing her on both cheeks and smiling were also plastered all over Riyad al-Solh Square in 2007 to keep memories fresh of the "felony" committed by the "clique" in power.

Lebanon at war: Lebanese perceptions of the government's performance
24–26 July 2006

	Yes	*No*	*Don't know*
1. Do you think that the political and diplomatic measures by the Lebanese government suffice to counter the offensive?	33.5%	64.3%	2.2%
2. Do you think the government has done all it can to help the refugees?	42.8%	54%	3.2%

Beirut Center for Research and Information (www.beirutcenter.info), *al-Safir*, 27 July 2007

The "Marjayoun affair" furnished another excuse for supporters of Hezbollah to stoke their antagonism towards the government. A few days after the Israeli attack on the Lebanese convoy that had left the town under a safe-conduct from Tel Aviv, several media sources reported that the acting minister of the interior, Ahmad Fatfat, a Sunni and member of the FC, apparently collaborated with the Israeli army. A video broadcast after the end of hostilities by an Israeli national channel did show the barracks commander, General Adnan Daoud, joking and having a friendly cup of tea with Israeli soldiers. Unlike the version originally put forward by Fatfat, it seems that the Israeli soldiers did not take the barracks by force but were fleeing, pursued by IRL fighters.[25] It seems certain that the Marjayoun barracks, being under the direct orders of the interior minister and not of the Lebanese force's regimental commanding officer, had been surrendered by the former when he ordered the barracks gate opened to the fleeing Israeli soldiers. This turned into a real soap opera that fed opposition suspicions that March 14 was collaborating, especially since Adnan Daoud was questioned by the Justice Department but Ahmad Fatfat emerged unscathed.

Comments and statements by some March 14 officials were also vexing, starting with those seeking to pin responsibility for the tragedy on Hezbollah and attempting to call it to account even before the end of hostilities. Charges that the IRL had launched Operation Truthful Pledge "on orders from Syria and/or Iran" aroused contempt for a class of politicians deemed "militia-like as it has always been" and "unable to understand that an armed group may have good reasons for launching attacks".[26] Despite statements by Samir Geagea, for whom the summer war had just demonstrated the ineffectiveness of Hezbollah's defensive strategy—meaning that the country's defence should be left to the army—the majority of Hezbollah supporters, sure of the IRL's effectiveness in the field as well as of the Lebanese army's inability to stand up to the enemy, emerged from the war even more convinced that the Resistance alone was capable of protecting Lebanon. Considering also that the Israeli army had proved that it could re-enter Lebanon at will, and keeping in mind the Israeli government's promise to "return in 2007", they were more convinced than ever that disarming the IRL would be "suicidal" (*intiḥārī*).

By the same token, the March 14 thesis of "unwavering support by the United States and France" turned out to be overblown. Speeches by some US officials, in particular by John Bolton, the American UN representative, outraged large segments of Lebanese society. A few days after the start of the conflict he argued that there was "no moral equivalence" between Israeli and Lebanese civilian casualties, the former being "victims of malicious terrorist acts" while an army killing the latter is "self-defence."[27] Fears about importation of the neocon "constructive chaos" into Lebanon were reawakened when Condoleezza Rice spoke on 21 July of a "new Middle East in the making" to justify not calling for a ceasefire, saying that it would mean otherwise a return to the "old Middle East".[28] In the eyes of Resistance supporters, the American "compromise of its principles" was confirmed by a *New Yorker* article published in the last days of the war that was reported on extensively in the Lebanese press. In it, the journalist Seymour Hersh "disclosed" the details of an Israeli–American agreement covering an Israeli project to attack Lebanon.[29] If the author is to be believed, and contrary to what the US government affirmed at the beginning of the conflict about its non-participation in Israeli military plans,[30] Washington apparently actually helped Tel Aviv prepare an offensive well before the Islamic Resistance's 12 July operation. Supposedly, the United States supported the project in the hope of observing an Israeli *modus operandi* that might serve as a possible template for a preventative American attack on Iran, a highly tempting idea for Washington at the time. The Israelis were then alleged to have been waiting for a "false pretext" which, once Hezbollah had provided it, would have permitted them to claim self-defence. Washington denied this version. As for Hezbollah's leadership, it did not hesitate to use the article to argue that the IRL in the end stole a march on the Israeli army, which had originally wanted to attack Lebanon in the autumn.

As for the European countries, in particular Great Britain and Germany, they once again appeared to lack independent will and to be "subject to American *diktat*". While

France was spared somewhat due to the efforts by President Jacques Chirac to end the conflict, it was blamed for certain gestures and words by its minister of foreign affairs.[31]

Lebanon at war: Lebanese perceptions of the United States
24–26 July 2006

	Yes	*No*	*Don't know*
1. Do you think that the United States and Israel will succeed in imposing their conditions for a ceasefire?	35.5%	56.9%	7.6%
2. Do you think the United States plays the role of unbiased mediator in this war?	7.8%	89.5%	2.7%
3. Do you think the United States has adopted a constructive position towards Lebanon in this war?	9.5%	85.6%	4.9%

Beirut Center for Research and Information (www.beirutcenter.info), *al-Safir*, 27 July 2007

The UN also appeared to live up to its prevailing image as operating on a "double standard". "As usual", it was perceived as incapable of resolving the situation, paralysed by a US government intent on giving priority to Israeli interests. In late July the UNSC's refusal to condemn the Qānā massacre attracted the ire of much of the Lebanese public. At news of the tragedy, emotional demonstrators in tears stormed United Nations House on Riyad al-Solh Square in Beirut, hurling rocks at the glass façade, smashing down the building's main door and quickly invading upper floors; they ransacked offices, ripped out doors, and threw things out the windows. They carried banners displaying slogans such as "Thank you America for the smart bombs that kill our children!" and protesters yelled "Feltman, get out now!"[32] The refusal of the UN to condemn Israeli attacks against its own outposts degraded its image that much more.[33] Resolution 1701, whose passage provided some reassurance, was nevertheless held to be very unsatisfactory, tailor-made for Israel. The text called for the unconditional release of the abducted Israeli soldiers, but merely talked of encouraging efforts to resolve the issue of Lebanese prisoners jailed in Israel. While it created concern by not demanding the immediate withdrawal of Israeli forces, it astonished by banning all attacks by Hezbollah but only offensive operations by Israel, suggesting that Tel Aviv should be allowed to continue defensive operations, a term considered subject to expedient interpretations.

Finally, where the Arab countries were concerned, the supporters of the Resistance already regarded Egypt, Saudi Arabia, and Jordan with suspicion, habitually attributing their conciliatory positions towards Israel and the United States to their supposed subservience to them both. The summer 2006 war reinforced this feeling. Several Lebanese newspapers published accounts of contacts during the conflict between "certain Arab countries" and Israel, under which the former were said to have encouraged the latter not to suspend its offensive until Hezbollah had been rendered completely harmless. Thus, during the conflict the Saudi government openly blamed the crisis on Hezbollah's leaders, described as "adventurers".[34] The Egyptian and Jordanian governments immediately adopted the same position.[35] These statements resonated all the more badly with Hezbollah's public because this marked the first time in the history of the Arab–Israeli conflict that Arab governments explicitly sided with Tel Aviv in a declared war against a Lebanese party.

The Resistance, object of admiration and pride

The Islamic Resistance, on the other hand, sparked admiration. The battles were closely followed day by day by its supporters, and the IRL's exploits were greeted with automatic-weapons fire as expressions of joy. The IRL's aggressiveness and its ability regularly to inflict heavy losses on an enemy deployed in force were promoted as a source of pride, renewing the bond of trust between the Islamic Resistance and its public. Roughly ten days after the start of hostilities, a survey found that more than 85 per cent of Lebanese at the time supported the Resistance's operations and that nearly 65 per cent thought Israel could not win.

Lebanon at war: Lebanese views of Israel and the IRL
24–26 July 2006

	Yes	*No*	*Don't know*
1. Did you support the capture of Israeli soldiers by the Resistance to use in exchange for Lebanese captives?	70.1%	29.9%	0%
2. Do you support the IRL's action against the Israeli aggression in Lebanon?	86.9%	11.8%	1.3%
3. In your opinion, will Israel succeed in defeating the Resistance?	28.4%	63.3%	8.3%

Beirut Center for Research and Information (www.beirutcenter.info), *al-Safir*, 27 July 2007

In the weeks following the end of the conflict, as the accounts by the fighters reached the media, people told each other of hand-to-hand fighting between the IRL and the Israeli army. They told how, at the height of the bombings and clashes, the *shabeb* (fighters) continued to provide services to the citizens, distributing water and bread in the bombed areas, organizing patrols around the clock in the deserted neighbourhoods to deter looting, mobilizing the party's technical people to change the locks on doors of apartment buildings and distributing duplicate keys to people on their return. All this further reinforced the image that Hezbollah was substantially different from the militias of the civil war years.[36]

However, there remained a residue of anxiety in the days after the war ended. There was some question whether the IRL had anticipated the potential Israeli military reaction when it made the move to kidnap the two soldiers on 12 July. Nasrallah acknowledged as much: "We absolutely would not have done this had we known it would lead to a war of such magnitude."[37] However, in March 2007 the Israeli prime minister acknowledged that Israel had planned to attack Lebanon well before 12 July, thus confirming the Seymour Hersh article. The conviction that the IRL won, if not unanimously held in Lebanese ranks, would be reinforced by the fact that, with time, both Israel and the West acknowledged the victory as such.

A symbiotic, strengthened pact

Beyond the situational reactions and appraisals by the Shiites of the 2006 conflict, the Thirty-Three-Day War occupies a special place in Hezbollah's mobilization trajectory. This stems from the conflict's profound effects, including an acceleration in the Shiite community's psychological liberation. The party's mobilization acquired a new resilience, a feeling that it would in the future be able to count on to sustain itself. More than the war itself, it was what the party's public, and especially the Shiites, would make of it, how they reworked its meaning independent of how the party leadership interpreted it, that explains the post-2006 solidification of the close ties between Hezbollah and its supporters.

A "victory secured by God"

In Shiite circles, any lingering doubts at the beginning of the conflict about the IRL's ability to counter a large-scale Israeli offensive were dispelled. There would thereafter be "nothing that the Resistance could not accomplish" (*al-Muqāwama qādira ʿalā kill shī*). The certainty was strengthened all the more because the IRL stood its ground alone (*wiqfit la-hālhā*), without even the support of the Lebanese population as a whole, against an Israeli army that enjoyed overwhelming support on the home front and was aided militarily and diplomatically by the United States and several European countries. Many observers—homegrown, Arab, but also Western and Israeli—conceded that the way the IRL fighters prevailed against their opponents was unexpected and difficult to fathom. Nasrallah spoke of a "divine victory" only after Hezbollah's public took the adjective literally and saw nothing less than God's direct hand in the Resistance's prowess. As a matter of fact, the rise in stories of heroic deeds was a novel phenomenon compared to 2000. God supposedly not only protected the Resistance during the battles, but the *imāms* themselves were said to have descended from Heaven in support of the fighters. In Baalbek and in the South, several people were quoted as having seen 'with their own eyes' a man with a face of light astride a white horse (a reference to *imām* Mahdī) charge the Israeli troops, or a second one, also mounted but brandishing the sword Dhū al-Fuqār (alluding to the *imām* ʿAlī). These witness accounts were numerous enough, incidentally, to be turned into a book in 2007.[38] A Hezbollah visual media supervisor, claiming that he had coined the slogan *Nasr min Allāh* ("A victory sent by God") that was paraded systematically in the party's iconography after the war, explains:

> We were asked to develop a communication campaign around the summer war. We then came up with the idea of a "divine victory", we were the ones who coined the slogan *Nasr min Allāh*.[39] Indeed, this war proved that material considerations, superior military technology—all the hardware—matter little when faced with faith and determination. If you think about it carefully, this war defies all rational understanding; nine fighters at ʿAytā al-Shaʿb stood up to the highly equipped Israeli army—it beggars belief! Who therefore but God could have given us this victory?[40]

The IRL fighters thus took on a new allure. In 2000, the martyrs in particular were eulogized as the ones who "gave their blood for their country". The fighters back then were referred to as courageous young men, coming from a humble people suffering under the occupation. They had everyone's gratitude and were looked upon as true heroes. But theirs was a proximate image, one imbued with familiarity to the public—that is, the image was that of a *shaʿbiyya* or popular resistance in the sense that they issued forth from society. In other words, they were still human. After 2006 the dead were still honoured, but this time people regarded the veterans with a special kind of esteem and sentiment. The combatants were elevated to become a caste not just of heroes but of the elect, touched by divine grace. The expression *rijāl Allāh*, the "men of God", is how the combatants described themselves in their letter to Nasrallah and which he echoed in his reply. The expression quickly became standard, and was repeated in books dedicated to the IRL fighters.[41]

"The sayyid": more acclaimed than ever

In tandem with the image of the Resistance, that of Hassan Nasrallah gained significantly in power and stature. During his television appearances he above all conveyed a strong impression by appearing calm, serene, and confident as the fighting raged.

Willner has written about the effect that the charismatic leader's calm and controlled bearing can produce during times of uncertainty, panic or chaos.[42] The episode that Shiites today refer to colloquially with the phrase "And now, on the high seas" (*'Wal-ān, fī 'ard al-bahr'*), formulated by Nasrallah during the conflict to announce the destruction in real time of an Israeli warship, undoubtedly left its mark on the collective mind. In the same vein, the statement with which he closed the same address—one of his first during the conflict—"Just as I have always promised you victory, I promise it to you once again" (*'Kamā kuntu a'idukum bil-nasr dā'iman, a'idukum bil-nasr mujaddadan'*) has become a creed, a statement of faith. In terms of image, 2006 saw Hezbollah continuing to be "the only party in Lebanon that does not lie", and Nasrallah more than ever as the one "who says what he does and does what he says".

This portrait of an oracular Nasrallah was reinforced by another, this time echoed by the Israeli political class and society themselves. Many accounts filtered through the press that gave the impression that the Israelis found the secretary-general of Hezbollah to be more reliable than their own political elite. Nasrallah had already called attention to this fact in one of his speeches when he warned the Israelis: "You Zionists, you say in polls that you believe me more than you believe your leaders. Today, I urge you to listen to me carefully and to believe me."[43] In fact, that evening, at the height of the war, all the Israeli TV channels broke away from an interview with Dan Halutz, chief of the Israeli General Staff, to broadcast Nasrallah's speech live.[44] One year after the war, a survey in Israel still showed that "the Israelis trust Hassan Nasrallah more than Ehud Olmert".[45] As already mentioned, the Hezbollah public took a great deal of pride in such recognition being accorded by the Israelis to their leader and his credibility.[46] So much so, that the Hezbollah website featured on its home page a daily digest of "Selected excerpts" from the Israeli press,[47] featuring translated articles containing references by Israeli authorities or analysts to the IRL's "superiority" over their army and their "grudging admiration" for Nasrallah.

This image of a visionary leader who "is never wrong", coupled with the surprise produced by the IRL's unexpected effectiveness on the ground during the Thirty-Three-Day War, including "surreal" victories in several battles ('Aytā al-Sha'b, Bint Jbeil, etc.), added a novel superhuman, crypto-divine dimension to the Nasrallah persona. There was great temptation after the war to see in him no less than the Mahdī himself. Only the mismatched given names—the Mahdī is called Muhammad—explains why the pairing did not happen. A *ta'bi'a* told me a few days after war's end, half in jest, half-seriously, that "Hassan Nasrallah is not the Mahdī, of course. But between us, what can the Mahdī have that Nasrallah does not?" Not quite seeing in Nasrallah the Messiah who must return to let justice reign on earth did not prevent large segments of the Shiite public from spontaneously seeing him instead as "herald" of the Mahdī's return. Shiite dogma was called to the rescue *a posteriori* to give the idea more heft: tradition has it that the Mahdī's arrival will be preceded by "signs", including a proliferation of conflicts. The "incredible but true" defeat of the Israeli army, the intervention by angels or even the *imāms* themselves in battles were all treated as such precursor signs. Better yet, the return of the Mahdī will be announced by a "Yemenite"; and it turns out that Hassan Nasrallah is of Yemeni descent. Some, without quite formulating it this way, were convinced that he had magical powers—another trait that Willner had remarked on as a quality usually attributed to charismatic leaders.[48] For example, a young woman named Rim Haydar, interviewed by al-Manār during the war, expressed her dream of obtaining Nasrallah's *ʿabāya* to wrap around her children, then cut it into pieces to give to the people around her. After the war, Nasrallah actually sent her one of his *ʿabāyas*, supposedly the one he wore during an interview with al-Jazeera on the day of the victory celebration.[49] A handover ceremony was then held by the party in Ms Haydar's native village. In the end, she could not muster the "courage" to cut up the precious cloak, so she exhibited it in her home and held an open house for "all those who wanted to come [touch it] to receive a blessing".[50]

"The sayyid" therefore entered a different category in 2006: no longer human, he was henceforth considered—consciously or subconsciously—as semi-divine. It became unthinkable for him to fail, inconceivable for him to make a mistake. While not belonging to the *imām* caste, he shared with them an exclusive quality: he is a *maʿsūm*, an "infallible". This meant that he could be trusted blindly in all domains—starting with that of politics.

Widespread popular homages to the Resistance

This evolution of the image of the Resistance manifested itself in various ways after the war. The world of music released pent-up emotions. Julia Boutros, a (Christian) singer already known for her songs in the 1990s in support of the occupied South and Palestine, turned Nasrallah's letter to the fighters into verse and then set it to music.[51] Bands close to Hezbollah produced a stream of albums singing the praises of the IRL, which were promoted with a slew of increasingly sophisticated music videos. Al-Manār and the Unit for Artistic Activities produced a sample of these called "flashes" (*flashshāt*) in immense quantities. These video clips, combining images of the war and powerful calls to action by Nasrallah against a background of martial music or popular songs with stirring melodies, were played in loops in stores, on the street, in public venues, on MP3 players, and car radios. *Halā yā saqr Lubnān!* (Be greeted, hawk of Lebanon!), a tune composed in Nasrallah's honour by Firqat al-Shimāl (the Group of the North), a Palestinian group originally known for writing wedding songs, became all the rage.[52] Photos and giant posters of Nasrallah could be seen on every wall in supporters' neighbourhoods, sporting an abundance of effusive slogans expressing gratitude, swearing loyalty, and extending wishes for a long life. Mobile phones and computers followed the trend: Nasrallah's image was the background for display screens. His speeches, resistance hymns, and popular songs newly composed in their honour were massively downloaded and shared. Key chains and wallets bearing the secretary-general's likeness, lighters engraved with the *Enta mīn?* of 2005, pins in the party colours, and other derivative objects abounded. In the spring of 2007 the face of Nasrallah in a frame encircled by zirconia occupied pride of place among gold medallions in jewellery-shop windows. In May 2008 a toy set came out featuring little plastic fighters, vans, and rocket launchers identical to the IRL's. One detail on the box stood out: painted a yellow reminiscent of the party's flag, it had "National Resistance" embossed on it.

How the Shiites see themselves and others

Publication of books dedicated to the war and the Resistance grew by massively, particularly in 2007 and 2008. Both within Hezbollah and in circles close to it, elaborate theorizing and systematization involving the concept of resistance made their first appearance.[53] The party and its followers thus worked on a redefinition of the various meanings that *muqāwama* (resistance) could assume, as well as *thaqāfat al-muqāwama* (culture of resistance) and *mujtamaʿ al-muqāwama* (resistance society), similarly reflecting on ways of expanding their applications in practice. This laid the official groundwork for what I will call the first "doctrine of resistance according to Hezbollah".

Hezbollah was not the only one engaged in theorizing. Many authors outside the party published their own texts and documentations of the war. Three themes recur throughout this literature.

The need to archive for posterity

The Liberation had already precipitated the publication of a number of books on the IRL victory that varied in form as well as approach but which, on the whole, treated the Liberation in its Lebanese context over a limited time span (1982–2000) or framed it within the Arab–Israeli conflict. The texts published after the 2006 war are very different. Much more numerous, they are mostly presented as archival collections—mainly compilations of articles or short, journalistic analyses lifted from national or Arab newspapers and magazines.[54] They are strikingly redundant. The war appears to have provoked a pressing need, widely shared, to leave a detailed written record of how it unfolded. More than the Liberation, it gave rise to a sense that Lebanon had just experienced something that went beyond the contextual. In fact, it was like a collective impulse to create a legacy (*turāth*), to keep and to pass on. By this token, the new wave of publications after 2006 is indicative of how far the gradual disappearance of the Shiite community's sense of inferiority had progressed: the community felt the need above all to express itself, to celebrate its achievements, and it felt sure enough of their significance to want to immortalize and pass them on.

The resistance, from conjunctural social feat to guiding historical principle

The Thirty-Three-Day War not only occasioned a greater expression of self-confidence by the Shiites, it acted as a catalyst, accelerating the healing of their communitarian sense of subjection. The construction of this new *turāth* is all the more interesting because it is clearly revisionist.[55] The books do not shrink from expressing views about the place of this heritage in the sweep of the nation's history. In the aftermath of the Liberation, the historian Amīn Mustafā placed the IRL in a history of the Lebanese resistance movements, themselves a subset of the national history. After 2006 the historians of the IRL rethought the organizational scheme to give its history pride of place among the stories of the various resistance movements. These now appear more like ante-resistances, or rough drafts of resistance that were mere preludes to *the* Resistance, the one that succeeded. The various initiatives and operations conducted against the occupier are presented as a group of strategies destined ultimately to culminate in the IRL and its achievements. Moreover, resistance action as a whole is assigned the central role in the national historical process, in effect becoming its backbone, with the rest of Lebanese history merely grafted onto it. The latter in its entirety is now summarized as a long tradition of resistance to all kinds of occupations and repressions. Continuity of resistance action, increasingly spread out along the national timeline, has been established: books, sometimes running to several volumes, constructed linkages between 2000 and 2006, then pushed progressively further back in time to string together the Sykes–Picot agreement (1916), the Balfour Promise (1917), the Liberation (2000) and the Thirty-Three-Day War (2006).[56]

From peripheral spectator to central actor and national identity incarnate

The Shiite community was soon itself recast as the centre of national life. This reinterpretation of the meaning of events stretching from Lebanon's creation to the period following the 2006 war, ignoring the traditional dichotomy between the Sunni and Maronite communities, de facto presents a changed "cast of communities" with the Shiites as the main protagonists. Several books published in late 2007 and in 2008 that dealt exclusively with the Shiite community's history explicitly positioned it at the heart of the national historical process. Some no longer traced the history of Lebanon from 1920, but, imitating the Maronite Phoenicianists and their ideological literature in this regard, placed the Shiites expressly and openly and, for the first time in an overtly revisionist approach,[57] at Mount Lebanon as the first inhabitants—and, by extension, at the core of Lebanese national identity itself.[58] It is telling that in 2007 for the first time a book appeared about the Shiites of Mount Lebanon, a forgotten part of a community considered until that point as having been extraneous to the historical process that created the nation.[59] The author explicitly recounted that the Shiites of Lebanon, before their community moved to the peripheries, had made their principal home in the mountainous heart of the country.

This reading of the post-2006 literature dealing with the conflict and the Shiite community is not based solely on written material. It is backed by observation of rapid, marked changes in the Shiite discourse about themselves—indeed, in their attitude. This has been especially evident among the young people: they have become increasingly relaxed, confident, positive, uninhibited, and less inclined to take a back seat to the other communities—especially the Sunnis and Maronites. In September 2008 I was present by chance at this exchange between two Hezbollah *taʿbiʾas* at the coffee machine in one of the party's facilities: one of them asked if "it is true that St Maron[60] was a Syrian"; the other answered "yes", but did not seem to convince the first one, who repeated the question. Receiving the same answer, spoken this time in a very emphatic tone, he asked a third time: "But the Maronites are Syrians, fundamentally?" Once again receiving an affirmative answer, the interrogator exclaimed, loud and clear:

> So they are really Syrians? But then why do they spend their time b***ting us with their "Lebanese origins", spitting on those who supposedly are not "true Lebanese", blah, blah, blah! Maronites are Syrians? Basically, you're telling me they're nothing but bumpkins!

Such a direct attack on another community, in a quasi-public venue, is shocking enough in itself. But what is really noteworthy here is not so much the confessional attack as its object and its logic: those witnessing the exchange heard nothing less than a challenge to the traditional hierarchy of Lebanese community representations that had the Maronites in first and the Shiites in last place. Following Independence in 1943, the challenges to this hierarchy usually triggered debates between Sunnis and Maronites, the former seeking to wring from the latter an *ex aequo* rank, while the Shiites were always sidelined in the discussions. Not insignificantly, the challenges in the vignette cited above rely on the same argument as the one the Maronite community uses to buttress its supremacy over the others. It also reveals a novel phenomenon whereby the original Lebanese identity is detached from the community that had always considered itself as the embodiment of that identity since Lebanon's founding, for the benefit of one that had previously been deemed less worthy of representing it.

As already argued, on the community representation scale the Shiites after the Liberation no longer considered themselves second-class citizens, but just as Lebanese as their compatriots. While the events of 2005 and March 14's behaviour had created a moment of disillusionment, 2006 signified both a leap forward and confirmation of the belief that the Shiites no longer needed recognition by their compatriots to think of themselves as "authentic Lebanese". It got better: after 2006 they began to think that they might ultimately even be "more Lebanese than the others". It is no coincidence that the 2005 *Enta mīn* speech was massively revived in Shiite circles after the Thirty-Three-Day War, particularly the passage that said *Shū qaddamt la heydā al-balad? Shū dahhayt la heydā al-balad*? (What did you offer this country?

What have you sacrificed for this country?) For the first time in the history of Lebanon, the Shiites began to openly question the degree of Lebanese identity and loyalty to the homeland of the other communities, and especially of the top two. The war of 2006 inaugurated a new relationship between the Shiites and the others in which the Shiites felt empowered to hold the others accountable. The stigma had been reversed: the Shiite was no longer a "Persian", the "pseudo-Lebanese" from the peripheries, the one "who still has not opted for Lebanon", whose Lebanese identity had yet to be proved. The Shiites, in fact, became those who had given the most for the country, the most patriotic Lebanese. Shiites, therefore, are not only done with swallowing the accusations of non-Lebanese identity regularly flung at them by March 14, they have become, in their own eyes, the 'Super Lebanese'. This tendency was strengthened by the "excommunication" with which March 14 struck the Shiites from late 2006 until the 2009 elections, which stimulated even further the evolution of their identity that was occurring as a result of the 2006 war. Shiites began to identify even more strongly with Hezbollah/IRL, and the sense of common alienation brought them even closer together. In other words, March 14's policy of rejecting the Shiites had the effect of turning the IRL and its achievements into a symbol of the community as a whole. A young Hezbollah Shiite militant said it best in the spring of 2008 to me: "If March 14 does not want what the IRL has to offer, fine, we'll just keep it for ourselves, and, in all honesty, so much the better."

The 2008 clashes as seen from both sides

Two years after the Thirty-Three-Day War, the events of May 2008 in turn left their mark on Lebanese minds on both sides. However, and as expected, these events have not been interpreted in the same way.

Hezbollah "removed from Lebanese identity" as never before
"Even the Israelis didn't do that!"

During the week of fighting, the March 14 political class produced speeches and communiqués that employed a number of paradigms. They described Hezbollah as a "militia", "gang", and "foreign army" that had "turned its weapons against the home front". Its operations were overtly and systematically described as "invasion" (*ijtiyāh*). Prime Minister Siniora did not hesitate to proclaim that "even the Israelis have not dared to do what Hezbollah did in Beirut". The interpretation of events took on an existential dimension, in which the future of Lebanon and its very identity were threatened. Hidden agendas were ascribed to the party, which was accused of trying to carry out a "putsch", a "coup d'état", on the pretext of nullifying the government's 6 May decisions. Various March 14 officials also accused the party of having acted on the orders of the Syrian and/or Iranian regimes in order to "bring the Syrians back to

Lebanon" and to "expand Iran's borders to the Mediterranean". More than ever since the beginning of the campaign to exclude the Shiites from Lebanese identity, Hezbollah was portrayed as a group foreign to the country and dedicated to its ruin.

Beirut's Sunnis in shock

The events of the week of 7 May gave the March 14 public, Beirut's Sunnis especially, a collective psychological shock. Unlike their Shiite co-religionists who, not very long ago, had faced the tempest of an Israeli offensive, Beirut's Sunnis had not seen violence for nearly twenty years. The events of May 2008, with their exchanges of fire, their militiamen and their snipers—and their dead—shook them profoundly. In the face of this calamity, the first reaction was incredulity and incomprehension. Most people "did not understand what happened" (the formula would be repeated insistently) and did not make the connection between the political developments and the appearance of AMAL and Hezbollah fighters in the street. The most common feeling was that "everything was fine, everything was normal, and, suddenly, they hit us". A second reaction, superimposed on the first, was anger directed against Hezbollah, and Shiites generally. Many witness accounts dwelled on a sense that betrayal and ingratitude had been visited on a population that, having "opened its doors to the Shiites displaced during the 2006 war", felt that it was being "thanked very badly" for it. On the discursive level, the events of May 2008 allowed the Sunni community's sectarianists to justify their animosity towards their Shiite compatriots; 7 May became, in a certain discourse, the pivotal event in what was presented as an official split in the Lebanese Muslim community. This was the beginning of a new grand narrative that fixed 7 May 2008 as day one of a legitimate Sunni resentment towards the Shiites. This rationalized feeling of hostility would reveal itself as highly mobilizing during the following year's parliamentary elections.

Like their politicians, March 14 supporters of all faiths regarded Hezbollah and AMAL's actions as an invasion of the capital and a turning of their weapons inward. They also perceived these actions as spontaneous and unpredictable—and thus capable of being repeated at any time. The anti-Shiite animosity, fuelled by anger at the violence perpetrated by AMAL and Hezbollah fighters, was thus also fed by the fear of a repetition. Hezbollah in particular was demonized, because supporters of the majority, unlike the opposition, failed to draw a distinction between the behaviour of its fighters and that of its allies. But even for those who did perceive this difference in behaviour, Hezbollah was not blameless. Perceived as the movement's engine, the party was accused of "not having kept its allies on a leash".[61]

The opposition's narratives

In general, opposition supporters viewed the majority's reactions as overkill, and the Shiites in particular reminded their compatriots of the extent of the damage their areas had suffered in 2006. The present situation, while "regrettable", was termed a "lesser evil" compared to what might have happened "within the context of an actual civil war". They pointed out that the total of 65 dead, 15 of them in Beirut, "is far from the 150,000 dead last time".[62] Blame for the events was laid entirely at the government's feet. On 6 May, when the cabinet made its decisions, many observers—not only those in the Shiite community—were taken aback: the government had obviously opted for confrontation with full knowledge of the implications.[63] It would have known that the IRL would not simply remain passive, that the Shiites in the army might desert (as they had done in the early 1980s in answering Nabih Berri's call), and that a part of the population might opt for civil disobedience. What made it all even less comprehensible was that, a few months earlier, the government had detected a Hezbollah network grid in Beirut and demanded that it be dismantled; an amicable settlement had been reached and the party had voluntarily taken down the cables in question.

The thesis that the decisions had been prompted from outside the country thus soon gained ground, especially since a relatively detailed version of the supposed foreign interference was widely circulated. In Hezbollah circles, the story was that the cabinet had contacted the US government, namely Condoleezza Rice, with Fouad Siniora supposedly having informed her that his government was thinking about launching a shock operation against Hezbollah. Rice allegedly replied: "Go for it, we will send you the *USS Cole* as backup." This American warship, when it had patrolled in Lebanese waters the previous February, had provoked Hezbollah's ire, especially when the American secretary of state declared that it had been stationed off Lebanon by the United States "to defend its interests and the interests of its allies".[64] It turned out that, shortly after the outbreak of the May 2008 events, the *USS Cole*, then operating in the Gulf, did head back to the Mediterranean, which it reached on 11 May.[65] In many people's eyes, this confirmed the thesis that the Americans had promised to intervene. All the more so since, in the following months, the March 14 politicians would make many references to their "disappointment" at the lack of "concrete" Western reaction, confessing to some that they had expected nothing less than military intervention.

Commentary and interpretations by March 14 leaders annoyed Hezbollah supporters in multiple ways. The events of 7 May first of all shattered the myth that "Hezbollah is the only force in Lebanon equipped with illegal weapons". The fighting had clearly revealed that the FC, just like the PSP, did not fight barehanded.[66] To those who criticized the closure of FC media as an infringement of civil liberties, March 8 retorted that "Hariri *père* was not afraid to shut TV channels that annoyed him", a reference to the MTV affair in 2002.[67] Two comments in particular came in for heavy criticism: Fouad Siniora's comparing of Hezbollah's actions to those of the Israelis and remarks by the Sunni Mufti of the Republic, Muhammad Rashid Kabbani, on the evening of 7 May to the effect that "the Sunnis were fed up", which struck the Shiites as nothing less than a role reversal. The insults hurled at the

Resistance were not well received, nor were speeches criminalizing it. The criticism was all the more unwelcome because it came from the very individuals suspected of having personally fomented the situation from the start. The scenarios involving Iran, Syria—or al-Qāʿida (*sic*)—just like the accusations of an attempted putsch and coup d'état, were dismissed as inventions intended to divert attention from the government's responsibility. Innuendos, starting with the use of the term "invasion", sounded to Shiite ears like the federalist paradigms advocated by March 14, which held that each community "must remain in its/their area(s)" thus echoing Walid Jumblatt's accusations of a Shiite "colonization" of Mount Lebanon.

Furthermore, and unlike March 14, which considered that the guilt for all the excesses committed was Hezbollah's, the Resistance public drew a very clear distinction between the party on the one hand and AMAL and SSNP on the other. The news that Hezbollah had from the beginning of the clashes ordered one of its brigades to the Michel Aoun quarter to protect it against a potential attack by the Lebanese Forces quickly circulated, and was repeatedly cited as proof of Hezbollah's loyalty to its allies—"starting with the Christians among them". Moreover, the positions held by Christians in the opposing forces were not targeted by the party's combatants. But above all, there was the fact that not only had the leadership of Hezbollah been widely reported to have declared *taklīf sharʿī* both the prohibition on entering private houses and apartments and on targeting civilians, but this could also be verified on the ground. The closing of the FC media by Hezbollah militants was done without physically harming the staff, whom the fighters immediately turned over to the army to be sent home. AMAL and SSNP were clearly identified as bearing responsibility for burning down some buildings and committing acts of vandalism. Within the Shiite community, people repeated that "AMAL are thugs (*zuʿrān*), this is not new" and "as for the Hezb, it conducted itself very well". A riddle made the rounds, illustrating the difference between the party and other opposition groups engaged in the fighting:

> How do you know, in Hamra [a Sunni district of Beirut], if it's AMAL or Hezb that entered an apartment? Answer: If the apartment is ransacked, the furniture trashed or stolen, the walls scorched, then it was AMAL. If everything is in place and there are two bearded guys, one of them vacuuming and the other dusting, and there's a note on the dining-room table that reads: "Sorry for the inconvenience," it's the Hezb!

Numerous anecdotes made the rounds about the "exemplary" discipline and behaviour of Hezbollah fighters:

> One of my colleagues is Druze. She and her husband were fervently pro-Jumblatt until the 7 May trouble. She told me how it was precisely the week of the 7th that she and her husband had chosen to spend a few days in the Mountain with their three children. When the trouble started, they were forced to hide in their building's shelter with neighbours and their families. This is what she told me: "Outside there were very loud

booms. Hezb and PSP were firing with B7s at each other. We damned Hezbollah and the Shiites to hell, and we all said that if Hezbollah won, we would be slaughtered on the spot. We were scared stiff. I clutched my youngest one to me, he was crying because he thought we were going to die. All of a sudden, it quieted down a bit outside and the sound of boots came on the stairs. The shelter door opened, and when we saw that it was bearded Hezb our hearts all stopped. Well, the first thing their leader said was: "Nobody panic, we're not going to kill anyone, calm down." Then he said, "Your 'friends' are firing at us from the fourth floor of the building opposite. To dislodge them would require us to fire on them from the roof of your building, but we don't want any of you to get hurt in the firefight. So you're all going to get out, right away, in an orderly manner and without yelling, and we'll put you in a sheltered spot until we're done." ... We went out, we took cover and for me now it's all over. When we got home, I dumped the calendar with the picture of Jumblatt's face on it."[68]

(*In French*) The second day when it got scary, I went by car to do some shopping in Sodeco [between East and West Beirut] and then tried to return home. I live in Tabaris [a beautiful Christian neighbourhood in East Beirut]. When I got to my neighbourhood, I saw that the road was blocked by some Hezb boys (*grimaces*). For an instant, I didn't know if I should reverse, or else what to do. Then I thought it would be best to approach them; you can always talk with Hezb guys. So I asked one of them, "Ahh, how do I get over there?" and I pointed toward Tabaris. He said to me: "Where do you live?" I didn't dare tell him Tabaris; it's a Lebanese Forces and Kataeb hole, and I didn't want him to think I was one of them. So I just said: "Well, just over there." He began to smile and he kept it up: "Where is over there? Tabaris?" I ended up telling myself that it would be better just to tell him the truth, but I didn't have time. The guy out of the blue said, "Listen, brother. If you're in the Lebanese Forces, you don't need to be afraid of me. I have strict orders not to mess with civilians.[69] So, just tell me roughly where you live and I'll point out the way around our checkpoints so you can barricade yourself at home." I was struck speechless. ... He did show me how to get back home.[70]

The sense of a protective Hezbollah, already prevalent, was reinforced: far from being the "gang" described by March 14, it appeared instead as "the saviour of the people", which had just prevented a great nationwide massacre (*al-majzara al-kbīreh*). Through the IRL and the war with Israel it had already acquired the image of the armed force protecting the country against external aggression; after May 2008 it earned another stripe as protector of the nation against internal threats and a safeguard against government by the "reckless". The feeling of having witnessed a role reversal was very strong and shared: while March 14 embodied the state and the law as its credo while excluding Hezbollah and the IRL, Hezbollah's public believed that the events of May 2008 had in fact shown March 14 and the government behaving like "thugs and militia" (*zuʿrān w-mīlīshyā*). Hezbollah, by 'snuffing out the spark of civil war (*taffā shuʿlat al-harb*)' and saving the lives of bystanders and residents, had conducted itself "like a government worthy of the name should have done". And it was more than a detail; there was also satisfaction among the Shiites at having "cleansed the community's honour" after having been insulted and isolated for over three years. The feeling of having witnessed a "well-deserved spanking" was widely shared, even in non-Shiite segments of the opposition (Christian in particular).[71]

Commentary in the opposition ranks on the events of May 2008

We [Shiites] were shot at in 1993 for Oslo,[72] and we said nothing; they shot at us in 2004 for electricity,[73] and we said nothing; they shot at us in Raml al-Ali[74] after the war, and then in December 2006 when we demonstrated in downtown Beirut,[75] ditto in January 2007,[76] and again in Shiyyah early in the year;[77] and every time we said nothing! Each time, the sayyid [Nasrallah] told us: "Everyone go home and no reprisals" and we obeyed! Precisely because we wanted to show that we were not savages and that we were devoted to civil peace! And the others, instead of appreciating it, considering it good of us, they saw it as weakness and continued shooting at us! How long do they think we will put up with getting shot at without objecting?! Well, then, now they've understood, it's all over!

Hezbollah supporter, Shiite, Baalbek, late May 2008.

Coup d'état, coup d'état ... Where's the coup d'état? Where is the take over of the Serail? We just wanted them [the March 14 government] to rescind their initial decisions [of May 6] and when that was done, the Hezb and AMAL withdrew from the streets voluntarily and turned them over to the army. In the history of mankind, have you ever come across an armed force that behaves like this? Withdrawing on its own? Imagine for a moment if it had been a militia like the Lebanese Forces or Kataeb instead of us! Do you think they would have been civilized like us? No, they would have done the usual: murdered people and raped girls.

Hezbollah supporter, Shiite, Baalbek, late May 2008.

It's not like they weren't warned. Ever since 2005, Hezbollah warns anyone who wants to touch its weapons. It always said that there would be no problem as long as they did not touch its weapons. So, what went through the government's head?

Hezbollah militant, Shiite, Baalbek, mid-May 2008.

That March 14 has some nerve. They openly call for war at the start of the year, trigger the civil war officially in the Council of Ministers. And when they finally get the spanking they've deserved for more than two years, they scream rape, and once it's over, they reinflate their feathers (*nafashō rīshun*) and go right on with their provocative speeches and insults!

Hezbollah supporter, Shiite, Baalbek, early June 2008.

You see, in 2005, when March 14 started up, you could see the mess in Iraq because of the Americans and the continuing tragedy in Palestine because of the Israelis. And we distrusted March 14. Their palling around with the Americans, the tale of the 'New Middle East', the 'positive chaos' or whatever, and March 14's alignment with the Bush gang ... we knew it all. We knew that the Americans would export the chaos to Lebanon through March 14. And now, here we have it. During the 2006 war, they collaborated with the Israelis. And there is Condoleezza Rice telling them: 'Declare the civil war, we are behind you.' And they do!

Hezbollah supporter, Shiite, Beirut, end of May 2008.

You can't possibly feel safe with people like that in power. They are crazy people. How can you remain calm when you know that from one day to the next your own government can decide on civil war on a whim in the Council of Ministers? When all it takes is for a moron like Jumblatt to put out a completely insane scenario to have the whole ensemble play his tune? Not only do these people not protect us, they put the people's lives in danger. Fortunately, the Hezb is there as a safeguard, if not, hey, at the beginning of May we would have been all dead. You see, [March 14] says it's the state, the state, they hit us over the head with that endlessly, but they behave like outlaws. And Hezbollah, which is supposedly the outlaw, acts the way a state worthy of the name should behave.

School teacher, Hezbollah supporter, Shiite, June 2008.

Let me tell you something. What happened is very unfortunate; but at the same time, let's hope that March 14 got the message, and that is that the Shiites won't keep their traps shut any longer. Muhammad Rashid Kabbani said that the Sunnis were fed up. He did not ask if the Shiites were fed up, among other things to be shot down like rabbits every time and get called all kinds of names without ever responding. Well, the good little Shiites who let themselves be insulted, treated like shoe shiners, savages, Persians without answering back, well, that's all over with. Here's the *big news* (*in English*): From now on, the Shiites are going to open their traps!

Business cadre, Shiite, Beirut, June 2008.

Jumblatt is complete scum. God knows I do not like Samir Geagea, but of March 14, he's the only one who had the right attitude, he took on Jumblatt, after all that business. Me, I'm Sunni and I am ashamed. Hariri, my leader in theory, not only didn't say anything to Jumblatt, who sent us "into the cannon's mouth" (*bi-būz al-madfaʿ*),[78] us Sunnis, but at Doha, he appeared together with him, hand in hand. It makes you want to vomit. Jumblatt dropped his bomb, and then he went to hide in the Mountain and left the Sunnis to take it in the face. You know what they said: on the day he released his asinine statements, he gave the keys to the PSP's offices in Beirut to the army and then quietly ordered all his followers to go to hide in the Mountain; to be perfectly clear, the guy knew exactly what he was doing. And what a coward! Just three firecrackers slam next door to him and there he is, in the arms of Arslan—hence Syria! Some hero! ... And the *beyk* [Jumblatt], didn't anyone tell him, this guy that kept on saying after the July [2006] war that Nasrallah had no right to decide alone on peace and war, did no one tell him he had no right to start a civil war by himself? Did he ask the point of view of his little buddies in March 14 to begin with, before his pathetic press conference where he dropped his s***t bomb? He couldn't ask Siniora first: 'Ah, Fouad, what do you think? Are you prepared to manage s***t like that in the Council of Ministers?' Or, ask Hariri if he was ready for the Beirut Sunnis to die in place of his Druze? Whose advice did he seek, apart from that of the Americans? And Hariri, after all those dead ... he said nothing, that's what. He didn't put his fist in his face either. 'Jumblatt is my brother,' he said. Note, he had also said that Pierre Gemayel was his brother, same as Sfeir, who is the 'conscience of Lebanon', so yes, of course. ... Hezbollah was right when it said that Hariri let himself be manipulated by Geagea and Jumblatt.

Leftist journalist, Sunni, Beirut, early June 2008.

It's Jumblatt's fault, yes, basically, in the sense that it was he who dropped the bomb and who put the Siniora government in the position of having to manage the mess that resulted, an unenviable situation and without any warning beforehand by Jumblatt. But it is just as much the government's fault; it didn't have to dive in head first. It would have been enough for them to say: "We will consider that next time" or "when the investigation is complete," since until proven otherwise, an inquiry was ongoing. That would have bought some time for making contact with Hezbollah and trying to settle things amicably. And this is the fault of March 14 generally, even of the moderates; I mean, for two years their hawks had been spewing anti-Shiite hatred, created provocations continuously, and no one in their camp told them to knock it off. March 14 is a non-integrated structure where anyone can say whatever comes to mind without coordinating with the others. Well, there it is. They just finished paying the price for it.

Lebanese university professor, Shiite, opposition supporter,
Beirut, early June 2008.

Some effects of Israeli threats and blockades

From 2006 on, Israeli planes flying over Lebanese territory, often daily, mock raids, violations of the Blue Line, incursions into Lebanese territory and Lebanese territorial waters, and abductions of Lebanese civilians in the border regions of the South (Halta, Shebaa, Ghajar areas) never ceased to make news. The Lebanese government appealed regularly to the UN, and called on friendly Western governments to pressure Tel Aviv, to no avail. The conviction grew ever stronger among Hezbollah's public that diplomatic channels were destined to fail. There was a strong perception of a "double standard", which has drained any hope of rebuilding confidence in international institutions:

> When Hezbollah captures an Israeli soldier, the whole world finds it normal and justified for Israel to demolish Lebanon and kill its sons, and it drafts resolutions ordering the release of the guy in question. When the Israelis enter Lebanon like it is their private playground and abduct civilians, nobody gives a damn.[79]

Despite a formal commitment by the American and French governments in 2006 to put pressure on Israel and have the Shebaa Farms put under international supervision, in 2018 they were still under Tel Aviv's authority. The Israeli army never pulled out of the village of Ghajar, which it had recaptured during the summer 2006 war. This recalcitrance has reopened wounds and revived bad memories, as many Lebanese saw it as a new occupation of their country.

The Hezbollah supporter circles are equally convinced that the Lebanese government is unable to defend the country and its people against Israel's destructive potential. This feeling has been strengthened by the knowledge that, while one of March 14's paradigms was that the army was just as capable as the IRL of defending the national territory—or would be, with training and above all the necessary weaponry—Tel Aviv has worked openly with Washington and European capitals to keep the Lebanese army from acquiring sufficient weapons. In June 2008, for example, the Israeli government blocked US aid to the Lebanese army amounting to $ 400 million.[80] In November the US government, at the request of the Israelis, put a hold on supplying heavy weapons, missiles, sophisticated tanks, planes, and advanced helicopters to the Lebanese military.[81] Ironically, Hezbollah benefits from this Israeli blockade by discrediting the logic of March 14 and positioning the IRL as the only armed force capable of defending the national territory.

Lastly, the discovery, starting in 2009, of spy networks paid for by Mossad heightened the paranoia that the Goldman affair had loosed in 2007. At the end of June that year an Israeli journalist, Lisa Goldman, managed to enter Lebanon travelling on a Canadian passport.[82] She took photographs and made a video featuring the Lebanese capital. Back in Tel Aviv, she was contacted by a television channel and commissioned to do a documentary for the first anniversary of the Thirty-Three-Day

War. In early July Goldman returned to Beirut incognito, where over three days she did a few interviews—some versions have it that a number of them were with members of Hezbollah—and took videos of several streets in the city and its southern suburbs. On 11 July she presented the results of her wanderings on the Channel 10 station. Always tuned in to Israeli media of all kinds, the Hezbollah leadership discovered, along with the Israeli viewers, the "enemy breakthrough" to the heart of its Beirut stronghold. Rebroadcast by al-Manār and al-Jazeera within twenty-four hours of the Israel showing, the affair caused a great stir on the Lebanese political and media scene.[83] The entire Shiite community was up in arms for several weeks. With speculation rife at the time about an imminent war of revenge promised by the Israeli army since the previous year, the regional context boosted the importance Hezbollah assigned to the "hostile" intrusion. The party took radical action. Internally, all cadres and militants were instructed to refuse any interview with a third party without first referring it to the Central Information Unit. This drastically reduced contact between the party and local as well as international observers. Previously accessible players ultimately became impossible to contact. Actions normally considered perfectly innocent became problematic. For example, anyone photographing Hezbollah posters or those relating to the Shiite community in public venues is now likely to be accosted by the party's security service. In late April 2007 they did, in fact, apprehend Karim Pakzad, the representative of the French Socialist Party to the Socialist Internationale, who was taking photos in a sensitive area in the southern suburbs.[84] The following August a French photographer[85] and two Brazilian journalists doing a report from an area under party surveillance were interrogated.[86] Instead of taking offence at these increasingly security-conscious procedures, Hezbollah followers have viewed them as justified, with some going so far as to become independent observers in their own neighbourhoods, keeping an eye on strangers and not hesitating to question them.[87]

The WikiLeaks revelations

Adding more embarrassing revelations about United States Middle East policy, the WikiLeaks site from December 2010 published a number of important American diplomatic cables, some of which related to Lebanon. The cables did name some members of March 8, AMAL and the FPM in particular,[88] but the damning commentary was mainly in the March 14 batch. Throughout the first half of 2011, compromising disclosures concerning the former majority proliferated. The moment was all the more untimely as it came when March 14 happened to have just lost both its stranglehold on parliament and the support of the Maronite Patriarch, Nasrallah Sfeir, replaced by the Vatican in March by one of his former assistants, Bishara al-Rai, who was thought to be more moderate.[89] The behind-the-scenes events of the Thirty-Three-Day War and the events of May 2008 ranked first in terms of "secrets" revealed. Hezbollah's accusations against March 14 at the end of the war were largely backed up: Minister of Defence Elias Murr allegedly had contact with the Israeli authorities, in which he is said to have provided "advice" to improve their effectiveness in the context of a future war. He is said to have expressly asked for the Christian areas not to be attacked, on the grounds that Christians "supported Israel [during its offensive] in 2006 until the Israeli army bombed bridges in Christian areas", adding that "should Israel again bomb this type of target in Shiite areas ... it will be Hezbollah's problem".[90] Several cables also revealed that the idea of a large-scale ground invasion, something the Israelis had balked at throughout the conflict before deciding on it only during the final days, was actually recommended by Walid Jumblatt and his right-hand man, the minister of telecommunications, Marwan Hamadeh. In mid-July, with the crisis in full swing, the vast majority of Maronite politicians in March 14—from Samir Geagea, to the Gemayels, father and son, Minister Nayla Moawad, MP Boutros Harb and even the MP and former minister Nassib Lahoud[91]—apparently told Jeffrey Feltman that they saw a need to prolong the war, "by seven to ten days" according to some, by "several weeks" according to others, "until Hezbollah is buried".[92]

Saad Hariri also allegedly promised the US ambassador to "f**k up Hezbollah" provided that the USA supplied weapons and money to FC.[93] In the logic of clientelist competition, then-prime minister Fouad Siniora in turn is said to have asked Saudi Arabia and Qatar not to pay the $500 million and $300 million respectively they had promised for rebuilding Lebanon. The reason was to keep these sums from being disbursed into the Fund for the South, a South Lebanon government development fund that Nabih Berri traditionally controlled.

Regarding the events of May 2008, it emerged that Elias Murr and Marwan Hamadeh had already urged the government to take steps against Hezbollah in April, after having presented a detailed report on the IRL's telephone lines to the cabinet. Fouad Siniora appears to have refused a head-on confrontation; instead, discussions with Hezbollah supposedly ensued during which the party is said to have made it clear that the dismantling of its telecom network by force would be tantamount to a declaration of war. In other words, when the government made its decisions on the night of 5 May it did so knowingly. Regardless of the happenings in May 2008, Hariri had apparently factored in an eventual military face-off with Hezbollah. According to Jumblatt, the former had pulled together nearly 1,500 militiamen in April 2008 on the advice of Ashraf Rifi, head of the Lebanese police. Given Siniora's reluctance to make any aggressive move, Jumblatt and Hamadeh in early May opted to force the government's hand by making the report public. On the night of the 5th, during the Council of Ministers session, Siniora and some ministers reportedly again spoke up for negotiations with Hezbollah, but Moawad, Hamadeh, Murr, and Jumblatt pressed for direct action. Following the deteriorating situation on the ground in ensuing days, Hariri is supposed to have come out quickly for suspending the contested decisions, while Geagea is said to have taken an opposing line. The latter apparently even asked the American embassy for weapons, claiming to have already formed a force of between 7,000 and 10,000 ready to do battle with Hezbollah. When the crisis was over, March 14 blamed Western governments, the USA in particular, for not directly supporting the action. While it was confirmed that the American warship *USS Cole*, when requested by March 14, was actually ordered to reverse course with the mission of intimidating March 8 and Damascus, the anti-Syrians would deem the operation to have too little impact.

The cables also added a series of illustrations of how the March 14 class sustained a militia logic, of how the government practises its depredations, of anti-Shiite sectarian comments and reports of conversations between Lebanese and Western officials casting doubt on just how neutral the work of the International Commission of Inquiry was. Among Hezbollah's supporters, these findings largely helped to burnish the party's image. Not only did they give a large amount of credit to the narratives of the party's leadership, but, more importantly, by not being followed by any charges against the persons named, they invalidated even further March 14's official line that Hezbollah was the "only obstacle" to the return of the rule of law. Instead, they gave the impression that March 14 itself was incapable of abiding by the law and institutional practices that it claims to stand for.

The STL and terrorism

By 2010, with threats of war between Israel and the IRL persisting, it seemed that Hezbollah's public had put its confidence in the Islamic Resistance's ability to stand up to possible renewed hostilities with the southern neighbour.

The Lebanese and the Islamic Resistance (February 2010)

	National median	*Sunni*	*Shiite*	*Christian*	*Druze*
1. Do you have faith in the capability of the Resistance to cope with any kind of Israeli aggression?					
Yes	84.1%	75.9%	98.1%	80%	86.9%
No	14.2%	20.4%	1.9%	18.3%	13.1%
No opinion	1.7%	3.7%	0%	1.7%	0%
2. Do you think that the Resistance's capabilities will deter Israel from attacking Lebanon in the future?					
Yes	73.7%	65.7%	86.1%	72.3%	69.6%
No	22.3%	26.8%	11.1%	26.3%	21.7%
No opinion	4%	7.5%	2.8%	1.4%	8.7%

3. Do you think there will be a deep split among Lebanese if Israel follows through on its threat to attack Lebanon?					
Yes	26.1%	29.6%	23.1%	25.8%	26.1%
No	70.2%	67.6%	71.3%	70.8%	69.6%
No opinion	3.7%	2.8%	5.6%	3.4%	4.3%
4. In your opinion, does a balance of terror between the Resistance and Israel encourage or discourage Israel from attacking?					
Encourages it	11%	13.9%	2.8%	14.6%	17.4%
Discourages it	81.7%	77.8%	93.5%	76.4%	73.9%
No opinion	7.3%	8.3%	3.7%	9%	8.7%
5. Do you think that Israel is in a position to launch a new war and to win it?					
Yes	16.8%	24.1%	1.9%	23.1%	13.1%
No	72.4%	64.8%	93.5%	63.6%	65.2%
No opinion	10.8 %	11.1%	4.6%	13.3%	21.7%

Beirut Center for Research and Information (www.beirutcenter.info), 19–20 February 2010.

On the other hand, confidence in the integrity of the STL was not what it should have been, and rumours of Hezbollah's involvement in the Rafic Hariri assassination did not convince the majority of the party's supporters. Intensive communication campaigns orchestrated by the party seem to have borne fruit. A telling example of this internalized suspicion towards the Tribunal was provided in late October 2010 in a private gynaecological clinic in the southern suburbs treating wives and daughters of Hezbollah members. When two Tribunal investigators presented themselves to demand the addresses and telephone numbers of seventeen of the clinic's patients from the doctor, who had been alerted to their impending visit, they were physically attacked by a dozen patients to keep them away from the files.[94]

The Lebanese and the STL (August 2010)

	National median	*Sunni*	*Shiite*	*Christian*	*Druze*
1. Do you think the evidence presented by Hassan Nasrallah will cause the STL to pursue the Israeli connection?					
Yes	73.5%	60%	90.8%	72.2%	65.2%

No	21.9%	35.2%	4.6%	24.1%	26.1%
No opinion	4.6%	4.8%	4.6%	3.7%	8.7%
2. Do you think the STL has integrity?					
Yes	31.4%	50.1%	3.2%	35.3%	39.1%
No	60.9%	37.4%	92.6%	58.4%	47.9%
No opinion	7.7%	12.5%	4.2%	6.3%	13%
3. What reasons ultimately cause you to doubt the STL's integrity?					
False witnesses	20.1%	50.1%	23%	23.1.8%	8.8%
Media leaks	7%	4.6%	17.5%	2.5%	0%
The arrest of the four generals	11.5%	8.3%	25.8%	6.8%	0%
The above three reasons	19.4%	5%	26.3%	23%	26.1%
No opinion	3%	3%	7.4%	3%	13%
4. Do you think the STL is being used as a tool against the IRL?					
Yes	60%	38.9%	88.9%	55.9%	52.2%
No	33.8%	52.8%	8.3%	37.9%	34.8%
No opinion	6.2%	8.3%	2.8%	6.2%	13%
5. Do you think that implicating Hezbollah in the Rafic Hariri assassination threatens civil peace?					
Yes	69.2%	54.6%	90.4%	63.4%	78.3%
No	27.6%	40.8%	6.4%	34.7%	17.4%
No opinion	3.2%	4.6%	3.2%	1.9%	4.3%
6. In your view which party is responsible for the assassination of Rafic Hariri?					
Israel	49.2%	37.5%	79.7%	38.7%	34.9%
Israel and the United States	10.6%	13.9%	5.5%	13%	0%
Syria	2%	2.8%	0%	3.1%	0%
Hezbollah	1.5%	2.8%	0%	1.2%	4.3%
Others, fundamentalist groups	6%	5.1%	6.5%	6.8%	4.3%
No opinion	30.7%	37.9%	8.3%	37.2%	56.5%

Beirut Center for Research and Information (www.beirutcenter.info), 11–14 August 2010.

Better yet, this conviction that the STL was being manipulated both domestically and from outside with the objective of harming Hezbollah and its reputation was a potent argument against any temptation to give credence to the series of accusations that had been hurled at the party since 2011. This applied to its putative involvement in the assassination attempts in Lebanon since then, as well as the EU's decision to classify its "military wing" as a terrorist organization. On this issue in particular, the condemnations formulated by the West and especially Israel against the party had always been viewed by Hezbollah supporters as amounting to defamation. It was also in July 2013 that word came from Buenos Aires that a Jewish former Argentine minister of the interior, Carlos Vladimir Corach, had been implicated in the planning of an attack in 1994 against a Jewish cultural centre that had been blamed on Hezbollah.[95] More generally, the integrity of the judicial systems of countries where the party had been suspected of planning attacks was methodically questioned, and Sofia with the Bourgas affair was no exception to the rule. If the accusations of terrorism against Hezbollah were usually shrugged off by its supporters, the EU's move against the IRL in the summer of 2013 aroused anger and disappointment. Europe, seen as the "rational" Western player, especially in comparison with North America, traditionally viewed as hostile to the Arab and Muslim world, was said to have proved its weakness, "making a fool of itself" (*jarrasit hālhā*).

Comments by Shiites on "the military arm of Hezbollah" being placed on the European Union's list of terrorist organizations

Europeans in general have always been weak reeds in front of the United States and Israel, but here they really made a mess. And that woman from the European Union [Angelina Eichhorst], the poor thing, trying to reassure us: "We will remove the Hezb later, it's temporary!" Give me a break. It was an injustice that put it on the list, so justice will scratch it from the list, maybe? And she tells us: "No, no, don't worry, it's only the armed branch"—the Resistance, the most respectable branch! And then right away she goes on to say: "It doesn't mean that if Israel attacks you we will not recognize Lebanon's right to defend itself and of the Resistance to react," and then she adds: "And we will support you!" Frankly, she takes us for a***s. Even when the Resistance was not terrorist in their eyes, the Westerners never supported it. Did they support us in 2006, did they? Their media and politicians didn't call us terrorists, really? And there, now that it's official and Hezbollah's on the list, we should feel reassured that the European Union will support the "terrorist Resistance" against Israel.

Shopkeeper with a son fighting in the ranks of the IRL, Baalbek, August 2013.

Sayyid Hassan [Nasrallah] was right. Act I: Resolution 1559; it did not work. Act II: national dialogue with March 14 to disarm the Resistance; that didn't work either. Act III: the 2006 war when Israel tried to do the job itself—failure.

Act IV: Resolution 1701, to have the Lebanese government and the international community disarm the Resistance on Israel's behalf; still not good. Act V: the Tribunal; still impossible to knock Hezbollah down. So now they [Westerners] decided to take the bull by the horns: even if they are unable to find Hezbollah at fault, they will punish it anyway, even without fault.

Engineer, Baalbek, August 2013.

Who cares. As Sayyid Hassan [Nasrallah] put it: "Take your list of terrorist organizations and blow your nose in it." Frankly, it won't change anything. They treated us like terrorists before. And if they want to boycott us, let them boycott. We're not going to budge an inch. First of all, we know what is Israel. We know every one of Israel's crimes, while in Europe they know nothing. Anyway, it's funny: Israel massacres, steals, practises racism, and makes light of international law every day—it is Israel that should be on the list of terrorist organizations. ... But no, as far as Europe is concerned, Israel is a civilized country, friendly, respectful of human rights, whatever you do, don't take any action against it and especially don't impose a boycott. ... When Israel assassinated Mabhouh using stolen Western passports, nothing, no retaliation, not a single Israeli ambassador was sent home.[96] So there, Hezbollah is accused without any evidence, just because Israel wants it—and *voilà* it's on the list of terrorist organizations. ... But what matters most is that we, we know what the Resistance is owed. And we know what we have achieved, the Liberation, the victory of 2006, our freedom, our dignity regained, our strength, we know who we owe it to. And we have not forgotten that nobody in the West has ever supported us. The [Westerners] did not support us before, they do not support us now, and they were not going to support us in the future, even without a terrorist listing. ... It won't change a thing. We will not change our mind about the Resistance because a band of cowards in Europe has put its name on a meaningless piece of paper. We're not the losers here, they are; they are the ones history will remember as people who took the side of injustice against justice. It is they who betray their so-called values of truth, democracy, justice, human rights—not us.

Teacher, Baalbek, July 2013.

Jihadist threat and recommunitarization

Lebanon's Shiites have two sets of reasons not to let themselves be seduced by the idea of Bashar al-Assad's regime in Syria falling. The first is political and relates to the dichotomy that pits the Islamic Resistance public against the March 14 forces on the domestic scene. Lebanese amalgams compounded from national, regional, and international political preferences automatically put the majority of Shiites in Syria's Baath camp. As already mentioned, the community overall does not necessarily admire the Syrian regime or even approve of its policies and its practices—they prefer it as a lesser evil to the American and/or Israeli options.[97] Attachment to the Resistance and to keeping it armed, viewed as the sole guarantee of national security in view of regular threats against it by Israel, naturally keeps the Shiites from wanting Assad to fall since it would jeopardize the IRL's interests.

But political alliances do not explain everything. In the 2010s, the Christians are not the only religious group worried about the rise of radical Sunni Islamism in the Levant and its inroads into Syrian opposition ranks. The Shiites, who know they are reviled by the Salafists on religious as well as political grounds, feel little sympathy for an anti-Assad coalition both aided by and composed of jihadist fundamentalists. The Iraqi example is still on everybody's mind. The kidnapping of Shiite pilgrims; news reports of a confessionalization of the Syria fighting; threats against Shiites uttered by certain groups in the Syrian opposition, even in the FSA's own communiqués; and the inability of the latter to control armed groups who claim allegiance to it have convinced the Shiites of Lebanon that they are under attack mainly because of their religious colouration. The al-Assir phenomenon, which was seen as a preview of the path their Sunni compatriots might have been tempted to take in the absence of a credible moderate Sunni leadership, also did its part in making them feel the need for self-protection.

At the beginning of this decade, bloody attacks targeting Shiite areas, including one on 15 August 2013 in the southern suburbs of Beirut that left almost 30 dead and over 300 injured, did not have the effect of demonstrating that the IRL's involvement in Syria was ultimately an error. There was a widespread belief that involvement only served as an excuse for the jihadist Sunnis and that Hezbollah, its territories, and, by extension, the Shiite community, would have been targeted even if the IRL had not fought alongside the Syrian army. Threats voiced by several groups in the Syrian rebellion were heard even before the 2013 battle of Qusayr, and the Syrian opposition made it only too clear that they had reckoned well before Qusayr, with or without proof, that Hezbollah was engaged in fighting in Syria. That was enough to keep a large majority of Lebanon's Shiites from believing that non-participation by the Islamic Resistance in the Syrian counter-revolution would have spared them the Syrian opposition's criticisms. In other words, far from convincing the Lebanese Shiites that dropping their support for Hezbollah would be in their interest, these perceptions actually brought them a little closer to it. They saw Hezbollah even more clearly as the one armed group shielding them against the threats looming over the community in the absence of a state capable of meeting its responsibility for preserving order and security.

Attacks against their areas have not provoked them—yet—into opting for open animosity towards their Sunni compatriots. What vocabulary they use to describe the instigators and perpetrators of the attacks is not a trivial matter: it does not include the term "Sunni"; instead, throughout the Shiite areas they adopt the circumlocution coined by the Hezbollah leadership, *irhābiyyīn takfiriyyīn*, literally "excommunicating terrorists". The jihadists are tagged as terrorists because they are depicted as not using the violence of legitimate war between fighters, but blind, barbaric violence against civilians. Calling them excommunicators is also a reference to Sunni *takfīrī* circles whose dogmatic radicalism does not recognize the Shiites as Muslims; the jihadists therefore are accused of fighting strictly for sectarian reasons. Their cause is doubly discredited, both as to motivation and means. Shiite narratives emphasize their refusal to declare war against an entire "sister in Islam" community, sending the message that Shiites distinguish between a Sunni majority with which they hope to live in peace and a fringe of this community even more reviled because it seems to be directed by Saudi Arabia. In August 2013, when an especially bloody double attack struck (Sunni) Tripoli, hospitals in Beirut's southern suburbs, which had themselves known a tragedy of comparable magnitude the previous week, immediately organized a blood-donation campaign for the capital of the North. An avalanche of messages of support directed to Sunni netizens flooded social media. "We are not Sunnis, we are not Shiites, we are all Lebanese", "We are one and the same people", "We are not enemies, our enemies are those who want us to believe that we are", etc. A slogan reposted by the hundreds gained currency, and was even posted on Hezbollah's website: *Min al-Dāhyeh ... hunā Trāblus* (Live from the southern suburbs ... here is Tripoli), in a clear reference to their common fate, was written, photographed, placarded on various media and produced in various formats against a variety of backgrounds.

Despite these good intentions, there remained a widely shared concern that the commitment to the country's stability would fade away over the medium or long term if both national and regional conditions inimical to civil peace should persist.

[illegible]

CONCLUSION

'They didn't know that it was impossible, so they did it.'

Mark Twain

'Never will we allow anyone to take us back to when we were shiners of shoes.'

Hassan Nasrallah, August 2006

"Lebanon's wars are others' wars on Lebanese soil," the Lebanese are too often inclined to say to foreign observers. However, this formula, salving consciences by its exonerating effect, falls short of revealing the primary sources of those conflicts. When dealing with a subject like Hezbollah, the temptation is even greater to make regional or international "others" the main participants. The overwhelming majority of analyses give centre stage to Iran, Syria, Israel, Saudi Arabia, France, and the United States, while giving short shrift to Hezbollah itself. This book, written from a perspective of recentring the object studied, differs from analyses favouring outside to inside as the guiding principle by being deliberately constructed from inside to outside: from Hezbollah, from the environment it originated in, from the space in which it evolved out towards the regional and the international. And the choice was made to fold in the latter two only to the extent that they contribute elements that explain the choices and positioning of the observed actor—and especially, of its relationship to its public.

Understanding the "Hezbollah" notion

The usual versions of the Hezbollah story agree in presenting it as an Islamist organization with a military wing that was created in 1982 following the second Israeli invasion of Lebanon by a revolutionary Iran determined to export its revolution to the entire Middle East. Hezbollah is depicted as having gone through a series of profound changes in identity, ideology, and strategy in thirty-five years of existence that led it to abandon its original position, a dissident radicalism fixated on replacing the Lebanese system with an Islamic government. The party is described as gradually having had a shift to pragmatism imposed on it by its regional mentors and becoming no better than a semi-nationalized political party, as its organic connections to the

Syrian and Iranian regimes trumped its allegiance to the homeland. The analysis is often coupled with attempts to understand the factors explaining these modulations in Hezbollah's practice and motivations over time, in an effort to reconstruct rationality of thought and action in an organization regarded as a puzzle and feared as an unpredictable actor.

The particulars presented in this book allow a more precise, more refined understanding of Hezbollah's nature as well as of its path. Without question, arrival of Israeli tanks in the Land of Cedars in June 1982 set in motion the mobilization of part of the militant Shiite world around a desire to take up arms against the invader. This drive initially translated into a very localized military organization, the Islamic Resistance in Lebanon (IRL) founded by two North Bekaa clerics, Subhī al-Tufaylī and ʿAbbās al-Mūsawī. Both had engaged for some years in militant action, particularly the struggle against Israel, the former distinguishing himself in revolutionary networks close to the Iranian regime, the latter by dedicating himself to mobilizing people of the Baalbek–al-Hermel region. Both differed in this respect from their co-religionists in Beirut, whether the militants of the AMAL movement or members of religious associations focused on a spiritual and quietist renewal of their community, who had already been active for some years. When the invasion happened, al-Tufaylī attempted to leverage his Iranian connections to set up the IRL and get logistical, financial, and organizational assistance from the Pasdaran. The request was initially refused by an Iranian leadership more interested in its dispute with Saddam Hussein than in exporting its newly Islamized political system. With tight restrictions imposed by both Tehran and Damascus prohibiting the Revolutionary Guards from participating in combat, a small contingent was assigned to train young men from the Bekaa funnelled to their camp by al-Mūsawī and his students. Also among the first to enlist were followers of Husayn al-Mūsawī, a disaffected former AMAL spokesman who had just founded AMAL al-Islāmiyya that August, precipitating the return of some AMAL cadres and militants to the Bekaa. It is only when travel again became possible, with the loosening of the Israeli stranglehold, that fighters from the Committee of Beirut Cadres, the Lebanese Union of Muslim Students, and other smaller associations active in the capital along with fighters from the South also swelled the ranks of the IRL. During the first months, a five-man council representing the main currents making up the IRL constituted a civilian counterpart. It was soon replaced by a small structure flanked by embryonic social institutions for mobilization, whose name was finally decided on in the spring of 1984: Hezbollah. Officially dedicated to the defence of the Resistance's social and political interests, Hezbollah was given responsibility for mobilization on the Resistance's behalf and for defusing threats against it cropping up on the domestic scene.

The composition of the Hezbollah leadership, which includes both clerics and laity, reflects the evolution of the party and its ideological choices. Thus, its founding fathers, still comprising the bulk of the ruling elite in 2018, bring together clerics who studied in Najaf and were close to the Iraqi Daʿwa of the 1970s, religious men who pursued their studies in Qom or developed affinities with Iranian revolutionary circles, lay people who fought alongside the Palestinian Fateh, and militants from religious associations whose military journey began at the battle of Khaldeh. These men have in common a commitment to the two constituent principles of the party's ideational identity: to serve the interests of the Resistance above all else; and submit to the principle of *wilāyat al-faqīh*.

In its over thirty-five years of existence, the party has evolved. But this evolution ultimately was one of means; it never carried over to its *raison d'être* or its universe of meaning. Its internal structure and its social institutions have been developed, have become specialized and more professional. Its relationship to society has become more supple. And, after some years interspersed with (rare) contretemps with certain state institutions, particularly the army, the party sent members to parliament and ministers into the government. However, these changes must be read correctly. Hezbollah has never been revolutionary in the sense of Western political science, never having attempted to overthrow the Lebanese regime or establish parallel state-like institutions. The party's actions and pronouncements are contextual retranslations of what it is able to conceive as the best strategy at a given point in time for accomplishing its mission—which always has been and remains defending the interests of the IRL. Thus, it opted for participation in the 1992 parliamentary elections when it was decided internally that the ballot was an opportunity that would let the Resistance's voice be heard in Parliament and obtain the support of government institutions for its cause. As long as the Syrian tutelage lasted, this task was eased because the Lebanese regime, then aligned with Syria, did not pose any threats to the party or the IRL. Starting in 2005, with power in the hands of what was seen as a "coterie" allied to an international community resolved to disarm the Resistance, the political dimension of Hezbollah's mission assumed supreme importance. During the few months spanning the time from the Syrian withdrawal to the 2006 war, the party tried to negotiate guarantees for the IRL, all the while not hesitating to engage in blocking manoeuvres against specific decisions by the government that it judged to be inimical to the interests of the Resistance. In the IRL leadership's eyes, 2006 clearly showed the full panoply of threats that can arise in the absence of support on the domestic scene. It is in this sense that Hezbollah's overinvestment in politics after the war should be understood. The domestic scene was not a substitute field of action but a source of threats that had to be held in check. Israel was no longer the only danger that had to be dealt with: in its war against the Israeli army, the IRL was also faced with the "treasonous actions" of March 14. Hence the fight, starting in the second half of 2006, both against the convening of an international criminal court and for obtaining a blocking minority within the government. The events of the week of 7 May 2008 were part of this logic: the IRL, overtly attacked by the government, could no longer leverage Hezbollah because the Shiite ministers were no longer in the government. The bridge that the party was supposed to provide on the political scene was no longer there. And while it would be possible, until 2008, to interpret Hezbollah's quest for a blocking minority as stemming from a desire to prevent the ICT from being set up and thereby serving the interests of its Syrian ally, the party's insistence on preserving this blocking minority after the tribunal's advent and the 2009 elections henceforth reflected its very real fear of the government again making decisions like those of 6 May 2008. The fall of the Hariri government in 2011 was no more than a footnote to this.

Understanding its mobilization

Just like Hezbollah's courses of action, the sources of its popularity have evolved over time. The party's image improved significantly in the early 1990s with the end of the war that it had fought for three years against AMAL, the beginning of the opening-up period, and the first military setbacks inflicted on Tel Aviv's troops since their partial withdrawal in 1985. Until Israel's presence in South Lebanon was at an end, Hezbollah was above all a *groupe de référence* around which anti-occupation partisans gravitated. Its followers saw it as the standard bearer at once of an anti-confessional patriotism and an incorruptibility that stood out in the political context of that era.

After Liberation, the grassroots of the party's mobilization underwent significant—and rapid—changes. In the first two decades of the twenty-first century, the increasing identification of its public with the party's cause is also explained by certain discourses and initiatives by the Other in its three different forms: local (March 14), regional (Israel, Saudi Arabia), and international (the international community). Interpreted as "mistakes" in circles close to Hezbollah, they immunized its followers against any temptation to desert to the ranks of rival parties. In a country with such polarized politics, antagonisms are framed as a zero-sum game. Setbacks suffered by one party do comfort the sympathizers of the opposite camp, who feel they are "on the right side of the barricade". In addition, Hezbollah's renewed successes, from the prisoner exchanges to the second victory over the Israeli army in 2006, and its dedication to civil peace, sometimes at what is perceived as a high cost, have regularly reinforced its image as the national saviour in the eyes of many Lebanese.

However, of all the factors sustaining the continued mobilization of the party over time, the strongest consists of a set of perceptions—more precisely, of the gradually developed and regularly refined meaning given to its actions and its achievements. The effect of these interpretations is especially durable because the party's followers have invested them with an identity shift that they firmly made their own. Indeed, in the decades 2000 and 2010, the collective Shiite sense of self-esteem experienced a rapid, marked upswing. In 2000, thinking that they had just demonstrated their commitment to the nation with the Liberation, the Shiites felt that they had achieved a place in the national consciousness equal to those of their compatriots from other communities. March 14's arrival on the scene in 2005, and the shock at its failure to validate their interpretation of the Liberation had the effect of a cold shower on the Shiites. But the disappointment was short-lived: fifteen months after the Syrian withdrawal, the achievements of the IRL in the summer of 2006 helped the community get over the setback. While the victory of 2006, like the Liberation in 2000, was also offered to all Lebanese, Hezbollah's public this time had no illusions about the reception that March 14 and its followers would accord to it. Convinced that it was a victory, and one "sent by God" at that, but having to claim it for themselves, the Resistance's Shiite followers developed a perception of the collective sectarian identity that was highly reasserted. No longer promoting a non-confessional vision of the common self and of the others, this interpretation restored a hierarchy of confessional groupings measured by patriotism and Lebaneseness, with Shiites in the pre-eminent position. The admiration, trust, and, especially, gratitude felt towards Hezbollah, without which such a liberation of the community identity and its ascendancy would have remained a long-term aspiration, undeniably constitutes the rock-solid base on which the party's mobilization can today rely.

Despite any scenario that might possibly harm Hezbollah's reputation, the transformation triggered in the collective image of the Shiite community by the party, in part unwittingly, is destined to endure. The Shiites of Lebanon find themselves now as the guardians of a military and identity heritage that, given the community's growth, we can liken to the already well-developed embryo of a new national identity. The simple demographic calculus that forecasts the existence of four Shiites in Lebanon to six non-Shiites and which, in a few years, could turn the Country of Cedars into another Middle Eastern Shiite country, gives an edge to the resistance-based concept of the national identity over that espoused by March 14. The Shiite community has an opportunity to reify the template for the first Lebanese nation, having, for the first time in the history of Lebanon, succeeded in proposing an inclusive and integrationist national identity buttressed by an endogenous Grand Narrative built around great founding events generated on Lebanese soil by Lebanese and for Lebanese—in other words, by an aconfessional patriotic logic. To date, nothing like this has ever succeeded in emerging, stifled by Maronite conservatism wedded to an exclusivist sectarian conception or reduced to a component of a larger aggregation (the Arab nation) by Sunni militancy and that of the left in general. While the collective identity of Maronite conservatism shrinks Lebanon's borders and that of pan-Arabism needs expanded ones, the resistant 'we' spoken for by Hezbollah is conceived on a territory of 10,452 square kilometres—Lebanon in its present official borders—devoid of confessionalized regions, accepting of any Lebanese provided they join the ranks of Resistance followers. It therefore supports a *vouloir vivre* as one—and not a communitarian acceptance of living side by side.

There is nevertheless no guarantee that this resistant 'we' will remain inclusive and anti-communitarian in the future. IRL and Hezbollah's successes did not only trigger a Lebanese neonationalism, they also stirred a Shiite pride, which, faced with stubborn sectarian rejection by March 14 and new identitarian orders triggered by events in tormented Syria, might be encouraged to fall back on itself and eventually mutate into a new sect-anchored nationalism. The temptation will be there, in the measure of the threats to Lebanon that may loom from its eastern neighbour, to opt for retreat into community for the purpose of collective protection and to compound its Shiite identity. There could emerge a new Lebanese people, with a Shiite majority that would define itself, as the Maronites did earlier, as the "true Lebanese", with members of other communities then susceptible of being relegated to the status of second-class citizens.

How to study a mobilization

The major role played by meaning and identity in sustaining Hezbollah's mobilization over time allows us to reaffirm the choice of a meaning-making approach as a suitable analytical perspective. If Hezbollah gave substance to the supports of an image—'supports' here being the Liberation and other accomplishments—the party could not anticipate how its public would appropriate this image. An approach that would focus solely on the mobilizing actor (and thus on the issuance) does not take into account the dimension generated by the mobilized themselves (thus by the reception). It is therefore possible to argue that this mobilized body is as much a participant in the mobilization as is the mobilizing party. It is both object and subject, recipient as well as producer of (part of) this mobilizing action aimed at itself. The process is more bottom-down than top-down.

In other words, studying a mobilization is a sociological approach whose analytical framework can only be determined depending on the question that the observer asks him/herself about his/her subject. They may be interested in the universe of meaning produced by the mobilizing actor and work from methods advocated by Rational Action Theory (RAT), exposing the discourse of the actor intent on mobilizing, the resources this actor invests to achieve it, and his actions. However, the analyst will not get to the causes of this mobilization; its sources, if they interest him/her, are to be found elsewhere—with the mobilized group. The latter has to be studied in a split fashion. The first is as recipient of two main streams, one addressed to it by the actor seeking to mobilize it and a second one that springs from the environment. But, while some of the stream's components excite the group's sensibility and have a mobilizing effect, others leave it indifferent. It is therefore necessary to recognize not all the inflows in the perception of the mobilized group but only those that it retains. It follows that the mobilized group must be understood as also being an actor in its own mobilization, because it also produces perceptions that act like mobilizing resources—even if the mobilized group is also their recipient. These perceptions are produced by integration and cross-linking of a part of the perceptions the mobilized group receives from the actor intent on mobilizing it and those it receives from the environment. The process is influenced by experiences or knowledge linked to the past, and unfolds in a framework of norms, values, and beliefs derived from multiple moral or cultural referents.

Hezbollah in the years to come

In November 2009 the leadership of Hezbollah produced its "second political document", presented as a revision of the Open Letter of 1985. Far from being a new charter, it is instead a situational statement designed to recall certain positions taken by the party.[1] It leaves no doubt that disarming the IRL is not envisaged; its role and function are characterized as

> a national necessity that will persist as long as the Israeli threat remains, as long as the enemy continues to covet our land and our water ... and as long as a strong and capable state is lacking. ... The permanent nature of the Israeli threat requires Lebanon to adopt a dual defensive posture, executed by a *popular Resistance* participating *in the defence of the country against any Israeli invasion* and a national army that protects the country and anchors its security and stability. [This calls for] a *complementary* process. ... The persistent Israeli threat against Lebanon ... *requires effort by the Resistance to give itself the means for staying strong and to build up its capabilities*—resorting to whatever will help it fulfil its duty and assume national responsibilities. The goal is to complete the mission: liberation of our land remaining under occupation, the Shebaa Farms, the heights of Kfarshuba and the Lebanese village of Ghajar; also the release of detainees, the recovery of the missing and of martyrs' bodies, and participation in the defence and protection of the land and the people.[2]

In other words, the role that the IRL assigns to itself is not about attacking Israel to liberate Palestine, just as it does not contemplate intervening in a framework of inter-Lebanese conflicts. However, it intends to maintain itself and keep its weaponry—indeed, augment it—in order to (i) liberate the rest of the Lebanese territory still occupied by Israel, and (ii) to defend the country against an attack coming from across the southern border. To the east, Syria's territory fragmenting gives Hezbollah as well as its Iranian ally a space in which the party's interests and those of the IRL in Bilād al-Shām will be preserved.

On the domestic front, the party leadership envisions pragmatic relations with the Lebanese government. The party is prepared to continue living under confessional rules for a time. It realizes that the probability of the non-Shiite political class (apart from the LCP) seriously studying the modalities of a transition to a one man, one vote system is virtually zero, given that it would mean a lessening of its power in favour of a Hezbollah backed by a demographic majority. In this type of perspective, the prospect of an Islamic state founded by Hezbollah in Lebanon finds itself further diminished. In January 2011 the party in any case announced a joint project for a "believing civil state"[3] with the Maronite Patriarchate; a year later, Hassan Nasrallah responded to the criticism levelled by Christians in March 14 against him for a 1982 speech in which he had pronounced himself in favour of an Islamic regime in Lebanon:

> In 1982, 1983, in the beginning, some of our brothers—I was one of them—gave lectures and speeches on the choice of an Islamic republic in Lebanon. ... But I would like to remind you that among the Christian leaders who today speak of a single state, a democratic state with interconfessional cohabitation, civil peace and living in unity, at the time spoke of a Christian national state, of division and of federalism![4]

By suggesting in this way that it will not work outside legal avenues to abolish confessionalism, the party leadership is just as clearly signalling that it will insist that everyone participates in the decision-making process. In this, it is in alignment with the rest of the political class, united around the rules of the game set at Taef.

That said, the party also reaffirmed in the 2009 Document what it sees as its right to review the outputs of the national decision-making process—and, by corollary, the right to veto government decisions that it does not agree with:

> While waiting for the Lebanese to succeed through a national dialogue in achieving ... the abolition of political confessionalism ... *consensual democracy remains the essential rule of government* in Lebanon because it is the effective retranslation of the spirit of the Constitution and the essence of the Pact for Communal Life. ...
>
> Consensual democracy is an appropriate political formula for real participation of all and a confidence-building factor for the country's constituent parts. It is a large part of launching the stage of building the benign state in whose shadow all citizens can feel that it exists for them.
>
> From that starting point, any approach to national affairs through the prism of the majority/minority remains subject to the achievement of historical and social conditions conducive to the practice of real democracy in the shadow of which the citizen is valued in and for himself.[5]

Meanwhile, despite the tense national and regional context, Hezbollah continues its work in service to the Islamic Resistance. Writing the national history based on patriotic values as understood by the party is still a work in progress. On the occasion of Ramadan in 2011 and 2012 al-Manār broadcast two seasons of a historical series produced by the party with the explicit title of *al-Ghālibūn* (The Victors), chronicling the Israeli occupation years and the efforts of IRL fighters. In February 2012 the website of the al-Mahdī scouts won the prize for best Arab scout website.[6] On 11 May 2012 the party organized a giant celebration in the southern suburbs of Beirut to mark the completion of the Waʿd (Promise) project, dedicated to the reconstruction of the capital's periphery demolished by Israeli bombs in 2006 and carried out by

Jihād al-Binā'. Five years after project started in May 2007, Hezbollah had fulfilled its commitment: the 270 apartment buildings in the Haret Hreik neighbourhood had been rebuilt, 3,941 apartments and 1,771 stores, warehouses, and offices were returned to their owners.[7] On this occasion, the former "Security Perimeter" in the suburbs' heart, so named once upon a time because it protected the core institutions of Hezbollah's central apparatus, was renamed the "Perimeter of Dignity". The project, completed at a cost of $400 million, eventually benefited 20,000 people.

NOTES

INTRODUCTION

1. The Christians are divided into Maronites, Greek Orthodox, Greek Catholics (Melkites), Orthodox Armenians (Gregorians), Armenian Catholics, Orthodox Syriacs (Jacobites), Eastern Nestorians, Chaldaeans, Latins, and Protestants. There are Sunni, Shia, Druze, Alawite or Ismaili Muslims. There is also a Jewish community. In September 1996, a twelfth Christian community was recognized (Orthodox Copt), bringing the number of officially recognized sects to eighteen.
2. For evident political reasons, no census has been taken since 1932, but many private estimates confirm a permanent increase in the Muslim share of the population. See Table 1.
3. Sabrina Mervin (ed.), *Les mondes chiites et l'Iran*, Paris: Karthala, Beirut: IFPO, 2007, p. 462.
4. Here used in contrast to military (not to religious).

1. ON THE ORIGINS OF HEZBOLLAH

1. See for example Fouad Ajami, *The Vanished Imam*, Ithaca: Cornell University Press, 1986; Sabrina Mervin, "Les yeux de Mūsā Sadr (1928–1978)", in Catherine Mayeur-Jaouen (ed.), *Saints et héros du Moyen-Orient contemporain*, Paris: Maisonneuve et Larose, 2002, p. 285; Augustus R. Norton, *Amal and the Shiʿa*, Austin: University of Texas Press, 1987, and *Hezbollah: A Short History*, Princeton: Princeton University Press, 2007; Roschanack Shaery-Eisenlohr, *Shiʿite Lebanon*, New York: Columbia University Press, 2008.
2. Sabrina Mervin's phrase.
3. Repeating here the formulation by Hānī Fahs (*al-Sharq al-Awsat*, 17 May 2008). Fahs (1946–2014) was a Shiite cleric who oscillated between a long-standing allegiance to Harakat al-Mahrūmīn and sympathy for March 14 during the second half of the 2000s.
4. This holds true for the Twelvers. The Ismailis trace a different descent from the seventh *imām*. For the Twelvers, he is Mūsā al-Kādhim; for the Ismailis, it is his brother Ismāʿīl.
5. For more details, see Sabrina Mervin, "Les autorités religieuses dans le chiisme duodécimain contemporain", *Archives de sciences sociales des religions*, no. 125 (January–March 2004), pp. 63–77.
6. Shiites can choose a *marjaʿ* who need not be of their nationality or dwell in their country. The *wakīl* is the representative of the *marjaʿ* in the various Shiite countries. He disseminates the *fatwās* and collects the *khums* on the *marjaʿ*'s behalf.
7. Other translations include "the regency of the doctor of the law", "the guidance of the

theologian–jurist", "the governorship of the jurist–theologian", and "the doctrine of the jurist–theologian". The most widely used formulation remains *wilāyat al-faqīh*.

8. Cited by Wajīh Kawtharānī, *Bayna fiqh al-islāh al-shīʿī wa-wilāyat al-faqīh* [Between Shiite reform jurisprudence and the government of the legal adviser], Beirut: Dār al-Nahār, 2007, p. 89–90. My emphasis.
9. Baqer Moin, *Khomeini: Life of the Ayatollah*, London: I. B. Tauris, 1999, p. 158.
10. Cited in Kawtharānī, *Bayna fiqh al-islāh al-shīʿī wa-wilāyat al-faqīh*, p. 90.
11. Even though, in theory, the *waliy* need not be Iranian.
12. Elizabeth Picard, *Liban, État de discorde*, Paris: Flammarion, 1988, p. 34.
13. ʿAlī Ahmad, *al-Muslimūn al-shīʿa fī Kisrwān wa Jubayl (1842–2006)* [The Shiite Muslims in the Kesruan and Jbeil (1842–2006)], Beirut: Dār al-Hādī, 2007, p. 7.
14. Saʿdūn Hamādeh, *Tārīkh al-Shīʿa fī Lubnān* [History of the Shiites in Lebanon], Beirut: Dār al-Khayyāl, 2008, vol. I, p. 34.
15. Ibid.
16. Kamal Salibi, *The Modern History of Lebanon*, London: Weidenfeld & Nicolson, 1965, p. xvi.
17. Ahmad, *al-Muslimūn al-shīʿa*, p. 26.
18. Norton, *Amal and the Shīʿa*, p. 14.
19. Picard, *Liban, Etat de discorde*, p. 160.
20. Institut International de Recherche et de Formation Education Culture et Développement.
21. Picard, *Liban, Etat de discorde*, p. 147.
22. Cited by Picard, ibid.
23. Mūsā al-Sadr, quoted in Houchang Chehabi (ed.), *Distant Relations*, London: I. B. Tauris, 2006, pp. 152–3.
24. Norton, *Amal and the Shīʿa*, pp. 17–18.
25. Ibid., p. 18.
26. Yann Richard, *L'Islam chi'ite*, Paris: Fayard, 1991, p. 15.
27. Picard, *Liban, Etat de discorde*, p. 159.
28. Ibid., p. 254, footnote 15.
29. See Introduction.
30. Norton, *Amal and the Shīʿa*, p. 19.
31. The principal "Islamo-leftist" grouping, which incorporated some fifteen organizations, among them the Progressive Socialist Party (PSP), the Lebanese Communist Party (LCP), the Communist Action Organization in Lebanon (CAOL), the Syrian Social Nationalist Party (SSNP), the Murābitūn, the Baathists, and AMAL.
32. For a global view of Mūsā al-Sadr's political trajectory see Ajami, *The Vanished Imam*; Husayn Sharafeddīn, *al-Imām al-sayyid Mūsā al-Sadr* [The *imām* Sayyid Mūsā al-Sadr], Beirut: Dār al-Arqām, 1996 and *al-Mashrūʿ al-watanī wal-nuhūd al-muqāwim ʿindal-imām Mūsā al-Sadr* [The national project and the resistance awakening of the *imām* Mūsā al-Sadr], Beirut: Dār al-Maʿārif al-Hikmiyya, 2007; Mervin, "Les yeux de Mūsā Sadr".
33. In 1963 the Lebanese government awarded him Lebanese citizenship in recognition of his positive attitude.

34. In September 1970 the Jordanian army attacked the PLO after it tried to overthrow the monarchy. The number of Palestinian victims is subject to debate, the figures cited variously ranging from 3,000 to 10,000 dead.
35. Regretting the phrase with the descent into civil war, he reformulated it as: "Yes, guns make the man, but only when turned against the occupier."
36. A border region in south-east Lebanon.
37. That he was favourably disposed towards the latter had already manifested itself earlier when Hafez al-Assad took power in Syria and became the first Alawite (Shiite) president in the history of the country (with its large Sunni majority). In early 1973 several cities protested at the fact that the Constitution then being amended did not specify Islam as the state religion; the regime learned a lesson from the revolt and sought religious cover. Al-Sadr, who then presided over the SSC, issued a *fatwā* declaring that "the Alawites are fully a branch of Islam".
38. On Saturday 6 December 1975, members of the Kataeb discovered the mutilated corpses of four of their comrades. Invading the quarters of downtown Beirut that were still untouched by the violence, they kidnapped and massacred several dozen of their Muslim compatriots in reprisal. E. Picard cites "several dozen anonymous passers-by" (*op. cit.*, p. 174); other sources mention 200 to 600 dead.
39. Starting in the second half of 1975, the Christian militias (Kataeb, the National Lebanese Party, and Lebanese Forces) "cleansed" their territories. In December the Muslims in Antelias and Sebnay (an eastern Beirut suburb) were expelled. In January 1976 the (Christian) Palestinian camp of Dbayyeh (East Beirut) came under Christian militia control and the shantytown of La Quarantaine was demolished after the massacres. In June the siege of the Palestinian refugee camp at Tall al-Zaʿtar (East Beirut) began. In August the last Muslim zones of East Beirut were cleansed, 100,000 Shiites were expelled from Nabʿa, 6,000 Palestinians from Jisr al-Bacha and 50,000 Palestinians and Lebanese from south of Tall al-Zaʿtar (Picard, *op.cit.*, p. 175).
40. Samir Kassir, "L'affirmation des chiites libanais", *Le Monde Diplomatique*, May 1985.
41. He was accused, among other things, of being in the pay of the American government.
42. Kassir, "L'affirmation".
43. On Mughniyyeh, see Chibli Mallat, *Shīʿi Thought from the South of Lebanon*, Oxford: Centre for Lebanese Studies, 1988; Richard, *L'Islam chīʿite*, pp. 158–62; Kawtharānī, *Bayna fiqh al-islāh al-shīʿī wa-wilāyat al-faqīh*, pp. 91–92.
44. Richard, *L'Islam chīʿite*, p. 158.
45. Ibid., p. 159.
46. On Fadlallāh, see Jamal Sankari, *Fadlallāh: The Making of a Radical Shīʿite Leader*, London: Saqi Books, 2005 and Munā Sukkariyyeh, *Muhammad Husayn Fadlallāh: ʿan sanawāt wa mawāqif wa shakhsiyyāt* [Muhammad Husayn Fadlallāh: stands taken and personalities through the years], Beirut: Dār al-Nahār, 2007.
47. Sabrina Mervin (ed.), *Le Hezbollah: état des lieux*, Paris: Sindbad–Actes Sud–IFPO, 2008, p. 279.

48. Sukkariyyeh, *Muhammad Husayn Fadlallāh*, p. 192.
49. Ibid.
50. Author's interview with one of the founders of al-Ittihād, 2007.
51. Ibid.
52. Ibid.
53. Ibid.
54. *al-Muntalaq*, March–April 1978, no. 2, p. 3.
55. He was hanged by the Iraqi regime in 1980.
56. See Hassan Nasrallah's account in Amīn Mustafā, *al-Muqāwama fī Lubnān (1948–2000)* [The resistance in Lebanon (1948–2000)], Beirut: Dār al-Hādī, 2003, p. 433.
57. In 1994 he was elected president of the SSC; his deputy, Sheikh ʿAbdel-Amīr Qabalān, became vice-president.
58. This biography of Shamseddīn relies on Shaery-Eisenlohr, *Shiʿite Lebanon*, pp. 34–7.
59. He was later re-connected with AMAL, from the 1990s.
60. *al-Safir*, 9 February 1979.
61. See the editions of *al-Muntalaq* between 1978 and 1982.
62. A municipality in Beirut's southern suburbs.
63. Author's interview with a founder of al-Ittihād, 2007.
64. See the special issues and articles of *al-Muntalaq* for this period.
65. *al-Muntalaq*, March–April 1980, no. 9, p. 3.
66. Ibid.
67. *al-Muntalaq*, July–August 1981, no. 15, p. 99.
68. *al-Shirāʿ*, 11 September 1989.
69. He would have been living in Lebanon at this time, then rejoined Khomeini during the latter's exile in France before returning to Lebanon: *al-Shirāʿ*, 15 December 1989.
70. See the articles he wrote in 1977 for *Mabādiʾ al-Islām*, an Islamic magazine published in Beirut.
71. Interview by al-Nahār with Sādiq al-Mūsawī, originally slated for publication in the 26 August 1984 edition but eventually spiked (my own files).
72. Ibid.
73. This presentation relies on the *al-Nahār* and *al-Safir* archives.
74. *al-Shirāʿ*, 23 July 1984; *al-Safir*, 14, 28, and 29 December 1984. From 2005 onwards Jūzū championed the defence of the Lebanese political system and advocated a virulent anti-Shiism.
75. The commentaries and analyses appeared almost daily between 1984 and the start of 1987.
76. See the group's tracts and communiqués.
77. Communiqué dated 22 April 1978, signed by Sādiq al-Mūsawī.
78. *al-Safir*, 10 December 1984.
79. "Lā li-nidhām al-aqalliyya al-mārūniyya, naʿam lil-jumhūriyya al-islāmiyya."
80. To these quotes would be added others by Montazeri, Rafsanjani, Khamenei, and Ardabīlī denouncing the fact that power in Lebanon was not in the hands of Muslims, with some of them calling for the overthrow of the Lebanese regime.

81. "The fighting is bound to intensify if the Maronite minority persists in clinging to power and its terrorist measures against the tyrannized Muslims" (*al-Safir*, 15 May 1985).
82. *al-Shirāʿ*, 17 May 1993.
83. Mustafā, *al-Muqāwama fi Lubnān*, p. 400.
84. Ibid., pp. 429–30.
85. Ibid., p. 401. For al-Mūsawī, see Chapter 2.
86. These details are drawn from the sole extant biography of al-Tufaylī, accessible in *Mawsūʿat Hizbillāh* [Encyclopaedia of Hezbollah], Beirut: Edito Creps, 2006, vol. III.
87. Shiite religious studies are organized in three cycles: the *Muqaddimāt* (Starters), the *Sutūh* (Surfaces) and the *Khārij* (Outside Research).
88. Author's interview with al-Tufaylī, 2008.
89. *Mawsūʿat Hizbillāh*, vol. III. The information should be treated with caution as the text does not cite sources.
90. Author's interview with al-Tufaylī, 2008.
91. Author's interview with al-Tufaylī, 2009.
92. Hasan ʿAbbās Nasrallāh, *al-Harakāt al-hizbiyya fi Baʿalbak* [The partisan movements in Baalbek], Beirut: Muʾassasat al-Wafāʾ, 1994, p. 161.
93. Ibid., p. 162.
94. Author's interview with al-Tufaylī, 2008.
95. The Iraqi Baath assassinated clerics of al-Daʿwa-Lebanon in Beirut, but also lay people, such as Hasan Sharrī, an AMAL cadre assassinated in October 1981.
96. Few biographies of ʿAbbās al-Mūsawī exist. Biographical brochures are routinely distributed by the Foundation of the Martyr on certain occasions organized by the party. Only three books and booklets endorsed by Hezbollah offer a fairly fleshed-out biography: Sheikh Muhammad Khātūn (a former student of al-Mūsawī), *Amīr al-qāfila* [The caravan prince], Beirut: Dār al-Walāʾ, 2002; Hiyyām Rizq and Muhammad Bazzī, *Sayyid al-qāda* [The sayyid of leaders], Beirut: Dār al-Amīr, 2002; and Fuʾād Merʿī, *Sayyid al-dhill al-akhdar* [The sayyid with the green shadow], Beirut: Jamʿiyyat al-Maʿārif al-Islāmiyya al-Thaqāfiyya, 2003. The biography put forward here is based in part on Khātūn's work, which remains the richest and most reliable source.
97. Khātūn, *Amīr al-qāfila*, pp. 11–12. Another version has it that Abū al-Fadl al-ʿAbbās also appeared to her proffering a child: Rizq and Bazzī, *Sayyid al-qāda*, p. 17.
98. Sukkariyyeh, *Muhammad Husayn Fadlallāh*, pp. 196–8.
99. Khātūn, *Amīr al-qāfila*, pp. 51–2.

2. HEZBOLLAH, CARRYING ON THE ISLAMIC RESISTANCE IN LEBANON

1. On the 1982 invasion see Ghassan al-Ezzi, *L'invasion israélienne du Liban*, Paris: L'Harmattan, 1990; Franklin Lamb (ed.), *Israel's War in Lebanon*, Nottingham: Russell Press Ltd., 1984; Picard, *Liban, Etat de discorde*, chapter 10; Ze'ev Schiff and Ehoud Ya'ari, *Israel's Lebanon War*, New York: Simon & Schuster, 1984.
2. *L'Armée du Liban-Sud*, Ministère des Affaires Étrangères et Européennes, Paris: Commission des Recours des Réfugiés, June 2001.

3. 1,000 according to A. R. Norton (*Amal and the Shiʿa*, p. 49); 2,000 according to Véronique Ruggirello (*Khiam: prison de la honte*, Paris: L'Harmattan, 2003, p. 51) and Chehabi (*Distant Relations*, p. 202).
4. Under his real name, Sabrī al-Bannā, he was a PLO militant and a rival to Yasser Arafat. He founded the Fatah Revolutionary Council in 1974. See Patrick Seale, *Abu Nidal: A Gun for Hire*, New York: Random House, 1992.
5. Jean-Pierre Alem and Patrick Bourrat, *Le Liban*, Paris: PUF, 1994 (5th edn.), p. 10. The evacuated Syrian soldiers were part of the Palestine Liberation Army (PLA), a component of the PLO.
6. It was organized by an SSNP militant, Habib Chartouni.
7. The invasion contravened UNSC Resolutions 515 and 516, approved the previous month.
8. An accounting of the massacres is difficult to arrive at. According to Alem and Bourrat, nearly 1,300 Palestinians and Lebanese were massacred (*Le Liban*, p. 103). Al-Ezzi estimates the number of victims between 2,000 and 4,000, saying that hurried mass burials distorted the count (*L'invasion israélienne du Liban*, p. 79). See also Amnon Kapeliouk, *Sabra et Chatila: enquête sur un massacre*, Paris: Seuil, 1982, and Bayan Nuwayhed al-Hout, *Sabra and Shatila: September 1982*, London: Pluto Press, 2004.
9. Picard, "La Guerre civile au Liban", *Encyclopédie en ligne des violences de masse*, available at www.massviolence.org, posted on 13 July 2012.
10. "The 1982 Israeli Invasion of Lebanon: The Casualties", *Race & Class*, vol. 24, no. 4 (1983), pp. 340–3.
11. *The Christian Science Monitor*, 14 October 1982.
12. Associated Press, 5 March 1991.
13. Mahmoud Soueid, *Israël au Liban: la fin de 30 ans d'occupation*? Paris: Revue d'études palestiniennes, 2000, p. 15.
14. Nearly all the lemon and apple plantations were deliberately burned by the Israeli army.
15. al-Ezzi, *L'invasion israélienne du Liban*, p. 152.
16. Chehabi, *Distant Relations*, p. 206.
17. Ibid., p. 212.
18. Mustafā, *al-Muqāwama fī Lubnān*, p. 402.
19. Ibid.
20. Ibid.
21. Ibid., p. 403.
22. There is a mistake in this testimony, as the Lebanese President at the time was not Amin Gemayel but Elias Sarkis.
23. Mustafā, *al-Muqāwama fī Lubnān*, pp. 403–4.
24. On 11 July 1982 a communiqué published in the newspaper *al-Safīr* announced the decision of one part of the Beirut cadres and of the AMAL military apparatus to continue the fight against the occupier and to reject the Committee of National Salvation.
25. A reference to the first name of his first-born son.
26. This biography of al-Mūsawī relies on *Mawsūʿat Hizbillāh*, vol. III.
27. Ibid. His election to this position came as the result of the dust-up at the fourth congress.

28. Communiqué by AMAL al-Islāmiyya, 16 August 1982.
29. See Chapter 3.
30. Mustafā, *al-Muqāwama fi Lubnān*, pp. 404–5.
31. A quarter in Beirut's southern suburbs.
32. The same.
33. Mustafā, *al-Muqāwama fi Lubnān*, p. 405.
34. A quarter in West Beirut.
35. The same.
36. Mustafā, *al-Muqāwama fi Lubnān*, p. 420–1.
37. Ibid., pp. 421–2.
38. Ibid., p. 423.
39. This part is adapted from Chehabi, *Distant Relations*, pp. 180–98.
40. It is impossible to state with certainty that the model of the "Muslim Student Association" was consciously adopted by al-Ittihād, but it is not unreasonable to think so given the similarity of the names that these associations bear (al-Jamʿiyya al-Islāmiyya lil-Talaba al-Jāmiʿiyyīn (Islamic Association for Students)—see *al-Muntalaq*, February–March 1982, no. 19, p. 51). Also in Beirut at the time there was Munadhdhamat al-Talaba al-Irāniyyīn al-Muslimīn fi Lubnān (the Organization of Iranian Muslim Students in Lebanon), with which al-Ittihād would jointly organize demonstrations (*al-Muntalaq*, April–May 1979, no. 4).
41. Nicholas Noe, *Voice of Hezbollah*, London: Verso, 2007, p. 118.
42. Montazeri is better known for his unusual personality and his stubborn militancy. Nicknamed "Ringo" for always carrying a revolver on his belt, this true revolutionary dreamed of an Islamic Internationale and travelled the world to support all anti-imperialist liberation movements, exhibiting special sympathy for Latin American movements. In late 1979 he tried to dispatch Iranian fighters to Lebanon, but the Lebanese government, supported by AMAL and a section of the clergy, lobbied the Iran regime to prevent their departure. See Chehabi, *Distant Relations*, p. 207.
43. The Islamic Revolutionary Guards or Pasdaran are an official paramilitary force in Iran, created by a Khomeini decree in May 1979. Their primary function is to "protect the Revolution and its works". In practice, the organization was created as a counterweight to the regular army, much of which is said to have remained loyal to the Shah. See Wilfried Buchta, *Who Rules Iran?*, Washington: Washington Institute for Near East Policy, 2000, pp. 67–71.
44. They did not stay there long because the Islamic Republic was proclaimed on 1 April.
45. Chehabi, *Distant Relations*, pp. 191–2.
46. Ibid., p. 197.
47. In March the two regimes signed a trade agreement assuring Syria of Iranian oil at a discount. Some weeks later the Syrian government closed one of Iraq's pipelines crossing Syrian territory, thus creating difficulties for Iran's enemy: Chehabi, *Distant Relations*, pp. 212–13.

48. Ibid., p. 214.
49. Ibid., pp. 214–15.
50. The exact number of Pasdaran stationed in Lebanon in 1982 is impossible to establish with certainty. It was 500 according to journalist Gilles Delafon (*Beyrouth: les soldats de l'islam*, Paris: Stock, 1989, p. 83), 1,000 according to Norton (*Amal and the Shiʿa*, p. 100), 1,500 according to Chehabi (*Distant Relations*, p. 216) and John Esposito (*The Islamic Threat*, New York: Oxford University Press, 1992, p. 147), and 2,000 according to Alem and Bourrat (*Le Liban*, p. 112).
51. The Bassij are an Iranian paramilitary organization set up in November 1979 by a Khomeini decree. It constitutes the second most important military force after the Pasdaran, under whose command it functions. In theory, its role is to "protect the Islamic Republic against American intervention from outside and from internal enemies". In practice, it seems to be dedicated to stifling any domestic dissent (Buchta, *Who Rules Iran?*, pp. 65–7).
52. Mohtashami-Pur, quoted by Muhammad Hasan Akhtarī in *al-Sharq al-Awsat*, 14 May 2008.
53. ʿAbdallāh Qasīr, a former cadre of AMAL and later a Hezbollah MP, spoke of the month of Ramadan and of the aid arriving then for the resisters surrounded in Beirut by Israeli troops and the Lebanese Forces at Khaldeh. Likewise, in the course of an interview that he granted me in 2009, Sheikh al-Tufaylī was positive that it was definitely in the month of Ramadan that the Pasdaran arrived in the Bekaa. As it turns out, that year the month of Ramadan fell between the end of June and the end of the third week in July.
54. Author's interview with al-Tufaylī, 2009.
55. Mustafā, *al-Muqāwama fi Lubnān*, p. 406.
56. See Chapter 5.
57. Chehabi, *Distant Relations*, p. 216.
58. On the concept of a "culture of resistance" see Chapter 4 and Part II.
59. Created in 1969, it stood for a Marxism tinged by Maoism and influenced by the Cuban and Vietnamese experiences.
60. Author's interviews, 2008, 2009.
61. Calculations based on voting lists of 2005.
62. At the time, equivalent to $3,550.
63. Mustafā, *al-Muqāwama fi Lubnān*, pp. 405–6.
64. See the preceding chapter. Al-Ittihād and the Association of the Muslim Ulema in the Bekaa are both action structures of al-Daʿwa (Mustafā, *al-Muqāwama fi Lubnān*, p. 433; author's interview with al-Tufaylī, 2009).
65. See the preceding chapter.
66. My emphasis. Nasrallah makes clear that Hezbollah was not created as an Islamist party augmented later by a military arm. The Hezbollah matrix is clearly that of a military organization designed to fight the occupation.
67. Mustafā, *al-Muqāwama fi Lubnān*, p. 426.
68. Hasan Fadlallāh, *al-Khiyār al-ākhar* [The other choice], Beirut: Dār al-Hādī, 1994, p. 41.
69. Ibid.

70. Ibid. The High Council for the Defence in Iran approved the idea of the Council of Lebanon in October 1982.
71. Nasrallāh, *al-Harakāt al-hizbiyya fī Baʿalbak*, p. 169.
72. Hassan Nasrallah quoted in Mustafā, *al-Muqāwama fī Lubnān*, p. 436.
73. The "Hezbollah" name had been in use for some time already, but next to other appellations that would soon disappear. Fadlallāh, *al-Khiyār al-ākhar*, p. 33.
74. Ibid.,p. 35.
75. Author's interview with al-Tufaylī, 2008.
76. Author's field observation.
77. Author's field observation.
78. Sura *al-Mujādala*, verse 22.
79. Sura *al-Māʾida*, verse 56.
80. Sura *al-Anfāl*, verse 60.
81. Author's interview with al-Tufaylī, 2008.
82. The agreement was never ratified by the Lebanese parliament.
83. "Lā ikrāha fil-dīn" (sura *al-Baqara*, verse 256).
84. Author interview with al-Tufaylī, 2008.
85. Hānī Fahs, *al-Sharq al-Awsat*, 17 May 2008.
86. In an article written in Harb's memory for *al-Muntalaq* (April 1984, no. 24), one reads that he held the view that "Islam is too large to be packaged in a party; a cleric must consecrate himself [to the whole of] the *ummah*, without joining any particular party". This shows that he was close to Shamseddīn who, as we have already seen, preferred not to join a group of militant clerics who subscribed to *wilāyat al-faqīh*.
87. This thesis was first proposed by Norton as "the Iraq Connection" (*Hezbollah*, p. 30), taken up by Laurence Louër as "the Najaf Connection" (*Chiisme et politique au Moyen-Orient*, Paris: Autrement, 2008, p. 32).
88. Author's interview with al-Tufaylī, 2009. On ʿAbdel-Karīm ʿUbayd, see pp. 55, 65.
89. Author's interview with al-Tufaylī, 2009.
90. *Mawsūʿat Hizbillāh*, vol. III.
91. Ibid. On al-Tawhīd see Michel Seurat, *L'État de barbarie*, Paris: Seuil, 1989, and Bernard Rougier, *Everyday Jihad*, Cambridge, MA: Harvard University Press, 2009.
92. See the presentation by Sheikh ʿAlī Khāzim (which seems to date from 1996–7) on the Association of Muslim Ulema in Lebanon website (www.tajamo.net, accessed 5 November 2009).
93. See ibid.
94. Ibid.
95. See the newspapers from that time. The SSC blamed the Association of Muslim Ulema in Lebanon after one of the young demonstrators, Muhammad Najdeh, was killed by security forces trying to keep the demonstration from getting out of hand.
96. *al-Nahār*, 23 May 1983.
97. See next chapter.
98. These pages on Rāghib Harb rely on one of his rare biographies, *Shaykh al-shuhadāʾ*

wa-amīr al-muqāwimīn [Sheikh of martyrs and prince of resisters], Beirut: Jamʿiyyat al-Maʿārif al-Islāmiyya al-Thaqāfiyya, 2003, and *al-Muntalaq*, April 1984, no. 24, p. 122.

99. He would only return at the end of July (Hasan Fadlallāh, *Harb al-irādāt* [The war of wills], Beirut: Dār al-Hādī, 1998, p. 103).
100. This most famous and regularly quoted phrase in Hezbollah iconography was uttered one evening at the feast of al-Adhā when Harb, surrounded by family, was talking on a rooftop with friends: some Israeli tanks had burst into the village, and a sharp discussion ensued with an officer. Harb refused to shake his hand when it was offered, declaring: "The stance [itself] is a weapon; shaking the hand [of the enemy] is to acknowledge [him]."
101. One day, his mother, worried about his whereabouts, took off in search of him and, on her finding him at the village entrance, weapon in hand, he is said to have rebuffed her with: "Mother, does it cost 25 piastres to enter Paradise?"
102. Hala Jaber, *Hezbollah: Born with a Vengeance*, New York: Columbia University Press, 1997, p. 18.
103. Ibid.
104. Cited in Soueid, *Israël au Liban*, p. 21, footnote 6: (iii) and (iv) refer to the fact that the question during the 1982 invasion was whether Lebanon would be dismembered and if Israel would annex South Lebanon; this fear was accentuated by the occupier's systematic confiscation of any home or premises left unoccupied several days in a row (the Israeli law regarding what Israel calls the "absent present").

3. TRAJECTORY OF AN ISLAM OF RESISTANCE

1. Jeroen Gunning, "Hizballah and the Logic of Political Participation", in Marianne Heiberg, Brendan O'Leary, and John Tirman (eds.), *Terror, Insurgency, and the State*, Philadelphia: University of Pennsylvania Press, 2007, p. 164.
2. al-Ezzi, *L'invasion israélienne du Liban*, p. 225. It was the same at the Zimrayya checkpoint. Private cars were no longer allowed to approach beyond a certain distance in front of the checkpoint; taxis with dual plates (Lebanese on one side of the checkpoint, Israeli on the other) served to carry those seeking to enter the occupied zone across the last section of road. They were dropped off at the checkpoint entrance, where everyone in turn would be subjected by members of the SLA to a detailed interrogation (children having to pass through before their parents), a body search, and a series of annoyances (personal recollections).
3. Some sources speak of 60,000 residents remaining. *L'Armée du Liban-Sud*.
4. This sketch of the SLA draws on *L'Armée du Liban-Sud*.
5. See p. 92.
6. Mustafā, *al-Muqāwama fi Lubnān*, p. 50.
7. Ibid., p. 51. According to the author of *L'Armée du Liban-Sud*, the AFL changed its name to the SLA in 1982 under orders from the Israeli authorities. Even so, I am using the date and the circumstances advanced by the historian Amīn Mustafā that other Lebanese sources corroborate, including Mahmoud Soueid, who also states that it was only after Haddad's death—hence, not before April 1984—that the militia would adopt its final name.

8. A refusal to cooperate was most often cause for expulsion; Ghassan al-Ezzi cites the cases of women who had repulsed the advances of militia men or of professors who refused to organize field trips to Israel for their students.
9. The village of Rīhān in 1984 is one example. Amnesty International and Human Rights Watch both cite the cases of Mārūn al-Rās and ʿAytā al-Shaʿb. In 1997 the former was emptied of all its inhabitants, and those of the latter were deported *en masse* to the Khyām prison (al-Ezzi, *L'invasion israélienne du Liban*, p. 225; *L'Armée du Liban-Sud*).
10. An example is furnished by the village of Suhmur in September 1984. With Israeli troops encircling the village, the SLA men rampaged through the hamlet, gathered nearly 300 men aged 16 to 39 and opened fire on them, killing 14 and wounding 25: al-Ezzi, *L'invasion israélienne du Liban*, p. 226.
11. This section on the prisons operated by the Israeli authorities or on their behalf is based on data provided by the president of the Lebanese Association for Prisoners and Liberated (LAPL) (author's interview, 2007), on ICRC reports, on the testimony of Souha Bechara (*Résistante*, Paris: JC Lattès, 2000), and the testimonies in the collection by V. Ruggirello (*Khiam*).
12. Author's interview with the president of the LAPL, 2007. The ICRC and Ruggirello (*Khiam*, p. 13) date the centre's opening to 1985. The Lebanese government's official statistic is 12,000 persons between 1978 and 2000 (*L'Orient-Le Jour* (henceforth *LOLJ*), 21 January 2000).
13. The ICRC disclosed that the Israeli occupation authorities informed it that they intended to close the Ansār camp in April 1985. At the time, it held nearly 1,800 prisoners (www.icrc.org, accessed 17 October 2009).
14. This was its appellation in South Lebanon.
15. "Administration was delegated to Lahd's men. This kept the Israelis from getting their hands dirty in the eyes of the international community. They erected barracks for the Israelis at some distance so they would not be associated with the prison. The interrogators and supervisors were Israeli, the administrative staff Lebanese and the tortures were inflicted by the Israelis and Lebanese both", author interview with the president of the LAPL, 2007. According to the ICRC, the Israeli soldiers and officers were in fact permanently stationed in the Khyām prison until 1995, when the ICRC made its first (rare) visits. It is after that that they actually moved to the barracks far from the prison.
16. Author's interview with the president of the LAPL, 2007. Several witnesses said that the Israeli authorities preferred the prisoners to die outside the prison walls for the sake of appearances.
17. Ibid.
18. *L'Armée du Liban-Sud.*
19. Ruggirello, *Khiam*, p. 84, 132.
20. Ibid., p. 13. "The Israelis have always denied any responsibility for this business by speaking of it as a 'problem between the Lebanese'", author's interview with the president of the LAPL, 2007.
21. This section is drawn from the presentation made on the subject by al-Ezzi (*L'invasion israélienne du Liban*, pp. 150–5).

22. Israeli goods sold in Lebanon cost 40–75 per cent less than their Lebanese equivalents.
23. Soueid, *Israël au Liban*, p. 20; personal recollection of the scandal that broke out when the Israeli pumps along the South Lebanon watercourses were discovered after the Israeli retreat in 2000.
24. A secular party founded in 1932 by Antoun Saadeh (Greek Orthodox); he advocated the reunification of the Levant countries in a Greater Syria. It is to this party that the Lebanese Resistance owes its second, and still famous, operation. It took place on 24 September 1982, when an SSNP militant, Khālid ʿAlwān, fired point blank at a group of Israeli soldiers sitting at a patio table in a café on Hamra Street in West Beirut, killing an officer and wounding two soldiers, before he disappeared into the alleys of the quarter (*al-Safir*, 12 March 2000).
25. Elias Atallah, a former member of the LCP Politburo, revealed that Soviet and Arab aid meant for the LNRF was cancelled from 1984 on and that, in 1985, the Syrian authorities insisted that the LNRF "clear in advance [its] military operations": Soueid, *Israël au Liban*, p. 23.
26. LCP cadres were assassinated during the second half of the 1980s. Among them were Selim Yammut (cadre), killed in 1985; Khalil Naous (journalist and member of the LCP Politburo) and Suheil Tawileh (member of the LCP Central Committee), in 1986; Mehdi Amel (intellectual) and Hussein Mruweh (intellectual), in 1987; and Hikmat al-Amin (cadre), who died in an attack on the Central Committee headquarters in 1989. Those responsible were never clearly identified, but fingers are routinely pointed at the Syrian regime and groups subservient to it. Hezbollah was suspected of having killed Amel and Mruweh, but the LCP executive also suspected Sunni fundamentalist groups at the time.
27. Soueid, *Israël au Liban*, p. 24.
28. Author's interview with this cadre, 2007.
29. Mustafā, *al-Muqāwama fī Lubnān*, p. 463.
30. *al-Safir*, 30 January 2016.
31. See the al-Nābulsī website (www.nabolsi.net., accessed 4 November 2009).
32. This biography of ʿAbdel-Muhsin Fadlallāh is taken from Fadlallāh, *Harb al-irādāt*, pp. 119–23.
33. His father was Sayyid Sadreddīn Fadlallāh (d.c. 1941).
34. ʿAbdel-Muhsin was married to Muhammad Husayn's sister.
35. After surviving seventeen assassination attempts instigated against him by the Israeli army, he succumbed to an illness in 1992, one month after ʿAbbās al-Mūsawī's assassination.
36. Mustafā, *al-Muqāwama fī Lubnān*, p. 463.
37. Ibid., p. 425.
38. Naʿīm Qāssem, *Hezbollah: la voie, l'expérience, l'avenir*, Beirut: Dar Albouraq, 2008, p. 68.
39. Ibid.
40. Ibid.
41. Mustafā, *al-Muqāwama fī Lubnān*, pp. 459–60.
42. Qāssem, *Hezbollah*, p. 141.
43. Georges Corm, *Le Proche-Orient éclaté 1956–2007*, Paris: Gallimard, 2007, p. 345.

44. This pertains to the commitment made by the party to liberate Lebanon from the Israeli occupation.
45. The issues of *al-ʿAhd* at the time were full of articles describing these interventions.
46. See the editions of *al-ʿAhd* subsequent to these events.
47. Author's interview with al-Tufaylī, 2008. Hassan Nasrallah also evoked this non-differentiation in the roles of armed fighter and cadre responsible on the ground for organizing and taking charge of demonstrations by the party (*al-Safir*, 5 September 2006).
48. Author's interview in the Bekaa region with original members of the IRL, 2007.
49. On hostage taking and Hezbollah see Jaber, *Hezbollah*; Magnus Ranstorp, *Hizb'Allah in Lebanon*, New York: St Martin's Press, 1997; and Robin Wright, *Sacred Rage*, New York: Touchstone Books, 1985.
50. He was also accused of taking part in the hijacking of TWA flight 847, on 14 June 1985, which the kidnappers, members of Islamic Jihād, used to demand that Israel release some 700 Shiite detainees. In an act of vengeance echoing the assassination of his brother by the Israeli army in 1984, Mughniyeh killed one of the passengers, an American navy diver.
51. As just one example of many, Husayn al-Mūsawī denied all responsibility by Hezbollah for the attacks and abductions, and added that "he would have liked very much for it to have been Hezbollah militants" but that "there was no cause to steal the merit earned by the brothers who did it" (*Ahzāb Lubnān: Hizbullāh 1982–2002* [The Lebanese parties: Hezbollah 1982–2002], Beirut: NBN, DVD, 2002).
52. Qāssem, *Hezbollah*, p. 137.
53. *The Washington Post*, 17 May 1985. A second article, published on 21 October 2001, mentioned that Ronald Reagan is said to have given his approval for a CIA operation supported by the Lebanese army and "foreigners". According to journalist Bob Woodward, President Reagan and the CIA were "advised" by Israel's Mossad and supported by the Saudi authorities.
54. According to Hala Jaber, eighty-seven foreign nationals were kidnapped in Lebanon, including seventeen Americans, fourteen Britons, fifteen French, seven Swiss, and seven Germans (*Hezbollah*, p. 113).
55. He was abducted on 19 July 1982 and freed on 21 July 1983.
56. Jaber, *Hezbollah*, p. 113.
57. A consortium created in 1973 and based in France, Eurodif was a uranium enrichment plant. In 1974 the Shah's regime bought a 10 per cent interest in return for investing up to $1 billion in the form of loans to France for the construction of the plant. Subsequently, Tehran acquired 25 per cent of Eurodif and thus had a blocking minority on the board of directors. With the Shah overthrown, the revolutionary regime wanted a refund, which France refused; France also attempted to prevent Iran from exercising its prerogatives as a shareholder in the consortium. The taking of French hostages in Lebanon in the 1980s was interpreted as an attempt by the Iranian regime to pressure the French government.
58. Marie Seurat, *Les Corbeaux d'Alep*, Paris: Gallimard, 1989.
59. Ranstorp, *Hizb'Allah in Lebanon*.
60. This was the case with the Hamādeh brothers, who abducted two German nationals to obtain their brother's release from a German jail.

61. Chehabi, *Distant Relations*, p. 291.
62. Tāriq al-Bishrī, *Manhaj al-nadhar fil-nudhum al-siyāsiyya al-muʿāsira fil-ʿālam al-islâmī* [Manual of the theory of contemporary political regimes of the Islamic world], Amman: Dār al-Shurūq lil-Nashr wal-Tawzīʿ, 2005.
63. This does not prove, *a priori*, that there is no internal debate on the issue. The fact is, however, that the subject does not appear in public discourse or in the literature of party intellectuals for internal use that can be purchased in some bookstores. The author's interviews on the subject with some of these intellectuals did not give rise to the impression that they have developed views on the concept of Islamic government.
64. See Chapter 11.
65. "Lebanon cannot be a detached Islamic state outside the project of the *ummah* ... It is not necessary to address the form of government or the distribution of power within it while Lebanon is still under Israeli occupation and domination of American power. It makes more sense for the Lebanese people to regain their freedom, so that [then] they can choose the regime that they want": Ibrāhīm Amīn al-Sayyid, *al-Shirāʿ*, 13 August 1982.
66. Sura *al-Baqara*, verse 256.
67. *Magazine*, 26 September 1986.
68. Hassan Nasrallah, "al-Sayyid Hasan Nasrallāh: al-sīra al-dhātiyya" [Sayyid Hassan Nasrallah: the autobiography], *al-Mustaqbal al-ʿArabī*, no. 331, September 2006, p. 118.
69. Unlike Shaʿbān's al-Tawḥīd in Tripoli.
70. A reference to the name of the hill on which it perches.
71. Amine Gemayel, *L'offense et le pardon*, Paris: Gallimard, 1988.
72. Author's field observation, confirmed by interviews (North Bekaa, 2007).
73. Chehabi, *Distant Relations*, pp. 288–9.
74. Ibid.
75. Khomeini's designated successor between 1979 and 1989, he was removed for having protested at the liquidation of 30,000 members of the People's Mujahedin in 1988.
76. Chehabi, *Distant Relations*, p. 228.
77. Alain Gresh and Dominique Vidal, *Les 100 clés du Proche-Orient*, Paris: Hachette, 2006, *s.v.* "Syria".
78. *al-ʿAhd*, no. 140, 29 Jumada al-Thani 1407 (March 1987).
79. Apart from the Sunnis, all the political groups challenged the Taef Agreement when it was announced. Under pressure from Damascus, most ultimately accepted the new rules of the game.
80. *al-Nahār*, 6 November 1989.
81. See Chapter 5 on *wilāyat al-faqīh*.
82. Aurélie Daher, alias Vito Romani, "Le Hezbollah, un instrument de la politique étrangère iranienne?" in Bernard Rougier (ed.), *Les diplomaties contestataires au Moyen-Orient*, *Les Cahiers de l'Orient*, no. 87, September 2007, p. 87.
83. Chehabi, *Distant Relations*, p. 305.
84. Ibid., pp. 290–1.
85. See Chapter 6.

86. See Chapter 4.
87. Aurélie Daher, "Le Hezbollah face aux clans et aux grandes familles de la Békaa-Nord", in Franck Mermier and Sabrina Mervin (eds.), *Leaders et partisans au Liban*, Paris: Karthala, 2012, p. 419–33.
88. Subhī al-Tufaylī, ʿAbbās al-Mūsawī, Naʿīm Qāsim, Muhammad Yazbek, Hassan Nasrallah, Husayn Kūrānī, Muhammad Raad, Muhammad Fneish, and Muhammad Yaghi (Fadlallāh, *Harb al-irādāt*, p. 96, footnote no. 2).
89. Ibid., p. 97. For the party's internal organization see Chapter 5.
90. From 1991 to 1993 he was allowed to remain on the consultative council, but really had no portfolio. In 1992 the council voted 10 to 2 to participate in the parliamentary elections. Al-Tufaylī cast one of the negative votes. During the 1995 congress he failed to be re-elected to the council. This falling out remained *sub rosa* until the summer of 1997, when al-Tufaylī launched the "Revolt of the Hungry" (*Thawrat al-Jiyāʿ*). He was officially expelled from the party in January 1998. For more on this see Aurélie Daher, "Subhī al-Tufaylī et la 'Révolte des Affamés'", in Mervin (ed.), *Le Hezbollah*, pp. 273–6.
91. Without specifying the type of government.
92. Fadlallāh, *al-Khiyār al-ākhar*, p. 96.
93. "From1982 to1990, no moves towards a political discussion or of high-level contact between Hezbollah and the Christian parties were recorded, with the exception of a few meetings on the sidelines in the Bekaa or in the southern Beirut suburbs. Those aside, the boycott on relations of any kind with the Christian parties, specifically with the Maronite [side], was global": ibid., p. 137.
94. See Chapter 6.
95. Rizq and Bazzī, *Sayyid al-qāda*, pp. 66–7.
96. Many party cadres were afraid that the Israeli army would take advantage of the occasion to assassinate him, and had tried to dissuade him from going to Jibshīt (Khātūn, *Amīr al-qāfila*, p. 148).
97. Ibid., pp. 147–8.
98. Rizq and Bazzī, *Sayyid al-qāda*, p. 63.
99. In the East, the question is routinely asked when leaving a person to meet a second one known to the first. Politeness demands an expression of concern to know if one can perhaps bear any sort of message from the first person to the second.
100. Rizq and Bazzī, *Sayyid al-qāda*, p. 63.
101. A village near Nabatiyeh.
102. A village in the *caza* of Zahrani.
103. Same.
104. Nasrallah was elected in February, and the parliamentary elections took place the following summer.
105. The principal champion of a theory of shifts by Hezbollah is Joseph Alagha.
106. James Piscatori, *Islam in a World of Nation States*, Cambridge, MA: Cambridge University Press, 1986, pp. 146–7.
107. A phrase used by a Hezbollah MP (author's interview, 2007).

108. A declaration by MP Muhammad Berjawi dated 29 June 1994, quoted by Dalal al-Bizri in *Islamistes, parlementaires et libanais: les interventions à l'Assemblée des élus de la Jamaʿa Islamiyya et du Hizb Allah, 1992–1996*, Beirut: Les Cahiers du CERMOC, 1999, no. 3, p. 13.
109. Mainly Druzes and Christians who had lost their homes during the civil war. They received aid from the government through a special fund, the Central Fund for the Displaced.
110. Shiite quarters in the capital that were cleared of their inhabitants by the Lebanese Forces when the war started. The government never took steps to compensate them.
111. *Bismillāh al-Rahmān al-Rahīm* (In the name of Allah the Most Gracious and Merciful). Islamists frequently use this pious phrase when they begin voicing an opinion.
112. Hezbollah's facilities are open on Fridays. Their holidays are Saturday and Sunday or Sunday and Monday. Regardless, from then until 1985, the party used both the Muslim calendar (and never adopted the Iranian calendar) and the Christian Gregorian calendar. It has only used the latter since then.
113. al-Bizri, *Islamistes, parlementaires et libanais*, p. 15.
114. Hezbollah's parliamentary caucus at the time had twelve members: eight from its own ranks and four allies.
115. Fadlallāh, *al-Khiyār al-ākhar*, p. 117.
116. In Baalbek, the Sheikh ʿAbdallāh barracks were handed over to the army in August 1992 and the Khomeini Hospital was moved in July 1999 in order to turn over the locations of the École Normale where it had been housed.
117. See Chapter 5.
118. Usually cited as an example is the resumption of the Baalbek Festival, suspended for a time by the war, where Lebanese, Arab, and Western artists perform dance of all kinds, operas, classical music, jazz, and rock, without encountering any opposition from the party.
119. See Chapter 6.
120. The IRL and the international wire services reported a total of fifteen Israeli dead. See Rizq and Bazzī, *Sayyid al-qāda*, pp. 85–8.
121. Mustafā, *al-Muqāwama fī Lubnān*, pp. 494–6.
122. Gunning, 'Hizballah,' p. 177.
123. Mustafā, *al-Muqāwama fī Lubnān*, p. 494.
124. Ibid., pp. 492–3.
125. Hence in violation of the April 1996 Accord. Cf. infra.
126. Qāssem, *Hezbollah*, p. 162.
127. This account is taken from ibid., pp. 189–90.
128. Ibid., p. 190.
129. This section is taken from ibid., pp. 150–4 and 156–61, and Soueid, *Israël au Liban*, pp. 17–18.
130. Quoted by Qāssem, *Hezbollah*, pp. 150–1.
131. Ibid., p. 151. This strategy, relied on during the 1982 invasion, would be recycled for the 2006 war (see Chapter 8).

132. This announcement was corrected in 1998: the Israeli General Staff admitted having lost twenty-six men in Lebanon in 1996.
133. Gilles Kepel, *Jihad*, Paris: Gallimard, 2003, chapter "Des illusions de la paix aux attentats-suicides".
134. One of the most useful aspects of the camera was its suitability for reviewing the way the Resistance forces performed after every operation. Clips of some of the IRL operations have been studied at Russian military schools. See Mustafā, *al-Muqāwama fī Lubnān*, pp. 478–487.
135. The post of al-Dabsheh, manned by Israelis and Lahdists, had been targeted by several attacks. One operation in particular, on 10 June 1996, was filmed by al-Jihād al-I'lāmī; its outcome was deliberately not published until after the Israeli General Staff and government had announced their version to the Israeli public. "No one can forget Yitzhak Rabin's embarrassment after denying that the post of al-Dabsheh had fallen ... when the very next day the broadcast video showed that what he had said was false": ibid., pp. 488–9.
136. One Resistance cameraman reported that "There are resisters whose mission is to kill soldiers and their collaborators; for us, the mission is to hit the entire Israeli society, by means of the image ... it is the morale of Israeli society that we are killing." Ibid., p. 488.
137. Ibid., p. 486.
138. Observed by the author during the late 1990s. Amīn Mustafā also mentions these (ibid., p. 490).
139. For example, the release of the video of the operation at Sujud, carried out in September 1998, caused quite a stir among the Israeli political and military classes. It shows a lone IRL fighter taking over an Israeli position for a time. Wielding a knife, he then fights an Israeli paratrooper, and slaps the soldier before taking off and returning unharmed from his mission. In Israel the scene was described as a "catastrophe" and "shameful" (ibid., p. 496; Soueid, *Israël au Liban*, p. 24).
140. One of the IRL military leaders recalled how "Israeli television would take up this idea of Hezbollah superiority in the media war. They evoked the stories of the Vietnamese people's heroism against the American Yankees. Alon Ben-David, the correspondent for the Israeli Channel 10 TV channel at the time, acknowledged that the war in Lebanon was different, that it was a media war in which Hezbollah had chalked up some resounding victories. He cited as example the role played by al-Manār, the TV channel affiliated with Hezbollah, in showing the realities on the ground. He recounted the Israeli army's psychological defeats and how badly they impacted the morale of the soldiers and their families and raised that of the Hezbollah fighters. This explains why Israeli warplanes went after party media the way they did" (Mustafā, *al-Muqāwama fī Lubnān*, pp. 489–90).
141. Soueid, *Israël au Liban*, p. 17.
142. *LOLJ*, 7 April 2000.
143. In February 2000, 75 per cent of Israelis were in favour: *LOLJ*, 11 February and 13 May 2000. In 2007 the last months of the occupation as lived by Israeli troops were made into

a movie, *Beaufort*, directed by Joseph Cedar, depicting the pervasive fear gripping the Israeli soldiers in South Lebanon.

144. *LOLJ*, 7 March 2000.
145. Ibid., 21 March 2000.
146. Ibid., 14 January 2000.
147. Ibid., 11 and 20 March 2000.
148. Ibid., 10 April 2000.
149. In 1983 the Israeli army pulled back from the Shuf; the evacuated areas were turned over to the fighters of the PSP instead of the Lebanese army, in hopes of getting Walid Jumblatt to support the Agreement of 17 May. Jumblatt, who had ordered that not a single bullet should be fired at the Israeli invader in order to "avoid bloodshed", let his militia settle accounts with the Kataeb and the Lebanese Forces that had moved into the region behind the Israeli tanks in the summer of 1982. The result was hundreds of massacred Christian villagers.
150. For examples see *LOLJ*, 10, 19, and 20 May 2000.
151. Ibid., 31 March, 5, 6, 22 and 28 April, and 19 May 2000.
152. Ibid., 17 April 2000.
153. Ibid., 10 April 2000.
154. Lahd was no longer able to enter the town (Qāssem, *Hezbollah*, pp. 172–3).
155. Damage was estimated to be at least $40 million, and Lebanon was not able to restore its normal electricity supply until four or five months later: *LOLJ*, 9 February 2000.
156. Ibid., 24 May 2000.
157. Ibid., 15 May 2000.
158. Personal recollections of televised images of the Israeli retreat in May of 2000. The Israeli daily's *Yediot Aharonot* front page headline on 24 May read "Mom, we're out of Lebanon!" See also *LOLJ*, 24 May 2000.
159. The prohibition would be qualified as *taklīf sharʿī*, "religious duty". See Chapter 5.
160. Rmeish and Ain Ebel especially. Some acts of looting perpetrated by civilians were reported at Marjayoun, the former SLA and Israeli army base, as well as in neighbouring Christian enclaves. The villa of Antoine Lahd would also be looted, but members of the SSNP made the thieves return their loot: *LOLJ*, 25 May 2000.
161. Ibid.
162. Ibid., 31 May 2000.
163. It would seem that the Israeli authorities never responded to their demands. Among the problems getting in the way was nationality, including that of children born in Israel after the withdrawal. In any event, the $175 million compensation was reduced to $60 million, and paid out only to SLA members who were refugees in Israel: ibid., 29 May 2000.
164. Ibid.
165. Ibid.
166. For several months, demonstrators threw rocks at Israeli soldiers posted on the other side of the border fence, which caused them to open fire in retaliation.
167. Karrūbī had supported the creation of Hezbollah during the early 1980s.

168. *LOLJ*, 26 May 2000.
169. Ibid.
170. Muhammad Qbaysī, *al-Shahāda wal-Tahrīr* [Martyrdom and Liberation], Beirut: Dār al-Hānī, 2000, p. 223.
171. Count taken from the list of these fighters.
172. Or 1,800 according to the IRL. See Mustafā, *al-Muqāwama fī Lubnān*, p. 497.
173. Qbaysī, *al-Shahāda wal-tahrīr*, p. 213.
174. Mustafā, *al-Muqāwama fī Lubnān*, p. 498.

4. HEZBOLLAH, A SOCIAL ENTREPRENEUR?

1. See, among others, Judith Palmer Harik, *Hezbollah: The Changing Face of Terrorism*, London: I. B. Tauris, 2004 and Nizar Hamzeh, *In the Path of Hizbullah*, New York: Syracuse University Press, 2004.
2. This section relies on *Mawsūʿat Hizbillāh*, vol. XI.
3. Literally: the Welfare Association of the Foundation of the Martyr.
4. See p. 102.
5. *al-ʿAhd*, 6 Rabi al-Thani 1405 H (30 December 1984), p. 4.
6. Author's interview with a Hezbollah cadre who worked on archiving martyr biographies for the centre, 2009; author's interview with Dr Kinda Chaïb, expert in Lebanese Shiism, 2009—see her doctoral dissertation: *La culture du martyre au Liban-Sud depuis la fin des années 1970*, Paris, Université Panthéon-Sorbonne, 2014.
7. See www.atharshohada.org.
8. See www.alshahid.org, accessed 23 August 2009.
9. See www.alshahid.org, accessed 4 July 2008.
10. For more on the al-Mahdī schools see pp. 37, 110.
11. Catherine Le Thomas, "Les scouts al-Mahdî", in Mervin (ed.), *Le Hezbollah*, p. 173. According to Le Thomas, in early 2007 just 46 out of 2,400 pupils were the children of martyrs.
12. In 2009 the institute was described as a "faculty": *kulliyyat al-Rasūl al-aʿdham* (www.alshahid.org, accessed 23 August 2009).
13. Author's field observations made in early 2009, especially around Baalbek.
14. See www.aljarha.net, accessed 23 August 2009.
15. *Mawsūʿat Hizbillāh*, vol. XI.
16. This description of LAPL is based on the author's interview with its president in 2007.
17. Author's interview with the president of the LAPL, 2007.
18. Ibid.
19. This section is based on information published on the Association's website (www.hayaa.net, accessed 23 August 2009).
20. Not to be confused with the Lebanese agency of the same name. There are no institutional ties between the two organizations.
21. See www.hayaa.net, accessed 24 July 2008.
22. IHC checks oral hygiene, hearing, eyes, speech and motor skills, digestive tract, urinary

and genital systems, skin health, food habits, and psychological well-being, as well as proper vaccinations.

23. Salāh Ghandūr was an IRL fighter.
24. See www.hayaa.net, accessed 24 July 1008.
25. During its joint operations with IRL or when rescuing civilians under Israeli bombardments, IHC lost medics, doctors, nurses, and volunteers. IHC and Civil Defence facilities and vehicles were targeted on several occasions by the Israeli air force: in 1993, and again in 1996 and 2006. IHC had 32 killed and 45 wounded during Israeli operations between 1984 and 1996.
26. The last time IHC's website was checked (late 2012), the numbers for the 2006 offensive had still not been posted.
27. This description draws on *Mawsūʿat Hizbillāh*, vol. XI.
28. *al-ʿAhd*, 22 Dhu al-Hijja 1408 H (6 August 1988), p. 6.
29. See p. 111 for more on the al-Mahdī scouts.
30. *al-Safir*, 12 March 1009.
31. *Mawsūʿat Hizbillāh*, vol. XI. The discrepancy between the two dates is perhaps due to the difference between the date the Committee came into being and when it obtained its licence from the Lebanese government (a large portion of Hezbollah's social welfare institutions were licensed in the late 1980s).
32. *al-Safir*, 12 March 2009.
33. Statement by CIRS about itself in a booklet distributed in early 2008.
34. The programmes are listed on the back of the donation receipt.
35. *al-Safir*, 12 March 2009.
36. *Mawsūʿat Hizbillāh*, vol. XI.
37. Ibid. Unfortunately the citation lacks a date.
38. The CIRS calendar was free to contributors for many years; it has been sold since 2008.
39. Hassan Nasrallah himself is invited to these *iftār*s every year.
40. Included are those held annually in Baalbek's Roman citadel and in Nabatiyeh. These events are so successful that in 2005 the CIRS organized the "Great National Zajal Festival" at Tyre (with a venue for lease that is larger than Nabatiyeh's), where the country's champions competed.
41. This description relies on two interviews with the author in 2007 with the head of the Association's PR department. The quotes are his.
42. The name appearing below the Association's logo is a translation of the Iranian name Lijnat Imdād al-Imām al-Khumaynī (the Imam Khomeini Charity Committee). The official name was changed by the Lebanese government when it granted the licence.
43. The Advisory Centre for Studies and Documentation is a research and archive centre belonging to Hezbollah. In the beginning its missions were restricted to social and developmental studies. See Chapter 5.
44. See www.alemdad.net, accessed 27 July 2008.
45. Before the 2006 war, during which it was destroyed, it had received more than 100.
46. Some locations were opened prior to 1999, but did not take in children with Down syn-

drome, only those with learning disabilities. Today, the centres admit both categories of children.

47. *al-Safir*, 15 February 2010.
48. Cited by Palmer Harik, *Hezbollah*, pp. 92–3.
49. *al-Safir*, 15 February 2010.
50. *Mawsūʿat Hizbillāh*, vol. XI.
51. Author's interview with the principal of an al-Mahdī school, 2007.
52. The calculation is based on numbers posted on www.almahdischools.org accessed 30 August 2009. It excludes the students of the school at Ouzai (not available) and of the school in Qom (outside Lebanon.)
53. Author's field observation. To illustrate, in 2007–8, Lebanon's top national brevet (certificate) holder was a female student at al-Mahdī Baalbek.
54. Author's interview with an official of the Mobilization Unit for Education, 2007.
55. Ibid.
56. Le Thomas, "Les scouts al-Mahdî", p. 173.
57. See www.almahdiscouts.org, accessed 23 August 2009.
58. Le Thomas, "Les scouts al-Mahdî", p. 173.
59. *al-Akhbār*, 21 April 2010.
60. Author's field observation.
61. Naʿīm Qāsim, *Mujtamaʿ al-muqāwama* [The resistance society], Beirut: Maʿhad al-Maʿārif al-Hikmiyya, 2008, p. 67.
62. Author's field observations made on several occasions between 2006 and 2009.
63. Author's interview, 2007.
64. Qāsim, *Mujtamaʿ al-muqāwama*, pp. 62–5.
65. "Hezbollah has found a way to overcome the obstacles that create a sharp separation between men's and women's roles on the political, social, and combat levels. It has also been able to create an effective division of concerns, bringing the woman out of the shadows, isolation, and confinement in the home, so she can influence the Resistance's social and developmental structures": ibid., p. 65.
66. On Units and Hezbollah's internal organization, see Chapter 5.
67. *LOLJ*, 20 April 2005.
68. See Chapter 5.
69. Author's interview with a Sports Mobilization official, 2007.
70. Same.
71. Club website: www.alahed.com.
72. Author's interview with a club manager, 2007.
73. Ibid.
74. "They thought the old name was too long...": ibid.
75. Another top Lebanese club.
76. It was started by editorial writer Joseph Samaha, who wanted to establish a daily newspaper to support the Resistance. He published his first issue in August 2006. For more on

this see Lea Müller-Funk, "The political influence of al-Akhbar in Lebanon: partisans in search for a daily?" Masters 2 thesis, Paris, Institut d'Études Politiques, 2009–10, 130 pp.

77. See www.alintiqad.com. The last print issue is dated 30 May 2008 (no. 1269).
78. This section is based on two articles published in *al-Safir* on 24 and 28 December 2004.
79. Even though al-Manār today is only an FAII (financially and administratively independent institution). See Chapter 5.
80. The other stations started their newscasts at 8 p.m.
81. See Chapter 2.
82. He succeeded ʿAlī-Akbar Mohtashami in this post, which he would occupy from 1986 to 1997.
83. M. H. Akhtarī, *al-Sharq al-Awsat*, 15 May 2008.
84. The information would not be published in the Official Gazette until November 1998.
85. The LBC is the premier Lebanese TV broadcaster, today pro-March 14.
86. Refer to Part II.
87. Author's interview with the chief executive of the Department of Information for the Bekaa, 2009.
88. Refers to a speech by Nasrallah at Bint Jbeil in 2000, where he declared the Israeli army to be flimsier than a "spider's web".
89. Author's field observation.
90. *Le Figaro*, 22 August 2010.
91. Janine Clark, *Islam, Charity, and Activism*, Bloomington: Indiana University Press, 2004.
92. Qāsim, *Mujtamaʿ al-muqāwama*, pp. 66–7.
93. As already mentioned, it is generally conceded that between 1989 and 2005, that is, during the Rafsanjani and Khatami presidencies, the Iranian authorities made serious cuts to Hezbollah's funding.
94. Following the death of the *marjaʿ* in July 2010, his son, Sayyid ʿAlī Fadlallāh, took over the leadership of his office and his welfare associations.
95. Author's interview with the head of public relations of al-Imdād, 2007.
96. Ibid.
97. Author's interview with a surgeon providing medical care in one of the IHC hospitals, where he charged only 20 per cent of his normal fee for services rendered.
98. The rural families supported by al-Imdād are larger (a minimum of seven people).
99. See Chapter 9 and the Conclusion.
100. See the programme's website: www.waad-rebuild.com.
101. Mentioned here would be the Fund for the Displaced and the Fund for the South, monopolized by PSP and AMAL, respectively. They serve to maintain sectarian clientelist networks.
102. *LOLJ*, 12 April 2006. The number is probably inflated, at least partly by the number of employee family members.
103. The salaried staff of al-Imdād, for example, which is classified as a "large association" (assessed as such by the head of public relations), totalled ninety-one persons in Lebanon.

Turnover is extremely low, the same as in the party's other institutions. Author's interview, 2007.

104. Ibid.
105. An expression used by a member of the party base during an interview with the author.
106. Iman Farag, "Croyance et intérêt: réflexion sur deux associations islamiques", in Iman Farag and Alain Roussillon (eds.), *Modernisation et nouvelles formes de mobilisation sociale II*, Cairo: CEDEJ, 1992, pp. 127–40; Clark, *Islam, Charity, and Activism*.
107. Author's interview with the vice-president of al-'Ahd, 2007.
108. Author's interview, al-Imdād, 2007.
109. See www.alshahid.org, accessed 23 August 2009.
110. A recent example would be that of the direction of al-Mahdī school in Baalbek, which had the highest-scoring student for the national diploma in Lebanon in the summer of 2008. It placarded the prize winner's photo on a large number of billboards in the region for more than a month.
111. Hezbollah highly recommends its militants to wear their hair short.
112. "When we offered the job to Jasper, the German media insisted on showing him packing his suitcase, saying goodbye to his family, and getting on the plane just in case he didn't make it back! He himself had a good laugh! He knew very well that our club was linked to Hezbollah, he did a search on the internet, but he took it as a challenge; sometimes the Europeans approach it that way, like a *challenge* (*laughs*) ... And then he couldn't get over how kind we are to him, how "civilized" we are." Author's interview, 2007.
113. See www.hayaa.net, accessed 23 August 2009. Of the remains recovered by Hezbollah, a good number were those of Lebanese fighters who did not belong to the party. Mostly they were Sunni or Christian combatants.
114. A point that even the Israeli commanders remarked on and saluted.

5. HEZBOLLAH'S INTERNAL ORGANIZATION

1. Among other differences, Hezbollah is not a brotherhood. For the Muslim Brotherhood structure see Richard Mitchell, *The Society of the Muslim Brothers*, Oxford: Oxford University Press, 1993 [1969], p. 164; Olivier Carré and Gérard Michaud (Michel Seurat), *Les Frères musulmans: 1928–1982*, Paris: L'Harmattan, 2001. On al-Qā'ida see Gilles Kepel et al., *al-Qaida dans le texte*, Paris: PUF, 2005.
2. Buchta, *Who Rules Iran?*, p. 69.
3. See Harakat Amal, *Al-nidhām al-asāsī 2002* [The Amal Movement, *The basic regime 2002*]. Cf. p. 350.
4. See Chapter 6.
5. This description of Hezbollah's relationship to the field is drawn from the author's interviews with three senior Hezbollah leaders, 2007.
6. On the grouping categories of the FSP see Maurice Duverger, *Les partis politiques*, Paris: Armand Colin, 1976, pp. 71–2.
7. Hezbollah does not employ the concept of *usra* (family), peculiar to the Muslim Brotherhood.
8. It is easy to see why the LCP's *firqa* category was not copied. Hezbollah lacks the ideological

rapport that tends to link the communist parties to the world of work and business. The comment also applies to AMAL.

9. The case could be made that the "sector" corresponds to "district" (also translatable in Arabic by *qitāʿ*) of the Pasdaran that Wilfried Buchta (*Who Rules Iran?*, p. 69) mentions.
10. Naʿīm Qāsim, *Hizbullāh: al-manhaj, al-tajriba, al-mustaqbal* [Hezbollah: the way, the experience, the future], Beirut: Dār al-Hādī, 2002, 4th edn, p. 87.
11. The description of these councils is based on a series of the author's interviews with Hezbollah cadre, 2007.
12. See pp. 132, 136–8 for more on the Executive Council.
13. Most authors are fond of using the term "Politburo" for Hezbollah's Political Council. While the literal translation is acceptable, drawing an equivalence between the two organs is not. The Politburo (of the CP) is a decision-making organ, while the Political Council (Hezbollah) is an advisory and public-relations organ. Today the usage of the term is even more inappropriate (this is a council and no longer a bureau.)
14. The deputies elected on party slates who are not members do not sit in this council.
15. *al-Safir*, 17 August 2004.
16. The Congress did not exist before 1989. It took place biennially from that year until 1995 (1989, 1991, 1993, and 1995).
17. In 2007, taking into account the threats regularly issued against Hezbollah by Israel starting in the autumn of 2006, the party resolved to postpone its Congress (author's interview, 2007).
18. Author's interview, 2007.
19. "The Congress itself does not decide who is going to head up this or that council. It leaves the choice of how to divide up the positions to the seven who were elected. The rationale is to have the posts allocated by agreement between the elected members so that no one finds himself heading up a Council that goes against the grain" (author's interview, 2007).
20. This is the case, for example, with Hāshim Safiyeddīn, routinely presented as Nasrallah's heir apparent, who has been chairing the Executive Council for a number of years.
21. "This was not always the case but is now because the deputy secretary's work does not consist only of doing the secretary-general's work when the latter is absent or indisposed. The deputy secretary is a veritable *aide de camp* to the secretary, who may delegate some of his prerogatives to him from time to time. It therefore makes sense to let the secretary choose his own deputy secretary" (author's interview, 2007).
22. Buchta, *Who Rules Iran?*, p. 69; Chehabi, *Distant Relations*, p. 216.
23. To illustrate, the Central Information Unit in the Bekaa becomes the Department of Information.
24. Its complete name is Ittihād al-Wafāʾ-lil-ʿummāl wal-mustakhdimīn fī Lubnān (the Confederation of Loyalty to the Workers and Beneficiaries of Lebanon; see www.syndialwafaa.org).
25. On-site observation between February 2006 and December 2007.
26. According to a manager in the GAU during this era: "GAU started up in 1983, but the

real work started during 1984. You could say the framework became operational in 1984" (author's interview, 2007).

27. Ibid.
28. Author's interview with an MUE cadre, 2007.
29. Ibid.
30. Ghassān Tāhā, *Shīʿat Lubnān* [The Shiites of Lebanon], Beirut: Maʿhad al-Maʿārif al-Hikmiyya, 2006, p. 322.
31. Nasrallāh, *al-Harakāt al-hizbiyya fī Baʿalbak*, p. 185.
32. This issue was dated 29 Ramadan 1404.
33. For more information on Hezbollah print media see Bashir Saade, *Hizbullah and the Politics of Remembrance*, Cambridge: Cambridge University Press, 2016.
34. See www.alnour.com.lb, accessed 21 July 2002.
35. *al-Sharq al-Awsat*, 22 July 2009.
36. Ibid., 15 May 2008.
37. Author's interview with a cadre in Hezbollah's communications apparatus, 2007.
38. There was, for example, a "Martyred Ulema" competition, organized with help from the Foundation of the Martyr in the early 2000s. Texts presented dealt with biographies of clerics who had fallen as martyrs in fighting the Israeli army or AMAL combatants. Some of these texts were published in the form of elegant miniature boxed book sets, such as *Silsilat "Umarāʾ al-nasr wal-Tahrīr"* ["The princes of victory and the Liberation" collection], 11 booklets, Beirut: Jamʿiyyat al-Maʿārif al-Islāmiyya al-Thaqāfiyya, 2003.
39. Author's interview with a senior Hezbollah official, 2007. More generally, as things stand now, it appears that the unit is the contact inside Hezbollah for the Lebanese security forces, and also for UNIFIL.
40. Author's interview with a senior Hezbollah official, 2007.
41. Author's interview with a manager in Sports Mobilization, 2007.
42. Author's interview with a senior Hezbollah official, 2007.
43. A large portion of the FAIIs started as small work groups of modest means, part of what was then called the Unit of [General] Activities. "Growing to considerable size subsequently and having been given more important roles, they were split off and given boards of directors to make them easier and more effective to manage. This is the case, for example, with the al-Mahdī schools or Jihād al-Bināʾ" (author's interview with a management cadre in a Hezbollah FAII, 2007).
44. ACSD archives publications in Arab, French, and English languages.
45. Duverger, *Les partis politiques*, p. 174.
46. This section relies on extensive author's interview with rank-and-file members of Hezbollah, between 2006 and 2007.
47. To recall: "The Resistance did not resort to the military mobilization of women and did not seek to train and prepare women for direct combat. ... The number of young [men] ready to fight sufficed ... so why then involve women in the hostilities? The idea was to give the women reserve status for specific requirements and particular conditions, which,

by the way, conforms to religious prescriptions that reserve combat for men and not women": Qāsim, *Mujtamaʿ al-muqāwama*, p. 67.

48. Nizar Hamzeh has mentioned two ways, one of which he described as "horizontal" (*In the Path of Hizbullah*, pp. 75–76). What he describes does exist, but does not lead to party membership. It is, however, a procedure to join not Hezbollah but an FAII—bodies whose employee complement has many non-party employees, as already mentioned. Applicants will eventually be allowed to take jobs as sound engineers with al-Nūr, work as graphic designers for al-Manār, or teach English in an al-Mahdī school, but they will not automatically become party members.
49. Author's interview with a member of the Hezbollah base, 2006.
50. "These precautions are explained by the difficulties these parties experienced at inception, including efforts by the police to plant "stool pigeons". Hence, control through sponsors, background investigations and final evaluation by the section": Duverger, *Les partis politiques*, p. 130.
51. "Members do not get membership cards, in the first place, because they are not the only ones working to achieve the party's goals and, furthermore, because we do not want them to define themselves by a membership card": Qāsim, *Mujtamaʿ al-muqāwama*, p. 86. Qāsim also states that the party is wary of "partisan ties [that] risk engendering an *esprit de corps* that would undermine unity with non-members who nevertheless subscribe to the party's objectives": ibid., p. 85.
52. "The socialist sections normally meet monthly or semi-monthly. The meeting however is not like that of the committee: it is not just an electoral tactic, but also one of political education": Duverger, *Les partis politiques*, p. 71.
53. "There is also the case of an old woman, whose son and daughter-in-law were killed during an Israeli shelling and who took over the children's education. She could not take them to school every day for lack of transport. Members in my neighbourhood learned of it and told our leader about it. We immediately contacted a taxi driver who did school transport and charged reasonable prices. So, we put the old woman in touch with him, and he wound up taking the children to school daily and bringing them home": author's interview, 2007.
54. Ibid.
55. As expressed by a rank-and-file member to the author in 2007.
56. Author's interview with a *taʿbiʾa*, 2006.
57. Duverger, *Les partis politiques*, p. 100.
58. Ibid.
59. Ibid., p. 101.
60. Ibid.
61. Ibid., p. 112.
62. Ibid., p. 102.
63. Quoted in ʿAbdallāh Qasīr, *Wilāyat al-faqīh*, Beirut: Imam Khomeini Cultural Centre, *Silsilat al-Muʾtamarāt wal-Nadawāt al-Fikriyya* collection, no. 4, January 2005, p. 65.
64. Qāsim, *Hizbullāh*, p. 78.
65. Ibid., pp. 77–80.

66. Ibid., p. 80.
67. Qasīr, *Wilāyat al-faqīh*, p. 66.
68. Qāsim, *Hizbullāh*, p. 283.
69. Qasīr, *Wilāyat al-faqīh*, p. 66.
70. Qāsim, *Hizbullāh*, p. 78.
71. Qasīr, *Wilāyat al-faqīh*, p. 67.
72. Qāsim, *Hizbullāh*, pp. 77–8.
73. Qasīr, *Wilāyat al-faqīh*, p. 68.
74. Ibid., pp. 67–8.
75. Ibid., p. 69.
76. Ibid.
77. Sometimes also translated as "religious duty".
78. Qasīr, *Wilāyat al-faqīh*, p. 69.
79. "Experience has shown that the exit of some [Hezbollah members] and attempts at secession [by other members] of the party do not succeed in creating partisan splits; they translate consistently into an exit [from the sphere] of *wilāya* and turn out to be isolated, exceptional cases that do not succeed in provoking turmoil inside the Hezbollah organization": ibid., pp. 69–70.
80. See Nasrallah's speeches on the eve of the 2005 parliamentary elections, or his speech of 17 June 2009, in which he acknowledges having resorted to the *taklīf sharʿī* at the 2005 elections. He nevertheless stresses the fact that "the one and only time we had to order *taklīf sharʿī* for our base was in 2005, namely for the sole reason that the results of the election could have led to the *fitna*. To avoid this *fitna*, we invoked *taklīf sharʿī* before our base; the only time we talked about *taklīf sharʿī* was when we had voted for them [certain March 14 candidates]." This speech is available in its entirety on the party's website at www.moqawama.org.
81. See Chapter 9.

6. THE HASSAN NASRALLAH PHENOMENON

1. Ann R. Willner, *The Spellbinders: Charismatic Political Leadership*, New Haven and London: Yale University Press, 1984.
2. Ibid., p. 60.
3. Ibid., p. 60, 63.
4. See www.nndb.com, accessed 11 July 2009.
5. Ibid.
6. "Man huwa al-sayyid Hasan Nasrallāh? [Who is Sayyid Hassan Nasrallāh?]", *Nidāʾ al-Watan*, 31 August 1993 (English version accessible in Noe, *Voice of Hezbollah*, pp. 116–43); Roula Mouaffak, "Sayyid Nasrallah raconte Hassan", *Magazine*, no. 2090, 28 November 1997; Hasan Nasrallah, "al-Sayyid Hasan Nasrallāh" (French version on the blog of Alain Gresh: http://blog.mondediplo.net/2006-08-22-Hassan-Nasrallah-par-lui-meme, 18 July 2009).
7. *Mawsūʿat Hizbillāh*, vol. III. This is also stated in his biography posted on the party's official website (www.moqawama.org) and in the multimedia biography *al-Sīra al-dhātiyya*

li-samāhat al-sayyid Hasan Nasrallāh [Biography of His Excellency Sayyid Hassan Nasrallah], Beirut, 2007, DVD produced by Mu'assasat Hanā International and distributed by the Lebanese Cultural Centre.

8. The document *Mustaqbal al-usūliyya fī al-ʿālam al-ʿarabī* [The future of fundamentalism in the Arab world], Beirut: al-Markaz al-ʿArabī lil-Maʿlūmāt, 1993, p. 107 and Tawfīq al-Madīnī, *Amal wa Hizbullāh, fī halabat al-mujābahāt al-mahalliya wal-iqlīmmiyya* [AMAL and Hezbollah in the arena of local and regional confrontations], Damascus: al-Ahālī lil-Tibāʿa wal-Nashr wal-Tawzīʿ, 1999, p. 173, both give a date of 1953.
9. Mouaffak, "Sayyid Nasrallah raconte Hassan".
10. The imam prays in front of (Arabic, *amām*) the faithful. The anecdote is taken from *The Washington Post*, 16 July 2006.
11. "Man huwa al-sayyid Hasan Nasrallāh?"
12. Nasrallāh, "al-Sayyid Hasan Nasrallāh".
13. *Mawsūʿat Hizbillāh*, vol. III.
14. "Man huwa al-sayyid Hasan Nasrallāh?"
15. Ibid.
16. Ibid.
17. Nasrallāh, "al-Sayyid Hasan Nasrallāh".
18. Ibid.
19. "Man huwa al-sayyid Hasan Nasrallāh?"
20. Nasrallāh, "al-Sayyid Hasan Nasrallāh".
21. *al-Sīrah al-dhātiyyah li-samāhat al-sayyid Hasan Nasrallāh*. Nasrallah contradicts himself on this point: in the autobiography he wrote in 2006, he maintains that he addressed al-Mūsawī in classical Arabic (Nasrallāh, "al-Sayyid Hasan Nasrallāh"). But thirteen years earlier, in an interview he gave to *Nidā' al-Watan*, he had asserted that he spoke with him in Iraqi-tinged Lebanese dialect.
22. Nasrallāh, "al-Sayyid Hasan Nasrallāh".
24. *Min al-Sadr ilā Nasrallāh* [From al-Sadr to Nasrallah], Beirut: Manshūrāt al-Ridā, 2007, p. 292.
25. In December1974 five ulema were hanged by the regime. These executions marked the start of a serious deterioration in relations between the Iraqi authorities and clerical circles. In February 1977 a march organized for ʿĀshūrā' in which several tens of thousands took part was broken up brutally by the army. Muhammad Bāqir al-Sadr was arrested in June 1979 and hanged in April 1980. See Pierre-Jean Luizard, *La question irakienne*, Paris: Fayard, 2002, Chapter 4.
26. "Man huwa al-sayyid Hasan Nasrallāh?"
27. A name sometimes used for the twelfth *imām*, *al-imām al-Mahdī*.
28. Mouaffak, "Sayyid Nasrallah raconte Hassan".
29. One of the IRL battalions.
30. Nasrallāh, "al-Sayyid Hasan Nasrallāh".
31. *al-Sīrah al-dhātiyyah li-samāhat al-sayyid Hasan Nasrallāh*.
32. Ibid.

33. Nasrallāh, "al-Sayyid Hasan Nasrallāh".
34. "Man huwa al-sayyid Hasan Nasrallāh?".
35. *Mawsūʿat Hizbillāh*, vol. III.
36. Mouaffak, "Sayyid Nasrallah raconte Hassan"; Nasrallāh, "al-Sayyid Hasan Nasrallāh".
37. "Man huwa al-sayyid Hasan Nasrallāh?"; Nasrallāh, "al-Sayyid Hasan Nasrallāh".
38. Nasrallāh, "al-Sayyid Hasan Nasrallāh".
39. *Mawsūʿat Hizbillāh*, vol. III. J. Palmer Harik, echoing M. Ranstorp, goes so far as to maintain that Nasrallah would have been elected secretary-general during the Congress, but the departing secretary-general, Subhī al-Tufaylī, is supposed to have protested at this decision so vehemently, threatening a split, that Nasrallah of his own accord withdrew in favour of his mentor, ʿAbbās al-Mūsawī (Ranstorp, *Hizb'Allah in Lebanon*, p. 75; Palmer Harik, *Hezbollah*, p. 59). This version of the Congress proceedings has nevertheless never been reported by the party, and al-Tufaylī himself denies it (author's interview with al-Tufaylī, 2008).
40. Nasrallāh, "al-Sayyid Hasan Nasrallāh".
41. Ibid.
42. These accusations became even more virulent after 1995, after Nasrallah's nomination for the post of *wakīl* to Khamenei.
43. Hamzeh, *In the Path of Hizbullah*, p. 69.
44. Personal recollection of the event.
45. Author's recollections and those of party supporters and others with whom I discussed the subject in the spring of 2008.
46. This was the first time that the IRL had fired rockets into northern Israel since it had first carried out attacks in its own name, that is, since 1984. The LNRF had taken responsibility for the most recent rocket salvo into Israeli territory. See al-Ezzi, *L'invasion israélienne du Liban*, p. 23.
47. As a fifty-year-old Shiite professor and former Nasserite phrased it (to the author) at the time.
48. See Chapter 3.
49. Even if, as already mentioned, this is partially incorrect.
50. See Chapter 3.
51. Even though a large number of these texts were cribbed from each other, at least in part if not entirely. See Nasrīn Idrīs, *ʿArīs aylūl* [The September bridegroom], Beirut: Dār al-Amīr, 2001; *Min al-Sadr ilā Nasrallāh*; and *Nasrallāh (Nasr [min] Allāh)* [Nasrallah (Victory from God)], Beirut: Manshūrāt al-Ridā, 2009.
52. This is Nasrallah's wife. Her eldest son being named Hādī, she is addressed as Umm Hādī, "mother of Hādī", as is customary in the East.
53. *Min al-Sadr ilā Nasrallāh*, pp. 344–5.
54. Ibid., pp. 345–6.
55. Ibid., pp. 368–9.
56. *al-Safir*, 16 September 1997.
57. Ibid.
58. *Min al-Sadr ilā Nasrallāh*, pp. 361–4.

59. See Chapter 3.
60. Qāsim, *Hizbullāh*, p. 175.
61. The entire speech is available in *Min al-Sadr ilā Nasrallāh*, pp. 351–8.
62. Willner, *The Spellbinders*, p. 92.
63. Qāsim, *Hizbullāh*, p. 174.
64. Ibid.
65. Worth mentioning at this point is an interview published by *Magazine*, the Lebanese French-language weekly. In this piece it is the man who intrigues, not his political opinion (Mouaffak, "Sayyid Nasrallah raconte Hassan"). It reads: "Charismatic, this man has a soul dipped in steel. He easily copes with an ever-present threat that would wreck the nerves of any ordinary citizen. He knows that, at any moment, Israel might try to liquidate him, his family, his wife, their children ... as was the case with his predecessor, Sayyed Abbas Mussaoui." The journalist describes Nasrallah "as morally very strong", portrays his attitude as "stoic," but "without any affectation" in the face of losing his son. "You wonder about it when you see him on TV and the direct contact confirms it: Hassan Nasrallah is a strong person. He impresses not by putting on airs—he is first of all very approachable—but by his logic, and his well-honed reasoning. He is a man of arguments whose strength of conviction is embellished with a frequent smile."
66. Ibid.
67. For example: "Will Hezbollah agree to recover Hādī's remains in exchange for the body of an Israeli soldier it is holding? The systematically incorrect Israeli understanding of the Arab world has led the Israeli leaders to formulate a theory that Hezbollah will be in a hurry to make the exchange. But a (correct) understanding of the Shiite community and Hezbollah's manner of operating leads in all certainty to the opposite conclusion: Hādī's remains will be the last ones that Hezbollah will claim as part of an exchange of whatever kind": *Haaretz*, 15 September 1997.
68. A Qur'an sura recited as a prayer by Muslims.
69. His image was considerably tarnished in certain Arab countries, starting with Syria, from 2011 on during the revolutions of the Arab Spring.
70. The IRL lost 1,373 fighters during the Israeli occupation.
71. Among the texts citing these nicknames, see "Dhātiyyat Nasrallāh" [Nasrallah's personality], in *Min al-Sadr ilā Nasrallāh*, pp. 332–7. The comparison with Che Guevara was also remarked upon by American journalist Robin Wright (*The Washington Post*, 16 July 2006).
72. Mouaffak, "Sayyid Nasrallah raconte Hassan".
73. "Nasrallāh, shakhsiyyatuhu" [Nasrallah. His Personality], in *Min al-Sadr ilā Nasrallāh*, pp. 294–8.
74. A reference to the fact that in Shiite history, it is Hussein who was the rebel and fighter, while Hassan was the resigned submissive.
75. An article took up this link between Nasrallah's first name and his handsomeness: "Nasrallāh, shakhsiyyatuhu".
76. One of the principles of colour theory holds that one way to emphasize a certain colour

component is by placing another colour close by that lacks that component. So, to make a green object in a painting look more yellow, the painter will place a blue object next to it.

77. Author's interview with a Hezbollah cadre, Beirut, April 2007.
78. Quoted in Sālim Shakkūr, *Nasrallāh, al-rajul alladhī yakhtasir ummah* [Nasrallah, the man who sums up a nation], Beirut: Manshūrāt al-Fajr, 2006, vol. I.
79. Willner, *The Spellbinders*, p. 7.
80. On the attempts to assassinate Nasrallah see the *al-Intiqād* dossier of 14 April 2006, no. 1157 and that of *al-Safir*, 29 December 2006.
81. See Chapter 3. The expression of this wish was followed a few months later by the creation of the LBRIO (Lebanese Brigades to Resist the Israeli Occupation).

7. "NEW MIDDLE EAST", "CEDAR REVOLUTION" (2000–2006)

1. Passed on 19 March 1978, following the first Israeli invasion. It required Tel Aviv to withdraw its troops from Lebanese territory and created the UN Interim Force in Lebanon (UNIFIL).
2. The Israeli army tried in this way to get information on one of its pilots, Ron Arad, whose plane was shot down over Lebanon in 1986 and whom Dīrānī would be responsible for guarding for several years. Tel Aviv also hoped to use the two men for recovering the bodies of three Israeli soldiers killed during fighting with the Syrian army in 1982.
3. *LOLJ*, 9 October 2000. The three Israeli soldiers were actually killed during the kidnapping operation. However, Hezbollah did not divulge this fact until the actual exchange later, not wanting to impair their bargaining leverage with the Israelis while negotiating the terms of an eventual exchange. The calculus was that Hezbollah could extract more concessions from the Israelis to release a greater number of prisoners in return for receiving the three Israeli soldiers alive instead of in body bags.
4. Ibid.
5. Ibid., 16 October 2000.
6. Ibid., 17 October 2000.
7. Ibid.
8. The date since then was added to the calendar of Hezbollah celebrations as the "Day of Liberty".
9. Ibid., 26 January 2004.
10. An allusion to the fact that Michel Seurat and William Higgins, suspected in the West of having been taken hostage by Hezbollah during the 1980s, had died for lack of medical care when ill.
11. Interview excerpted in *LOLJ*, 29 January 2004.
12. *LOLJ*, 17 and 18 July 2008. He was killed (most probably) in an Israeli airstrike targeting the building where he lived in Damascus, Syria, on 19 December 2015.
13. He was accused of having collected information on gas and electrical power plants and infrastructure plans "of a kind to threaten the national security of the Jewish state". His Jewish mother's family had emigrated to Israel in 1967. Born the following year, he had left Lebanon after the war, ostensibly seeking work and a better future (*LOLJ* in its 28 May

2008 issue stated that he left during the Israeli invasion of 1982; in its 31 May edition, however, the daily has him leaving for Israel in 1990, which is not consistent with his age at the time.) He married an Israeli Jewish woman of Russian origin. He gave up his Israeli citizenship after his conviction. His mother remained in Lebanon and always refused any association with Israel, openly supporting the IRL instead.

14. His was a complex case in view of the fact that Tel Aviv denied holding him in any of its jails, while an association of Lebanese captives and Hezbollah believed him to be held prisoner there.
15. *LOLJ*, 30 January 2004.
16. A play on the name of the 2006 Operation Truthful Pledge. See Chapter 8.
17. In early October 1988 the Lebanese Forces occupied North Metn, the Gemayel fiefdom, and took control of the region's military positions. Amin Gemayel was placed under house arrest.
18. In March 1989 the general launched a "War of Liberation" against the Syrian army. The clashes only ended when the Arab League succeeded in negotiating a ceasefire on 23 September. The six-month War of Liberation left more than 1,000 dead, 5,000 wounded, and damages estimated at a billion US dollars.
19. To all appearances, the assassination was perpetrated by Samir Geagea's Lebanese Forces as part of competition between Maronite forces.
20. Under the Syrians, the Christians of the KRM or the Lebanese Forces expressed their discontent, first by boycotting the 1992 elections and then, to a lesser extent, those of 1996 and 2000.
21. *LOLJ*, 1 May 2001.
22. *LOLJ*, 28 May 2004.
23. *al-Safir*, 17 June 2004. The Hezbollah leadership demanded an investigation through the CGTL. Concluding that the response was unsatisfactory, Hezbollah withdrew from the Federation the following month.
24. *LOLJ*, 17 September 2001.
25. Ibid.
26. "1. Arrest terrorists in your territory and bring them to justice; 2. Stop the movement of terrorists to and from your country; 3. Disclose your information on terrorists to your partners in the international community; 4. Hand over or expel persons whose extradition is sought by third countries; 5. Adopt an uncompromising language against terrorism, regardless of its stated objectives; 6. Support initiatives in the international fight against terrorism under United Nations auspices and other international bodies; 7. End all accommodation of states or entities that support terrorism": ibid., 19 September 2001.
27. The hijacking was claimed at the time by an "Organization of the World's Oppressed", which Western intelligence agencies considered to be a Hezbollah front.
28. *LOLJ*, 6 November 2001.
29. Ibid., 10 November 2001.
30. Ibid., 15 December 2001.
31. Ibid., 12 January 2002.

32. Ibid., 15 January 2002.
33. Ibid., 22 January 2002.
34. Ibid., and 8 August 2002.
35. Speech by Richard Armitage to the United States Institute of Peace Conference, 5 September 2002.
36. *LOLJ*, 10 September 2002.
37. Ibid., 11 September 2002.
38. Ibid., 3 July 2002.
39. Ibid., 12 January 2002.
40. Ibid., 20 June 2002.
41. Ibid., 12 March 2002.
42. Ibid., 20 June 2002.
43. For more details see Olivier Koch, "'L'affaire *al-Manār*' en France", in Mervin (ed.), *Le Hezbollah*, pp. 47–64.
44. Author's field observation, 2005.
45. This vote took place following testimony before the Congress by Michel Aoun in September 2003, during which he vehemently attacked Syrian policy in Lebanon.
46. *LOLJ*, 3 September 2004.
47. The final count was 18 dead and 220 wounded: ibid., 23 February 2005.
48. Ibid., 15 February 2005.
49. The square was so named in memory of the Arab nationalists who were hanged there by the Ottomans on 6 May 1916.
50. Although he is close to the Syrian regime, his positions on the domestic political scene remain moderately aligned with those of Damascus.
51. *LOLJ*, 7 March 2005.
52. According to some reports there were 400,000: ibid., 9 March 2005.
53. Ibid., 15 March 2005.
54. For example, see the speech by Bahia Hariri, Rafic's sister, partially reprinted in ibid.
55. See the reportage on the day's events in ibid.
56. After the 2006 war it would be Hezbollah's turn to call March 14 "Israeli agents".
57. *LOLJ*, 19 January 2005.
58. News at 8 p.m., LBCI, 9 March 2005. My emphasis.
59. No newspaper reported this part of the speech. However, a number of articles referred to it, such as the one in *al-Nahār* of 17 March 2005 reporting on the demonstration that the remark provoked in Nabatiyeh some days later.
60. *LOLJ*, 9 March 2005.
61. The best example are texts by the journalist Samir Kassir, who was assassinated on 2 June 2005. Some of them have been collected in Samir Kassir, *Liban: un printemps inachevé*, Paris: Actes Sud, 2006.
62. In particular, military families and supporters of military circles had difficulty finding Geagea's newly legalistic image credible: the War of Liberation in the late 1980s, during which the Lebanese army led by Michel Aoun had faced a Syrian army supported by

Geagea's Lebanese Forces, created in these circles—especially Christian ones—the image of a clear demarcation between a legalistic Christianism represented by Aoun (lumped together with the institution that he commanded back then) and a militant Christianism embodied by Geagea that was hostile to the state.

63. *LOLJ*, 12 May 2005.
64. Telecommunications was a key ministry for the majority, for the Commission of Inquiry would soon use its archives and documentation—in particular, SIM cards and telephone logs—in its efforts to identify Rafic Hariri's assassins.
65. Starting the first week of July, for "reasons of security", and following the "discovery of arms trafficking from Lebanon to Syria", Damascus slowed the crossing by Lebanese trucks over the Syria–Lebanon border, sometimes holding them up for weeks. The blockade soon expanded to Lebanon's territorial waters, with several Lebanese fishermen arrested. Then, in the spring, the Syrian regime demanded that Lebanon "pay penalties for the abuses committed against Syrian workers".
66. See Nasrallah's speech on 8 March 2005, available on the party's website: www.moqawama.org.
67. *LOLJ*, 21 July 2005.
68. Ibid., 25 July 2005. Here referring to the naturalization of Palestinian refugees in Lebanon.
69. This indulgence would not be repeated the following year: the deteriorating relationship between Hezbollah and the government encouraged the latter to restore 25 May to the list of official state holidays.
70. *Le Figaro*, 20 July 2005; *LOLJ*, 21 July 2005.
71. Some among the Israeli leadership had already stated, a short time after the assassination, that Hezbollah was implicated in Hariri's murder: *LOLJ*, 17 February 2005.
72. Ibid., 27 August 2005.
73. Ibid., 19 October 2005.
74. Ibid., 21 October 2005.
75. Ibid., 28 October 2005.
76. *al-Safir*, 11 November 2005.
77. Nasrallah acknowledged in an interview on 23 December that the discord had its real roots in Resolution 1559 (*LOLJ*, 24 December 2005).
78. Ibid., 7 November 2005.
79. Ibid., 18 November 2005.
80. Speech dated 25 November 2005. An excerpt can be found in *LOLJ*, 26 November 2005.
81. In early December the Commission was expected to be working for at least another six months on the investigation. Hence, in the eyes of the party leadership, there was no need for haste in setting up an ICT. Hezbollah tried to beat March 14 at its own game by stating that "the problem of the Lebanese judiciary has always been in the investigation, not in the judgment". The party was thus saying that it was prepared to accept an international inquiry to make it a credible investigation, then having the trial conducted by the Lebanese legal system, thus providing an opportunity, according to the party, to "rebuild the rule of law"—one of the main slogans of March 14—whereas going the ICT route would "deal a blow to the Lebanese judicial system": ibid., 5 December 2005.

82. Ibid., 2 December 2005.
83. President of 'Ulamā' Jabal 'Āmil, an association of Shiite clerics close to Hezbollah. See Chapter 1.
84. *LOLJ*, 21 December 2005.
85. Ibid., 3 February 2006.
86. Ibid., 15 and 24 February 2005.
87. Ibid. and 25 July 2005.
88. Ibid., 7 September 2005.
89. Ibid., 17 December 2005.
90. See Chapter 10.
91. *LOLJ*, 16 January 2006. Several days later, faced by a very marked reaction in the party, he backtracked by claiming he had meant "the arms of Rafic Hariri's assassins and of the pro-Syrian Palestinian militias". During meetings of the Dialogue Table in the spring of 2006, however, he confessed to Nasrallah that he had indeed been talking about the IRL's weapons.
92. Ibid., 13 February 2006.
93. Ibid., 9 and 16 January 2006.
94. Ibid., 16 January 2006 and 27 December 2007.
95. See Chapter 9.
96. Arriving in Beirut on 7 May, he favoured his admirers, come to welcome him with noisy enthusiasm, with a "Hey, shut the f**k up!", shocking both those present and television viewers (*LOLJ*, 9 May 2005). On being interviewed, he referred to the capital as "East Beirut" and "West Beirut", two terms harking back to the civil war period (when the capital was divided into two zones with different confessional majorities that waged war against each other), which the Lebanese had stopped using since the capital's reunification as Bayrūt al-Kubrā, Greater Beirut, after the war.
97. Here "March 14" refers to the Syrian withdrawal—not the Sunni–Maronite reconciliation that Aoun considered as embodied in the spontaneous assembly of 14 February.
98. *LOLJ*, 7 June 2005. Koraytem is the neighborhood where Hariri (Sunni) lives in Beirut and Mukhtara is the village where Jumblatt (Druze) resides in the Shuf.
99. During the parliamentary elections, Aoun chose to present his candidacy and that of his partisans not on opposition lists but on rival lists alongside certain pro-Syrian parties.

8. THE THIRTY-THREE-DAY WAR: 12 JULY–14 AUGUST 2006

1. *LOLJ*, 22 July 2006.
2. The operation initially was to be called "Freedom for Samir Quntar and his fellow prisoners", but the name was judged to be too long.
3. The Israeli version claiming that the kidnapping took place on Israel's territory would play in the Western press. Some accounts suggest that the patrol was on Israeli territory, came under fire from Lebanon, and an IRL commando squad then crossed the border for a few minutes to snatch the two soldiers (*LOLJ*, 14 July 2006). In its defence, the party always maintained that the operation was conducted in Lebanon, a version supported by Lebanese

law enforcement, and also by UNIFIL: "According to the Lebanese police, two Israeli soldiers were captured on Lebanese territory, in the Aita al-Shaab region, near the border with Israel, where an Israeli unit had penetrated in mid-morning" (*Le Monde*, 12 July 2006).

4. *LOLJ*, 15 July 2006.
5. Ibid., 13 July 2006.
6. *al-Safir*, 13 July 2006.
7. The operation was initially called "Just Punishment", but was renamed soon after the start.
8. In Lebanon it was called the July War (Harb Tammūz), in Israel the Second Lebanese War, and on al-Jazeera the Sixth Israeli–Arab War.
9. I spent the entire war in Baalbeck, one of the conflict's hottest spots. The account in this chapter relies on official data in the Lebanese daily newspapers and various academic studies and articles. But it mainly employs participant observation and material that I gathered during the conflict.
10. *LOLJ*, 2 August 2010.
11. Ibid.
12. See pp. 213, 297.
13. *LOLJ*, 14 July 2006.
14. Ibid., 19 July 2006.
15. Ibid., 21 July 2006.
16. *al-Safir*, 21 July 2006.
17. *LOLJ*, 17 and 27 July 2006.
18. Ibid., 7 August 2006.
19. In the city of Baalbek the Sheikh Habīb and al-ʿAsayra quarters, for example, supposedly adjoining a handful of houses belonging to Hezbollah cadres, were entirely destroyed and seeded with cluster bombs. No Hezbollah cadre lost his life there (most having evacuated the city even before hostilities began), while civilians who had nothing to do with the party perished by the dozen.
20. *al-Safir*, 26 July 2006.
21. Reported in the Lebanese press and television.
22. *LOLJ*, 31 July 2006.
23. The story of the Marjayoun barracks had several versions.
24. *LOLJ*, 19 and 20 July 2006.
25. 230 rockets on 2 August (ibid., 3 August 2006) and 250 on 11 August (ibid., 12 August 2006).
26. See www.moqawama.org.
27. *LOLJ*, 7 August 2006.
28. Ibid., 11 August 2006. An Egyptian commentator on al-Jazeera told of the discovery by the Israeli army of these tunnels during the ground offensive: "The Israeli soldiers could not figure out where the Hezbollah fighters that ambushed them came from, to the point where they thought they emerged from the sewers!" (Personal log).
29. *LOLJ*, 20 July 2006.

30. Ibid.
31. Ibid.
32. Ibid., 21 July 2006.
33. The Israeli army in subsequent weeks conducted a series of sweeps into villages such as Kfar Kila, Taybeh, Deir Mimas, Adayseh, Hula, and Mays al-Jabal. Each time, the IRL stood its ground.
34. *LOLJ*, 27 July 2006.
35. Ibid., 10 August 2006.
36. An expression coined by the Lebanese press. A Merkava is an Israeli tank.
37. *al-Safir*, 13 August 2006; *LOLJ*, 14 August 2006 ("On the first day of the ground operation ... twenty-four Israeli soldiers were killed. It turned into the bloodiest day for the Israeli army since the start of fighting in Lebanon on 12 July").
38. *Libération*, 11 August 2008. Lebanese and Arab television stations both reported this number. *Le Monde*, on 14 August, mentioned 30,000 soldiers.
39. "We estimate that Hezbollah lost on the order of 600 combatants and we suspect that another 600 were wounded, so 1,000 to 1,200 out of 2,500, announced ... Shimon Peres, after the war": *LOLJ*, 16 August 2006.
40. The exact number of IRL combatants is unknown. Circles close to Hezbollah estimate them at around 5,000.
41. Others were stationed in the country's other Shiite towns and villages, to make sure they were defended in case of attack.
42. See Chapters 10 and 12.
43. *LOLJ*, 25 July 2006.
44. On 16 August it was possible to read in *LOLJ*: "'After the end of hostilities, Israel continued its psychological war against Hezbollah with air drops over Lebanon of thousands of car air fresheners mocking its leader, Hassan Nasrallah,' reported *Yediot Aharonot* yesterday. Sayyid Nasrallah's head wearing his famous black turban emerges above these air fresheners that are shaped like a Lebanese cedar and below is written in Arabic: 'You can recover the scent of cedar if you rid yourself of the one who destroyed Lebanon,' the newspaper reported next to a photo. The Israeli Air Force dropped 25,000 of these air fresheners."
45. Author's field observation.
46. These messages were written in poor Arabic, and some words are unclear.
47. The Masnaʿ passage is the main crossing point between Lebanon and Syria. It is located near Chtoura (Central Bekaa).
48. Ironically, the holes in the highway are the ones made by the Israeli army.
49. *LOLJ*, 13 July 2006. From 13 July on, after rockets landed on Haifa, Israeli defence minister Amir Peretz vowed to "break Hezbollah" and declared that Israel would not permit it to return to the positions occupied along the border before start of the conflict (ibid., 14 July 2006). Some days later, he clarified that he would no longer tolerate the presence of Hezbollah fighters near the border (ibid., 20 July 2006).
50. Ibid., 15 July 2006.
51. Ibid., 24 July 2006.

52. Ibid.
53. Ibid.
54. Ibid.
55. Ibid.
56. Ibid., 25 July 2006.
57. Ibid.
58. Ibid., 27 July 2006.
59. Ibid., 10 August 2006.
60. Ibid., 14 August 2006. My emphasis.
61. Ibid., 14 and 29 August 2006.
62. Ibid., 13 July 2006.
63. Ibid., 17 July 2006.
64. "1. A commitment to release Lebanese and Israeli prisoners through the channel of the International Committee of the Red Cross; 2. Withdrawal of the Israeli army behind the "Blue Line" (drawn by the UN between Lebanon and Israel) and the return of displaced persons to their villages; 3. An undertaking by the Security Council to place the Shebaa Farms sector under United Nations jurisdiction; 4. Extending the authority of the Lebanese government in its territory through deployment of its own legitimate armed forces; 5. Reinforcing the number, equipment, mandate and scope of operations of the international UN forces operating in southern Lebanon in so far as necessary to carry out urgent humanitarian and rescue operations; 6. A UN commitment to implement the Armistice Agreement signed by Lebanon and Israel in 1949; 7. The international community's commitment to support Lebanon on all levels and help it bear the tremendous burden resulting from the human, social and economic tragedy that has afflicted it": ibid., 27 July 2006.
65. "The head of the PSP accuses Damascus of trying to "lay hands" on the country" (ibid., 14 July 2006); "Lebanon is held hostage to orders from Syria, says Hamadeh" (ibid.); "Jumblatt: 'Assad has managed to sow chaos in Lebanon, I congratulate him'" (ibid., 20 July 2006); "Geagea: 'The timing of the battle is bound to a regional agenda'"(ibid., 24 July 2006); "Hamadeh: 'The beginning of an Iranian–American conflict'" (ibid., 29 July 2006); "'Syria wants to regain international stature with Lebanese blood'"(ibid., 5 August 2006); "Gemayel: "Tehran wants to influence the Israeli–Arab conflict"" (ibid., 7 August 2006).
66. Ibid., 15 July 2006.
67. Ibid., 19 July and 5 August 2006.
68. Ibid., 19 July 2006.
69. It would transfer these weapons through the United Kingdom: al-Arabiya, News at 2 p.m., 29 July 2006.
70. "'Yesterday in Rome, we indeed received the green light to continue our operations until Hezbollah is no longer present in southern Lebanon and is disarmed,' stated Haim Ramon, the Israeli minister of justice, on military radio": *LOLJ*, 28 July 2006.
71. Ibid., 1 August 2006.
72. Tony Blair and Angela Merkel threw their support behind an end to the hostilities "as soon as possible": ibid.

73. Ibid.
74. For the reasons for this, see Chapter 11.
75. The American authorities supported the Israeli refusal to withdraw from South Lebanon until after the deployment of an international force, while the Lebanese government demanded its departure as soon as the ceasefire was proclaimed: *LOLJ*, 7 August 2006.
76. "An Israeli official Thurdsay evening underlined that the issue of the Shebaa Farms should not be part of the resolution project ... 'This resolution project has been distorted as a result of the intervention by Lebanon under pressure from Hezbollah. The discussions have begun to look like haggling with a Lebanese rug merchant. We will not fall into this trap,' stated M. Pazner to AFP": ibid., 12 August 2006.
77. Ibid., 8 September 2006.
78. Ibid., 8 August 2006.
79. The end to hostilities was officially planned for 08.00 a.m. (Beirut and Tel Aviv time). In Baalbek it was not until 08.45 that the last Israeli aeroplane stopped shelling the town and turned south. Author's field observation.
80. *LOLJ*, 15 August 2006.
81. This refers to those fleeing from northern Israel towards the south; it is the first time that Israelis in such numbers had to flee deep into their country under the IRL threat.
82. *Report of the Commission of Inquiry on Lebanon pursuant to Human Rights Council resolution* S-2/1* (http://www.cggl.org/publicdocs/20061205HRC.pdf, accessed 15 October 2010). These numbers would later be revised upward, particularly after explosions of cluster bombs that continued to kill and injure people in Lebanon. AFP reported in a note dated 4 April 2008 that between the end of the war and April 2008, 40 people were killed and 252 wounded by Israeli bombs that had been scattered in 2006.
83. *LOLJ*, 15 August 2006.
84. Ibid.
85. Ibid., 18 August 2006.
86. Associated Press, 15 December 2006; a ratio of 1:2 of soldiers to fighters.
87. *LOLJ*, 16 August 2006.
88. Ibid., 15 August 2006.
89. Michel Goya, "Dix millions de dollars le milicien", *Politique étrangère*, no. l, Spring 2007, p. 192.
90. See Uri Benziman, "Shell shock", *Haaretz*, 24 December 2006.
91. Goya, "Dix millions de dollars le milicien".
92. *LOLJ*, 14 August 2006.
93. Of the initial 15,000 troops planned for the new UNIFIL (the number was lowered at the end of October to between "6,000 and 7,000 men total"), Italy planned first to send 3,000 soldiers, then 2,000; France, 2,000; Germany a maximum of 2,400, including 1,500 naval personnel; and Spain, 950 (ibid., 16, 22, 26, and 29 August and 21 September 2006).
94. See Chapter 3.
95. *LOLJ*, 18 August 2006; *al-Safir*, 22 August 2006.
96. *LOLJ*, 23 August 2006.

97. Ibid., 28 August 2006.
98. As the attacks by Sunni Islamist networks on the Blue Helmets proved in June and July 2007 and again in January 2008.
99. *LOLJ*, 7 August 2006.
100. Hervé Pierre, *Le Hezbollah: un acteur incontournable de la scène internationale?* Paris: L'Harmattan, 2008, p. 22.
101. *LOLJ*, 28 August 2006.
102. The most distant town reached by IRL Katushyas was Afula, south of Haifa, 90 kilometres from the border.
103. "'What we did was insane and monstrous. We carpeted entire villages with cluster bombs.' These words come from a commander of the Israeli army who yesterday confirmed to the Israeli daily *Haaretz* that his forces used cluster and phosphorus bombs and shells. The commander said that more than 1,800 cluster bombs containing a total of 1.2 million bomblets were dropped over Lebanon. ... The United Nations estimates that some 40 per cent of the bombs (nearly 500,000 mines) did not explode on impact, presenting risk for people that they will be exposed to for a long time, added the newspaper" (*LOLJ*, 13 September 2006). "It will take thirty million dollars and a little over a year to clean up southern Lebanon" (ibid., 27 September 2006).

9. ESCALATION, COLLAPSE, AND TEMPORARY STATUS QUO: AUGUST 2006—JANUARY 2011

1. The slogan appeared in this form originally, but a few weeks after the war it was reformulated as *Nasr(un) min Allāh* (a victory sent by God), which allowed plays on words in Hezbollah communication campaigns and on Nasrallah's name (*Nasr Allāh*, God's victory).
2. For a few months after the war there was a debate in Lebanon, in Israel, and in the West on the question of who had emerged as the victor, Hezbollah or the Israeli army.
3. See Chapter 11.
4. Halutz was accused of insider trading. Parliament called for his dismissal.
5. See p. 305.
6. *LOLJ*, 16 August 2006.
7. Ibid., 17 August 2006.
8. Ibid., 9 March 2007.
9. The same information was relayed by the Lebanese press in the summer about certain Arab governments, with suspicion then falling on Jordan and Egypt.
10. Names do appear in the interim version filed in April 2007, but it was not published. Two *Haaretz* journalists, Amos Harel and Avi Issacharoff, also confirmed the connection between a portion of March 14 and the Israeli government, in *34 Days: Israel, Hezbollah, and the War in Lebanon*, Basingstoke: Palgrave Macmillan, 2008, pp. 98 and 109.
11. *LOLJ*, 29 August 2006.
12. Ibid., 9 March 2007.
13. Ibid., 20 January 2009.

14. In the 21 August *LOLJ* edition, it says: "Helicopters had dropped off the commandos Friday night in the mountains, about twenty kilometres from Boudai. Dressed in Lebanese uniforms and driving vehicles, including a Humvee, painted like those of the Lebanese army, they were able to operate with impunity for several hours. But just outside Boudai, a Hezbollah sentinel stopped the convoy. The "Lebanese soldiers" told him in Arabic that they were on the same side, but their accent gave them away. The guard gave the alert and the battle began." A *ta'bi'a* who was at the site after the clash told me: "The repeated circling around the school roused the party's security services in the area, who found it odd that an army patrol would be roaming alone so determinedly in the area. Our buddies called the command post at the military barracks in Baalbek, running the licence plate number by them. The reply came as 'No record of this plate; not one of our vehicles.' The *shabeb* [fighters] immediately understood what was happening and went after the Israelis. When the Israelis saw that they were being pursued, they called their side but help did not come in time. We launched a rocket against the commandos; we killed one and wounded two others."
15. *LOLJ*, 21 August 2006.
16. Ibid.
17. Ibid., 4 September 2006.
18. This village, oddly, is divided in two: the northern part, reoccupied by the Israeli army in 2006, is in Lebanese territory; the southern half is part of the Golan. The villagers are mainly Alawites and consider themselves Syrians.
19. These are still continuing.
20. See, among others, *LOLJ*, 15 July and 13 and 22 August 2008.
21. Ibid., 7 August 2008.
22. Ibid., 7 and 9 August 2008.
23. Ibid., 7 August 2008.
24. Ibid., 20 and 21 July and 4 October 2008.
25. See, for example, "IDF plans to use disproportionate force in next war", *Haaretz*, 6 October 2008.
26. *LOLJ*, 14 February 2009.
27. Ibid., 18 July 2008.
28. Ibid., 12 November 2008. Observed in Baalbek by the author.
29. Ibid.
30. The Lebanese government and UNIFIL investigators corroborated this.
31. Observation made by the author in January 2009 in Baalbek.
32. *LOLJ*, 3 November 2008.
33. Author's interview with a *ta'bi'a*, 2009.
34. They were accused of "collaboration with Israel, entering Israeli territory without prior authorization, and weapons possession without permits". They admitted having worked for the Israeli government for more than fifteen years: *LOLJ*, 15 and 25 April and 12 May 2009.
35. Ibid., 13 May 2009.

36. Ibid., 17 and 21 May 2009. Homsi began working for Israel in early 2006. He was told to get information on three Israeli soldiers who disappeared during the battle at Sultan Yakub in 1982. He was also supposed to try to get a meeting with Nasrallah so that Mossad would know how to get to the secretary-general.
37. Ibid., 21 May 2009.
38. Ibid., 18 May 2009.
39. Ibid., 22 May 2009.
40. Adib Allam and his family are Christians.
41. Speech dated 22 May 2009, www.moqawama.org.
42. *LOLJ*, 13 September 2006.
43. Ibid., 19 August 2006.
44. Ibid., 22 August 2006.
45. Ibid., 17 August, 6 and 11 September 2006.
46. An article in *The New Yorker* (14 August 2006) by the journalist Seymour Hersh revealed the existence of an Israeli–American agreement dating back to several months before the conflict on an Israeli plan to attack Lebanon. An article published in Britain in *The New Statesman* and echoed by *al-Safir* in its 5 August issue had already argued that Israel had finalized its plans before the kidnapping of the two soldiers and informed both the US government and Tony Blair of its intentions to launch an offensive against its northern neighbour.
47. *LOLJ*, 13 September 2006.
48. Even the Lebanese government found itself in an uncomfortable position, the chancellor's word validating the reservations already expressed by Hezbollah concerning German participation, when the Lebanese government had been its foremost advocate. At the immense gathering organized in Beirut's southern suburbs by Hezbollah the following week to celebrate the "Divine Victory", Nasrallah sent a warning: "They [UNIFIL] come to impose a maritime blockade, for what? Is it to protect Lebanon? No; anyway, the German chancellor herself said it: the German navy has a historic role of protecting the right of Israel to exist. They come by sea, want to circle around Lebanon's skies and besiege its borders. I say to them: lay siege, seal off the borders, the ocean, the sky; it will in no way weaken the will of the Resistance or its weapons. We just fought a thirty-three-day war and were ready to fight for much longer than that. What we deployed during the war is only an infinitesimal part of our capabilities": *al-Safir*, 23 September 2006.
49. *LOLJ*, 17 August 2006.
50. This estimate does not include either the indirect losses or the lost earning suffered by Lebanon's economy (ibid., 18 August 2006).
51. *al-Safir*, 17 August 2006.
52. *LOLJ*, 14 July 2006.
53. Ibid., 16 July 2006.
54. Ibid., 18 August 2006.
55. *al-Safir*, 26 August 2006.
56. *LOLJ*, 5 September 2006.

57. Ibid., 3 October 2006.
58. *al-Safir*, 9 September 2006. Actually, there is no proof that Sadirat Iran finances Hezbollah. But, according to Nizar Hamzeh, Sadirat Iran is the bank where Hezbollah keeps most of its accounts, putting them beyond the reach of the pressures the United States could bring to bear against the Lebanese government to freeze the party's assets (*In the Path of Hizbullah*, p. 65).
59. *LOLJ*, 26 September 2006. Iran counter-attacked by filing a complaint against the United States with the IMF.
60. *al-Safir*, 28 September 2006.
61. Ibid., 30 September 2006.
62. Ibid., 6 October 2006.
63. *LOLJ*, 12 October 2006.
64. *al-Safir*, 22 August 2006.
65. Ibid., 6 November 2006.
66. *LOLJ*, 15 August 2006.
67. The party disbursed $10,000 per family in the Baalbek region (ibid., 21 August 2006) and $20,000 in the southern suburbs (ibid., 18 August 2006).
68. From the programme's slogan.
69. The Baalbek Qur'an school was shut in 1998 after clashes between Hezbollah and the Lebanese army on the one hand, and Subhī al-Tufaylī's movement on the other, when the army shelled the school's campus. On 14 August 2006 Hezbollah reopened it and made 100 apartments available to families who had lost their homes during the summer conflict (*al-Safir*, 16 August 2006).
70. Ibid., 5 and 7 September 2006.
71. Ibid., 6 September 2006.
72. My thanks to Dr Mouna Harb (American University of Beirut) for having shared this observation with me.
73. *LOLJ*, 28 August 2006.
74. *al-Safir*, 29 August 2006.
75. *LOLJ*, 30 August 2006.
76. Ibid., 26 July 2006.
77. al-Arabiya, News at 1 p.m., 22 July 2006.
78. *LOLJ*, 22 September 2006.
79. Ibid., 19 September 2006.
80. *al-Safir*, 6 October 2006.
81. Ibid., 2 November 2006.
82. *LOLJ*, 23 October 2006.
83. Ibid., 29 December 2006.
84. Ibid., 31 August and 23 October 2006.
85. *33 yawm min al-nār* [33 Days of Fire], Beirut: Tārīkh al-ʿArab wal-ʿĀlam, 2006, p. 100.
86. Ibid.
87. *LOLJ*, 1 August 2006.

88. *al-Safir*, 6 October 2006.
89. Ibid., 12 October 2006. The conferences Paris I (February 2001), Paris II (November 2002), and Paris III (January 2007) were international conferences for supporting the Lebanese debt.
90. A public agency reporting to the prime minister, responsible for reconstruction and land management.
91. *al-Safir*, 24 August 2006.
92. Ibid., 7 October 2006; *LOLJ*, 9 and 10 October 2006.
93. His alleged collaboration falls within the story of the Marjayoun convoy. See Chapter 11.
94. *LOLJ*, 2 November 2006.
95. Ibid., 9 January 2007.
96. Ibid., 13 November 2006. The Shiite community was indeed no longer represented in the government.
97. The square in the centre of Beirut in front of the parliament.
98. *LOLJ*, 5 April 2007.
99. Ibid., 21 October 2006.
100. Ibid., 19 October 2006.
101. "'So let them go, we can form a government without them,' asserts Aoun": ibid., 30 October 2006.
102. "Chehayeb [a PSP Druze MP]: 'To their street we will oppose ours, and in answer to their bullets we will not wave ... roses'": ibid.
103. The blocking third allows the party that holds it to oust a government provided that it can talk one-third plus one ministers into resigning.
104. When the tribunal's preliminary draft was signed by the truncated government, Hezbollah expressed reservations "regarding form but not the substance": *LOLJ*, 14 November 2006.
105. The party of Sleiman Frangieh, Maronite leader and March 8 partisan.
106. The party of Talal Arslan, Druze leader and March 8 partisan.
107. *LOLJ*, 4 and 5 December 2006.
108. "Downtown, the Christmas tree is festooned with the people's grievances. For the demonstrators, the celebration unfolds under the sign of tolerance and accepting of the other": ibid., 20 December 2006.
109. Ibid., 23 December 2006.
110. Ibid., 24 January 2007.
111. Ibid.
112. Nasrallah ordered his followers to return home, with a formal admonishment not to engage in reprisals. The flare-ups on the second day having started at the Arab University, Hezbollah's leadership hired dozens of mini-bus drivers to take non-Shiite students regardless of political orientation home at the party's expense, even as far as the heights of the Mountain that overlook the capital. "On 25 January, when things got heated at the Arab University around 10 or 11 a.m. and when there were three fatalities already, we received phone calls from there asking us what we were going to do. The Arab

University is in a Sunni zone; if a Shiite were to be killed there, we couldn't guarantee that there would not immediately be reprisals in Hadath, the campus in "our" zone. Hezbollah's student committees immediately rented vans at their expense: Sunni students were taken to their homes, Christian students to theirs in Baabda and Hadath, and Druzes to shelter in the Mountain. Today still, with mid-March behind us, we still receive phone calls from parents thanking us": author's interview with a cadre of the Mobilization Unit for Education, 2007. The account was confirmed by the author's field investigation in 2007.

113. The working concept was to form a government of twenty-four or thirty individuals. It remained to decide how many portfolios to allocate to each of the political factions (March 14, opposition, "independents").
114. The opposition insisted on a quorum of two-thirds of the parliament, counting on a difference in number of seats between the two camps as too small to guarantee this ratio, especially after Pierre Gemayel (minister of industry and son of Amin) was assassinated in November 2006, and Walid Eido (a Sunni FC MP) and then Antoine Ghanem (a Kataeb MP) were killed, in June and September 2007 respectively. For the same reasons, the majority favoured an absolute majority.
115. Aoun meant to stand for the presidency of the Republic, but the majority balked and Hezbollah did not officially support his candidacy back then.
116. Sleiman started out as the opposition's candidate—more precisely, Bashar al-Assad's, but his profile was agreeable to Hezbollah—and he did not have majority support. The opposition then scored a masterstroke: completely unexpectedly, it dithered, then did an about-face, opposing Sleiman. By doing this, they got the majority to come to Sleiman's defence and to ultimately present him as its candidate. The opposition then insisted on first getting an agreement "on a certain number of points" (the tribunal, the blocking minority, and maintaining IRL's armed status) before the presidential election took place, while the majority insisted on having the presidential election before any other discussion.
117. Lebanon had already experienced this kind of situation following Amin Gemayel's term, when the presidential office remained unoccupied from late 1988 until the end of 1989.
118. Patriarch Nasrallah Sfeir, *LOLJ*, 26 April 2007.
119. Ibid., 18 December 2006 and 31 July 2007, 15 February 2008.
120. Ibid., 24 January and 28 May 2007.
121. Ibid., 27 December 2006.
122. Ibid., 13 November 2007.
123. Ibid., 5 January 2007.
124. Ibid., 12 January 2007.
125. Ibid., 25 September 2007, 19 February 2008.
126. Ibid., 30 January 2007.
127. Ibid., 29 December 2006.
128. Ibid., 8 January 2007.
129. Ibid., 16 October 2006.

130. The campaign was financed by USAID and designed by Saatchi & Saatchi. See Mervin (ed.), *Le Hezbollah*, p. 230.
131. A space in Beirut reserved for fairs and celebrations.
132. From 2005 on, the political parties had taken on "colours": yellow stood for Hezbollah, orange for FPM, blue for FC, red for the LCP, etc. These politicized colours were internalized to such a degree that the colour of a garment, albeit worn innocently, could provoke aggressive reactions. The opposition's decision to sign its posters with a rainbow was designed to tweak the nose of March 14 and the sectarianism it stoked at the time.
133. This alludes to the fact that the election law did not provide for an exact representation of the political powers on the ground: it thus awarded a majority of seats to March 14 despite a majority of the votes cast by all confessions having come out in favour of March 8.
134. About €150.
135. See "The government outdone", above.
136. "It seems that the international tribunal is the exposed nerve of the Lebanese crisis, with one camp insisting that it be convened ... with the other side, of which a majority is not Lebanese, want[ing] to stymie its formation and to move on": *LOLJ*, 4 January 2007.
137. Ibid., 23 January 2010.
138. Ibid., 10 January 2010.
139. Ibid.
140. Ibid., 28 January 2008.
141. *al-Mustaqbal*, 8 February 2008.
142. *LOLJ*, 11 February 2008.
143. See below.
144. Ibid., 3 May 2008.
145. Ibid.
146. Ibid.
147. Ibid., 5 May 2008. He appealed to the Arab countries to join him in standing up to the "Iranian expansion".
148. *al-Mustaqbal*, 7 May 2008.
149. *LOLJ*, 9 May 2008.
150. *al-Akhbār*, 6 May 2008.
151. This section is based on the *LOLJ* and *al-Safir* editions of 8, 9, and 10 May 2008.
152. *LOLJ*, 6 May 2008.
153. After it had been evacuated.
154. The editor-in-chief, Salah Salam, is from the Salam family of Beirut (Sunni, pro-March 14).
155. Its editor in chief, Hassan Sabra, is pro-March 14.
156. *LOLJ*, 11 May 2008.
157. *L'Express*, 15 May 2008.
158. *LOLJ*, 6 August 2008. My emphasis.
159. The first Syrian ambassador arrived in Lebanon in late May 2009.

160. *LOLJ*, 4 September 2008.
161. Ibid., 3 September 2008.
162. Ibid., 13 March 2009.
163. Ibid., 7 March 2009.
164. Ibid., 7 February 2008.
165. Ibid., 8 May 2009.
166. Ibid.
167. Ibid., 2 March 2009.
168. Two Abdel-Aal brothers, members of the Ahbash group, had been liberated on 25 February, *i.e.*, a few days before the STL got under way.
169. The Israeli government had until then always categorically refused to free Quntar.
170. This was a Falasha (Ethiopian) soldier who drowned; his body had been washed up on the Lebanese coast and was recovered by the IRL. See *LOLJ*, 16 October 2007.
171. Nasīm Nisr, Samir Quntar, and three fighters captured during the 2006 war.
172. Ridwān was Mughniyeh's *nom de guerre*.
173. *LOLJ*, 16 July 2008.
174. Ibid., 17 July 2008. My emphasis.
175. Ibid., 8 and 16 May 2009.
176. Ibid., 27 May 2009.
177. Ibid., 8 June 2009. These were unusual sentiments in the mouth of the patriarch, the Arab identity of Lebanon being a concept to which the conservative Christians had always been hostile. Actually, he was not referring to the Arabism of progressive circles but the anti-Iranianism of the March 14 radicals. The speech echoed paradigms of a "Persian" Lebanon developed by Jumblatt and Hamadeh in 2007–8.
178. Sixty-eight seats for March 14 and three for independents close to the movement.
179. "Today, we can say that two great lies have dropped. First, certain parties of the majority have not ceased saying that the opposition does not want the elections to take place, or that the opposition will mount an assault on the polling stations if the results are not to our advantage. They have even stated that we would not accept the results of the election. ... The second great lie ... is the one that says that the elections cannot be held while the opposition keeps its weapons. Today is Monday, and here we are, the lie has dropped. Our weapons are not to keep certain individuals from power; they only are for resisting, and that proves that the Resistance is healthy. We accept the results in a sporting, democratic spirit. We accept the fact that the rival camp has obtained a majority of the seats in Parliament": *LOLJ*, 9 June 2009.
180. "With 865,012 voters, the Lebanese opposition obtained more than 54.9% of votes, supplanting the current majority that only got 680,000 votes, or 45.1% of the 1,575,617 Lebanese voters who cast a ballot": www.almanar.com.lb, 9 June 2009.
181. *LOLJ*, 13 June 2009.
182. Ibid., 27 November 2009.
183. *al-Akhbār* (6 May 2008) reported that Jumblatt was said to have threatened to pull his ministers out of the government if it did not dismiss Shuqair from his post and take on the IRL's network.

184. The News at 8 p.m., LBC, 11 May 2008.
185. *LOLJ*, 16 July 2008.
186. Ibid., 17 July 2008.
187. The News at 2 p.m., LBC, 17 July 2008.
188. *LOLJ*, 18 July 2008.
189. Ibid., 4 August 2008. My emphasis. However, Jumblatt had raised doubts in the spring of 2006 about the Shebaa Farms being Lebanese, and had urged their liberation through diplomatic channels only.
190. Ibid., 28 July 2008.
191. Ibid., 14 April 2009.
192. Ibid., 21 April 2009.
193. Lebanese isolationism designates the attitude prevailing among Christian conservatives during the 1960s and 1970s, particularly disassociation from the Palestinian cause.
194. *LOLJ*, 23 March 2009.
195. Ibid., 28 March 2009.
196. Ibid., 1 and 2 April 2010.

10. THE SPECIAL TRIBUNAL FOR LEBANON AND THE SYRIAN CONFLICT

1. Report posted on the UN website.
2. Ibid.
3. Ibid.
4. Hariri had ceased to be prime minister in September.
5. The group also goes by the name Association of Charitable Works.
6. *LOLJ*, 31 December 2005.
7. Ibid., 23 July 2005.
8. Al-Siddiq had put into play those close to the Syrian president and maintained that Hariri's assassination had been the object of a plot concocted beginning in September 2004. "Thus," explains the magazine, "Siddiq, 42 years of age, affirmed he had left Beirut a month before the attack, before admitting in September that he had taken part in preparing the bombing attack that killed the former prime minister": ibid., 23 October 2005.
9. "They offered me money, a house, and a car. They proposed sending me to France for surgery to change my facial appearance." He talked about having been tortured in Lebanon so that he would accuse Maher al-Assad and Assef Shawkat, and he point-blank accused Fares Khashan, a reporter for *al-Mustaqbal* and Future TV, "of having forced him to say specific things to the investigators". He is supposed also to have been "in contact with Americans and Israelis": ibid., 29 November 2005.
10. At the time, May Chidiac had already been the victim of a car-bomb attack that left her seriously injured; Gebran Tueni was assassinated fifteen days before Hussam changed his story.
11. *LOLJ*, 24 February 2006.
12. "Russia and China wish to have this article amended, considering that it constitutes a challenge and a grave danger and that Washington will have recourse to it so that any Lebanese

or Syrian official may be extradited, given that the charge of a "crime against humanity" explodes all immunities, however sovereignist they may be, and allows the tribunal to summon whomever it wishes and no one will be able to escape it": ibid., 18 October 2006.

13. Ibid., 18 December 2006.
14. Ibid., 24 December 2006.
15. Ibid., 30 May and 2 June 2007.
16. *The Jerusalem Post*, 31 July 2010.
17. See https://www.youtube.com/watch?v=76EiK9DzRTQ and https://www.youtube.com/.watch?v=3j60KcCX948, 10 October 2012.
18. Saad Hariri had named al-Hassan head of the ISF in 2006, casting doubt on the latter's responsibility for assassinating Hariri's father.
19. On the 16th, 22nd, and 25th. The speeches can be read on www.moqawama.org.
20. Since 2005 the ISF had been considered in Lebanon as clients of the Hariri family.
21. *AFP*, 2 November 2010; *LOLJ*, 12 November 2012.
22. *LOLJ*, 29 November 2010.
23. The first act would have been passage of Resolution 1559; the second the period following the assassination of Rafic Hariri during which March 14 tried to negotiate the Resistance into disarming; the third the war of 2006; and the fourth the decisions by the government on 6 May 2008, "after reaching agreement with the United States". The speech is available on Hezbollah's website at www.moqawama.org.
24. The content of these cables is set out in the next chapter.
25. Al-Siddiq, however, had by then already been discredited by the Commission itself.
26. See http://mplbelgique.wordpress.com, 20 February 2011.
27. The speech can be read on the Hezbollah website: www.moqawama.org.
28. According to him, "when the STL began its work, the Commission of Inquiry's investigators and equipement had been evacuated; the tribunal has only a single office in Lebanon, and all the material was shipped from Beirut airport—except for ninety-seven computers transferred to Israel."
29. A profile that Hezbollah and numerous other parts of civil society had already pointed to in the past as a sign of the STL's bias.
30. See the next chapter.
31. Even so, it had some difficulty keeping the lid on individual positions that some ministers took, particularly the minister of foreign affairs, Adnan Mansour, who openly sided with the Assad regime at the start of 2013.
32. See p. 270.
33. After the Hula massacre that left 108 dead in May 2012, France, Germany, Great Britain, the Netherlands, Spain, Italy, and Bulgaria sent the Syrian ambassadors home. The United States, Canada, Australia, and Japan did likewise. Tunisia had already sent the Syrian ambassador back in February. Morocco would do the same in July.
34. United Nations and UNHCR websites, on 2 October 2012 and 8 March 2013 respectively; *LOLJ*, 15 July 2013.
35. In the autumn of 2013 there was talk of a million Syrian refugees in Lebanon (equivalent to 25 per cent of the Lebanese population) and a million and a half in early 2015.

36. At first, the army tracked down the opposition fighters and sent them back to Syria, but soon chose to limit its interventions to—soft—attempts to curtail the arms traffic.
37. It claimed that "several arms and ammunition caches were set up in Lebanese sectors bordering Syria. These were illegally transported to Lebanon by sea and by air, with some countries using the pretext of humanitarian shipments to Syrians displaced in Lebanon as a cover for transferring arms and ammunition that are then smuggled into Syria." The complaint alleges that "[there are] centres operated by Salafist groups and the FC in Lebanese regions bordering Syria, that were converted into bases for Syrian terrorists affiliated with al-Qāʿida and the Muslim Brotherhood who infiltrate into Syria from Lebanese territory for the purpose of conducting criminal activities before returning to these bases. Their wounded are cared for under fictitious names in hospitals and clinics belonging to these groups and financed by countries such as Qatar and Saudi Arabia. ... Some fifty terrorists use forged identity documents bearing the UN logo to pass through the Lebanese army's roadblocks in transporting various weapons." The complaint goes on to claim that there are reports of "Colonel Riad el-Assaad, who defected from the Syrian Army, recently having set foot on Lebanese territory in order to create a buffer zone along the Syrian border": *LOLJ*, 6 January 2012.
38. Ibid., 3 January 2012.
39. Ibid., 5 January 2012.
40. Ibid., 3 February 2012.
41. That is to say, with the war waged by the Christian conservative militias against Palestinian factions, progressive Lebanese groups, and then the Syrian army in an effort aimed at preserving the confessional system and a crypto-federalist decentralization conforming to a homogenized conception of sectarian territories.
42. *LOLJ*, 15 February 2012.
43. In April 2013, in a commentary that would be classed as a "*fatwā* for murder and provocation" by the Syrian Druze clergy, he went so far as to decree that it was "legitimate to spill the blood of pro-Assad Druzes".
44. *al-Diyār*, 1 October 2012.
45. The spillover of the conflict to Lebanon and the excesses of certain radical groups in the Syrian opposition, however, led March 14 to change its mind starting in 2013.
46. *LOLJ*, 14 February 2012.
47. *The New York Times*, 6 October 2012.
48. According to the communiqué, "Saad Hariri personally put Okab Sakr in charge of monitoring developments in Syria and coordinating with [Syrian] opposition political forces regarding media and political support by the FC for the people who fall victim to the killing machine run by the Syrian regime": *LOLJ*, 18 October 2012.
49. On 23 October 2011 Tunisian Islamists won 89 seats out of 217.
50. In late October 2011 the president of the Libyan National Council, Mustafa Abdeljalil, announced that the new Constitution and legislation of Libya would be based on *sharīʿa*. In January 2012 the Egyptian Islamist MPs took the oath after their own style, inserting religious phrases in it and, in February, an Islamist MP made the call to prayer right there in the chamber.

51. *LOLJ*, 6 January and 21 May 2012.
52. In the spring of 2007, a pursuit initiated by the Lebanese army against the members of an Islamist group, Fateh al-Islam, in Tripoli degenerated into a battle lasting a little over three months (20 May to 2 September) between the military and Fateh al-Islam, which was entrenched in the Palestinian refugee camp of Nahr al-Bared. On a psychological level, the event would above all mark the first real awareness among the Lebanese population of the existence of radical Sunni Islamic networks in the country.
53. The presence of al-Qāʿida in Lebanon is dissected by Bernard Rougier in *Everyday Jihad*, Cambridge: Harvard University Press, 2009 and *The Sunni Tragedy in the Middle East*, Princeton: Princeton University Press, 2015.
54. Bakri had been expelled after the July attacks in London.
55. *Le Parisien*, 24 July 2012.
56. See www.tayyar.org, 30 August 2012.
57. See "The Assyrophobia" of Christians in the Aounist current, discussed in *al-Akhbār*, 6 March 2012.
58. The demonstration had been organized in the wake of the publication of caricatures of the Prophet Muhammad in the Copenhagen daily *Jyllands-Posten*.
59. Ghaleb Abu Zeinab, the Hezbollah cadre responsible for relations with Christian groups, and Ali Fayyad, a party MP, thus attended the first mass celebrated by the Pope with the new cardinals.
60. An illustration of the popular disaffection for the Hezbollah secretary-general in Syrian opposition circles is the criticism addressed to him by the actress May Skaff in February 2012, when she offered him the choice of either "pulling his *shabbīha* (hoodlums) from Syria or return[ing] the money" that she had collected during the summer of 2006 to aid Lebanese refugees in Syria. See http://english.alarabiya.net/articles/2012/02/22/196322.html, 22 February 2012.
61. al-Arabiya, 2 December 2011.
62. *LOLJ*, 6 December 2011.
63. Videos were posted on YouTube showing fighters described as being from Hezbollah units riding on Syrian army tanks. Analysis done on this footage provides no proof that these are in fact members of the party. In fact, there are positive indications that they are not (Syrian accents, beards of the "Salafi" type, etc.).
64. *The Times*, 26 January 2012.
65. See www.naharnet.com (*al-Nahār*), 18 January 2012.
66. See www.mediarabe.info, 23 January 2012.
67. *LOLJ*, 1 February 2012.
68. Some sources mentioned the fact that the abductors believed that Hezbollah militants, relatives of Nasrallah, even his youngest son, were part of the group. It quickly turned out that in fact this was not the case. Negotiations for a release were under way when Nasrallah, in a speech on 25 May, described "the kidnapping of innocents an odious deed that will do damage to the aims [of the Syrian opposition] and will harm [its] cause", before thanking President Assad and the Lebanese government for their efforts in trying to obtain the pilgrims' release. This last point antagonized the kidnappers, who suspended the talks and

demanded an apology. Nasrallah refused, demanding that they release "the innocents who have nothing to do with the present conflict between those responsible for the abduction and Hezbollah". Each party stood firm, and the hostages were not released until October 2013.

69. *LOLJ* (online version), 16 September 2012.
70. Ibid. (online version), 21 January 2012.
71. See www.moqawama.org, accessed 26 January 2012.
72. *LOLJ* (online version), 18 October 2012.
73. From 2011 on, March 14 tended to blame Hezbollah for every assassination attempt in the country. Thus, when Samir Geagea then Boutros Harb claimed to have escaped attempted assassinations in April and July 2012 respectively, and then Wissam al-Hassan was killed by a car bomb in October of the same year, numerous people inside the former majority immediately accused Hezbollah before any investigation. In fact, no proof of its involvement has ever been found.
74. *LOLJ* (online version), 9 October 2012.
75. See www.moqawama.org, 9 October 2012.
76. *LOLJ*, 3 October 2012.
77. Ibid., 8 October 2012.
78. Ibid., 8 and 12 October 2012. According to sources in Baalbek, he was killed by a rocket that hit his home.
79. In Arabic, the concept of *jihād* refers actually to the notion of "effort" and is prescribed in Islam in two forms: the "minor *jihād*"—*al-jihād al-asghar*—which means fighting "infidels", and the "major *jihād*"—*al-jihād al-akbar*—which relates to the individual psychological struggle that all faithful wage against their shortcomings with the goal of moral betterment.
80. This unusual situation stems from a drawing of borders between Lebanon and Syria that was never completed. Large swaths of territory thus find themselves placed under a sovereignty that does not accord with the citizenships of the people living there. In the border regions near al-Hermel, entire villages, although inhabited by Lebanese, have always been under Syrian sovereign control.
81. See www.moqawama.org, 11 October 2012. His version of events was confirmed by an investigation conducted by the BBC several days later: see www.bbc.co.uk, 26 October 2012.
82. *al-Joumhouriya*, 3 September 2012.
83. *LOLJ*, 9 October 2012.
84. *The Telegraph*, 19 January 2012.
85. See www.tayyar.org, 3 October 2012.
86. *al-Akhbār*, 20 May 2013; *Le Figaro*, 29 May 2013; *Daily Star*, 4 June 2013; *Haaretz*, 5 June 2013.
87. Author's interviews with Hezbollah officials, Beirut, 2015. The number of IRL combatants fighting in Syria in 2015 was between 4,500 and 5,000.
88. *LOLJ*, 3 June 2013. The number cited by Minister of Foreign Affairs Laurent Fabius hardly

seems credible, given the total number of men in the Islamic Resistance and its reluctance to leave Lebanon stripped of the majority of its fighters when it feared a possible Israeli attack on the country.

89. Ironically, it favoured the same strategy as that of the Israeli army in 1978, when the latter carved out a buffer zone in South Lebanon that it "cleansed" of all armed Palestinian presence, hoping to stop rocket launches into northern Galilee and to prevent incursions into Israel by Palestinian combatants from Lebanese territory.
90. No one took responsibility for the attack, but suspicion fell on the Syrian regime or groups close to it. Some media outlets in August 2013 claimed that, although a tiny Sunni group in the Syrian opposition laid claim to the first attack in Rueiss, the two attacks (Beirut southern suburbs and Tripoli) were perpetrated by the same people.
91. However, these barriers disappeared a few weeks later, Hezbollah turning back over to government forces the responsibility for ensuring security in the party's areas.
92. *LOLJ*, 13 January 2012. Saad Hariri answered a greeting addressed to him by the Israeli official in a friendly fashion, at which condemnation rained down on his Twitter and Facebook accounts for what was perceived as an act of collaboration at worst and a regrettable blunder at best.
93. Parliament having been blocked by Nabih Berri starting in 2007, it did not sign off on the Siniora government's expenditure. The amount of off-budget expenditures for 2006–9 reached $11 billion. The FPM accused the FC of misappropriation if not outright theft for clientelist purposes, turning a blind eye to the $6 billion off-budget expenditure by the Mikati government that the FPM thought merited different treatment. It is nevertheless true that, in terms of image, the affair severely damaged March 14, and especially the FC.
94. *LOLJ* and *al-Akhbār*, 15 March 2012.
95. *LOLJ*, 18 September 2012.
96. Ibid.
97. In the wake of Wissam al-Hassan's murder, the TV host Marcel Ghanem invited al-Assir onto his show on LBC, March 14's flagship TV channel, to comment on the event.
98. In Lebanon, the mufti of the Republic remains dependent on the government's president.
99. The Lebanese Brigades to Resist the Israeli Occupation, a multiconfessional appendage of the IRL. See Chapter 3.
100. The notion of a Sunni *ihbāt* had been raised some years previously in the writings of sociologists (Rougier, *Everyday Jihad*), but it had only come into vogue recently. The March 8 media had talked it up for several months before the attack on al-Assir's HQ, but it was this and the Sunni community's reactions that prompted media close to March 14 to resort to the concept in turn. For examples, see *al-Akhbār*, 4 February 2013; *LOLJ*, 10 June 2013; and *al-Hayāt*, 30 June 2013.
101. This was even more so because certain Western intelligence services active in Lebanon during the years in question were sometimes the object of manipulation by local actors wanting to use them in battling the party. See for example how the CIA was duped by

the Lebanese Forces when the latter was organizing the attempt on Muhammad Husayn Fadlallāh's life in 1985. See Chapter 3.

102. See the retrospective of the affair in *Le Monde*, 26–27 February 2015.
103. World Jewish Congress, "Former Argentine minister investigated in connection with AMIA bombing", 2 July 2013, www.worldjewishcongress.org/en/news/former-argentine-minister-investigated-in-connection-with-amia-bombing, accessed 4 July 2016; www.timesofisrael, 1 July 2013.
104. *Haaretz*, 4 January 2014.
105. He was released a few months later for lack of evidence of involvement in preparing attacks.
106. "Hezbollah is Blamed for Attack on Israeli Tourists in Bulgaria", *The New York Times*, 19 July 2012; "Holding Iran Accountable for Terrorist Attacks", *The Washington Post*, 20 July 2012.
107. See www.timesofisrael.com, 20 July 2013. It was later said that he was "French and Lebanese".
108. *The New York Times*, 9 August 2012.
109. *Le Figaro*, 7 February 2013; *LOLJ*, 14 February 2013.
110. *Le Figaro*, 7 February 2013; *LOLJ* (online version), 6 February 2013.
111. Private interview with author, May 2015.
112. "Israel Pins Bombing on Hezbollah to Get EU Terror Ruling", IPS News, 24 July 2012; "Bulgarian Charge of Hezbollah Bombing Was an 'Assumption'", IPS News, 7 February 2013; "Bulgarian Revelations Explode Hezbollah 'Hypothesis'", IPS News, 18 February 2013. Porter had already critiqued the accusation levelled against Hezbollah in 1992: "Argentine Report Casts Doubt on Iran Role in '94 Bombing", IPS News, 13 November 2006; "Bush's Iran/Argentina Terror Frame-Up", *The Nation*, 18 January 2008.
113. *al-Nahār*, 10 February 2013.
114. *LOLJ*, 6 February 2013.
115. "Taking into account the decisions made by Hezbollah and the fact that it has very harshly fought against the people of Syria, I confirm that France will submit a proposal to register Hezbollah's military branch on the [EU's] list of terrorist organizations. ... You have not only seen Hezbollah engage fully in Syria but also seen it take responsibility for its engagement": France 24, 23 May 2013.
116. *LOLJ*, 23 July 2013.
117. The *New York Times* shared this perspective, reasoning that the decision was part of a "carrot-and-stick" strategy used by the European Union towards Israel for the Palestinian dossier: "Europe's Carrot-and-Stick Approach to Israel Includes Blacklisting Hezbollah", 19 July 2013.
118. *LOLJ*, 25 July 2013.
119. Ibid., 26 July 2013.
120. Ibid., 27 July 2013. This was criticized on two levels. The battle of Qusayr being perceived as the real reason for Hezbollah's blacklisting, the Burgas affair was seen as a pretext hastily wrapped in a manufactured credibility.

121. In early June the Grand Mufti of Saudi Arabia, Abdel Aziz al-Sheikh, exhorted "all political and religious men to take serious measures against this repugnant sectarian group [Hezbollah] and all who support it", hailing the call to *jihād* issued against the party a few days earlier by the Egyptian preacher Yussef al-Qardawi: ibid., 7 June 2013.
122. Starting with the expulsion without warning of Shiites of Lebanese nationality from their territories.
123. On 14 June Princes Saud al-Faysal and Bandar ben Sultan, respectively the Saudi minister of foreign affairs and director of intelligence, visited Paris in a move to mobilize against the involvement by Hezbollah and Iran in Syria.
124. *LOLJ*, 27 July 2013.
125. Ibid., 24 July 2013.
126. See www.moqawama.org and www.lebanonfiles.com, 26 July 2013. See also the next chapter.

11. HEZBOLLAH IN THE EYES OF ITS PUBLIC

1. The assertions made in this chapter concerning the perceptions of Hezbollah by its public—and by the Shiites in particular—are based on my field observation, hundreds of interviews, participant observation, and an exhaustive reading of news accounts.
2. I retain vivid memories of the disruptions of social life engendered by the fighting between AMAL and Hezbollah in the late 1980s in the Baalbek–al-Hermel area: difficulty in entering and leaving the city without prior notice for reasons of security, interrupted schooling, catastrophic shop closings during battles, travelling on dirt paths to bypass main roads held by fighters, flight by known militants and supporters on both sides for fear of reprisals, etc.
3. Many militia leaders who extorted civilians and robbed both private companies and state institutions during the civil war years made their way into the political class after the war. The late 1990s and early 2000s were punctuated by episodes of embezzlement and diversion of public funds in which several Lebanese politicians were implicated, starting with individuals close to Prime Minister Rafic Hariri. Hezbollah's profile, beyond reproach when it came to corruption, was slightly marred in the late 2000s. At the time, scandals involving people close to the party included the Ezzedine case in 2009 when several party officials were cheated by a trusted businessman, or the Yazbek case, in 2011, when the son of Sheikh Muhammad Yazbek, a member of the Shūrā, was discovered to be trafficking arms to the Syrian rebels. The rigour with which the party leadership has consistently managed these cases has so far prevented them from damaging its image with its public.
4. Palmer Harik, *Hezbollah*, p. 121.
5. The Lebanese National Movement, led by Druze leader Kamal Jumblatt.
6. That is, confessional non-mixing on the geographical level. Sunnis, on the whole, had no territorial mixing problem before 2005. In the view of Hezbollah supporters, the Druze community was spared despite the "massacres of the Mountain" in 1983 by the fact that its main party, the PSP, remained dominated by an anti-confessional logic until the assassination of Kamal Jumblatt in 1977, and that the killings were usually perceived as arising from "retaliation", not an ideology that advocated a "confessional cleansing" in principle.

7. In particular, the population in Hezbollah areas tends to think of persons (shopkeepers and civil servants) who are party members or close to it as more honest than others. Hence, individuals will take their business or turn to them more readily than other persons in case of need.
8. An example would be Simon Haddad, "The Origins of Popular Support for Lebanon's Hezbollah", *Studies in Conflict and Terrorism*, vol. 29, no. 1, January–February 2006, pp. 21–34.
9. Following the death of Fadlallāh in early July 2010, a field study carried out by the author the following August, delving into which *marja*ʿ his followers would turn to, revealed that it would primarily be Sayyid ʿAlī Sistānī, although most respondents intended to continue to rely on the *fatwā*s of Fadlallāh as long as no new decrees were called for.
10. The Liberation speech, www.moqawama.org.
11. The outbreak of the July 2006 war would prove that feeling to be unjustified.
12. 2005 and the ensuing years would prove to what extent that feeling was wrong.
13. *LOLJ*, 5 January 2006.
14. See, for example, Walid Jumblatt's declaration: "My enemy at present is not Israel, it is the Syrian regime": ibid., 21 January 2006.
15. Through their insistence on having Hezbollah take part in the government, the Ministerial Statement, etc.
16. *LOLJ*, 21 February 2006.
17. This meeting was organized in May 2006, just before the summer war. Bolton's pronouncements during the war presented an opportunity for Hezbollah to remind the FC of the "error" that this tribute represented.
18. *LOLJ*, 24 February 2005.
19. The events of May 2008 would be interpreted as the realization of this fear.
20. This is especially noticeable in relations among Christians, where numerous FPM partisans support Aoun in remembrance of those killed by the Kataeb or the Lebanese Forces.
21. *al-Nahār*, 17 March 2005.
22. Though the *Bass Māt Watan* programme had already mocked several other political personalities of all stripes.
23. An example is the response by Tzipi Livni to Fouad Siniora when the latter, in describing the extent of human and material damage wreaked by the Israeli army to Arab leaders convened in emergency session in Beirut in early August, buckled under the pressure and burst into tears in public. The Israeli minister, in a tone the Lebanese would find cavalier, invited him to "dry his tears and [to] work toward a New Middle East". The Lebanese press, starting with the pro-March 14 and anti-Hezbollah dailies, published scathing pieces directed at the Israeli minister (for example: "To Cry a Thousand Times" and "Eyes Filled with Rage", in *LOLJ*, 9 August 2006).
24. Personal log book. The Israeli helicopters did not leave Baalbek until about 4.30 in the morning, so the messages would have been sent before they landed in Israel.
25. *LOLJ*, 17 and 18 August 2006; *al-Safir*, 17 August 2006.
26. In this case, the liberation of political prisoners.

27. "I think it would be a mistake to ascribe moral equivalence to civilians who die as the direct result of malicious terrorist acts and the deaths of civilians that are a tragic and unfortunate consequence of military actions dictated by self-defence. In our moral and legal system, there is a huge difference between different acts according to the intentions that motivate them and there is no comparison between the act of taking civilian targets deliberately ... and the very unfortunate consequence of self-defence": *LOLJ*, 20 July 2006.
28. Ibid., 22 and 26 July 2006.
29. *The New Yorker*, 14 August 2006.
30. *LOLJ*, 22 July 2006.
31. Philippe Douste-Blazy received the families of two kidnapped soldiers and declared that it was necessary to "first disarm Hezbollah, then see about arranging a ceasefire next." Ibid., 25 July 2006.
32. Ibid., 31 July 2006. Jeffrey Feltman was the American ambassador to Lebanon from August 2004 to August 2008.
33. None of the attacks—even lethal ones—by the Israeli army against UN and UNIFIL posts were condemned.
34. *LOLJ*, 15 July 2006.
35. Ibid., 15 and 27 July 2006.
36. The press was full of stories in the same vein. At the end of August this appeared: "For the people of Bint Jbeil the "*shababs*" [Hezbollah's fighters] are true heroes. Everyone talks about them, but no one can identify them. 'They appear as soon as you need them and never ask for anything in return. They are discreet and courageous and appear out of nowhere,' says Fatima. 'One day, I took a few things from my house before it is demolished, and I wanted to take them to the storage. But the bags were heavy and I have a lame leg. Suddenly, a young man came to help me. He carried the bags and once we got there, he left without a word. I didn't see him again. I really would have liked to thank him.'": ibid., 29 August 2006.
37. Interview with Nasrallah, New TV, 27 August 2006.
38. Jaʿfar al-ʿAttār, *al-Harb al-ustūra bayna Hizbillāh wal-kayān al-sahyūnī* [The legendary war between Hezbollah and the Zionist entity], Beirut: Sharikat al-Khalīj lil-Tibāʿa wal-Nashr, 2006.
39. As a matter of fact, the expression *Nasr min Allāh*, taken from the Qur'an, was previously used by a Lebanese poet in a homage to the Iranian Revolution published in *al-Muntalaq* in 1979 (no. 5, Ramadan 1399 H., July–August 1979). However, there is no indication that the speaker knew this.
40. Author's interview, 2007.
41. Examples: Muhsin al-Mūsawī, *Asrār wa karāmāt rijāl Allāh fī Karbalāʾ al-Waʿd al-sādiq* [Secrets and glories of the men of God in the Karbala of Operation Truthful Pledge], Beirut: Dār al-Kitāb al-ʿArabī, 2007; Mājid al-Zubaydī, *Rijāl Allāh wal-Nasr al-ilāhī* [The men of God and the Divine Victory], Beirut: Muʾassasat al-Hudā al-Islāmiyya, 2007.
42. "Composure or presence of mind carried to the extreme is another characteristic capable

of creating awe in observers. Self-control is frequently seen as a manifestation of latent power, and self-control or composure under conditions of stress, challenge, or danger, where most men would be expected to be thrown off the balance, can seem somewhat inhuman": Willner, *The Spellbinders*, p. 142.

43. *al-Safir*, 15 July 2006.
44. Ibid.
45. *LOLJ*, 30 July 2007.
46. See Chapter 6.
47. "Muqtatafāt ʿibriyya" was the title for several years before it was renamed "Iʿlām al-aduww" (The Enemy's Media).
48. See Chapter 6.
49. *al-Nahār* (Sunday supplement), 6 December 2006.
50. *al-Safir*, 19 September 2006.
51. The song's title is "al-Waʿd al-sādiq", taken from the IRL operation of 12 July 2006.
52. For information on the song, the group, and Israeli reactions, see http://netzoo.net/the-hawk-of-lebanon/ (13 June 2009).
53. Examples: *Thaqāfat al-muqāwama* [The culture of resistance], Beirut: Dār al-Hādī, 2006; *al-Intisār al-muqāwim* [The resistant victory], Beirut: al-Markaz al-Islāmī lil-Dirāsāt al-Fikriyya, 2007; *Qiyam al-muqāwama* [The values of the resistance], Beirut: Dār al-Hādī, 2008; Tāhā ʿAbdel-Rahmān, *al-Hadātha wal-muqāwama* [Modernity and resistance], Beirut: Maʿhad al-Maʿārif al-Hikmiyya, 2007; Samīr Shams, *Thaqāfat al-muqāwama* [The culture of resistance], Beirut: n.p., 2007; Hasan Jābir, *al-Muqāwama fī mīzān al-istrātījyā* [The Resistance in the balance of strategy], Beirut: Dār al-Hādī, 2007; Qāsim, *Mujtamaʿ al-muqāwama*.
54. *al-Waʿd al-sādiq: harb tammūz 2006* [Truthful Pledge: the war of July 2006], Beirut: Lebanese Cultural Centre, 2007, 6 vols.; *Harb kasr al-irāda bayn al-Muqāwama wal-mashrūʿ al-sahyū-amirīkī* [The war of wills between the Resistance and the American–Zionist project], Beirut: Arab Scientific Publishers, 2007; *33 yawm harb ʿalā Lubnān* [33 days of war against Lebanon], Beirut: Centre des Études Palestiniennes, 2007 (trans. from Hebrew); *Yawmiyyāt al-harb al-isrāʾīliyya ʿalā Lubnān 2006* [Journal of the Israeli war of 2006 against Lebanon], Beirut: al-Markaz al-ʿArabī lil-Maʿlūmāt, 2006.
55. In the neutral sense of the word, referring to the fact that it challenges the usual versions.
56. Jaʿfar ʿAtrīsī, *Hizbullāh yajurr ʿarabat al-Tārīkh* [Hezbollah, the engine of history], Beirut: Dār al-Safwa, 2007.
57. Again, in the neutral sense of the term.
58. Hamādeh, *Tārīkh al-Shīʿa fī Lubnān*.
59. ʿAlī Rāghib Haydar Ahmad, *al-Muslimūn al-Shīʿa fī Kisrwān wa Jubayl (1842–2006)* [The Shiite Muslims in Kesruan and Jbeil (1842–2006)], Beirut: Dār al-Hādī, 2007.
60. St Maron (Mār Mārūn), a Syrian monk from the Antioch region (dc. 410), to whom the Maronite community owes its name.
61. The question of coordination between Hezbollah and its allies in the field remained one of the obscure points in the sequence of events.

62. A reference to the civil war (1975–90).
63. "As one member of the majority put it, it is no exaggeration to say that the ministers that night had split into "hawks" and "doves". ... MP Saad Hariri and then Walid Jumblatt quickly realized that a real blunder had been made," said a parliamentary source. "It is hard not to wonder, however, how such a decision could be a mistake when it has been discussed for over ten hours. Today, it is ... legitimate to ask why this country's leaders could have consciously chosen to adopt a policy that they were not able to carry through, to adhere to." The question, according to this MP, was "why some ministers more than others pushed the Cabinet to make these decisions and then, like magic, disappeared from the radar. It's bizarre." All the more bizarre since Hezbollah had issued a clear warning, just days before 5 May, stressing that "no one will touch" its telecommunications network, a statement confirmed by an authoritative source. According to this source, the army's commander, Michel Sleiman, had from the start advised the government to hand over the telecom network dossier to him, along with the one for the Shuqair reassignment, because, "as far as he was concerned, any decision the government made on these two matters would be tantamount to war". The source went on to say that "the events took the army by surprise because there were no advance warnings of that type of security problem in Beirut" (*LOLJ*, 16 May 2008). The newspaper *al-Safir*, for its part, blamed both sides equally and criticized the government in particular for arrogating this decision to itself when it should have been nothing more than a caretaker government. It concluded by saying that either the government decided on its own, which made it dangerous, or was following external orders and was continuing the 2006 war on Israel and the West's behalf. Even the daily *al-Nahār*, the majority's flagship newspaper, from 11 May reproachfully posed the question why the government did not wait for the results of the inquiry before taking a decision.
64. *LOLJ*, 29 February 2008.
65. Ibid., 12 May 2008.
66. Author's interviews with opposition combatants in June 2008 revealed that the FC fighters had access to American state-of-the-art materiel; some AMAL cadres benefited from this by trading their old Russian automatic rifles for American ones they stole from FC facilities. Numerous witnesses reported "sixty or so tanks" deployed by the PSP in the heights of Beirut and use by the latter of Russian truck-mounted machine guns and B7 rocket launchers in combat in the Mountain.
67. In August 2002 the government of Rafic Hariri filed charges against MTV for "damaging relations with Syria and the dignity of the Chief of State". The real reasons behind these indictments, however, are said to have been related to a personal problem between Rafic Hariri and Gabriel Murr, the network's owner and a candidate that summer in the by-elections in Metn with the opposition's support. A month later the network was permanently shut down "for violations of the electoral law". The opposition voiced its anger in parliament as well as on the street. The network's employees, demonstrating in Ashrafiyeh, were beaten up by the ISF.
68. Testimony by a thirty-year-old opposition follower, with a Shiite father and Sunni mother, but distanced from Hezbollah, from Baalbek.

69. Reference to the *taklīf sharʿī* decreed by Nasrallah.
70. Testimony by a young man, thirty years old, distanced from both sides, Maronite, student, native Beirutian.
71. Including in FPM ranks.
72. At a demonstration in Beirut protesting against the signing of the Oslo Accords. See Chapter 3.
73. See Chapter 7.
74. See Chapter 9.
75. Reference to the murder of a young AMAL militant in a Beirut Sunni neighbourhood two days after the start of the opposition's sit-in. See Chapter 9.
76. See Chapter 9.
77. See Chapter 9.
78. Lebanese expression meaning "He sent us in the enemy's line of fire."
79. Words of a Shiite from Baalbek after yet another abduction by Israel of a Lebanese shepherd along the border in January 2008. The resentment at the perceived lack of fairness shown by the international community was widely shared.
80. *LOLJ*, 23 June 2008.
81. Ibid., 27 November 2008. The Israelis had argued that the arms and material supplied could be diverted to Hezbollah.
82. Anyone with Israeli citizenship, or who has visited Israel (i.e. with an Israeli stamp on their passport), is legally prohibited from entering Lebanon.
83. Israeli television gave the impression that the interview with Goldman was being conducted live ("Channel 10 Report from Beirut"). In the eyes of Hezbollah and the Shiite community, Goldman's travels to Lebanon were intrusions in the southern suburbs by a "Zionist" who, under cover of a "camouflage" passport, took pictures of potential use to Mossad and the Israeli army. Goldman also meant trouble for Beirut since the state of war between Lebanon and Israel legally prohibits the presence of Israeli citizens in Lebanon. The minister of information at the time, Ghazi Aridi, was forced to justify himself.
84. Nasrallah clarified that his home appeared in these photos (*LOLJ*, 29 and 30 April 2008). The affair caused even more of a stir because Pakzad was driven to the suburbs and encouraged to take pictures by PSP cadres, which was interpreted in Hezbollah circles as a provocative act. PSP appears to have manipulated Pakzad "for the sole purpose of tarnishing the party's image".
85. *LOLJ*, 19 August 2008.
86. Ibid., 22 August 2008.
87. Observed by author on site.
88. Certain comments by leaders of both organizations, formulated in the presence of the American ambassador in connection with the IRL initiative, were harsh on Hezbollah.
89. Officially, the changeover took place in March 2011 following Sfeir's retirement. However, it appeared that this was a dismissal disguised as a resignation. Several analyses, supported by WikiLeaks, have suggested the Vatican's dissatisfaction with the way Sfeir limited his actions to defending the interests of March 14's Christian class at the expense of unity in

Lebanese Christian ranks and of safeguarding Syria's Christians. Rai's first step was to arrange a reconciliation between Bkerké and the FPM. He was also careful not to resort to the anti-Shiite sectarian language of his predecessor. On the Syrian issue, he advocated a political solution and that Lebanon keep its distance from the conflict next door.

90. WikiLeaks, cable 08BEIRUT372.
91. For decades, Nassib Lahoud had embodied a moderate and anti-confessional Maronitism.
92. This feeling was apparently commented on by the French ambassador Bernard Emié as follows: "March 14 is waiting for the Israelis to do the dirty work" (WikiLeaks, cable 06BEIRUT2413.) Olmert's cabinet reversed this division of roles at the end of the war, seeing in the passage of 1701, as already mentioned, a means for Tel Aviv to let March 14—abetted by the international community—accomplish what the Israeli army had just failed to do.
93. WikiLeaks, cable 06BEIRUT2706.
94. *LOLJ*, 18 October 2010.
95. As mentioned previously, the Iranian and Argentine governments decided to reopen the file in October 2012 and resume the inquiry in full.
96. Mahmud al-Mabhouh, a Hamas cadre, was assassinated in January 2010, in all likelihood by the Mossad on orders of the Israeli government. The suspects were carrying forged European and Australian passports. Tel Aviv found itself accused of violation of sovereignty.
97. See the article in *al-Balad* dated 1 June 2012: "The Shiites do not support Assad."

CONCLUSION

1. The full text is available at www.moqawama.org, 9 June 2010.
2. My emphasis.
3. *al-Akhbār*, 3 January 2011.
4. See www.muqawama.org, 7 February 2012.
5. Ibid.
6. Ibid.
7. *LOLJ*, 11 May 2012.

BIBLIOGRAPHY

Books and articles in English/French

AbuKhalil, As'ad, "Ideology and Practice of Hizballah in Lebanon: Islamization of Leninist Organizational Principles", *Middle Eastern Studies*, Vol. 27, No. 3, July 1991, pp. 390–403.

Achcar, Gilbert and Michel Warschawski, *La guerre des 33 jours. La guerre d'Israël contre le Hezbollah au Liban et ses conséquences*, Paris: La Discorde Textuel, 2006.

Ajami, Fouad, *The Vanished Imam*, Ithaca: Cornell University Press, 1986.

Alagha, Joseph, *The Shifts in Hizbullah's Ideology: Religious Ideology, Political Ideology, and Political Program*, Amsterdam: Amsterdam University Press, 2006.

——— *Hizbullah's Documents*, Amsterdam: Amsterdam University Press, 2011.

——— *Hizbullah's Identity Construction*, Amsterdam: Amsterdam University Press, 2011.

——— *Hizbullah's DNA and the Arab Spring*, New Delhi: K W Publishers Pvt Ltd, 2012.

Alem, Jean-Pierre and Patrick Bourrat, *Le Liban*, Paris: PUF, 1994 (5th edition).

Avon, Dominique and Anaïs-Trissa Khatchadourian, *Le Hezbollah. De la doctrine à l'action: une histoire du "parti de Dieu"*, Paris: Seuil, 2010.

Azani, Eitan, *Hezbollah: The Story of the Party of God, from Revolution to Institutionalization*, New York: Palgrave Macmillan, Middle East in Focus Series, 2009.

Bahout, Joseph, "Liban: les élections législatives de l'été 1992", *Maghreb–Machrek*, No. 139, Jan-Mar. 1993, pp. 53–84.

Béchara, Souha, *Résistante*, Paris: JC Lattès, 2000.

Bizri (al-), Dalal, *Islamistes, parlementaires et libanais. Les interventions à l'Assemblée des élus de la Jama'a Islamiyya et du Hizb Allah (1992–1996)*, Beirut: Les Cahiers du CERMOC, No. 3, 1999.

Blanford, Nicholas, *Warriors of God: Inside Hezbollah's Thirty-Year Struggle Against Israel*, London: Random House, 2011.

Buchta, Wilfried, *Who Rules Iran? The Structure of Power in the Islamic Republic*, Washington D.C.: The Washington Institute for Near East Policy & Konrad Adenauer Stiftung, 2000.

Cambanis, Thanassis, *A Privilege to Die: Inside Hezbollah's Legions and Their Endless War Against Israel*, New York: The Free Press, 2010.

Carré, Olivier, *Septembre noir*, Paris: Complexe, 1980.

Carré, Olivier and Michel Seurat (alias Gérard Michaux), *Les Frères musulmans. Égypte et Syrie, 1928–1982*, Paris: L'Harmattan, 2001.

Chalabi, Tamara, *The Shi'is of Jabal 'Amil and the New Lebanon: Community and Nation-State, 1918–1943*, Basingstoke: Palgrave Macmillan, 2006.

Charara, Walid and Frédéric Domont, *Le Hezbollah, un mouvement islamo-nationaliste*, Paris: Fayard, 2004.

Chehabi, Houchang E. (ed.), *Distant Relations: Iran and Lebanon in the Last 500 Years*, London: I. B. Tauris, 2006.

Clark, Janine, "Social Movement Theory and Patron-Clientelism: Islamic Social Institutions and the Middle Class in Egypt, Jordan, and Yemen", *Comparative Political Studies*, Vol. 37. No. 8, Oct. 2004, pp. 941–968.

——— *Islam, Charity, and Activism: Middle-Class Networks and Social Welfare in Egypt, Jordan, and Yemen*, Bloomington, IN: Indiana University Press, 2004.

Corm, Georges, *Liban. Les guerres de l'Europe et de l'Orient (1840–1992)*, Paris: Gallimard-Folio Actuel, 1992.

——— *Le Liban contemporain. Histoire et société*, Paris: La Découverte, 2003.

——— *Le Proche-Orient éclaté (1956–2007)*, Paris: Gallimard-Folio Histoire, 2007.

Daher, Aurélie (alias Vito Romani), "Le Hezbollah, un instrument de la politique étrangère iranienne?", in Bernard Rougier (ed.), "Les diplomaties contestataires au Moyen-Orient", *Les Cahiers de l'Orient*, No. 87, Sept. 2007, pp. 79–96.

Daher, Aurélie, "Le Hezbollah face aux clans et aux grandes familles de la Bekaa-Nord: les élections municipales de 2004 dans la ville de Baalbek", in Franck Mermier and Sabrina Mervin (eds.), *Leaders et partisans au Liban*, Paris and Beirut: Karthala and Institut Français du Proche-Orient, 2012, pp. 419–433.

Deeb, Lara, *An Enchanted Modern: Gender and Public Piety in Shi'i Lebanon*, Princeton, NJ: Princeton University Press, 2006.

Dekker, Ted and Carl Medearis, *Tea With Hezbollah: Sitting at the Enemies' Table*, New York: Doubleday Religion, 2010.

Desportes, Vincent, *La guerre probable*, Paris: Economica, 2007.

Donati, Caroline, "Le Liban sud. Le retrait israélien", *Maghreb–Machrek*, No. 168, April–June 2000, pp. 125–155.

Ezzi (al-), Ghassan, *L'invasion israélienne du Liban. Origines, finalités et effets pervers*, Paris: L'Harmattan, 1990.

Farag, Iman and Alain Roussillon (eds), *Modernisation et nouvelles formes de mobilisation sociale. Volume II: Égypte-Turquie*, Cairo: Cedej, 1992.

Fayyad, Ali, *Fragile States: Dilemmas of Stability in Lebanon and the Arab World*, Oxford: Intrac, 2008.

Fisk, Robert, *Pity the Nation: The Abduction of Lebanon*, New York: Thunder's Mouth Press, 2002.

Goodarzi, Jubin M., *Syria and Iran: Diplomatic Alliance and Power Politics in the Middle East*, London: I. B. Tauris, 2006.

Goya, Michel, "Dix millions de dollars le milicien. La crise du modèle occidental de guerre limitée de haute technologie", *Politique étrangère*, No. 1, spring 2007, pp. 191–202.

Haddad, Simon, "The Origins of Popular Support for Lebanon's Hezbollah", *Studies in Conflict and Terrorism*, Vol. 29, No. 1, Jan-Feb. 2006, pp. 21–34.

Hamzeh, A. Nizar, "Lebanon's Hizbullah: From Islamic Revolution to Parliamentary Accommodation", *Third World Quarterly*, Vol. 14, No. 2, 1993, pp. 321–337.

—— "Clan Conflicts, Hezbollah and the Lebanese State", *The Journal of Social, Political, and Economic Studies*, Vol. 19, No. 4, winter 1994, pp. 433–446.

—— "The Role of Hizbullah in Conflict Management Within Lebanon's Shia Community", in Paul Salem (ed.), *Conflict Resolution in the Arab World: Selected Essays*, Beirut: American University of Beirut, 1997, pp. 93–118.

—— *In the Path of Hizbullah*, New York: Syracuse University Press, 2004.

Harel, Amos and Avi Issacharoff, *34 Days: Israel, Hezbollah, and the War in Lebanon*, Basingstoke: Palgrave Macmillan, 2008.

Hūt (al-), Bayān Nuwayhid, *Sabra and Shatila: September 1982*, London and Ann Arbor, MI: Pluto Press, 2004.

International Crisis Group, "Israël/Hezbollah/Liban: Éviter un regain de la violence", *Middle East Report*, No. 59, 1 Nov. 2006.

—— "Le Hezbollah et la crise libanaise", *Middle East Report*, No. 69, 10 Oct. 2007.

Jaber, Hala, *Hezbollah: Born with a Vengeance*, New York: Columbia University Press, 1997.

Johnson, Michael, *Class and Client in Beirut: The Sunni Muslim Community and the Lebanese State (1840–1985)*, New Jersey: Ithaca Press, 1986.

Jorisch, Avi, *Beacon of Hatred: Inside Hizballah's al-Manar Television*, Washington D.C.: The Washington Institute for Near East Policy, 2004.

Kapeliouk, Amnon, *Sabra et Chatila. Enquête sur un massacre*, Paris: Seuil, 1982.

Kassir, Samir, *La guerre du Liban. De la dissension nationale au conflit régional (1975–1982)*, Paris and Beirut: Karthala and CERMOC, 1994.

—— *Liban: un printemps inachevé*, Paris: Actes Sud, 2006.

Katzman, Kenneth, *The Warriors of Islam: Iran's Revolutionary Guards*, Boulder, CO: Westview Press, 1993.

Kepel, Gilles, *Jihad. Expansion et déclin de l'islamisme*, Paris: Gallimard, 2003 (2000).

Khatib, Lina, Dina Matar and Atef Alshaer, *The Hizbullah Phenomenon: Politics and Communication*, London: Hurst, 2014.

Kramer, Martin (ed.), *Shi'ism, Resistance and Revolution*, Boulder, CO: Westview Press, 1987.

—— "Hezbollah's Vision of the West", Washington D.C.: The Washington Institute for Near East Policy, Policy Papers, No. 16, 1989.

—— "The Moral Logic of Hizbullah", in Walter Reich (ed.), *Origins of Terrorism: Psychologies, Ideologies, Theories, States of Mind*, Cambridge: Cambridge University Press, 1990, pp. 131–157.

Kurzman, Charles, *The Unthinkable Revolution in Iran*, London: Harvard University Press, 2004.

Leenders, Reinoud, "Hizbollah: Rebel Without a Cause?", International Crisis Group, 30 Jul. 2003.

—— "How the Rebel Regained His Cause: Hizbullah & the Sixth Arab-Israeli War", *MIT Electronic Journal of Middle East Studies*, Vol. 6, No. 2, Summer 2006.

Lefort, Bruno, "Être jeune au Hezbollah. Étude sur la section étudiante du 'parti de Dieu'", *Revue internationale et stratégique*, No. 66, 2007, pp. 25–36.

Maasri, Zeina, *Off the Wall: Political Posters of the Lebanese Civil War*, London: I. B. Tauris, 2009.

Makovsky, David and Jeffrey White, "Lessons and Implications of the Israel-Hizballah War: A Preliminary Assessment", Washington D.C.: The Washington Institute for Near East Policy, Policy Focus, No. 60, Oct. 2006.

Mallat, Chibli, "Shi'i Thought from the South of Lebanon", Oxford: Centre for Lebanese Studies, 1988.

Mayeur-Jaouen, Catherine (ed.), *Saints et héros du Moyen-Orient contemporain*, Paris: Maisonneuve et Larose, 2002.

Mermier, Franck and Sabrina Mervin (eds), *Leaders et partisans au Liban*, Paris and Beirut: Karthala and Institut Français du Proche-Orient, 2012.

Mermier, Franck and Elizabeth Picard (eds), *Liban. Une guerre de 33 jours*, Paris: La Découverte, 2007.

Mervin, Sabrina (ed.), "Les autorités religieuses dans le chiisme duodécimain contemporain", *Archives de sciences sociales des religions*, No. 25, Jan.–Mar. 2004, pp. 63–77.

—— *Les mondes chiites et l'Iran*, Paris and Beirut: Karthala and Institut Français du Proche-Orient, 2007.

—— *Le Hezbollah. État des lieux*, Paris: Sindbad Actes Sud, 2008.

Mitchell, Richard P., *The Society of the Muslim Brothers*, Oxford: Oxford University Press, 1993.

Moaffak, Roula, "Sayyed Nasrallah raconte Hassan", *Magazine* (Beirut), 28 Nov. 1997, pp. 10–16.

Moroy, Franck, "Le sport comme adjuvant à l'action politique. Le cas du Hezbollah à Beyrouth", *Politix*, Vol. 13, No. 50, 2000, pp. 93–106.

Nassif, Nicolas, "Les élections législatives de l'été 2000", *Maghreb–Machrek*, No. 169, July–Sep. 2000, p. 116–127.

Nassif Tar Kovacs, Fadia, *Les rumeurs dans la guerre du Liban. Les mots de la violence*, Paris: CNRS, 2002.

Noe, Nicholas (ed.), *Voice of Hezbollah: The Statements of Sayyed Hassan Nasrallah*, London: Verso, 2007.

Norton, Augustus Richard, "Shi'ism and Social Protest in Lebanon", in Juan Cole, and Nikki Keddie (eds), *Shi'ism and Social Protest*, New Haven, CT and London: Yale University Press, 1986, pp. 156–178.

—— *Amal and the Shi'a: Struggle for the Soul of Lebanon*, Austin, TX: University of Texas Press, 1987.

—— "Lebanon: The Internal Conflict and the Iranian Connection", in Esposito, John L. (ed.), *The Iranian Revolution: Its Global Impact*, Miami, FL: Florida International University Press, 1990, pp. 116–167.

——— "Hizballah: From Radicalism to Pragmatism", *Middle East Policy*, Vol. 5, No. 4, Jan. 1998, pp. 147–158.

——— *Hizbullah of Lebanon: Extremist Ideals vs. Mundane Politics*, New York: Council of Foreign Relations, 1999.

——— "Hizballah and the Israeli Withdrawal from Southern Lebanon", *Journal of Palestine Studies*, Vol. 30, No. 1, 2000, pp. 22–35.

——— "Hizballah Through the Fog of the Lebanon War", *Journal of Palestine Studies*, Vol. 36, No. 1, 2006, pp. 54–70.

——— "Why Hizbullah is Winning", *Middle East Journal*, Vol. 61, No. 1, 2007, pp. 145–149.

——— *Hezbollah: A Short Story*, Princeton, NJ: Princeton University Press, 2014 (updated edition).

Palmer Harik, Judith, "Between Islam and the System: Sources and Implications of Popular Support for Lebanon's Hizballah", *Journal of Conflict Resolution*, Vol. 40, No. 1, Mar. 1996, pp. 41–67.

——— *Hezbollah: The Changing Face of Terrorism*, London: I. B. Tauris, 2004.

Perrin, Jean-Pierre and Chantal Rayes, "Hezbollah: Y a-t-il une vie après le retrait d'Israël? Entretien avec Hassan Nasrallah", *Politique internationale*, No. 88, 2000, pp. 109–117.

Picard, Élizabeth and Bernard Rougier (eds), "Le Liban dix ans après la guerre", *Maghreb-Machrek*, No. 169, Jul-Sep. 2000.

Picard, Élizabeth, *Liban, État de discorde. Des fondations aux guerres fratricides*, Paris: Flammarion, 1988.

——— "Les habits neufs du communautarisme libanais", *Cultures et Conflits*, Vol. 3, No.15/16, 1994, pp. 49–70.

——— "Les dynamiques politiques des chrétiens au Liban: Changement de statut et crise du leadership", *Maghreb–Machrek*, No. 153, Jul–Sep. 1996, pp. 3–21.

——— "Autorité et sourveraineté de l'État à l'épreuve du Liban Sud", *Maghreb–Machrek*, No.169, Jul–Sep. 2000, pp. 32–42.

Pierre, Hervé, *Le Hezbollah, un acteur incontournable de la scène internationale?*, Paris: L'Harmattan, Chaos International Series, 2008.

Piscatori, James P., *Islam in a World of Nation-States*, Cambridge: Cambridge University Press, 1986.

Qassem, Naim, *Hizbullah: The Story from Within*, London: Saqi Books, 2005.

Ranstorp, Magnus, *Hizb'Allah in Lebanon: The Politics of the Western Hostage Crisis*, New York: St Martin's Press, 1996.

Richard, Yann, *L'islam chi'ite. Croyances et idéologies*, Paris: Fayard, 1991.

Rosiny, Stephan. "Hizb Allah: An Islamic Way to Modernity?", in Makrides Vasilios, Rüpke Jörg and Ferdinand Kasten (eds), *Religionen im Konflikt*, Münster: Aschendorff, 2005, pp. 128–145.

Rougier, Bernard (ed.), "Liban: les élections législatives de l'été 1996", *Maghreb–Machrek*, No. 155, Jan-Mar. 1997, pp. 119–130.

——— *Le jihad au quotidien*, Paris: PUF, 2004.

—— "Les camps palestiniens du Liban. La Syrie, le Hezbollah et le nouveau pouvoir libanais face aux attentes internationales", *Transcontinentales*, No. 1, 2nd semester 2005, pp. 51–84.

—— "La guerre d'Israël contre le Hezbollah et la défaite de l'État libanais", *La Documentation française, Afrique du Nord Moyen-Orient*, No. 5244/5245, 2006/2007, pp. 67–94.

—— *Qu'est-ce que le salafisme?*, Paris: PUF, 2008.

Ruggirello, Véronique, *Khiam, prison de la honte*, Paris: L'Harmattan, 2003.

Saad-Ghorayeb, Amal, *Hizbu'llah: Politics and Religion*, London: Pluto Press, 2002.

Sankari, Jamal, *Fadlallah: The Making of a Radical Shi'ite Leader*, London: Saqi Books, 2005.

Schiff, Ze'ev and Ehud Ya'ari, *Israel's Lebanon War*, New York: Simon and Schuster, 1984.

Seurat, Michel, *L'État de barbarie*, Paris: Seuil, 1989.

Shaery-Eisenlohr, Roschanack, *Shi'ite Lebanon: Transnational Religion and the Making of National Identities*, New York: Columbia University Press, 2008.

Sneifer-Perri, Régina, *Guerres maronites, 1975–1990*, Paris: L'Harmattan, 1995.

Soueid, Mahmoud, *Israël au Liban. La fin de 30 ans d'occupation?*, Paris: Revue d'études Palestiniennes, 2000.

Sueur, Emilie, "Les chiites du Liban: comment ils se perçoivent", *Confluences Méditerranée*, No. 61, Spring 2007, pp. 31–39.

Vers la Troisième République... Elections 2009. Programme du Courant Patriotique Libre. Beirut, s.e.

Wright, Robin, *Sacred Rage: The Wrath of Militant Islam*, New York: Touchstone, 1985.

—— *In the Name of God: The Khomeini Decade*, London: Bloomsbury, 1990.

Books and articles in Arabic

'Abdel-Rahmān, Tāhā, *Al-hadātha wal-Muqāwama*, Beirut: Ma'had al-Ma'ārif al-Hikmiyya, 2007.

'Ammār, 'Abdel-Majīd, *Tawāzun al-ru'b fil-harb al-maftūha*, Beirut: Dār al-Kitāb al-Hadīth, 2002.

'Atrīsī (al-), Ja'far Hasan, *Hizbullāh. Al-khiyār al-as'ab wa damānat al-watan al-kubrā*, Beirut: Dār al-Mahajja al-Baydā', 2005.

—— *Hizbullāh yajurr 'arabat al-Tārīkh*, Beirut: Dār al-Safwa, 2007.

'Attār (al-), Ja'far, *Al-harb al-ustūra bayna Hizbillāh wal-kayān al-sahyūnī: Harb tammūz 2006*, Beirut: Sharikat al-Khalīj lil-Tibā'a wal-Nashr, 2006.

'Atwī, Muhammad, *Al-khatar al-sahyūnī 'alā Lubnān*, Beirut: Dār al-Hādī, 2002.

—— *Hurūb Isrā'īl al-muqbila*, Beirut: Dār al-Hādī, 2002.

'Ulayyiq, Nāsir Hasan, *Falsafat al-istishhād: Allāh wal-watan fī khitāb al-Muqāwama al-islāmiyya*, Beirut: Dār al-Mawāsim, 2004.

'Ulayyiq, Rāmī, *Tarīq al-nahl: Jumhūriyyat Rāmī 'Ulayyiq*, Beirut: Manshūrāt Tarīq al-Nahl, 2008.

Abū Hudbah, Ahmad, *33 yawm harb 'alā Lubnān: Atwal al-hurūb wa aktharuhā fashalan wa taklīfan*, Beirut: al-Dār al-'Arabiyya lil-'Ulūm, 2007.

Abū al-Nasr, Fadīl, *Hizbullāh: Haqā'iq wa ab'ād*, Beirut: al-Sharika al-'Ālamiyya lil-Kitāb, 2003.

Ahmad, Rif'at Sayyid, *Hasan Nasrallāh: Thā'ir min-al-janūb*, Beirut, Damascus and Cairo: Dār al-Kitāb al-'Arabī, 2006.

—— *Hassan Nasrallah, Al-Wa'd al-Sādiq wa malhamat al-Nasr al-Ilāhī*, Beirut, Damascus and Cairo: Dār al-Kitāb al-'Arabī, 2007.

Al-Intisār al-muqāwim, *Hawiyyat al-intisār wa tadā'iyyātuh al-istrātījiyya*, Beirut: Al-Markaz al-Islāmī lil-Dirāsāt al-Fikriyya, 2007.

Al-Wa'd al-Sādiq, *Harb tammūz 2006: Hikāyat sha'b wa Muqāwama*, Beirut: The Lebanese Cultural Center, 6 volumes, 2007.

Amīn (al-), Rāmī, *Yā 'Alī... Lam na'ud ahl al-Janūb/How I was orphaned by Hezbollah: The Personal Testimony of a Young Shia Journalist Living in Dahiyeh*, Beirut: Hayya Bina, No. 8, February 2008.

Asadollahi, Masood, *Al-islāmiyyūn fī mujtama' ta'addudiy*, Beirut: Arab Scientific Publishers, 2004.

Ballūq, Lānā H, *Al-fāris al-'arabī: Sīrat hayāt al-sayyid Hasan Nasrallāh min al-wilāda hattā al-qiyāda*, Beirut: Dar al-Mahajja al-Baydā', n.d. (2008).

Balqazīz, 'Abdul-Ilāh, *Hizbullāh: Min al-Tahrīr ilā al-rad' (1982–2006)*, Beirut: Arab Unity Studies Center, 2006.

Baydūn, Ahmad, *Hādhihi al-harb... Mihnat Lubnān al-mutamādiya fī bayānayn*, Beirut: Dār al-Sāqī, 2007.

Bazzī, Muhammad Husayn, *Hākadha takallama Nasrallāh*, Beirut: Dār al-Amīr, 2004.

—— *Al-Wa'd al-Sādiq: Yawmiyyāt al-harb al-sādisa*, Beirut: Dār al-Amīr, 2006.

Bishrī (al-), Tāriq, *Manhaj al-nadhar fil-nudhum al-siyāsiyya al-mu'asira fil-'ālam al-islāmī*, Amman: Dār al-Shurūq lil-Nashr wal-Tawzī', 2005.

Dāhir, 'Adnān Muhsin and Riyād Ghannām, *Al-mu'jam al-niyābī al-lubnānī (1861–2006)*, Beirut: Dār Bilāl, 2007.

Duhaynī, 'Abdel-Hasan, *Nihāyat Isrā'īl: Haqīqa, lā wahm*, Beirut: Dār al-Hādī, 2002.

Elyās, Salīm, *Al-Wa'd al-Sādiq. Sumūd sha'b wa Muqāwama*, Beirut: s.e., 2006, 2 volumes and DVD.

Fadlallāh, Hasan, *Al-khiyār al-ākhar: Hizbullāh: Al-sīra al-dhātiyya wal-mawqif*, Beirut: Dār al-Hādī, 1994.

—— *Harb al-irādāt: Sirā' al-Muqāwama wal-ihtilāl al-isrā'īlī fī Lubnān*, Beirut: Dār al-Hādī, 1998.

—— *Suqūt al-wahm: Hazīmat al-ihtilāl wa-intisār al-Muqāwama fī Lubnān*, Beirut: Dār al-Hādī, 2001.

Fadlallāh, Muhammad Husayn, *Khitāb al-Muqāwama wal-nasr fī muwājahat al-harb al-isrā'īliyya 'alā Lubnān, tammūz 2006*, Beirut: Dār al-Malāk, 2006.

—— *'An sanawāt wa mawāqif wa shakhsiyyāt*, Beirut: Dār al-Nahār, 2007.

Fajr al-intisār, *Al-harb al-'arabiyya al-isrā'īliyya al-sādisa*, Cairo, Damascus and Beirut: Dār al-Kitāb al-'Arabī, 2006.

Fakhrī, Abū 'Imād, *Al-Intisār, rabī' al-janūb al-muqāwim: Fakhr, majd, 'izza, karāma*, Beirut: Dār al-Mahajja al-Baydā', 2008.

Fayyād, Munā, *Ma'nā an takūna lubnāniyyan*, Beirut: al-Dār al-'Arabiyya lil-'Ulūm, 2008.

Hamādeh, Hasan, *Sirr al-intisār*, Beirut: Dār al-Hādī, 2001.

—— *Sadā al-intisār*, Beirut: Dār al-Hādī, 2004.

—— *Rijāl Allāh: Al-manhaj al-islāhī wa binā' al-dhāt al-insāniyya*, Beirut: Dār al-Hādī, 2007.

Hamādeh, Sa'dūn, *Tārīkh al-Shī'a fī Lubnān. Al-mujallad al-awwal: Al-hukm al-shī'ī fī Lubnān*, Beirut: Dār al-Khayyāl, 2008.

—— *Tārīkh al-Shī'a fī Lubnān. Al-mujallad al-thānī: Tahjīr al-Shī'a min Jabal Lubnān*, Beirut: Dār al-Khayyāl, 2008.

Hammūd, 'Abdel-Halīm, *"Isrā'īl" wa Hizbullāh: Al-harb al-nafsiyya*, Beirut: Dār wa Maktabat al-Hilāl, 2007.

—— *Al-Wa'd al-Sādiq: Ustūra tahzim "ustūra"*, Beirut: Dār wa Maktabat al-Hilāl, 2007.

Harb kasr al-irādah baynal-Muqāwama wal-mashrū' al-sahyū-amirikī, Beirut: Arab Scientific Publishers, 2007.

Haydar Ahmad, 'Alī Rāghib, *Al-muslimūn al-shī'a fī Kisrwān wa Jubayl: siyāsiyyan, tārīkhiyyan, ijtimā'iyyan, bil wathā'iq wal suwar (1842–2006)*, Beirut: Dār al-Hādī, 2007.

Hezbollah Media Central Unit, *Safahāt 'izz fī kitāb al-Ummah*, Beirut, 1993, 1994, 1995, 1996, 1997, 1998, 1999, 2000.

Hilmī Zādeh, Hamīd, *Zaman al-Husayn*, Beirut: Mu'assasat al-Balāgh, 2007.

Idrīs, Nasrīn, *'Arīs aylūl: Qissat al-shahīd Hādī Hasan Narallāh*, Beirut: Dār al-Amīr, 2001.

Ishtāy, Shawkat, *Al-shuyū'iyyūn wal-Katā'ib: Tajribat al-tarbiya al-hizbiyya fī Lubnān*, Beirut: Mu'assasat al-Intishār al-'Arabī, 1997.

Jābir, Hasan, *Al-Muqāwama fī mīzān al-istrātījyā*, Beirut: Dār al-Hādī, 2007.

Khadra, Sāmī, *Al-Khā'ibūn*, Beirut: Focus Advs, 2006.

Khātūn, Muhammad 'Alī, *Amīr al-qāfila. Al-sīra al-dhātiyya li-sayyid shuhadā' al-Muqāwama al-islāmiyya al-sayyid 'Abbās al-Mūsawī*, Beirut: Dār al-Walā', 2002.

Khawāja, Muhammad, *Al-Harb al-Sādisa: Al-nasr al-sa'b*, Beirut: Bisān, 2006.

Kūrānī (al-), *Tarīqat Hizbillāh fil-'amal al-islāmī*, s.l.: al-Mu'assasa al-'Ālamiyya, 1406 H, 1985/1986.

—— 'Alī, *'Asr al-Dhuhūr*, Beirut: Dār al-Mahajja al-Baydā', 2004.

Kūrānī, Muhammad Amīn, *Al-judhūr al-tārīkhiyya lil-Muqāwama al-islāmiyya fī Jabal 'Āmil*, Beirut: Dār al-Hādī, 2005.

Lahhām (al-), Sa'īd and Muhammad Qudayh (eds), *Mawsū'at al-Wa'd al-Sādiq: Yawmiyyāt intisār Tammūz*, Beirut: Nadhīr 'Abbūd, 12 volumes, 2007.

Madīnī (al-), Tawfīq, *Amal wa Hizbullāh, fī halabat al-mujābahāt al-mahalliyya wal-iqlīmiyya*, Damascus: Al-Ahālī lil-Tibā'a wal-Nashr wal-Tawzī', 1999.

Mahmūd, Arwā, *Qitāl Hizbillāh. Al-dīn fī muwājahat Isrā'īl: Kayf intasara Hizbullāh fī harb tammūz 2006*, Beirut: Dār al-Amīr, 2008.

Mājid, Ahmad, *Al-khitāb 'indal-sayyid Hasan Nasrallāh*, Beirut: Ma'had al-Ma'ārif al-Hikmiyya, 2007.

Makārim, 'Izzeddīn 'Abdel-Karīm, *Wa mā baddalū tabdīlan: Khawātir muqāwima*, Beirut: Dār al-Amīr, 2007.

Mawsū'a, Nasrallāh, al-rajul alladhī yakhtasir umma, Beirut: Manshūrāt al-Fajr, 3 volumes, 2006.

Mawsū'at Hizbillāh, Al-Muqāwama wal-Tahrīr, Beirut: Edito Creps, 12 volumes, photo album and DVD, 2006.

Min al-Sadr ilā Nasrallāh, Masīrat Muqāwama wa sīrat rajulayn, Beirut: Manshūrāt al-Ridā, 2007.

Muhsin, Muhammad and 'Abbās Muzannar, *Sūrat al-Muqāwama fil-i'lām: Hizbullāh wa tahrīr janūb Lubnān*, Beirut: The Center for Strategic Studies, Research and Documentation, 2001.

Mustafā, Amīn, *Al-Muqāwama fī Lubnān, 1948–2000*, Beirut: Dār al-Hādī, 2003.

——— *Al-i'sār: Waqā'i' wa asrār al-intisār al-thānī li-Hizbillāh 'alā Isrā'īl*, Beirut: Dār al-Hādī, 2007.

Nābulsī (al-), 'Abbās, *Ru'b al-silāh: Asrār al-qudra al-'askariyya li-Hizbillāh*, Beirut: Dār Iwān, 2007.

Nadwa, *Al-mashrū' al-watanī wal-nuhūd al-muqāwim 'indal-imām Mūsā al-Sadr*, Beirut: Markaz al-Hadāra lil-Dirāsāt al-Irāniyya al-'Arabiyya, Dār al-Ma'ārif al-Hikmiyya, 2007.

Nahwa al-Jumhūriyya al-thālitha... Intikhābāt 2009: Burnāmij al-Tayyār al-Watanī al-Hurr, Beirut: s.e., 2009.

Nasr (min) Allāh, Beirut: Manshūrāt al-Ridā, 2009.

Nasr, Mawsū'at Adab al-Muqāwama, *Qalam Rasās: Silsilat al-qisas al-qasīra, al-jiz' al-awwal*, Beirut: al-Jam'iyya al-Lubnāniyya lil-Funūn, Risālāt, 2009.

Nasrallāh, Hasan'Abbās, *Al-harakāt al-hizbiyya fī Ba'alabak*, Beirut: Mu'assasat al-Wafā', 1994.

——— *Tārīkh Ba'alabak: Al-tārīkh al-siyāsī wal-iqtisādī*, Baalbeck: Qamar al-'Ashīra, 2005.

——— *Tārīkh Ba'alabak: Al-hayāt al-fikriyya*, Baalbeck: Qamar al-'Ashīra, 2005.

——— *Al-hayāt al-ijtimā'iyya fī Ba'alabak: Turāth madīna wa thaqāfat sha'b*, Beirut: Dār al-Qāri', 2009.

Nasrallah, Hassan, "Al-sayyid Hasan Nasrallāh: al-sīra al-dhātiyya", *al-Mustaqbal al-'Arabī*, No. 331, Sep. 2006, pp. 113–118.

Nasrallāh, Muhammad-Jawād, *Hurūf muqāwima: Shi'r*, Beirut: Dār al-Hādī, 2007.

Ni'ma, Muhammad, *Nasrullāh, Ustūrat al-'Arab*, Beirut: Dār al-Quds, s.d.

Nūrī (al-) Mūsawī (al-), Muhsin, *Asrār wa karāmāt rijāl Allāh fī Karbalā' al-Wa'd al-Sādiq*, Beirut: Dār al-Kitāb al-'Arabī: Dār al-Muttaqīn, 2007.

Qāsim, Na'īm, *Hizbullāh, Al-manhaj, al-tajriba, al-mustaqbal*, Beirut: Dār al-Hādī, 2002.

——— *Mujtama' al-Muqāwama: Irādat al-shahāda wa sinā'at al-nasr*, Beirut: Ma'had al-Ma'ārif al-Hikmiyya, 2008.

Qatīt, Hishām Āl, *Al-bayānāt wal-fatāwā al-mu'ayyida lil-Muqāwama al-islāmiyya fī Lubnān*, Beirut: Dār Salūnī, Mu'assasat al-Balāgh, 2006.

——— *Thalātha wa thalāthūn yawman ahdathat burkānan fī Isrā'īl*, Beirut: Dār Salūnī, 2006.

Qazzī, Fāyiz, *Min Hasan Nasrallāh ilā Mishāl 'Awn: Qirā'a siyāsiyya li-Hizbillāh*, Beirut: Riad El-Rayyes Books, 2009.

Qbaysī, Hasan Mahmūd, *Al-inhidār wal-indihār: Min wa'd Balfūr ilāl-Wa'd al-Sādiq*, vol. I and II, Beirut: Mu'assasat al-'Arwa al-Wathqā, 2007.

Qbaysī, Muhammad Ahmad, *Al-shahāda wal-Tahrīr*, Beirut: Dār al-Hānī, 2000.

——— *Al-Harb al-sādisa: Al-sumūd wal-intisār*, Beirut: Dār al-Hādī, 2007.

Qiyam al-Muqāwama, Khiyār al-shahāda wal-hayāt, Beirut: Dār al-Hādī: Ma'had al-Ma'ārif al-Hikmiyya, 2008.

Qudsī 'Āmilī (al-), Muhammad, *Al-Malhama al-Kubrā: Ayyām al-Wa'd al-Sādiq*, Beirut: Dār al-Walā', 2006.

Rikābī (al-), 'Abdel-Amīr and Nahid Hattar, *Al-Muqāwama al-lubnāniyya taqra' abwāb al-Tārīkh: Yawmiyyāt al-harb*, Amman: Ward Editions, 2006.

Rizk, Hiyām and Muhammad Husayn Bazzī, *Sayyid al-qāda: Qissat sayyid shuhadā' al-Muqāwama al-islāmiyya, sayyid 'Abbās al-Mūsawī*, Beirut: Dār al-Amīr, 2002.

Sa'd, 'Abdō, *Al-intikhābāt al-niyābiyya li'ām 2005: Qirā'āt wa natā'ij*, Beirut: Markaz Bayrūt lil-Abhāth wal-Ma'lūmāt, 2005.

Salāmeh, Husayn, *Hizbullāh fil-'aql al-isrā'īlī*, Beirut: Markaz al-Istishārāt wal-Buhūth, 2006.

Salmān, Talāl, *Sīra dhātiyya li-haraka muqāwima 'arabiyya muntasira*, Beirut: s.e., n.d.

Sāyigh (al-), Nasrī, *Hiwār al-hufāt wal-'aqārib. Difā'an 'an al-Muqāwama*, Beirut: Riad El-Rayyes Books, 2007.

Shams, Samīr, *Thaqāfat al-muqāwama*, Beirut: s.e., 2007.

Shamseddīn, Muhammad Mahdī, *Al-wasāyā*, Beirut: Dār al-Nahār, 2002.

Sharafeddīn, Husayn, *Al-imām al-sayyid Mūsā al-Sadr. Mahattāt tārīkhiyya: Irān, al-Najaf, Lubnān*, Tyre and Beirut: Dār al-Arqām, 1996.

Sharāra, Rita, *Shib'ā awwalan*, Beirut: Shimali & Shimali SLA, 2005.

Sharāra, Waddāh, *Dawlat Hizbillāh: Lubnān mujtama'an islāmiyyan*, Beirut: Dār al-Nahār, 2006 (4th edition).

Shaykh al-shuhadā' wa-amīr al-muqāwimīn, Qissat shaykh al-shuhadā' al-shaykh Rāghib Harb, Beirut: Jam'iyyat al-Ma'ārif al-Islāmiyya al-Thaqāfiyya, 2003.

Shehādeh, Ahmad Husayn, *Mughāmarāt Hizbillāh wal-mustaqbal al-'arabī al-jadīd*, Beirut: al-Adyān lil-Dirāsāt wal-Tawthīq, 2006.

Sherrō, Jean, *Al-fidirāliyya hiya al-hall*, Beirut: n.e., 2007.

Shidyāq, 'Imād, *Al-Muqāwama wa sayyiduhā Hasan Nasrallāh*, Beirut: Al-Maktaba al-Hadītha, 2006.

Shqayr, Faraj Ahmad, *Al-Muqāwama al-islāmiyya wa mashrū' istinhād al-Umma*, Beirut: Dār al-Hādī, 2005.

Sobelman, Daniel, *Qawā'id jadīda lil-lu'ba: Isrā'īl wa Hizbullāh ba'd al-insihāb min Lubnān*, 'Ayn al-Tīneh and Beirut: Arab Scientific Publishers and Matābi' al-Dār al-'Arabiyya lil-'Ulūm, 2004.

Sulaymān Sa'b, Laure, *Intikhābāt 2005*, Beirut: Carlos Frères Editions, 2005.

Surūr, 'Alī, *Al-Khyām, Shahādāt hayya min al-irhāb al-sahyūnī*, Beirut: Manshūrāt Tajammu' Mu'taqalī Ansār, 1988.

Tāhā, Ghassān Fawzī, *Shī'at Lubnān: al-'ashīra, al-hizb, al-dawla. Ba'albak-al-Hirmil namūdhajan*, Beirut: Ma'had al-Ma'ārif al-Hikmiyya, 2006.

Thaqāfat al-Muqāwama, Tahaddiyāt al-wāqi' wa-āfāq al-mustaqbal, Beirut: Muntadā al-Fikr al-Lubnānī, Dār al-Hādī, 2006.

Tuéni, Gebran, *Bil-hibri wål-damm: Istiqlāliyyāt*, Beirut: Dār al-Nahār, 2006.

Tuéni, Ghassan, *Al-Janūb 2006: Al-Muqāwama, al-harb wal-silm, al-Mīthāq*, Beirut: Dār al-Nahār, 2006.

Wakīm, Najāh, *Al-ayādī al-sūd*, Beirut: Sharikat at-Matbū'āt lil-Tawzī' wal-Nashr, 2003.

Wilāyat al-faqīh, Qirā'āt fil-mabānī, al hudūd wal-tajriba, Beirut: The Imām Khomeini Cultural Center, Silsilat al-Mu'tamarāt wal-Nadawāt al-Fikriyya collection, No. 4, Jan 2005.

Yawmiyyāt al-harb al-isrā'īliyya 'alā Lubnān, Al-nasr al-mukhaddab, Beirut: al-Safīr, al-Markaz al-'Arabī lil-Ma'lūmāt, 2006.

Yazbik, Sa'dī, *Ayyām lā tunsā: Harb Tammūz 2006 wa-ab'āduhā*, Beirut: al-Dār al-Islāmiyya, 2007.

Zaytūn, 'Alī Mahdī, *'Āshūrā' wa khitāb al-Muqāwama al-islāmiyya: Al-sayyid Hasan Nasrallāh namūdhajan*, Beirut: Ma'had al-Ma'ārif al-Hikmiyya, 2007.

Zubaydī (al-), Mājid Nāsir, *Karāmāt al-Wa'd al-Sādiq*, Beirut: Dār al-Mahajja al-Baydā', 2007.

——— *Rijāl Allāh wal-Nasr al-ilāhī*, Beirut: Mu'assasat al-Hudā al-Islāmiyya, 2007.

25 *Ayyār: Yawm bi-qāmat Umma*, Beirut: Dār al-Walā', 2001.

33 *yawman min al-nār, Al-harb 'alā Lubnān, bidāya am nihāya?*, Beirut: Tārīkh al-'Arab wal-'Ālam, 2006.

Theses and doctoral dissertations (indicative bibliography)

Chaib, Kinda, *La culture du martyre au Liban Sud depuis la fin des années 1970*, Doctoral dissertation, History, Paris: Paris I Panthéon-Sorbonne, 2014.

Ghoussoub, Dani, *Le rôle du confessionnalisme dans la vie institutionnelle libanaise*, Doctoral dissertation, Public Law, Lyon: Lyon III Jean Moulin University, 2007.

Le Thomas, Catherine, *Mobiliser la communauté. L'émergence d'un secteur éducatif chiite depuis les années 1960 au Liban*, Doctoral dissertation, Political Science, Paris: Institut d'études politiques, 2009.

Lefort, Bruno, *Engagement partisan et construction identitaire: le cas des étudiants membres du Hezbollah dans le Liban contemporain*, Thesis, Master 2, Comparative Politics, Aix-Marseille University, Institut de recherches et d'études sur le monde arabe et musulman, 2005–2006.

Müller-Funk, Lea, *The Political Influence of Al-Akhbar in Lebanon. Partisans in Search for a Daily*, Thesis, Master 2, Comparative Politics, Paris: Institut d'études politiques, 2009–2010.

Theory and manuals (indicative bibliography)

Bayat, Asef, "Islamism and Social Movement Theory", *Third World Quarterly*, Vol. 26, No. 6, 2005, pp. 891–908.

Casas-Cortés, María Isabel, Michal Osterweil and Dana E. Powell, "Blurring Boundaries: Recognizing Knowledge-Practices in the Study of Social Movements", *Anthropological Quarterly*, Vol. 81, No. 1, winter 2008, pp. 17–58.

Cefaï, Daniel, *Pourquoi se mobilise-t-on? Les théories de l'action collective*, Paris: La Découverte, 2007.

BIBLIOGRAPHY

Davis, Gerald F. et al. (eds), *Social Movements and Organization Theory*, Cambridge: Cambridge University Press, 2005.

Duverger, Maurice, *Les partis politiques*, Paris: Armand Colin, 1976.

Holland, Dorothy, Gretchen Fox and Vinci Daro, "Social Movements and Collective Identity: A Decentered, Dialogic View", *Anthropological Quarterly*, Vol. 81, No. 1, 2008, pp. 95–126.

Kurzman, Charles, "Meaning-Making in Social Movements", *Anthropological Quarterly*, Vol. 81, No. 1, 2008, pp. 5–15.

Lavau, Georges, *À quoi sert le Parti communiste français?*, Paris: Fayard, 1981.

Lijphart, Arend, *Democracy in Plural Societies: A Comparative Exploration*, New Haven, CT and London: Yale University Press, 1977.

Park, Robert E., *Introduction to the Science of Sociology*, Chicago, IL: University of Chicago Press, 1921 (1969).

Snow, David A. and Robert D. Benford, "Ideology, Frame Resonance, and Participant Mobilization", *International Social Movement Research*, Vol. 1, 1988, pp. 197–217.

—— "Framing Processes and Social Movements: An Overview and Assessment", *Annual Review of Sociology*, Vol. 26, No. 1, Aug. 2000, pp. 611–639.

Snow, David et al., "Frame Alignment Processes, Micromobilization, and Movement Participation", *American Sociological Review*, Vol. 51, No. 4, 1986, pp. 464–481.

Snow, David, Sarah Soule and Hanspeter Kriesi (eds), *The Blackwell Companion to Social Movements*, Oxford: Blackwell, 2003.

Wedeen, Lisa, *Ambiguities of Domination: Politics, Rhetoric, and Symbols in Contemporary Syria*, Chicago, IL: University of Chicago Press, 1999.

Willner, Ann R., *The Spellbinders: Charismatic Political Leadership*, New Haven, CT and London: Yale University Press, 1984.

INDEX

INDEX

INDEX